Communications
in Computer and Information Science   1375

More information about this series at http://www.springer.com/series/7899

Raian Ali · Hermann Kaindl ·
Leszek A. Maciaszek (Eds.)

Evaluation of Novel Approaches to Software Engineering

15th International Conference, ENASE 2020
Prague, Czech Republic, May 5–6, 2020
Revised Selected Papers

 Springer

Editors
Raian Ali
Hamad Bin Khalifa University
Doha, Qatar

Hermann Kaindl
TU Wien
Vienna, Austria

Leszek A. Maciaszek
Wrocław University of Economics Institute
of Business Informatics
Wrocław, Poland

Department of Computing
Macquarie University
Sydney, Australia

ISSN 1865-0929   ISSN 1865-0937 (electronic)
Communications in Computer and Information Science
ISBN 978-3-030-70005-8   ISBN 978-3-030-70006-5 (eBook)
https://doi.org/10.1007/978-3-030-70006-5

This Springer imprint is published by the registered company Springer Nature Switzerland AG
The registered company address is: Gewerbestrasse 11, 6330 Cham, Switzerland

Preface

The present book includes extended and revised versions of a set of selected papers from the 15th International Conference on Evaluation of Novel Approaches to Software Engineering (ENASE 2020), held as an online event from May 5 to 6, 2020.

ENASE 2020 received 96 paper submissions from 30 countries, of which 20% are finally included in this book as extended versions. These papers were selected by the event chairs and their selection is based on a number of criteria that include the classifications and comments provided by the program committee members, the session chairs' assessment and also the program chairs' global view of all papers included in the technical program. The authors of selected papers were then invited to submit a revised and extended version of their paper having at least 30% innovative material. In addition, an extended version of a paper from ENASE 2019 and a keynote paper of ENASE 2020 are included in this book.

The mission of ENASE (Evaluation of Novel Approaches to Software Engineering) is to be a prime international forum to discuss and publish research findings and IT industry experiences with relation to novel approaches to software engineering. The conference acknowledges evolution in systems and software thinking due to contemporary shifts of computing paradigms to e-services, cloud computing, mobile connectivity, business processes, and societal participation. By publishing the latest research on novel approaches to software engineering and by evaluating them against systems and software quality criteria, ENASE conferences advance knowledge and research in software engineering, including and emphasizing service-oriented, business-process–driven, and ubiquitous mobile computing. ENASE aims at identifying the most hopeful trends and proposing new directions for consideration by researchers and practitioners involved in large-scale systems and software development, integration, deployment, delivery, maintenance and evolution.

The papers included in this book contribute to the understanding of relevant trends of current research on novel approaches to software engineering for the development and maintenance of systems and applications, specifically with relation to: business process management and engineering, requirements engineering, ontology engineering, software architecture, aspect-oriented programming, parallel programming support, automated program repair, software patterns, cloud services, middleware, model-based software engineering, security risks, functional safety, big data, open-source software, energy-efficient software design, IoT systems development, and self-adaptive systems.

We would like to thank all the authors for their contributions and the reviewers for ensuring the quality of this publication.

May 2020

Raian Ali
Hermann Kaindl
Leszek A. Maciaszek

Organization

Conference Chair

Leszek Maciaszek   Wroclaw University of Economics, Poland
                          and Macquarie University, Australia

Program Co-chairs

Raian Ali   Hamad Bin Khalifa University, Qatar
Hermann Kaindl   TU Wien, Austria

Program Committee

Marco Aiello   University of Stuttgart, Germany
Frederic Andres   National Institute of Informatics, Japan
Issa Atoum   The World Islamic Sciences and Education University,
                          Jordan
Richard Banach   University of Manchester, UK
Jan Blech   Aalto University, Finland
Iuliana Bocicor   Babeş-Bolyai University, Romania
Jessie Carbonnel   LIRMM, CNRS and University of Montpellier, France
Glauco Carneiro   Universidade Salvador (UNIFACS), Brazil
Ruzanna Chitchyan   University of Bristol, UK
William Chu   Tunghai University, Taiwan, Republic of China
Rebeca Cortázar   University of Deusto, Spain
Guglielmo De Angelis   CNR - IASI, Italy
Fatma Dhaou   FSEG Tunis El Manar, Tunisia
Sophie Ebersold   IRIT, France
Angelina Espinoza   University College Cork (UCC), Ireland
Vladimir Estivill-Castro Griffith University, Australia
Anna Fasolino   Università degli Studi di Napoli Federico II, Italy
Maria Ferreira   Universidade Portucalense, Portugal
Tarik Fissaa   ENSIAS Mohammed V University Rabat, Morocco
Stéphane Galland   Université de Technologie de Belfort-Montbéliard,
                          France
Claude Godart   University of Lorraine, France
José-María   Universidad de Alcalá, Spain
  Gutiérrez-Martínez
Hatim Hafiddi   INPT, Morocco
Peter Herrmann   NTNU, Norway
Lom Hillah   LIP6 (CNRS, Sorbonne Université), France
Mirjana Ivanović   University of Novi Sad, Serbia

Stefan Jablonski	University of Bayreuth, Germany
Stanisław Jarząbek	Bialystok University of Technology, Poland
Dongwon Jeong	Kunsan National University, Korea, Republic of
Özgür Kafalı	University of Kent, UK
Georgia Kapitsaki	University of Cyprus, Cyprus
Osama Khaled	The American University in Cairo, Egypt
Siau-Cheng Khoo	National University of Singapore, Singapore
Diana Kirk	The University of Auckland, New Zealand
Piotr Kosiuczenko	WAT, Poland
Jurgita Lieponienė	Panevezys Applied Sciences University, Lithuania
Jorge López	Airbus Defense and Space, France
Ivan Luković	University of Novi Sad, Serbia
Lech Madeyski	Wroclaw University of Science and Technology, Poland
Nazim Madhavji	University of Western Ontario, Canada
Johnny Marques	Instituto Tecnológico de Aeronáutica, Brazil
Patricia Martín-Rodilla	University of A Coruña, Spain
Francesco Mercaldo	National Research Council of Italy (CNR), Italy
Breno Miranda	Federal University of Pernambuco, Brazil
Arthur-Jozsef Molnar	Babeş-Bolyai University, Romania
Ines Mouakher	University of Tunis El Manar, Tunisia
Pornsiri Muenchaisri	Chulalongkorn University, Thailand
Malcolm Munro	Durham University, UK
Cornelius Ncube	The British University in Dubai, UAE
Andrzej Niesler	Wroclaw University of Economics, Poland
Zsuzsanna Onet-Marian	Babeş-Bolyai University, Romania
Janis Osis	Riga Technical University, Latvia
Meriem Ouederni	IRIT/INPT, France
Mourad Oussalah	Laboratoire Lina CNRS Fre 2729, University of Nantes, France
Siew Hock Ow	University of Malaya, Malaysia
Claus Pahl	Free University of Bozen-Bolzano, Italy
Ricardo Pérez-Castillo	Instituto de Tecnologías y Sistemas de Información (ITSI), University of Castilla-La Mancha, Spain
Dana Petcu	West University of Timişoara, Romania
Alexander Poth	Volkswagen Aktiengesellschaft, Germany
Deepika Prakash	NIIT University, India
Naveen Prakash	IIITD, India
Adam Przybyłek	Gdansk University of Technology, Poland
Elke Pulvermüller	Osnabrück University, Germany
Łukasz Radliński	West Pomeranian University of Technology in Szczecin, Poland
Philippe Roose	LIUPPA/IUT de Bayonne/UPPA, France
Irina Rychkova	Université Paris 1 Panthéon-Sorbonne, France
Camille Salinesi	Université Paris 1 Panthéon-Sorbonne, France
Antonella Santone	University of Molise, Italy

Markus Schatten	University of Zagreb, Croatia
Rainer Schmidt	Munich University of Applied Sciences, Germany
Richa Sharma	Lock Haven University, USA
Josep Silva	Universitat Politècnica de València, Spain
Michał Śmiałek	Warsaw University of Technology, Poland
Ioana Sora	Politehnica University of Timişoara, Romania
Andreas Speck	Christian-Albrecht University of Kiel, Germany
Maria Spichkova	RMIT University, Australia
Witold Staniszkis	Rodan Development, Poland
Chang-ai Sun	University of Science and Technology Beijing, China
Jakub Swacha	University of Szczecin, Poland
Stephanie Teufel	University of Fribourg, Switzerland
Hanh Nhi Tran	University of Toulouse, France
Christos Troussas	University of West Attica, Greece
Feng-Jian Wang	National Chiao Tung University, Taiwan, Republic of China
Bernhard Westfechtel	University of Bayreuth, Germany
Danny Weyns	KU Leuven, Belgium
Martin Wirsing	Ludwig-Maximilians-Universität München, Germany
Igor Wojnicki	AGH University of Science and Technology, Poland
Michalis Xenos	University of Patras, Greece
Nina Yevtushenko	Ivannikov Institute for System Programming of RAS, Russian Federation
Alfred Zimmermann	Reutlingen University, Germany

Additional Reviewers

Natalia Kushik	Telecom SudParis, France
Abdelfetah Saadi	Houari Boumediene University of Science and Technology, Algeria

Invited Speakers

Xavier Franch	Universitat Politècnica de Catalunya, Spain
Alon Halevy	Facebook AI, USA
Stanisław Jarząbek	Bialystok University of Technology, Poland

Contents

Service Science and Business Information Systems

Resilient Process Modeling and Execution Using Process Graphs

Frank Nordemann[1(✉)], Ralf Tönjes[1], Elke Pulvermüller[2], and Heiko Tapken[1]

[1] Faculty of Engineering and Computer Science,
Osnabrück University of Applied Sciences,
Albrechtstr. 30, 49076 Osnabrück, Germany
{f.nordemann,r.toenjes,h.tapken}@hs-osnabrueck.de
[2] Institute of Computer Science, University of Osnabrück,
Wachsbleiche 27, 49090 Osnabrück, Germany
elke.pulvermueller@informatik.uni-osnabrueck.de

Abstract. Unreliable communication challenges the execution of business processes. Operation breaks down due to intermittent, delayed or completely failing connectivity. The widely used Business Model and Notation 2.0 (BPMN) provides limited flexibility to address connectivity-related issues and misses a technique to verify process resilience. This paper presents a graph-based approach to identify resilient process paths in BPMN business processes. After a process-to-graph transition, graph-based search algorithms such as shortest-path and all-paths are applied to list resilient configurations. Evaluation of the approach confirms reasonable performance requirements, good scalability characteristics, and a significant resilience improvement. Recommendations for the practical insert of algorithms and metrics conclude the paper.

Keywords: BPMN · Business process resilience · Directed acyclic graphs · Unreliable communication environments

1 Introduction

Resilient modeling and execution of business processes can be a challenging task. Depending on the scenario and application environment, communication conditions between process participants may change over time. BPMN, the major process definition language in the industry, does not focus on modeling and maintaining resilient operation in terms of communication. For instance, there are no options to verify resilient operation of a process at design time. The integration of alternatives for failing message flows is often cumbersome and inflexible. Domain experts are unsure whether or not processes will work as expected. This results in breaking process executions, especially in unreliable communication environments.

Based on the concepts of *resilient BPMN (rBPMN)*, a BPMN metamodel extension for unreliable environments, a graph-based approach to identify

© Springer Nature Switzerland AG 2021
R. Ali et al. (Eds.): ENASE 2020, CCIS 1375, pp. 3–23, 2021.
https://doi.org/10.1007/978-3-030-70006-5_1

resilient process paths is introduced. While the transition of process models to directed acyclic graphs is explained in depth in [19], this paper focuses on the evaluation of the graph-based resilience analysis of business processes. The evaluation observes the performance requirements and scalability characteristics of graph-based search algorithms operating on typical process graphs. Resilience of identified paths is evaluated using scenario-driven metrics, recommendations are provided for the practical insert of the approach. The main research contributions of the paper include:

1. Implementation of a process graph generator for resilience evaluation.
2. Evaluation of graph algorithm performance requirements/scalability characteristics on different devices.
3. Resilience evaluation of identified paths using scenario-driven metrics.
4. Recommendations for the practical insert of graph algorithms and resilience metrics.

The paper is organized as follows: Challenges of resilient process operation are outlined in Sect. 2, including a brief introduction of *rBPMN*. Section 3 describes the transition of process models to directed graphs and the algorithms to identify resilient process paths. The approach is evaluated in Sect. 4, followed by a discussion of evaluation results and recommendations for practical usage in Sect. 5. Section 6 presents related work before a conclusion is presented in Sect. 7.

2   Challenges of Resilient Process Operation

This section outlines the shortcomings of BPMN when modeling and executing processes taking place in unreliable communication environments. Furthermore, *rBPMN* and its resilience strategies are introduced.

2.1   Business Model and Notation 2.0

BPMN 2.0 is one of the most prominent process definition languages in the industry. Its metamodel allows to use a variety of modeling elements in different application areas. If needed, an extension/adaptation of the metamodel is possible.

Unreliable communication challenges resilient process operation. Processes may break down due to intermittent, delayed, or broken connectivity between process participants. BPMN was not explicitly designed to handle unreliable communication. Domain experts often end up in cumbersome and time-consuming process modeling. Many models only provide limited flexibility to address connectivity issues. No mechanisms to verify resilient process design exist, resulting in failing process executions.

The shortcomings of BPMN in aspects of addressing connectivity issues are elaborated in the example presented in Fig. 1. A process *Ex1* is calling service functionality from a third party participant. Since message flows may fail due to connectivity issues, alternatives for the service call have been implemented by a domain expert.

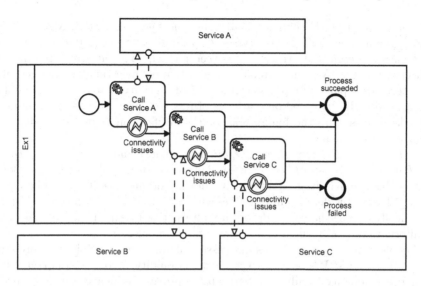

Fig. 1. Process *Ex1* with limited flexibility, modeled in BPMN.

The process model only includes limited flexibility: If a service is not available, the next service is chosen. The sequence order of calling services is fixed. If no service is callable, the process will fail. Instead of using interrupting error events, gateways could be used to design the service choice in an agile way. However, modeling effort would increase rapidly to intercept and to react on failing message flows. The resulting process could still break down if no service is available. As further outlined in [18], other modeling elements such as business rule tasks can enhance the flexibility of process models. However, the required knowledge about handing and modeling connectivity issues rises. The focus of the actual model shifts from the original objective of the application domain to handling technical aspects of communication. Furthermore, a domain expert is not able to verify the model for reasons of resilience optimization.

2.2   Resilient BPMN

The metamodel extension *resilient BPMN (rBPMN)* adds new modeling elements to the BPMN tool palette addressing the issues of unreliable communication. The modeling elements are depicted in Fig. 2.

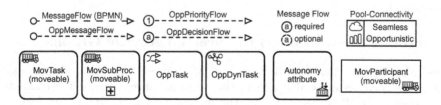

Fig. 2. Modeling elements introduced by *resilient BPMN (rBPMN)*.

First of all, *rBPMN* extends traditional message flows of BPMN to integrate opportunistic message flow types. *Opportunistic message flows (OppMessageFlows)* represent data transfers between participants which may fail due to connectivity issues. A scenario-related description of the estimated connectivity characteristics is part of OppMessageFlows. Connectivity characteristics may be *i)* estimated or be *ii)* based on statistics of previous process runs. The connectivity descriptions are the foundation for the verification of process resilience, elaborated subsequently.

Opportunistic Priority Flows (OppPriorityFlows) and *Opportunistic Decision Flows (OppDecisionFlows)* are specializations of OppMessageFlows. Both types enable the definition of alternatives for failing message flows. While OppPriorityFlows allow defining alternatives with fixed priorities, OppDecisionFlows dynamically choose the most appropriate alternative based on characteristics of the alternatives (e.g. resilience, accuracy of operation, cost).

Complete prevention of breaking message flows is not possible in many scenarios. Hence, *rBPMN* allows to move functionality across participants. By moving functionality locally to a participant, process resilience is ensured even if message flows break down. *Movable Tasks, Sub-Processes* and *Participants (MovTasks, MovSubProc., MovParticipants)* offer functionality, which may be used by *Opportunistic Tasks (OppTaks/OppDynTasks)*. OppDynTasks further extend process flexibility by adding dynamically appearing participants, which have not been explicitly modeled before, as alternatives. Finally, annotations allow to indicate locally moved functionality, the connectivity type of participants, and to label message flows as required or optional.

OppMessageFlows and its derivatives are associated with scenario-related connectivity descriptions. A description includes expected characteristics like the minimum and mean bandwidth as well as the possibility and timeout frame for communication outages. Additional descriptions map out the message properties (e.g. message size, message interval) and the required Quality of Service (QoS, e.g. delivery time, failure probability). Correlating the connectivity, message and QoS descriptions allows to state whether or not a message can be sent successfully. Calculations also allow predicting how likely the transfer is to fail. Background information about resilience calculations of message flows and the depicted *rBPMN* elements of Fig. 2 can be found in [18].

Resilience calculations in [18] only consider message flows and do not present a process-wide resilience analysis. Besides, the paper misses mechanisms to automate the resilience analysis and to compare different resilient process paths. These facts motivate the graph-based resilience approach developed in [19] and evaluated in this paper.

3   From Process Models to Directed Acyclic Graphs

Resilience metrics, the transition from BPMN process models to graphs, and the graph analysis are elaborated in this section. Since many of the contents have been originally covered in [19], the presentation is shortened and focuses on reader understanding for the remaining paper parts.

3.1   Resilience Metrics

A communication-resilient process will not fail its operation in case of connectivity failures. But, what is the right way to measure resilience? Can resilient process configurations be compared to each other? Is one process path *more resilient* than another? Is it possible to rank paths according to their resilience?

Whether a process path is resilient or not depends on the edges part of the path. If a single edge (representing a message flow) is non-resilient based on *rBPMN's* calculation, the whole path will be non-resilient. Unforeseen changes of communication characteristics at runtime may turn a path from resilient to non-resilient.

A path includes a number of edges $n \in \mathbb{N}$ between process start and end. The range of weight values representing resilience calculation results can be defined according to the scenario requirements. An edge weight may be a value $R_e \in \mathbb{R}$, a normalized value $R_e \in \mathbb{R} | 0 \leq R_e \leq 1$ or an inverted, normalized value $R_e \in \mathbb{R} | 0 \leq R_e \leq 1$. Inverted values are useful when applying shortest-path algorithms, which find the path with the minimum total edge weight.

Most scenarios require to differentiate resilient paths from each other. An option is to apply the shortest-path approach by summarizing the edge weights along the path, and to pick the path with best total weight value $R_t = \sum_{i=1}^{n} R_{e_i}$. However, the chosen path probably includes non-resilient edges depending on the concrete characteristics of the process graph.

If resilient operation is the main factor, the path which is most unlikely to change to non-resilient operation due to unforeseen scenario behavior is desired. A concept is to choose the path with the best path level $R_l = min(R_{e_1}, ..., R_{e_n})$, which represents the minimum edge weight along the path. Another option is to calculate the total distance to non-resilient edges R_d along the path. Here, the ranking of resilient paths is possible by prioritizing the path with the highest distance to non-resilient operation. In scenarios missing a resilient process path, R_d may help to find a path that barely misses resilient operation.

Other metrics such as the average $R_a = R_t/n$ and maximum edge weight $R_{max} = max(R_{e_1}, ..., R_{e_n})$ or the range of the path $R_r = R_{max} - R_l$ are useful to understand the characteristics of the applied scenario. Keep in mind that inverting edge weights also requires to invert metrics (e.g. $min \rightarrow max$). The evaluation in this paper focuses on metrics for the total path weight R_t, the path level R_l, and the path distance R_d.

3.2   Transition Rules

Applying graph-based search algorithms on process models requires to translate models into a graphs first. An example process *Ex2* is provided in Fig. 3. *Ex2* includes XOR-gateways to either call *P1* using *T1* or to execute *T2*, which requires no communication to another participant.

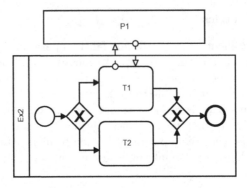

Fig. 3. Process example *Ex2*.

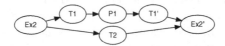

Fig. 4. Process graph of *Ex2*.

The corresponding process graph of *Ex2* is depicted in Fig. 4. It is an Acyclic Directed Graph (DAG) with a start vertex *Ex2* and an end vertex *Ex2'*. Two paths exist between both vertices: The upper path follows *T1*, and within *T1* the participant *P1* is called. The lower path simply calls *T2* and ends the process.

The graph transition completes with the addition of edge weights representing calculated resilience values. Two message flows that may fail are part of the process: A service at *P1* is requested and a reply is sent back to *T1*. The corresponding results of *rBPMN's* resilience calculations are assigned to these two edges. All other edges are assigned with resilient edge weights since they are not exposed to unreliable communication.

A graph analysis of *Ex2* will find at least one resilient process path (*Ex2* → *T2* → *Ex2'*). The second path using *T1* may be identified as resilient if the connectivity between *T1* and *P1* is adequate.

The transition of process example *Ex2* is fairly simple. Including BPMN elements such as inclusive gateways, parallel gateways with merging XOR-gateways, multi-instance activities, (interrupting) events, loops, and alternatives for message flows into process models leads to a much more complex transition procedure. Decisions have to be taken if a process path needs to be separated/split or extended. A detailed description of the process-to-graph transition including a list of transition rules is provided by [19].

3.3 Graph Analysis

Graph-based search algorithms can find resilient process paths in a graph. The following options should be considered for analysis.

Shortest-Path. Shortest-path algorithms are typically used to find the graph path with minimum cost. Therefore, edge weights along a path are summarized and the path with the minimum total weight is selected. Different shortest-path algorithms like Dijkstra, Bellman-Ford and A* are available.

All-Paths. All-paths algorithms find all available paths between a source and a destination vertex. The provided list of paths is an optimal input for resilience metrics, which may identify the path with best path level R_l or best path distance R_d. If useful, it is also possible to combine metrics. For instance: If multiple paths with the best path level R_l exist, the best total path weight R_t can be selected.

Shortest-Path on Adjusted Graph. Shortest-path algorithms do not prevent the inclusion of non-resilient edges in the chosen path. Removing non-resilient edges from the graph before analysis leads to finding a resilient path, if one is available. However, an analysis can also result in finding no path, since edges have been removed from the graph.

4 Evaluation

This section evaluates the usage of graph-based search algorithms for the identification of resilient process paths. A broad variety of possible process graphs is analyzed. The evaluations' focus is on identifying performance/time requirements to run the algorithms as well as their scalability in growing graphs. Furthermore, the resilience of identified process paths is evaluated in regard to operation in unreliable environments.

4.1 Evaluation Scenario

Processes often include a variety of participants, geographically distributed across the area of application. The technical configuration of the participants/their devices may be represented by Cloud-Systems, PCs, smartphones, sensors, and actors. Since many processes in unreliable communication environments use performance-restricted devices, the evaluation is performed on a *Raspberry Pi Zero WH*. This Raspberry-configuration features an ARM-1GHz-processor (BCM 2835 SOC) and 512 MB of RAM.

The software measuring the performance requirements is written in Java and executed on the Raspberry using the OpenJDK Runtime Environment 1.8. The JGraphT-Library [13] provides the implementations for graph-based search algorithms used in the evaluation.

4.2 Generation of Process Graphs

Depending on the objectives and application areas, business processes differ in their characteristics in terms of structure and size.

While the concrete structure of different processes varies, most include a number of decision points. Based on the configuration and the value of process variables, one path or another is chosen. In a graph, these decision points are represented by multiple edges originating from a common vertex and splitting the path to the process end. When analyzing graph-based search algorithms, the number of graph decision points is the challenging aspect. Path sequences avoiding decision points do not affect their performance significantly. Hence, these sequences are not considered in this evaluation.

A process graph generator has been designed and implemented for the evaluation of process resilience. The generator builds up a graph by splitting paths at each following vertex. To reflect the varying sizes of possible process graphs, horizontal and vertical graph layers (H-Layers/V-Layers) are introduced. H-Layers define how often a path is split (horizontally) at a vertex. In other words, H-Layers describe the number of outgoing edges of a vertex.

Additionally, V-Layers configure the number of follow-up vertices in which the process path is split by outgoing edges. After the defined number of V-Layers, the following vertical layers are used to merge the previously separated paths again. This results in a DAG with a starting and an ending vertex, including a high number of different process paths.

During the graph generation, a random weight value $R_e \in \mathbb{R} | 0 \leq R_e \leq 1$ is assigned to every created edge. The weights represent normalized and inverted resilience values. Inversion allows to easily comply with shortest-path algorithms. In regard to resilience, a low weight has the meaning of a high resilience value and vice versa. The threshold until what value a weight is considered to be resilient is adjusted during different types of analysis in the evaluation.

The graph generation process with a continuous H-Layer of 2 is illustrated in Figs. 5, 6, 7 and 8. Increasing the number of V-Layers quickly increases the number of decision points in the graph. The graphs generated in this evaluation include up to 7 V-Layers. However, the majority of business processes is expected to use up to 5 V-Layers. Table 1 illustrates the number of vertices, number of edges, and the edge-vertex-ratio in graphs with different H-Layers and V-Layers.

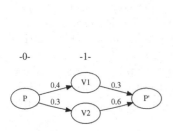

Fig. 5. A generated process graph with 1 V-Layer.

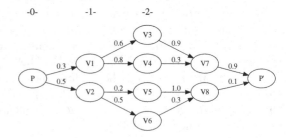

Fig. 6. Process graph with 2 V-Layers.

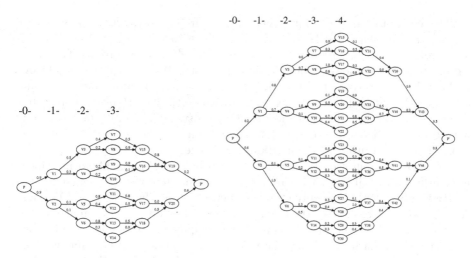

Fig. 7. Graph with 3 V-Layers.   **Fig. 8.** Graph with 4 V-Layers.

Table 1. Characteristics of generated graphs.

H-Layers	V-Layers	Vertices	Edges	Edge-Vertex-Ratio
2	1	4	4	1.0
2	2	10	12	1.2
2	3	22	28	1.27
2	4	46	60	1.31
2	5	94	124	1.32
2	6	190	252	1.33
2	7	382	508	1.33
3	3	53	78	1.47
3	4	161	240	1.49
4	3	106	168	1.58
4	4	426	680	1.60

4.3   Performance Analysis

The performance requirements are identified by measuring the time of a path
search operation. Time frames required to create new graph objects and to allocate memory for them are excluded for reasons of comparability. The H-Layer is
configured to a value of 2, resulting in two outgoing edges of every splitting vertex. The number of V-Layers varies throughout the performance analysis. The
JGraphT implementations of the shortest-path algorithms Dijkstra, Bellman-
Ford, and A* as well as an all-paths algorithm based on Dijkstra are part of the
evaluation.

The computation times for a path search from process start to end are depicted in Figs. 9 and 10. The charts are based on 1000 repetitions per V-Layer and algorithm, the lines represent the mean values of these repetitions. The evaluation indicates the lowest computation time for Dijkstra, followed closely by Bellman-Ford. Starting at V-Layers around 5 to 6, A* requires more computation time compared to the other two shortest-path algorithms. This may be due to A* requiring a list of vertices as it's heuristic, where only start and end have been provided. At V-Layers 1 to 4, only minor differences exist between shortest-path algorithms. Computations finish after 4 ms on average.

The most computation time was consumed by the all-paths algorithm since it identifies all available paths from start to end. However, the difference to shortest-path calculations only starts to increase radically at 5 to 7 V-Layers. At V-Layers of 1 to 4, all-paths calculations end after up to 10 ms on average.

A closer look at the distribution of the computation times is provided by Figs. 11 and 12. Each box encapsulates 50% of the measured time frame values, the median is depicted by a (green) line within each box. The whiskers on top and at the bottom of a box show the distribution of remaining values according to [23], outliers are omitted.

The boxplot in Fig. 11 illustrates computation times at 7 V-Layers. Times for the all-paths algorithm show a distribution around 75 to 120 ms. The shortest-path algorithms take roughly 10% of that computation time (10–30 ms). At 4 V-Layers, the all-paths algorithm is able to operate in a closer range to the shortest-path algorithms (cf. Fig. 12). Computation times stay below 12 ms.

Figure 13 depicts computation times for Dijkstra at V-Layers 1 to 7. While computation times are about equal for graphs with up to 2 V-Layers (cf. Fig. 14), the effort increases consistently with growing V-Layers. However, computation times stay below 15 ms at all V-Layers in the evaluation.

The corresponding Cumulative Distribution Function (CDF) and Kernel Density Estimations (KDE) for V-Layers 7 and 4 are illustrated in Figs. 15, 16, 17 and 18. Again, differences in required computation times at V-Layer 7 are identifiable between A* and all-paths compared to Dijkstra/Bellman-Ford. The distribution of all-paths computation times varies more than the times of the other algorithms. At V-Layer 4, some minor differences exist between the shortest-path algorithms.

Summarizing the results for the computation time evaluation of the different algorithms indicates minor differences at V-Layers 1 to 4. At V-Layers 5 to 7, the gap between shortest-path and all-paths algorithms grows increasingly.

4.4 Resilience Analysis

Shortest-path algorithms calculate the lowest cost by summarizing the edge weights of a path. As described in Sect. 3.3, this may not be optimal. The question arises if the path level R_l or the path distance R_d are a better choice to measure and optimize resilience. Besides, the removal of non-resilient edges before shortest-path calculations seems to be promising. These aspects are evaluated subsequently.

The all-paths algorithm returns a list of possible graph paths between start and end of the process. Using this list, a path with an increased path level R_l compared to the path level provided by a shortest-path analysis may be identified. Depending on the scenario-based definition of resilient edges, an increased path level may result in a resilient path compared to a non-resilient shortest-path.

Figure 19 compares the path level R_l of an all-paths and a Dijkstra shortest-path analysis. While the total path weight R_t is lower ($\rightarrow$ better) for Dijkstra, the path level R_l is lower ($\rightarrow$ better) for the all-paths analysis. The boxplot in Fig. 20 illustrates the path level distribution for V-Layers 1 to 7. The all-paths-variant can optimize the path level within limits. Depending on the resilient edge definition this may result in a resilient all-paths choice against a non-resilient shortest-path.

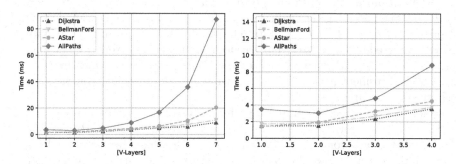

Fig. 9. Path computation times. **Fig. 10.** Computation times close-up.

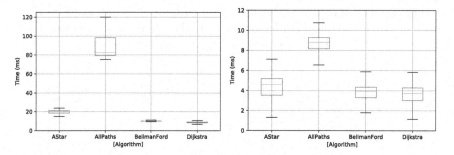

Fig. 11. Distribution of computation times at 7 V-Layers. (Colour figure online) **Fig. 12.** Distribution of computation times at 4 V-Layers. (Colour figure online)

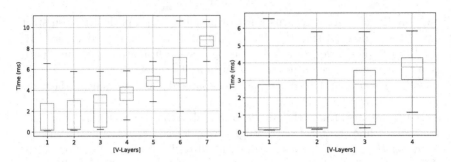

Fig. 13. Distribution of computation times for Dijkstra.

Fig. 14. Close-up of computation time distribution for Dijkstra.

Another optimization approach is to minimize the total distance to resilient edges R_d (cf. Sect. 3.3). For the evaluation in Fig. 21 and Fig. 22, edges are defined as resilient for $R_e \in \mathbb{R} | 0 \le R_e \le 0.75$. The charts indicate an optimized path distance compared to the shortest-path, especially at high V-Layers. The median in the boxplot of Fig. 22 remains at 0 for the all-paths analysis, which maps to at least 50% of resilient paths. This is a considerable improvement compared to the shortest-path outcomes.

Besides selecting paths from an all-paths analysis list based on chosen metrics, shortest-path algorithms can be tweaked to increase resilience. By deleting all non-resilient edges from a graph before a shortest-path analysis, the resulting path will represent a resilient configuration. However, there may not necessarily be a path in the adjusted graph anymore.

Figure 23 and Fig. 24 illustrate the total path weights R_t and path levels R_l for Dijkstra operating on an adjusted graph without non-resilient edges and operating on an unmodified graph. Again, a resilient edge was configured as $R_e \in \mathbb{R} | 0 \le R_e \le 0.75$. The charts indicate improvements for R_t and R_l.

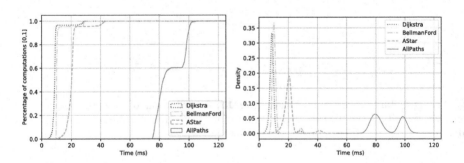

Fig. 15. CDF at 7 V-Layers.

Fig. 16. KDE at 7 V-Layers.

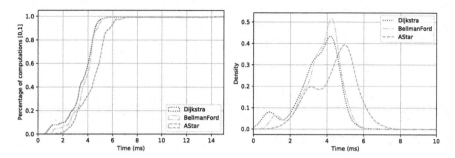

Fig. 17. CDF at 4 V-Layers.   **Fig. 18.** KDE at 4 V-Layers.

The most relevant aspect to compare the different approaches is to measure the resilience of the identified paths. Resilient edge values of $R_e \in \mathbb{R} | 0 \leq R_e \leq 0.75$ and $R_e \in \mathbb{R} | 0 \leq R_e \leq 0.5$ have been chosen for the evaluation. The number of non-resilient paths within a test out of 1000 runs is depicted in Fig. 25 and Fig. 26. The lines of a Dijkstra analysis based on an adjusted graph and two all-paths analysis (based on path level R_l/path distance R_d) are compared to a Dijkstra analysis on the original graph. In both charts, the all-paths analysis and the Dijkstra adjusted graph analysis map on the same line. Results show a significant improvement by reducing the number of non-resilient paths. However, the improvements are minor when using a resilient edge value of 0.5.

Since the comparison between the optimized analysis variants shows no difference in terms of their resilience, it is unclear which analysis should be preferred. A comparison of the computation times of the optimized analysis methods with their original Dijkstra and all-paths variants is depicted in Fig. 27 and Fig. 28. The results indicate a slightly larger computation time for the adjusted Dijkstra analysis compared to Dijkstra on an unmodified graph. This is due to additional effort for removing non-resilient edges from the graph. However, this is only valid for up to 4 V-Layers. At higher V-Layers, the adjusted variant saves computation time since many possible, but non-resilient paths have already been removed by

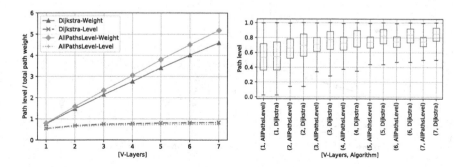

Fig. 19. Optimizing the path level R_l.   **Fig. 20.** Distribution of R_l.

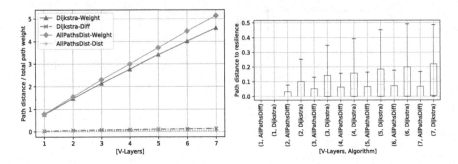

Fig. 21. Path distance R_d.   **Fig. 22.** Distribution of R_d.

deleting corresponding edges. The additional computation effort for the two all-paths-based variants is minor. A difference between all-paths and all-paths-level can be hardly identified in Fig. 27 and Fig. 28.

4.5 Scalability Analysis

The scalability of using graph-based search algorithms to find resilient paths in process graphs is indicated by the Figures presenting the computation times at different V-Layers in Sect. 4.3. This section continues the evaluation by further increasing the graph size and adding a second, more powerful computation device.

In addition to evaluations based on an H-Layer of 2, analysis for H-Layers of 3 and 4 have been added. An Apple MacBook Pro (Early 2015) with a 3,1 GHz Dual-Core Intel Core i7 processor and 16 GB of RAM acts as a second device. The Java Runtime Environment is configured to only use 0.5 GB of the available RAM.

The charts for the extended analysis on the Raspberry Pi Zero are depicted in Fig. 29 and Fig. 30. The Raspberry is challenged at a growing number of vertices

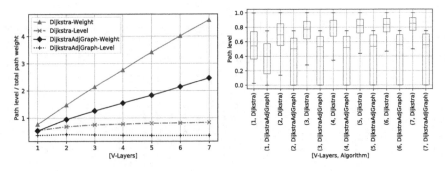

Fig. 23. Dijkstra operating on unmodified and on adjusted graphs.   **Fig. 24.** R_l-Distribution of Dijkstra variants.

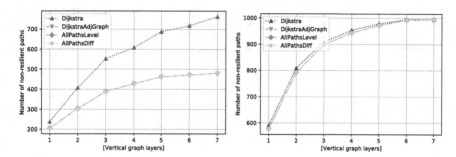

Fig. 25. Resilient edge $R_e \in \mathbb{R}|0 \leq R_e \leq 0.75$.

Fig. 26. Resilient edge $R_e \in \mathbb{R}|0 \leq R_e \leq 0.5$.

and edges. Dijkstra shortest-path computations may take up to 1 s on average, while all-paths computations may require up to 12 s.

The performance of the MacBook Pro is illustrated in Fig. 31 and Fig. 32. Computations for all-paths may take up to 250 ms on average for an H-Layer of 4. However, the results indicate that the MacBook Pro is not challenged by graphs with high amounts of vertices and edges. This is especially the case for shortest-path algorithms.

5 Discussion and Recommendations

The results of the evaluation executed on a Raspberry Pi Zero WH indicate no performance and scalability issues when computing resilient paths in typical process graphs. The computation effort for all-paths algorithms is significantly higher compared to shortest-path algorithms, especially in large graphs. However, the required average time frame of about 90 ms for an all-paths calculation at V-Layer 7 is comparatively small. In particular, this is true if a process employs full-feature BPM runtime engines which usually show higher performance demands. The extended evaluation with even larger graphs on a

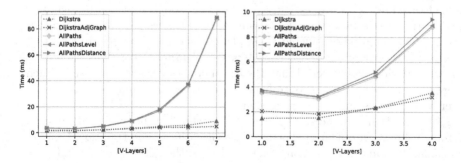

Fig. 27. Path computation times.

Fig. 28. Close-up of comp. times.

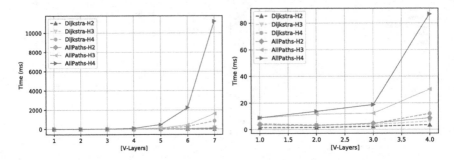

Fig. 29. Computation times on Raspberry Pi Zero WH.

Fig. 30. Close-up of computation times on Raspberry Pi Zero WH.

Raspberry Pi Zero WH and a MacBook Pro demonstrates the scalability of the graph-based resilience analysis. If computation time is not highly critical, a low-performance device such as the Raspberry may be used. In other scenarios, a more powerful device is suggested to speed up computation time.

Comparing the different shortest-path algorithms Dijkstra, Bellman-Ford, and A* shows minor differences at V-Layers 1 to 5. Noticeable differences can be identified between A* and Dijkstra/Bellman-Ford at V-Layers 6 and 7. This may be due to A* requiring provision of vertices as a heuristic, and only the start and end vertex were provided. In practice, selecting a shortest-path algorithm may be based on available implementations and implementation effort.

It is believed that the majority of process graphs will not exceed the number of 46 vertices/60 edges (e.g. 2 H-Layers/4 V-Layers). At least, this was determined for the OPeRAte research project [22]. OPeRAte orchestrates process chains in the area of agriculture, where multiple actors cooperate in unreliable communication environments (e.g. on farms and fields). The agricultural process chains including slurry applications and maize harvest scenarios typically range between V-Layers 2 to 4 with an H-Layer of 2. Here, a Raspberry Pi Zero WH would fully address the performance requirements.

Computations for a resilient process path may be repeated multiple times during process runtime. Communication conditions may change over time, resulting in changed resilience values/corresponding edge weights. Scenarios including a high variability or new processes missing solid statistics are prone to recalculations. This should be considered when planning performance requirements.

A more critical performance consideration of graph algorithms should be done when devices less powerful than the Raspberry Pi Zero WH are used. When using sensors, actors, or microcontrollers, computation times may be significantly larger with impacts on process operation.

The evaluation of process resilience with defined values for resilient edge weights outlines a problem of shortest-path algorithms. The traditional way of minimizing cost may include non-resilient edges in the path, resulting in failing processes. Since all shortest-path algorithms follow the same objective, there is no difference in the chosen process path among them.

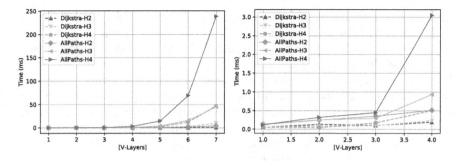

Fig. 31. Computation times on MacBook Pro.

Fig. 32. Close-up of computation times on MacBook Pro.

Analyzing the path list examined by an all-paths algorithm may result in finding *more resilient* process paths. Choosing the path with the best path level R_l is reducing the number of non-resilient paths. Considering the path with the best path distance R_d represents another possibility. Although there is no difference in resilience optimization between path level and path distance in this evaluation, other scenarios may show different outcomes. The additional computation effort for both all-paths variants is reasonable.

There is also a possibility to benefit from the reduced computation effort of a shortest-path analysis and to identify resilient paths at the same time. By removing non-resilient edges from the process graph prior to a shortest-path algorithm, no unreliable edges are chosen as part of the shortest-path anymore. The Dijkstra-Adjusted-Graph procedure is able to keep up with the two all-paths variants in terms of reducing non-resilient process paths. However, this approach may not be able to identify any path between start and end. This is not recommended for dynamic scenarios with changing communication conditions, where a previously considered non-resilient path may become resilient over time.

In general, it is recommended to examine the resilience of a process at design time. Resilience may be estimated by using statistics about communication conditions from previous process executions. In the case of new or dynamically changing scenarios, it is suggested to include a buffer into the resilience estimation values. If the conditions are worse than expected, there is still a chance that the included buffer takes over the difference.

Design time analysis also helps to get familiar with the concrete scenario characteristics. This eases to decide which resilience metric and graph-based algorithm fulfill the requirements best. Finally, the process itself may be adapted if the danger for non-resilient operation is too high.

The all-paths algorithm using the best path level and the Adjusted-Graph-Dijkstra approach operated well in the evaluation. Both reduced the number of non-resilient paths in the analysis and seem to be a good choice for many application areas. If computation time is critical, the Dijkstra algorithm operating on an adjusted graph without any non-resilient edges has to be preferred. The computation effort for the adjusted Dijkstra is less compared to all-paths algorithms, especially for high V-Layers. Adjusted Dijkstra is also a good choice when there is solid knowledge about the resilience behavior of edge weights in a scenario. The approach may be a suboptimal choice in dynamic scenarios since there is a possibility of not finding any path.

In addition, the path level seems to be a good indicator to enhance resilience. Choosing the path with minimum distance to resilience may also work well for scenarios that do not find any resilient process path. The advantage of an all-paths analysis is to have all available options on hand. If performance requirements are less strict, a combination of different metrics to choose the best available path may be an optimal, scenario-based solution.

As a recommendation, an all-paths analysis with selected metrics should be compared to shortest-path analysis at design time. Identification of scenario characteristics and the suitability of different metrics support the development of a performance-optimized approach for runtime analysis. Using the graph-based approach, automation of the resilience analysis at process runtime is possible. In scenarios that have a high chance of becoming non-resilient, a warning may be sent to the user about expected connectivity-issues in the future.

While resilience may be an important aspect of many business processes, there are often other aspects to consider for process execution. A typical example is provided in [20], which presents a graph-based approach to find an optimal process path in terms of resilience, accuracy, cost, and time. The same applies to the evaluation results of this paper: Edges do not have to describe the resilience between activities and participants in unreliable communication environments, but basically can be used for any aspect relevant to a process.

6   Related Work

The Business Process Model and Notation has been in the interest of research and industry since its first release in 2004. The second version was released in 2011 [21] and is part of numerous publications and products, such as commercial BPMN runtime engines. It has been extended in various ways for different use cases [4], such as the Internet of Things [6,17] and Cyber Physical Systems [3,12]. It is applied in Wireless Sensor Networks [25] and was extended to inspect and include Quality of Information [10,14].

Business process resilience is a major topic in the literature. Different aspects of resilient operation are considered. An important topic is the reliability of tasks and processes [1,2,24]. Effects of human, nun-human and ambient assisted living behavior are studied [9,15]. Compensation of faulty tasks for process service plan execution is addressed [16].

Business processes and DAG's have been part of other publications in the past. In general, the publications map activities to graph vertices and sequence flows/message flows to graph edges. Mostly, XOR-gateways are translated by separating a graph path in different outgoing edges of a vertex. The translation of other modeling elements differs. Specifically, parallel and inclusive gateways, merging XOR-gateways splitting the BPMN token, multi-instance activities, loops and events are often not addressed or are translated following the objectives of the concrete approach. Furthermore, the process definition language of choice and the kinds of applied algorithms are divers.

[8] elaborates a transition procedure based on formal semantics for mapping BPMN processes to Petri Nets. The objective is to apply existing process analysis methods available for Perti Nets. The same authors extend the approach for task and control flow similarity checking of processes in [7]. The application of performance optimization techniques originating from the area of databases motivates [11] to translate processes to directed graphs. The optimization procedure reorders activities and tries to parallelize process parts. Finally, [5] advises on human activities by using DAG's.

None of the listed publications focuses on analyzing and optimizing process operation in terms of communication-resilient execution. To the best of the author's knowledge, no publication translates processes to graphs to apply graph-based search algorithms for finding and verifying resilient process operation. The process-to-graph transition differs from existing approaches due to the objective off a connectivity-related resilience analysis.

7   Conclusion

Graph-based search algorithms can be used along scenario-driven metrics to analyze the resilience of business processes. Based on process-to-graph transition rules for BPMN processes, resilience requirements and characteristics of a scenario are determined at design time. Following, suitable resilience metrics and graph algorithms are selected for application at process runtime.

Shortest-path algorithms like Dijkstra and Bellman-Ford performed with minimum computation time in the evaluation. The evaluation shows that the identified shortest-path not necessarily is an ideal choice.

An all-paths analysis requires more computation time in large graphs. The resulting path list helps to compare the variety of available paths with resilience metrics to pick the most appropriate path. Considering a path with the highest path level reduced the number of non-resilient paths significantly in the evaluation. The same outcome is provided by operating a shortest-path algorithm on an adjusted graph. Removing all non-resilient edges from the graph prior to graph analysis leads to a higher amount of resilient shortest-path.

The presented graph-based approach may be adapted for non-communication- oriented aspects of processes. Examples are process characteristics such as accuracy, cost, and time.

References

1. Bocciarelli, P., D'Ambrogio, A.: A BPMN extension for modeling non functional properties of business processes. In: Proceedings of the 2011 Symposium on Theory of Modeling & Simulation, pp. 160–168. Society for Computer Simulation International (2011)

2. Bocciarelli, P., D'Ambrogio, A., Giglio, A., Paglia, E.: Simulation-based performance and reliability analysis of business processes. In: Proceedings of the 2014 Winter Simulation Conference, pp. 3012–3023. IEEE Press (2014)

3. Bocciarelli, P., D'Ambrogio, A., Giglio, A., Paglia, E.: A BPMN extension for modeling cyber-physical-production-systems in the context of Industry 4.0. In: 14th International Conference on Networking, Sensing and Control (ICNSC), pp. 599–604. IEEE (2017)

4. Braun, R., Esswein, W.: Classification of domain-specific BPMN extensions. In: Frank, U., Loucopoulos, P., Pastor, Ó., Petrounias, I. (eds.) PoEM 2014. LNBIP, vol. 197, pp. 42–57. Springer, Heidelberg (2014). https://doi.org/10.1007/978-3-662-45501-2_4

5. Ceballos, H.G., Flores-Solorio, V., Garcia, J.P.: A probabilistic BPMN normal form to model and advise human activities. In: Baldoni, M., Baresi, L., Dastani, M. (eds.) EMAS 2015. LNCS (LNAI), vol. 9318, pp. 51–69. Springer, Cham (2015). https://doi.org/10.1007/978-3-319-26184-3_4

6. Chiu, H.H., Wang, M.S.: A study of IoT-aware business process modeling. Int. J. Model. Optim. **3**(3), 238 (2013)

7. Dijkman, R., Dumas, M., García-Bañuelos, L.: Graph matching algorithms for business process model similarity search. In: Dayal, U., Eder, J., Koehler, J., Reijers, H.A. (eds.) BPM 2009. LNCS, vol. 5701, pp. 48–63. Springer, Heidelberg (2009). https://doi.org/10.1007/978-3-642-03848-8_5

8. Dijkman, R.M., Dumas, M., Ouyang, C.: Formal semantics and automated analysis of BPMN process models. Preprint 7115 (2007)

9. Domingos, D., Respício, A., Martinho, R.: Using resource reliability in BPMN processes. Procedia Comput. Sci. **100**, 1280–1288 (2016)

10. Domingos, D., Respício, A., Martinho, R.: Reliability of IoT-aware BPMN healthcare processes. In: Virtual and Mobile Healthcare: Breakthroughs in Research and Practice, pp. 793–821. IGI Global (2020)

11. Gounaris, A.: Towards automated performance optimization of BPMN business processes. In: Ivanović, M., et al. (eds.) ADBIS 2016. CCIS, vol. 637, pp. 19–28. Springer, Cham (2016). https://doi.org/10.1007/978-3-319-44066-8_2

12. Graja, I., Kallel, S., Guermouche, N., Kacem, A.H.: BPMN4CPS: a BPMN extension for modeling cyber-physical systems. In: 25th International Conference on Enabling Technologies: Infrastructure for Collaborative Enterprises (WETICE), pp. 152–157. IEEE (2016)

13. JGraphT-Library: Java library of graph theory data structures and algorithms (2020). https://jgrapht.org. Accessed 31 Aug 2020

14. Martinho, R., Domingos, D.: Quality of information and access cost of IoT resources in BPMN processes. Procedia Technol. **16**, 737–744 (2014)

15. Martinho, R., Domingos, D., Respício, A.: Evaluating the reliability of ambient-assisted living business processes. In: ICEIS (2), pp. 528–536 (2016)

16. Mazzola, L., Kapahnke, P., Waibel, P., Hochreiner, C., Klusch, M.: FCE4BPMN: on-demand QoS-based optimised process model execution in the cloud. In: 2017 International Conference on Engineering, Technology and Innovation (ICE/ITMC), pp. 305–314. IEEE (2017)

17. Meyer, S., Ruppen, A., Magerkurth, C.: Internet of Things-aware process modeling: integrating IoT devices as business process resources. In: Salinesi, C., Norrie, M.C., Pastor, Ó. (eds.) CAiSE 2013. LNCS, vol. 7908, pp. 84–98. Springer, Heidelberg (2013). https://doi.org/10.1007/978-3-642-38709-8_6

18. Nordemann, F., Tönjes, R., Pulvermüller, E.: Resilient BPMN: robust process modeling in unreliable communication environments. In: 8th International Conference on Model-Driven Engineering and Software Development (MODELSWARD). Scitepress (2020)
19. Nordemann, F., Tönjes, R., Pulvermüller, E., Tapken, H.: A graph-based approach for process robustness in unreliable communication environments. In: 15th International Conference on Evaluation of Novel Approaches to Software Engineering (ENASE). Scitepress (2020)
20. Nordemann, F., Tönjes, R., Pulvermüller, E., Tapken, H.: Graph-based multi-criteria optimization for business processes. In: Shishkov, B. (ed.) BMSD 2020. LNBIP, vol. 391, pp. 69–83. Springer, Cham (2020). https://doi.org/10.1007/978-3-030-52306-0_5
21. Object Management Group (OMG): Business Process Model and Notation (BPMN) 2.0 Specification (2011). www.omg.org/spec/BPMN/2.0/About-BPMN. Accessed 21 June 2020
22. OPeRAte: Osnabrueck University of Applied Sciences: OPeRAte research project (2019). http://operate.edvsz.hs-osnabrueck.de. Accessed 03 Sept 2019
23. Pandas-Framework: Description of boxplots (2020). https://pandas.pydata.org/pandas-docs/stable/reference/api/pandas.DataFrame.boxplot.html. Accessed 31 Aug 2020
24. Respício, A., Domingos, D.: Reliability of BPMN business processes. Procedia Comput. Sci. **64**, 643–650 (2015)
25. Sungur, C.T., Spiess, P., Oertel, N., Kopp, O.: Extending BPMN for wireless sensor networks. In: 2013 IEEE 15th Conference on Business Informatics, pp. 109–116. IEEE (2013)

Application of Fuzzy Logic to Evaluate the Performance of Business Process Models

Mariem Kchaou[✉], Wiem Khlif[✉], and Faiez Gargouri[✉]

Mir@cl Laboratory, University of Sfax, Sfax, Tunisia
mariem.kcha@gmail.com, wiem.khlif@gmail.com,
faiez.gargouri@isims.usf.tn

Abstract. Performance is one of the major topics for organizations seeking continuous improvements. Evidently, evaluating the performance of business process model is a necessary step to reduce time, cost and to indicate whether the company goals are successfully achieved or not. In the literature, several researchers refers to different techniques that aim at improving a BP model performance. Some approaches assist BP designers to develop high-performance models while others propose measures to assess the performance. This paper adopts performance measures and targets models represented in Business Process Modeling and Notation (BPMN). It proposes a methodology based on fuzzy logic along with a tool system developed under eclipse to evaluate the performance of business process models in terms of characteristics related to the actor (i.e. availability, suitability and cost) and characteristics related to BPMN elements (i.e. time behaviour, cost). The preliminary experimental evaluation of the proposed system shows encouraging results.

Keywords: Business process · Performance measures · Fuzzy logic · Thresholds · Characteristics related to BPMN elements · Characteristics related to the actor

1 Introduction

Business process performance is vital for organizations seeking continuous improvements. Obviously, the business process performance is highly influenced by decisions taken during the modelling phase. This justifies the motivation of several researchers to invest in finding solutions to define, manage and evaluate the performance of a business process model.

In the literature, different solutions have been proposed to assess BP model's performance. These solutions are based on two trends of approaches: those based on the application of formal verification methods [13] or those centered on the use of a set of performance measures calculated on the BP model [9, 11, 14].

The first trend provides for the verification of performance properties like measurement process and feedback process [13]. However, their application stills delayed by their time and cost. In addition, they are unable to express any qualitative analysis of

© Springer Nature Switzerland AG 2021
R. Ali et al. (Eds.): ENASE 2020, CCIS 1375, pp. 24–50, 2021.
https://doi.org/10.1007/978-3-030-70006-5_2

the model in terms of time behaviour and cost of BPMN elements; and availability, suitability and cost of the actor. These characteristics influence the BP performance.

In the second trend, several researchers conduct a qualitative evaluation of BP models by proposing a set of performance measures that are calculated either on the BP model (i.e., [11, 12]), or the simulated BP model [2, 7]. These measures are exploited to evaluate several quality characteristics [4, 16] or to predict the BP performance (case of simulated model assessment) [2, 7].

Since the variety of measures, several researchers proposed frameworks to assess BP model [11, 12, 21]. The main challenge is the lack of consensus about threshold values of the performance measures, which are needed to interpret/evaluate a BP model's performance.

This paper, which is a revised and extended version of our paper presented at the 15th International Conference on Evaluation of Novel Approaches to Software Engineering (ENASE 2020) [10], overcomes the problem of threshold identification based on fuzzy logic methodology which asses the BP performance in terms of characteristics related to the actor and characteristics related to BPMN elements.

The proposed methodology followed two major phases: threshold identification and fuzzy logic application. First, it applies data mining precisely decision tree in order to define approximate thresholds for each performance measure. These thresholds permit the designer to interpret the characteristic associated to the actor (i.e., availability, suitability or cost levels) and those related to the Business Process Modelling Notation (BPMN) elements (i.e., time behaviour, and cost levels). To this end, we used a database baptized "Business Process Database"[1], developed by our Mir@cl laboratory team which contains 100 business processes of organizations operating in different sectors. Then we annotate the collected processes by temporal and semantic information in conjunction with design instructors from IT department of our university (considered as experts).

The approximate thresholds produced in the first phase are considered as the input of the second phase. The latter uses the fuzzy logic [22] in order to obtain precise thresholds values.

The proposed methodology is developed in a tool called "FuzzPer" that help to assess the performance of BPMN models in terms of availability, suitability and cost of the actor; and time behaviour and cost of BPMN elements. To illustrate the efficiency of our performance tool, we rely on two types of experimental evaluation. The former is accomplished with students while the second is done through the proposed tool. These preliminary experimental evaluations of the proposed tool display encouraging results.

In summary, this paper presents three contributions: the first one expresses the imprecise thresholds determination for performance measures in terms of characteristics related to the actor (i.e., availability, suitability and its cost) and characteristics related to BPMN elements (i.e., time behaviour, cost). The second one handles the imprecise nature of the identified thresholds by applying fuzzy logic. The third one develops a tool that supports the proposed methodology.

The remainder of this chapter is organized as follows: Sect. 2 summarizes existing related works on the BP performance measures. In Sect. 3, we present the proposed

---

[1] https://sites.google.com/site/kchaoumariemsi/resources.

methodology mining measures thresholds. Section 4 expresses how we apply fuzzy logic to support the imprecise thresholds. Section 5 illustrates the developed system of BP model performance assessment. Section 6 evaluates the proposed system through two types of experiments. Section 7 identifies threats to the validity of our methodology. Finally, Sect. 8 summarizes the presented work and outlines its extensions.

2 Related Work

In this section, we introduce the BP measures used for assessing BP performance. They are classified into two categories: measures related to the actor characteristics and measures associated to BPMN elements characteristics.

Based on their formula, the presented measures below can be calculated and then each one has its corresponding value. Depending on this criterion, we keep all of them for the determination of their thresholds.

2.1 Measures Related to the Actor Characteristics

To evaluate the performance of an actor, [9, 11] propose measures related to the actor characteristics such as availability, suitability and cost.

By definition, availability is the capability of the actor to be able to perform the activity in the required unit of time. Suitability expresses the skills that cover his qualification, expertise, social competence, skills, motivation and performance ability. The cost is expressed as a price or monetary value.

The following measures evaluate the availability and suitability of the actor:

- *Planned Production Time of an Actor to Perform an Activity ($PPT_{Act}(A)$)*: is calculated by subtracting the Actor's breaks from Shift time.

$$PPT_{Act}(A) = ShT_{Act}(A)\_BR_{Act}(A) \tag{1}$$

- *Working Time Spent by an Actor to Perform an Activity ($WT_{Act}(A)$)*: is calculated by the difference between the Planned Production Time and Stop Time (the time where the actor was intended to work but was not due to unplanned or planned stops).

$$WT_{Act}(A) = PPT_{Act}(A)\_ST_{Act}(A) \tag{2}$$

- *Total Working Time Spent by an Actor in a Lane per Day ($TWTDay_{Act}(L)$)*: the sum of working time spent, in a day, by an actor in the corresponding lane.

$$TWTDay_{Act}(L) = \sum_{p=1}^{f} WT_{Act}(A_p) \tag{3}$$

- *Total Working Time Spent by an Actor in the whole Process per Day ($TWTDay_{Act}(P)$)*: the sum of working time spent by an actor in all lanes in the process.

$$TWTDay_{Act}(P) = \sum_{k=1}^{q} TWTDay_{Act}(L_k) \tag{4}$$

- *Performance of an Actor per Day (PerDay$_{Act}$)*: compares the working Time spent by an actor per day to the Ideal Cycle Time which is defined as the theoretical minimum time to perform an activity by an actor.

$$Per\,Day_{Act} = \frac{TWT\,Day_{Act}}{ICT\,Day_{Act}} \tag{5}$$

- *Availability of an Actor in a Day (AVDay$_{Act}$)*: is calculated as the ratio of Working Time spent by an actor to Planned Production Time.

$$AVDay_{Act} = \frac{TWTDay_{Act}}{PPTDay_{Act}} \tag{6}$$

- *Ratio of Defected Activities by an Actor per day (RDA$_{Act}$)*: is calculated by the Total Number of Defected Activities performed by an actor divided by the Total number of Activities performed by the same actor.

$$RDA_{Act} = \frac{TDADay_{Act}}{TADay_{Act}} \tag{7}$$

- *Ratio of Good Activities Performed by an Actor (RGA$_{Act}$)*: is calculated by the Total Number of Good Activities realized by an actor in a day divided by the Total number of Activities performed by the same actor in one day.

$$RGA_{Act} = \frac{TGADay_{Act}}{TADay_{Act}} \tag{8}$$

In addition, several measures are proposed in [9, 11] to assess the cost of an actor such as

- Cost of an actor in a Lane per Day (CosDay$_{Act}$(L)) which is calculated by the product of the total working time spent by an Actor in a Lane per Day (TWTDay$_{Act}$(L)) and its actual Labour Costs per Hour (LCH$_{Act}$).

$$CosDay_{Act}(L) = TWTDay_{Act}(L) * LCH_{Act} \tag{9}$$

- *Cost of an actor in a Pool per Day (CosDay$_{Act}$(P))* which is determined by the product of the total working time spent by an Actor in a Pool per Day (TWTDay$_{Act}$(P)) and its actual Labour Costs per Hour (LCH$_{Act}$).

$$CosDay_{Act}(P) = TWTDay_{Act}(P) * LCH_{Act} \tag{10}$$

2.2 Measures Related to BPMN Elements Characteristics

Time behaviour and cost are the characteristics of BPMN elements to evaluate the performance efficiency [6].

By definition, time behaviour is defined as the appropriate transport time between different BPMN elements and processing times when executed; while cost expresses the price or monetary value related to BPMN elements.

[9, 11] propose the following measures to assess the time behaviour of BPMN elements:

- *Gateway Duration (GD (Gateway))* represents the duration of a gateway.

$$GD = ETG - STG \tag{11}$$

Where ETG represents End Time of a Gateway and STG represents Start Time of a Gateway.
- *Sequence Flow Duration (SeqFD)* represents the transfer time between BPMN elements (activity, gateway and event).

$$SeqFD = ST(BPMN\ element_{i+1}) - ET(BPMN\ element_i) \tag{12}$$

Where ST: Start Time, ET: End Time.

In addition, [14] present other temporal measures such as *Activity/Process Duration (AD)* which is calculated by the difference between the end time of the activity (Process) and the start time.

$$AD = ETA - STA \tag{13}$$

Where ETA represents End Time of an Activity and STA represents Start Time of an Activity.

On the other hand, [9, 11] proposed a set of measures to evaluate the cost of BPMN elements such as

- *Cost of an Activity Realized by an Actor (CA_{Act})* is calculated by the product of the actor actual Labour Costs per Hour and the working time spent by an Actor to perform an Activity.

$$CA_{Act} = LCH_{Act} * WT_{Act}(A) \tag{14}$$

- *Cost of a Gateway (CosGat(Gatway))* represents the product of the gateway duration and the actor's actual Labour Costs per Hour (LCHAct).

$$CosGat_{Act} = GD * LCH_{Act} \tag{15}$$

- *Cost of a Sequence Flow (CosSeqF$_{Act}$)* expresses the product of the Sequence Flow Duration (SeqFD) and the actor's actual Labour Costs per Hour (LCHAct).

$$CosSeqF_{Act} = LCH_{Act} * SeqFD \tag{16}$$

Table 5, 7 and 8 display respectively the usability of the presented measures to evaluate the actor characteristics and BPMN element characteristics. However, to our knowledge, there is no works that focus on the determination of measures thresholds values.

3 Design Methodology for Thresholds Determination

Figure 1 illustrates our methodology for determining approximate thresholds related to performance measures. It aims to evaluate the performance of business process models in terms of characteristics related to the actor (i.e., availability, suitability and its cost) and to BPMN elements (i.e., time behaviour, cost). This methodology is organized in two major activities: "Analyze Data" and "Validate Data".

The "Analyze data" activity goes through three stages: 1) Collect a set of BPMN models that we annotated by semantic information covering the cost, organizational aspect, and temporal constraints related to the actor and BPMN elements, 2) Prepare these models through creating matrices related to actors and to BPMN elements to evaluate their characteristics and 3) Apply Data mining to build decision trees using WEKA system. The latter is based on algorithms that construct decision trees.

The "Validate Data" activity is composed of two activities: Training Database based Validation and Test Database based Validation.

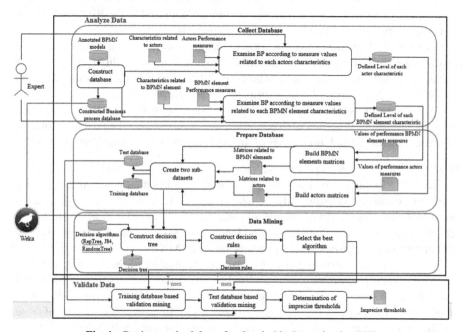

Fig. 1. Design methodology for thresholds determination [10].

3.1 Analyze Data

The Analyze data activity is composed of three major stages: the first one collects data based on a set of business process models annotated by semantic information that covers the cost, organizational aspect, and temporal constraints related to the actor and BPMN elements. The second step prepares data through creating matrices related to actors and to BPMN elements to evaluate their characteristics and the third one apply data mining technique to build decision trees using WEKA system. The latter is based on algorithms that construct decision trees.

Collect Database. As a part of research of our Mir@cl laboratory, we collect around 100 BPMN models having small/medium size. The collected BPMN models belong to different organizations (banks, healthcare, institutions, commercial enterprises, etc.) in order to guarantee that our methodology is generic. Next, we annotate them by temporal constraints and semantic information (cost and organizational aspects) associated to the actor and BPMN elements. For more details, reader can refer to [9, 11]. The main objective of this information is to evaluate the actor and BPMN elements characteristics.

Then, we examined business processes with design instructors from IT department of our university according to measures values related to each characteristics associated to the actor and to BPMN elements. The objective is to organize them according to the level of each characteristic related to the actor and BPMN elements.

To end this purpose, we organized ourselves into two groups. First, each one examine 50 processes in term of characteristics related to the actor and to the BPMN elements. Then, we verify the cross-validation process among two groups.

Finally, to evaluate the process in terms of characteristics associated to the actor, we classified the "Business Process Database" in two levels of availability (actor is always available and rarely available), two levels of suitability (having the best skills and having low skills) and three levels of cost (expensive, acceptable and cheap).

To assess business processes based on the BPMN elements characteristics, we organized the "Business Process Database" into three levels of time behaviour (minimal, normal and maximal) and three levels of the cost (expensive, acceptable and cheap).

Prepare Data. In order to prepare data for the next stage, we produce nine matrices based on the "Business Process Database". Three matrices are dedicated to the actor in order to evaluate his availability, suitability and cost; while the rest is devoted to the BPMN elements (activity, gateway and sequence flow) in order to assess their time behavior and cost. These matrices take as input performance measures values and the level of each characteristics related to actors and to BPMN elements.

Each row in each matrix expresses the actor (respectively BPMN element); and each column depicts a performance measure used to assess the availability, suitability and cost of the actor (respectively time behaviour and cost of BPMN elements). The corresponding case representing the intersection of row and column details the values of these performance measures calculated for a specific actor (respectively BPMN elements).

The last column of each matrix represents the level of each actor characteristic (respectively BPMN element). For example, the last column of each matrix associated to the actor expresses the level of each characteristic: his availability (i.e., actor is always available and rarely available), suitability (i.e., having the best skills and having low skills) and cost (i.e., expensive, acceptable and cheap); Whereas the last column of each matrix related to BPMN elements depicts levels of their characteristic time behaviour (i.e., minimal, normal and maximal) and cost (i.e., expensive, acceptable and cheap).

The elaborated matrices are used to create two sub-datasets: one for learning "Training Dataset" and one for testing needs "Test Dataset". The first one includes 70% of the "Business Process Database" while the second one comprises the rest of the "Business Process Database". The percentage choice is justified by the fact that the "Training Dataset" is the one on which we train and fit our model to adjust thresholds. Whereas "Test Dataset" is used only to assess the BP performance.

Data Mining. To identify thresholds for performance measures from the "Business Process Database", we used in the first step decision trees and in the second step decision rules. For more details about decision trees readers are referred to [15, 17].

To create decision trees, we use the training dataset which contains the values of the performance measures calculated for a specific actor (respectively BPMN elements). The required nine decision trees is classified into three for the actor characteristics (Availability, suitability and cost) and six for BPMN elements characteristics (time behaviour and cost), we used WEKA system [5]. The latter is a collection of machine learning algorithms for data mining tasks. It contains tools for data pre-processing, classification, regression, clustering, association rules, and visualization. WEKA is based on algorithms (J48, RandomTree, REPTree, etc.) that construct decision trees.

We note that the J48 algorithm is an implementation of C4.5 algorithm [1]. It produces decision tree classification for a given dataset by recursive division of the data. It works with the process of starting from leaves that overall formed tree and do a backward toward the root.

The RepTree uses the regression tree logic and creates multiple trees in different iterations. After that, it selects best one from all generated trees.

The Random Tree is a supervised classifier; it is an ensemble learning algorithm that generates many individual learners. It employs a bagging idea to produce a random set of data for constructing a decision tree.

In our work, we apply all of the algorithms, and then we select the best one which have a lower error rate based on the validation phase (Sect. 3.2).

3.2 Validate Data

To assess the quality of a prediction model, we used the following ratios: (17) precision, (18) Recall, (19) F-measure and (20) Global Error Rate. Next, we select the most popular and best algorithms (J48, RandomTree and REPTree) according to the values of the calculated ratios.

$$\text{Precision} = \frac{\text{CorrectEntitiesFound}}{\text{TotalEntitiesFound}} \tag{17}$$

$$\text{Recall} = \frac{\text{CorrectEntitiesFound}}{\text{TotalCorrectEntities}} \tag{18}$$

$$\text{F\_mesure} = 2 * \frac{\text{Precision} * \text{Recall}}{\text{Precision} + \text{Recall}} \tag{19}$$

$$\text{GlobalErrorRate} = 1 - \frac{\text{CorrectEntitiesFound}}{\text{TotalEntities}} \tag{20}$$

Training Database Based Validation Mining. We calculate the ratios after testing the resulting decision trees based on characteristics trees related to the actor (availability, suitability and cost), and also based on characteristics trees associated to BPMN elements (time behaviour and cost). In this section, we applied decision trees on the "Training Database".

Table 1 indicated that we realized very acceptable results with REPTree algorithm, for assessing the BP model actor characteristics. Concerning the availability, the values of precision, recall and F-measure are 94.5%, 94.1% and 94.2% while the global error is equal to 5.8%. In addition, regarding the suitability, the values of precision, recall and F-measure are 76.4%, 76.5% and 76.3% while the error is equal to 2.3%. To evaluate the cost, the values of precision, recall and F-measure are 98.6%, 98.5% and 98.5% while the global error rate is 1.4%.

Table 1. J48 vs RandomTree vs REPTree for decision tree of availability, suitability and cost of the actor using the "Training Database" [10].

Ratios	Availability			Suitability			Cost		
	J48	RandomTree	REPTree	J48	RandomTree	REPTree	J48	RandomTree	REPTree
Precision	0,815	0,869	0,945	0,748	0,724	0,764	0,972	0,986	0,986
Recall	0,824	0,863	0,941	0,706	0,725	0,765	0,971	0,985	0,985
F-Measure	0,808	0,866	0,942	0,704	0,724	0,763	0,971	0,985	0,985
Global error rate	0.176	0.137	0.058	0.029	0.027	0.023	0.029	0.014	0.014

Table 2 displays that we reached very acceptable results with REPTree algorithm, for evaluating BPMN elements characteristics. To evaluate each characteristic, we calculate for each one the values of precision, recall and F-measure and the corresponding errors.

Table 2. J48 vs RandomTree vs REPTree for decision tree of time behaviour and cost of each BPMN element using the "Training Database" [10].

BPMN elements	Ratios	Time behaviour			Cost		
		J48	RandomTree	REPTree	J48	RandomTree	REPTree
Activity	Precision	0,987	0,987	0,991	0,968	0,964	0,969
	Recall	0,986	0,986	0,991	0,968	0,964	0,968
	F-Measure	0,986	0,986	0,991	0,968	0,964	0,968
	Global error rate	0,013	0,013	0,009	0.031	0.036	0.031
Gateway	Precision	0,989	0,989	0,989	0,955	0,932	0,980
	Recall	0,988	0,988	0,988	0,955	0,932	0,977
	F-Measure	0,988	0,988	0,988	0,955	0,931	0,978
	Global error rate	0,011	0,011	0,011	0.045	0.068	0.022
Sequence Flow	Precision	0,980	0,975	0,980	0,967	0,983	0,983
	Recall	0,980	0,975	0,980	0,964	0,982	0,982
	F-Measure	0,980	0,975	0,980	0,964	0,982	0,982
	Global error rate	0,020	0,025	0,020	0.035	0.017	0.017

Test Database based Validation Mining. To assess the performance of the proposed decision tree and select the best algorithm provided by WEKA, we used the "Test Database" which is extracted from the "Business Process Database".

Then, we evaluate the level of each characteristic related to the actor and BPMN elements by applying each decision tree to all BPs of the "Test Database". Then, we compare this evaluation to that elaborated by design instructors from IT department of our university. The objective behind is to compare the obtained decision trees with design instructors judgment and therefore, to determine the error rate of our decision trees.

Tables 3 and 4 show the values of the ratios presented in Sect. 3.2 for evaluating the performance of the proposed characteristics of decision trees (availability, suitability and the cost of the actor and time behavior and cost of BPMN elements).

Table 3 depicts that we reached very acceptable results using the "Test Database" with REPTree algorithm, for evaluating the actor characteristics. Concerning the availability, the values of precision, recall and F-measure are 91.7%, 91.7% and 91.7% while the global error is equal to 8.3%. In addition, regarding the suitability, the values of precision, recall and F-measure are 87%, 86.7% and 86.7% while the error is equal to 1.3%. To evaluate the cost, the values of precision, recall and F-measure are 96.5%, 96.2% and 96.2% while the global error rate is 3.8%.

Table 3. J48 vs RandomTree vs REPTree for decision tree of availability, suitability and cost of the actor using the "Test Database" [10].

Ratios	Availability			Suitability			Cost		
	J48	RandomTree	REPTree	J48	RandomTree	REPTree	J48	RandomTree	REPTree
Precision	0,917	0,887	0,9	0,702	0,634	0,870	0,889	0,923	0,965
Recall	0,917	0,875	0,917	0,700	0,633	0,867	0,885	0,923	0,962
F-Measure	0,917	0,879	0,917	0,700	0,627	0,867	0,884	0,923	0,962
Global error rate	0.083	0.125	0.083	0.030	0.036	0.013	0.115	0.076	0.038

In addition, based on Table 4, we deduce that the achieved results with REPTree algorithm are very acceptable, for evaluating BPMN elements characteristics. To assess each characteristic, we calculate for each one the values of precision, recall and F-measure and the corresponding errors.

Table 4. J48 vs RandomTree vs REPTree for decision tree of time behaviour and cost of each BPMN element using the "Test Database" [10].

BPMN elements	Ratios	Time behaviour			Cost		
		J48	RandomTree	REPTree	J48	RandomTree	REPTree
Activity	Precision	0,987	0,987	0,991	0,968	0,964	0,969
	Recall	0,986	0,986	0,991	0,968	0,964	0,968
	F-Measure	0,986	0,986	0,991	0,968	0,964	0,968
	Global error rate	0,013	0,013	0,009	0.031	0.036	0.031
Gateway	Precision	0,989	0,989	0,989	0,955	0,932	0,980
	Recall	0,988	0,988	0,988	0,955	0,932	0,977
	F-Measure	0,988	0,988	0,988	0,955	0,931	0,978
	Global error rate	0,011	0,011	0,011	0.045	0.068	0.022
Sequence Flow	Precision	0,932	0,979	0,979	0,946	0,946	0,946
	Recall	0,932	0,977	0,977	0,946	0,946	0,946
	F-Measure	0,931	0,977	0,977	0,946	0,946	0,946
	Global error rate	0,068	0.022	0.022	0.054	0.054	0.054

3.3 Discussion

According to the level of availability, suitability and cost of the actor (respectively time behaviour and cost levels of each BPMN element), we used decision trees to classify actors (respectively BPMN element), extracted from "Business Process Database". This classification is based on the values of the used performance measures.

In addition, we used these decision trees in order to define a set of decision rules and performance measures thresholds to evaluate the characteristics related to the actor such as availability, suitability and cost (respectively the characteristics associated to the BPMN element such as the time behaviour and cost of each BPMN element).

Evaluation of Actor Characteristics Levels. Table 5 shows the defined thresholds values and their interpretations which are determined by design instructors from IT department of our university.

Table 6 displays an excerpt of the decision rules which specify the performance measures values for each characteristic level of the actor.

Evaluation of BPMN Elements Characteristics Levels. Table 7 presents the defined thresholds and the corresponding linguistic interpretations for the assessment of the time behaviour characteristic associated to each BPMN elements (activity, gateway and sequence flow), which are determined by design instructors from IT department of our university.

Table 5. Identified thresholds values for the evaluation of the characteristics related to the actor [10].

Characteristics	Performance measures	Threshold	Linguistic interpretation
Availability	$PPT_{Act}(A)$	$PPTAct(A) < 5$	Low
		$5 \leq PPTAct(A) < 7$	Moderate
		$7 \leq PPTAct(A) < 9$	High
		$PPTAct(A) \geq 9$	Very high
	$WT_{Act}(A)$	$WT_{Act}(A) < 3$	Low
		$WT_{Act}(A) \geq 3$	High
	$PerDay_{Act}$	$PerDay_{Act} < 78$	Low
		$PerDay_{Act} \geq 78$	High
	$AVDay_{Act}$	$AVDayact < 72.5$	Low
		$AVDayact \geq 72.5$	High
Suitability	$PPT_{Act}(A)$	$PPTAct(A) < 12.5$	Low
		$12.5 \leq PPTAct(A) < 17.5$	Moderate
		$17.5 \leq PPTAct(A) < 25$	High
		$PPTAct(A) \geq 25$	Very high
	$WT_{Act}(A)$	$WT_{Act}(A) < 3$	Very low
		$3 \leq WT_{Act}(A) < 10.5$	Low
		$10.5 \leq WT_{Act}(A) < 12.5$	Moderate
		$12.5 \leq WT_{Act}(A) < 21$	High
		$WT_{Act}(A) \geq 21$	Very high
	$TWTDay_{Act}(L)$	$TWTDay_{Act}(L) < 17.5$	Low
		$17.5 \leq TWTDay_{Act}(L) < 24.5$	Moderate
		$TWTDay_{Act}(L) \geq 24.5$	High
	$TWTDay_{Act}(P)$	$TWTDay_{Act}(P) < 60$	Low
		$TWTDay_{Act}(P) \geq 60$	High
	$PerDay_{Act}$	$PerDay_{Act} < 79.2$	Low
		$PerDay_{Act} \geq 79.2$	High
	$AVDay_{Act}$	$AVDayact < 72.5$	Low
		$AVDayact \geq 72.5$	High
	$RGAAct$	$RGAAct < 37.5$	Low
		$37.5 \leq RGAAct < 75$	Moderate

(*continued*)

Table 5. (*continued*)

Characteristics	Performance measures	Threshold	Linguistic interpretation
		RGAAct ≥ 75	High
	RDAAct	RDAAct < 58.3	Low
		RDAAct ≥ 58.3	High
Cost	CosDayAct(L)	CosDayAct(L) < 4.8	Low
		4.8 ≤ CosDayAct(L) < 9	Moderate
		CosDayAct(L) ≥ 9	High
	CosDayAct(P)	CosDayAct(P) < 10.16	Low
		CosDayAct(P) ≥ 10.16	High

Table 6. Extract of decision rules to assess the level of actor's characteristics [10].

Characteristics	Rule	Decision rules
Availability	R1	If (AVDayact < 72.5 and PPTAct(A) < 9 and WTAct(A) < 3) then the actor is rarely available
	R2	If (AVDayact < 72.5 and PPTAct(A) ≥ 9 and PerDayAct ≥ 78 and TWTDayAct(L) < 15.5) then the actor is always available
	R3	If (AVDayact ≥ 72.5 and PPTAct(A) < 7 and PPTAct(A) < 5) then the actor is always available
Suitability	R1	If (PerDayAct < 79.2 and RDAAct < 58.3 and WTAct(A) < 3) then the actor has low skills
	R2	If (PerDayAct < 79.2 and RDAAct < 58.3 and WTAct(A) ≥ 3 and AVDayact < 72.5) then the actor has low skills
	R3	If (PerDayAct ≥ 79.2 and 37.5 < RGAAct < 75 and WTAct(A) < 12.5) then the actor has low skills
Cost	R1	If CosDayAct(L) < 4.8 then the cost of the actor is Cheap
	R2	If CosDayAct(L) ≥ 4.8 and CosDayAct(P) < 10.16:then the cost of the actor is Acceptable
	R3	If CosDayAct(L) < 9 and CosDayAct(P) ≥ 10.16 then the cost of the actor is Acceptable

Table 8 shows the defined thresholds and the corresponding linguistic interpretations for the assessment of the cost characteristic related to each BPMN elements (activity, gateway and sequence flow).

Table 9 illustrates an extract of decision rules that determine the time behaviour level of each BPMN element according to the values of performance measures.

Table 7. Identified thresholds values for the evaluation of the time behaviour characteristic related to BPMN elements.

BPMN elements	Performance measures		Time behaviour	
			Threshold	Linguistic interpretation
Activity	AD	Activity	AD < 6.5	Low
			$6.5 \leq AD < 14.5$	Moderate
			$AD \geq 14.5$	High
		Process	AD < 19.5	Low
			$19.5 \leq AD < 28.5$	Moderate
			$AD \geq 28.5$	High
Gateway	GD		GD < 2.5	Low
			$2.5 \leq GD < 4.5$	Moderate
			$GD \geq 4.5$	High
Sequence Flow	SeqFD		SeqFD < 4.5	Low
			$4.5 \leq SeqFD < 8$	Moderate
			$SeqFD \geq 8$	High

Table 8. Identified thresholds values for the evaluation of the cost characteristic related to BPMN elements.

BPMN elements	Performance measures		Cost	
			Threshold	Linguistic interpretation
Activity	CA_{Act}	Activity	$CA_{Act} < 4.92$	Low
			$4.92 \leq CA_{Act} < 10$	Moderate
			$CA_{Act} \geq 10$	High
		Process	$CA_{Act} < 18.67$	Low
			$8.67 < CA_{Act} \leq 24.95$	Moderate
			$CA_{Act} \geq 24.95$	High
Gateway	CosGat(Gateway)		CosGat < 0.45	Low
			$0.45 \leq CosGat < 0.97$	Moderate
			$CosGat \geq 0.97$	High
Sequence Flow	CosSeqF		CosSeqF < 0.45	Low
			$0.45 \leq CosSeqF < 0.99$	Moderate
			$CosSeqF \geq 0.99$	High

Table 9. Extract of decision rules to assess the level of each time behaviour's BPMN element.

BPMN elements		Rule	Time behaviour
Activity	Activity	R1	If AD < 6.5 then the time of the activity is Minimal
		R2	If $6.5 \leq$ AD < 14.5 then the time of the activity is Normal
		R3	If AD $\geq$ 14.5 then the time of the activity is Maximal
	Process	R1	If AD < 19.5 then the time of the process is Minimal
		R2	If $19.5 \leq$ AD < 28.5 then the time of the process is Normal
		R3	If AD $\geq$ 28.5 then the time of the process is Maximal
Gateway		R1	If GD < 2.5 then the time of the gateway is Minimal
		R2	If GD $\geq$ 2.5 then the time of the gateway is Normal
		R3	If GD $\geq$ 4.5 then the time of the gateway is Maximal
Sequence Flow		R1	If SeqFD < 4.5 then the time of the sequence flow is Minimal
		R2	If $4.5 \leq$ SeqFD < 8 then the time of the sequence flow is Normal
		R3	If SeqFD $\geq$ 8 then the time of the sequence flow is Maximal

Table 10 illustrates an extract of decision rules that identify the level of each BPMN element cost.

Table 10. Extract of decision rules to assess the level of each cost's BPMN element.

BPMN elements		Rule	Cost
Activity	Activity	R1	If CA_{Act} < 4.92 then the cost of the activity is Cheap
		R2	If $4.92 \leq CA_{Act}$ < 10 then the cost of the activity is Acceptable
		R3	If $CA_{Act} \geq$ 10 then the cost of the activity is Expensive
	Process	R1	If CA_{Act} < 18.67 then the cost of the process is Cheap
		R2	If $18.67 < CA_{Act} \leq$ 24.95 then the cost of the process is Acceptable
		R3	If $CA_{Act} \geq$ 24.95 then the cost of the process is Expensive
Gateway		R1	If GD < 2.5 then the cost of the gateway is Minimal
		R2	If $2.5 \leq$ GD < 4.5 then the cost of the gateway is Normal
		R3	If GD $\geq$ 4.5 then the cost of the gateway is Maximal
Sequence Flow		R1	If CosSeqF < 0.45 then the cost of the sequence flow is Cheap
		R2	If $0.45 \leq$ CosSeqF < 0.99 then the cost of the sequence flow is Acceptable
		R3	If CosSeqF $\geq$ 0.99 then the cost of the sequence flow is Expensive

In summary, the obtained thresholds are persist and imprecise because they are predisposed by the judgment of design instructors from IT department of our university when we collect the database. In order to manage this problem, we use the fuzzy logic which is details in the next section.

4 Fuzzy Logic for BP Performance Assessment

Fuzzy Logic is an appropriate approach for handling approximate and imprecise values like those for the performance measures thresholds. Fuzzy-logic application goes through three stages: fuzzification, inference and defuzzification.

Fuzzification is the process of converting a crisp input value representing the performance measures to a fuzzy membership function expressing linguistic values (i.e., High, Moderate and Low). The inference used the decision rules presented in Sect. 3.3 to obtain a set of fuzzy decision rules written in a linguistically natural language.

The defuzzification produces crisp values of each performance measure as well as the degree of certainty using the one of the technique proposed in the literature.

In this section, we present in detail how we use the fuzzy logic to evaluate the performance of BP.

4.1 Fuzzification

Fuzzification transforms crisp values of performance measures representing the input variables into linguistic values that express fuzzy sets. This transformation is realized thanks to the membership functions that are determined based on the identified approximate thresholds (Sect. 3.3). One membership function is proposed for each possible fuzzy set per performance measure.

The first part of Fig. 2 expresses the membership without fuzzification. In this part, the two values (x and y) express the approximate thresholds obtained based on the use of decision trees and fuzzy sets that are defined in different intervals. These intervals are determined by design instructors from IT department of our university (i.e., Low, Moderate and High).

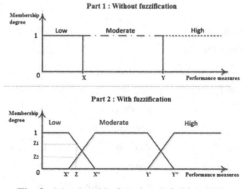

Fig. 2. Membership function definition [10].

Figure 2 illustrates that each performance measure value, which has a membership degree equals to 1, belongs only to a single fuzzy set.

This situation is true if the identified thresholds are exact and precise. Nevertheless, since this case cannot be applied, we use in this paper, the membership function with fuzzification reflects the ranges by different design instructors from IT department of our university. It is depicted in the second part of Fig. 2. In this part, the design instructors defined four values (x', x'', y', y'') for each performance measure. Each value inside the interval $[x', x'']$ and $[y', y'']$ fits respectively in two fuzzy sets with different membership degrees. For instance, the value "z" belongs to the two fuzzy sets "Low" and "Moderate" with membership degree of "z1" and "z2".

4.2 Inference

The inference step used a set of fuzzy decision rules written in a linguistically natural language. A fuzzy rule is a simple IF-THEN rule with a condition and a conclusion. It should be written based on the following syntax: "if D is X and/or E is Y then F is Z". D and E represent the input variables, F is the output variable and X, Y, Z are their corresponding linguistic values.

These rules are crucial to determine the values of the output variables representing levels of the actor characteristics (his availability, suitability and cost) and levels of each BPMN element characteristics (time behavior and cost) based on the input values expressing the set of performance measures.

To obtain the fuzzy rules, we start by using the set of decision rules obtained from the decision tree (Sect. 3.3). We changed the crisp values of performance measures with their corresponding linguistic values and rewrote the rules according to the syntax defined above. Table 11 shows the total number of defined fuzzy rules for each actor's and BPMN element characteristic.

Table 11. Total number of defined fuzzy rules for the actor characteristic and those corresponding to BPMN elements [10].

			Total number of fuzzy rules
Actor	Availability		50
	Suitability		207
	Cost		15
BPMN element	Time behaviour	Activity	12
		Gateway	6
		Sequence Flow	6
	Cost	Activity	12
		Gateway	6
		Sequence Flow	6

Table 12 represents an excerpt of the identified fuzzy decision rules for the actor characteristics such as availability, suitability and cost.

Table 12. Extract of fuzzy decision rules to evaluate the level of availability, suitability and cost of the actor [10].

Fuzzy rule	Fuzzy decision rules		
	Availability	Suitability	Cost
FR1	If (AVDayact is low and PPTAct(A) is High and WTAct(A) is low) then the AvailabilityLevel is rarely available	If (PerDayAct is low and RDAAct is low and WTAct(A) is very low) then the SuitabilityLevel is having low skills	If CosDayAct(L) is low then the CostLevel is Cheap
FR2	If (AVDayact is low and PPTAct(A) is Very high and PerDayAct is High) then the AvailabilityLevel is always available	If (PerDayAct is low and RDAAct is low and WTAct(A) is low and AVDayact is low) then the SuitabilityLevel is having low skills	If CosDayAct(L) is moderate and CosDayAct(P) is low then the CostLevel is Acceptable
FR3	If (AVDayact is high and PPTAct(A) is Moderate) then the AvailabilityLevel is always available	If (PerDayAct is low and RDAAct is low and WTAct(A) is low and AVDayact is high and TWTDayAct(L) is low) then the SuitabilityLevel is having low skills	If CosDayAct(L) is moderate and CosDayAct(P) is high then the CostLevel is Acceptable

Table 13 shows an excerpt of the identified fuzzy decision rules for the time behaviour of each BPMN element (activity, gateway and sequence flow).

Table 13. Extract of fuzzy decision rules to evaluate the level of time behavior corresponding to each BPMN element.

BPMN elements		Fuzzy rule	Time behaviour
Activity	Activity	FR1	If AD is low then the TimeBehaviorLevel is Minimal
		FR2	If AD is moderate then the TimeBehaviorLevel is Normal
		FR3	If AD is high then the TimeBehaviorLevel is Maximal
	Process	FR1	If AD is low then the TimeBehaviorLevel is Minimal
		FR2	If AD is moderate then the TimeBehaviorLevel is Normal
		FR3	If AD is high then the TimeBehaviorLevel is Maximal
Gateway		FR1	If GD is low then the TimeBehaviorLevel is Minimal
		FR2	If GD is moderate then the TimeBehaviorLevel is Normal
		FR3	If GD is high then the TimeBehaviorLevel is Maximal
Sequence flow		FR1	If SeqFD is low then the TimeBehaviorLevel is Minimal
		FR2	If SeqFD is moderate then the TimeBehaviorLevel is Normal
		FR3	If SeqFD is high then the TimeBehaviorLevel is Maximal

Table 14 displays an excerpt of the identified fuzzy decision rules for the cost of each BPMN element (activity, gateway and sequence flow).

Table 14. Extract of fuzzy decision rules to evaluate the level of cost associated to each BPMN element.

BPMN elements		Fuzzy rule	Cost
Activity	Activity	FR1	If CA_{Act} is low then the CostLevel is Cheap
		FR2	If CA_{Act} is moderate then the CostLevel is Acceptable
		FR3	If CA_{Act} is high then the CostLevel is Expensive
	Process	FR1	If CA_{Act} is low then the CostLevel is Cheap
		FR2	If CA_{Act} is moderate then the CostLevel is Acceptable
		FR3	If CA_{Act} is high then the CostLevel is Expensive
Gateway		FR1	If CosGat is low then the CostLevel is Cheap
		FR2	If CosGat is moderate then the CostLevel is Acceptable
		FR3	If CosGat is high then the CostLevel is Expensive
Sequence flow		FR1	If CosSeqF is low then the CostLevel is Cheap
		FR2	If CosSeqF is moderate then the CostLevel is Acceptable
		FR3	If CosSeqF is high then the CostLevel is Expensive

4.3 Defuzzification

Defuzzification is the process of producing a quantifiable result in crisp logic, given fuzzy sets and corresponding membership degrees. This conversion is ensured thanks to a set of membership functions that we defined based on several rules that transform a number of variables into a fuzzy result, that is, the result is described in terms of membership in fuzzy sets.

Several defuzzification techniques are proposed in the literature such as Center Of Gravity (COG), Centroid Of Area (COA), Mean Of Maximum (MOM), Center Of Sums (COS), etc. We use the Center Of Sums (COS) since it is faster than many defuzzification methods that are presently in use. In addition, the method is not restricted to symmetric membership functions. The defuzzified value X* of the output variable is given by Eq. 21:

$$X^* = \frac{\sum_{i=1}^{M} x_i * \sum_{j=1}^{m} \mu\, A_j(X_i)}{\sum_{j=1}^{m} \mu\, A_j(X_i)} \tag{21}$$

Where m is the number of fuzzy sets, M represents the number of fuzzy variables and expresses the membership function for the j-th fuzzy sets.

Defuzzification determines the level of each actor and BPMN element characteristic as well as the degree of certainty of each level. For example, an actor can be estimated as the most suitable having best skills with a certainty degree of 80%.

5 FuzzyPer: Fuzzy Performance Tool

We have developed a tool, bapized "FuzzPer" which supports our methodology for evaluating the actor characteristics (suitability, availability and cost of the actor) and assessing the BPMN elements characteristics (time behaviour and cost time of each BPMN element). Our tool is implemented in Java as an EclipseTM plug-in [3]. It is composed of four main modules: Extractor, Measures calculator, Decision Maker and Fuzzy-logic control. The functional architecture of this tool is presented in Fig. 3.

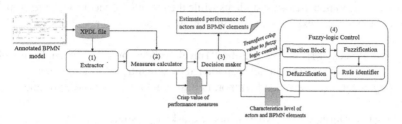

Fig. 3. Architecture of "FuzzPer" tool [10].

The extractor takes as input a business process modeled by BIZAGI tool [8] transformed into XPDL file [18]. Based on the generated file, the information extracted by the extractor reflects the semantic (cost and organizational aspects), temporal and the structural information. This information involves all BPMN elements contained in the business process model and the actors. The use of the standard ensures that our tool can be integrated within any other modeling tool that supports this standard.

The measures calculator takes as input the XPDL file, calculates and displays the crisp values of each used performance measures for estimating either the cost or time of each BPMN elements or the suitability, availability and cost of the actor.

The Decision Maker takes the crisp values of performance measures representing the input variables and transfers them to the fuzzy control module. This module runs the Fuzzy Control Language (FCL) for approximating the performance of the actor and BPMN elements.

Fuzzy-logic Control is implemented in Fuzzy Control Language (FCL) which is a standard for Fuzzy Control Programming. It was standardized by IEC 61131–7. FCL is composed of four main modules: Function Block Interface, Fuzzification, Rule identifier, Defuzzification.

- Function Block Interface: defines input and output parameters.
- Fuzzification: converts the input variables which represents crisp values of performance measures into linguistic values (fuzzy sets) using the membership functions. The latter are determined based on the identified approximate thresholds.
- Rule Identifier: defines the level of the actor characteristic (his availability, suitability and cost), and the level of each BPMN element characteristic (time behavior and cost) using a set of fuzzy decision rules written in a linguistically natural language (Sect. 4.2).
- Defuzzification: determines the level of availability, suitability and cost of the actor and the level of time behaviour and cost of each BPMN element as well as the degree of certainty of this level using the Center Of Sums (COS) technique (Sect. 4.3).

Based on the obtained result provided by the Defuzziification, the decision maker estimates the performance of the actor and BPMN elements.

6 Experiments

In order to validate our methodology, we rely on two types of experimental evaluation. The former is accomplished with students while the second is done through the proposed "FuzzPer" tool. These experiments use the following additional resources:

- Business Process Model: we use the "Travel Agency process" example modelled with BPMN in Fig. 4. The model is annotated by semantic information that covers the cost, organizational aspect and temporal constraints related to the actor and BPMN elements.
- Participants: During these experiments, we asked 50 students to evaluate the actor characteristics (availability, suitability and cost) and to assess BPMN elements characteristics (time behaviour and cost of each BPMN element).
- Actor characteristics exercise[2]: students should answer to a set of questions to assess the performance of the actor. The questions are classified into three categories: those that related to the availability of the actor, those focus on the suitability of the actor and those associated to the actor cost. Finally, each student should choose the level of each actor characteristic (i.e., availability, suitability and cost). For instance, the actor is always available or rarely available.
- BPMN elements characteristics exercise (See footnote 2): students had to evaluate the time behaviour of each BPMN element (the time performing an activity, the time of make decision and the transfer time) and the cost of each one (the cost of an activity, the cost of make decision and the cost of the transfer time). Finally, each one select the time level and the cost level of each BPMN element. For instance, the activity's cost is cheap, acceptable or expensive.

Experiment 1: Figure 5 represents the number of correct and incorrect answers for the actor characteristics exercise. In this figure, 75% of the responses are correct. The result expresses that the majority of students can evaluate the performance of the actor. This result is also established based on their answers to the last question for each category of the first exercise, which is about the availability, suitability and cost of the actor.

---

[2] https://sites.google.com/site/kchaoumariemsint/resources.

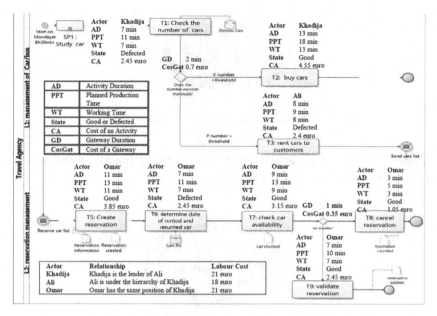

Fig. 4. "Travel Agency process" example [10].

Fig. 5. Correct and incorrect answers for the actor characteristics exercise.

Indeed, Fig. 6 displays that 78% of students considered the actor as always available, 22% as rarely available.

Fig. 6. Students' judgments about the availability levels.

In addition, Fig. 7 shows that 69% of students considered the actor as has low skills, 31% as has best skills. They show that a good number of students have correctly assess competences of actors.

Fig. 7. Students' judgments about the suitability levels.

Furthermore, Fig. 8 represents that 52% of students considered the actors as expensive, 29% as acceptable, and 19% as cheap.

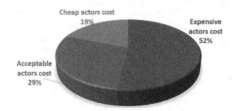

Fig. 8. Students' judgments about the cost levels.

Figure 9 shows the number of correct and incorrect answers for the BPMN elements characteristics exercise. In this figure, 67% of the responses are correct. Based on this result, we can deduce that the majority of students can evaluate the performance of BPMN elements. This result is also established based on their responses to the last question for each category of the second exercise, which is about the time behaviour and cost of BPMN elements.

Fig. 9. Correct and incorrect answers for the BPMN elements characteristics exercise.

Indeed, Fig. 10 depicts students' judgments about the characteristics levels of activities. 61% of students consider the time of activities in the BPMN model as normal, 23% as maximal and 16% as minimal (see Fig. 10 (a)). In addition, 74% of students considered activities as expensive, 16% as acceptable, and 10% as cheap (see Fig. 10 (b)).

Experiment 2: Uses our tool to estimate the actor characteristics levels and the BPMN element characteristics levels of the business process model illustrated in Fig. 4.

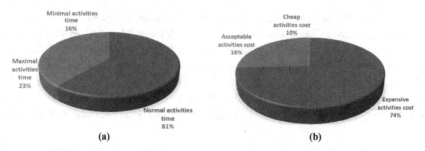

Fig. 10. Students' judgments about the characteristics levels of activities.

Our BPMN model is annotated by temporal constraints and semantic information (cost and organizational aspects).

Considering the limited space, we present an example of the actor characteristic (suitability) and an example of BPMN element characteristic such as the time behaviour of an activity.

If the designer selects *"Measures calculator thresholds"* menu and then "Performance *measures"* and choose the actor *"Omar"* with the *"Suitability"* characteristics, then the system displays the numeric values and their linguistics interpretations of different performance measures used for assessing the suitability of the actor. It also displays the estimated level of suitability.

For instance, the estimated suitability level of the actor *"Omar"* is *"Having Low Skills with a certainty degree of 63%"*. Figure 11 displays the interface for actor suitability evaluation.

Measures Calculator Threshold		
Measures Categories		**Characteristics**
○ Structural Measures		Suitability ▾
⦿ Performance Measures		
○ BPMN elements	Activity ▾	
⦿ Actor	Omar ▾	

Measures	Numeric values	Linguistic values
RDAAct : Actor Omar | Day Monday	20.0 %	Low
RGAAct : Actor Omar | Day Monday	80.0 %	High
PPTAct : Actor Omar | Task T7: check car availability	13 minutes	Moderate
PPTAct : Actor Omar | Task T9: validate reservation	10 minutes	Low
PPTAct : Actor Omar | Task T8: cancel reservation	5 minutes	Low
PPTAct : Actor Omar | Task T5: Create reservation	13 minutes	Moderate
PPTAct : Actor Omar | Task T6: determine date of rented and returned car	11 minutes	Low
WTAct : Actor Omar | Task T7: check car availability	9 minutes	Low
WTAct : Actor Omar | Task T9: validate reservation	7 minutes	Low
WTAct : Actor Omar | Task T8: cancel reservation	3 minutes	Low
WTAct : Actor Omar | Task T5: Create reservation	11 minutes	Moderate
WTAct : Actor Omar | Task T6: determine date of rented and returned car	7 minutes	Low
TWTDayPoolAct : Actor Omar | Pool Travel Agency | Day Monday	37 minutes	Low
TWTDayPoolAct : Actor Omar | Pool Travel Agency | Day Monday	37 minutes	High
PerAct : Actor Omar | Day Monday	68.51852 %	Low
AVAct : Actor Omar | Day Monday	71.15385 %	Low

Interept   The Suitability Level of the Actor Omar is: Having low Skills with a certainty degree of 63%

Fig. 11. Availability characteristic assessment interface [10].

In addition, if the designer selects "*Measures calculator thresholds*" menu and then "*Performance measures*" and choose the BPMN element "*Activity*" with the "*Time behavior*" characteristic, then the system displays the numeric values and their linguistics interpretations corresponding to the different activities used for assessing the time behaviour. It also displays the estimated level of time behaviour.

For instance, the estimated time behaviour level of the BPMN element "*Activity*" is "*Normal with a certainty degree of 67%*". Figure 12 presents the interface for the activity evaluation.

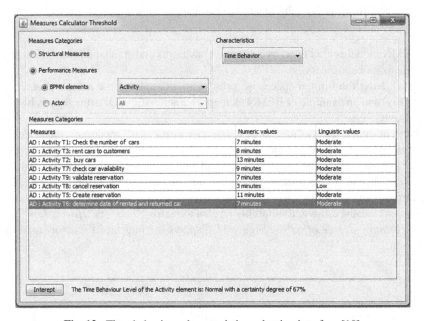

Fig. 12. Time behaviour characteristic evaluation interface [10].

Based on answers of students to the suitability questions, experiments reveal that the suitability of actors as having low skills. This result is conform with the assessment realized by "FuzzPer", which reflects that the actors in the presented BP model as "having low skills". As the same, regarding the time behaviour, students consider the time of activities in the BPMN model "Travel agency process" as "normal".

These compliant results demonstrate that our methodology provides promising results that should be shown based on further experiments.

7   Threats to Validity

This study, as every other empirical business process study, is subject to two type of threats: internal, external [20].

The internal validity threats are related to the following issues: The first issue is the use of three algorithms (J48, RandomTree and REPTree) to find the imprecise thresholds using our methodology. We chose REPTree algorithm for finding threshold values as it is the one that yielded the best results. Of course, we should find other algorithms to determine more objectively the values of thresholds. The second issue is that although the annotation of BPMN models are listed in the datasets used, these information has not been tested. Therefore, some errors may not have been discovered in some BPMN models. Considering this, our thresholds could have found faults that are yet undiscovered.

The external validity is related to the limited number of the used databases (one database). Our study covers only BPMN models having small/medium size. This means that the findings of this study cannot be generalized to all BPMN models, particularly those having complex size. Further tests on many other BP from different domains would be needed to generalize obtained results.

8 Conclusion

BP modeling is crucial for enterprises seeking to improve their performance. In this context, several researchers refers to different techniques that aim at improving a BP model performance [19, 21]. Some approaches assist BP designers to develop high-performance models while others propose measures to assess the performance [9, 11, 14]. However, despite all these initiatives, there is a lack of consensus about the used performance measures, their thresholds, etc.

To tackle these challenges, we proposed, in this paper, a fuzzy-based approach for assessing the performance of BPMN-based BP models with emphasis on two categories of characteristics: actor characteristics and BPMN elements characteristics. The approach is based on a set of performance measures such as Activity Duration (AD), Performance of an Actor per Day (PerDay$_{Act}$), etc. In addition, for a concise interpretation of the performance measures, the approach uses data mining techniques (decision tree) to determine thresholds that high-performance BP models should attain and/or maintain. The use of fuzzy logic aims at dealing with the approximate and imprecise nature of the obtained thresholds.

Furthermore, we automated the assessment process with a Java-based tool that calculates the values of the different metrics. Based on these values the tool determines levels of the actor's availability, suitability and cost; and levels of BPMN element's time behaviour and cost.

The preliminary experiments' results are very supportive of mixing data mining and fuzzy logic for better assessment of BP model performance.

In terms of future work, we focus on three main axes: 1) examine the integration of other performance measures and characteristics, like fault tolerance and maturity, into our methodology 2) Developing recommendations to BP engineers for higher performance BP models, And 3) validate the proposed fuzzy methodology for BP performance evaluation through some real case studies with business experts.

References

1. Chen, J., Wang, X., Zhai, J.: Pruning decision tree using genetic algorithms. In: International Conference on Artificial Intelligence and Computational Intelligence, pp. 244–248 (2009)

2. D'Ambrogio, A., Paglia, E., Bocciarelli, P., Giglio, A.: Towards performance-oriented perfective evolution of BPMN models. In: 49th International Conference on Spring Simulation Multi-Conference, SpringSim 2016, p. 15 (2016)
3. Eclipse Specification (2011). www.eclipse.org/documentation
4. Gonzalez-Lopez, F., Bustos, G.: Business process architecture design methodologies - a literature review. Int. J. Bus. Process Manag. 1317–1334 (2019)
5. Hall, M., Frank, E., Holmes, G., Pfahringer, B., Reutemann, P., Witten, I.H.: The weka data mining software: an update. ACM SIGKDD Explor. Newsl. 10–18 (2009)
6. Heinrich, R., Paech, B.: Defining the quality of business processes. In: 4th International Conference of Modellierung, Modellierung 2010, pp. 133–148 (2010)
7. Heinrich, R.: Aligning business process quality and information system quality. Ph.D. thesis (2013)
8. ISO/IEC 19510: information technology - object management group business process model and notation (2013)
9. Kchaou, M., Khlif, W., Gargouri, F.: Temporal, semantic and structural aspects-based transformation rules for refactoring BPMN model. In: The 16th International Joint Conference on e-Business and Telecommunications, Prague, Czech Republic, pp. 133–144 (2019)
10. Kchaou, M., Khlif, W., Gargouri, F.: A methodology for determination of performance measures thresholds for business process. In: The 15th International Conference on Evaluation of Novel Approaches to Software Engineering, pp. 144–157 (2020)
11. Khlif, W., Kchaou, M., Gargouri, F.: A framework for evaluating business process performance. In: The 14th International Conference on Software Technologies, pp. 371–383 (2019)
12. Kis, I., Bachhofner, S., Di Ciccio, C., Mendling, J.: Towards a data-driven framework for measuring process performance. In: Reinhartz-Berger, I., Gulden, J., Nurcan, S., Guédria, W., Bera, P. (eds.) BPMDS/EMMSAD -2017. LNBIP, vol. 287, pp. 3–18. Springer, Cham (2017). https://doi.org/10.1007/978-3-319-59466-8_1
13. Kluza, K., Nalepa, G.: Formal model of business processes integrated with business rules. Inf. Syst. Front. 21(5), 1167–1185 (2018). https://doi.org/10.1007/s10796-018-9826-y
14. Lanz, A., Reichert, M., Weber, B.: Process time patterns: a formal foundation. Int. J. Inf. Syst. 57, 38–68 (2016)
15. Quinlan, J.R.: Induction of decision trees. Mach. Learn. 1(1), 81–106 (1986)
16. Razzaq, S., et al.: Knowledge management, organizational commitment and knowledge-worker performance. Int. J. Bus. Process Manag. 25, 923–947 (2019)
17. Safavian, S.R., Landgrebe, D.: A survey of decision tree classifier methodology. IEEE Trans. Syst. Man Cybern. 21(3), 660–674 (1991)
18. Shapiro, R.M.: XPDL 2.0: Integrating process interchange and BPMN, pp. 183–194 (2006)
19. van der Aa, H., del-Río-Ortega, A., Resinas, M., Leopold, H., Ruiz-Cortés, A., Mendling, J., Reijers, H.: Narrowing the business-IT gap in process performance measurement. In: Nurcan, S., Soffer, P., Bajec, M., Eder, J. (eds.) CAiSE 2016. LNCS, vol. 9694, pp. 543–557. Springer, Cham (2016). https://doi.org/10.1007/978-3-319-39696-5_33
20. Wohlin, C., Runeson, P., Höst, M., Ohlsson, M.C., Regnell, B., Wesslén, A.: Experimentation in Software Engineering: An Introduction. Academic Publishers, Kluwer (2000)
21. Wynn, M.T., Low, W.Z., Nauta, W.: A framework for cost-aware process management: generation of accurate and timely management accounting cost reports. In: Asia-Pacific Conference on Conceptual Modelling, APCCM'9, pp. 79–88 (2013).
22. Zadeh, L.: Is there a need for fuzzy logic? Inf. Sci. 178(13), 2751–2779 (2008). https://doi.org/10.1016/j.ins.2008.02.012

Cloud Services Discovery Assistant for Business Process Development

Hamdi Gabsi$^{(\boxtimes)}$, Rim Drira, and Henda Hajjami Ben Ghezala

RIADI Laboratory, National School of Computer Sciences,
University of Manouba, La Manouba, Tunisia
{hamdi.gabsi,rim.drira,henda.benghezala}@ensi-uma.tn

Abstract. Business Process (BP) development can be defined as the process of constructing a workflow application by composing a set of services performing BP's activities. In this respect, cloud services prove indispensable to build business applications with higher performance, lower operating cost, and faster time-to-market. The crucial challenge facing several companies in cloud-based BP development is to effectively address the business activities and cloud services matching issue. Formerly, we present this issue as a discovery challenge of suitable cloud services performing abstract BP's activities. Business activities are generally named and described with non-standard format based on natural language and subjective terminology. In parallel, the great variety and the exponential proliferation of cloud services over the Web introduce several functionally similar offers with heterogeneous descriptions. Therefore, efficient and accurate cloud service discovery performing business activities requires a high level of expertise and a steep documentation curve. To address this challenge, firstly, we offer a publicly available cloud data-set, named ULID (Unified cLoud servIces Data-set), where services offered by different cloud providers are collected, unified and classified based on their functional features. Secondly, we introduce the concept of cloud-aware BP by proposing a Domain-Specific Language (DSL) named "BP4Cloud" to enrich BP modeling and specify cloud services requirements. Based on ULID data set and "BP4Cloud" language we propose an Activity-Services Matching algorithm that automates the discovery of cloud services performing BP's activities. As a part of the evaluation, we set up by clarifying the specification of BP4Cloud elements through a proof of concept implementation applied on a real BP. Then, we proceed by evaluating the precision and recall of our Activity-Service Matching algorithm.

Keywords: Cloud services discovery · Business process development · Natural language processing · Activity-service matching algorithm

1 Introduction

Cloud services are becoming the prominent paradigm for business process development. A business process can be defined as the combination of a set of activ-

© Springer Nature Switzerland AG 2021
R. Ali et al. (Eds.): ENASE 2020, CCIS 1375, pp. 51–80, 2021.
https://doi.org/10.1007/978-3-030-70006-5_3

ities which are performed in coordination within an organizational and technical environment. These activities jointly realize a business goal [1]. The BP development leads to define a workflow application which consists of coordinated executions of multiple activities that require access to high performance IT services [1]. For this reason a great interest has been paid to cloud computing environments which provide a dynamic provisioning of on demand shared IT services based on a pay-as-you-go model. The increasing interest for cloud services in business process development has led to an expeditious diversity of provided services to cover all the needs. Nonetheless, this diversity brings several challenges, essentially, the business activities and cloud services matching which can be defined as a discovery issue. In fact, the discovery process is defined as the process of detecting automatically or semi-automatically services performing business activities and delivering their related information [2]. Cloud services discovery is considered as a challenging task for different reasons. First, cloud providers often publish their services descriptions, pricing policies, and Service Level Agreement (SLA) rules on their portals in various and heterogeneous formats. Therefore, most of the available cloud services come with non-standard format (e.g., HTML documentation and textual descriptions). To deal with this heterogeneity, a steep documentation curve is required to clearly identify relevant services' functional features and compare several offers. Second, cloud services are continuously evolving (the update of existing services and the emergence of new services), handling this evolution during the discovery process is known to be a challenging task for business applications' developers. Several studies have been carried out to address these challenges using different approaches such as semantic-based approach [3] and syntactic-based approaches [4]. Through investigating different research studies, two main observations are deduced. First, the discovery scope cloud services is often limited to some services that are published in a specific description standard such as OWL-S [3] or Web Services Description Language (WSDL) [6]. This limitation is impractical since it expects available cloud services to have semantic tagged descriptions or WSDL describing files, which is not the case in a real-world scenario. Therefore, a general approach that ensures an automatic discovery of cloud services without making any assumptions about cloud services description language is needed. Second, the discovery of concrete cloud service performing an abstract business activity needs an alignment between the business activity requirements and cloud service specifications, this challenge can be defined as a business and IT alignment. Unfortunately, the business and IT alignment is not clearly conducted in several research studies [7]. As a result of which many cloud services relevant to the request may not be considered in the service discovery process. The above mentioned observations are, practically, conducted, in our work, through three main perspectives presenting our contributions.

- We handle the business and IT alignment by assisting the cloud resources requirements specification during BP modeling, thus we introduce the concept of cloud-aware BP. We propose a semantic enrichment of business activities description realized in full compliance with the standard Business Process

Model and Notation (BPMN) to cover both business and technical requirements and pave the way to the cloud services discovery step.

- We propose a cloud data-set, named ULID (Unified cLoud servIces Data-set), where services offered by different cloud providers are collected, unified and classified based on their functional features without making any assumptions about cloud services description language.
- We propose a discovery approach based on an activity-services matching algorithm ensuring the discovery of relevant cloud services performing business activities.
- We demonstrate the effectiveness of the proposed algorithm through experimental validation.

The present work is a comprehensive extension to our previous work [8]. We expand the discovery approach presented in [8] in order to assist SMEs and startups in cloud-based business process development. Precisely, we present three extensions to our initial discovery approach and demonstrate the improved framework that encompasses the enhancements of our cloud services discovery process. First, we consider, in this work, BP's activities as developer's requirements instead of keyword-based queries defined in [8]. This fact requires modeling business and technical requirements with regard to cloud services discovery process. Therefore, we propose a Domain-Specific Language (DSL) named "BP4Cloud" defining the concept of cloud-aware business process that ensures the enrichment of BP modeling. Second, we enrich the cloud services meta-model proposed in [8] in order to present relevant cloud services meta-data needed to define the service-activity matching. Third, considering BP's activities as discovery queries expects several improvements of our discovery approach to be suitable to the context cloud-based business process development. Therefore, we propose a new Activity-Services Matching algorithm that automates the discovery of cloud services performing business activities. The remainder of this paper is organized as follows: Sect. 2 presents the problem statement. In Sect. 3, we details our discovery assistant. Section 4 illustrates the evaluation of our work. In Sect. 5, we discuss the related work. Section 6 concludes the paper and outlines our ongoing works.

2   Problem Statement

Our main focus in this paper is to assist the discovery of cloud services required for BPs development. To effectively achieve our purpose, we propose to outline a substantial interaction between business designers and technical developers during the resources modeling and resources discovery. The resources modeling presents the specification of abstract entities that carry out the work related to activities which are in our context cloud services [1]. The resources discovery presents the identification of concrete cloud services needed to (i) the deployment and (ii) the performing of abstract BP's activities. The deployment of the BP requires identifying suitable infrastructure and platform services. These services provide virtualized resources and software tools needed for business development.

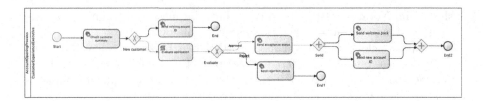

Fig. 1. BPMN process example.

The performing of BP activities requires a matching between abstract business activities and concrete software services. To illustrate, let us suppose the following scenario presented in Fig. 1. This scenario describes a simple BPMN process for online bank accounts opening: which initiates with an application request sent from a customer.

The first activity consists on checking the customer summary, if a similar request is already in process, his/her request will be rejected. Otherwise, the process evaluates the customer application, if the application is approved, a provisional account Id is generated and sent. In order to develop the bank account opening process using cloud service, two major steps should be conducted: First, we need to define technical cloud resources, essentially, IaaS and PaaS requirements. For instance, the evaluation application activity requires a computing resource to evaluate the customer's application. The check customer summary activity requires a database server to verify if the customer has already an account Id. The whole process may require a load-balancer to distribute the application traffic across the allocated compute resources. However, BPMN, which is the most used standard for the high-level description of BPs, supports neither the modeling of the required cloud resources nor their configuration features. This fact presents an important challenge for business designers. The second step consists of the discovery of software services performing abstract activities. For instance, the sending account Id activity can be performed by a service which sends notifications or emails. Our main purpose is to assist business designers in the above-mentioned steps.

3   Cloud Services Discovery Assistant

Our proposed cloud services discovery assistant is based mainly on three basic steps. First, we define a cloud aware business process based on our DSL "BP4Cloud" which enriches BP modeling in order to assist cloud services discovery. Second, we propose a centralized data-set that references scattered cloud services regardless of their providers and their heterogeneous descriptions in unified data-set publicly available. Third, we propose an activity-service matching algorithm in order to identify relevant cloud services satisfying technical and business requirements of business activities. An overview of our proposed discovery approach is presented in Fig. 2. Each step is detailed in the next sections.

3.1   BP4Cloud Language

BP4Cloud consists of a set of extension elements that allow the attachment of cloud resource perspectives to the BPMN standard. BP4Cloud comprises various aspects of specification namely, business specification and technical specification. The technical specification presents cloud services, mainly IaaS "Infrastructure as a Services" and PaaS "Platform as a Services" services, allowing to define the run-time environment responsible of business process execution. The business specification aims to assist SaaS "Software as a Service" services discovery to perform abstract business activities.

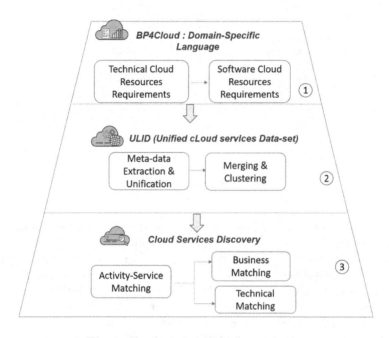

Fig. 2. Cloud services discovery assistant.

Technical Cloud Resources Specification. The technical specifications define the cloud infrastructure ensuring the execution of the business process. Figure 3 illustrates the meta model presenting the technical specifications.

The "infrastructure-requirements" meta-class presents the requirements in terms of compute capacity, storage devices and network resources necessary to perform business activities in the cloud. We present the "compute", "storage" and "network" meta-classes inheriting from the "infrastructure-requirements" meta-class. The "compute" meta-class is used to specify the computation capacities required to deploy and execute business activities. This class defines the configuration of servers and virtual machines offering highly scalable compute

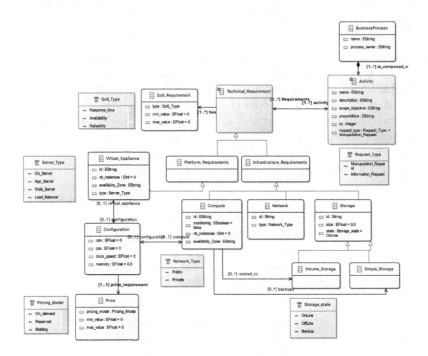

Fig. 3. BP4Cloud meta-model.

capacities that can be adjusted on demand. We assist business designers in specifying the configuration of cloud computing capabilities through the "configuration" meta-class. We define the following configuration attributes; the machine's RAM memory, internal storage capacity, clock frequency, and number of virtual CPUs. We provide default values for these configuration attributes ensuring the specification of a medium virtual machine to perform a given business activity. The virtual machine proposed by default is characterized by a RAM memory of 8 Gb, an internal storage capacity of 16 Gb, a clock frequency of 10,000 Mbit/s and a number of virtual CPU equal to 2. The "storage" meta-class defines the storage of data exchanged between business activities. The goal of this class is to assist business designers in modeling cloud resources presenting data backup based on business process flow control. Indeed, depending on the flow control model, an appropriate type of storage will be recommended. The parallel or conditional flow control models present an exchange of data in a shared way between different activities, this fact requires a temporary online storage. For a sequential flow control model, the data exchanged between the activities can be private, this requires permanent storage or archiving, so we recommend a "backup" or archiving type storage. The "Network" meta-class presents network resources providing communication mechanisms between different actors of the business process. It ensures an exchange of several information presenting the execution state of business activities. We support the specification of network resources as well as their characteristics such as bandwidth and through-put through the "Network" meta-class. The "platform-requirements" meta-class provides hardware and software tools for the implementation and execution of business activities. It offers middleware components, such as; web server, appli-cation server, databases, ensuring the development, customization and testing of business activities. Our goal is to help business designers define the technical specifications necessary to model the business process execution infrastructure in the cloud. We consider business designers to be non-cloud experts with an inter-mediate level of expertise. Therefore, these specifications have been presented in a simple way by defining basic cloud resources which can be exhaustively extended.

Business Cloud Resources Specification. Business specifications are used to enrich the modeling of activities to support the discovery of cloud services. In practice, these services are identified using our proposed Activity-Services Matching algorithm. To improve the performance and the results of the algo-rithm, we need accurate specifications related to the business logic of BP's activ-ities. For these reasons, we introduce the Business Logic meta-class which clas-sifies activities according to their business logic. This classification is basically inspired by Workflow Pattern Activity (WPA) [9]. We take advantage of cloud services categories detailed in ULID in order to assist services discovery by iden-tifying f a set of cloud services sharing the same business context as the activities. Figure 4 presents the "Business-Logic" meta-class.

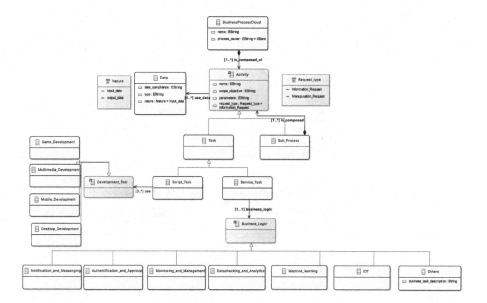

Fig. 4. Business-logic meta-class.

3.2   ULID: Unified cLoud ServIces Data-Set

After modeling the required cloud services using BP4Cloud, we propose a unified cloud services data-set "ULID" presenting a centralized source of services to efficiently assist the discovery process. We present ULID construction's steps dealing with several cloud services proprieties.

First, we manage the heterogeneous nature of cloud service by properly extracting relevant services capabilities from ambiguous services' descriptions. To do so, we propose an automated process for services 'capability extraction in order to identify services' functional features. Based on these features, we define a services' functional clustering to unify functionally similar services. Thus, we can reduce the search scope and we improve the response time of the discovery process.

Second, we deal with the huge diversity of scattered cloud services by proposing a structured main source that provides relevant services meta-data and avoids laborious documentation task in several providers web portals. In that respect, we introduce ULID which presents a centralized cloud service data-set to which the business designer has access to.

Last but not least, we manage the dynamic evolution of cloud services by regularly updating our data-set. Based on each commitment presented previously, we present ULID construction steps. In fact, Our data-set is based on three main steps which are: Meta-data Extraction & Unification, Merging & Clustering and Update detection. We give further details about these steps in the next sections.

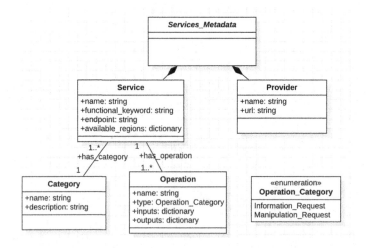

Fig. 5. Meta-model of cloud services meta-data.

Meta-data Extraction and Unification. This step aims to collect cloud services meta-data which are scattered in HTML pages of cloud providers web portals. To do so, we use a HTML parser to harvest relevant cloud services meta-data from these portals. The collected meta-data is stored in conformance with a unified meta-model of services description given in Fig. 5. Our meta-model defines relevant services meta-data that can facilitate services discovery and assist selection decisions.

The class "Service" provides the name, the description, the endpoint and the available regions of the service. Each cloud service has a category and offers multiple operations. A service's operation has a category that can be information request (IR) or manipulation request (MR). Information requests (IR) aim to retrieve diverse information regarding a particular request such as get attributes(), list methods() etc. Manipulation requests (MR) present several modification functions such as: create(), recommend(). The class "Provider" presents information related to the service's provider.

Identifying services functional features is considered as an important pillar in cloud services discovery. In order to automatically extract relevant keywords presenting the functional features of cloud services, we use a natural language processing tool named Stanford Parser [10]. The Stanford Parser can identify the grammatical structure of each sentence of service descriptions by creating grammatical relations or type dependencies among elements in the sentence. These dependencies are called Stanford Dependencies SDs [10]. In our work, we model keywords as a set of binary relations $<action, object>$, where action denotes the functional feature of the service. Object denotes the entities affected by the action. Then, we use the SD sets to properly identify the grammatical relations between $<action, object>$. In fact, each SD is a binary relation between a governor (also known as a regent or a head) and a dependent [10].

To illustrate, let's suppose this sentence "This service offers compute capacity in order to deploy workloads in a public cloud". We use the following SD:

- Relation direct object: dobj(governor, dependent) generally appears in the active voice, in which the governor is a verb, and the dependent is a noun or noun phrase as the direct object of governor. In our case, we obtain dobj(offers, capacity) and dobj(deploy, workloads).
- Relation adverbial clause modifier: advcl(governor, dependent), an adverbial clause modifier of a verb phrase or sentence is a clause modifying the verb (consequence, conditional clause, purpose clause, etc.). For instance, advcl(offers, deploy).
- Relation prepositional modifier: prep(governor, dependent), is any prepositional phrase that serves to modify the meaning of the verb, adjective, noun, or even another preposition. In our case, we obtain prep_in(deploy, cloud).

The basic keywords extracted above may not present relevant functional features semantics. For example, the pair {offers, capacity}, we expect that it is {offers, compute capacity}. Likewise, the pair {deploy, cloud} was expected to be {deploy, public cloud}. Therefore, the semantic extension of the basic extracted keywords is necessary. The semantic extension mainly refers to the noun part of the service functional feature. In fact, the semantic extension of nouns mainly includes qualifiers, adjectives, nouns, gerunds, and adverbs. Through the analysis of the text description of cloud services, we note that qualifiers, adverbs do not provide the semantic information, we need only a few adjectives to contain useful business semantic information. Therefore, we consider nouns and gerunds as modifiers for semantically extending the keywords. In the Stanford Parser, we mainly consider the noun compound modifier; nn(governor, dependent) relationship, which indicates that both the governor and dependent are nouns, and dependent is treated as a modifier to modify the governor.

Finally, we created a stop-word list to remove the meaningless functional features which contain verbs such as "allow, get, can, helps, etc.". We presented in our previous work [8], a real example tested on a text description of a compute service offered by AWS [11] (Fig. 6).

```
[('is', 'web service'), ('provides', 'compute capacity')]
[('make', 'computing easier')]
[('obtain', 'capacity'), ('configure', 'capacity')]
[('provides', 'computing environment')]
[('reduce', 'time'), ('scale', 'capacity')]
[('pay', 'capacity use')]
[('build', ' applications')]
[('includes', 'instances')]
[('use', 'Micro instances')]
[('increase', 'capacity'), ('decrease', 'capacity')]
[('commission', ' instances')]
[('maintain', ' availability'), ('scale', 'fleet'), ('maximize', 'performance'), ('minimize', 'cost')]
[('scale', ' services'), ('use', 'AWS Auto Scaling')]
[Finished in 1.4s]
```

Fig. 6. Functional keywords extraction [8].

Merging and Clustering. We classify services referenced in our data-set in unified categories. Our main purpose, in this step, is to provide unified services categories regardless of cloud providers. These categories are basically inspired by Workflow Pattern Activity (WPA) [9]. WAP describes a business function frequently found in BPs. Thom et al. [12] performed a manual analysis to identify relevant WAPs as well as their cooccurrences within a collection of 214 real wold BPs. Based on the frequency of appearance and potential reuse of a business function in the analyzed models, the authors define seven WPAs which are: Approval, Question-answer, Uni/Bi-directional Performative, Information Request, Notification, and Decision Making. Therefore, we offer a classification of cloud services inspired by WPAs in order to create a relationship of correspondence based on the business aspect between the activities of a business process and the cloud services. As a result, we ensure a pre-selection of a set of cloud services sharing the same business context as the activities, this fact can improve the performance and accuracy of our discovery algorithm. To do so, first of all, we extract appropriate keywords expressing the functional features of services categories as explained previously for services description. Second, we calculate the semantic similarity between each pair of categories based on extracted keywords and WPAs keywords descriptions. Finally, we gather categories into clusters using a modified K-means clustering algorithm. We detail each step as the following:

Classes Similarity Computation: We base our clustering approach on the following heuristic: *Services' categories over different providers tend to respond to the same business requirements if they share the same or similar keywords describing their functional features.*

After identifying categories' functional features which are the set of pairs $<action, object>$, we calculate the similarity $SC_{(C_1,C_2)}$ between services categories over different providers. We denote $C_i = \{p_{i1}, p_{i2}, p_{i3}, ..., p_{in}\}$ a category's functional features, where p_{in} is the pair $<action, object>$ and $|C_i|$ the cardinality of C_i, (the number of pairs p_i).

The similarity $SC_{(C_1,C_2)}$ is inspired from [13]. Indeed, the authors prove the relevance of the proposed similarity formula in the context of words pairs similarity. The main asset of this work is defining similarity in information theoretic terms which ensure the universality of the similarity measure. The main issue of many similarity measures is that each of them is tied to a particular application or assumes a particular domain model. Dealing with this issue, the proposed similarity measure has significantly improved words' pairs similarity. The similarity formula $SC_{(C_1,C_2)}$ presents the sum of the similarities between each pair p_{1i} of C_1, and the pairs $\{p_{2_1}, p_{2_2}, p_{2_3}, ..., p_{2_n}\}$ of C_2, normalized by the cardinality of C_1. Formally, we obtain;

$$SC_{(C_1,C_2)} = \frac{\sum_{i=1}^{|C_1|}\left(\frac{\sum_{j=1}^{|C_2|} S(p_{1i},p_{2j})}{|C_2|}\right)}{|C_1|} \tag{1}$$

where $S(p_{1i}, p_{2j})$ is the pairs similarity. We define the pairs similarity as follows:

- Let A_1 and A_2 respectively denote the actions in the pair p_1 and p_2.
- O_{i1} and O_{i2} respectively denote objects in the pair p_1 and p_2.
- w_1, w_2 denote the weight of the action part and the object part. We suppose that some predefined action has a higher weight such as; offer, provide, deliver, etc. These weights are defined by the developers.
- m is the minimum number of objects of the pair p_1 and p_2 $(min\_number\_objects(p_1, p_2))$ whereas n is the maximum number of objects of the pair p_1 and p_2 $(max\_number\_objects(p_1, p_2))$.

The pair similarity is calculated as:

$$S_{(p_1,p_2)} = w_1 S_{(A_1,A_2)} + w_2 \frac{\sum_{i=1}^{m} S_{(O_{i1},O_{i2})}}{n} \tag{2}$$

where $S_{(O_{i1},O_{i2})}$ is words similarity. We use Jacard Similarity Coefficient to calculate the word similarity. In fact, the Jaccard coefficient measures similarity between finite sample sets, and is defined as the size of the union divided by the size of the intersection of the sample sets.

$$J(E,F) = \frac{E \cup F}{E \cap F} \tag{3}$$

where E and F are two given sets of words. We create a feature set F(w) for each word 'w' (i.e for each object which is presented by a word in our context) containing the synonym set, generic word and interpretation of the word w. F(w) is created using BabelNet [14]. Based on [13], we define the similarity between the two words as follows:

$$S_{(w_1,w_2)} = \frac{2 \times I(F(w_1) \cap F(w_2))}{I(F(w_1)) + I(F(w_2))} \qquad (4)$$

where $I(S)$ represents the amount of information contained in a set of features S. $I(S)$ is calculated as:

$$I(S) = - \sum_{f \in S} log P(f) \qquad (5)$$

The probability $P(f)$ can be estimated by the percentage of words that have the feature f among the set of words that have the same part of speech in the entire BabelNet library database. When two words have the same feature set, then the maximum similarity is 1. The minimum similarity is 0 when the intersection of two words' features is empty.

Modified K-means Clustering Algorithm: The K-means algorithm is an algorithm widely used in the field of data mining. It aims to partition n elements (observations) into k clusters presented by k data centroids. Usually, k-means uses the Euclidean distance or Manhattan distance to assign each observation to the nearest cluster. We propose a modified K-means algorithm in order to have meaningful clusters and enhance the basic K-means algorithm results.

To do so, first, we left frequent and rare words unclustered. This fact is approved by the (Information Retrieval) IR community in order to have the best performance in automatic query expansion and avoids over-fitting.

Second, we enhance the cohesion and correlation conditions defined in the basic K-means algorithm by quantifying the cohesion and correlation of clusters based on our semantic functional similarity instead of Euclidean distances used in the basic K-means algorithm. The Euclidean distance is not consistent in our context because it does not provide meaningful information related to semantic similarity.

Third, to ensure that we obtain clusters with high cohesion, we only add an item (in our case a services' category) to a cluster if it satisfies a stricter condition, called cohesion condition. Given a cluster C, an item 'i' is called a kernel item if it is closely similar to at least half of the remaining items in C. Our cohesion condition requires that all the items in the cluster be kernel items. Formally;

$$i \in C \Rightarrow ||\forall j \in C, i \neq j, Sim(i,j) \geq \frac{||C|| - 1}{2} \qquad (6)$$

We illustrate the major steps of the modified K-means algorithm as follows.

To keep our data-set up-to-date and manage the dynamic evolution of cloud services, we verify, first, if a cloud provider offers a services update's detection API. In this case, we take advantage of this API by using an agent-based system able to execute existing update's APIs. Otherwise we revisit providers' web

---

Algorithm 1. Modified K-means Algorithm.

Input: classes scopes set $(S = s_1, ..., s_n)$
Input: k the number of clusters
  Let $sim(s_1, s_2)$be the similarity function
  Let $C = c_1, c_2, ..., c_k$ (set of cluster centroids)
  Let $L = L(s_i)|i = 1, 2, ..., n$ (set of cluster labels)
  for all $c_i inC$ **do**
    $c_i \leftarrow s_j$Initialize Centroid (c_i)
  end for
  for all $s_i inS$ **do**
    $l(c_i) \leftarrow index_{max_S im(s_i, c_j)}$
  end for
  $Centroid_{Change} \leftarrow False$
  $cohesion_{condition()} \leftarrow True$
  while $Until(Centroid_C hange \land Verify(cohesion_c ondition())) == True$ **do**
    for all $c_i inC$ **do**
      $UpdateCentroid(c_i)$
    end for
    for all $s_i inS$ **do**
      $M \leftarrow index_{max_S im(s_i, c_j)}$
      if $M <> l(s_i)$ **then**
        $l(s_i) \leftarrow M$
        $Centroid_C hange < - - True$
      end if
      $Verify(cohesion_{condition(s_i, s_l)})$
      $lin(1, 2, ..., n)l <> i$
    end for
    $lin(1, 2, ..., n)l <> i$
  end while

---

portal periodically using the web scraper to detect new cloud services or those
frequently updated. After updating ULID, we apply the clustering algorithm in
order to assign each new service to the suitable cluster.

3.3 Activity-Services Matching Algorithm

After modeling the required cloud resources, we need to particularly discover
concrete services that will be invoked to perform BP's activities. To do so, we
propose the Activity-Services Matching algorithm which is accomplished through
two main steps: the technical matching and the business matching. Figure 7
illustrates an overview of the matching algorithm steps.

Technical Matching. The main purpose of the technical matching is discovering the infrastructure environment based on technical requirements specified by
BP4Cloud. To do so, we establish, first, a mapping relationship between "agnostic cloud resources" specified in BP4Cloud and "concrete cloud resources" referenced in ULID. Figure 8 illustrates this mapping. However, this is not enough to

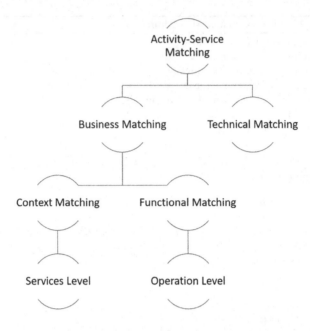

Fig. 7. Matching algorithm steps.

precisely define the infrastructure environment. Indeed, IaaS services need to be correctly configured. Several and conflicting criteria have to be considered such as VCPU, RAM, etc. No single service exceeds all other services in all criteria but each service may be better in terms of some of the criteria. Therefore, we consider IaaS services discovery and configuration as a MultiCriteria Decision Making (MCDM) problem. In our previous works [15] and [16], we have clearly addressed the technical matching.

Business Matching. The business matching is conducted through two steps. The context matching and the functional matching. Figure 9 illustrates the business matching steps.

Context Matching. The context matching discovers cloud services sharing the same business context as BP's activity. To identify the business context of BP's activities, we annotate each activity by scope and objective that clearly define the business context such as Send Notification, Database Access. The scope and objective are defined by the business designer. Defining the business context of a CS is more challenging due to its heterogeneous description and the abundant use of adjectives for commercial purposes. To deal with this challenge, we extract relevant keywords presenting the functional features of cloud services from its provided descriptions in supplier's web portals. To do so, we use the meta-data Extraction & Unification component of ULID allowing

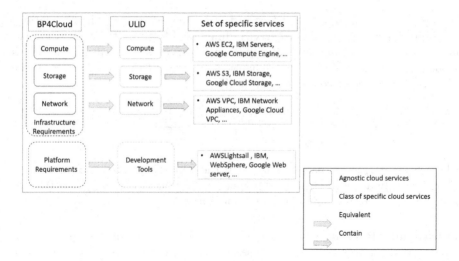

Fig. 8. Technical matching.

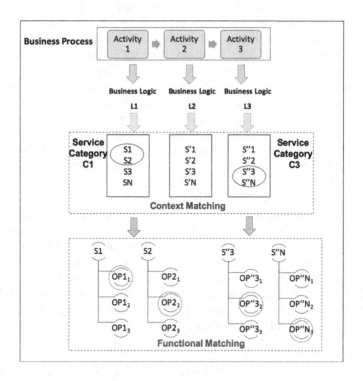

Fig. 9. Business matching.

the properly extract functional keywords modeled as a set of binary relations $<action, object>$. After defining services functional features, the context matching is based on the semantic similarity between service's keywords and activity's scope and objective. We use the semantic similarity $SIM_{(S_1, A_1)}$ detailed in the Merging & Clustering component of ULID.

$$SIM_{(S_1, A_1)} = \frac{\sum_{i=1}^{|S_1|} \left(\frac{\sum_{j=1}^{|A_1|} SIM(s_{1i}, a_{1j})}{|A_1|} \right)}{|S_1|}$$

where $S(s_{1i}, a_{1j})$ is the pairs similarity. If the semantic similarity $SIM(S_1, A_1)$ is greater than a specific threshold (experimentally fixed in our work as 0.5), S_i is considered as candidate for the functional matching.

Functional Matching. The output of the context matching is a set of candidate cloud services that share the same business context as the activity. The functional matching aims to identify the CS's operations that can perform the BP's activity. Inspired by [17], we perform the functional matching by evaluating how a service operation fulfills an activity requirement. This is performed by answering two symmetric questions: (1) how the activity can fulfill required inputs for the service operation; and (2) how the service operation can fulfill expected outputs of the activity. To do so, first, we classify cloud services operations and business activities into two categories: information request (IR) and manipulation request (MR). Based on this classification, we identify candidate operations according to the activity request type. We define a matched operation if two main elements are verified: a matched context and matched inputs/outputs. A matched context is defined through two steps. First, we take advantage of the structure of cloud services operations' naming, which is typically a pair $<action\ object>$, to calculate the semantic similarity between the operation and the activity's action. If this similarity is greater than a fixed threshold, the second step consists on verifying if the operation's object is a generic word of the activity's object, that means the activity's object satisfies the relationship "is a" an operation's object. We consider an operation is a candidate for the inputs/outputs matching if it satisfies the two above-mentioned conditions. The input/output matching consists of a matching level and matching degree. The matching degree consists of four elements: SIF: Service's operation Input Fulfillment, AIR: Activity's Input Redundancy, AOF: activity's Output Fulfillment, and SOR: Service's operation Output Redundancy. SIF and AOF are, respectively, the ratio of the fulfillment of the service operation's inputs and activity's outputs by the activity's inputs and service operation's outputs. AIR and SOR are, respectively, the ratio of redundancy (unused) of the activity inputs and service operation outputs in fulfilling the service operation inputs and activity outputs. SIF, AIR, AOF, and SOR have values in [0.1]. Formally:

$$SIF = \frac{matched\,inputs\,count}{Operation\,input\,size}$$

$$SOR = \frac{Unusedoperationoutputs}{Operationoutputsize}$$

$$AIR = \frac{Unusedactivityinputs}{Activityinputssize}$$

$$AOF = \frac{matchedoutputscount}{Activityoutputssize}$$

A match level can be precise, over, partial, or mismatch and it is specified based on SIF, AIR, AOF, and SOR in the following rules:

- Precise: if $(SIF = 1 \wedge AOF = 1) \wedge (AIR = 0 \wedge SOR = 0)$
- Over if $(SIF = 1 \wedge AOF = 1) \wedge (AIR > 0 \vee SOR > 0)$
- Partial if $(SIF >= iMT \wedge SIF < 1) \wedge (AOF >= oMT \wedge AOF < 1)$
- Mismatch if $SIF < iMT \vee AOF < oMT$

iMT and oMT are customized matching thresholds for the ratio of fulfillment of service operation inputs and activity outputs by activity inputs and service operation outputs, respectively. Depending on particular business context, we can set suitable values for iMT and oMT to get more or less partial matched services, e.g. they can be set to 0.5. The match degree is based on how much fulfillment of data elements between an activity and a service operation. If there are more than one service operations which are matched with the activity then the list of matched service operations is sorted according to the following rules:

1. precise>over>partial>mismatch
2. If two operations are both over match then
   (a) The smaller the value SOR is the better the matched operation is.
   (b) If they have the same value SOR then the smaller the value AIR is the better the matched operation is.
3. If two operations are both partial match then
   (a) The larger the value AOF is the better the matched operation is.
   (b) If they have the same value AOF then the larger the value SIF is the better the matched operation is.
   (c) If they have the same values AOF and SIF then we apply the rules of the values SOR and AIR as in case of over match above.
4. If two operations are both mismatch then they are considered as the same.

Algorithm 2 illustrates the Acitivity-Services Matching Algorithm.

4   Application and Performance Analysis

In order to illustrate our discovery assistant, we set up, firstly, by clarifying the specification of BP4Cloud elements applied on the use case, "Online Bank Accounts Opening". Then, we evaluate each step of ULID construction process as well as the modified K-means clustering algorithm. Finally, we proceed evaluating the overall performance of our Activity Service Matching Algorithm.

Algorithm 2. Acitivity-Services Matching Algorithm.

Input: Business Activity A

  Let S be a Cloud Service

  Let CS be set of the Candidate Services

  {Context Matching}

  Select S where $S.Class == A.BusinessLogic$

  if $Sim(A.Scope_{objective}, S.Keywords_{set}) >= 0.5$ **then**

    $Add(Candidate_{services}, S)$

  end if **{Functional Matching}**

  for all $SinCandidate_{Services}$ **do**

    Select $S.Operations_{Set} where A.Request_{Type} == S.Operation_{Category}$

    if $SSim(A.Verb, S.Operation_{Verb}) >= 0.7$ **then**

      if $A.Object is_a(S.Operation_{Object})$ **then**

        $Add(Candidate_{Operaton}, S.Operation)$

      end if

    end if

  end for

  $matchCount = 0$

  $unusedCount = 0$

  for all $opinCandidate_{Opereration}$ **do**

    for all $inpinop.Input_{set}$ **do**

      $m = match(inp, A.input)$ (the match function checks the compatibility between data types.)

      if $m <> "mismatch"$ **then**

        $matchCount ++$

      end if

    end for

  end for

  for all $a_i input in A.input$ **do**

    if $a_i input.used == "false"$ **then**

      $unusedCount ++$

    end if

  end for

  $Sif = matchCount/S.Input.size()$

  $unusedCount/A.Input.size()$

  if $Sif == 1 \wedge Air == 0$ **then**

    $matchingInput.Level = "precise"$

  else if $Sif == 1 \wedge Air > 0$ **then**

    $matchingInput.Level = "over"$

  else if $Sif < 1 \wedge Sif >= iMT(0,5)$ **then**

    $matchingInput.Level = "partial"$

  else if $Sif < iMT(0,5)$ **then**

    $matchingInput.Level = "mismatch"$

  end if { We apply the same algorithm for matching the outputs as matching the inputs}

  if $(matchingInput.Level == "precise" \wedge matchingOuput.Level == "precise"$ **then**

    $matchingOperation.Level == "precise"$

  else if $matchingInput.Level == "precise" \wedge matchingOutput.Level == "over"$ **then**

    $(matchingInput.Level = "over"$

  else if $matchingInput.Level == "partial" \wedge matchingOutput.Level <> "mismatch"$ **then**

    $(matchingInput.Level = "partial"$

  else if $matchingInput.Level == "mismatch" \vee matchingOutput.Level == "mismatch"$ **then**

    $(matchingInput.Level = "mismatch"$

  end if

4.1 BP4Cloud Evaluation

We present an extract of BP4Cloud file specifying the activity "Check customer summary" requirements. The activity requires a compute server, as IaaS requirement, and a database server as PaaS requirements. Its business logic is "Datachecking_and_Analytics".

```
1   <is_composed_of
2       xsi:type="CloudBusinessProcess:Service_Task"
3       name="Check customer summary"
4       description="Verify if a customer has already made an
              application earlier"
5       key_words="Check summary" , "Verify application", "Validate
              Summary"
6       preconditins=""
7       effects=""
8       id="1">
9       <use_data
10          href="Data.xmi#/" input_data_type="String" output_data_type="
              Boolean"/>
11      <requirements
12          xsi:type="CloudBusinessProcess:Data_Base_Server"
13          href="Data_Base_Server.xmi#/">
14      <requirements
15          xsi:type="CloudBusinessProcess:Compute"
16          href="Compute.xmi#/" id="1" vmsize="Meduim">
17      <business_logic
18          href="Datachecking_and_Analytics.xmi#/"/>
```

To practically evaluate our specification, we measure the complexity of two process models, one using the standard BPMN and the other using BPMN extended by BP4Cloud. The complexity of a process model can be defined as the degree to which a BP is difficult to analyze and understand. [18]. Huber et al. [18], propose to categorize BP complexity metrics. We consider the following metrics:

- The number of activities and control-flow elements in a process metric (NOAC). It counts the activities and control-flow elements of a process, which are the gateways in BPMN.
- McCabe's Cyclomatic Complexity metric (MCC) measures the number of control paths through the process. MCC is defined to be $e - n + 2$, where e is the number of edges and n is the number of nodes in the control flow graph.
- Control-flow Complexity metric (CFC) is defined as the number of mental states that have to be considered when a designer develops a process. It is calculated as $C_{XOR} + C_{OR} + C_{AND}$, where C_{XOR} is complexity of XOR-split (equals to number of branches that can be taken), C_{OR} complexity of OR-split (equals to number of states that may arise from the execution of the split), and C_{AND} complexity of AND-split (always equals 1). The higher the value of C_{XOR}, C_{OR}, and C_{AND}, the more complex is the process design.

The online bank accounts opening process designed using BP4Cloud has the same control-flow elements (NOAC), activities elements (NOA, control paths (MCC) (in our use case e=15 and n=15) and the control-flows (CFC). Using the presented metrics, we can clearly demonstrate that using BP4Cloud is not in any view more complex. In fact, BP4Cloud does neither modify the control-flow elements of the BP nor its activities.

4.2 ULID Construction Component Evaluation

To ensure a proper evaluation of ULID construction component, essentially, the merging & clustering step, we proceed by an external evaluation, namely, the clustering results are evaluated based on data that was not used for the clustering, such as known class labels and external benchmarks. These types of evaluation methods measure how close the clustering is to the predetermined benchmark classes [19]. To do so, we test the UCC on a real data-set presenting Azure Microsoft cloud services. The test-set is composed of 205 cloud services offered by Azure Microsoft [20]. It is created by parsing Azure Microsoft web portal [20] and collecting services meta-data.

Services Functional Keywords Extraction. By analyzing the description of 205 services using the Stanford Parser, it is worth pointing that the functional keywords extraction highly depends on the terms used by the service providers in describing their services. In some cases, we obtain non-meaningful pairs $<action, object>$ due to the abundant use of adjectives for commercial purpose. In our case, we obtained 14 non-meaningful pairs. In order to verify the effectiveness of our method of extracting functional keywords (pairs $<action, object>$), we randomly selected 50 services as experimental data. We ask five developers to manually extract the sets of functional keywords pairs for each service, and compare them to the sets of functional keywords pairs automatically extracted. We evaluate the experimental results by calculating the precision and recall rate. The formula of the precision and recall rates are defined as follows:

$$Precision = \frac{S_A \cap S_M}{S_A} \qquad Recall = \frac{S_A \cap S_M}{S_M} \qquad (7)$$

$$F_1 = \frac{2 \times Precision \times Recall}{Precision + Recall} \qquad (8)$$

Where S_M represents the set of functional keywords pairs that is extracted manually, S_A denotes the set of functional keywords pairs that is automatically extracted. Based on [8], we present the Table 1 that shows the experimental results (for reason of space restraint, we display a sample of five sets). For the extraction result, we have 0,7 as precision average, 0,98 as recall average and 0.817 as F- Measure average.

From Table 1, it can be concluded that the results of the functional keywords extracted by developers are different. The reason is that each developer has a

Table 1. Extracted functional keywords results [8].

Automatically extracted set of functional keywords pairs	Manually Extracted set of functional keywords pairs	Precision	Recall	F- Measure
S_1 : {<$Create, Virtual\_machine$>}	S_1 : {<$Create, Virtual\_machine$>}	1	1	1
S_2 : {<$Create, Mobile\_application$>, <$Build, Mobile\_application$>, <$Deploy, Mobile\_application$>}	S_2 : {<$Create, Mobile\_application$>, <$Deploy, Mobile\_application$>}	0,67	1	0,8
S_3 : {<$Detect, Human\_faces$>, <$Identify, People$>, <$Organize, images$>, <$Compare, Image$>, <$Verify, Features$>, <$Provide, Face\_algorithm$>}	S_3 : {<$Detect, Human\_faces$>, <$Identify, People$>, <$Compare, Image$>, <$Verify, Features$>, <$Provide, Face\_algorithm$>}	0,83	1	0,9
S_4 : {<$Create, Data\_pipelines$>, <$Monitor, Data\_pipelines$>, <$Orchestrate, workflows$>}	S_4 : {<$Create, Data\_pipelines$>, <$Monitor, Data\_pipelines$>, <$Accelerate, Data\_integration$>, <$Orchestrate, workflows$>}	0,75	1	0,86
S_5 : {<$Protect, Data$>, <$Provide, Backup$>}	S_5 : {<$Protect, Data$>, <$Provide, Backup$>}	1	1	1

different understanding of services description. The recall rate of the extracted results is almost close to 1.0. This shows that the automatically extracted sets of functional keywords pairs can cover all the keywords sets of each service. The precision average of the extraction results is 0,7, lower than the recall rate. The F-measure average is 0.817. This means that the automatically extracted functional keywords pairs provides acceptable results, but it leaves scope for enhancements due to the non- standardized description used by services providers.

Modified K-Means Clustering Algorithm. While presenting our approach, we mention that we take advantage of the proposed services categories already offered by services providers. Thus, we applied our clustering algorithm on services' categories to unify them over different providers. Our approach remains accurate if we apply it directly on cloud services, namely we cluster services instead of services' categories. In that respect, we test our clustering algorithm on the test-set composed of 205 services offered by Azure Microsoft [20]. These services are functionally clustered, by the provider, in 18 categories (Machine learning, Analytics, Compute, Management services, etc) which present the predetermined benchmark classes.

We use the Purity of the Cluster as a metric to analyze the effectiveness of the modified K-means algorithm [19]. The following is the definition of cluster purity: suppose that D is the set of services to be clustered and C is the result of a clustering on D. $C_i \in C$ denotes a cluster in C, whereas S denotes the standard classification result on D, $s \in S$ denotes a class s in S, p_i denotes the largest number of services in the cluster C_i which are in common with s. The cluster purity CP (C_i) is defined as:

$$CP(C_i) = \frac{1}{|C_i|} max(p_i) \tag{9}$$

The clustering purity of the whole set of service to be clustered is defined as:

$$CP(C) = \sum_{i=1}^{C} \frac{|C_i|}{|D|} CP(C_i) \tag{10}$$

We set up our modified K-means algorithm on $k = 18$. Figure 10 presents the clusters returned by the algorithm. To correctly interpret our results, inspired by [8] we compare the purity values given by our algorithm to those given by he basic K-means algorithm. Table 2 shows the clustering results.

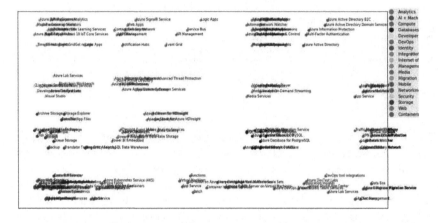

Fig. 10. Services clustering results [8].

Using the modified K-means algorithm, the number of services in each cluster is slightly different from that obtained according to the pre-classified services. This difference is due to some confusing descriptions basically for services in the integration and management tools clusters as well for the security and identity clusters. This explains the reason why the CP value is not very high for these clusters.

In light of the clustering results, we have 0,78 as purity value. It is worth mentioning that the proposed modifications (the cohesion condition, the weak correlation and the semantic similarity function) made on the basic K-means algorithm have contributed to better purity values (0,78 instead of 0,60).

4.3   Activity-Service Matching Algorithm Evaluation

In order to evaluate the effectiveness of our algorithm, experiments were conducted to evaluate its precision and recall on the BP presented in the problem statement section. The precision evaluates the capability of the algorithm to retrieve top-ranked services that are most relevant to the activity. The recall evaluates the capability of the algorithm to get all the relevant cloud services [21].

Formally;

$$P = \frac{|S_{Rel}|}{|S_{Ret}|} \qquad R = \frac{|S_{Rel}|}{|Rel|}$$

Table 2. Cluster purity results [8].

Cluster results	Central service of cluster	Number of services	Purity values	Basic K-means purity
Cluster 1: Analytics	Azure Analysis Services	15	0,87	0,67
Cluster 2: Compute	Virtual Machines	13	0,85	0,62
Cluster 3: Containers	Container Registry	7	1	0,57
Cluster 4: Databases	Azure Database	11	0,91	0,72
Cluster 5: AI + Machine Learning	Machine Learning Services	31	0,90	0,65
Cluster 6: Developer Tools	Azure Lab Services	9	1	0,67
Cluster 7: DevOps	Azure DevOps Projects	8	0,88	0,63
Cluster 8: Identity	Azure Active Directory	6	0,67	0,50
Cluster 9: Integration	Event Grid	5	0,60	0,40
Cluster 10: Web	Web Apps	7	0,86	0,57
Cluster 11: Storage	Storage	13	0,92	0,69
Cluster 12: Security	Security Center	11	0,55	0,42
Cluster 13: Networking	Virtual Network	13	0,85	0,62
Cluster 14: Mobile	Mobile Apps	8	0,88	0,50
Cluster 15: Migration	Azure Migrate	5	1	0,60
Cluster 16: Media	Media Services	8	1	0,75
Cluster 17: Management Tools	Azure Managed Application	21	0,67	0,48
Cluster 18: Internet of Things	IoT Central	14	0,92	0,64
		Clustering Purity	0,78	0,60

$$P_k = \frac{|S_{Rel,k}|}{k} \qquad P_r = P_{|Rel|} = \frac{|S_{Rel,|Rel|}|}{|Rel|}$$

where Rel denotes the set of relevant services, S_{Ret} is the set of retuned services, S_{Rel} is the set of returned relevant services and $S_{Rel,k}$ is the set of relevant services in the top k returned services. Among the above metrics, P_r is considered to most precisely capture the precision and ranking quality of the algorithm. We also plotted the recall/precision curve (R-P curve). In an R-P curve figure, the X-axis represents recall, and the Y-axis represents precision. An ideal discovery result presents a horizontal curve with a high precision value. The R-P curve is considered by the IR community as the most informative graph showing the effectiveness of the discovery algorithm [21].

In order to evaluate our proposed algorithm, we asked several BP designers and technical developers who are familiar with cloud services uses to identify the relevant services meeting the business activities. Table 3 illustrates the online bank account process results. For reason of space restraint, we display some relevant services related to the activities "check customer summary" and "send account id".

We evaluated the precision of the proposed services and report the average top-2, top-5, and top-10 precision. To ensure the top-10 precision is meaningful, we selected activities for which we can identify more than 15 relevant services over different providers. Figure 11 illustrates the results. The top-2, top-5, and top-10 precisions related to the context matching of our algorithm are, respectively, 91%, 87%, 74%. The precision related to the functional matching can be 1 or 0. Finding the suitable operation performing the activity is considered as 1 in terms of precision value, else the precision is estimated to 0.

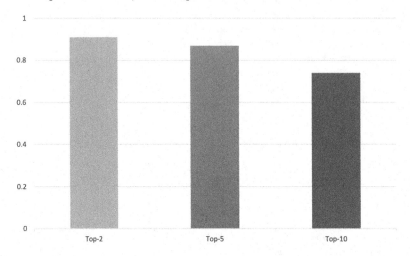

Fig. 11. Top-k precision for retrieved services.

The evaluation demonstrates that taking into account the context of both the business process and activity using their business features during the context matching can effectively provide acceptable precision values (91%, 87%), which means, we can identify suitable candidate services. The discovery of suitable service operation can more challenging since the functional matching involves different matching level. The inputs/outputs matching is considered as the main important step to validate if a candidate operation can perform the activity.

We plot the average R-P curves to illustrate the overall performance of the matching algorithm. As mentioned previously, an appropriate discovery result has a horizontal curve with a high precision value. Typically, precision and recall are inversely related, ie. as precision increases, recall falls and vice-versa. A balance between these two needs to be achieved. As presented in our previous work [8], Fig. 12 illustrates that for a recall average equals to 0,63 we have 0,85 as precision value. As an example, for the service activity "Check customer summary", we have 20 services considered as relevant in ULIT i.e $|Rel| = 20$, the matching algorithm returns a total of 16 services i.e $|S_{Ret}| = 16$, among them 13 services are considered relevant i.e $|S_{Rel}| = 12$. We obtain a precision value $P = 13/16 = 0,81$ and a recall value $R = 13/20 = 0,65$.

It is worth pointing out that in some cases, depending on particular context, high precision at the cost of a recall or high recall with lower precision can be chosen. Thus, evaluating a matching algorithm for services discovery must be related to the purpose of the discovery. In our case a compromise between the recall and the precision values is necessary. Therefore, we can announce the proposed algorithm provides accurate results for cloud services discovery.

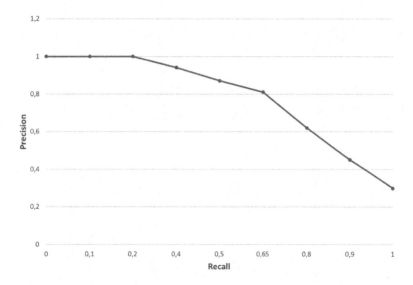

Fig. 12. R-P curves [8].

5   Related Work

Despite various efforts made to assist cloud services discovery for business process development, several challenges remain for further investigation, particularly business activities and cloud services matching. This matching is considered as a discovery challenge. In that respect, the research efforts can be presented in two different points of view, namely: architecture view and matchmaking view [3]. From one side, the architecture view is divided into centralized and decentralized. The centralized architecture depends on one central node that provides a complete view of all cloud services being offered in the market. This architecture can be achieved by proposing a cloud services registry or using cloud broker platforms. Actually, several cloud broker platforms have been proposed. Jrad et al.[23] developed a cloud broker system to select cloud services based on the user QoS requirements and SLA attributes. The authors developed a utility-based algorithm for matching user functional and non-functional requirements to SLA attributes of cloud providers. Rajganesh et al. [24] proposed a broker based cloud computing framework for enabling the users to specify their services requirements in terms of numerical representation. With respect to the user specification, the proposed broker constructs the cloud ontology to represent the available services from the service repository. The appropriate services are represented using semantic network which enables the user to know about the available services as per their posted requirements. It is worth pointing that, even though cloud broker platforms can provide assistance in the discovery process, most of them are based on an additional layer between the provider and the final cloud user which can complicate the service's delivery chain and certainly increase the services' cost. In our work, we aim to propose an assistance

Table 3. Activity-Services Matching algorithm Evaluation.

Activity	Scope/Objective	Relevant Services	Returned Services	Context Matching	SIM (S.KW, A.Scope)	Business Matching
				Extracted keywords		Returned Operation
Check summary	Database Access/Availability Check	Amazon SimpleDB Amazon DynamoDB Amazon RDS Amazon Aurora Amazon Neptune Amazon Redshift Oracle Database	Amazon SimpleDB	('query', 'data items') ('storing', 'data items') ('serving', 'requests')	0.796	Query()
			Amazon RDS	('query', 'data items') ('replicate', 'databases') ('scale', 'database setup')	0.796	–
			Amazon DynamoDB	('handle', 'requests') ('Create', 'table') ('handle', 'data')	0.642	Query()
			Amazon Neptune	('build', 'queries') ('querying', 'database')	0.597	Select ()
			Oracle Database	('retrieve', 'information')	0.503	Query()
Send account ID	Send/ Receive Message	Amazon SQS Amazon SNS Amazon SimpleMail Amazon WorkMail IBM BlueMix Twilio IBM BlueMix SendGrid	Amazon SQS	('send', 'messages') ('receive', 'messages') ('losing', 'messages')	1	Send Message()
			Amazon SNS	('fan out', 'messages') ('fan out', 'notifications')	0.674	Publish()
			Amazon SimpleMail	('send', 'email') ('send', 'marketing') ('integrate', 'email clients')	0,791	Send Email()
			Amazon WorkMail	('access', 'business email') ('use', 'email journaling') ('encrypt', 'data')	0.562	Send Message()

framework which allow business designer to fulfill seamless discovery process without any intermediaries, so that, they can better assume their decisions, and control their budgets. The centralized architecture can be achieved using public registries such as Musabah et al. [25] who provided a centralized cloud service repository. The authors propose a harvesting module to extract data from the web and make it available to different file format. The harvesting module uses an algorithm for learning the HTML structure of a web page. This work requires the user to determine specific control parameters such as targeted web page URL and the required information from in the targeted web page. Moreover, the collected data sets lack main service information such as services' description and operations. From another side, the matchmaking view is divided into syntactic-based and semantic-based. The semantic-based matchmaking approaches are based on semantic description to automate the discovery and selection process. [3] proposed a cloud services ontology with automated reasoning to support services discovery and selection. However, the discovery scope, in this work, is depending on the pre-existence of providers specific ontologies (OWL-S services description files) that require mapping techniques to coordinate the difference between agnostic (abstract) and vendor dependent concepts to support interoperability. Even though many semantic approaches are scientifically interesting [3], they require that the business designers have intimate knowledge of semantic services and related description and implementation details which makes their usage difficult. Moreover, from the service requestor's perspective, the requestor may not be aware of all the knowledge that constitutes the domain ontology. Specifically, the service requestor may not be aware of all the terms related to the service request. As a result of which many services relevant to the request may not be considered in the service discovery process. The syntactic-based approaches are, generally, based on WSDL description of cloud services. [6] proposed a clustering algorithm based on similarity between users query concepts and functional description parameters of cloud services expressed in a WSDL document. Despite the high precision values found in this work, generally assuming that the candidate cloud services are described using WSDL files, is considered as impractical limitation. In [26], the authors proposed the use of BPSim, which is a standard that provides a framework for structural and capacity analysis of BP models specified by the use of BPMN or XPDL (XML Process Definition Language). However, it is limited to introduce BPMN extensions to enhance its expressive capabilities without considering the runtime environment. In fact, the resource perspective may change depending on the runtime environment, notably, cloud environments require specific resources that are different from other runtime environments. The analysis of several research studies illustrates the main motivations of our proposal which are:

- First, the relevance of a centralized architecture that references scattered cloud services regardless of their providers and their heterogeneous descriptions in unified data-set. This fact can practically assist the developers in a seamless search for relevant cloud services.

- Second, the need to integrate cloud services requirements specification during business process modeling in order to handle the business and IT alignment.
- Third, the need for an efficient matching approach which does not make any assumptions, such as particular standard or specific semantic representation, about the description language of available cloud services.

6   Conclusion

This paper aims to provide efficient support to discover cloud services required for business process development. To achieve our aim, we define a cloud-aware BP by proposing BP4Cloud which is a BPMN extension that supports the design of cloud resource perspective requirements. BP4Cloud offers a solution for coordinating cloud resources between business designers and technical developers. Following the modeling of the required cloud resource, we propose a public cloud service data-set named ULID which is available on [22]. ULID services are classified according to their functional features using our clustering algorithm. We used ULID in our Activity-Services Matching algorithm to assist technical developers in discovering the required cloud services. Our proposed algorithm is conducted through two steps; the context matching which aims to discover services that share the same business context as the business activity and the business matching which aims to identify the suitable operation performing the activity. Our experimental evaluation has demonstrated that the Activity-Services Matching algorithm can potentially assist technical developers owing to its precision. Although we believe that our algorithm leaves scope for a range of enhancements, yet it provides suitable results. As ongoing work, we intend to conduct the composition of the discovered cloud resources in order to develop the cloud workflow application.

References

1. Carrillo, A., Sobrevilla, M.: BPM in the cloud: a systematic literature review. In: Software Engineering (cs.SE) (2017)
2. Sun, L., Dong, H., Khadeer, F., Hussain, Hussain, O.K., Chang, E.: Cloud service selection: state of the-art and future research directions. J. Netw. Comput. Appl. **45**, 134–150 (2014)
3. Martino, B.D., Pascarella, J., Nacchia, S., Maisto, S.A., Iannucci, P., Cerr, F.: Cloud services categories identification from requirements specifications. In: International Conference on Advanced Information Networking and Applications Workshop, vol. 1, pp. 436–441 (2018)
4. Lizarralde, I., Mateos, C., Rodriguez, J.M., Zunino, A.: Exploiting named entity recognition for improving syntactic-based web service discovery. J. Inf. Sci. **45**, 9–12 (2018)
5. Bey, K.B., Nacer, H., Boudaren, M.E.Y., Benhammadi, F.: A novel clustering-based approach for SaaS services discovery in cloud environment. In: Proceedings of the 19th International Conference on Enterprise Information Systems, vol. 1, pp. 546–553. SciTePress (2017)

6. Nacer, A.A., Godart, C., Rosinosky, G., Taria, A., Youcef, S.: Business process outsourcing to the cloud: balancing costs with security risks. Comput. Ind. **104**, 59–74 (2019)
7. Nagarajan, R., Thirunavukarasu, R., Selvamuthukumaran: Cloud broker framework for infrastructure service discovery using semantic network. Int. J. Intell. Eng. Syst. **11**, 11–19 (2018)
8. Gabsi, H., Drira, R., Ghezala, H.H.B.: Cloud services discovery and selection assistant. In: Evaluation of Novel Approaches to Software Engineering, pp. 158–169 (2020)
9. Workflow Resource Patterns (2018). http://www.workflowpatterns.com/patterns/resource/. Accessed 02 Sept 2020
10. Marneffe, M.-C., Manning, C.D.: The stanford typed dependencies representation. In: Proceedings of the Workshop on Cross-Framework and Cross-Domain Parser Evaluation, pp. 1–8 (2015)
11. Amazon compute service description (2020). https://aws.amazon.com/ec2/?nc1=h_ls. Accessed 05 Sept 2020
12. Lucineia, T., Manfred, R., Iochpe, C.: Activity patterns in process-aware information systems: basic concepts and empirical evidence. Int. J. Bus. Process Integr. Manag. **4**, 93–110 (2009)
13. Lin, D.: An information-theoretic definition of similarity. In: 15th International Conference on Machine Learning, pp. 296–304 (1998)
14. Pamungkas, E.W., Sarno, R., Munif, A.: B-BabelNet: business-specific lexical database for improving semantic analysis of business process models. In: Proceedings of the workshop on Cross-Framework and Cross-Domain Parser Evaluation, vol. 15, pp. 407–414 (2017)
15. Gabsi, H., Drira, R., Ghezala, H.H.B.: Personalized IaaS services selection based on multi-criteria decision making approach and recommender systems. In: International Conference on Internet and Web Applications and Services, pp. 5–12 (2018). ISBN 978-1- 61208-651-4
16. Gabsi, H., Drira, R., Ghezala, H.H.B.: A hybrid approach for personalized and optimized IaaS services selection. Int. J. Adv. Intell. Syst. (2019)
17. Tran, V.X., Punthee Ranurak, S., Tsuji, H.: A new service matching definition and algorithm with SAWSDL. In: IEEE International Conference on Digital Ecosystems and Technologies, vol. 1, pp. 371–376 (2009)
18. Huber, J., Polančič, G., Kocbek, M., Jošt, G.: Towards the component-based approach for evaluating process diagram complexity. In: Shishkov, B. (ed.) BMSD 2018. LNBIP, vol. 319, pp. 260–269. Springer, Cham (2018). https://doi.org/10.1007/978-3-319-94214-8_17
19. Rendan, E., Abundez, I., Arizmendi, A., Quiroz, E.M.: Internal versus external cluster validation indexes. Int. J. Adv. Intell. Syst. **1** (2011)
20. Microsoft Azure Services (2020). https://azure.microsoft.com/en-us/services/. Accessed 05 Sept 2020
21. Davis, J., Goadrich, M.: The relationship between precision-recall and ROC curves. In: International Conference on Machine Learning, pp. 233–240 (2006)
22. ULID (2020). https://doi.org/10.17632/7cy9zb9wtp.2. Accessed 05 Sept 2020
23. Jrad, F., Tao, J., Streit, A., Knapper, R., Flath, C.: A utility based approach for customised cloud service selection. Int. J. Comput. Sci. Eng. **10**, 32–44 (2015)
24. Rajganesh Nagarajan, R.T., Selvamuthukumaran: A cloud broker framework for infrastructure service discovery using semantic network. Int. J. Intell. Eng. Syst. **11**, 11–19 (2018)

25. Alkalbani, A.M., Hussain, W., Kim, J.Y.: A centralised cloud services repository (CCSR) framework for optimal cloud service advertisement discovery from heterogenous web portals. IEEE Access **7**, 128213–128223 (2019)
26. Heidari, F., Loucopoulo, P., Frances Brazier, J.B.: A meta-metamodel for seven business process modeling languages. In: IEEE Conference on Business Informatics, pp. 216–221 (2013)

Software Engineering

Data-Driven Requirements Engineering: A Guided Tour

Xavier Franch(✉)

UPC-BarcelonaTech, Universitat Politècnica de Catalunya, Barcelona, Spain
franch@essi.upc.edu

Abstract. Data-driven approaches are becoming dominant in almost every single software engineering activity, and requirements engineering is not the exception. The analysis of data coming from several sources may indeed become an extremely useful input to requirements elicitation and management. However, benefits do not come for free. Techniques such as natural language processing and machine learning are difficult to master and require high-quality data and specific competences from different fields, whilst their generalization remains as a challenge. This paper introduces the main concepts behind data-driven requirements engineering, provides an overview of the state of the art in the field and identifies the main challenges to be addressed.

Keywords: Requirements engineering · Data-driven requirements engineering · Feedback · Natural language processing · Software analytics · Monitoring · Decision-making · Release planning

1 Introduction

Identifying, documenting and managing requirements has been part of engineering tasks from old times. In the realm of software systems, requirements engineering (RE) [1] as a discipline originated more than 40 years ago [2]. The importance of managing requirements properly became evident very soon. Several studies quantified the cost of fixing errors to be about 10–100 times greater in later phases of software development and maintenance than in the requirements phase [3, 4]. This observation motivated the fast emergence of research related to requirements and the consolidation of RE as a well-established software engineering area on its own.

In recent years, we still find evidence that RE plays a central role in software project success. Requirements understanding and "-ilities" (non-functional requirements) are reported to be the most influential factors on cost[1] and in the particular case of non-functional requirements, failure to satisfy them can be catastrophic (resulting in a system worse than useless) [5]. Industry reports go along the same direction. For instance, the Project Management Institute (PMI) reported that inaccurate requirements management

---

[1] Quote from Ricardo Valerdi (U. Arizona & SpaceX) slides in seminar "Cost Estimation in Systems Engineering" given at UPC-BarcelonaTech, Sept. 2017.

© Springer Nature Switzerland AG 2021
R. Ali et al. (Eds.): ENASE 2020, CCIS 1375, pp. 83–105, 2021.
https://doi.org/10.1007/978-3-030-70006-5_4

is the primary cause of unsuccessful projects (i.e., not meeting their original goals and business objectives) almost half of the times (47%) [6].

Given that requirements are aimed to express needs of all system's stakeholders, the question that arises is: how to ensure that a system is delivering the right value to its stakeholders? Among the several directions of research addressing this question, data-driven RE is a prominent, emerging strand of research. Data-driven RE adopts a different perspective than traditional RE methods, shifting the focus from the interaction with the stakeholders at system design time, to the exploitation of runtime data.

2 An Overall View of Data-Driven Requirements Engineering

The term data-driven requirements engineering (DDRE) was proposed to the community in a seminal paper by Maalej et al. published in 2016 [7], in which they defined DDRE as "RE by the masses and for the masses". The main motivation for DDRE is to take profit of the existence of large amounts of data in the form of feedback to guide requirement engineers in their decisions about what requirements to include in subsequent system releases. While the concept of feedback is very generic and exists from long ago [8, 9] (e.g., in the form of issues stored in an issue tracker in open source projects), it has been with the emergence of applications for mobile devices (apps) that feedback has gained momentum. Apps' users can easily comment and provide their opinions through adequate feedback gathering mechanisms in app stores [10] while gathering data about system usage is also commonplace today.

DDRE conveys the need of a continuous cycle to make actionable the gathered data. This is illustrated in Fig. 1, which adapts the cycle proposed in the Q-Rapids project [11, 12]. At the topmost left part of the figure we find the set of requirements for the software system, which can be stored in a product backlog or some other format (even a word file). Requirements are prioritized in a way that a software development team implements a subset of them in the next release (possibly after refining them into concrete development tasks). Again, this can be done in different ways depending on the software development process, ranging from a traditional process to an agile one, even in the extreme a continuous software development process [13] where the concept of release gets diluted and instead, requirements are continuously selected and implemented.

Once the (latest release of the) software system is deployed, users will use it for their own purposes. While they use it, some data can be collected in a transparent manner, through usage logs, system monitors and similar instruments. These data are known as implicit feedback, since their gathering does not require the explicit intervention of the user. Besides, the user can provide explicit feedback provided that some communication channels are available. Explicit feedback will be often textual, although other modalities exist.

Feedback can be seen as a stream of data with potential to deliver insights that ideally can be made actionable. Therefore, the DDRE cycle inherently includes an activity for data analysis. The capabilities provided by this activity are a key point in every DDRE approach. Typically, this activity will clean, combine and analyse the feedback in order to compute values for factors or indicators, uncover patterns of behaviour, raise alerts, etc. In the ideal case, these consolidated data are rendered through a software analytics tool. Beyond advanced visualization techniques, this type of tool offers diverse capabilities to support requirement engineers in deciding upon new or modified (even removed) requirements, which are eventually implemented, generating new data for the next iteration in the cycle.

In the following sections, we examine the key elements of this cycle.

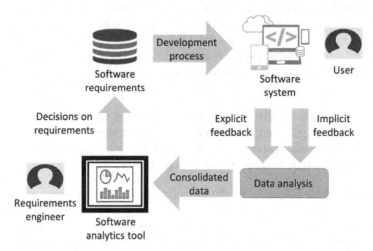

Fig. 1. The data-driven Requirements Engineering cycle (adapted from [11]).

3   Explicit Feedback Management

Explicit feedback is the term that denotes the feedback directly provided by the system's users. User involvement is what differentiates explicit feedback from implicit feedback: users may choose if and when to provide such type of feedback. It is worth to mention that many researchers still use the traditional term "user feedback" with the meaning of explicit feedback. However, we find "explicit feedback" more accurate and less prone to ambiguity.

Roughly speaking, explicit feedback management comprises two phases: gathering and analysis.

3.1   Explicit Feedback Gathering

Explicit feedback gathering is determined by the following characteristics.

Types of Explicit Feedback. As it happens with requirements themselves, explicit feedback is most usually provided in natural language. But differently than requirements, the language used in explicit feedback is normally unstructured, eventually with typos or careless grammar, including emoticons or punctuation signs to emphasise the message given, and hints and clues that makes difficult its analysis [14]. In addition, explicit feedback may be multi-modal, i.e. may include images (photos, screenshots, …), audio recordings, videos or other attachments. Together with text, or alternatively to text, explicit feedback may include some type of evaluation, through ratings (typically using stars or a number) or emoticons.

Communication Channel. In order to be processable in a DDRE cycle, the communication channel needs to be persistent and accessible for easy processing. In the case of apps, app stores are the most popular channel nowadays. Forums, ticket systems and social media (typically Twitter) are also widely used, although the difficulty of discriminating the information increases. There are also tools in the market such as UserVoice[2] and Usabilla[3] aimed at adding feedback channels to existing software systems or web pages.

Communication Style. Whilst the typical style is push, in which the user has the lead and decides when to provide the feedback, we may find also the pull style, in which the system prompts the user at designated moments, either a fixed moment (e.g., Skype when finalizing a call) or when some condition happens.

Advanced Features. For instance, the capability given to requirement engineers or developers to rate the quality of the given explicit feedback, which may help to identify the most valuable users from the perspective of feedback provision. Also, the possibility to establish a bidirectional feedback channel in which the requirements engineer may interact with the user, to ask for clarifications or more details on the feedback initially given.

3.2 Explicit Feedback Analysis

Given that, as said above, explicit feedback consists mostly of text written in natural language, we focus on this type of feedback in the rest of the subsection.

The complexity of dealing with natural language is well known from many decades ago. As a response to this difficulty, the research area of natural language processing (NLP) emerged in the late 40 s. NLP explores how computers can be used to understand and manipulate natural language text or speech to do useful things [15]. Many disciplines have used and are increasingly using NLP with different purposes, and RE is one of them [16, 17]. NLP techniques in RE research are complemented with machine learning (ML), which allows learning from data (in different variations, which may involve the human in the loop, e.g. supervised learning [18]).

In RE, NLP is used for undertaking different types of analysis. In this paper, we cover three of them:

- Categorization: the supervised grouping of feedback items into predefined categories.
- Sentiment analysis: the capability of understanding the person's intention behind her feedback.

---

[2] https://usabilla.com/.

[3] https://www.uservoice.com/.

- Topic modelling: the unsupervised organization of feedback items into one or more thematic topics.

All of these activities have a common need, namely the need of preprocessing the natural language text that forms the feedback communicated explicitly by the user.

Preprocessing. The main purpose of preprocessing is transforming a stream of characters that form a piece of text, in our case the explicit feedback provided by a user, into a syntactic structure formed by lexical units. This activity is typically broken into the following steps:

- Tokenization, which splits a stream of text into a list of words or phrases (the tokens) [19]. Stop words like "the", "an" or "with" are usually removed (some authors consider stop words removal as a step on its own). Stop words are either predefined or are computed analysing their frequency, discrimination power and prediction capability [20].
- Stemming or Lemmatization, both aimed at reducing variant forms into a base form (for instance, past/present/future of a verb; plural/singular of a noun). While stemming basically "cuts" suffixes [21], lemmatization is able to find inflections of variant forms (e.g., "be" and "was"), looking up headwords in a dictionary [22]. Lemmatization is not always convenient, e.g. the use of verb tenses may help classifying a feedback item into bug or feature request.
- Part-of-speech (PoS) tagging [23], segments the sentence into syntactic units with tags as "adjective" or "verb"). It can be followed by a parsing step that creates a parse tree showing the syntactic nature of the text.

All these techniques face several challenges. For instance, tokenization needs to handle multi-word terms. For PoS tagging, the main problem is to determine the right tags for those words that allow for more than one; for instance, the word "back" that can be labelled as a noun, as a verb or as part of a phrasal verb.

Once the text is preprocessed, we can further apply other techniques over the resulting syntactic structure.

Categorization. The classical example of categorization in the field of explicit feedback analysis is the classification of an explicit feedback item as bug report of feature request. For instance, Morales et al. proposed a categorization technique [24] based on speech-act analysis [25]. This technique first gathers feedback from discussions held in online media (e.g., forums). Then it applies a preprocessing pipeline based on the techniques mentioned above, first removing noisy text and then annotating the resulting input with speech-acts using lexico-syntactic rules. Last, it runs some ML algorithms over the annotated sentence in order to classify the feedback into three possible categories: new feature request, enhancement request or bug report.

This simple categorization can be further elaborated using finer-grained classification schemas. For instance, Guzman et al. implemented a detailed classification of twitter opinions on software [26]. Their classification schema shows that feedback can be related not only to particular features (shortcoming, strength, request) or bug reports, but also general feedback as "General praise", "Software price" and others. Furthermore, their schema proposes some general-purpose categories: "Noise" (which means "impossible to process", e.g. too many illegible symbols), "Unclear" (ambiguous), "Unrelated" (valid tweet but out of scope of the study) and "Other" (valid but it cannot be classified in the predefined categories).

Sentiment Analysis. It is the process of deciding if a piece of text expresses a particular affect or mood [27].

Current approaches to sentiment analysis combine the use of dictionaries and other syntactic elements [28] with machine learning or even deep learning techniques [29]. Guzmán and Maalej [30] proposed an approach based on the assignment of quantitative values to different sentence tokens that compose an explicit feedback item. In the general case, a sentence may combine positive and negative messages (e.g., "had fun using it before but now it is really horrible: (help!!)"). Therefore, the individual values are combined into two values, the aggregated positive score and the aggregated negative score. Constructs as booster words ("really"), emoticons and punctuation emphasis are crucial in this assignment of values.

In DDRE, sentiment analysis may help requirement engineers to understand the general position of the user. For instance, consider the sentences "pleeeeeeease add an unlike button and I will love you forever!!" and "uploading pictures with the app is so annoying!" [30]. While both of them are stating some dissatisfaction (asking for an additional feature the first, and complaining about a feature the second), the tone is very different and sentiment analysis will show that the first user is basically happy with the system while the second one is really complaining.

Topic Modelling. This type of unsupervised analysis identifies the topics that best describe a corpus of knowledge, where each topic is a repeating pattern of co-occurring terms in such corpus, described by a probability distribution of words (i.e., the probability that a word pertains to a topic) [31].

Topic modelling is well known in information retrieval for the analysis of large documents, e.g. in order to recommend contents to readers of newspapers [32], but it has spread into software engineering in general, and RE in particular [33]. The most popular algorithm used to identify the topics and their words is Latent Dirichlet Allocation (LDA) [34], where the word "latent" means that the distribution emerges during the analysis by statistical inference. Results are not unique and in fact, one of the most challenging issues on putting LDA into action is parameterization. There are several parameters to determine: number of topics, number of words per topic, number of iterations in the LDA algorithm for convergence, and others. Another challenging property of LDA is instability meaning that it suffers from "order effects", i.e. the output of the algorithm may depend on the order in which the terms are processed. Given these problems, other algorithms have been formulated, such as the Biterm Topic Model (BTM) [35] that models topics by exploring word-word (i.e., biterm) patterns. BTM has overperformed LDA in the context of short texts [33], which is a typical situation in explicit feedback.

Putting All Together. All of the techniques above and others that are not covered in this paper (e.g., summarization [36, 37]) deal with a particular NLP-related activity, but usually it is necessary to combine them in order to achieve a research goal. For instance, the ultimate goal of Guzman and Maalej's paper cited above [30] is to identify the positive or negative sentiment that users may have with respect to app features. They used two apps as examples, Pinterest in Android and Dropbox in iOS, mined reviews in their app stores and computed the number of positive and negative reviews they found for these features. In order to get these results, they built the workflow presented in Fig. 2. From the user reviews, they extracted titles and comments and initiated two parallel paths. On the one hand, for each review, they applied the sentiment analysis technique outlined above (without preprocessing, in order not to eliminate for instance stop words or other elements that may convey emotions). On the other hand, they extracted the features in the review by preprocessing their contents first and then extracting fine-grained features. Last, their grouped the fine-grained features into high-level features using topic modelling, combining adequately the sentiment scores. This example is representative of the type of solutions prevalent in explicit feedback analysis.

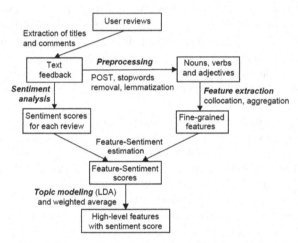

Fig. 2. Guzman and Maalej's approach to sentiment analysis in app reviews (as appears in [30]).

It is also worth to mention the existence of a large number of libraries of components that implement some of the algorithms mentioned here, e.g. Standford CoreNLP toolkit [38][4], NLTK[5] and GenSim[6] (for similarity analysis).

4 Implicit Feedback Management

Implicit feedback is the term that denotes the feedback gathered from the system usage as it is used by their users. The main difference with explicit feedback, as said, is that

---

[4] https://stanfordnlp.github.io/CoreNLP/.

[5] https://www.nltk.org/.

[6] https://pypi.org/project/gensim/.

data comes from the users without their explicit communication, but with their explicit consent. This unobtrusiveness is the main advantage over explicit feedback, although instrumentation is generally more complex.

The origins of implicit feedback come from the information retrieval discipline, where implicit feedback techniques are used for query expansion and user profiling in information retrieval tasks [39]. Also, the concept was heavily used in the web page ranking [40]. In software engineering, implicit feedback is having a momentum in the last years. For instance, with the advent of the Internet of Things and smart cities, sensors are continuously gathering data from users and their context. Also, big corporations and governments are going in the direction of collecting more and more information from citizens, and responses to crisis such as COVID-19 are increasing this trend [41]. In the rest of the section, we focus on the use of implicit feedback in DDRE.

4.1 Types of Implicit Feedback

The first type of implicit feedback we mention is quality of service (QoS). This is an old topic emerging in the 70 s–80 s in the areas of networking, real-time applications and middleware, adopted in the 2000s in the fields of service-oriented computing [42] and cloud-based systems [43], but still it plays an important role for analysing contemporary systems. QoS include attributes as response time, availability and security, which can provide very useful information to understand which parts of the system need improvement.

The second type is usage data. It may include the individual clicks of the users [44], telemetry[7], interactions with the user interface and navigational paths (clickthroughs) [45]. Usage data can be especially useful for detecting patterns of behaviour that may serve to discover unused functionalities or different ways to organize the user interface more fit to the real needs of the system users.

We mention a third type of data, non-verbal human data that can be sensed through appropriate sensors [46]. The most popular technique is eye tracking [47], but we can also mention gesture, heartrate, face muscles, etc.

Different types of feedback may be combined. For instance, Joachims et al. report an empirical study in which clickthroughs and eye-tracking are combined to achieve better results in web page ranking [48].

4.2 Gathering Implicit Feedback

Implicit feedback is usually stored in logs. Logs are files that contain a trace of the behaviour of the user when using the system, in the form of implicit feedback of any of the types mentioned above. Each entry in the log represents an interaction. The data fields that compose an entry are not standard but we will usually find: the timestamp, the user ID, the event type, the type of element, the URL or endpoint invoked, etc. From these logs, some typical observations are: which functionalities are most used, which navigational paths prevail (or not, even if expected), which calls result often in error codes, etc. This information may be enriched with QoS (which may require some

---

[7] https://firefox-source-docs.mozilla.org/toolkit/components/telemetry/index.html.

additional monitoring infrastructure, e.g. in the case of cloud-based systems [49]). All in all, this is valuable input for understanding functionalities that are problematic, features that are missing (e.g., because the users often follow bizarre navigational paths), features that can eventually be merged (because they are always used one after the other), etc.

4.3 Importance of Context

When analysing feedback, context is utterly important. Both the response of a user and the behaviour of the system can be strongly influenced by some contextual characteristic. For instance, a system may have a good user interface as a web application but a terrible user interface in its version for mobile phones. Although context can be provided explicitly, the usual case is that it is collected as part of the system's implicit feedback, using the same gathering instruments and channels.

Context is a very wide term and includes classical concepts as time and location, but also others as user's profile and type of device for the connection. Therefore, a great amount of context ontologies has been devised especially in the field of context-aware computing and self-adaptive systems [50], which can be used as a basis to implement the concept of context in an implicit feedback gathering and analysis approach.

From the point of view of RE, there are some approaches that deal with context by defining contextual requirements [51]. A contextual requirement is a requirement whose satisfaction is guarded by a condition that represents a context. The context is operationalized as a function over a set of context variables. Each variable is sensed through one or more monitors whose values are gathered with a monitoring infrastructure. While the concept of contextual requirement is clear and intuitive, many challenges arise, as dealing with uncertainty [52] and in general, discovering unknown unknowns [53] (e.g., context conditions that are not known in advance).

4.4 Combining Explicit and Implicit Feedback

We have seen that explicit and implicit feedback are very different in nature. Explicit feedback is mostly related (still) to natural language, while (contextual) implicit feedback has to be mainly with analysing streams of data stored in logs. However, they are two different kinds of input for the main purpose: to gather feedback from the user in order to understand the actual use and acceptance of the system. The natural question that arises is: may these two types of feedback be combined into one single input? For instance, if a user provides an explicit complaint about a concrete functionality of the system, it may be useful to have available as many implicitly collected data as possible. Maybe the user entered the review in a moment where the network experienced some downtime, or maybe she was using a particular type of device that does not support well this functionality.

This mixed approach is a hot topic of investigation in the field. One example is the FAME approach [54], which implements two streams for data acquisition (see Fig. 3): explicit feedback using feedback forms, and runtime events in the form of logs that were captured by a monitoring infrastructure. Since implicit feedback comes as a continuous flow, FAME uses a data lake to ensure performance. Both streams are combined in a component that uses domain ontologies [55] to be able to match concepts and inform the requirements engineer in order to elicit new requirements.

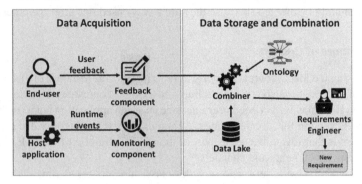

Fig. 3. The ontology-based FAME approach to integrated explicit and implicit feedback analysis (as appearing in [54]).

As a particular case on this combination of explicit and implicit feedback, we find the concept of crowd-based RE. As defined by Groen et al., crowd-based RE "is an umbrella term for automated or semiautomated approaches to gather and analyse information from a crowd to derive validated user requirements" [56]. Implicit feedback is aggregated to multi-modal explicit feedback similarly as done in the FAME approach [54] (Fig. 4).

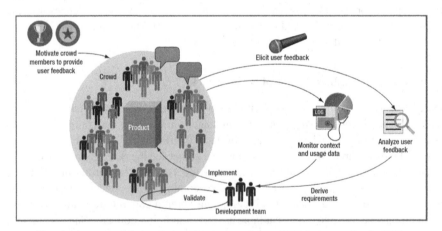

Fig. 4. Actors and their relationships in crowd-based RE (as appearing in [56]).

Other approaches to combine explicit and implicit feedback in DDRE exist. Wüest et al. follow a different strategy, in which implicit feedback is used as a trigger for explicit feedback [57]. Their argument is that this approach will engage users to provide more explicit feedback, and it will be provided when some situation uncovered by the implicit feedback requires to be analysed. It remains as a challenge to transfer these approaches into industry projects, which still rely mainly on explicit feedback [58].

5 Decision-Making

As Fig. 1 shows, once feedback is gathered and analysed, requirements engineers still need some support to make informed decisions. There are two key dimensions to decision-making in DDRE. First, to visualize the data in an actionable manner and to have at hand techniques for further analysis; to this end, requirements engineers may use software analytic tools. Second, to arrange these decisions in the form of a software release plan.

5.1 Software Analytic Tools

According to the outcome of the Dagstuhl Seminar 14261, software analytics is "to utilize data-driven approaches to obtain insightful and actionable information to help software practitioners with their data related tasks" [59]. This very generic definition accommodates a large variety of tools, some of them heavily used by the software engineering community during the development process, e.g. SonarQube[8].

Buse and Zimmermann defined several guidelines for software analytics tools, such as easiness of use and interactivity [60]. In addition, they suggested to map indicators to features, and this links well to DDRE: when applied to DDRE, the ultimate goal of a software analytics tool is to assist in the evolution of a requirements specification. This means suggesting new requirements, or modifying existing ones (e.g., by enforcing some threshold in a quality requirement, or by changing the priority or business value of a requirement).

To obtain the aforementioned indicators, it is necessary to aggregate the data that was gathered as feedback into more elaborated attributes until we reach a level of indicator. These indicators convey actionable information for requirements engineers, e.g. product quality, time to market or business value. Usually, the aggregation is multi-level and can be conducted bottom-up using the classical concept of quality model as driver [61]. For instance, the Q-Rapids dashboard (a software analytics tool aimed at eliciting quality requirements) [62] builds upon the Quamoco approach to software quality model construction [63]. Quamoco proposes the use of utility functions and weighted sums in order to define qualitative values for these quality factors. In Q-Rapids, top-level indicators are visualized in a gauge form with three values (ok, warning and failure) depending on their distance to a given threshold.

The Q-Rapids dashboard also implements several techniques suggested by Buse and Zimmermann [60], among which we can mention:

- Visualization capabilities as drill-down navigation, from one indicator to the quality factors that compose it.
- Analysis of trends and summarization of results, to understand the direction of a software project.
- Prediction of the evolution of a particular indicator or some of the quality factors used to compute it [64].

---

[8] https://www.sonarqube.org/.

- Definition and triggering of alerts, to report underperformance or (in combined use with prediction) to anticipate future threshold violations.
- Simulation through what-if analysis, using sliders to understand the effects of changes in factors' values over the indicators.

Oriol et al. propose to associate mitigation actions to alerts triggered by underperforming quality factors, so that these mitigation actions operate over the requirements specification [65]. The new requirements are proposed to the requirements engineer as instantiations of requirements patterns stored in a catalogue [66]. Possible instantiations of the patterns with a description of their consequences are presented to the requirements engineer through the software analytics tool. With a similar aim of identifying requirements, Dalpiaz and Parente proposed the RE-SWOT method [67]. RE-SWOT aims at eliciting requirements from app store reviews through competitor analysis. Results are presented to the requirements engineer by means of a dashboard that visualizes a Strengths-Weaknessess-Opportunities-Threats analysis of identified features.

5.2 Release Planning

The next activity in order to close the data-driven cycle is deciding how to allocate the requirements that have emerged or changed, to the next or even further system releases. The problem of software release planning is well known in software engineering [68, 69] and can be stated as follows: given a set of requirements to be allocated, and a set of constraints in terms of resources, budget, and similar criteria, maximize some utility or multi-objective function and thus design a release plan, where every requirement has a release assigned (or eventually remains undecided or is even discarded) [70].

When applied to DDRE, feedback becomes the critical object that guides release planning. Having an app's release strategy is a factor that affects the ongoing success of mobile apps [71]. For instance, Villaroel et al. [72] propose a technique that processes feedback by forming clusters of related reviews (bug reports and new feature suggestions) and then prioritizes the clusters according to their: (i) number of reviews, (ii) average rating, (iii) difference of cluster average rating and app average rating, (iv) difference of ratings assigned by users who reviewed older releases of the app, and (v) number of different devices from which users reported reviews (which is a basic but still useful combination of explicit and implicit feedback).

Maalej et al. [7, 73] mention other possible ways to adapt usual release planning approaches to DDRE characteristics: involving an increasing number of stakeholders in the process (from single person to group-based process), relying on real-time and rigorous data analytics instead of intuition, or allowing stakeholders to play a more proactive role. Several techniques to involve the right stakeholders have been proposed, mainly in relation to gamification [74], but also others as applying the concept of liquid democracy to requirements engineering [75], so that a stakeholder can nominate others to rank a requirement on her behalf when she is not knowledgeable on the requirement's facet.

6 Challenges

In this section we outline some challenges ahead for DDRE, both from research and from practical perspective.

Integration with Data-oriented Analysis Cycles. The first challenge is to be able to integrate DDRE with existing development processes. Given the data-driven nature, companies may need to adopt some data management method, e.g. CRISP-DM [76]. CRISP-DM was formulated in the early 2000s as a cycle aimed at supporting data scientists in making data actionable through several well-defined stages: business understanding, data understanding, preparation, modelling, evaluation and deployment. Reconciling DDRE and CRISP-DM is a research direction that has been already subject of attention [77].

Integration with Other Software Engineering Approaches. Beyond integration with data-oriented approaches, DDRE needs to be integrated also in the software life cycle. DDRE is usually connected to agile approaches [78] but we can imagine integration with other processes. For instance, Franch et al. [79] explore the integration of DDRE into a model-driven development software life cycle, where the generation of the feedback gathering infrastructure is integrated with the generation of the system itself, supporting thus evolution of the embedded mechanisms as the system requirements evolve.

User Motivation and Trust. While implicit feedback mainly depends on the availability of a feedback gathering infrastructure (although of course privacy concerns are also a challenge to consider), explicit feedback requires the engagement of users. Gamification is the most usual strategy to motivate users to provide explicit feedback [80], although it has shown mixed results in this field; instead, tangible incentives can be more attractive to users (e.g., in the gaming domain, alpha/beta players get early versions of games). A problem in the opposite direction to having scarce data is the reliability of the explicit feedback given. Especially in the app market, the fight against fake reviews has become critical. A recent empirical study by Martens and Maalej analysed thoroughly the business behind fake reviews, ultimately revealing their significant impact [81].

Context-Driven Feedback Gathering. To make any feedback management approach fully contextual, the feedback gathering instruments themselves need to adapt to context. For instance, the frequency of monitoring can decrease when the device executing the system is running out of battery, or on the contrary, it can be increased when it comes to monitoring the behaviour of a problematic feature. Approaches for context-driven implicit feedback gathering exist in the form of adaptive monitoring infrastructures [82]. For explicit feedback, Almaliki et al. use the concept of *Persona* [83] to gather explicit feedback depending on the profile of the user [84].

Analysis of Implicit Feedback. The analysis of usage logs faces several recurrent challenges. First, data is usually noisy, both in terms of log entries that are useless, and fields that are not useful for the purpose of DDRE. Second, data is often incomplete, so that fields may be missing or may be too coarse-grained to be useful. Third, the concept of session is not always evident. Sessions are useful because they represent chunks of work of a user, and it is convenient to delimit them in the log files. Fourth, as applications evolve, so should do log files, but then it is difficult to analyse them along time. Fifth, data collection should be non-intrusive and as minimal as possible according to the objectives sought. Last but not least, anonymization is critical and required by law.

Use of Domain Knowledge. While DDRE is based on analysing as much data as possible, it remains a challenge to investigate whether it can be effectively leveraged using domain knowledge. For instance, we have already mentioned in Sect. 4.4 the use of domain ontologies for matching explicit and implicit feedback concepts [54]. If we look into the details, this domain ontology bridges both worlds through some connecting concepts, for instance *TimeStamp*, *User* and *Application*.

Adoption by Companies. In the addition to the research-oriented challenges above, other more practical barriers emerge for companies to adopt DDRE [62, 85]. We may classify them into three categories:

- **Organizational.** First, the general concept of DDRE needs to be tailored to every company. For instance, the indicators to be used for decision-making will be ultimately determined by both the business priorities of the company and the availability of data. Second, integration with the company way of working, since it cannot be expected that a company will completely change its current processes and practices. Last, aligning the vocabulary, which may seem not so important at a first glance, but it becomes an important impediment, especially when it comes to discuss about particular types of quality requirements.
- **Value-Related.** Two complementary challenges are: providing explanations (informative dashboards and generation of reports, for instance), and transparency, allowing decision-makers to drill from recommendations in terms of requirements or decisions, down to data.
- **Technological.** Given that it is necessary to implement a software infrastructure to gather, analyse and decide upon feedback, the technology needs to be as less invasive as possible, simplifying the installation of the tool and making efficient its configuration.

7   Discussion

7.1   Related Areas

While DDRE is a recent research direction, it is clear from this guided tour that it benefits from consolidated results produced in other software engineering areas that exist for many years, some of them already mentioned. We highlight:

- **User-Centred Design.** This area emerged in the 70 s [86] and originated the concept of user feedback. For instance, as early as in 1971, Hansen reported the following in the design of a text editor called Emily: "A log is kept of all user interactions, user errors, and system errors. There is a command to let the user type a message to be put in the log and this message is followed by a row of asterisks. When the user is frustrated he can push a 'sympathy' button. In response, Emily displays at random one of ten sympathetic messages. More importantly, frustration is noted in the log and the system designer can examine the user's preceding actions to find out where his understanding differed from the system implementation" [87].

- **Process Mining.** The area of process mining appeared in the mid-90 s under the label of process discovery, and more related to software process and workflow technologies [88, 89]. These approaches used event-based logs to capture the actions that occurred during the execution of the process [90]. In the early 2000s, there was a shift of focus into business process and information systems [91] and service design [92]. Techniques appearing in these areas [93] can be used in DDRE.
- **Mining Software Repositories.** Software repositories, such as issue and bug tracking systems and project management tools, are a valuable source of information that can be used to understand software development practices and uncover software quality issues [94]. It is used for many purposes like fault prediction, productivity analysis, impact analysis and in general, product and process dynamics [95]. In the last years, given the large amounts of data to be processed and the complexity to analyze them, there is a corpus of knowledge delivering increasingly sophisticated analysis solutions [96]. Connection to DDRE appears especially when considering software repositories' data as a possible source for software quality defects, which can eventually generate internal quality requirements (related to maintainability, portability, etc.) [61].
- **Service Monitoring.** With the advent of service-oriented computing in the early 2000s [97], one of the areas of research was that of service monitoring. Oriol et al. surveyed the different areas in which monitoring is important, and remarkably monitoring quality of service is one of them [98]. An ample body of research on this topic appeared, with special emphasis on using the monitoring infrastructure for checking service level agreements [99] and even suggesting explanations or repair rules when those agreements were violated [100].
- **Requirements Monitoring.** The concept of requirements monitoring emerged in the mid-90 s [101] and is still present in the RE area [102]. Requirements monitoring has been frequently used over goal-oriented models, for instance in the context of self-adaptive systems [103] and obstacle resolution [104]. This concept can also be connected with DDRE, by considering requirements monitoring as part of the software analytics activities, and especially focusing on monitoring of user requirements [105].

It is also worth to mention the relationship of DDRE with the topic of online controlled experimentation [106]. This approach to software product development proposes to collect data from users based in two competing versions that differ in a particular feature [107]. It is a generalization of the concept of A/B testing and shares several principles with DDRE, as the need of quality data and the convenience to establish necessary competencies [108].

Other areas not part of software engineering, as information retrieval or linguistics, have also had an influence to DDRE, as shown in this paper.

7.2 Lessons Learned

The concepts presented in this paper have been applied in the last years in several EU collaborative projects (Q-Rapids [109], SUPERSEDE [110] and OpenReq [111]) where large corporations and small-medium enterprises have adopted DDRE at some extent. Some observations arising from these projects follow:

- DDRE is not for free. Adopting DDRE requires both adapting organizational processes and mindset and developing some infrastructure in order to make it happen.
- DDRE is different for every company. There are not two companies adopting the proposed DDRE approach in the same way. This means that DDRE needs to define general process with high customization capabilities. Situational method engineering [112] can be helpful in dealing with such diversity, as we have explored in one of these projects, SUPERSEDE [113].
- DDRE requires expertise in terms of specialized roles, e.g. data scientists accompanying the requirements engineers and software engineers.
- DDRE needs to be implemented in an incremental way, in order to gradually master its intricacies and complexities, and create awareness in the organization.
- DDRE requires full transparency. Decisions made during data-informed software analysis need to be clearly justified [114] and with a rationale behind such that the requirements engineer can understand the decision and then accept or decline, or elaborate further.

8 Conclusions

In this paper, we have presented a guided tour to data-driven requirements engineering (DDRE). The main message is that DDRE offers a great opportunity for delivering more business value to systems' stakeholders by evolving the system according to the real needs elicited through the analysis of the gathered feedback and tool-supported decision-making. In line with Ebert et al. [77], we can say that those companies that do not consider data from system usage in their development processes are increasingly putting themselves at competitive disadvantage.

DDRE changes the focus of traditional requirements engineering from human-oriented to data-oriented, although this does not mean that it can replace completely the existing requirements engineering management approaches and in particular, data will still need to be analysed and validated by humans. First, data (mainly represented by feedback) is agnostic per se, and therefore interpretation by humans is still necessary, even if machine learning techniques are adopted. This is why we have presented the decision-making process as tool-supported but not as automatic. Second, in order to gather feedback, an initial system needs to be made available to users. Requirements for this minimal viable product need to be gather without data, i.e. using traditional requirement elicitation and prioritization techniques [1].

Considering the paragraph above, and the challenges and lessons learned enumerated in previous sections, we can conclude that it may not be appropriate to blindly adopt DDRE in the context of some companies or systems. At the end, DDRE is another approach that composes the requirements engineer toolbox, adding some new activities to those that are more traditional [115], to be used wisely in the right moment with the right customization.

Acknowledgment. This work is partially supported by the GENESIS project, funded by the Spanish Ministerio de Ciencia e Innovación under contract TIN2016-79269-R. The author wants to deeply thank Fabiano Dalpiaz, Silverio Martínez-Fernández and Marc Oriol for their comments and suggestions over a first draft of the paper.

References

1. Pohl, K.: Requirements Engineering: Fundamentals, Principles and Techniques. Springer, Heidelberg (2010)
2. Ross, D.T. (ed): Special Collection on Requirement Analysis. IEEE Trans. Softw. Eng. **SE-3**(1), 2–84 (1977)
3. Boehm, B.: Software engineering. IEEE Trans. Comput. **C-25**(12), 1226–1241 (1976)
4. Kuffel, W.: Extra time saves money. Comput. Lang. (1990)
5. Spinellis, D.: Code Quality – The Open Source Perspective. Pearson (2006)
6. PMI: Pulse of the Profession® In-Depth Report: Requirements Management—A Core Competency for Project and Program Success (2014). https://www.pmi.org/-/media/pmi/docume nts/public/pdf/learning/thought-leadership/pulse/requirements-management.pdf
7. Maalej, W., Nayebi, M., Johann, T., Ruhe, G.: Toward data-driven requirements engineering. IEEE Softw. **33**(1), 48–54 (2016)
8. Lucas, H.C.: A user-oriented approach to systems design. In: Proceedings of the 26th Annual Conference of the Association for Computing Machinery (ACM), pp. 325–338. ACM Press (1971)
9. Trotter, P.: User feedback and how to get it. In: Proceedings of the 4th Annual Conference on User Services (SIGUCCS), pp. 130–132. ACM Press (1976)
10. Pagano, D., Maalej, W.: User feedback in the appstore: an empirical study. In: Proceedings of the 21st International Requirements Engineering Conference (RE), pp. 125–134. IEEE Press (2013)
11. Guzmán, L., Oriol, M., Rodríguez, P., Franch, X., Jedlitschka, A., Oivo, M.: How can quality awareness support rapid software development? – A research preview. In: Grünbacher, P., Perini, A. (eds.) REFSQ 2017. LNCS, vol. 10153, pp. 167–173. Springer, Cham (2017). https://doi.org/10.1007/978-3-319-54045-0_12
12. Franch, X., et al.: Data-driven requirements engineering in agile projects: the Q-rapids approach. In: Proceedings of the 25th International Requirements Engineering Conference Workshops (REW), pp. 411–414. IEEE Computer Society (2017)
13. Fitzgerald, B., Stol, K.J.: Continuous software engineering: a roadmap and agenda. J. Syst. Softw. **123**, 176–189 (2017)
14. Hosseini, M., Groen, E.C., Shahri, A., Ali, R.: CRAFT: a crowd-annotated feedback technique. In: Proceedings of the IEEE 25th International Requirements Engineering Conference Workshops (REW), pp. 170–175 (2017)
15. Chowdhury, G.: Natural language processing. Ann. Rev. Inf. Sci. Technol. **37**, 51–89 (2003)

16. Zhao, L., et al.: Natural language processing (NLP) for requirements engineering: a systematic mapping study. arXiv:2004.01099v2 [cs.SE] (2020)
17. Dalpiaz, F., Ferrari, A., Franch, X., Palomares, C.: Natural language processing for requirements engineering; the best is yet to come. IEEE Softw. **35**(5), 115–119 (2018)
18. El Shawi, R., Maher, M., Sakr, S.: Automated machine learning: state-of-the-art and open challenges. arXiv:1906.02287v2 [cs.LG] (2019)
19. Webster, J.J., Kit, C.: Tokenization as the initial phase in NLP. In: Proceedings of the 14th Conference on Computational Linguistics (COLING),vol. 4, pp. 1106–1110. ACM Press (1992)
20. Ladani, D.J., Desai, N.P.: Stopword identification and removal techniques on TC and IR applications: a survey. In: Proceedings of the 6th International Conference on Advanced Computing and Communication Systems (ICACCS), pp. 466–472. IEEE Press (2020)
21. Singh, J., Gupta, V.: A systematic review of text stemming techniques. Artif. Intell. Rev. **48**, 157–217 (2017). https://doi.org/10.1007/s10462-016-9498-2
22. Balakrishnan, V., Lloyd-Yemoh, E.: Stemming and lemmatization: a comparison of retrieval performances. Lect. Notes Softw. Eng. **2**(3), 262–267 (2014)
23. Abney, S.: Part-of-speech tagging and partial parsing. In: Young, S., Bloothooft, G. (eds.) Corpus-Based Methods in Language and Speech Processing. Text, Speech and Language Technology, vol. 2, pp. 118–136. Springer, Heidelberg (1997). https://doi.org/10.1007/978-94-017-1183-8_4
24. Morales-Ramirez, I., Kifetew, F.M., Perini, A.: Speech-acts based analysis for requirements discovery from online discussions. Inf. Syst. **86**, 94–112 (2019)
25. Searle, J.R.: Speech Acts: An Essay in the Philosophy of Language. Cambridge University Press, Cambridge (1969)
26. Guzman, E., Alkadhi, R., Seyff, N.: A needle in a haystack: what do twitter users say about software? In: Proceedings of the 24th International Requirements Engineering Conference (RE), pp. 96–105. IEEE Computer Society (2016)
27. Nasukawa, T., Yi, J.: Sentiment analysis: capturing favorability using natural language processing. In: Proceedings of the 2nd international Conference on Knowledge Capture (K-CAP), pp. 70–77. ACM Press (2003)
28. Taboada, M., Brooke, J., Tofiloski, M., Voll, K., Stede, M.: Lexicon-based methods for sentiment analysis. Comput. Linguist. **37**(2), 267–307 (2011)
29. Zhang, L., Wang, S., Liu, B.: Deep learning for sentiment analysis: a survey. Data Min. Knowl. Discov. **8**(4), e1253 (2018)
30. Guzman, E., Maalej, W.: How do users like this feature? A fine grained sentiment analysis of app reviews. In: Proceedings of the 22nd International Requirements Engineering Conference (RE), pp. 153–162. IEEE Computer Society (2014)
31. Wallach, H.M.: Topic modeling: beyond bag-of-words. In: Proceedings of the 23rd International Conference on Machine Learning (ICML), pp. 977–984. ACM Press (2006)
32. Jacobi, C., van Atteveldt, W., Welbers, K.: Quantitative analysis of large amounts of journalistic texts using topic modelling. Digit. J. **4**(1), 89–106 (2016)
33. Abad, Z.S.H., Karras, O., Ghazi, P., Glinz, M., Ruhe, G., Schneider, K.: What works better? A study of classifying requirements. arXiv:1707.02358 [cs.SE] (2017)
34. Blei, D.M., Ng, A.Y., Jordan, M.I.: Latent Dirichlet allocation. J. Mach. Learn. Res. **3**, 993–1022 (2003)
35. Yan, X., Guo, J., Lan, Y., Cheng, X.: A biterm topic model for short texts. In Proceedings of the 22nd International Conference on World Wide Web (WWW), pp. 1445–1456. ACM press (2013)
36. Nenkova, A., McKeown, K.: A survey of text summarization techniques. In: Aggarwal, C., Zhai, C. (eds.) Mining Text Data, pp. 43–76. Springer, Heidelberg (2012). https://doi.org/10.1007/978-1-4614-3223-4_3

37. Allahyari, M., et al.: Text summarization techniques: a brief survey. arXiv:1707.02268v3 [cs.CL] (2017)
38. Manning, C.D., Surdeanu, M., Bauer, J., Finkel, J., Bethard, S.J., McClosky, D.: The stanford CoreNLP natural language processing toolkit. In: Proceedings of the 52nd Annual Meeting of the Association for Computational Linguistics: System Demonstrations (ACL), pp. 55–60 (2014)
39. Kelly, D., Teevan, J.: Implicit feedback for inferring user preference: a bibliography. ACM SIGIR Forum **37**(2), 18–28 (2003)
40. Agichtein, E., Brill, E., Dumais, S.: Improving web search ranking by incorporating user behavior information. In: Proceedings of the 29th Annual International ACM SIGIR Conference on Research and Development in Information Retrieval (SIGIR), pp. 19–26. ACM Press (2006)
41. Carvalho, V.M., et al.: Tracking the Covid-19 crisis with high-resolution transaction data. CEPR Discussion Paper No. DP14642 (2020)
42. Papazoglou, M.P., Georgakopoulos, D.: Introduction: service-oriented computing. Communun. ACM **46**(1), 24–28 (2003)
43. Abdelmaboud, A., Jawawi, D.N.A., Ghani, I., Elsafi, A., Kitchenham, B.: Quality of service approaches in cloud computing: a systematic mapping study. J. Syst. Softw. **101**, 159–179 (2015)
44. Janes, A.: Non-distracting, continuous collection of software development process data. In: Nalepa, G.J., Baumeister, J. (eds.) Synergies Between Knowledge Engineering and Software Engineering. AISC, vol. 626, pp. 275–294. Springer, Cham (2018). https://doi.org/10.1007/978-3-319-64161-4_13
45. Joachims, T.: Optimizing search engines using clickthrough data. In: Proceedings of the 8th ACM SIGKDD International Conference on Knowledge Discovery and Data Mining (KDD), pp. 133–142. ACM Press (2002)
46. Harrigan, J., Rosenthal, R., Scherer, K. (eds.): The New Handbook of Methods in Nonverbal Behavior Research. Oxford University Press, Oxford (2005)
47. Sharafi, Z., Soh, Z., Guéhéneuc, Y.-G.: A systematic literature review on the usage of eye-tracking in software engineering. Inf. Softw. Technol. **67**, 79–107 (2015)
48. Joachims, T., Granka, L., Pan, B., Hembrooke, H., Gay, G.: Accurately interpreting clickthrough data as implicit feedback. In: Proceedings of the 28th Annual International ACM SIGIR Conference on Research and Development in Information Retrieval (SIGIR), pp. 154–161. ACM Press (2005)
49. Kertesz, A., et al.: Enhancing federated cloud management with an integrated service monitoring approach. J. Grid Comput. **11**(4), 699–720 (2013). https://doi.org/10.1007/s10723-013-9269-0
50. Cabrera, O., Franch, X., Marco, J.: Ontology-based context modeling in service-oriented computing: a systematic mapping. Data Knowl. Eng. **110**, 24–53 (2017)
51. Ali, R., Dalpiaz, F., Giorgini, P.: Reasoning with contextual requirements: detecting inconsistency and conflicts. Inf. Softw. Technol. **55**, 35–57 (2013)
52. Knauss, A., Damian, D.E., Franch, X., Rook, A., Müller, H.A., Thomo, A.: ACon: a learning-based approach to deal with uncertainty in contextual requirements at runtime. Inf. Softw. Technol. **70**, 85–99 (2016)
53. Sutcliffe, A., Sawyer, P.: Requirements elicitation: towards the unknown unknowns. In Proceedings of the 21st International Requirements Engineering Conference (RE), pp. 92–104. IEEE Press (2013)
54. Oriol, M., et al.: FAME: supporting continuous requirements elicitation by combining user feedback and monitoring. In: Proceedings of the 26th International Requirements Engineering Conference (RE), pp. 217–227. IEEE Computer Society (2018)

55. McDaniel, M., Storey, V.C.: Evaluating domain ontologies: clarification, classification, and challenges. ACM Comput. Surv. **52**(4), Article 70 (2019)
56. Groen, E.C., et al.: The crowd in requirements engineering: the landscape and challenges. IEEE Softw. **34**(2), 44–52 (2017)
57. Wüest, D., Fotrousi, F., Fricker, S.: Combining monitoring and autonomous feedback requests to elicit actionable knowledge of system use. In: Knauss, E., Goedicke, M. (eds.) REFSQ 2019. LNCS, vol. 11412, pp. 209–225. Springer, Cham (2019). https://doi.org/10. 1007/978-3-030-15538-4_16
58. Johanssen, J.O., Kleebaum, A., Bruegge, B., Paech, B.: How do practitioners capture and utilize user feedback during continuous software engineering? In: Proceedings of the 27th International Requirements Engineering Conference (RE), pp. 153–164. IEEE Press (2019)
59. Gall, H., Menzies, T., Williams, L., Zimmermann, T. (eds.): Software development analytics. Dagstuhl Rep. **4**(6), 64–83 (2014)
60. Buse, R.P.L., Zimmermann, T.: Information needs for software development analytics. In: Proceedings of the 34th International Conference on Software Engineering (ICSE), pp. 987–996. IEEE Press (2012)
61. The ISO Organization: ISO/IEC 25010:2011 –Systems and Software Engineering—Systems and Software Quality Requirements and Evaluation (SQuaRE)—System and Software Quality Models (2011)
62. Martínez-Fernández, S., et al.: Continuously assessing and improving software quality with software analytics tools: a case study. IEEE Access **7**, 68219–68239 (2019)
63. Wagner, S., et al.: Operationalised product quality models and assessment: the quamoco approach. Inf. Softw. Technol. **62**, 101–123 (2015)
64. Choraś, M., Kozik, R., Pawlicki, M., Hołubowicz, W., Franch, X.: Software development metrics prediction using time series methods. In: Saeed, K., Chaki, R., Janev, V. (eds.) CISIM 2019. LNCS, vol. 11703, pp. 311–323. Springer, Cham (2019). https://doi.org/10.1007/978-3-030-28957-7_26
65. Oriol, M., et al.: Data-driven and tool-supported elicitation of quality requirements in agile companies. Softw. Qual. J. **28**(3), 931–963 (2020). https://doi.org/10.1007/s11219-020-095 09-y. (in press)
66. Renault, S., Mendez-Bonilla, O., Franch, X., Quer, C.: PABRE: pattern-based requirements elicitation. In: Proceedings of the 3rd International Conference on Research Challenges in Information Science (RCIS), pp. 81–92. IEEE Press (2009)
67. Dalpiaz, F., Parente, M.: RE-SWOT: from user feedback to requirements via competitor analysis. In: Knauss, E., Goedicke, M. (eds.) REFSQ 2019. LNCS, vol. 11412, pp. 55–70. Springer, Cham (2019). https://doi.org/10.1007/978-3-030-15538-4_4
68. Svahnberg, M., Gorschek, T., Feldt, R., Torkar, R., Saleem, S.B., Shafique, M.U.: A systematic review on strategic release planning models. Inf. Softw. Technol. **52**(3), 237–248 (2010)
69. Ameller, D., Farré, C., Franch, X., Rufian, G.: A survey on software release planning models. In: Abrahamsson, P., Jedlitschka, A., Nguyen Duc, A., Felderer, M., Amasaki, S., Mikkonen, T. (eds.) PROFES 2016. LNCS, vol. 10027, pp. 48–65. Springer, Cham (2016). https://doi. org/10.1007/978-3-319-49094-6_4
70. Greer, D., Ruhe, G.: Software release planning: an evolutionary and iterative approach. Inf. Softw. Technol. **46**(4), 243–253 (2004)
71. Nayebi, M., Adams, B., Ruhe, G.: Release practices for mobile apps – what do users and developers think? In: Proceedings of the 23rd International Conference on Software Analysis, Evolution, and Reengineering (SANER), pp. 552–562 (2016)
72. Villarroel, L., Bavota, G., Russo, B., Oliveto, R., di Penta, M.: Release planning of mobile apps based on user reviews. In: Proceedings of the 38th International Conference on Software Engineering (ICSE), pp. 14–24. IEEE Computer Society (2016)

73. Maalej, W., Nayebi, M., Ruhe, G.: Data-driven requirements engineering - an update. In: Proceedings of the IEEE/ACM 41st International Conference on Software Engineering: Software Engineering in Practice (ICSE-SEIP), pp. 289–290 (2019)
74. Kifetew, F.M., et al.: Gamifying collaborative prioritization: does pointsification work? In: Proceedings of the 25th International Requirements Engineering Conference (RE), pp. 322–331. IEEE Press (2017)
75. Johann, T., Maalej, W.: Democratic mass participation of users in requirements engineering? In: Proceedings of the 23rd International Requirements Engineering Conference (RE), pp. 256–261. IEEE Press (2015)
76. Shearer, C.: The CRISP-DM model: the new blueprint for data mining. J. Data Warehous. 4(5), 13–22 (2000)
77. Ebert, C., Heidrich, J., Martinez-Fernandez, S., Trendowicz, A.: Data science: technologies for better software. IEEE Softw. 36(6), 66–72 (2019)
78. Svensson, R.B., Feldt, R., Torkar, R.: The unfulfilled potential of data-driven decision making in agile software development. In: Kruchten, P., Fraser, S., Coallier, F. (eds.) XP 2019. LNBIP, vol. 355, pp. 69–85. Springer, Cham (2019). https://doi.org/10.1007/978-3-030-19034-7_5
79. Franch, X., et al.: Towards integrating data-driven requirements engineering into the software development process: a vision paper. In: Madhavji, N., Pasquale, L., Ferrari, A., Gnesi, S. (eds.) REFSQ 2020. LNCS, vol. 12045, pp. 135–142. Springer, Cham (2020). https://doi.org/10.1007/978-3-030-44429-7_10
80. Dalpiaz, F., Snijders, R., Brinkkemper, S., Hosseini, M., Shahri, A., Ali, R.: Engaging the crowd of stakeholders in requirements engineering via gamification. In: Stieglitz, S., Lattemann, C., Robra-Bissantz, S., Zarnekow, R., Brockmann, T. (eds.) Gamification. PI, pp. 123–135. Springer, Cham (2017). https://doi.org/10.1007/978-3-319-45557-0_9
81. Martens, D., Maalej, W.: Towards detecting and understanding fake reviews in app stores. Empir. Eng. 24, 3316–3355 (2019). https://doi.org/10.1007/s10664-019-09706-9
82. Zavala, E., Franch, X., Marco, J.: Adaptive monitoring: a systematic mapping. Inf. Softw. Technol. 105, 161–189 (2019)
83. Pruitt, J., Grudin, J.: Personas: practice and theory. In: Proceedings of the 2003 Conference on Designing for User Experiences (DUX), pp. 1–15. ACM Press (2003)
84. Almaliki, M., Ncube, C., Ali, R.: Adaptive software-based feedback acquisition: a persona-based design. In: Proceedings of the 9th International Conference on Research Challenges in Information Science (RCIS), pp. 100–111. IEEE Press (2015)
85. Choras, M., et al.: Measuring and improving agile processes in a small-size software development company. IEEE Access 8, 78452–78466 (2020)
86. Kling, R.: The organizational context of user-centered software designs. MIS Q. 1(4), 41–52 (1977)
87. Hansen, W.J.: User engineering principles for interactive systems. In: Proceedings of the Fall Joint Computer Conference (AFIPS), pp. 523–532. ACM Press (1971)
88. Cook, J.E., Wolf, A.L.: Automating process discovery through event-data analysis. In: Proceedings of the 17th International Conference on Software Engineering (ICSE), pp. 73–82. IEEE Press (1995)
89. Agrawal, R., Gunopulos, D., Leymann, F.: Mining process models from workflow logs. In: Schek, H.-J., Alonso, G., Saltor, F., Ramos, I. (eds.) EDBT 1998. LNCS, vol. 1377, pp. 467–483. Springer, Heidelberg (1998). https://doi.org/10.1007/BFb0101003
90. Wolf, A.L., Rosenblum, D.S.: A study in software process data capture and analysis. In: Proceedings of the 2nd International Conference on the Software Process-Continuous Software Process Improvement (SPCON), pp. 115–124. IEEE Press (1993)
91. van der Aalst, W.: Process Mining: Discovery, Conformance and Enhancement of Business Processes. Springer, Heidelberg (2011). https://doi.org/10.1007/978-3-642-19345-3

92. van der Aalst, W.: Service mining: using process mining to discover, check, and improve service behavior. IEEE Trans. Serv. Comput. **6**(4), 525–535 (2013)
93. Garcia, C.D.S., et al.: Process mining techniques and applications – a systematic mapping study. Expert Syst. Appl. **133**, 260–295 (2019)
94. Hassan, A.E.: Mining software repositories to assist developers and support managers. In: Proceedings of the 22nd IEEE International Conference on Software Maintenance (ICSM), pp. 339–342. IEEE Press (2006)
95. Kagdi, H., Collard, M.L., Maletic, J.I.: A survey and taxonomy of approaches for mining software repositories in the context of software evolution. J. Softw. Evol. Process **19**(2), 77–131 (2007)
96. Bird, C., Menzies, T., Zimmermann, T.: The Art and Science of Analyzing Software Data. Elsevier, Amsterdam (2016)
97. Papazoglou, M.P., Georgakopoulos, D.: Introduction: service-oriented computing. Commun. ACM **46**(10), 24–28 (2003)
98. Oriol, M., Franch, X., Marco, J.: Monitoring the service-based system lifecycle with SALMon. Expert Syst. Appl. **42**(19), 6507–6521 (2015)
99. Comuzzi, M., Kotsokalis, C., Spanoudakis, G., Yahyapour, R.: Establishing and monitoring SLAs in complex service based systems. In: Proceedings of the 2009 IEEE International Conference on Web Services (ICWS), pp. 783–790. IEEE Press (2009)
100. Müller, C., et al.: Comprehensive explanation of SLA violations at runtime. IEEE Trans. Serv. Comput. **7**(2), 168–183 (2014)
101. Fickas, S., Feather, M.S.: Requirements monitoring in dynamic environments. In: Proceedings of the 2nd IEEE International Symposium on Requirements Engineering (ISRE), pp. 140–147. IEEE Press (1995)
102. Vierhauser, M., Rabiser, R., Grünbacher, P.: Requirements monitoring frameworks: a systematic review. Inf. Softw. Technol. **80**, 89–109 (2016)
103. Oriol, M., Qureshi, N.A., Franch, X., Perini, A., Marco, J.: Requirements monitoring for adaptive service-based applications. In: Regnell, B., Damian, D. (eds.) REFSQ 2012. LNCS, vol. 7195, pp. 280–287. Springer, Heidelberg (2012). https://doi.org/10.1007/978-3-642-28714-5_25
104. Cailliau, A., van Lamsweerde, A.: Runtime monitoring and resolution of probabilistic obstacles to system goals. ACM Trans. Auton. Adapt. Syst. **14**(1), Article 3 (2019)
105. Robinson, W.N.: Seeking quality through user-goal monitoring. IEEE Softw. **26**(5), 58–65 (2009)
106. Kohavi, R., Deng, A., Frasca, B., Walker, T., Xu, Y., Pohlmann, N.: Online controlled experiments at large scale. In: Proceedings of the 19th ACM SIGKDD International Conference on Knowledge Discovery and Data Mining (KDD), pp. 1168–1176. ACM Press (2013)
107. Fabijan, A., Dmitriev, P., McFarland, C., Vermeer, L., Holmström Olsson, H., Bosch, J.: Experimentation growth: evolving trustworthy A/B testing capabilities in online software companies. J. Softw. Evol. Process. **30**, e2113 (2018)
108. Lindgren, E., Münch, J.: Raising the odds of success: the current state of experimentation in product development. Inf. Softw. Technol. **77**, 80–91 (2016)
109. Franch, X., Lopez, L., Martínez-Fernández, S., Oriol, M., Rodríguez, P., Trendowicz, A.: Quality-aware rapid software development project: the Q-rapids project. In: Mazzara, M., Bruel, J.-M., Meyer, B., Petrenko, A. (eds.) TOOLS 2019. LNCS, vol. 11771, pp. 378–392. Springer, Cham (2019). https://doi.org/10.1007/978-3-030-29852-4_32
110. Perini, A.: Data-driven requirements engineering. The SUPERSEDE way. In: Lossio-Ventura, J.A., Muñante, D., Alatrista-Salas, H. (eds.) SIMBig 2018. CCIS, vol. 898, pp. 13–18. Springer, Cham (2019). https://doi.org/10.1007/978-3-030-11680-4_3

111. Felfernig, A., Stetinger, M., Falkner, A., Atas, M., Franch, X., Palomares, C.: OpenReq: recommender systems in requirements engineering. In: Proceedings of the International Workshop on Recommender Systems and Social Network Analysis (RS-SNA), pp. 1–4. CEUR 2025 (2017)
112. Henderson-Sellers, B., Ralyté, J., Ågerfalk, P., Rossi, M.: Situational Method Engineering. Springer, Heidelberg (2014). https://doi.org/10.1007/978-3-642-41467-1
113. Franch, X., et al.: A situational approach for the definition and tailoring of a data-driven software evolution method. In: Krogstie, J., Reijers, H.A. (eds.) CAiSE 2018. LNCS, vol. 10816, pp. 603–618. Springer, Cham (2018). https://doi.org/10.1007/978-3-319-91563-0_37
114. Dam, H.K., Tran, T., Ghose, A.: Explainable software analytics. In: Proceedings of the 40th International Conference on Software Engineering: New Ideas and Emerging Results (ICSE-NIER), pp. 53–56. ACM Press (2018)
115. Franch, X., Palomares, C., Gorschek, T.: On the requirements engineer role. Commun. ACM (in press). http://dx.doi.org/10.1145/3418292

BiDaML in Practice: Collaborative Modeling of Big Data Analytics Application Requirements

Hourieh Khalajzadeh[1]([envelope]), Andrew J. Simmons[2], Tarun Verma[1],
Mohamed Abdelrazek[2], John Grundy[1], John Hosking[3], Qiang He[4],
Prasanna Ratnakanthan[5], Adil Zia[5], and Meng Law[5]

[1] Monash University, Clayton, VIC 3800, Australia
{hourieh.khalajzadeh,john.grundy}@monash.edu, tver0005@student.monash.edu
[2] Deakin University, Burwood, VIC 3125, Australia
{a.simmons,mohamed.abdelrazek}@deakin.edu.au
[3] University of Auckland, Auckland 1010, New Zealand
j.hosking@auckland.ac.nz
[4] Swinburne University, Hawthorn, VIC 3122, Australia
qhe@swin.edu.au
[5] Alfred Health, Melbourne, VIC 3000, Australia
{P.Ratnakanthan,A.Zia,Meng.Law}@alfred.org.au
https://www.monash.edu/it/humanise-lab

Abstract. Using data analytics to improve industrial planning and operations has become increasingly popular and data scientists are more and more in demand. However, complex data analytics-based software development is challenging. It involves many new roles lacking in traditional software engineering teams – e.g. data scientists and data engineers; use of sophisticated machine learning (ML) approaches replacing many programming tasks; uncertainty inherent in the models; as well as interfacing with models to fulfill software functionalities. These challenges make communication and collaboration within the team and with external stakeholders challenging. In this paper, we describe our experiences in applying our BiDaML (Big Data Analytics Modeling Languages) approach to several large-scale industrial projects. We used our BiDaML modeling toolset that brings all stakeholders around one tool to specify, model and document their big data applications. We report our experience in using and evaluating this tool on three real-world, large-scale applications with teams from: realas.com – a property price prediction website for home buyers; VicRoads – a project seeking to build a digital twin (simulated model) of Victoria's transport network updated in real-time by a stream of sensor data from inductive loop detectors at traffic intersections; and the Alfred Hospital – Intracranial hemorrhage (ICH) prediction through Computed Tomography (CT) Scans. These show that our approach successfully supports complex data analytics software development in industrial settings.

© Springer Nature Switzerland AG 2021
R. Ali et al. (Eds.): ENASE 2020, CCIS 1375, pp. 106–129, 2021.
https://doi.org/10.1007/978-3-030-70006-5_5

Keywords: Big data analytics · Big data modeling · Big data toolkits · BiDaML · Domain specific visual languages · End-user tools

1   Introduction

Big data analytics applications have become increasingly widespread in business [18,24]. However, building such software systems requires considering roles from many different skill backgrounds compared to traditional software development teams. Therefore, it is not straightforward to manage collaborations, teamwork and task specification. Nor is it easy to choose a language that is communicable for the diverse range of users from programmers and analysts to business managers. Such systems require complex, ML-based approaches, deployed at scale and that undergo rapid evolution, as business goals change and new data sources become available. A challenge reported by data scientists in [17] is that it is hard to convey the resulting insights to leaders and stakeholders in an effective manner and to convince teams that data science approaches are in fact helpful. Moreover, results of a large-scale survey [28] of data science workers show that even though they engage in extensive collaboration across all stages of data science work, there are gaps in the usage of collaborative tools. In order to successfully develop such big data analytics systems, a range of perspectives, tasks and interactions need to be taken into consideration [11]:

- Business perspective, including management need for the solution;
- Domain experts, who understand the various datasets available and how analysis of these can lead to usable value;
- Target end-users of the data analytics solution, i.e. the data visualizations produced - sometimes this is business management and/or domain experts, and sometimes other end users e.g. business staff, planners, customers and/or suppliers;
- Data analysts who have deep knowledge of available analytics toolsets to integrate, harmonize, analyze and visualize complex data;
- Data scientists or ML experts who have the expertise to deploy sophisticated ML software solutions;
- Software engineers with expertise to deploy solutions on large scale hardware for data management and computation, and end-user devices for data presentation;
- and Cloud computing architects who deploy and maintain large-scale solutions and datasets.

Existing ML-oriented tools only cover the technical ML and data science part of such problems, i.e. a very small part of the data analytics software engineering life cycle [25]. Current frameworks do not adequately capture multiple stakeholder perspectives and business requirements and link these to support the development of domain models. In this paper, we discuss the challenges in multidisciplinary data analytics teams. We then report on our experiences using our BiDaML approach [10,12,14], to help stakeholders to collaborate (using visual diagrams) in specifying, modeling and documenting what and how the software should perform. BiDaML is a suite of domain-specific visual languages (DSVL) that we created to support the teams through the development of data analytics systems. Different visual languages support modeling of complex, big data software at differing levels of abstraction, using big data analytics domain constructs, and can be translated into big data solutions using Model-Driven Engineering (MDE)-based partial code generation. We also describe our experience working on three different industry use-cases to model and capture the requirements of their big data analytics applications. This paper is an extended version of an earlier one that appeared at ENASE 2020 [14]. The key contributions of this paper include:

– Important new insights into the key challenges in developing big data software solutions;
– Validating these challenges though three large, real-world data intensive industry projects and reporting on the experiences of using our approach for these usecases, and
– Identifying key future directions for researchers in the field of data analytics software development.

The rest of this paper is organized as follows. Section 2 presents our three large scale real world data intensive system examples. Section 3 provides key background and related work analysis. Section 4 outlines our approach to tackling such challenging big data system development and Sect. 5 presents the results of our industry case studies. Section 6 presents the results of research studies conducted to evaluate the usability of the BiDaML notations and tools. Section 7 discusses key findings and key future work directions, while Sect. 8 summarizes conclusions from this work.

2   Our Motivating Industrial Case Studies

In this section, we will show examples of real world data analytics projects to discuss some of the problems data scientists and software engineers face during the solution design process.

2.1   ANZ REALas

REALas[1] is a property price prediction website owned by the Australia and New Zealand Banking Group (ANZ). Launched in 2011, REALas claims to provide Australia's most accurate price predictions on properties listed for sale. ANZ had acquired Australian property start-up REALas to help home buyers access better information about the Australian property market in 2017. Being acquired by ANZ means more users and customers, and consequently, more data, leading to the need for an updated algorithm and retrained models, and therefore a need for

---

[1] https://realas.com/.

data scientists. In this use-case, a complex new model needed to be developed to improve the accuracy and coverage of the property price prediction model. The project team originally comprised a project leader, a business manager, a product owner, three software engineers, and one data scientist. There were an existing working website and an ML model, as well as a dataset purchased from a third party. Two new data analysts/scientists were appointed to this project in order to create new models and integrate them with the existing website. The solution had initially been developed without the use of our tool, and the challenges the team faced to communicate and collaborate through the process was a key motivation for our research. Data scientists initially lacked an understanding of the existing dataset and solution as well as domain knowledge. Therefore, it took them some time to be able to start the project. Communicating progress to the business manager and other members of the team was another challenge. With the REALas team, we used our tool to document the process from business analysis and domain knowledge collection to deployment of final models.

2.2   VicRoads

VicRoads[2], the Victorian road traffic authority, utilizes the Sydney Coordinated Adaptive Traffic System (SCATS) to monitor, control and optimize traffic intersections. Transport researchers within the Monash University Civil Engineering department sought to build a traffic data platform that would ingest a real-time feed of SCATS data from VicRoads and integrate it with other transport datasets such as public transport travel history and traffic incidents reported through social media. Initially, the Civil Engineering department consulted with a software outsourcing company, who proposed a platform composed of industry standard big data tools. However, the software outsourcing company lacked understanding of the datasets and intended use of the platform, thus were unable to begin work on the project. Furthermore, it was unclear who would maintain the computing infrastructure, monitor data quality, and integrate new data sources after the initial phase of the project. We worked with transport researchers and used our tool to document the intended software solution workflow from data ingestion to traffic simulation and visualization. This allowed us to assist in the formation of an alternative software solution making better use of systems and services already available.

2.3   Alfred Hospital and Monash Clinical Data Science

In this project, a group of radiologists, researchers and executives from Alfred hospital have used AI for predicting Intracranial hemorrhage (ICH), pulmonary embolism, spine/rib fractures, lung nodules/cancer through CT Scans, work traditionally done by radiologists. These AI platforms would enable them to prioritize the CT Scans based on the results and forward them to the radiologist for

---

[2] https://www.vicroads.vic.gov.au/traffic-and-road-use/traffic-management/traffic-signals/scats.

an urgent double check and follow up. Hence, a CT Scan with positive outcome could be reported in a few minutes instead of a few days. The team wanted to analyze the data before and after using the AI platform and based on the turnaround time (TAT) and cost analysis decide whether to continue using the AI platform or not. Human radiologists would then also spend more time interrogating scans which have been flagged to be abnormal by AI, and perhaps less time on scans analysed as normal. These clinical AI algorithms have already been found to detect abnormalities that have been missed by human radiologists, even though as that time, they did have some false positives. Currently with another AI clinical product used to detect lung nodules, the AI has in a few months detected 4–5 nodules which radiologists have missed. They were looking towards improving these models to provide near human or supra-human accuracy. However, due to the diversity of the team, it was difficult to communicate the medical terms to the data analysts and software engineers, and the analysis methods and software requirements and solution choices to the radiologists and the executive team. We used our approach with clinical, data science and software team members to model and document steps and plan further key project stages.

3   Data Analytics Software Development Challenges and Related Works

As illustrated using our motivating examples, there is no trace back to the business needs/requirements that triggered the project. Furthermore, communicating and reusing existing big data analytics information and models is shown to be a challenge for many companies new to data analytics. Users need to be able to collaborate with each other through different views and aspects of the problem and possible solutions. Current practices and tools do not cover most activities of data analytics design, especially the critical business requirements. Most current tools focus on low-level data analytics process design, coding and basic visualization of results and they mostly assume data is in a form amenable to processing. In reality, most data items are in different formats and not clean or integrated, and great effort is needed to source the data, integrate, harmonize, pre-process and cleanse it. Only a few off-the-shelf ML tools offer the ability for the data science expert to embed new code and expand algorithms and provide visualizations for their needs. Data processing and ML tasks are only a small component in the building blocks necessary to build real-world deployable data analytics systems [25]. These tasks only cover a small part of data and ML operations and deployment of models. Business and management modeling tools usually do not support many key data analytics steps including data pre-processing and ML steps. There is a need to capture the high-level goals and requirements for different users such as domain expert, business analyst, data analyst, data scientist, software engineer, and end-users and relate them to low level diagrams and capture details such as different tasks for different users, requirements, objectives, etc. Finally, most of the tools covering ML steps require data science and programming knowledge to embed code and change features based on the user requirements.

3.1 Key Challenges

Data analytics are widely used in different organizations to improve decision making. Developing big data software solutions to support an organization's data analytics needs requires a multidisciplinary team of data analysts, data scientists, domain experts, business managers, software engineers, etc. Domain experts, business analysts and business managers do not necessarily have a background in data science and programming, and therefore, they do not know how to convert their problem to a data analytics problem, where to start the project from and how to use the myriad of existing data science tools. Similarly, data scientists may be able to create small, bespoke solutions but lack software engineering skills to scale solutions. Software engineers generally lack detailed data science and domain expertise. As identified in [9,11], while many techniques and tools exist to support the development of such solutions, they have many limitations. In general, developing big data software solutions suffers from several key challenges.

Challenge 1 (C#1): *Domain Experts, Business Analysts and Business Managers Do Not have a Background in Data Science and Programming.* Domain experts and business users of big data analytics solutions know the target domain, the data in the domain and the intended benefits from the solution. However, they lack the expertise to design and develop, and sometimes to adequately understand such solutions.

Challenge 2 (C#2): *Data Analysts, Data Scientists and Software Engineers do Not have Domain Knowledge.* Data analytics is applied to a variety of different applications from health and education to finance and banking, and data scientists with technical data science and programming background do not necessarily have a background in any of the applications they work on. Therefore, it takes some time for them to collect background knowledge, get familiar with the domain, what has been done so far, the existing solutions, etc.

Challenge 3 (C#3): *Data Scientists Lack Software Engineering Expertise.* Data analysts and data scientists are an emerging IT workforce and are to describe a problem domain, analyze domain data, extract insights, apply ML models, do evaluations and deploy models. However, most do not have many of the skills of software engineers, including solution architecture, coding and large-scale data analytics software deployment. Often data science models lack ways to describe these aspects of the solution requirements and do not scale.

Challenge 4 (C#4): *Lack of a Common Language between Team Members.* Domain experts, business analysts and business managers have a high-level knowledge of the problem, objectives, requirements, users, etc. while data analysts and data scientists are more from a technical background with expertise in data science and programming. Communicating and collaborating between users from different backgrounds is a bottleneck in data analytics application development. Data scientists spend most of their time preparing data to make it usable by downstream modeling algorithms. There are no communicable models or outputs for different stakeholders to enable mutual understanding and agreement.

Challenge 5 (C#5): *Evolution of the Solution is Poorly Supported.* After the solution is developed and deployed, emerging new data, changing business needs and usage of the application all typically result in a need to update and re-train the models to improve performance. However, the data science group originally employed to develop the initial solution is often disbanded upon completion, leaving others to attempt to maintain their models. In contrast to software artifacts, the processes and decisions involved in gathering, cleansing and analyzing data are rarely fully documented even in scientific research [2], let alone industry projects with tight deadlines and limited resources for producing documentation.

Challenge 6 (C#6): *Re-using of the Existing Solutions is Not Feasible.* Whether a new group of data scientists is appointed to update and improve out-of-date models and software or the team is left struggling with it, traditional documentation approaches mean it will take a long time for the new team to understand the existing model, as different data scientists have their own method of modeling and programming. In addition, as they often use specific tools, it is not normally the case for them to spend time understanding and modifying the existing solutions. Often, the new team ends up creating new models and therefore repeating all these steps and facing all the same problems again. This is not only a problem within a single group but in different parts of organizations, where data analytics solutions are created without common models being shared and reused.

3.2   Related Work

There are many data analytics tools available, such as Azure ML Studio[3], Amazon AWS ML[4], Google Cloud ML[5], and BigML[6] as reviewed in [11]. However, these tools only cover a few phases of DataOps, AIOps, and DevOps and none

---

[3] https://studio.azureml.net/.
[4] https://aws.amazon.com/machine-learning/.
[5] https://cloud.google.com/ai-platform.
[6] https://bigml.com/.

cover business problem description, requirements analysis and design. Moreover, since most end-users have limited technical data science and programming knowledge, they usually struggle using these tools. Some DSVLs have been developed for supporting enterprise service modeling and generation using end-user friendly metaphors. An integrated visual notation for business process modeling is presented and developed in [19] using a novel tree-based overlay structure that effectively mitigates complexity problems. MaramaAIC [8] provides end-to-end support between requirements engineers and their clients for the validation and improvement of the requirements inconsistencies. SDLTool [16] provides statistician end-users with a visual language environment for complex statistical survey design/implementation. These tools provide environments supporting end-users in different domains. However, they do not support data analytics processes, techniques, data and requirements, and do not target end-users for such applications. Scientific workflows are widely recognized as useful models to describe, manage, and share complex scientific analyses and tools have been designed and developed for designing, reusing, and sharing such workflows. Kepler [20] and Taverna [27] are Java-based open source software systems for designing, executing, reusing, evolving, archiving, and sharing scientific workflows to help scientists, analysts, and computer programmers. VisTrails [5] is a Python/Qt-based open-source scientific workflow and provenance management system supporting simulation, data exploration and visualization. It can be combined with existing systems and libraries as well as your own packages/modules. Finally, Workspace [6], built on the Qt toolkit, is a powerful, cross-platform scientific workflow framework enabling collaboration and software reuse and streamlining delivery of software for commercial and research purposes. Users can easily create, collaborate and reproduce scientific workflows, develop custom user interfaces for different customers, write their own specialized plug-ins, and scale their computation using Workspace's remote/parallel task scheduling engine. Different projects can be built on top of these drag and drop based graphical tools and these tools are used in a variety of applications and domains. However, they only offer a limited number of data analysis steps and no data analytics and ML capabilities and libraries. Finally, some software tools implement algorithms specific to a given graphical model such as Infer.NET [21]. This approach for implementing data analytics techniques is called a model-based approach to ML [3]. An initial conceptualization of a domain specific modeling language supporting code generation from visual representations of probabilistic models for big data analytics is presented in [4] by extending the analysis of the Infer.NET. However, it is in very early stages and does not cover many of the data analytics steps in real-world problems.

4 Our Approach

Since the exisitng big data analytics tools provide only low-level data science solution design, despite many other steps being involved in solution development, a high-level presentation of the steps to capture, represent, and communicate the business requirements analysis and design, data pre-processing, high-level data analysis process, solution deployment and data visualization is presented in [10,14].

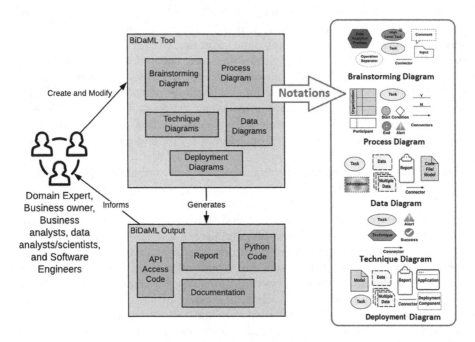

Fig. 1. BiDaML notations (from [14]).

4.1 BiDaML Visual Language

BiDaML, presented in [10] and extended in [12,14], is a set of domain-specific visual languages using different diagram types at different levels of abstraction to support key aspects of big data analytics. Overview of the BiDaML app-roach, high level to low level diagrams, and their notations are shown in Fig. 1. A brainstorming diagram is defined for every data analytics project. Then, at a lower level to include more details and involve the participants, we use a pro-cess diagram. Every operation in a process diagram can be further extended by technique and data diagrams, and then, the technique and data diagrams are connected to a result output diagram. Finally, the deployment diagram, defined for every data analytics problem, models deployment related details at a low level. The updated diagrams presented in [12] include:

Brainstorming Diagram. A data analytics brainstorming diagram's scope covers the entirety of a data analytics project expressed at a high-level. There are no rules as to how abstractly or explicitly a context is expanded. The diagram overviews a data analytics project in terms of the specific problem it is associated with, and the task and subtasks to solve the specific problem. It supports interactive brainstorming to identify key aspects of a data analytics project such as its requirements implications, analytical methodologies and specific tasks. Brainstorming diagram comprises an icon representing the data analytics problem, tasks which the problem is associated with, a hierarchy of sub-tasks for each task, and finally the specific information about sub-systems used or produced. We group the building blocks of an AI-powered system into four groups: Domain and business-related activities (BusinessOps); data-related activities (DataOps); artificial intelligence and ML-related activities (AIOps); and development and deployment activities (DevOps).

Process Diagram. The key business processes in a data analytics application are shown in a process diagram. We adapt the Business Process Modeling Notation (BPMN) [23] to specify big data analytics processes at several levels of abstraction. Process diagrams support business process management, for both technical users such as data analysts, data scientists, and software engineers as well as non-technical users such as domain experts, business users and customers, by providing a notation that is intuitive to business users, yet able to represent complex process semantics. In this diagram type, we use different "pools" for different organizations and different "swim lanes" for the people involved in the process within the same organization. Different layers are also defined based on different tasks such as business-related tasks (BusinessOps), technical (DataOps and AIOps), and operational tasks (DevOps and application-based tasks). Preparation of data items or different events trigger other events and redirect the process to the other users in the same or different pool.

Technique Diagram. Data analytics technique diagrams extend the brainstorming diagram to low-level detail specific to different big data analytics tasks and sub-tasks. For every sub-task, the process is broken down into the specific stages and the technique used to solve a specific sub-task specified.

Data Diagram. To document the data and artifacts consumed and produced in different phases described by each of the above diagrams, one or more low-level data diagrams are created. Data diagrams support the design of data and artifacts collection processes. They represent the structured and semi-structured data items involved in the data analytics project in different steps. A high-level data diagram can be represented by connecting the low-level diagrams for different BusinessOps, DataOps, AIOps, and DevOps. We initially had an output diagram to represent the reports and outputs, that has eventually been merged with data diagram.

Deployment Diagram. Deployment diagrams represent the software artifacts and the deployment components and specify the deployment related details. In the deployment diagram, we focus on distributed cloud platforms, services, and frameworks rather than individual nodes/devices. We had initially adopted the deployment diagram concepts from the context of Unified Modeling Language (UML) that has eventually changed to our new deployment representation. Details can be found in [12].

4.2   BiDaML Support Tool

We have developed an integrated design environment for creating BiDaML diagrams. The tool support aims to provide a platform for efficiently producing BiDaML visual models and to facilitate their creation, display, editing, storage, code generation and integration with other tools. We have used MetaEdit+ Workbench [26] to implement our tool. Using MetaEdit+, we have created the objects and relationships defined as the notational elements for all the diagrams, different rules on how to connect the objects using the relationships, and how to define low level sub-graphs for the high level diagrams. Figures 2 and 3 show examples of BiDaML tool in use for creating brainstorming diagram and an overview of all the diagrams. They show the outputs generated from the tool including Python code and word document.

4.3   BiDaML-Web

We have implemented a web based auto layout user interface for BiDaML. BiDaML-web[7] [15] uses Node.js as a runtime environment that executes

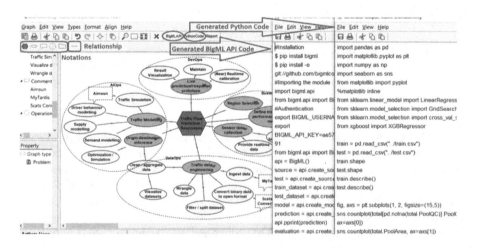

Fig. 2. Brainstorming diagram created in BiDaML tool for the traffic analysis example and snippets of the generated Python code (from [13]).

---

[7] https://bidaml.web.app/.

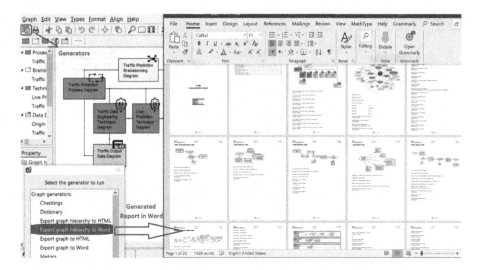

Fig. 3. Overview of all the diagrams created in BiDaML tool for the traffic analysis example and the final report in word generated from the overview diagram (from [13]).

JavaScript and for server-side scripting. The application uses Vue.js which is a JavaScript framework for building user interfaces. Our web-based implementation of BiDaML[8] is based on the auto-layout web-based tool vue-graphViz[9] [7] which includes features to adjust placement of items to avoid clutter (such as lines crossing symbols on the graph) in order to improve readability. Hosting of the application, Real-time database, Google Analytics, and authentication services have been also been implemented using Firebase's APIs. We include a set of quick-start questions to help the user rapidly generate the initial diagram with minimal clicks, then provide a minimal interface through which the user can modify the diagram as needed. To increase the user's awareness of relevant algorithms and datasets specific to their problem, we utilise Papers with Code and Google/Kaggle Datasets Search for recommending algorithms and datasets. Finally, our tool includes a technique recommender in order to help end users decide which techniques are appropriate given their dataset, and to consider questions such as the type of prediction or classification task, and whether they have access to sufficient labelled data. An example of using BiDaML-web for creating a brainstorming diagram for the property price prediction is shown in Fig. 4.

---

[8] https://github.com/tarunverma23/bidaml.

[9] https://github.com/yusufades/vue-graphViz.

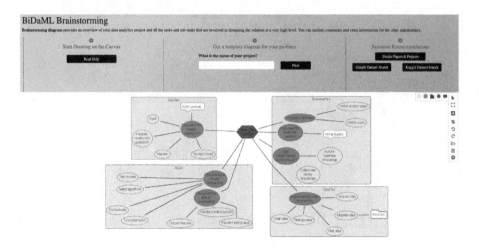

Fig. 4. BiDaML-web used for creating a brainstorming diagram for the property price prediction example.

5   BiDaML in Industry Practice

In this section, as the main contribution of this paper, we report on the experiences using our tool in three industry projects to validate the challenges we identified earlier as well as evaluating the usability and suitability of our approach in a real setting. We used our tool in 3 different real-world industry problems. In each case, we create a high-level view of an existing problem and use it to uncover assumptions and allow communications and collaborations to successfully evolve in a measured manner.

ANZ REALas. Our tool was used to model REALas development from initial requirement analysis and data collection through the entire life cycle of its deployment. The first issue *(C#1)* appeared when the team was unable to develop data analytics solutions or update the existing models due to the lack of necessary knowledge and therefore appointed new data scientists to work on it. There was no documentation available from the existing models, and the data scientist who had developed the existing model was not available to work on the project, therefore data scientists needed to spend hours talking to the existing members, and going through the existing source code, where available, to understand the existing solution. Moreover, new data scientists were not from finance and banking backgrounds and needed to go through documents in different formats, and dataset dictionaries to understand the concepts *(C#2)*.

Since there was no common language *(C#4)*, it took a long time for them to transfer information and convert them from domain knowledge to data science knowledge. Moreover, new data scientists needed to spend weeks to even months to analyze the existing dataset, clean and wrangle datasets, acquire more datasets, integrate all these models and try many new features to be able to improve the existing model since data scientists spend most of their time preparing data. However, due to the lack of a platform or common language, they could not share and communicate their progress with the business manager/leader/owner. Data scientists finally recreated new models instead of reusing and modifying the existing models due to the lack of documentation and also since there was no common framework and they had to use a different platform than used for the existing models *(C#6)*. They eventually created a new model to replace the existing model and finally had communicable results. They still needed to integrate it with the website, requiring software engineers in the final step *(C#3)*. However, this was not the end of the story for the team, and the models needed to be later updated and retrained after a while, and therefore, the need for updated models, new data scientists, and another round of all these challenges *(C#5)*.

We used our tool to redesign the whole project, in order to communicate and collaborate through the project, as well as automatically document all the above development steps. A brainstorming diagram was designed in the first place to help all the stakeholders fully understand and communicate the steps and existing solutions through a visualized drag-and-drop based platform. Once agreements were made on all the steps, a process diagram was created to assign the tasks to the existing stakeholders. These two steps only took a few hours from the whole team, and they could also incrementally modify these two during the process. Data scientists were now fully aware of the domain knowledge, background of the project and existing models and could further leave comments and ask questions if further information was required.

In the next step, data scientists worked on the data and ML parts, however this time, needed to visually record and keep track of the data items, artefacts, models, reports, etc. that they tried, whether they were successful, failed, or were just being planned. This made it easy for them to communicate their progress and also reach agreement on the results. Our tool has a code generation feature that could help data scientists start from a template instead of starting from scratch. Our tool provides a way to automatically document and embed their code templates for future usage. They gradually developed new models, and finally, worked with software engineers on a deployment diagram to define where and how to deploy the items generated in different steps. The new method was efficient in the way it took less time for the stakeholders to communicate and collaborate, and the step-by-step automatic documentation made the solution reusable for future reference. Based on the product owner's feedback *"this tool would have been helpful to understand and communicate the complexity of a new ML project within an organisation. It would assist the wider team to collaborate with data scientists and improve the outputs of the process"*.

Examples of some of the diagrams generated throughout the process are shown in Fig. 5. A full list of the diagrams and the generated report is available in [1]. In Fig. 5, a brainstorming diagram shows high-level tasks designed for the problem and how they are divided based on the nature of the operations (BusinessOps, DataOps, AIOps and DevOps). For instance, "price prediction website deployment" is a high-level DataOps task consisting of lower-level tasks such as "store", that is later supported by the "Real Estate MySQL DB" component on top of an AWS Cloud DB Server shown in the deployment diagram. Report data diagram enables agreement on the reports expected to be generated or shown on the website.

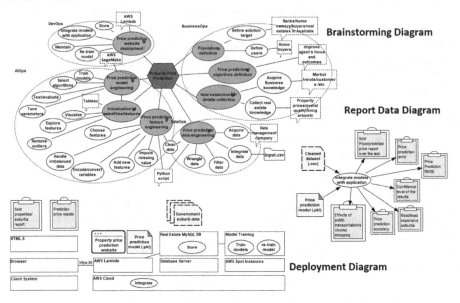

Fig. 5. Examples of the diagrams created for the property price prediction use-case.

VicRoads. In this use-case, there was a need to formally capture detailed requirements for a traffic data platform that would ingest a real-time stream of traffic data received from VicRoads (the Victorian road transport authority), integrate this with other transport data sources, and support modeling and visualization of the transport network at a state-wide level. The first issues (*C#1* and *C#3*) arose in the initiation of the project. The project leader and traffic modeling experts identified the need for a big data platform. However, without a background in software engineering or familiarity with modern data science tools, they were unable to determine whether the technology stack offered by the software outsourcing company would meet their needs.

The second issue *(C#2)* arose in requirements elicitation; the software outsourcing company lacked understanding of the domain and thus did not understand what tasks were required of them. To overcome the communication difficulties, a meeting was arranged between the project leader, the traffic modeling expert, a data engineer/visualization designer, the project team from the software outsourcing company, and the eResearch High Performance Computing services team. However, the lack of a common language *(C#4)* meant that communication could only take place at a high-level rather than at the level of detail necessary to initiate direct technical action. The software outsourcing company produced a plan for the software they intended to deploy; however, no plan existed for who would monitor and maintain the software and systems after deployment *(C#5)*, such as responding to faults in real-time data ingestion or adding support for new types of data. To justify the cost and time investment into the project, the project leader wanted to be able to reuse *(C#6)* the platform for related projects, such as a smart city. However, it was unclear whether the work invested in the design of the transport data platform could be reused in other projects.

We performed in-depth interviews with the project leader and traffic modeling expert, then used our tool to document the entire data analytics workflow including data ingestion, transport modeling, and result visualization. The traffic prediction brainstorming diagram was initially created as a handwritten sketc.h on paper, then later recreated using the tool. The process diagram, technique diagram, data diagram, and deployment diagram were created directly using the tool. While most diagram types took only 15–30 minutes to create, the process diagram proved the most time consuming, taking almost 3 h due to the need to detail tasks to integrate each system and determine roles of individuals (we have since simplified the process diagram notation in order to streamline the process). As our tool forces the user to consider all phases of the project, the modeling process helped reveal gaps in planning that required attention. Notably, no budget or personnel had been assigned to maintain the system after initial deployment, integrate new data sources, and monitor data quality/security. Indeed, in the process diagram, we were forced to label both the organization and participant for these tasks as To Be Determined (TBD).

We presented the diagrams to the traffic modeling expert for feedback. This took place over a course of an hour session, in which we presented each diagram in the tool. The tool supported live corrections to the diagrams such as creation, modification or reassignment of tasks as we discussed the diagrams with the traffic modeling expert. Feedback from the expert was positive: *"I think you have a good understanding of the business... how do you know about all of this? I think this is very interesting, very impressive what you are proposing. It covers a lot of work that needs to be done."* While the expert stated that the diagrams were helpful to *"figure out all the processes and what tasks need to be done"* they were reluctant to use our tool to communicate with external stakeholders in other organizations: *"to use this tool, it will be likely not possible, because they [the other organizations involved] have their own process, they don't want to follow a new one"*. We subsequently presented printouts of the diagrams to the project leader who expressed some uncertainty about the purpose of the notation; however, noted that an adaptation of the data diagrams as a means to document data provenance (i.e. the ability to trace the origins of data analysis results back to raw data used) would be *"very useful"*.

Examples of the diagrams generated throughout the process are shown in Fig. 6. A full list of the diagrams and the generated report is available in [1]. For instance, the "Simulation Data Diagram" shows that the Origin-Destination Matrix (where vehicles enter the traffic network and where they travel to) used for traffic modeling is partially derived from "15 min Volume Average" sensor data fed into an optimization/simulation process to find the most likely Origin-Destination matrix given the reported sensor readings. Documenting this using our approach can assist future users of the resultant Origin-Destination Matrix to better understand the original source of their data and to recompute the result. For the purpose of live traffic prediction, it was desired to automatically recompute the Origin-Destination Matrix from recent data. The "Live Prediction Technique Diagram" shows the consideration of different techniques to achieve this. Periodic re-execution of the workflow every 5 to 15 min emerged as an option to facilitate live predictions without requiring traffic modeling experts to have a software engineering background.

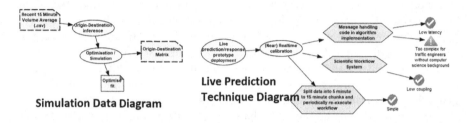

Fig. 6. Examples of the diagrams created for the VicRoads use-case.

Alfred Hospital and Monash Clinical Data Science. The team at the Alfred hospital needed to analyze data before and after using an AI platform to decide whether to continue using the tool or not. The team consisted of radiologists and medical researchers without a background in data analytics. The AI platform provider claimed that by using the AI platform they would be able to reduce the TAT time from days to minutes. Without a background in data analytics and ML they would not be able to collect, integrate, cleanse, analyze and compare the results after using the AI platform and ensure the AI platform was able to meet their requirements *(C#1)*. They decided to talk to a data analysis researcher to discuss the possible solutions, however, the data analysis researcher had no background in medical and radiology terms and concepts and communicating the requirements was a challenge *(C#2)* as there initially was a lack of a common language between these people *(C#4)*. Deploying the final software *(C#3)*, who would be responsible for different tasks *(C#5)* and whether they could reuse the analysis for the future projects *(C#6)* were other challenges they would face if they wanted to continue the project with no clear definition and documentation of the detailed tasks.

We briefly introduced our tool to the team and since it seemed to be a well-designed fit for the project due to the diverse nature of the stakeholders, we decided to use the tool to model and analyze the requirements and capture the details. We had an initial one-hour meeting with one of the radiologists and started developing the models and collecting a deep understanding of the project,

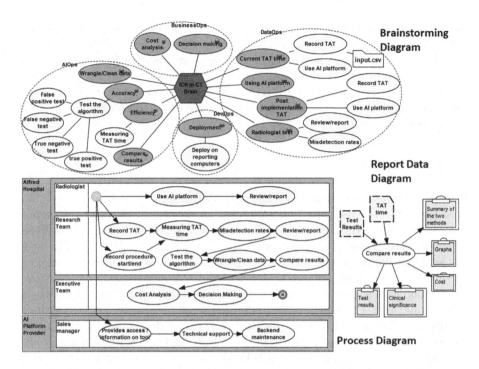

Fig. 7. Examples of the diagrams created for the alfred hospital use-case.

requirements, concepts, and objectives through the brainstorming diagram. Then we spent almost 30 min to document the entire data analytics workflow including data collection and wrangling, comparing the methods, making the final decision and deploying the final product through process, technique, data and deployment diagrams. Since we needed to deeply think about all the details and plans, the tool forced us to consider all phases and details of the project. We then organized a follow-up meeting with the team from the hospital, including two radiologists and the team leader and presented the diagrams for their feedback. The meeting took 30 min. During the meeting, we modified the organizations and users involved as well as the expected reports and outcomes and the infrastructure in the deployment diagram. Going through the diagrams made us think about these and plan for them. We then shared the report generated from the tool with the team for their feedback.

Feedback from the team was that *"BiDaML offered a simplified visual on different components of the project. These diagrams could be circulated to the project team and would clarify the workflow, requirements, aims and endpoints of each role and the entire project. In large-scale projects, BiDaML would be of even greater benefit, with involvement of multiple teams all working towards a common goal"*. However, *"The user interface seemed quite challenging to navigate. However, this could be easily negated with appropriate training and instructional material"*. Examples of the diagrams generated throughout the process are shown in Fig. 7. A full list of the diagrams and the generated report is available in [1]. For instance, the process diagram, as one of the high-level diagrams generated for this example, clarified that there are three groups from the hospital involved in this project, and there are currently no data analysts involved in the project and the research team are recording TAT, testing the algorithm, planning to compare the results, etc. before the executive team decides on purchasing the AI platform or not.

6   Evaluation

In addition to our experiences of using BiDaML in practice within Sect. 5, we have evaluated the usability and suitability of our visual languages and tool suite in two ways (preliminary results originally reported in [10,14] and the comprehensive extended experiments originally presented in [12,15]). The first was an extensive physics of notations evaluation [22]. This was a useful end-user perspective evaluation without having to involve a large-scale usability trial. The second was a series of user studies to understand how easy BiDaML is to learn and use. The user studies performed were: a cognitive walkthrough of the original BiDaML support tool with several target domain expert end-users, including data scientists and software engineers, as test participants; a group user study to compare handwritten BiDaML diagrams to other notations; and finally a user study of BiDaML-web.

6.1   Physics of Notations Evaluation

Semiotic clarity specifies that a diagram should not have symbol redundancy, overload, excess and deficit. All our visual symbols in BiDaML have 1:1 correspondence to their referred concepts. Perceptual discriminability is primarily determined by the visual distance between symbols. All our symbols in BiDaML use different shapes as their main visual variable, plus redundant coding such as color and/or textual annotation. Semantic transparency identifies the extent to which the meaning of a symbol should be inferred from its appearance. In BiDaML, icons are used to represent visual symbols and minimize the use of abstract geometrical shapes. Complexity management restricts a diagram to have as few visual elements as possible to reduce its diagrammatic complexity. We used hierarchical views in BiDaML for representation and as our future work, we will add the feature for users to hide visual construct details for complex diagrams. Cognitive integration identifies that the information from separate diagrams should be assembled into a coherent mental representation of a system; and it should be as simple as possible to navigate between diagrams. All the diagrams in BiDaML have a hierarchical tree-based structure relationship.

Visual expressiveness defines a range of visual variables to be used, resulting in a perceptually enriched representation that exploits multiple visual communication channels and maximizes computational offloading. Various visual variables, such as shape, color, orientation, texture, etc. are used in designing

BiDaML visual symbols. Dual coding means that textual encoding should also be used, as it is most effective when used in a supporting role. In BiDaML, all visual symbols have a textual annotation. Graphic economy discusses that the number of different visual symbols should be cognitively manageable. As few visual symbols as possible are used in BiDaML. Cognitive fit means that the diagram needs to have different visual dialects for different tasks or users. All the symbols in BiDaML are usable for different users and tasks. However, in the future, we will provide different views for different users in our BiDaML support tool, and users will be able to navigate between views based on their requirements.

6.2   Cognitive Walk-Through of BiDaML Support Tool

We asked 3 data scientists and 2 software engineers (all experienced in big data analytics) to carry out a task-based end-user evaluation of BiDaML. The objective was to assess how easy it is to learn to use the visual models and how efficiently it can solve the diagram complexity problem. BiDaML diagrams were briefly introduced to the participants who were then asked to perform three pre-defined modeling tasks. The first was to design BusinessOps, DataOps, AIOps, or DevOps part of a brainstorming diagram for a data analytics problem of their choice from scratch. In the second, each participant was given a process diagram and asked to explain it, comment on the information represented and provide suggestions to improve it. The third involved participants designing a technique diagram related to a specific task of the data analytics problem they chose for the first part of the evaluation.

Overall, user feedback from the participants indicated that BiDaML is very straightforward to use and understand. Users felt they could easily communicate with other team members and managers and present their ideas, techniques, expected outcomes and progress in a common language during the project before the final solution. They liked how different layers and operations are differentiated. Moreover, they could capture and understand business requirements and expectations and make agreements on requirements, outcomes, and results through the project. These could then be linked clearly to lower-level data, technique and output diagrams. Using this feedback we have made some minor changes to our diagrams such as the shape and order of some notations, and the relationships between different objects. However, several limitations and potential improvements have also been identified in our evaluations. Some users prefer to see technique and data diagrams components altogether in a single diagram, while some others prefer to have these separate. Moreover, in the process diagram, some users prefer to only see the operations related to their tasks and directly related tasks. Finally, one of the users wanted to differentiate between tasks/operations that are done by humans versus a tool. In future tool updates, we will provide different views for different users and will allow users to hide/unhide different components of the diagrams based on their preference. Moreover, in our future code generation plan, we will separate different tasks based on whether they are conducted by humans or tools.

6.3 Group User Study of Handwritten BiDaML Diagrams

To address limitations of the first user study, we performed a second user evaluation in a more structured manner, with feedback collected anonymously. In order to evaluate the suitability of the BiDaML notation for new users in a diversity of scenarios, the participants were asked to create BiDaML diagrams to model the project of their choice. Moreover, to see how BiDaML compared to other notations, participants were asked to create both a BiDaML diagram as well as diagram using another notation, then share their diagrams with other participants. The results of our study, reported in [12], showed that users prefer BiDaML for supporting complex data analytics solution modeling more than other modeling languages.

6.4 BiDaML-Web User Study

To evaluate BiDaML-web, we performed a user study with a group of 16 end-users. Given we had conducted comprehensive evaluations of BiDaML notations and its comparison in our previous works [10,12], we only evaluated the auto-layout web based user interface and the recommender tools in this study. Our aim was to evaluate the usability of BiDaML-web and whether users paid attention to recommendations and found the code, paper, project and dataset recommendations, helpful. In this study (originally reported in [15]), we first introduced the BiDaML concept, notations, and diagrams and then asked a group of 16 data analysts, data scientists, domain experts and software engineers to use BiDaMl-web tool to model and describe a project of their choice. We finally asked participants to fill in a questionnaire and asked to rate whether BiDaML-web is easy to understand/learn/use and how they found the recommender tool. The group study consisted of 9 PhD students, and 7 academic staff. 8 participants categorised themselves as software engineers, 4 as data analysts/scientists, 5 as Domain expert/business analyst/business manager, and 2 as "other" (some participants identified as multiple categories). The distribution of data analytics/data science experience was: 7 participants with less than 1 year; 2 participants with 2 years; 2 participant with 3 years; and 5 participants with 5 to 9 years. The distribution of programming experience was: 2 participants with 0–1 year, 1 participant with 1 year, 3 participants with 2 years, 2 participants with 3 years, 2 participants with 4 years, 2 participants with 5 to 9 years, and 4 participants with 10 or more years. Study participants found the integrated recommender tools helpful, and also responded positively to the tool overall, as detailed in [15]. The primary reasons selected were "it made me think of details that I never noticed" (9 of 16) and "introduced resources I wasn't aware of" (9 of 16); it was possible for a participant to select multiple reasons or provide a custom response to this question.

7 Discussions

We applied our approach on three different real world usecases to validate these challenges as well as our approach in a real setting. Our aim was to evaluate and gain experience with applying our method to conduct requirements analysis and modeling part of complex data analytics applications. We have found that our method: has been practical to a variety of real-world large-scale applications. It helped communication and collaboration between team members from different backgrounds by providing a common platform with mutual language *(C#1–C#4)*. It also helped identify and agree on details in the early stages *(C#5)*. Thus our tool can reduce costs and improve the speed of business understanding by addressing these details during the requirement analysis stage. It also provided automatic documentation that can be re-used for retraining and updating of the models *(C#6)*. Based on our radiologist users' experience: *"As the frequency of multidisciplinary, collaborative projects is increasing, there is a clear benefit with the use of BiDaML as a tool for designing data analytics processes. Furthermore, the automatic code generation capabilities of BiDaML would greatly aid those who do not have experience in large-scale data analysis. We do see use of BiDaML in this specific project and would be interested in seeing its results"*. There are some notable issues we faced while working with industrial partners on these data analytics requirement engineering problems. Our tool can be accessed by all the stakeholders in different geographical locations. However, our intervention has been required so far, as our original BiDaML tool depends on MetaEdit+ modeling development tool [26] and a license required to be purchased by users. Users make benefits of the early requirement engineering part. However, they continue using existing tools and programming languages to develop the ML and application development parts once they have completed the requirement analysis, modeling and planning part of the project. To overcome the first issue, we re-implemented the tool as a stand-alone web-based tool that users can work on individually without us being required to manage the modeling part. To overcome the second, we aim to develop recommendations and integrations for popular existing tools to encourage users to continue using our approach through the entire development of the final product. We see considerable scope for providing back end integration with data analytics tools such as Azure ML Studio, RapidMiner, KNIME, etc. Our tool can be used at an abstract level during requirements analysis and design, and then connect to different tools at a low-level. Therefore, our DSVLs can be used to design, implement and control a data analytics solution.

8   Conclusions

We have identified several key challenges in data analytics software engineering, compared to traditional software teams and processes. We described our BiDaML domain-specific visual-language based technique for requirements modeling and documentation of big data analytics systems. Our experience in three different real-world case studies in finance, transportation and health has been that our method is easy to apply to diverse real-world large-scale applications and greatly assisted us in identifying the requirements as well as domain and business knowledge that will potentially lead to improvements in planning and developing the software. Additionally, an initial web-based interface for BiDaML is presented and evaluated in this paper. Being able to successfully apply our practical method in designing and analyzing different big data analytics applications encouraged us to further extend BiDaML as a stand-alone web-based tool and connect it to the existing ML recommendation toolboxes as a step toward realising our vision of an integrated end-to-end modelling platform for big data solutions.

Acknowledgements. Support for this work from ARC Discovery Projects DP170101932 and from ARC Laureate Program FL190100035 is gratefully acknowledged. We would also like to acknowledge Prof. Hai Vu and Dr. Nam Hoang from the Monash Institute of Transport Studies for their collaboration, and thank the Department of Transport (VicRoads) for sharing the transport data.

References

1. BiDaML big data analytics modeling languages. http://bidaml.visualmodel.org/
2. Baker, M.: 1,500 scientists lift the lid on reproducibility (2016)
3. Bishop, C.M.: Model-based machine learning. Philos. Trans. Roy. Soc. A: Math. Phys. Eng. Sci. **371**(1984), 20120222 (2013)
4. Breuker, D.: Towards model-driven engineering for big data analytics-an exploratory analysis of domain-specific languages for machine learning. In: 2014 47th Hawaii International Conference on System Sciences, pp. 758–767. IEEE (2014)
5. Callahan, S.P., Freire, J., Santos, E., Scheidegger, C.E., Silva, C.T., Vo, H.T.: VisTrails: visualization meets data management. In: Proceedings of the 2006 ACM SIGMOD International Conference on Management of Data, pp. 745–747 (2006)
6. Cleary, P., Thomas, D., Bolger, M., Hetherton, L., Rucinski, C., Watkins, D.: Using workspace to automate workflow processes for modelling and simulation in engineering. in 'modsim2015. In: 21st International Congress on Modelling and Simulation', Broadbeach, Queensland, Australia, pp. 669–675 (2015)
7. Dwyer, T., Marriott, K., Wybrow, M.: Dunnart: a constraint-based network diagram authoring tool. In: Tollis, I.G., Patrignani, M. (eds.) GD 2008. LNCS, vol. 5417, pp. 420–431. Springer, Heidelberg (2009). https://doi.org/10.1007/978-3-642-00219-9_41
8. Kamalrudin, M., Hosking, J., Grundy, J.: MaramaAIC: tool support for consistency management and validation of requirements. Autom. Softw. Eng. **24**(1), 1–45 (2017)
9. Khalajzadeh, H., Abdelrazek, M., Grundy, J., Hosking, J., He, Q.: A survey of current end-user data analytics tool support. In: 2018 IEEE International Congress on Big Data (BigData Congress), pp. 41–48. IEEE (2018)
10. Khalajzadeh, H., Abdelrazek, M., Grundy, J., Hosking, J., He, Q.: BiDaML: a suite of visual languages for supporting end-user data analytics. In: 2019 IEEE International Congress on Big Data (BigDataCongress), pp. 93–97. IEEE (2019)
11. Khalajzadeh, H., Abdelrazek, M., Grundy, J., Hosking, J., He, Q.: Survey and analysis of current end-user data analytics tool support. IEEE Trans. Big Data (01), 1 (2019). https://doi.org/10.1109/TBDATA.2019.2921774

12. Khalajzadeh, H., Simmons, A.J., Abdelrazek, M., Grundy, J., Hosking, J., He, Q.: An end-to-end model-based approach to support big data analytics development. J. Comput. Lang. **58**, 100964 (2020)
13. Khalajzadeh, H., Simmons, A.J., Abdelrazek, M., Grundy, J., Hosking, J., He, Q.: End-user-oriented tool support for modeling data analytics requirements. In: 2020 IEEE Symposium on Visual Languages and Human-Centric Computing (VL/HCC), pp. 1–4. IEEE (2020)
14. Khalajzadeh, H., Simmons, A.J., Abdelrazek, M., Grundy, J., Hosking, J.G., He, Q.: Visual languages for supporting big data analytics development. In: ENASE, pp. 15–26 (2020)
15. Khalajzadeh, H., Verma, T., Simmons, A.J., Grundy, J., Abdelrazek, M., Hosking, J.: User-centred tooling for the modelling of big data applications. In: MODELS 2020: ACM/IEEE International Conference on Model Driven Engineering Languages and Systems. ACM (2020)
16. Kim, C.H., Grundy, J., Hosking, J.: A suite of visual languages for model-driven development of statistical surveys and services. J. Vis. Lang. Comput. **26**, 99–125 (2015)
17. Kim, M., Zimmermann, T., DeLine, R., Begel, A.: Data scientists in software teams: state of the art and challenges. IEEE Trans. Software Eng. **44**(11), 1024–1038 (2017)
18. Landset, S., Khoshgoftaar, T.M., Richter, A.N., Hasanin, T.: A survey of open source tools for machine learning with big data in the Hadoop ecosystem. J. Big Data **2**(1), 24 (2015)
19. Li, L., Grundy, J., Hosking, J.: A visual language and environment for enterprise system modelling and automation. J. Vis. Lang. Comput. **25**(4), 253–277 (2014)
20. Ludäscher, B., et al.: Scientific workflow management and the Kepler system. Concurr. Comput.: Pract. Exp. **18**(10), 1039–1065 (2006)
21. Minka, T., Winn, J., Guiver, J., Knowles, D.: Infer.net 2.4, 2010. Microsoft research Cambridge (2010)
22. Moody, D.: The "physics" of notations: toward a scientific basis for constructing visual notations in software engineering. IEEE Trans. Softw. Eng. **35**(6), 756–779 (2009)
23. OMG: Business process model and notation (BPMN) (2011). https://www.omg.org/spec/BPMN/2.0/
24. Portugal, I., Alencar, P., Cowan, D.: A preliminary survey on domain-specific languages for machine learning in big data. In: 2016 IEEE International Conference on Software Science, Technology and Engineering (SWSTE), pp. 108–110. IEEE (2016)
25. Sculley, D., et al.: Hidden technical debt in machine learning systems. In: Advances in Neural Information Processing Systems, pp. 2503–2511 (2015)
26. Tolvanen, J.P., Rossi, M.: MetaEdit+ defining and using domain-specific modeling languages and code generators. In: Companion of the 18th Annual ACM SIGPLAN Conference on Object-Oriented Programming, Systems, Languages, and Applications, pp. 92–93 (2003)
27. Wolstencroft, K., et al.: The taverna workflow suite: designing and executing workflows of web services on the desktop, web or in the cloud. Nucleic Acids Res. **41**(W1), W557–W561 (2013)
28. Zhang, A.X., Muller, M., Wang, D.: How do data science workers collaborate? Roles, workflows, and tools. arXiv preprint arXiv:2001.06684 (2020)

Challenges and Decisions in WOBCompute Design, a P2P Computing System Architecture

Levente Filep$^{(\boxtimes)}$ (iD)

Faculty of Mathematics and Computer Science, Babeş-Bolyai University,
Cluj-Napoca, Romania
f.levi@cs.ubbcluj.ro

Abstract. In the field of large-scale computing, Cloud Computing Services gained popularity due to their low cost and availability. Alternatives exist in the form of distributed computing systems, most of which combine existing, cheap, commodity hardware into clusters of computing and storage resources. Most of these implementations are Client-Server model-based. Decentralized solutions employ a form of Peer-to-Peer (P2P) design, however, without major benefits besides the decentralized task coordination, and due to increased design complexity compared to the Client-Server models, these implementations haven't gained widespread popularity. In this paper, the architecture of WOBCompute is presented, which is P2P based, and features decentralized task coordination, the possibility of workload transfer via checkpoints, and task tracking and location queries with the possibility of messaging between parallel branches of a distributed application. Architecture design considerations and choices are also presented. The overlay of the P2P system is a super-peer driven clusters organized into an extended star topology. Using backup super-peers, and distributing the cluster members between them, the size and stability of the clusters are improved; query and lookup messages are limited to only the super-peers and the topology employed reduces the longest message path. The complexity of the system mandates the use of a middleware, which hides these and provides a simplified interface for a distributed application to take advantage of the computing resources, being a combination of in-house computing devices, personal or volunteer donated resources, as well as Cloud-based VMs.

Keywords: Peer-to-peer networks · Super-peer topology · Distributed computing · Middleware · P2P computing architecture

1 Introduction

Harnessing cheap computing resources is the focus of many distributed computing systems that gained popularity in the past couple of decades. With the

© Springer Nature Switzerland AG 2021
R. Ali et al. (Eds.): ENASE 2020, CCIS 1375, pp. 130–153, 2021.
https://doi.org/10.1007/978-3-030-70006-5_6

advent of Cloud Computing Services and its ever-cheaper prices and availability, this has gained popularity in the large-scale computing landscape. Nonetheless, this is out of reach of some individuals or small research groups. For them, an alternative solution is combining existing, cheap commodity hardware resources into computational clusters. These can be in the form of grid computing, volunteer computing (VC), etc. [14].

VC frameworks utilize a specialized middleware for harnessing idle computing resources within a preset allowed limit from volunteer machines. Such a middleware can also be deployed with the combination of in-house computer networks and even Cloud VMs. Depending on the model of asymmetric communication between the participating hardware, such frameworks can implement either a centralized architecture such as the Client-Server, or a decentralized one such as the Peer-to-Peer (P2P) model.

The overwhelming majority of popular solutions are fully centralized in nature. Here, centralized server(s) are responsible for task coordination, namely the creation, deployment, and result collection. Participating nodes (clients) download and execute the tasks, and the results are sent back to the centralized servers. Decentralized solutions, on the other hand, utilize some form of P2P architecture. Here, each node participates in both task execution, as well as task coordination. Meanwhile, hybrid approaches utilize P2P architecture with some centralized elements (e.g. centralized storage servers for workload, etc.).

Comparing these types of architectures, the centralized ones, due to their reduced complexity, are the easiest to implement and deploy. The most popular and widespread framework is BOINC [2]. The downside of such implementation is the server bottleneck, namely, with the growing number of participating parties, more and more servers are needed to handle the task coordination in a timely manner, which in turn increases the cost of framework ownership. This is not necessarily a problem, since the cheap computing resources offset the cost of these servers. Even if P2P based solutions can eliminate this bottleneck, due to their increased design complexity and without additional benefits [14], these never gained popularity and widespread.

Task coordination, workload tracking, remote checkpointing with recovery, and messaging are implementable on the Client-Server model using high-performance centralized servers. However, in the P2P model, these can be offloaded and implemented in a distributed manner, which can be a cost-effective solution.

This paper presents the architecture of WOBCompute, a P2P based computing system architecture. The network topology employs hierarchical and structured elements in the form of super-peers and clustering, with the organization of these clusters into an extended star topology. An additional benefit of the system is the possibility of communication between the parallel tasks, which is achieved using a decentralized task tracking (location tracking and query) mechanism to first find the location of a task and then to exchange messages. The system also features task object relocation in the form of checkpoint migration, and remote backups and recovery. For deployment in a combination of existing computer networks and even volunteer machines, it harnesses idle resources. Such a system comes with enormous complexity in maintaining network structure and providing the above functionalities, therefore it features a middleware that hides this complexity from the computing applications and provides a simple interface for application developers.

This paper extends the previously published paper [10] with more in-depth explanation and additional content. The capacity based selection is discussed and evaluated, a new selection method based on predicted node availability is also present and discussed. The simulation results of these methods and their impact on network overlay is presented, compared, and discussed. Computing application design for this framework is discussed. The main logic of such an application is present and discussed. While this paper presents the architecture design, the original concept model the framework is based on was presented in [9].

2   Related Work

Nowadays, the usage of P2P architecture is common in data networks, such as streaming or data sharing, however, in computing networks, as opposed to the Client-Server architecture, arguably due to the implementation and design complexities, it has not gained widespread interest.

2.1   P2P Computing Systems

Despite less attention in the literature, P2P architecture has influenced several computing system designs. CompuP2P [12] is a lightweight architecture for internet computing; ad hoc Grid [22] is a self-organizing computing grid based on OurGrid [3] middleware; HP2PC [11] is a system proposal with a hierarchically distributed P2P architecture; P2P-HTC [16] is high throughput computing system utilizing Cassandra (a distributed DHT based database) for a distributed queue based scheduling with FCFS (First Come First Served) scheduling policy; DisCoP [4] is also a P2P based system that utilizes idle resource harnessing and a clustered topology for efficient resource search within. In another paper [6] a computing system for overlay network was proposed that uses centralized trackers on top of the overlay system which can be responsible for task scheduling and workload location tracking.

2.2   P2P Topologies

The P2P architecture organizes the participating nodes (peers) into a virtual topology on top of the physical one. The structure of this topology is a direct result of the rules used to connect the nodes. We can classify these into two main categories: structured and unstructured. An unstructured topology is easy to build and maintain, however, resource query is inefficient as query messages must reach all nodes, therefore, without some form of centralized data-service, some structure is desired to improve on resource availability and search speed [19].

DHT based topologies are also a form of structure. Chord [21] organizes the nodes into a ring topology and uses finger tables for improved search efficiency. Tapestry [26] introduced the concept of backup neighbor nodes for better availability in case of node failures.

Other topologies have been proposed with complex structures, such as the AFT [17], which is an adaptive and self-organizing topology, and uses a circle having multiple rings on it to organize the nodes into; a topology that provides fast resource location.

2.3   Clustering and Super-Peers

Clustering consists of organizing several peers into clusters. Each of these having a cluster leader, called a super-peer, that indexes the resources of all member peers, thus the search can be limited only to this single node. This concept exploits the heterogeneity of a P2P system by introducing a two-level hierarchy of peers: super-peers and regular peers (or members). The super-peer concept was proposed for several topologies over the years, such as for the Gnutella protocol [25], or even recently for file sharing system search [23].

However, the concept of super-peer introduces one-point of failure into the topology, namely, if this node fails, the entire cluster fails, requiring the members to be reorganized into the overlay. As a solution, the notion of super-peer with redundancy was proposed and evaluated [24], where the authors concluded that this technique has no significant impact on the overall bandwidth usage. Since the connection capacity of nodes is limited, cluster splitting was also proposed for handling an increased number of connecting nodes, and cluster merging in case of decreasing node numbers; however, no exact solution was presented on how to perform these operations.

Several studies have focused on the reliability of super-peer based topologies. In [15], the authors find that a super-peer ratio of less than 5% sharply decreases reliability. Such topologies are also vulnerable to churn [8]. Churn is a phenomenon when a large number of continuously connecting and disconnecting nodes can divide the network into isolated parts. For data survivability in such cases, data replication was proposed [18].

Super-peer election is the process of electing a node into the role of a super-peer. P2P systems are often described as where peers are equal, but this is not the case as each node differs in computational performance, storage availability, and bandwidth [5,13], which affect the selection of super-peers and topology bootstrapping. Several election methods exist, but usually, they are system-specific or are not carried out in a distributed manner [20]. For instance, in the gossip-based SG-2 protocol [13] a proximity-based election is proposed utilizing a node associated latency distance. However, the most straight-forward election type is a connection capacity-based with cutoff threshold values that are system-related, such as bandwidth, available storage space, etc. With the constant change in participating peers, the maintained super-peer based topology is highly dynamic in nature [13].

3   System Architecture

WOBCompute is a P2P based computing system. The base model was presented in a previous paper [9], but for context, its main characteristics will be summarized here:

- Task (or workload) coordination (creation, deployment, result collection) is offloaded from centralized servers to the peers. Each task starts as a whole and it is split based on requests by idle nodes. The splitting, thus the creation of workload is handled by the application itself. A workload request contains the hardware characteristics of the requester so that the workload can be split accordingly. This, in turn, can offer a better, decentralized load balancing. Completed workload result collection occurs at the parent workload, and is also handled by the application itself.
- The computation of a workload can be suspended (checkpoint creation), stored, or transferred to another node where computation can be resumed. Checkpointing is strictly an application-specific job, which then is stored by the system. The use of periodic checkpoints allows the possibility of partial result recovery. The recovered workload can be resumed on any node having the required hardware capabilities.
- Workload tracking and query features are essential for the above points, namely to query the status of a workload (for computation status, location, communication purposes) and recover it from backup if it's lost.
- Possibility of initiating communication between parallel branches of the application, using location query to first determine the task location address.

Since WOB creation is controlled by the application, at any stage of the computation, if a sufficiently large part of this can be parallelized, then a new WOB can be created and launched into the network for parallel execution on a different node (given there are free nodes with the required hardware capabilities to accept it).

Node bandwidth can be arbitrary, especially when dealing with volunteer participants, therefore checkpointing should only contain the minimal set of data, from which computation can be resumed at another node with the required hardware capabilities. Besides bandwidth, latency is also arbitrary in a P2P system. As the system allows the communication between tasks, any application taking advantage of this must be latency tolerant.

To improve search efficiency, and backup availability, a super-peer based clustering was proposed. Super-peers are also referred to as supervisors in the system model, as they perform additional functions compared to regular peers.

For achieving the above objectives, in the previous paper [9] the notion of workload unit was extended to workload objects, which contains additional data fields, such as: unique identifier (ID), application identifier, parent and children identifier (for result merging), checkpoint data (allows the transfer and continuation of computation), boundary information (identify data-set boundaries; if required), estimated total and remaining computational effort, state of computation, result data (partial or complete computation result) and metadata (application-specific use). The chosen data format to represent a WOB structure is JSON. Besides being human-readable, it has wide-spread support in many programming languages. Since the WOB only contains workload related data, malicious code injection is not possible here.

It must be mentioned, that when a node exits the network, the computed WOB is suspended and stored at its supervisor. These stored WOBs are prioritized in workload requests, meaning, if a super-peer has a stored WOB, it will not forward the request further but will offer the stored WOB instead to the requester node [9]. This reduces the fragmentation of the main workload while also easing the load on the indexing and backup storage.

3.1 Topology Considerations

Choosing an appropriate topology is an important design factor in a P2P system as it must suit the functionalities provided by the system. Starting from the base model, we need a search protocol for WOB queries (status and location) and a storage system for backups.

As it was mentioned, WOBs can migrate from node to node, child WOB objects are constantly created (by workload request; and if a workload can be further split) and removed when the result is processed at their parent WOBs. Furthermore, new workloads can be injected into the network, which undergoes the same process. As WOB creation is driven by requests, a request must reach each node. This presents a problem: as the overall project computation nears its end, more and more nodes will become idle, hence a proportional number of workload request messages will be sent out, which in turn can overwhelm the network. A solution would be the possibility to limit the spread of this type of message but without a centralized tracker. Several efficient topologies ware proposed and demonstrated to be both resilient and efficient in search, for instance, the ADP, however, none of these offer the possibility for request message cutoff.

3.2 Clustering

Given the previously mentioned considerations, foremost, clustering offers the better solution. With the indexing of WOBs present in a cluster, a query message is limited only to the super-peer. Furthermore, if idle nodes are present in the cluster (the cluster is "starved" of workload), the super-peer can cut off any workload request messages. In other words, the bigger the cluster, the more efficient are the WOB requests and searches.

Cluster Stability. As also proposed in the literature, backup super-peers can significantly improve cluster stability, and also comes with an additional benefit, as we can balance the member nodes between the primary supervisor and its backups [9], the size of the cluster can be dramatically increased. Connections to other clusters, as illustrated in Fig. 1, is also handled by a super-peer. To improve cluster stability, this paper further refines the base-model.

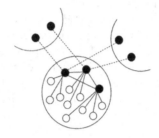

Fig. 1. Cluster topology with interconnection [10].

An isolated node can be defined as the node whose super-peer fails but the node is not relocated to another backup super-peer, therefore it becomes isolated from the topology and must reconnect to the network to join a different cluster. While the reconnecting process is ongoing, the node cannot receive workload requests. Nonetheless, the WOB location query still works as the WOB in question is still located on the respective node, thus the location address is valid.

Temporary increasing super-peer capacity until a new backup super-peer is elected may not be a viable solution as nodes with limited connection bandwidth or hardware capability can be overwhelmed. This, in turn, can cause them to become unresponsive, leading to further failures in the topology. As a solution, a reserved connection capacity is proposed, which can temporarily accommodate member nodes (either newly connecting ones or from an exited supervisor) until a new backup supervisor is elected.

Connection capacity of a node only referrers to the permanent connections: between supervisors and supervisor-members. Cluster supervisors are interconnected using a mesh topology. These connections are maintained during the participation of any node in the system as it's more efficient for constant message delivery, and it's also used as a heartbeat for detecting peer failures. The system allows for messaging between tasks, but these are handled as temporary connections only. Therefore, the total connection capacity of a super-peer can be defined as:

$$C_T = C_S + C_R + C_N \tag{1}$$

where C_T denotes the total capacity (minus the inter-cluster connection if present), C_S the number of connections to all other supervisors within the cluster, C_R is the reserved capacity, and C_N the leftover capacity available for regular member connections [10]. As cluster members are balanced between the supervisors, we can notice that the overall cluster capacity increases with each new supervisor, however, there is also an upper limit of cluster size, influenced by the average super-peer capacity.

Using a uniform capacity of 100 (fairly regular setting on BitTorrent clients) for each node and a C_R value of 0.1 (10%) of C_T, as illustrated in Fig. 2, a C_S value of 0.45 (45%) of super-peer connections allocated capacity produces the optimal cluster size, namely, a size of 2070. Above this percentage, due to the mash interconnection between the super-peers, the available capacity remaining for member connection decreases, thus the maximum cluster size also decreases.

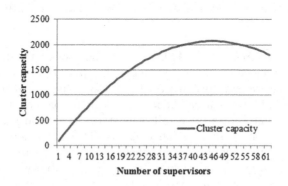

Fig. 2. Super-peer count influence on cluster size [10].

Super-Peer Promotion. A new backup super-peer election is triggered when all existing supervisors exhaust their available C_N capacity, but only if the C_S threshold is not yet reached; otherwise, the cluster is marked as "full" and further cluster entries are rejected. The promotion process consists of the selection process from available candidates and integrating the selected node into the super-peer hierarchy. The process is handles by the primary supervisor and consists of the following steps:

1. Score each candidate; select the one with the best core
2. Notify candidate of promotion; candidate changes its status to supervisor
3. All other supervisors are notified of the promotion; each initiates a permanent connection with the new supervisor

If any steps fail, the candidate is marked to be excluded from further selections in its current session, and the process is repeated.

Super-Peer Election. The super-peer election is the automated process where a new super-peer is selected for promotion within a cluster.

Capacity Based Selection (CapS). In the super-peer election, the capacity-based selection (*CapS*), as the name suggests, consists of selecting the highest capacity node to maximize cluster size. With higher capacity, the reserved capacity also increases which allows more nodes to be temporarily connected, for instance when a supervisor exits and its connected members are redistributed between the remaining super-peers. The reserved capacity value can be tuned to accommodate for a certain number of nodes, for example, to accommodate for the connected members of the largest capacity super-peer to lower the chance for isolated nodes, but at the cost of additional complexity to cluster maintenance.

A downside of this type of selection is the possibility of selecting the seemingly best node, only for that node to exit the network shortly afterward. In other words, this selection method does not give any guaranty regarding the node's future availability.

Predicted Availability Selection (PAS). As mentioned before, the disadvantage of CapS selection is the occurrence of selecting high capacity peers with low on-line time or in other words, low availability. The selection process can be improved if the future availability of a candidate node can be predicted. The basis of this idea is to assume that a node will behave, or better said will be available in similar pattern to its past availability history. To avoid generating too much data, we can use a simple hourly patter, where each value denotes the probability of a node being online. We can define this as the availability pattern function $AvPt(N_i, d, h) \subseteq [0..1]$ where h represents the hours of a day with values between $[0..23]$ and d represents the day of a week with values between $[0..6]$. Since $AvPt$ represents the average observed probability of a node availability over the same time periods, the $AvPt(N_i, d, h) = 1$ means the node was online the whole time in the given time-period. However, a $AvPt(N_i, d, h) = 0.5$ translates to either a node was online at one week and offline in the next, or is regularly online half the time in the given time-interval.

Using the $AvPt$ function in the election process, we can assign a score to each candidate node in the following manner:

$$Score(N_i) = \sum_{hr}^{\substack{hr \leq 23 \\ AvPt(N_i, d, hr) \neq 0}} ((TClAv - ClAvPt(hr)) * AvPt(N_i, d, hr)) \quad (2)$$

where N_i represents the i-th candidate node, and the cluster availability pattern is defined as:

$$ClAvPt(hr) = \sum_i AvPt(S_i, d, h) \quad (3)$$

where S_i represents the i-th super-peer and is always the current day of week, and total cluster availability is:

$$TClAv = \sum_{hr}^{h \leq 23} ClAvPt(h) \quad (4)$$

In other words, the *Score* function (Formula 2) rewards those candidate nodes that a have high probability of availability where the cluster has a lower one. For any given hour, this score is calculated by multiplying its $AvPt$ value with the cluster availability value (Formula 3) with respect to the total cluster availability value (Formula 4). This translates to higher scores for the candidate nodes that have a better contribution to cluster availability.

In the selection process, we only care about the probability that a candidate node will be available from the current time forward, therefore, the represents the hours from now on until a maximum of 24 h or until the $AvPt$ returns 0 (meaning the node was never observed to be available in that specific time-interval). When $AvPt(...) = 0$ is found, the score calculation is terminated, and the final score is the current summed value. Even if the node returns to the network after that it may not join the same cluster, and furthermore if exits, another super-peer can be elected in its place, therefore, the score is evaluated only until a 0 value in the $AvPt$ function.

It must be noted that nodes can be in different time zones, therefore, if not considering only the future availability, the score calculation algorithm would need to compensate for the shifts in the hour parameter. To avoid this, the cluster members regularly send the pattern of availability for the next 24 h.

The election method can also fail, for instance, if the cluster is comprised of nodes without a history of availability pattern or all candidate nodes is predicted to go offline. In the case of each candidate node having a score of 0, we can fall back to the *CapS* method. If all nodes go offline, then the cluster will become defunct and dismembered.

The selection method can be extended with additional parameters, for instance, if we have a ranking system, then the rank of the node can also be taken into account.

One downside of this idea relates to the availability of pattern data. Given the gateway assignment algorithm of joining nodes to clusters, a node is unlikely to join the same cluster as previously a member of. This means that a single cluster cannot store the availability pattern for any given node. Without overloading the gateway with database for the availability patterns, or employing a distributed database, we can only rely on the middleware to transmit this information. As this information is stored on the node itself, it can be subject to manipulation.

Supervisor Demotion. As previously discussed, a higher number of supervisors is beneficial for the cluster. On the other hand, maintaining the WOB indexes and backups up to date requires storage space and an update message for each change to be passed to each supervisor. Therefore, if the size of a cluster shrinks, it is also beneficial to reduce the supervisor count. The threshold value for triggering demotion highly depends on the number of connection and disconnecting nodes, so no exact values can be given. Nonetheless, an average value below $0.5C_N$ with a minimum of 3 supervisors seems to work sufficiently well in simulations. A good strategy is to demote the supervisor with the least amount of contribution to the cluster, namely, the one with the lowest score.

3.3   Overall Topology

With the most important aspects of clustering discussed, the question remains on how to interconnect these. As query speed is impacted by the number of hops a message takes, the goal is to minimize this, subsequently, minimize the maximum path between any two clusters.

A mash topology would be the best solution, as it interconnects each cluster; however, the connection capacity of nodes makes this topology impractical when dealing with a large number of clusters. The next best one is the extended star topology [1], which is frequently employed in LAN design; however, here each node is a single point of failure, meaning, if one fails, all subsequently connected nodes are isolated. In our case, however, this is less of an issue, since the topology nodes are whole clusters, which are more resilient due to the backup supervisors. By using a maximum of 10 child clusters, this topology can quickly organize a large number of clusters with a minimum path length.

DHT Consideration. Regarding search, DHT based solutions have proven to be extremely efficient. In the current model, the number of new entries and updates into the DHT can far exceed the number of queries, however, their exact number is highly dependent on the type of the distributed application and its workload. The above statement is only an assumption; the performance of a DHT system under such conditions was not tested experimentally. If the newly created WOBs are located within the same cluster, then the parent-child related location queries only take a single hoop, otherwise, the worst-case scenario is the longest path in the topology. The question is how this tradeoff compares to a DHT implementation.

Choosing this form of topology does not exclude further improvements. For example, for search improvement on a very large overlay, a DHT system can still be implemented on top of the clusters, as these have high reliability. Roughly put, a cluster would participate as a DHT node, represented by its super-peers, meaning that a super-peer will actively handle search requests while other super-peers serve as its backup.

Network Gateways. Although the model eliminates the need for centralized servers, the network requires an entry point for new nodes to connect through, which will be referred to as the network gateway. The gateway also plays an essential role in bootstrapping the network, maintaining the topology, and has the following functions:

- assigning connecting nodes to clusters
- isolated nodes and clusters can use the gateway to reconnect to the topology
- acts as failsafe storage for WOBs and their backups (if all nodes exit)
- new WOBs are injected, while results are collected through it
- auxiliary functions, such as data collection for statistics, project progress, etc.

As no persistent connection is required to be maintained to the gateway, this can be implemented as a web application. Update messages can be accomplished using a simple HTTP protocol. Another benefit of web implementation is the possibility of scaling, if required, using well-established techniques.

The topology is maintained by prioritizing the assignment of newly connecting nodes to the lower level but not yet saturated clusters. This ensures that the existing clusters are filled before creating any new ones, thus maintaining their number at a minimum. Algorithm 1 presents the node connection mechanism.

In normal operation, the gateway answer contains a list of supervisors for the target cluster for the node to attempt a connection with. This method is more reliable than just sending one address, as one may be temporarily unavailable, requiring the restart of the connection process.

Algorithm 1. Node connection mechanism.

```
1  success, answer ← QueryGateway()              // Query the gateway
2  // If failed, attempt previous cluster
3  if !success then
4  |   if len(PrevSups) > 0 then
5  |   |   success ← AttemptToConnect(PrevSups)
6  |   |   if !success then
7  |   |   |   Wait()
8  |   |   |   Reconnect()
9  |   else
10 |   |   if answer.wait then
11 |   |   |   Wait()
12 |   |   |   Reconnect()
13 // Check for the bootstrap command
14 if answer.bootstrap then
15 |   CreateCluster with answer.ClusterID
16 |   Set Node to Supervisor status
17 |   UpdateGateway()
18 else
19 |   // Attempt connection to any supervisor from SupList
20 |   success ← AttemptConnect(answer.SupList)
21 |   if !success then
22 |   |   Reconnect()
```

For the gateway to answer, it stores a list of active clusters, their level (how far is from the root cluster), and whether it's overloaded or not. Moreover, for each cluster, a list of active supervisors is stored. Each cluster is responsible for updating the gateway about its status and free supervisors, thus maintaining an up-to-date information.

Bootstrapping is the process of creating the initial overlay. If no prior clusters exist, then the gateway will answer a bootstrapping message with an initial ClusterID and will await the cluster update message from the node or timeout.

Meanwhile, all other nodes are given a wait status, to allow for the initial node to enter supervisor mode and initialize the cluster data. If the timeout occurs, then the bootstrapping process is repeated.

Regarding volunteers who donate their resources to a specific project, using the same overlay for multiple projects is unfair, as it forces them to participate in maintaining the topology of other projects. Also, smaller overlays improve the search and workload request efficiency as fewer clusters must be queried. Therefore, each project has its own independent overlay, with their own gateways. However, this does not exclude a node from participating in multiple projects at the same time.

Cluster Splitting. Cluster capacity limit is considered reached when C_S (no more supervisor election is possible) and C_N is exhausted. In such cases, if possible, we split the current cluster, create a child cluster, and migrate a certain number of supervisors and members over. A less intensive operation is to move just one supervisor and its connected members. A cluster splitting is followed by updating the WOB indexes and backups, setting up the primary and backup interconnections, selecting backup supervisors, plus updating the gateway. Cluster splitting is not possible when the maximum number of child clusters is reached. In this case, new join requests are rejected.

Cluster Merging. If the total members count within a cluster falls below a minimum threshold, we can consider the cluster defunct and begin a merging operation with its parent. The threshold value depends on the frequency of connecting and disconnecting nodes, however, a value of 5 worked sufficiently well in simulations. Depending on whether the cluster in question is a leaf in the overlay or not, there are two ways to carry out the merging operation.

Leaf Clusters. The merging operation is always carried out with the parent cluster. The stored WOB backups and members are transferred to the parent, followed by the dismemberment of the cluster and gateway update.

Branch Clusters. Rather than merging with the parent, one of the child clusters is absorbed. In other words, one of the child clusters is forced to merge with the cluster in question, while child cluster connections (if any) are carried over. Normally this should be a rear case, as the connection algorithm favors the branch clusters, meaning that the leaf clusters should empty first.

3.4   Communication and Messages

Data communication between nodes is through TCP protocol, and messages are encoded into a JSON structure. To reduce bandwidth utilization, and if both parties support it (determined at handshake), communication is compressed using ZLIB [27]. Generic message fields are presented in Table 1. Depending on the type of message, some fields can be omitted.

A separate *NodeID* (*SenderID*, *DestID*) is used for relaying messages to nodes behind a NAT; this id also identifies nodes between IP address changes. *NodeID* is generated by hashing the OS provided machine-id. Message types are prefixed according to their type, which helps with faster routing within the middleware without needing to parse the payload. Given their role, the messages can be grouped as:

- Cluster specific messages (prefixed "CL_") are used for cluster operations, such as supervisor entry request, election, demotion, node migration, balancing, splitting and merging, and also WOB index and backup updates.
- WOB related messages (prefixed "WOB_"), which contains the workload request, offer, accept, transfer, query, query answer, backup, location update, and any affiliated acknowledge (ACK) messages.
- Peer messages (prefixed "NODE_"), which include messages such as handshake, capacity advertisement, status update, and so on.
- Application-specific message (prefixed "APP_"), which are passed directly to the distributed application running on the node, and can be used for arbitrary purposes.

Although messages can be sent to nodes behind NAT via a connected supervisor, these nodes are not allowed to become supervisors unless a port forwarding is set up from the external IP address. Otherwise, as no direct external connection can be made, they cannot contribute to maintaining the network topology.

Table 1. Message wrapper structure [10].

Field	Description
ApplicationID	Distributed app unique ID
Message UUID	Unique message identifier
MessageType	Type of message
SenderID	Sender node unique identifier
SenderAddress	Sender node IP:Port
DestID	Destination node unique identifier
DestAddress	Destination node IP:Port
Relayed	Set to 1 if message was relayed by a super-peer, otherwise 0 or not present
Payload	Contents of message

3.5   Middleware

The presented system employs specialized middleware to harness idle resources. This process is achieved by strictly controlling the distributed application resource usage (app) by imposing limits on it. Therefore, the middleware is responsible for monitoring the available resources on a node, such as CPU, GPU, etc.

Probably the most important role of the middleware is to hide the system complexities from the app and provide a simple interface for its app-related functionalities, which is the task coordination and app messaging. The other network features and their operation, such as clustering and topology organization, WOB indexing, and backup storage is hidden from the app itself.

Nonetheless, the middleware itself generates some additional communication and computing overhead.

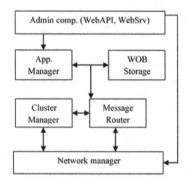

Fig. 3. Middleware internal structure [10].

For easy maintainability and separation of the code, as illustrated in Fig. 3, the middleware is broken up into components, each with its own distinct function, managing own data and threads. A "component linker" provides a reference to each component, thus allowing function calls between them. Next, the function of the components is summarized.

Network Manager. Responsible for maintaining all connections (both permanent and temporary), and handles transmitting and receiving of messages. Incoming messages are forwarded to the *MessageRouter*; however, outbound messages are sent by other components by directly calling the send functions from this component using the component link. This reduces the need to process the messages before sending them.

The component also abstracts the connections by encapsulating all connection related data into a Node structure. At the other components, it's sufficient to only use *NodeID* to refer to connected nodes as the rest of the address (IP, Port, and source address) in messages are filled automatically if left empty. Furthermore, a broken connection is also handled here and notification is sent to *ClusterManager*.

Message Router. This component is responsible for routing the incoming messages received from the *NetworkManager* to the corresponding component. A small amount of logic is incorporated here for two reasons: the first one is to decide which message handler function to call from a component, which avoids a second message type check at the destination component; the second is that some messages overlap multiple components. Such an example would be the handling of the workload request message, where, first the WOB Storage is checked for any stored WOBs and if one found, then an appropriate response message will be sent; if none found, the message is forwarded to the *AppManager* and the *ClusterManager*.

Relaying messages is another function of this component. This is decided by checking the *DestID* against the current *NodeID*. If they don't match, then *NetworkManager* is queried for the given *DestID*, and if the node is found, the message is relayed. This is a solution to message nodes behind NAT, however, a large number of messages can overwhelm the supervisor.

Cluster Manager. If the node is a supervisor, then this component handles all supervisor functions, such as maintaining WOB indexing, responding to search queries, and storing WOBs (utilizing the *WOBStorage* component), synchronizing between supervisors using differential update messages (only changes are advertised), balancing, and so on. However, if the node is just a regular member, then this component is only responsible for maintaining the supervisor connection and advertising capacity and status.

Workload requests forwarding is also handled here. If the cluster is not "starved", then the request is forwarded to all supervisors, which in turn forwards it to their connected nodes. The message is also forwarded to each cluster that is not "starved".

Cluster status updates, namely, "starved" or "workload available", are broadcast to adjected clusters, thus, a limitation in the number of workload requests and their propagation can be achieved.

WOB Storage. Handles the effective storage of WOB objects, their backups, and transfers with associated ACK messages. If the node gets disconnected from the network, the WOB backup, and in case of a shutdown, the suspended WOB, is stored here. On reconnect, a consistency check is performed for any stored WOBs, as these might have been recovered, thus they are outdated and can be removed. For any received WOBs, a location update message is sent out.

Application Manager. The primary responsibility of this component is the application scheduling (starting, suspending, or stopping) but also monitoring and imposing resource usage limits based on settings received from the *Admin-Component*. A secondary role is the regular checkpoint request to the app, creating the backup WOB and dispatching this to the supervisor. An optional role, based on the computing application setting, is the workload management, namely, acquiring the workload, notifying the app on a lost child or parent WOB, and acquiring completed child WOBs and forwarding to the app for processing their results. For any received WOB, a location update message is sent, updating its location in the cluster's index.

Application properties are defined in the project configuration file. This contains the download link, install, run, and uninstall commands, which are executed by this component.

Admin Component. With the combination of the Project Manager and Web-server parts, this component is responsible for administration related tasks, such as adding projects, downloading and storing applications and related configuration, and providing the middleware admin interface. Remote access is also an option via a WebAPI secured by a configured security key or predefined allowed IPs to use in group management; in this case, the local administration page can be disabled.

Application Side Middleware and API. For ease of application development, a small app-side middleware is provided, which translated messages into callback functions and provides an API on which a developer can build on. The app-side middleware can be skipped, thus messages can be directly handled (Fig. 4).

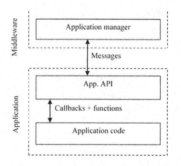

Fig. 4. Middleware internal structure [10].

The app-middleware intercepts the following type of messages to which offers callback functions for the app to register to:

- Workload related: receive offers and select one, receive WOB object, receive a workload request from another node
- App related: allow computing, suspend computation, quit request
- Checkpoint request
- Handle child WOB completion (the child WOB is transferred to the parent, which then can extract and process its results)

- Handle missing WOB notification (child or parent)
- Application specific message
- Handle location query answer messages
- Handle generic messages (for futureproof purposes, called for any other messages forwarded to the app but not handled in the above points)

The more important messages and API callbacks ware enumerated in the previous paper [10], and due to their large number, they will not be enumerated again in this paper. The next section, Application design, will shed more light on the related operating principles.

3.6 Application Design

As in many computing systems, an application must collaborate with the middleware. To support a multitude of programming languages, the choice was to handle the app-middleware communication through a TCP channel on "localhost". Due to the low frequency of messages, the benefit outweighs the associated overhead. The startup of the application consists of connecting to this channel and completing the handshake with the middleware.

The application design for this system reflects the operational principles of the base model. The main loop of a sample application, as presented in the skeleton Algorithm 2, starts with the acquiring of a workload, which then is computed until finished or the middleware asks to suspend work or to quit.

Algorithm 2. Application main logic.

```
 1 Set up API callbacks or message listener
 2 Main:
 3    InitWorkload()
 4    Acquire any required hardware resource (eg. GPU)
 5    // Effective computation cycle
 6    while CanCompute and !Completed do
 7        Compute workload chunk
 8        if available workload size changed then
 9            Notify middleware
10    end
11    Release any required hardware resource
12    Create a checkpoint                    // Pack data into WOB
13    if Completed then
14        WOBFinished()          // Notify middleware, offload WOB
15    if !AppExitRequested then
16        Goto Main                          // Repeat the process
```

The *InitWorkload* abbreviated part is responsible for acquiring the WOB. The process starts by sending the workload request message to the middleware. This completes the message with the hardware capability of the node and dispatches it to the network. The node side of the middleware then awaits the offers (or times out), which then are packed into a response message for the app. From there, it's the app's decision which one to select, generate the ACK message for the selection, and dispatch it. If no failure occurs, the WOB is received next, and the app can extract the necessary data for the computation.

The *CanCompute* basically can be just a bool variable, which is set to false when the middleware sends the suspend or quit message. If the computation cannot be done in distinct pieces, then adequate checks of CanCompute must be performed within. The middleware gives a threshold time for the app to send the checkpoint and exit, which, if crossed, will forcefully terminate the app, causing any not checkpointed results to be lost.

The system offers the possibility of passing application-specific messages; however, these messages are passed through the middleware, thus they have a higher overhead when compared to direct message exchange. For frequent messaging, a better option would be the use of MPI [7] or a similar protocol, bypassing the middleware. Location query can be used to first acquire the address of the target node.

4   Simulation Results

In this chapter, the results of topology and election simulation are presented and discussed.

4.1   Topology Simulations

The evaluation of the topology model was conducted using a custom, purpose-built simulator. To simulate real-life VC participation, each node joining the network was assigned, at random, a different connection capacity. The enter and exit times of each node was generated using an estimated online pattern of computers per week. Since this pattern differs very little between the weekdays, one pattern was used for these and one pattern for the weekends, as illustrated in Fig. 5. The online patterns ware obtained from a local internet provider.

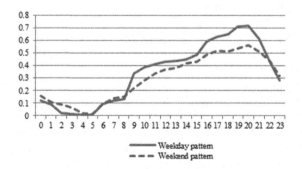

Fig. 5. Node online patterns [10].

Simulation parameters are presented in Table 2. In practice, node capacity is adjusted to reflect the physical bandwidth, therefore, connection bandwidth is assumed adequate to each node's connection capacity.

Table 2. Simulation parameters [10].

Parameter	Value
Number of nodes	50,000
Node capacity (C_T)	Random from: 50, 75, 100, 125, 150
Reserved cap. (C_R)	0.1
Min. supervisors	3
Max. supervisors	0.45 of $Min(C_t)$ Sup.
Cluster split threshold	0.9
Cluster interconnection	2

The presented results were obtained by running the simulation for two weeks (simulation time). As illustrated in Fig. 6, at the end of the simulation, the obtained results ware: peak number of online nodes: 35,995, isolated nodes: 264, total clusters formed 85 and defunct clusters: 79. Due to the joining methodology (Algorithm 1), the first clusters to become defunct ware the leaf clusters. The branch clusters had enough members to survive a large number of nightly exiting nodes.

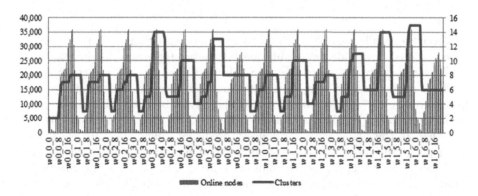

Fig. 6. Topology simulation result [10].

The advantages of the presented clustering technique becomes apparent as almost 36,000 nodes ware organized in as little as 8 clusters (average cluster size: 4,499, smallest: 4,489, largest: 4,501) with the longest messaging path of 3 hops. On the opposing side, in the worst-case scenario was 15 clusters (average size:

2, 399, smallest: 2, 360, largest: 2, 406) and 5 hops for the longest path. During the simulation, no isolated clusters ware observed. Nonetheless, this can occur due to catastrophic physical network failures.

4.2   Election Impact Simulation

Table 3 presents the simulation result extracted data averages from the same period of two weeks (simulation time). The result was obtained from a number of 10 simulations with the capacity-based (*CapS*), and an additional 10 simulations using predicted node availability selection type (*PAS*). The availability pattern for each node was pre-generated and reused at each simulation, which did not guaranty that the node will be available, but only an increased chance of this.

A threshold value for the node score (Formula 2) was experimented with, meaning, that a contribution to the cluster's availability at a specific hour was only accounted if the cluster availability at that moment was below this threshold, however, this approach didn't yield any significant benefits.

Table 3. Result comparison of CapS and PAS methods.

Election type	Cluster size AVG	Number of clusters AVG	Min	Max	AVG. number of elections	Isolated nodes
CapS	2, 391.74 ($\sigma : 60.75$)	7.47 ($\sigma : 0.31$)	3	16	258, 672.33	207.50 ($\sigma : 38.62$)
PAS	2, 135.29 ($\sigma : 124.28$)	8.54 ($\sigma : 0.55$)	3	23	211, 034.83	24.83 ($\sigma 28.08$)

From the results presented in Table 3, we can observe that super-peer election based on predicted node availability has both advantages and disadvantages.

As for the advantages of the *PAS* selection type, we observe the number of elections decrease by 22.57% and the number of isolated nodes is reduced by an average of 735.57% (with $\sigma : 28.08$). It is to be noted that 2 out of 10 simulations had a number of 0 isolated nodes. This can be explained by the fact that as the nodes with the longest predicted online time are elected as super-peers, the regular cluster members disconnect first, thus the cluster size is gradually reducing, easing the connection load on the supervisors. Therefore, as super-peers disconnect, the reduced number of connected nodes can easily be distributed among the remaining super-peers without exceeding their maximum capacity.

As for the disadvantages of the *PAS* selection type, as the simulation results indicate it, the average size of the clusters is reduced by 12.01%, and the maximum number of clusters that the overlay can organize the same number of nodes is increased by 23.53% (from an average of 15.17 to 19.83). This can easily be explained by the fact that as the "most reliable" nodes are selected instead of the ones with the highest capacity, therefore the clusters can hold fewer members, thus more clusters are needed to accommodate all connected nodes; hence, instead of 16 clusters, 23 was required.

The number of clusters at night hours usually decreased to only 3–6. This happens as the new nodes are connecting to the"prime" clusters, the leaf clusters are emptying and become defunct, and removed from the topology. As the number of clusters increased, subsequently the number of defunct clusters also increased, which translates to more backup WOBs to be transferred between clusters. In conclusion, the availability based super-peer election offers the advantage of reducing the number of elections, thus the message number and data-transfer when synchronizing the new supervisors, and the number of isolated nodes, translating to better cluster stability.

5   Conclusions

This work contains the design consideration, discussions, and evaluation of the more important characteristics of the presented P2P system architecture.

P2P topology is influenced by system operations, especially by the decentralized task coordination, the ability to suspend, migrate, resume and recover WOBs, remote backup and storage, WOB location tracking, and affiliated search mechanism. To improve on search efficiency, and location indexing, a super-peer driver clustering was chosen. With the use of backup super-peers and the balancing of the connected members between them, both the availability and size of the clusters are increased. To reduce the average length of message paths, which directly impact the search speed, the clusters are arranged into an extended star topology. The stability of the topology is maintained by prioritizing the lower level clusters regarding the distribution of connecting nodes.

All features of WOBCompute, including the task tracking and location query, and remote checkpointing with workload recovery, can also be implemented using the centralized Client-Server model. However, in the CS model, the increase in network size leads to the inevitable increase in server-side hardware requirements, thus an increasing associated cost in maintaining the system; this being the primary motivation of developing decentralized architectural systems.

The multitude of functions required for system operation leads to the inevitable complexity increase. This mandates the use of middleware to hide these complexities and provide a simple interface for the distributed application and its developers. Even so, the applications are more complex in nature compared to those using computing systems based on the Client-Server model. This complexity is balanced by the system's features mentioned above. With idle resource harnessing, the system offers the possibility to combine in-house computing devices with volunteer donated resourced, and even with Cloud VMs.

References

1. Akers, S.B., Harel, D., Krishnamurthy, B.: The star graph: an attractive alternative to the n-cube. In: Proceedings of International Conference on Parallel Processing, pp. 393–400 (1987)
2. Anderson, DP.: Boinc: A system for public-resource computing and storage. In: Proceedings of the 5th IEEE/ACM International Workshop, Pittsburgh, PA, USA, pp. 4–10 (2004). https://doi.org/10.1109/GRID.2004.14
3. Andrade, N., Cirne, W., Brasileiro, F., Roisenberg, P.: OurGrid: an approach to easily assemble grids with equitable resource sharing. In: Feitelson, D., Rudolph, L., Schwiegelshohn, U. (eds.) JSSPP 2003. LNCS, vol. 2862, pp. 61–86. Springer, Heidelberg (2003). https://doi.org/10.1007/10968987_4
4. Castellà, D., Solsona, F., Giné, F.: DisCoP: a P2P framework for managing and searching computing markets. J. Grid Comput. **13**(1), 115–137 (2014). https://doi.org/10.1007/s10723-014-9318-3
5. Chandra, J., Mitra, B., Ganguly, N.: Effect of constraints on superpeer topologies. In: 2013 Proceedings IEEE INFOCOM, pp. 60–64. IEEE, Turin (2013). https://doi.org/10.1109/INFCOM.2013.6566735
6. Chmaj, G., Walkowiak, K.: A P2P computing system for overlay networks. Future Gener. Comput. Syst. **29**(1), 242–249 (2013). https://doi.org/10.1016/j.future.2010.11.009
7. CORPORATE The MPI Forum: MPI: a message passing interface. In: Proceedings of the 1993 ACM/IEEE Conference on Supercomputing (Supercomputing 1993), pp. 878–883. Association for Computing Machinery, New York (1993). https://doi.org/10.1145/169627.16985
8. De, S., Barik, M.S., Banerjee, I.: Goal based threat modeling for peer-to-peer cloud. Proc. Comput. Sci. **89**, 64–72 (2016). https://doi.org/10.1016/j.procs.2016.06.010
9. Filep, L.: Model for improved load balancing in volunteer computing platforms. In: Themistocleous, M., Rupino da Cunha, P. (eds.) EMCIS 2018. LNBIP, vol. 341, pp. 131–143. Springer, Cham (2019). https://doi.org/10.1007/978-3-030-11395-7_13
10. Filep, L.: WOBCompute: architecture and design considerations of a P2P computing system. In: Proceedings of the 15th International Conference on Evaluation of Novel Approaches to Software Engineering - Volume 1: ENASE, pp. 39–49. SciTePress (2020). https://doi.org/10.5220/0009343100390049
11. Gomathi, S., Manimegalai, D.: Hierarchically distributed peer-to-peer architecture for computational grid. In: 2013 International Conference on Green High Performance Computing (ICGHPC), pp. 1–4. IEEE, Nagercoil (2013). https://doi.org/10.1109/ICGHPC.2013.6533906
12. Gupta, R., Sekhri, V., Somani, A.: CompuP2P: an architecture for internet computing using peer-to-peer networks. IEEE Trans. Parallel Distrib. Syst. **17**(11), 1306–1320 (2006). https://doi.org/10.1109/TPDS.2006.149
13. Jesi, G.P., Montresor, A., Babaoglu, O.: Proximity-aware superpeer overlay topologies. In: Keller, A., Martin-Flatin, J.-P. (eds.) SelfMan 2006. LNCS, vol. 3996, pp. 43–57. Springer, Heidelberg (2006). https://doi.org/10.1007/11767886_4
14. Lavoie, E., Hendren, L.: Personal volunteer computing. In: Proceedings of the 16th ACM International Conference on Computing Frontiers (CF 2019), New York, NY, USA, pp. 240–246 (2019). https://doi.org/10.1145/3310273.3322819
15. Mitra, B., Ghose, S., Ganguly, N., Peruani, F.: Stability analysis of peer-to-peer networks against churn. Pramana **71**(2), 263–273 (2008). https://doi.org/10.1007/s12043-008-0159-0

16. Pérez-Miguel, C., Miguel-Alonso, J., Mendiburu, A.: High throughput computing over peer-to-peer networks. Future Gener. Comput. Syst. **29**(1), 352–360 (2013). https://doi.org/10.1016/j.future.2011.08.011

17. Poenaru, A., Istrate, R., Pop, F.: AFT: adaptive and fault tolerant peer-to-peer overlay - a user-centric solution for data sharing. Future Gener. Comput. Syst. **80**, 583–595 (2016). https://doi.org/10.1016/j.future.2016.05.022

18. Qi, X., Qiang, M., Liu, L.: A balanced strategy to improve data invulnerability in structured P2P system. Peer-to-Peer Netw. Appl. **13**(1), 368–387 (2019). https://doi.org/10.1007/s12083-019-00773-9

19. Ratnasamy, S., Francis, P., Handley, M., Karp, R., Shenker, S.: A scalable content-addressable network. SIGCOMM Comput. Commun. Rev. **31**(4), 161–172 (2001). https://doi.org/10.1145/964723.383072

20. Sacha, J.: Exploiting heterogeneity in peer-to-peer systems using gradient topologies, Doctor of Philosophy (Computer Science) (2009)

21. Stoica, I., Morris, R., Karger, D., Kaashoek, M.F., Balakrishnan, H.: Chord - a scalable peer-to-peer lookup service for internet applications. SIGCOMM Comput. Commun. Rev. **31**(4), 149–160 (2001). https://doi.org/10.1145/964723.383071

22. Tiburcio, P.G.S., Spohn, M.A.: Ad hoc grid: an adaptive and self-organizing peer-to-peer computing grid. In: 2010 10th IEEE International Conference on Computer and Information Technology, pp. 225–232. IEEE, Bradford (2010). https://doi.org/10.1109/CIT.2010.504

23. Vimal, S., Srivatsa, S.K.: A file sharing system in peer-to-peer network by a nearness-sensible method. Int. J. Reason.-Based Intell. Syst. (IJRIS) **11**(4) (2019). https://doi.org/10.1504/IJRIS.2019.103510

24. Yang, B., Garcia-Molina, H.: Designing a super-peer network. In: Proceedings 19th International Conference on Data Engineering, pp. 49–60. IEEE, Bangalore (2003). https://doi.org/10.1109/icde.2003.1260781

25. Ye, F., Zuo, F., Zhang, S.: Routing algorithm based on Gnutella model. In: Cai, Z., Li, Z., Kang, Z., Liu, Y. (eds.) ISICA 2009. CCIS, vol. 51, pp. 9–15. Springer, Heidelberg (2009). https://doi.org/10.1007/978-3-642-04962-0_2

26. Zhao, H., Huang, L., Stribling, R., Rhea, S.C., Joseph, A.D., Kubiatowicz, J.D.: Tapestry - a resilient global-scale overlay for service deployment. IEEE J. Sel. Areas Commun. **22**, 41–53 (2004). https://doi.org/10.1109/JSAC.2003.818784

27. zlib Library. http://zlib.net/index.html. Accessed 25 Aug 2020

Reflections on the Design of Parallel Programming Frameworks

Virginia Niculescu[1]([✉]), Adrian Sterca[1], and Frédéric Loulergue[2]

[1] Faculty of Mathematics and Computer Science, Babeş-Bolyai University,
Cluj-Napoca, Romania
{virginia.niculescu,adrian.sterca}@ubbcluj.ro
[2] University of Orleans, LIFO, Orléans, France
frederic.loulergue@univ-orleans.fr

Abstract. Since parallel programming is much more complex and difficult than sequential programming, it is more challenging to achieve the same software quality in a parallel context. High-level parallel programming models, if implemented as software frameworks, could increase productivity and reliability.

Important requirements such as extensibility and adaptability for different platforms are required for such a framework, and this paper reflects on these requirements and their relation to the software engineering methodologies that could put them in practice. All these are exemplified on a Java framework – JPLF; this is a high-level parallel programming approach being based on the model brought by the *PowerLists* associated theories, and it respects the analysed requirements. The design of JPLF is analysed by explaining the design choices and highlighting the design patterns and design principles applied.

Keywords: Parallel programming · Frameworks · Software engineering · Separation of concerns · Design patterns · Recursive data structures

1 Introduction

Nowadays, in order to leverage the full computing power of current processors and also because the computing demand is increasing more and more, parallel programming is used in almost all software applications. Parallel programming requires considerably more skills than sequential programming since it introduces an additional layer of complexity and new types of errors. One way to master this complexity is to use frameworks and specialized APIs that make the programmers more productive in writing quality software. Besides performance, these should also provide reliability and flexibility that assures support for various system paradigms.

R. Ali et al. (Eds.): ENASE 2020, CCIS 1375, pp. 154–181, 2021.
https://doi.org/10.1007/978-3-030-70006-5_7

Since the frameworks for parallel programming are generally built around models of parallel computation, the analysis of requirements for an efficient framework has to start from the general requirements of a good model of parallel computation. We intend to provide in this paper an analysis of these requirements in relation to the software engineering that allow us to put them in practice. A general architecture is proposed for this kind of frameworks – MEDUGA (Model-Executors-DataManager-UserInteracter-GranularityBalancer-metricsAnalyser). This design is exemplified on a concrete framework –*JPLF: Java Parallel Lists Framework* [27,30]. This paper is an extension of the conference paper [28], in which the patterns and software development principles used for the JPLF implementation were analysed.

By being based on the *PowerList* theory introduced by J. Misra [25], JPLF is a high-level parallel programming framework that allows building parallel programs that follow the multi-way divide-and-conquer parallel programming skeleton with good execution performances both on shared and distributed memory architectures.

The provided shared memory execution is based on thread pools; the current implementation uses a Java `ForkJoinPool` executor [40], but others could be used too. For distributed memory systems, we considered MPI (Message Passing Interface) [39] in order to distribute processing units on computing nodes. So, JPLF is a multiparadigm framework that supports both multi-threading in a shared memory context and multi-processing in a distributed memory context, and it is open for other types of execution systems, too.

Allowing the support of multiple paradigms requires the framework to be flexible and extensible. In order to achieve these characteristics, the framework was implemented following object-oriented design principles. More specifically, we have employed separations of concerns in order to facilitate changing the low-level storage and the parallel execution environment, and in order to overcome the challenges brought by the multiparadigm support, we have used different design patterns, decoupling patterns having a defining role.

Outline: The remaining of the paper is organized as follows. First we analyse the general requirements for an efficient parallel programming framework in Sect. 2. Section 3 is devoted to a complex analysis of the JPLF framework design and implementation. Related work is discussed in Sect. 4. We give the conclusions and the specification of further work in Sect. 5.

2 Requirements for a Multiparadigm Parallel Programming Framework

In [36] Skillicorn and Talia analyse the usefulness requirements for a model of parallel computation. This kind of models should address both abstraction and effectiveness, which are summarized in a set of specific requirements: abstractness, software development methodology, architecture independence, cost measures, no preferred scale of granularity, efficiently implementable.

In computer programming, a model is seen as an abstract machine providing certain operations to the programming level above and requiring implementations for each of these operations on all of the architectures below. It is designed to separate software-development concerns from effective execution. We need models because we need both abstraction to assure easy development, but also stability to assure reliability. In general, models are valuable if they are theoretically consistent, fit the real world, and have predictive power.

A software framework is considered an integrated collection of components that collaborate to produce a reusable architecture for a family of related applications. A software framework provides software with generic functionality that can be specialized by additional user-written code, and thus providing application-specific software. It provides a structured way to build and deploy applications from a particular area or domain, and the use of frameworks has been shown to be effective in improving software productivity and quality. In parallel programming they are very important due to the complexity of the parallel execution that make parallel programming writing difficult and error prone. In contrast to libraries, frameworks are characterized by: inversion of control – the flow of control is not dictated by the user, but by the framework; default behaviour; extensibility – through concrete software extension points (usually entitled "hotspots"); non-modifiable code (usually entitled "frozen-spots") [20,34].

In relation to the models of computation, software frameworks come with a more empirical meaning, as they have the role to put the models into practice. They come as a further layer in the development process, providing the structure needed to implement and use a model.

So, in order to build a useful parallel programming framework, we have to rely on a model of parallel computation and provide the context of a concrete implementation for it. This means that we should carefully analyze the requirements of a model for parallel computation and the challenges imposed by the need to put them into practice on actual systems.

2.1   Requirements for a Model of Parallel Computation

We will analyse the requirements stated in [36], and based on them we emphasize what further requirements are implied for the corresponding frameworks.

– *Easy to Understand and Program.* A model should be easy to understand in order to secure a large mass of programmers that could embrace it. If parallel programming models are able to hide the complexities and offer an easy interface, they have a greater chance of being adopted. Parallel execution is a very complex process and a model must hide most of the execution details from programmers in order to allow productivity and reliability. In the same time it is well known that the most challenging issue, for such a computational model is to find a good trade-off between abstraction/readability and performance/efficiency [11].

The corresponding frameworks should provide well defined constructs that assure easy definition of the computation. Generic code facilitates this very much, but also creational patterns (e.g.. *Abstract Factory* or *Builder*) could provide mechanisms that allow the user to easily define correct and efficient programs inside the framework.

– *Architecture-Independence.* Parallel systems are not only very different and non-homogeneous, but are also highly modifiable, being in a continuous process of improvement. We may notice here the big change brought by the GPU devices that modified a lot the world of parallel implementators. So, the models should be independent on this low level of execution, but this rises big challenges for the parallel programming frameworks based on models.

There are now, many parallel systems that define many computation paradigms, each having particular characteristics. The most used architecture classes are shared-memory, and distributed memory systems, together with their hybrid variants. The hybrid variants may include very important accelerators, as GPUs and FPGAs, that introduce other computing paradigms.

A very clear separation between the level of specification and definition of the computation and the execution level should be provided by the framework. The model provides the tasks, and the 'executors', that are separately defined, should have the ability of executing the tasks in an efficient way. These executors represent a "hot-spot" in the framework, since they should be specialized for different platforms, and/or improved in time.

– *Software Development Methodology.* This is needed because rising the level of abstraction leads to a gap between the semantic structure of the program, and the detailed structure required for its execution. In order to bridge this gap a solid semantic foundation on which transformation techniques can be built is needed. Correctness by construction is very important in the parallel programming setting, since in this case debugging is a very difficult task. This requirement is intrinsically related to the abstract machine defined by the model.

The concrete execution should be provided by the framework, and if the model provides a good development methodology, this could be used for the executors definition. They should assure correct execution of the task generated inside the model for different types of parallel system.

– *Guaranteed Performance.* Even if it is not expected to extract absolutely all the performance potential when implementing a model on a particular architecture, the model should assure the possibility to obtain a good implementation on each architecture type. If the corresponding abstract machine associated to the model imposes restrictions about the data access, communications, or other low level computational aspects, then it doesn't qualify as a good general model.

Also, the model doesn't have to impose certain levels of granularity since the systems could come with different scales of dependencies on granularity.

A framework built based on a model has to be flexible enough to provide the possibility to improve and adapt the execution to new conditions brought by various systems. This requires flexibility and adaptability. The model being theoretical, could and should emphasize the maximum level of parallelism for a computation. But this maximum level of parallelism could lead to a very fine granularity that may not be appropriate for the concrete system. The adaptation of the task granularity to different system granularity levels is very important and the framework should tackle this issue, by providing a functionality that could inject the desired level of granularity.

Another important issue in achieving performance is related to data management. Parallel computation is in many cases related to huge volumes of data that have to be read, computed and stored. The computation defined inside the model should be connected to the data, and these operations could have a huge impact on the final cost of computation. Considering the impact of data management on computational costs, this has to be reflected in a well defined framework component, that could be transformed and improved in time.

- *Cost Measures.* The most important goal in a parallel program design and construct is increasing the performance. Execution time is the most important of the concerns, but there are others such as processor utilization or even the development costs that are important too. They all describe the cost of a program, and the model should provide cost measures. At the abstract level, the model provides measures that are independent on the concrete execution level, but these measures should be parameterized well enough, such that they are able to assess the real costs that could be achieved on real machines. Since the best solution is many times obtained through empirical tests (and not only based on a theoretical analysis inside the model), it would be desirable for the framework to provide functions that automatically gives the evaluation of some metrics – e.g. number of certain functions calls, number of threads/processes created, execution time, etc. – and correlate them with some concrete platform system parameters.

By summarizing the previous requirements, we may emphasise the main components of the architecture of a good framework for parallel programming:

- *Model* – the implementation of the model of parallel computation that satisfies the specified requirements;
- *Executors* – a component that treats the execution on different types of parallel systems;
- *Data Manager* – a data management component that deals with data acquisition and management;
- *User Interacter* – a component that facilitates the easy development of new programs inside the framework.
- *Granularity Balancer* – a component able to adjust the granularity of the tasks that should be executed by the executors.
- *Metrics Analyser* – a component that could automatically provide cost measures of the execution in order to evaluate the performance.

The model should be efficiently connected with the other components: it provides the necessary information (e.g. executors receive tasks), but also uses the components functionality when needed (e.g. receive data from Data

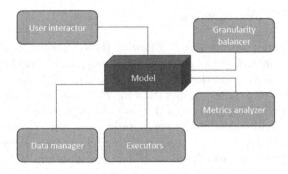

Fig. 1. MEDUGA - architecture scheme of a framework built based on a model of parallel computation.

Manager). The defined components represent the "hot-spots" of the framework. Figure 1 emphasises the proposed architecture of a framework for parallel programming – MEDUGA – Model-Executors-DataManager-UserInteracter-GranularityBalancer-MetricsAnalyser. This architecture could assure a good level of extensibility (through the component), but also stability (through the model).

2.2 The Importance on Relying on Software Engineering Methodologies and Patterns

In general, software engineering methodologies proved to be essential in the development of quality software of any kind. In order to satisfy the analysed requirements, the development of a framework that is based on a model of parallel computation, even more important than in the sequential case, must rely on appropriate software engineering methodologies, due to the complexity of such systems.

Parallel programming emphasizes specific parallel programming patterns and they are mainly related to the parallel programming paradigms that have been inventoried [23]. The model should provide well defined relations with these patterns, and their possible implementations. Many popular parallel computation models are defined based on skeletons [3], which structure and simplify the computational process. They are in direct connection to the parallel design patterns, which offer essential advantages in the development of software processes. They could provide the necessary flexibility and adaptability much needed in this case.

Besides the parallel programming patterns, general design patterns used in the common software design and software development methodologies are also important because the framework should assure correct separation of concerns, flexibility, adaptability and extensibility.

3   The *JPLF* Framework

The JPLF framework has been built following the requirements analysed in the previous section. *PowerList* and associated theories [17, 25] have been selected as a model of computation, and this model was proved to fulfill the general requirements for a model of parallel computation in [26]. *PowerLists* allow an efficient and correct derivation of programs of divide-and-conquer type; *PList* extensions allow multi-way divide-and-conquer computation, but also "embarrassingly parallel computation" [12]. Extensions with *PowerArrays*, resp. *PArrays* are possible, in order to move to multidimensional data organisation.

3.1   *PowerList* Theory as a Model of Parallel Computation

The theory of *Powerlists* data structures introduced by J. Misra [25] offers an elegant way for defining divide-and-conquer programs at a high level of abstraction. This is especially due to the fact that the index notations are not used, and because it allows reasoning about the algorithm correctness based on a formal defined algebra.

A *PowerList* is a linear data structure with elements of the same type, with the specific characteristic that the length of a *PowerList* is always a power of two. The functions on *PowerLists* are defined recursively by splitting their arguments based on two deconstruction operators (tie and zip).

Similar theories such as *ParLists* and *PLists* were defined [17], for working also with lists with non power-of-two lengths, and divide-and-conquer functions that split the problem in any number of subproblems. They extend the set of computation skeletons that could be defined using these data structures.

Besides the fact the inside these theories we have a solid software methodology that allows proving program correctness, the main advantage and specificity of the *PowerList* is the fact that there are two constructors (and correspondingly two desconstructors) that could be used: two *similar Powerlists* (with the same length and type), p and q, can be combined into a new, double length, power list data structure, in two different ways:

- using the operator *tie*, written $p \mid q$, the result containing elements from p followed by elements from q,
- using the operator *zip*, written $p \natural q$, the result containing elements from p and q, alternatively taken.

To prove the correctness of properties on *PowerLists* a structural induction principle is used: this considers a base case (for singletons), and two possible variants for the inductive step: one based on the *tie* operator, and the other based on *zip*.

Functions are defined based on the same principle. As a *PowerList* is either a singleton (a list with one element), or a combination of two *PowerLists*, a *PowerList* function can be defined recursively by cases. For example, the high order function *map*, which applies a scalar function to each element of a *PowerList* is defined as follows:

$$map(f, [a]) = [f(a)]$$
$$map(f, p \mid q) = map(f, p) \mid map(f, q) \tag{1}$$

The classical *reduce* function could be defined in a similar manner.

For both *map* and *reduce*, alternative definitions based on the *zip* operator could also be given. These could be useful if - depending on the memory allocation, and access – one could be more efficient than the other.

Moreover, the existence of the two decosntruction operators could be essential for the definition of certain functions. An important example is represented by the algorithm that computes the Fast Fourier Transform defined by Cooley and Tukey [4]; this has a very simple *PowerList* representation, which has been proved correct in [25]:

$$fft([a]) = [a]$$
$$fft(p \natural q) = (P + u \times Q) \mid (P - u \times Q) \tag{2}$$

where $P = fft(p)$, $Q = fft(q)$ and $u = powers(p)$. The result of the function $powers(p)$ is the *PowerList* $(w^0, w^1, .., w^{n-1})$ where n is the length of p and w is the $(2 \times n)$th principal root of 1.

The operators $+$ and $\times$ used in the *fft* definition are extension of the binary addition and multiplication operators on *PowerLists*. They have simple definitions that consider as an input two similar *PowerLists*, and specify that the elements on the similar positions are combined using the corresponding scalar operator.

The parallelism of the functions is implicitly defined: each application of a deconstruction operator (*zip* or *tie*) implies two independent computations that may be performed independently in two processes (programs) that could run in parallel. So, we obtain a tree decomposition, which is specific to divide-and-conquer programs. The existence of two decomposition operators eases the definition of different programs, but at the same time may induce some problems when these high-level programs have to be implemented on concrete parallel machines.

The *PList* data structure was introduced in order to develop programs for the recursive problems which can be divided into any number of subproblems, numbers that could be different from one level to another [17]. It is a generalisation of the *PowerList* data structure and it has also three constructors: one that creates singletons from simple elements, one based on concatenation of several lists, and the other based on alternative combining of the lists. The corresponding operators are $[.]$, (n-way $\mid$), and (n-way $\natural$); for a positive n, the (n-way $\mid$) takes n similar *PList* and returns their concatenation, and the (n-way $\natural$) returns their interleaving.

In *PList* algebra, ordered quantifications are needed to express the lists' construction. The expression

$$[\mid i : i \in \overline{n} : p.i]$$

is a closed form for the application of the n-way operator $|$, on the $PLists$ $p.i, i \in \overline{n}$ in order. The range $i \in \overline{n}$ means that the terms of the expression are written from 0 trough $n-1$ in the numeric order.

The $PList$ axioms, also define the existence of a unique decomposition of a $PList$ using constructors operators. Functions over $PList$ are defined using two arguments. The first argument is a list of arities: $PosList$, and the second is the $PList$ argument (if there are more than one $PList$ argument, they all must have the same length).

Usually the arity list is formed of the prime factors obtained through the decomposition of the list length into prime factors. Still, we may combine these factors, if convenient. The functions could be defined only if the product of the numbers in the arity list is equal to the $PList$ argument length. If the arity list is reduced to one element – the $PList$ argument length – the decomposition is done only once, and we arrive to an 'embarrassingly parallel computation' type.

We illustrate $PList$ functions' definitions with a simple example: the *reduction* function that computes the reduction of all elements of a $PList$ using an associative binary operator $\oplus$:

$$
\begin{aligned}
defined.red(\oplus).l.p & \equiv prod.l = length.p \\
red(\oplus).[].[a] & = a \\
red(\oplus).(x \triangleright l).[|i : i \in x : p.i] & = (\oplus i : 0 \leq i < x : red(\oplus).l.(p.i))
\end{aligned}
\tag{3}
$$

where $prod.l$ computes the product of the elements of list l, $length.p$ is length of p, $[]$ denotes the empty list, and $\triangleright$ denotes cons operator on simple lists. This function could also be defined using the $\natural$ operator because the $\oplus$ operator is associative.

The existence of the two decomposition operators differentiates these theories from other list theories, and also represents an important advantage in defining many parallel algorithms.

3.2 *JPLF* Design and Implementation

We will present in this section some details about the design and implementation of the major components of the framework.

Model Implementation. The main elements of the model are interconnected, although they have different responsibilities, such as:

- data structures implementations,
- functions implementations.

Design Choice 1. *Impose separate definitions for these elements allowing them vary independently.*

The motivation of this design choice is that separation of concerns enables independent modifications and extensions of the components by providing alternative options for storage or for execution.

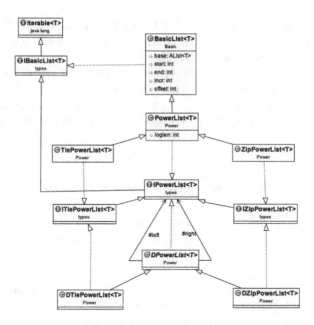

Fig. 2. The class diagram of the classes corresponding to lists implementation [28].

PowerList Data Structures. The type used when dealing with simple basic lists is IBasicList. In relation to the *PowerList* theory, this type is also used as a unitary super-type of specific types defined inside the theory. The framework extension with types that match the *PList* and *ParList* data structures is also enabled by this.

Design Choice 2. *Use the pattern* Bridge [10] *to decouple the definition of the special lists' types from their storage. Storage could be:*

- *a classical predefined list container where all the elements of a list are stored, but this doesn't necessarily mean that two neighbor elements of the same list are actually stored into neighbor locations in this storage: some byte distance could exist between the locations of the two elements;*
- *a list of sub-storages (containers) that are combined using* tie *or* zip *depending on the list type (*Composite *storage).*

The storage part belongs to the **DataManager** *component of the framework, since it may vary from one platform to another, and could be extended, too.*

The reason for this design decision is to allow the same storage being used in different ways, but most importantly to avoid the data being copied when a split operation is applied. This is a very important design decision that influences dramatically the obtained performance for the *PowerList* functions execution.

The result of splitting a *PowerList* is formed by two similar sub-lists but the initial list storage could remain the same for both sub-lists having only the *storage information* updated (in order to avoid element copy). Having a list (*l*), the *storage information* $SI(l)$ is composed of: the reference to the storage container `base`, the start index `start`, the end index `end`, the increment `incr`.

From a given list with storage information $SI(list) = $ (`base`,`start`,`end`,`incr`), two sub-lists (`left_list` and `right_list`) will be created when either *tie* and *zip* deconstruction operators are applied. The two sub-lists have the same storage container `base` and correspondent updated values for (`start`, `end`, `incr`).

Op.	Side	SI
tie	Left	base, start, (start+end)/2, incr
	Right	base, (start+end)/2, end, incr
zip	Left	base, start, end-incr, incr*2
	Right	base, start+incr, end, incr*2

If we have a *PList* instead of a *PowerList* the splitting operation could be defined similarly by updating `SI` for each new created sub-list. If we split the list into p sub-lists then the kth $(0 \le k < p)$ sub-list has $size = (end - start)/p$ and SI is:

Op.	Sub-List	SI
tie	kth	base, start+size*(k/p),
		start+size*((k+1)/p), incr
zip	kth	base, start+k*incr,
		end-(p-k-1)*incr, incr*k

The operators *tie* and *zip* are the two characteristic operations used to split a list, but they could also be used as constructors. This is reflected into the constructors definition.

There are two main specializations of the `PowerList` type: `TiePowerList` and `ZipPowerList`. Polymorphic definitions of the splitting and combining operations are defined for each of these types, which determine which operator is used. Since a PowerList could also be seen as a composition of two other PowerLists, two specializations with similar names: `DTiePowerList` and `DZipPowerList` are defined in order to allow the definition of a *PowerList* from two sub-lists that don't share the same storage. This is particularly important for executions on distributed memory platforms. The *Composite* design pattern is used for this. The corresponding list data structure types are depicted in the class diagram shown in Fig. 2.

PowerList Functions. A *PowerList* function is expressed in our model by specifying the *tie* or *zip* deconstruction operators for splitting the *PowerList* arguments and by a composing operator in case the result is also a *PowerList*.

Design Choice 3. *Use a type driven implementation for* PowerList *functions: if an argument's type is* `TiePowerList`, *then the* tie *operator is used for splitting that argument, and if an argument's type is* `ZipPowerList`, *the* zip *operator is used for it.*

This is possible because for the considered *PowerList* functions, one *PowerList* argument is always split by using the same operator (and so it preserves its type – a `TiePowerList` or a `ZipPowerList`). In case the result is a *PowerList*, the same operator (depending on the concrete type) is also used at each step of the construction of the result.

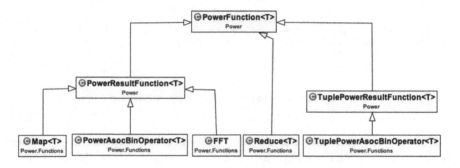

Fig. 3. The class diagram of classes corresponding to functions on PowerLists and their execution [28].

PowerList functions may have more than one *PowerList* argument, each having a particular type: `TiePowerList` or `ZipPowerList`. The *PowerList* functions don't need to explicitly specify the deconstruction operators. They are determined by the arguments' types: the *tie* operator is automatically used for `TiePowerLists` and the *zip* operator is used in case the type is `ZipPowerLists`. It is very important when invoking a specific function, to call it in such a way that the types of its actual parameters are the appropriate types expected by the specific splitting operators. The two methods `toTiePowerList` and `toZipPowerList`, provided by the `PowerList` class, transform a general `PowerList` into a specific one.

The result of a *PowerList* function could be either a singleton or a *PowerList*. For the functions that return a *PowerList*, a specialization is defined – `PowerResultFunction` – for which the result list type is specified. This is important in order to specify the operator used for composing the result.

Design Choice 4. *In order to support the implementation of the divide-and-conquer functions over* PowerLists, *use the* Template Method *pattern* [10].

The divide-and-conquer solving strategy is implemented in the template method `compute` of the `PowerFunction` class. `PowerFunction`'s `compute` method code snippet is presented in Fig. 4.

The primitive methods:

- `combine`
- `basic_case`
- `create_right_function` and `create_left_function`

are the only ones that need to be implemented in order to define a new *PowerList* function.

```
public Object compute() {
 if (test_basic_case())
  result = basic_case();
 else { split_arg();
    PowerFunction<T> left = create_left_function();
    PowerFunction<T> right = create_right_function();
    Object res_left = left.compute();
    Object res_right = right.compute();
    result = combine(res_left, res_right); }
 return result;
}
```

Fig. 4. The template method `compute` for *PowerList* function computation.

For the `create_right_function` and `create_left_function` functions we should provide specialized implementations to guarantee that the newly created sub-functions (left and right) correspond to the function being computed. For the other two, there are implicit definitions in order to free the user from providing implementations for all of them. For example, for *map* we have to provide a definition only for `basic_case`, whereas only a `combine` implementation is required for *reduce*.

The function `test_basic_case` implicitly verifies if the *PowerList* argument is a singleton, but there is the possibility to override this method and force an end of the recursion before singleton lists are encountered.

The `compute` method should be overridden only for functions that do not follow the classical definition of the divide-and-conquer pattern on *PowerLists*.

Figure 3 emphasizes the classes used for *PowerList* functions and some concrete implemented functions: `Map`, `Reduce`, `FFT`. The class `PowerAssocBinOperator` corresponds to associative binary operators (e.g.. $+, *$ etc.) extended to *PowerLists*. `TuplePowerResultFunction` has been defined in order to allow the definition of tuple functions, which combine a group of functions that have the same input lists and a similar structure of computation. Combining the computations of such kind of functions could lead to important improvements of the performance. For example, if we need to compute extended *PowerList* operators $< +, *, -, / >$ on the same pair of input arguments, they could be combined and computed in a single computation stream. This has been used for the FFT computation case [29].

3.3   Executors

Multithreading Executors. The simple sequential execution of a *PowerList* function is done simply by invoking the corresponding `compute` method.

In order to allow further modifications or specializations, the definition of the parallel execution of a *PowerList* function is done separately. The executors' supertype is the `IPowerFunctionExecutor` interface that covers the responsibility of executing a *PowerList* function. This type provides a `compute` method and also the methods for setting and getting the function that is going to be executed. Any function that complies with the defined divide-and-conquer pattern could be used for such an execution.

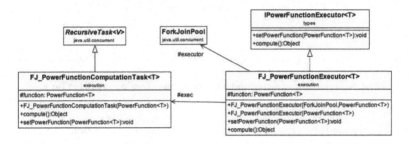

Fig. 5. The class diagram of classes corresponding to the multithreading executions based on ForkJoinPool.

Design Choice 5. *Define separate executor classes that rely on the same operations as the primitive methods used for the* PowerList *function definition.*

The class `FJ_PowerFunctionExecutor` relies on the `ForkJoinPool` Java executor, which is an implementation of the `ExecutorService` interface. Figure 5 shows the implemented classes corresponding to the multithreading executions based on `ForkJoinPool`. A `FJ_PowerFunctionExecutor` uses a `ForkJoinPool` to execute a `FJ_PowerFunctionComputationTask` that is created to compute a *PowerList* function. The simple definition of the recursive tasks that we choose to execute in parallel is enabled by this executor: new parallel tasks are created each time a split operation is done.

As the *PowerLists* functions are built based on the `Template Method` pattern, the implementation of the `compute` method of the `FJ_PowerFunctionComputa tionTask` is done similarly. The same skeleton, is used in this implementation, too. The code of the `compute` template method inside the `FJ_Power FunctionComputationTask` is shown in the code snippet of Fig. 6.

In this example, separate execution tasks wrap the two `PowerFunctions` that have been created inside the `compute` method of the `PowerFunction` class (`right` and `left`). A forked execution is called for the task `right_function_exec`, while the calling task is the one computing the `left_function_exec` task.

```
public Object compute() {
  Object result =null;
  if (function.test_basic_case()){ result = function.basic_case(); }
  else{
    function.split_arg();
    PowerFunction<T> left_function =   function.create_left_function();
    PowerFunction<T> right_function =   function.create_right_function();
    //wrap the functions into recursive tasks
    if (recursion_depth == 0){ result = function.compute(); }
    else{
      FJ_PowerFunctionComputationTask<T> left_function_exec =
      new FJ_PowerFunctionComputationTask<T>(left_function, recursion_depth-1);
      FJ_PowerFunctionComputationTask<T> right_function_exec =
      new FJ_PowerFunctionComputationTask<T>(right_function, recursion_depth-1)
          ;
      right_function_exec.fork();
      Object result_left = left_function_exec.compute();
      Object result_right = right_function_exec.join();
      result = function.combine(result_left, result_right);
    }
  }
  return result;
}
```

Fig. 6. The `compute` method in `PowerFunctionComputationTask`.

In order to define other kinds of executors, we need to define a new class that implements `IPowerFunctionExecutor`, and define its `compute` method based on the methods defined by the `PowerFunction` class.

MPI Execution. The ability to use multiple cluster nodes for execution could be attained by introducing MPI based execution of the functions [27]. This assures the needed scalability for a framework that works with regular data sets of very large sizes.

The command for launching a MPI execution has, generally the following is:

`mpirun -n 20 TestPowerListReduce_MPI`

where the `-n` argument defines the number of MPI processes (20 is just an example) that are going to be created. It could be easily observed that the MPI execution is radically different from the multithreading execution: each process executes the same Java code and the differentiation is done through the `process_rank` and the `number_of_processes` variables that are used in the implementing code.

The advantage brought by list splitting and combining without element moving (just changing the storage information `SI`), which is possible for the execution on shared memory systems, is no longer possible for the distributed memory execution paradigm. On a distributed memory system, based on an MPI execution, the list splitting and combining costs could not be kept so small because data communication between processes (sometimes on different machines) is needed. Since the cost for data communication is much higher than the simple computation costs, we had to analyze very carefully when this communication could be avoided.

During the *PowerList* functions computation when we apply the definition of the function on non-singleton input lists, each input list is split into two new lists. In order to distribute the work, we need to transfer one part of the split data to another process. Similarly, the combining stage could also need communication, since for combining stages, we need to apply operations on the corresponding results of the two recursive calls.

For identifying the cases when the data communication could be avoided, the phases of PowerList function computation were analyzed in details:

1. *Descending/splitting phase* that includes the operations for splitting the list arguments and the additional operations, if they exist.
2. *Leaf phase* that is formed only by the operations executed on singletons.
3. *Ascending/combining phase* that includes the operations for combining the list arguments and the additional operations, if they exist.

The complexity of each of these stages is different for particular functions.

For example, for *map*, *reduce* or even for *fft*, the descending phase does not include any additional operations. It has only the role of distributing the input data to the processing elements. The input data is not transformed during this process.

There are very few functions where the input is transformed during the descending phase. For some of these cases it is possible to apply some function transformation—as tupling—in order to reduce the additional computations. This had been investigated in [29].

Similarly, we may analyze the functions for which the combining phase implies only data composition (as *map*) or also some additional operations (as *reduce*).

Through the combination of these situations we obtained the following classes of functions:

1. *splitting $\equiv$ data_distribution*
   The class of functions for which the splitting phase needs only data distribution.
   Examples: *map, reduce, fft*
2. *splitting $\not\equiv$ data_distribution*
   The class of functions for which the splitting phase needs also additional computation besides the data distribution.
   Example: $f(p\natural q) = f(p+q)\natural f(p-q)$
3. *combining $\equiv$ data_composition*
   The class of functions for which the combining phase needs only the data composition based on the construction operator (*tie* or *zip*) being applied to the results obtained in the leaves.
   Example: *map*

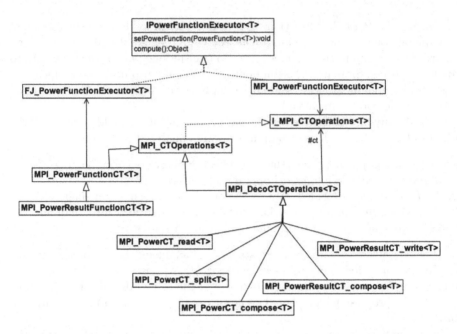

Fig. 7. The classes used for different types of execution of a PowerList function [28].

4. *combining* ≢ *data_composition*
   The class of functions for which the combining phase needs specific computation used in order to obtain the final result.
   Examples: *reduce, fft.*

One direct solution to treat these function classes as efficiently as possible would be to define distinct types for each of them. But the challenge was that these classes are not disjunctive. The solution was to split the function execution into sections, instead of defining different types of functions.

Design Choice 6. *Decompose the execution of the PowerList function into phases: reading, splitting, leaf, combining, and writing.*
Apply the Template method *pattern in order to allow the specified phases to vary independently.*
Apply the Decorator *pattern* [10] *in order to add specific corresponding cases.*

The Fig. 7 emphasizes the operations' types corresponding to the different phases. For MPI execution, we associated a different computational task (CT) for each phase. The computational tasks are defined as decorators, they are specific to each phase, and they are different for functions that return PowerLists by those that return simple types (`PowerResultFunction` vs. `PowerFunction`):

- `MPI_PowerCT_split`,
- `MPI_PowerCT_compose`, resp. `MPI_PowerResultCT_compose`,

- MPI_PowerCT_read,
- MPI_PowerResultCT_write.

Some details about the implementations of these classes are presented in Fig. 8. The class MPI_CTOperations provides a compute template method and empty implementations for the different step operations: read, split, compose, ... (details are given in Fig. 9).

The leaf operation encapsulates the effective computation that is performed in each process. It can be based on multithreading and this is why it could use FJ_PowerFunctionExecutor (the association between MPI_PowerFunctionCT and FJ_PowerFunctionExecutor). Hence, an MPI execution is implicitly a combination of MPI and multithreading execution.

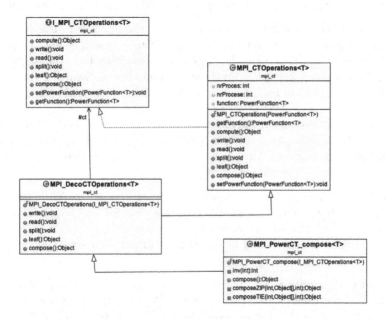

Fig. 8. Implementation details of some of the classes involved in the definition of MPI execution [28].

```
// compute method of MPI_CTOperations class
public Object compute(){
   Object result;
   read();
   split();
   result = leaf();
   result = compose();
   write();
   return result;
}
```

Fig. 9. The template method compute for MPI execution.

The `compose` operations in `MPI_PowerCT_compose` and `MPI_PowerResultCT_compose` are defined based on the `combine` operation of the wrapped PowerList function.

The input/output data for domain decomposition of parallel applications are in general very large, and so these are usually stored into files. This introduces other new phases in the computation function if reading and writing are added as additional phases (case 1), or if they are combined with splitting (respectively combining phases; in this case they introduce new variations of the computation function phases) (case 2).

If the data are taken from a file, then:

case 1: a reading is done by the process 0, followed by an implementation of the decomposition phase based on MPI communications;
case 2: concurrent file reads of the appropriate data are done by each process.

The possibility of having concurrent reads of the input data is given by the fact that each process needs to read data from different positions in the input file, and also because the data depends on known parameters: the type of the input data (`TiePowerList` or `ZipPowerList`), the total number of elements, the number of processes, the rank of each process, and the data element size (expressed in bytes).

The difficulty raised from the fact that all the framework's classes are , while almost all MPI Java implementations used only simple data types to be used in communication operations. The chosen solution was to use byte array transformations of the data through *serialization*.

Design Choice 7. *Use the* Broker *design pattern in order to define specialized classes for reading and writing data (FileReaderWriter) and for serializing/deserializing the data (ByteSerialization).*
*These specialised classes belong to the **DataManger** component of the framework.*

When the decomposition is based on the *tie* operator, reading a file is very simple and direct: each process receives a `filePointer` that depends on its rank and which represents the starting point for reading; all processes read the same number of data elements.

When the decomposition is based on the *zip* operator, file reading requires more complex operations: each process receives a starting `filePointer` and a number of data elements that should be read, but for each reading, another seek operation should be done. The starting `filePointer` is based on the bit reverse (to the right) operation applied on the process number.

For example, for a list equal to $[1, 2, 3, 4, 5, 6, 7, 8]$ a *zip* decomposition on 4 processes leads to the following distribution: $[[1, 5], [3, 7], [2, 6], [4, 8]]$.

In order to fuse the combining phase together with the writing, we applied a similar strategy. The conditions that allow concurrent writing are: the output file should already be created and each process writes values on different positions, these positions are computed based on the process rank, the operator type, the total number of elements, the number of processes, and the data element size.

In order to use this MPI extension of the framework, we don't need to define specific MPI functions for each *PowerList* function. We just define an executor by adding the needed decorators for each specific function: a `read` operation, or a `split` operation, and a `compose` operation or a `write` operation, etc. The order in which they are added is not important. At the same time, the operations: `read`, `write`, `compose`, etc. are based on the primitive operations defined for each *PowerList* function (which are used in the `compute` template method). Also, they are dependent on the total number of processes and the rank of each process.

To give better insights of the MPI execution we will present the case of the `Reduce` function (Sect. 3.1). The following test case considers a reduction on a list of matrices using addition. The code snippet in Figure 10 emphasizes what is needed for the MPI execution of the `Reduce` function.

```
ArrayList<Matrix> base = new ArrayList<Matrix>(n);
AsocBinOperator<Matrix> op = new SumOperator<Matrix>();
TiePowerList<Matrix> pow_list = new TiePowerList<Matrix>(base,0, n-1, 1);
PowerFunction<Matrix> mf = new Power.Functions.Reduce(op, pow_list);
int [] sizes = new int[1]; sizes[0] = n;
int [] elem_sizes = new int[1];
elem_sizes[0] = ByteSerialization.byte_serialization_len(new Matrix(0));
String [] files = new String[1];
files[0] = "date_matrix.in";
MPI_CTOperations<Matrix> exec =
  new MPI_PowerCT_compose<Matrix>(
    new MPI_PowerCT_read<Matrix>(
      new MPI_PowerFunctionCT<Matrix>(
        mf, ForkJoinPool.commonPool()
      ), files, sizes, elem_sizes
    )
  );
Object result = exec.compute();
```

Fig. 10. The MPI execution of the `Reduce` function.

3.4 Granularity Balancer

In an ideal case, the execution of parallel programs defined based on *PowerLists* implies the decomposition of the input data using the *tie* or *zip* operator and each application of *tie* and *zip* creates two new processes running in parallel, such that for each element of the input list, there will be a corresponding parallel process.

If we consider the `FJ_PowerFunctionExecutor`, this executor implicitly creates a new task that handles the `right_part_function`. So, the number of created tasks grows linearly with the data size. This leads to a logarithmic time-complexity that depends on the *loglen* of the input list.

Adopting this fine granularity of creating a parallel process per element may hinder the performance of the whole program. One possible improvement would be to bound the number of parallel tasks/processes, i.e. to specify a certain level until which a new parallel task is created:

Design Choice 8. *Introduce an argument –* `recursion_depth` *– for the Executor constructors; the default value of this argument is equal to the logarithmic length of the input list (loglen l) and the associated precondition specifies that its value should be less or equal to loglen l. When a new recursive parallel task is created this new task will receive a* `recursion_depth` *decremented with 1. The recursion stops when this* `recursion_depth` *reaches zero.*

This solution will lead to a parallel recursive decomposition until a certain level and then each task will simply execute the corresponding *PowerList* function sequentially.

In the same time, there are situations when for a sequential computation of the requested problem, a non recursive variant is more efficient than the recursive one. For example, for *map*, an efficient sequential execution will just iterate through the values of the input list and apply the argument function. The equivalent recursive variant (Eq. 1) is not so efficient since recursion comes with additional costs.

In this case we have to transform the input list by performing a data distribution. A list of length n is transformed into a list of p sub-lists, each having n/p elements. If the sub-lists have the type `BasicList` then the corresponding `BasicListFunction` is called. In the framework, this responsibility is solved by the following design decision:

Design Choice 9. *Define a* `Transformer` *class that has the following responsibilities:*

– *transforming a list of atomic elements into a list of sub-lists and,*
– *transforming a list of sub-lists into a list of atomic elements (flat operation).*

How the sub-lists are computed depends on the two operators `tie` *and* `zip`, *and the transformation should preserve the same storage of the elements.*

   For the `Transformer` *class implementation, the* Singleton *pattern [10] should be used.*

The transformation described above does not imply any element copy andit preserves the same storage container for the list. Every new list created has p `BasicList` elements with the same storage. On creation, the storage information SI is initialized for each new sub-list according to which decomposition operator was used (*tie* or *zip*) to create this new sub-list. The time-complexity associated to this operation is $O(p)$. The `Transformer` class has the following important functions:

– `toTieDepthList` and `toZipDepthList`,
– `toTieFlatList` and `toZipFlatList`.

The execution model for these lists of sub-lists is very similar and only differs for the basic case. If an element of a singleton list, that corresponds to the basic case is a sub-list (i.e. has the `IBasicList` type), a simple sequential execution of the function on that sub-list is called. Sequential execution of functions on sub-lists is implicitly based on recursion which is not very efficient in Java. If an equivalent function defined over IBasicList (based on iterations) could be defined, then this should be used instead.

3.5   User Interactor

In order to define a new program/function, the user only needs to specialize the functions: combine; basic_case; create_right_function and create_left_function; as it was described in Sect. 3.2. For the first two functions there are implicit definitions, such that they should be overwritten, only when combine is not a simple concatenation, and when basic_case is different from the identity function.

As specified before, *PowerList* functions don't have to explicitly specify the deconstruction operators since they are determined by the arguments' types; this simplifies a lot the definition of new functions. For the parallel execution, different executor types could be used and the user has to choose one depending on the available platform.

```
int limit =1<<5 ; // size of the list
// function to be applied on each element
Function f = new SquareFunctionFieldElem<Matrix>(new Matrix(1));
ArrayList<Matrix> base = new ArrayList<Matrix>(limit); //storage of the list
// populate the list
//[...]
//sequential execution
//define the list for sequential computation
BasicList<Matrix> list = new BasicList<Matrix>(base, 0, limit-1);
//sequential function definition
BasicListResultFunction<Matrix> bmf =  new Basic.Functions.Map<Matrix>(f,
    list);
//iterative sequential computation
Object result = bmf.compute();
//mulithreading execution
//define the list for parallel computation
TiePowerList<Matrix> pow_list = new TiePowerList<Matrix>(base,0, limit-1);
//parallel function definition
PowerResultFunction<Matrix> mf =
    new Power.Functions.Map<Matrix>(f, pow_list);
//recursive sequential computation
Object result = mf.compute();
//executor definition
FJ_PowerFunctionExecutor<Matrix> executor = new FJ_PowerFunctionExecutor<
    Matrix>(mf);
// parallel multithreading computation
result = executor.compute();
```

Fig. 11. Sequential and multithreading execution of Map function – squaring applied on a list of matrices.

In Fig. 11 we present the steps needed to execute the *map* function, which applies a square function on a list of matrices; the sequential execution based on an iterative list traversal is directed by the use of the BasicList type, recursive sequential execution is directed by the TiePowerList (ZipPowerLis also could be used), and for parallel multithreading execution, an executor based on Java `ForkJoinPool` is created, and the function is executed through it.

As it can be noticed from the code represented in Fig. 10, for an MPI execution of a *PowerList* function we only need to specify the 'decorators', and the files' characteristics (if it is the case). The general form of a *Powerlist* function has a list of *PowerLists* arguments. The reading should be possible for any number of *PowerLists* arguments. This is why we have arrays for the files' names and lists' and elements' sizes. For *reduce* we have only one input list.

Design Choice 10. *Apply the* Factory Method *pattern* [10] *in order to simplify the specifications/creation of the most common functions.*

The most common functions as *map*, *reduce*, or *scan* are provided by the framework since they have many applications, and many other functions could be obtained through their composition.

3.6   Metrics Analyser

For testing, we have used external scripts (under Linux OS) that allow us to executes several times one program with different parameters: number of MPI processes, number of threads of each process, recursion granularity, and depth of the data list (as explained in Sect. 3.4). The performance results were written into files. The parameterization has been done through command line arguments, and so, we may consider that we have used a very simple form of dependency injection.

3.7   Extensions

For *PList*, the functions and their possible multiparadigm executors are defined in a similar way to those for *PowerList*. *PList* is a generalization of *PowerList* allowing the splitting and the composition to be done into/from more than two sub-lists. So, instead of having the two functions: `create_right_function` and `create_left_function`, we need to have an array of (sub)functions. Still, the same principles and patterns are applied as in the *PowerList* case.

PowerArrays and *PArrays* are defined similarly to the unidimensional counterparts, and so are their corresponding functions, too. Including their implementation into the framework could be done based on the same principles as those followed for *PLists*.

4   Related Work

Algorithmic skeletons are considered an important approach in defining high level parallel models [3,32]. *PowerLists* and their associated theory could be used as a foundation for a domain decomposition divide-and-conquer skeleton based approach.

There are numerous algorithmic skeleton programming approaches. Most often, they are implemented as libraries for a host language. This languages include functional languages such a Haskell [22] with skeletons implemented using its GpH extension [13]. Multi-paradigm programming languages such as OCaml [24] are also considered: OCamlP3L [5] and its successor Sklml offer a set of a few data and task parallel skeletons and parmap [7]. Although OCaml is a functional, imperative and object oriented language, only the functional and imperative paradigms are used in these libraries.

Object-oriented programming languages such as C++, Java, or even Python are host languages for high-level parallel programming approaches. Very often object-oriented features are used in a very functional programming style. Basically classes for data structures are used in the abstract data-type style, with a type and its operations, sometimes only non-mutable. This is the approach taken by the PySke library for Python [33] that relies on a rewriting approach for optimization [21]. The patterns used for the design of JPLF, are also mostly absent from many C++ skeleton libraries such as Quaff [8] or OSL [18]. These libraries focus on the template feature of C++ to enable optimization at compile time though template meta-programming [38]. Still, there are also very complex C++ skeleton based frameworks – e.g. FastFlow [6] – that are built using a layered architecture and which target networked multi-cores possibly equipped with GPUs systems.

Java is one of the programming languages chosen often for implementing structured parallel programming environments that use skeletons as their foundation. The first skeleton based programming environment developed in Java, which exploits macro-data flow implementation techniques, is the RMI-based *Lithium* [1]. *Calcium* (based on ProActive, a Grid middleware) [2] and *Skandium* [19] (multi-core oriented) are two others Java skeleton frameworks. Compared with the aforementioned frameworks, JPLF could be used on both shared and distributed memory platforms.

Unrelated to architectural concerns, but related to the implementation of JPLF is that Java has been considered as a supported language by some MPI implementations which offer Java bindings. Such implementations are OpenMPI [37] and Intel MPI [41]. There are also 100% pure Java implementations of MPI such as MPJ Express [14,35]. Although there are some syntactic differences between them, all of these implementations are suitable for MPI execution. We have also used Intel Java MPI and MPJ Express and the obtained results were similar.

There are many works that emphasize the need of using well defined software engineering concepts and methodologies for increasing the reliability and productivity in parallel software development [15,16,23,31]. They refer either methodologies as I. Foster in [9], or patterns as the high impact book "A Pattern Language for Parallel Programming" [23], or both. Structured approaches are necessary since the technologies are various, there are many execution platforms, and also, the parallel software development is difficult.

5   Conclusions and Further Work

Starting from an analysis of the requirements for a reliable parallel programming framework, we tried to identify the main components of such a framework and we arrived to an architecture that is based on a model of parallel computation, but contains also well defined "hot-spot"s as components – MEDUGA (Model-Executors-DataManager-UserInteractor-GranularityBalancer-metricsAnalyser).

We emphasized also how this was applied on the development of a concrete framework - JPLF.

The JPLF framework has been architectured using design patterns. Based on the proposed architecture, new concrete problems can be easily implemented and resolved in parallel. Also, the framework could be easily extended with additional data structures (such as ParList or PowerArray [17]).

The most important benefit of the framework's internal architecture is that the parallel execution is controlled independently of the *PowerList* function definition. Primitive operations are the foundation for the executors' definitions, this allowing multiple execution variants for the same *PowerList* program. For example, sequential execution, MPI execution, multithreading using `ForkJoinPool` execution or some other execution model can be easily implemented. If we have a definition of a PowerList function we may use it for multithreading or MPI execution without any other specific adaptation of that particular function.

For the MPI computation model it was mandatory to properly manage the computation steps of a *PowerList* function: *descend, leaf*, and *ascend*. These computation steps were defined within a *Decorator* pattern based approach.

Many frameworks are oriented either on shared memory or on distributed memory platforms. The possibility to use the same base of computation and associate the execution variants depending on the concrete execution systems brings important advantages.

The separation of concerns principle has been intensively used. This facilitated the data-structures' behavior to be separated from their storage, and to ensure the separation of the definition of functions from their execution.

As further work we propose to enhance the metrics analyser component of the framework by allowing the injection of some metrics evaluation into the computation. Through this, the computation would be augmented with the required metrics computation.

Several executions have to be done, overhead regions identification could improve the performance very much, resource utilization evaluation (e.g. number of threads that are created/used) may improve the efficiency, etc.

As we presented in Sect. 4 there are many parallel programming libraries (that could be assimilated to frameworks), which are based on skeletons, and which provide implementations of the considered parallel skeletons on different systems. It would be interesting to investigate the measure in which they have been built following software engineering methodologies that assure the expected levels of software quality. How this aspects affect the performance, but also maintainability is another interesting subject of study.

References

1. Aldinucci, M., Danelutto, M., Teti, P.: An advanced environment supporting structured parallel programming in Java. Future Gener. Comput. Syst. **19**(5), 611–626 (2003)
2. Caromel, D., Leyton, M.: Fine tuning algorithmic skeletons. In: Kermarrec, A.-M., Bougé, L., Priol, T. (eds.) Euro-Par 2007. LNCS, vol. 4641, pp. 72–81. Springer, Heidelberg (2007). https://doi.org/10.1007/978-3-540-74466-5_9
3. Cole, M.: Algorithmic Skeletons: Structured Management of Parallel Computation. MIT Press, Cambridge (1991)
4. Cooley, J., Tukey, J.: An algorithm for the machine calculation of complex fourier series. Math. Comput. **19**(90), 297–301 (1965)
5. Cosmo, R.D., Li, Z., Pelagatti, S., Weis, P.: Skeletal parallel programming with OcamlP3l 2.0. Par. Proc. Lett. **18**(1), 149–164 (2008)
6. Danelutto, M., Torquati, M.: Structured parallel programming with "core" Fast-Flow. In: Zsók, V., Horváth, Z., Csató, L. (eds.) CEFP 2013. LNCS, vol. 8606, pp. 29–75. Springer, Cham (2015). https://doi.org/10.1007/978-3-319-15940-9_2
7. Di Cosmo, R., Danelutto, M.: A "minimal disruption" skeleton experiment: seamless map & reduce embedding in OCaml. In: Proceedings of the International Conference on Computational Science, vol. 9, pp. 1837–1846. Elsevier (2012)
8. Falcou, J., Sérot, J., Chateau, T., Lapresté, J.T.: QUAFF: efficient C++ design for parallel skeletons. Parallel Comput. **32**, 604–615 (2006)
9. Foster, I.: Designing and Building Parallel Programs: Concepts and Tools for Parallel Software Engineering. Addison-Wesley Longman Publishing Co., Inc., Boston (1995)
10. Gamma, E., Helm, R., Johnson, R., Vlissides, J.: Design Patterns: Elements of Reusable Object-oriented Software. Addison-Wesley Longman Publishing Co., Inc., Boston (1995)
11. Gorlatch, S., Lengauer, C.: Abstraction and performance in the design of parallel programs: an overview of the sat approach. Acta Inf. **36**(9–10), 761–803 (2000)
12. Grama, A., Gupta, A., Karypis, G., Kumar, V.: Introduction to Parallel Computing. Addison Wesley, Boston (2003)
13. Hammond, K., Rebón Portillo, Á.J.: HaskSkel: algorithmic skeletons in haskell. In: Koopman, P., Clack, C. (eds.) IFL 1999. LNCS, vol. 1868, pp. 181–198. Springer, Heidelberg (2000). https://doi.org/10.1007/10722298_11
14. Javed, A., Qamar, B., Jameel, M., Shafi, A., Carpenter, B.: Towards scalable Java HPC with hybrid and native communication devices in MPJ Express. Int. J. Parallel Prog. **44**(6), 1142–1172 (2016). https://doi.org/10.1007/s10766-015-0375-4
15. Jelly, I., Gorton, I.: Software engineering for parallel systems. Inf. Softw. Technol. **36**(7), 381–396 (1994). Software Engineering for Parallel Systems
16. Kiefer, M.A., Warzel, D., Tichy, W.: An empirical study on parallelism in modern open-source projects. In: SEPS 2015 (2015)
17. Kornerup, J.: Data structures for parallel recursion. Ph.D. dissertation, University of Texas (1997)
18. Légaux, J., Loulergue, F., Jubertie, S.: OSL: an algorithmic skeleton library with exceptions. In: Proceedings of the International Conference on Computational Science, pp. 260–269. Elsevier, Barcelona (2013)
19. Leyton, M., Piquer, J.M.: Skandium: multi-core programming with algorithmic skeletons. In: 18th Euromicro Conference on Parallel, Distributed and Network-based Processing (PDP), pp. 289–296. IEEE Computer Society (2010)

20. Lopes, S.F., Afonso, F., Tavares, A., Monteiro, J.: Framework characteristics - a starting point for addressing reuse difficulties. In: 2009 Fourth International Conference on Software Engineering Advances, pp. 256–264 (2009)

21. Loulergue, F., Philippe, J.: Automatic optimization of python skeletal parallel programs. In: Wen, S., Zomaya, A., Yang, L.T. (eds.) ICA3PP 2019. LNCS, vol. 11944, pp. 183–197. Springer, Cham (2020). https://doi.org/10.1007/978-3-030-38991-8_13

22. Marlow, S. (ed.): Haskell 2010 language report (2010). https://www.haskell.org/definition/haskell2010.pdf

23. Massingill, B.L., Mattson, T.G., Sanders, B.A.: A Pattern Language for Parallel Programming. Software Patterns Series. Addison Wesley, Boston (2004)

24. Minsky, Y.: OCaml for the masses. Commun. ACM **54**(11), 53–58 (2011)

25. Misra, J.: Powerlist: a structure for parallel recursion. ACM Trans. Program. Lang. Syst. **16**(6), 1737–1767 (1994)

26. Niculescu, V.: Pares - a model for parallel recursive programs. Roman. J. Inf. Sci. Technol. (ROMJIST) **14**, 159–182 (2012)

27. Niculescu, V., Bufnea, D., Sterca, A.: MPI scaling up for powerlist based parallel programs. In: 27th Euromicro International Conference on Parallel, Distributed and Network-Based Processing, PDP 2019, Pavia, Italy, 13–15 February 2019, pp. 199–204. IEEE (2019)

28. Niculescu., V., Loulergue., F., Bufnea., D., Sterca., A.: Pattern-driven design of a multiparadigm parallel programming framework. In: Proceedings of the 15th International Conference on Evaluation of Novel Approaches to Software Engineering - Volume 1: ENASE, pp. 50–61. INSTICC, SciTePress (2020)

29. Niculescu, V., Loulergue., F.: Transforming powerlist based divide&conquer programs for an improved execution model. J. Supercomput. **76** (2020)

30. Niculescu, V., Loulergue, F., Bufnea, D., Sterca, A.: A Java framework for high level parallel programming using powerlists. In: 18th International Conference on Parallel and Distributed Computing, Applications and Technologies, PDCAT 2017, Taipei, Taiwan, 18–20 December 2017, pp. 255–262. IEEE (2017)

31. Pankratius, V.: Software engineering in the era of parallelism. In: KIT-Nachwuchswissenschaftler-Symposium (2010)

32. Pelagatti, S.: Structured Development of Parallel Programs. Taylor & Francis (1998)

33. Philippe, J., Loulergue, F.: PySke: algorithmic skeletons for Python. In: International Conference on High Performance Computing and Simulation (HPCS), pp. 40–47. IEEE (2019)

34. Pressman, R.: Software Engineering: A Practitioner's Approach, 7th edn. McGraw-Hill Science, New York (2009)

35. Qamar, B., Javed, A., Jameel, M., Shafi, A., Carpenter, B.: Design and implementation of hybrid and native communication devices for Java HPC. In: Proceedings of ICCS 2014, Cairns, Queensland, Australia, 10–12 June 2014, pp. 184–197 (2014)

36. Skillicorn, D.B., Talia, D.: Models and languages for parallel computation. ACM Comput. Surv. **30**(2), 123–169 (1998)

37. Vega-Gisbert, O., Román, J.E., Squyres, J.M.: Design and implementation of Java bindings in Open MPI. Parallel Comput. **59**, 1–20 (2016)

38. Veldhuizen, T.: Techniques for scientific C++. Computer science technical report 542, Indiana University (2000)

39. X***: MPI: A message-passing interface standard. https://www.mpi-forum.org/docs/mpi-3.1/mpi31-report.pdf. Accessed 20 Nov 2019

40. X***: Oracle: The Java tutorials: ForkJoinPool. https://docs.oracle.com/javase/tutorial/essential/concurrency/forkjoin.html. Accessed 20 Nov 2019
41. X***: Intel MPI library developer reference for Linux OS: Java bindings for MPI-2 routines (2019). https://software.intel.com/en-us/mpi-developer-reference-linux-java-bindings-for-mpi-2-routines. Accessed 20 Nov 2019

Energy-Aware Pattern Framework: The Energy-Efficiency Challenge for Embedded Systems from a Software Design Perspective

Marco Schaarschmidt[1]([✉]) [ID], Michael Uelschen[1] [ID], Elke Pulvermüller[2], and Clemens Westerkamp[1]

[1] Faculty of Engineering and Computer Science,
University of Applied Sciences Osnabrück, Osnabrück, Germany
`{m.schaarschmidt,m.uelschen,c.westerkamp}@hs-osnabrueck.de`
[2] Software Engineering Research Group, University of Osnabrück,
Osnabrück, Germany
`elke.pulvermueller@informatik.uni-osnabrueck.de`

Abstract. Driven by the success of Internet of Things, the number of embedded systems is constantly increasing. Reducing power consumption and improving energy efficiency are among the key challenges for battery-powered embedded systems. Additionally, threats like climate change clearly illustrate the need for systems with low resource usages. Due to the impact of software applications on the system's power consumption, it is important to optimize the software design even in early development phases. The important role of the software layer is often overlooked because energy consumption is commonly associated with the hardware layer. As a result, existing research mainly focuses on energy optimization at the hardware level, while only limited research has been published on energy optimization at the software design level. This work presents a novel approach to propose an energy-aware software design pattern framework description, which takes power consumption and time behavior into account. We evaluate the expressiveness of the framework by defining design patterns, which use elaborated power-saving strategies for various hardware components to reduce the overall energy consumption of an embedded system. Furthermore, we introduce a dimensionless numerical efficiency factor to make energy savings quantifiable and a comparison for design patterns applied in various use cases possible.

Keywords: Embedded software engineering · Embedded systems · Software design pattern · Energy efficiency · Power consumption

1 Introduction

Embedded systems are nowadays ubiquitous, due to advances in high-performance hardware and new fields of applications, such as Internet of Things (IoT)

© Springer Nature Switzerland AG 2021
R. Ali et al. (Eds.): ENASE 2020, CCIS 1375, pp. 182–207, 2021.
https://doi.org/10.1007/978-3-030-70006-5_8

and Industrial Internet of Things (IIoT). IoT itself has a huge potential in solving parts of the climate change by addressing environmental issues like water and air pollution [1]. It is obvious that those systems should be economical in the use of resources itself. But not only because of the climate change debate, power consumption, energy efficiency, real-time behavior, durability, and maintainability are important Non-Functional Requirements (NFR) in the design process of an embedded system. For battery-operated systems, energy efficiency is a challenging problem and often the bottleneck in the development process [5], especially when they operate at places that are difficult to maintain (e.g. buried underground [12]). From a software perspective, the complexity of tasks is constantly increasing, which results in more detailed and complex software architecture. The control flow (e.g. access and utilization of hardware components) and algorithms of software applications have a direct impact on the energy efficiency of the system. Pang et al. [25] stated, that software developers often have a good understanding of the application and hardware platform. However, when it comes to energy efficiency, they often have limited knowledge of how an application consumes energy as well as best practices for reducing power consumption. In the process of software development, design patterns are documented best practice solutions for recurring problems. During the software design and architecture phase, significant energy savings can be achieved [35]. However, to the best of our knowledge, there is only limited work towards design patterns, which include NFR like energy efficiency and power consumption of a system in their description. To address the gap between software design patterns and hardware designs, the following contributions are presented in this paper:

- To take the complete system into account, we identify and describe power-related characteristics of hardware components. This can also be addressed by software applications.
- As part of our framework, we define the tow metrics *energy balance EB_P* and *efficiency factor η_P*. EB_P represents the difference between the ability to save energy and additional energy consumption. η_P describes a quantitative estimation of the efficiency of energy savings. We also propose a uniform *power-timing diagram* to outline the behavior of each design pattern.
- We revise and update our framework, first published in [32], and extend our pattern catalog by adding two new energy-aware design pattern descriptions.

The remainder of this paper is organized as follows: Sect. 2 summarizes existing research related to our approach. Section 3 presents an overview of power consumption characteristics, the impact of software on those characteristics and the definitions of the design pattern framework. A pattern catalog to evaluate the framework is part of Sect. 4. Section 5 discusses the advantages and limitations of our proposed design pattern framework. A conclusion is provided in Sect. 6.

2 Related Work

Power analysis and power optimization can be addressed at various levels of hardware and software design domains, as shown in Fig. 1. From a software

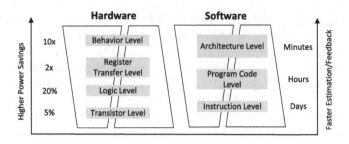

Fig. 1. Power reduction and analysis efficiency, adapted from [35].

perspective, optimizations can be performed on *Architecture Level, Program Code Level* and *Instruction Level*. They are equivalent to various hardware levels starting from *Transistor Level* to *Behavior Level*. Tan *et al.* [35] mentioned that optimizations on the *Architecture Level*, as the most abstract level, lead to significantly higher power savings. At the same time, applying and evaluating changes regarding energy optimization takes less time compared to lower levels. This paper focuses on a energy efficiency analysis at the software design level as part of the *Architecture Level*, while other work like [13] and [28] covers the system-related part of the *Architecture Level* like networks and cloud systems.

Software design patterns are typically used to address challenges during the process of software development. They describe generic and programming language independent proven best practice solutions for recurring problems. The work of Gamma *et al.* [11], commonly known as Gang of Four (GoF), describe basic and widely accepted best practices for software design problems in object-oriented software development. Their work includes concepts for structural, behavioral and creational related problems without limitation to a specific technology or programming language. The main drawback in [11] is the lack of fields for typical NFRs, such as power consumption and time behavior, which are important aspects of embedded systems. In common representations [7,8], only time-related aspects are slightly addressed for a subset of patterns without relation to power consumption. The approach in [4] extends common representations to consider safety aspects as part of NFRs in the pattern description for safety-critical applications. Several approaches target the challenge of analyzing and improving energy efficiency focusing on software development and design patterns to lower the overall power consumption of a system. There are also approaches to optimize design pattern on lower levels and close to the instruction level, as described in Fig. 1. Litke *et al.* [18] analyzed the consumption and performance of software designs before and after design patterns (e.g. Factory Method, Observer, and Adapter) are applied to an embedded system. Maleki *et al.* [19] compare the power consumption of different GoF design patterns. Feitosa *et al.* [10] propagate alternative pattern solutions with lower power consumption. The main reason for energy-efficiency differences in [10,19] is due to the usage of overloading, inheritance, virtual functions and dynamic binding in each alternative pattern solution. However, these techniques are programming language-specific and the effect on power consumption also depends on the compiler settings. Noureddine & Rajan [21] improve energy efficiency by optimizing design patterns at compile time by taking specific aspects of programming languages like memory management and compiler optimizations automatically into account. Abdulsalam et al. [2] mentioned, that changing the programming languages and compiler settings can heavily influence the overall performance and the impact on energy efficiency of the software in particular. Additionally, all aforementioned optimizations are targeting the efficiency of the used processor. For embedded systems, especially IoT devices with multiple sensors, LEDs, and wireless communication capabilities, the processor is not the main energy consumer of the system [38,40]. Bunse & Höpfner [6] stated, that optimization of source code during compile time is often inefficient because the usage of existing resources cannot be predicted. The strategy of accessing and using connected resources (e.g. peripheral devices) is an important factor when it comes to energy efficiency for embedded systems. Even though hardware and software must fulfill the same NFRs, typical design patterns are strictly divided into software- and hardware-based patterns [4]. To take a complete system and the close relationship between software and hardware into account, a more general approach is required to describe the impact of energy efficiency for embedded systems from a software perspective. Reinfurt et al. [29,30] propose a pattern framework describing more abstract design patterns for IoT devices. Their work addresses energy efficiency by considering energy supply, energy harvesting, and energy-saving approaches in software architectures at system level of IoT ecosystems (e.g. server systems and infrastructure). The optimization of a single IoT node from a software perspective is not covered by their work. However, to the best of our knowledge, the aforementioned work is not taking the close connection between the software and hardware layer into consideration and there is no approach to include power consumption and time behavior as two closely related NFRs in the definition of software design patterns.

3   Approach

This section describes the updated and extended approach, based on our previous work [32]. First, we describe the calculation of power consumption for different peripheral devices of an embedded system. Afterward in Sect. 3.2, we outline how the software can influence the parameters proposed in the previous Sect. 3.1 to close the gap between the hardware and software layers. Section 3.3 introduces the design pattern framework as the basic template for all energy-aware design pattern of the pattern catalog described in Sect. 4.

3.1   Power Consumption of Embedded Systems

This chapter contains the definition of power consumption as part of the energy consumption for embedded systems. Modern embedded systems can be highly complex devices consisting of several different components like actuators (e.g.

Table 1. Average power consumption of hardware components taken from datasheets.

Device	Power consumption
NXP LPC54114 (ARM Cortex M4 & M0+ dual-core MCU)	Active: 32.67 mW Sleep: 2.97 mW
ams TSL2591 Digital Light Sensor	0.825 mW
Bosch BME280 Sensor (Indoor Navigation)	1.14 mW
Bosch BMM150 Geomagnetic Sensor	11.76 mW
Futurlec Red LED (0805 SMD)	40 mW
Melexis MLX90640 Far Infrared Thermal Sensor	66 mW
Atmel WINC1500-MR210PA IEEE 802.11 b/g/n	TX: 880.2 mW, RX: 297 mW

motors, LEDs, and displays), sensors, and radio modules. As mentioned in [38, 40], the processor of an embedded system is not the main energy consumer by default. Table 1 contains examples of components with their average power consumption. More complex sensors can exceed the power consumption of the processor by the factor 2 and communication interfaces like the WINC1500-MR210PA in transfer mode by factor 27.

Optimization approaches must consider each component of a system individually. Therefore, the total energy consumption E_{tot} defines the power consumption for a given time interval $[0, T]$ can be calculated as:

$$E_{tot} = \int_0^T \left(\underbrace{\sum_{i=1}^n P_{dyn}^i(t) + P_{stat}^i(t)}_{complex} + \underbrace{\sum_{j=1}^m V^j(t) \cdot I^j(t)}_{simple} \right) dt \qquad (1)$$

In general, possible energy optimization approaches depend on the characteristics of peripheral devices. The categories of simple and complex components were defined in our previous work [32]. *Complex components* are based on CMOS technology and are clock-driven. Their power consumption contains a static part P_{stat}, which is the leakage current of transistors [15], and a dynamic part $P_{dyn} = n \cdot C \cdot V^2 \cdot f$ [26] with n as the number of transistors, C as the capacitance, V as the supply voltage, and f as the operating frequency. The power consumption for *simple components* is defined as $P = V \cdot I$ and can only be optimized by adjusting the voltage V and electric current I. If more components are used, power consumption optimizations from a software perspective can be a challenging task. Furthermore, optimization regarding overall energy consumption cannot be analyzed in isolation, because of its impact on other requirements like temporal behavior.

3.2   Impact of Software on Power Characteristics

This chapter discusses the impact of a software application on energy-related parameters (c.f. Sect. 3.1) to address the overall energy consumption during

execution by reducing the power consumption of individual hardware components. In general, typical *energy bugs* in software applications like *unnecessary
wait cycles* and *misusage of peripheral devices* can lead to a higher power consumption. The misusage can also heavily influence the overall power consumption (c.f. Table 1) no matter how optimized the application executing on the
processor is. Both problem domains can be addressed by energy-aware design
patterns described with our framework. The following power characteristics can
be influenced by a software application:

1. *Voltage (V)*: Adjusting the voltage V of the system and single components.
   Alternatively, turn off the power from separated parts of the system, which
   requires hardware layer support. Software applications do not always have
   control over those features (e.g. Dynamic Voltage Scaling) [17, 24].
2. *Frequency (f)*: Adjusting the operation frequency of components (e.g. processors, sensors) in particular situations. This requires support from the hardware layer and is not always directly manageable by the application. Techniques like Dynamic Frequency Scaling (DFS) [27] are not or only partially
   supported by low-costs and low-end processors (e.g. ARM Cortex M family).
3. *Capacity (n · C)*: Controlling the active states of components and functional
   units. A strategy to control components can be implemented statically before
   compilation or executed dynamically during runtime.
4. *Time (t)*: The parameter (t) targets the time a system or component is operating in active mode with high power consumption. The software application
   can minimize the total runtime by reducing the workload, using effective
   algorithms, and optimizing control flows.

The impact of energy-aware design patterns on each of the presented parameters
can be outlined and included in the description based on the proposed design
pattern framework in Sect. 3.3. By this, the gap between the software design
layer and the hardware layer can be addressed.

3.3   Energy-Aware Design Pattern Framework

This section describes our framework for the specification of energy-aware software design patterns. The framework is intended to meet the following goals:

1. Create a uniform template to describe the key elements of energy-aware
   design patterns without dependencies on programming languages and specific peripheral devices.
2. Provide a section to describe the impact on power consumption using the
   proposed power characteristics (c.f. Sect. 3.2) in order to address the gap
   between hardware and software layers.
3. Include a uniform graphical description of the behavior resulting from applying a design pattern w.r.t. power consumption and time behavior aspects.

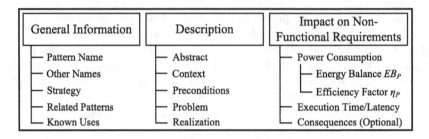

Fig. 2. Energy-aware design pattern framework structure, adapted from [32].

The design of the framework is related to the concepts proposed in [4] but modified to take power consumption instead of safety aspects into account. Additionally, the decoupling of hardware and software for power consumption is removed. The structure of the proposed framework description is divided into the three main parts *General Information*, *Description*, and *Impact on Non-Functional Requirements*, as shown in Fig. 2.

General Information: This part describes the meta-information of a design pattern and contains the following elements:

- *Pattern Name*: A unique name that identifies the design pattern.
- *Other Names*: Existing other well-known names (e.g. from other disciplines or domains).
- *Strategy*: A description of how power consumption parameters (c.f. Sect. 3.3) are addressed and influenced by the design pattern.
- *Related Patterns*: Names of other design patterns realizing the same or a closely related concept, if available.
- *Known Uses*: Other domains or disciplines (e.g. electrical engineering) or existing solutions using this design pattern successfully.

Description: This part covers the basic definitions of the design pattern concept and general conditions for an effective utilization. The structure is based on [11] and contains the following elements:

- *Abstract*: A short description of the pattern to provide a first overview.
- *Context*: Description of the situation in which this pattern can be applied.
- *Preconditions*: Conditions including requirements and properties of the underlying hardware architecture, which must be fulfilled to apply the pattern successfully.
- *Problem*: Description of the problem to be solved by this design pattern. The problem statement should be expressed as a question.
- *Realization*: Contains a description of the implementation details. As a graphical representation of the implementation details, Unified Modeling Language (UML) [23] diagrams (e.g. structure, class, and object diagrams) can

be added to the textual description. Additionally, other UML diagrams like state, timing, activity, or sequence diagrams can be used to define aspects of the implementation.

Impact on Non-functional Requirements: This section describes the impact on power consumption, execution time as energy-related NFRs, and consequences like development costs or modifiability. Design patterns addressing energy-related problems can have a negative influence on other NFR like execution time. Furthermore, this results in a trade-off between additional energy overhead and total energy savings.

- *Power Consumption*: For a unified description, we introduce the *energy balance* EB_P and the *efficiency factor* η_P to describe the impact on power consumption. EB_P indicates possible savings, where a higher value of EB_P suggests greater possible savings. η_P enables a quantitative evaluation of the efficiency of energy savings (effort-saving ratio). $\eta_P \geq 1$ means a design pattern applied in a specific situation saves energy without additional effort. Otherwise, when a design pattern is not effective and does not save energy, $\eta_P \leq 0$. Values within $]0,1[$ describe a trade-off between additional energy overhead and energy savings. A *power-timing diagram* is added to the description to outline the behavior of a design pattern.
- *Execution Time/Latency*: Describes the impact of a design pattern on the execution time and additional latencies.
- *Consequences*: Drawbacks and side-effects regarding the behavior and control flow as well as additional hardware requirements. This can lead to adaptations, which must be addressed by the software developer.

4   Introduction of the Pattern Catalog

In this section, we use the design pattern framework introduced in Sect. 3.3 as a template to describe energy-aware design patterns. The pattern catalog contains a total of six different energy-aware design patterns. Four are revised and extended versions of design patterns presented in [32], while two are newly introduced in this paper. Each description contains a uniform *power-timing diagram* as a graphical representation of the behavior related to power consumption, computation power, and execution time. Based on this diagram, design patterns are evaluated with the proposed metrics EB_P and η_P, described in Sect. 3.3.

4.1   Pattern: Energy-Aware Sampling (EAS)

General Information
Other Names: Adaptive Sampling (proposed in [33]) or Energy-Aware Switching when this pattern is used for a processor (c.f. *Strategy* description).

Strategy: Energy-Aware Sampling (EAS) influences the time t a peripheral device is operating in an active state. By lowering the sampling rate (respectively the active time), a peripheral device can be inactive for longer periods and the processor can enter a lower power state. Increasing the sampling rate increases the power consumption of the component due to a longer active period. This pattern can also be used to switch periodically between a processor's active and low power states.

Related Patterns: *Cost-Aware Sampling* and Quality of *Service Based Sampling* as two specializations of the generic EAS pattern are described in [20]. The first pattern adapts the sampling rate according to energy consumption, memory size, and communication bandwidth, while the second pattern affects the sampling rate based on transmission network performance.

Known Uses: A dynamically adapting sampling frequency is used in [33] to save approx. 31% of the system's battery energy during a three months continuous water quality monitoring period.

Description
Abstract: The main purpose of EAS is to adjust the sample rate of peripheral devices or to switch between the power modes of processors. The sample rate itself has a strong impact on the power consumption of the system [36]. When EAS is used in combination with a sensor, the lowest sample frequency f_{sample} should be $f_{sample} > 2 \cdot f_{max}$ to extract all the necessary information [16].

Context: This pattern is highly suitable for periodic systems (e.g. constant sampling rates) without interrupts. EAS can be used for peripheral devices in situations when signal characteristics are known and algorithms for data processing can handle varying sample rates. For processors, EAS can be applied when the application flow contains a high percentage of idling time.

Preconditions: Peripheral devices addressed by this pattern must have the capabilities to adjust the sampling rate. When used in combination with a processor, a dynamic change of power states must be supported.

Problem: How can the energy consumption of a system be optimized by adjusting the sample rate of a peripheral device or by reducing the active state duration of a processor?

Realization: EAS has a minimal impact on the software application. A static adjustment of the sample rate for peripheral devices can be achieved during the startup process of software applications. If the adjustment is supposed to vary during runtime, further software components (e.g. algorithms, data transmissions) need to be considered. When EAS is used to adjust the active time of processors, parts of the application containing idling times need to be identified. For those parts, the processor can be set to a lower power state.

Impact on Non-functional Requirements
Figure 3 shows the *power-timing diagram* for the basic definition of EAS applied on a processor without considering peripheral devices and sensors.

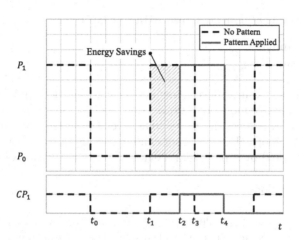

Fig. 3. EAS power characteristics [32].

Energy Consumption: The power consumption is defined in the upper part of Fig. 3, where the sleep mode is defined as P_0 and the normal mode as P_1. The lower part represents the computing power, where CP_1 described the computing power in normal mode. The power (duty) cycle for such applications is defined as:

$$D = \frac{c}{T} \qquad\qquad c = t_3 - t_1 \qquad\qquad T = t_3 - t_0 \qquad (2)$$

$$D' = \frac{c}{T'} \qquad\qquad T' = t_4 - t_0 \qquad\qquad\qquad (3)$$

with the duration c when the processor is in normal mode and T as the overall period. When EAS is applied, a new period $T' > T$ is defined, leading to a new relaxed power cycle D'. EB_P can be calculated using the Eq. (2)–(3) and $\Delta P_{10} = P_1 - P_0$. When taking other peripheral devices like sensors into account, Eq. (4) needs to be extended, which is beyond the scope of this paper.

$$\begin{aligned} EB_P &= E_{normal} - E_{relaxed} \\ &= (D \cdot \Delta P_{10}) - (D' \cdot \Delta P_{10}) \qquad (4) \\ &= \Delta P_{10}\,(D - D') \end{aligned}$$

There exists a linear relationship between relaxing the duty cycle and energy savings. Since additional power or computing power effort is not required, the *efficiency factor* can be defined as $\eta_P = 1$.

Execution Time/Latency: The execution time of a software application is effected, when adapting the duty cycle. Furthermore, periodic latencies like waiting periods during measurements of a sensor can be reduced.

Consequences: When using EAS to adjust the reading of a sensor, the number of total data points, and the accuracy of the sampled signal decreases.

4.2   Pattern: Event-Based Computing (EBC)

General Information
Other Names: None

Strategy: Processors can achieve a low energy consumption by minimizing the time spent in an active mode and maximizing the time operating in a low power mode. This pattern reduces the active *time* (t) of a processor by using interrupts instead of polling loops. The processor can instead operate in a low power mode and will be triggered by a peripheral device when an event occurs.

Related Patterns: None

Known Uses: In event-based development, internal and external interrupts can be used to trigger specific software functions which can cause spontaneous behavioral changes. Peripheral devices like an analog-to-digital converter (ADC) and external devices (e.g. NXP CLRC663 plus [22]) are using interrupts to signal the host processor when thresholds are reached or changes detected.

Description
Abstract: The Event-Based Computing (EBC) design pattern optimizes the power consumption of the processor by replacing polling loops in the software application with interrupt implementations. Interrupts can be used by internal and external peripheral devices to indicated state changes directly. They serve as triggers for events and cause a spontaneous change in the state of a software application. Peripheral devices can operate without intervening the processor, which only needs to be active for data processing purposes.

Context: EBC can be used when a software application has to react to events caused by a peripheral device. This pattern is suitable for time-critical systems.

Preconditions: This pattern requires peripheral devices with interrupt support and build-in trigger functionalities e.g. ADCs combined with comparators or external devices (e.g. NXP CLRC663 plus).

Problem: How can a system be able to process discrete events but remain in a low power state most of the time?

Realization: Polling forces the application to constantly query peripheral devices. This behavior produces wait cycles and keeps the processor in active mode permanently, which leads to a significantly increased power consumption. Avoidable wait cycles can be replaced by interrupts and interrupt service routines (ISR). An application can enable the processor to enter a low power mode and configure peripherals to wake up the processor if necessary.

Impact on Non-functional Requirements

Figure 4 outlines the basic power characteristics of the EBC design pattern.

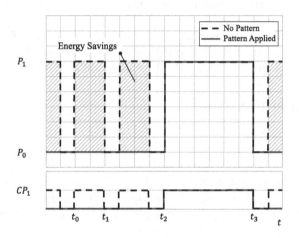

Fig. 4. EBC power characteristics.

Energy Consumption: The upper part of Fig. 4 contains the power levels P_0 for the low power mode and P_1 for the active mode of a processor. When no pattern is applied, the application in this basic example constantly queries a peripheral device at a fixed interval. For a better understanding of the behavior, we introduce the terms *miss* and *hit*. A *miss* is defined as a polling operation where the result does not lead to a behavioral change of the application (e.g. a following data processing). In case of a hit, the result exceeds an internal threshold and the data from a peripheral device leads to computationally intensive operations. When this pattern is applied, the processor will be notified and can query peripheral devices if necessary and directly start computationally intensive operations. To reduce complexity, the duration of a hit and the interrupt solution are equal. The following declarations are required to describe the behavior:

$$\Delta t_{miss} = t_1 - t_0 \qquad \Delta t_{hit} = \Delta t_{interrupt} = t_2 - t_3 \qquad \Delta P_{10} = P_1 - P_0 \qquad (5)$$

In Eq. 6, n defines the number of polling requests which do not lead to further data processing (*miss*). Energy savings result from the avoidance of such polling requests. The *efficiency factor* $\eta_P = 1$ since the basic implementation of this pattern doesn't produce additional power-related overhead, if $\Delta t_{hit} = \Delta t_{interrupt}$.

$$E_{polling} = n \cdot (\Delta t_{miss} \cdot \Delta P_{10}) + \Delta t_{hit} \cdot \Delta P_{10} \tag{6}$$

$$E_{interrupt} = \Delta t_{hit} \cdot \Delta P_{10} \tag{7}$$

$$EB_P = E_{polling} - E_{interrupt} = n \cdot (\Delta t_{miss} \cdot \Delta P_{10}) \tag{8}$$

Execution Time/Latency: Changing from a polling to an event-based approach has no negative effect on time-behavior. Event-driven software applications are suitable for real-time requirements. Because the processor operates in a low power mode in this basic example, additional overhead based on context switching when handling interrupts is not considered.

Consequences: Interrupts generally causing changes in the workflow and structure of the application, which has to be considered. Pin-based interrupts require additional wires or lines which can lead to hardware design changes.

4.3   Pattern: PowerMonitor

General Information
Other Names: None

Strategy: The PowerMonitor design pattern [37] reduces the active *time* (t) of a peripheral device and the overall *capacity* ($n \cdot C$) of the system. It automatically disables all peripheral devices and interfaces which are no longer in use or requested by any part of the application.

Related Patterns: None

Known Uses: Known as power-gating [14], the principle of this design pattern is used at the block level of the integrated circuit design (hardware layer).

Description
Abstract: This design pattern considers the power consumption properties of internal peripheral devices of a system on a chip (SoC) and external peripheral devices. This also includes interfaces with various devices connected to it. The centralized approach allows a deep knowledge of devices and can disable or change their power modes dynamically when they are temporarily not needed.

Context: The PowerMonitor can be used when an application has to periodically access peripheral interfaces and devices. It can also be applied when a centralized and fine-grained hardware access control has to be achieved.

Preconditions: The software application requires access of all considered interfaces (e.g. I^{2}C) and must have the capability to disable and enable external devices (e.g. sensors and actuators) as well as clocks of functional units.

Problem: How can a software application with a fine-grained dynamic power consumption strategy be implemented, which only enables peripheral devices on request? Additionally, how can conflicts between sleep modes (e.g. preventing software from being executed) and use cases with continuous tasks be addressed?

Realization: A reference implementation follows a template meta-programming approach is described in our previous work [37].

Impact on Non-functional Requirements

The *power-timing diagram* in Fig. 5 sketches the power characteristics of the PowerMonitor design pattern.

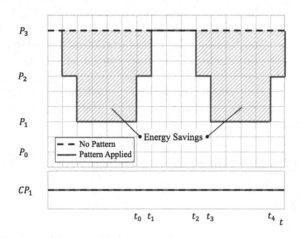

Fig. 5. PowerMonitor power characteristics [32].

Energy Consumption: In this example we assume, that the considered functional unit and the peripheral device are disabled before t_0. This state is denoted as P_1. At first, the functional unit (e.g. I^{2}C) to access devices is enabled at t_0. Afterwards at t_1, the peripheral device (e.g. sensor connected via I^{2}C) gets enabled. The following declarations are required to describe the behavior:

$$T = t_4 - t_0 \qquad \Delta P_{21} = P_2 - P_1 \qquad \Delta P_{31} = P_3 - P_1 \qquad (9)$$
$$\Delta t_{10} = t_1 - t_0 \qquad \Delta t_{21} = t_2 - t_1 \qquad \Delta t_{32} = t_3 - t_2 \qquad (10)$$

For the time frame Δt_{21}, the application can use the device without any loss of functionality. During Δt_{21} the power consumption level is P_3. After utilization, the PowerMonitor dynamically disables the external device and the functional unit while the power consumption drops back to the previous level P_1. Possible energy savings can be calculated using Eq. (9)–(10) and are related on the power consumption of the SoC's functional unit ΔP_{21} and the external device ΔP_{31}.

$$
\begin{aligned}
E_{normal} &= T \cdot \Delta P_{31} \\
E_{monitor} &= \underbrace{(\Delta t_{10} + \Delta t_{32}) \cdot \Delta P_{21}}_{\approx 0} + \Delta t_{21} \cdot \Delta P_{31} \\
EB_P &= E_{normal} - E_{monitor} \\
&= \Delta P_{31} \cdot (T - \Delta t_{21})
\end{aligned}
\tag{11}
$$

The first part of $E_{monitor}$ can be ignored since enabling functional units usually takes only a few clock cycles. The computing power (lower part of Fig. 5) is not affected by this pattern and remains constant at level CP_1. The *efficiency factor* $\eta_P = 1$ because the basic concept does not require additional energy.

Execution Time/Latency: Additional latencies are caused by application overhead and during switching affected hardware on and off. These kinds of latencies cannot be generalized because they depend on the specific implementation of the software application and hardware layer characteristics. Therefore, latencies are not considered in the description of the basic concept shown in Fig. 5.

Consequences: Switching peripheral devices on and off in a short interval can lead to increased power consumption, e.g. by re-establishing a radio connection or the preheating phase of gas sensors.

4.4   Pattern: Direct Memory Access Delegation (DMAD)

General Information
Other Names: None

Strategy: The process of transferring a huge amount of data can take a long time and depends on the clock settings of the used transfer bus, the source's reading speed as well as the destination's writing speed. During this transfer time, the processor core is operating in active mode. The strategy of this pattern is to use the Direct Memory Access (DMA) peripheral to handle the data and memory transfer without the usage of a processor, which can be set to a low power mode to reduce power consumption. This leads to a lower overall capacity $(n \cdot C)$ if devices can be turned off completely. Additionally, DMA transfer is usually faster, which also reduces the active time t of a system.

Related Patterns: None

Known Uses: High Speed Serial Port [9] describes a hardware interface design pattern where the DMA is used to transfer data between a serial device and memory without intervention of the processor.

Description

Abstract: The Direct Memory Access Delegation (DMAD) pattern optimizes the power consumption of a system by using the DMA for data transfers between peripheral devices and memory units. The processor, which would otherwise be responsible for the communication, can be set to a lower power mode.

Context: This design pattern is highly suitable for use cases, where larger data transfers or continuous data streams need to be processed automatically. The processor can be set to a low power state if no other application workload has to be computed for the data transfer period. This pattern should also be considered if a high-speed data transfer up to 100 Mbps is needed since a DMA needs fewer clock cycles compared to a processor.

Preconditions: This design pattern requires a processor with DMA capability.

Problem: How can data be transferred between peripheral devices or memory units without using the processor?

Realization: DMAD is independent of the software application but depends on the hardware platform and the wiring of the DMA. DMA controllers and interrupts are typically configured during the application's initialization phase. The processor only needs to respond to those interrupts and ISRs which for example are triggered when a data transfer task by the DMA is finished. Common use cases are audio and video data streams and continuous ADC values, which can be directly transferred into the memory or to other peripheral devices.

Impact on Non-functional Requirements

Figure 6 outlines the power characteristics of the DMAD design pattern.

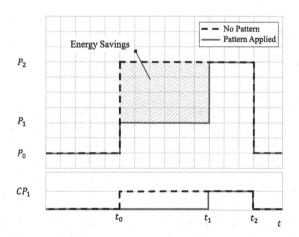

Fig. 6. DMAD power characteristics.

Energy Consumption: For a basic understanding of the impact on power consumption and time behavior, the *power-timing diagram* describes only a simplified use case. The upper part in Fig. 6 shows the temporal behavior and the power consumption levels of the pattern. P_0 is defined as the state where the processor core and DMA are operating in a low power mode. In P_1 the DMA is active and in P_2 the processor is operating. For simplification, the configuration overhead and possible power consumption when the DMA is idling are ignored. To calculating the *energy balance* EB_P, we define:

$$\Delta P_{10} = P_1 - P_0 \qquad\qquad \Delta P_{20} = P_2 - P_0 \qquad (12)$$

$$\Delta t_{10} = t_1 - t_0 \qquad\qquad \Delta t_{20} = t_2 - t_0 \qquad (13)$$

For this pattern EB_P can be calculated using Eq. (12)–(13):

$$EB_P = E_{normal} - E_{dma} \qquad (14)$$

$$= (\Delta t_{20} \cdot \Delta P_{20}) - (\Delta t_{10} \cdot \Delta P_{10} + \Delta t_{21} \cdot \Delta P_{20}) \qquad (15)$$

$$= \Delta t_{10} \cdot (\Delta P_{20} - \Delta P_{10}) \qquad (16)$$

Since DMAD not require additional power consumption or computing power effort, the *efficiency factor* can be defined as $\eta_P = 1$.

Execution Time/Latency: Due to the use of the DMA, this pattern accelerates the data transfer which has a positive impact on the overall execution time. Furthermore, the processor core can use the number of cycles saved for other tasks.

Consequences: An additional overhead is caused by the configuration of the DMA device. For example, if only a few data values have to be read from the ADC, additional processor cycles for setting up the DMA controller neutralize the effect of the design pattern. In addition, the structure of the application has to be reviewed to support interrupts.

4.5   Pattern: Mirroring

General Information
Other Names: None

Strategy: This design pattern describes strategies to lower the time (t) and capacity ($n \cdot C$) (cf. Sect. 3.2) of a system by shifting the application (partly) between processor cores during runtime. The execution time of compute-intensive parts can be reduced by migrating from an energy-efficient to a high-performance core. When a significant amount of idle time exists, tasks can be moved from a high-performance to an energy-efficient core.

Related Patterns: If multiple cores are used simultaneously for a short period of time to finish the workload earlier, it corresponds to the *Race-To-Sleep* design pattern (c.f. Sect. 4.6).

Known Uses: ARM's big.LITTLE describes a technology for heterogeneous multiprocessor architectures. With this architecture, ARM is able to assign threads either to a high-performance or energy-efficiency core depending on the expected computational intensity [39].

Description
Abstract: The Mirroring design pattern is able to migrate an application or parts of the workload (tasks) between processor cores with different levels of power consumption. It can be adapted for heterogeneous and multi-core processors.

Context: Developing energy-efficient applications in situations where the underlying hardware architecture contains multiple cores and the execution environment of tasks can be controlled dynamically.

Preconditions: A typical configuration consists of a fast, high-performance processor core alongside a slower, energy-efficient core. Each processor/core must be able to communicate with other processors/cores (e.g. signaling) and to change the operation mode or the operating frequency during runtime.

Problem: How can a software application or parts of the application (tasks) be switched dynamically between individual cores of a multi-core system or processors during runtime to increase energy efficiency?

Realization: The concept of this pattern can be applied to different processor architectures. A proposed software-based implementation was presented in [32]. With support of technologies like ARM's big.LITTLE, tasks can be switched between cores without the need to extend parts of the software design.

Impact on Non-functional Requirements
Figure 7 outlines the basic power characteristics of the Mirroring design pattern. *Energy Consumption*: The purpose of this pattern is to optimize the power consumption by dynamically controlling different cores of a processor or multiple processors of a system. The impact on power consumption depends on how the cores are controlled. Figure 7 shows the *power-timing diagram* as an example for a dual-core processor consisting of an energy-efficient core and a high-performance core. The use case describes a migration of a task running on a high-performance core to an energy-efficient core. The upper part of Fig. 7 describes the power consumption P of the processor, with P_0 if both cores are in sleep mode, P_1 if the energy-efficient core is active, P_2 if the high-performance core is active and P_3 if both cores are active. The computing power CP is defined as CP_1 for the energy-efficient core, CP_2 for the high-performance core, and CP_3 as the computing power for both cores. The mirroring of a task starts at t_0. The application moves relevant tasks from the high-performance to the energy-efficient core. During this time frame, both cores are active and causing a power-consumption overhead. At t_1, the high-performance core is set into a low

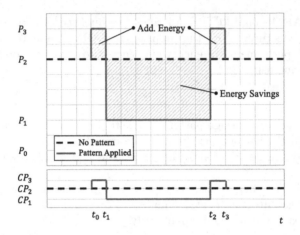

Fig. 7. Mirroring power characteristics.

power mode. Between t_1 and t_2, the system is utilizing the low-power core. At t_2, the process of task mirroring by shifting back to the high-performance core. We define:

$$\Delta t_{10} = t_1 - t_0 \qquad \Delta t_{21} = t_2 - t_1 \qquad \Delta t_{32} = t_3 - t_2 \qquad (17)$$

$$\Delta P_{21} = P_2 - P_1 \qquad \Delta P_{32} = P_3 - P_2 \qquad (18)$$

$$\frac{\Delta P_{32}}{\Delta P_{21}} = q_P < 1 \qquad \frac{\Delta t_{10}}{\Delta t_{21}} = q_t < 1 \qquad (19)$$

and assume that $\Delta t_{32} = \Delta t_{10}$. Using Eq. (17)–(19), EB_P can be calculated:

$$\begin{aligned} EB_P &= E_{save} - E_{add} \\ &= \Delta P_{21} \cdot \Delta t_{21} - 2 \cdot \Delta P_{32} \cdot \Delta t_{10} \qquad (20) \\ &= \Delta P_{21} \cdot \Delta t_{21} (1 - 2 \cdot q_P q_t) \end{aligned}$$

The *efficiency factor* is specified as $\eta_P = (1 - 2 \cdot q_P q_t)$. For a given $q_p = 0.125$ and $q_t = 0.1$, *efficiency factor* can be calculated as $\eta_P = 0.975$. The efficiency of this design pattern highly depends on the application's workflow as well as processor characteristics. Each change of a state (e.g. go-to-sleep and wake-up) consumes energy by the process of loading and unloading transistors, which has to be considered in the application design [38].

Execution Time/Latency: This pattern impacts the execution time in two different ways. The first impact is related to the overhead during the execution of the application responsible for the task control. The second impact is caused by the migration process itself. Additionally, if a task is moved between two differently clocked cores, the execution time can be shortened or extended.

Consequences: This pattern can be modified to assign m different tasks to n cores ($m \geq n$) . Development costs are low if processors/cores have the same architecture, compiler, and programming language. If source code for a task has to be ported from e.g. C++ to Assembler, the development costs will increase due to the variety of implementations for the same task.

4.6   Pattern: Race-To-Sleep

General Information
Other Names: Race-To-Idle, Race-To-Halt, Race-To-Zero, Race-To-Black.

Strategy: Race-To-Sleep can be applied in two basic variants to influence the time behavior (t). In a single-core environment, the processor uses the highest possible operating frequency to compute the application workload as fast as possible. After the associated task is finished, the processor switches to a low-power state to save energy. The second variation is defined for a multi-core environment, where the application can be split and executed on different processor cores.

Related Patterns: When applied to a single-core environment, the concepts is equal to DFS [27].

Known Uses: The basic concept of this pattern is used for speed scaling in [3]. A multi-core scenario is described in [31].

Description
Abstract: This design pattern can influence the dynamic part P_{dyn} and static part P_{stat} of the power consumption described in Sect. 3.1. The implementation type depends on processor characteristics and the application structure. Computing-intensive applications can profit especially from this pattern. In single-core usage, the highest possible operating frequency can be used. Applied on a multi-core processor, the application can be split and executed on different processor cores.

Context: Race-To-Sleep can be used in situations where applications are computationally intensive or contain computational intensive sections.

Preconditions: The processor must be able to change the frequency during run-time when used in single-core environments. In multi-core setups for parallel processing, software developers must ensure, that the application can be (partly) parallelized and does not induct bottlenecks due to serialization.

Problem: How can an application be computed as fast as possible while also maximizing the time a system can operate in a low-power mode?

Realization: The basic concept of this design pattern can be applied by adjusting the frequency or by splitting the workload to different cores. Frequency alteration has to be supported by the operating system or has to be implemented using software libraries and advanced algorithms. A simple approach can be achieved by measuring the current workload or using provided performance counters of the processor. For a dual-core processor, a fork-join approach can be used to split the workload and speed-up the computation.

Impact on Non-functional Requirements
The impact of this pattern is demonstrated using a dual-core processor example.

Energy Consumption: The upper part of the *power-timing diagram* (Fig. 8) shows the temporal behavior of the pattern with the power consumption levels P_0 for the low-power or sleep mode, P_1 for the normal mode, and P_2 for the race mode. In this example, only one processor core is active in P_1 while in P_2 both cores are used.

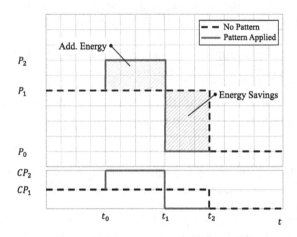

Fig. 8. Race-To-Sleep power characteristics [32].

When a single-core processor is used, P_2 defines the mode where the maximum frequency is used. In the lower part of Fig. 8, CP_1 describes the computing power for the normal mode and CP_2 for the race mode. The time between t_0 and t_1 specifies the active time of the race mode while t_2 defines the beginning of the sleep mode. With this pattern applied, the application enters race mode at t_0, where the computing power and power consumption, are increased. When the computation is finished, the application switches back to the sleep mode at t_1. To calculate the effectiveness, the following declarations and assumptions are required:

$$\Delta P_{10} = P_1 - P_0 \qquad \Delta P_{21} = P_2 - P_1 \qquad \Delta P_{21} < \Delta P_{10} \qquad (21)$$

$$\Delta t_{10} = t_1 - t_0 \qquad \Delta t_{21} = t_2 - t_1 \qquad \Delta t_{10} \geq \Delta t_{21} \qquad (22)$$

$$\frac{\Delta P_{21}}{\Delta P_{10}} = q_P < 1 \qquad \frac{\Delta t_{10}}{\Delta t_{21}} = q_t \geq 1 \qquad (23)$$

q_P is defined as the quotient between the power consumption and q_t as the quotient between the duration of the race mode P_2 and normal mode P_1. EB_P can be calculated using Eq. (21–23) and is positive if the energy savings are larger than the additional energy required to finish the computing earlier.

$$EB_P = E_{save} - E_{add} \qquad (24)$$

$$= \Delta P_{10} \cdot \Delta t_{21} - \Delta P_{21} \cdot \Delta t_{10} \qquad (25)$$

$$= \Delta P_{10} \cdot \Delta t_{21}(1 - q_P q_t) \qquad (26)$$

The *efficiency factor* η_P can be defined as $(1 - q_P q_t)$. As an extension of our previous work, we evaluate our model using Amdahl's law [26] which describes the execution time of an application when switching from a sequential to a parallel approach. The speedup S can be defined as:

$$S = \frac{T_S}{T_P} = \frac{1}{f + \frac{1-f}{p}} \qquad (27)$$

T_S is defined as the sequential execution time, f is the sequentially performed proportion of an algorithm with $0 \leq f \leq 1$, p defines the number of used processor cores and T_P the parallel execution time with $T_P = f \cdot T_S + (1 \cdot f)/p \cdot T_S$. Those definitions can be used to redefine some of our calculations:

$$\Delta t_{20} = T_S \qquad \Delta t_{10} = T_P \qquad (28)$$

$$\frac{\Delta P_{21}}{\Delta P_{10}} = g \cdot (p - 1) = q_P \qquad \frac{\Delta t_{10}}{\Delta t_{21}} = \frac{T_P}{T_S - T_P} = \frac{1}{S - 1} = q_t \qquad (29)$$

$g = [0, 1]$ is defined as the relative proportion $(\frac{\Delta P_{21}}{\Delta P_{10}})$ of the power consumption of an additional processor core.

$$EB_P = (\Delta P_{10} \cdot (T_S - S_P)) - (\Delta P_{10} \cdot g \cdot (p - 1) \cdot T_P) \qquad (30)$$

$$= \Delta P_{10} \cdot (T_S - T_P)(1 - q_P \cdot \frac{T_P}{T_S - T_P}) \qquad (31)$$

$$= \Delta P_{10} \cdot \Delta t_{21}(1 - q_P \cdot q_t) \qquad (32)$$

$$\eta_P = 1 - g \cdot (p - 1) \cdot \frac{1}{(S - 1)} = 1 - q_P \cdot q_t \qquad (33)$$

Considering the MPC8641 multi-core system [34] as an example. The additional energy consumption is 30% ($g = 0.3$) higher compared to a single-core usage. With an overhead of 10% (non-parallelizable part of the application) $f = 0.1$ and a dual core setup ($p = 2$), the following calculations for η_P can be performed.

$$S = \frac{1}{0.1 + 0.45} = 1.81 \implies q_t \approx 1.2, \; q_p = 0.3 \qquad (34)$$

$$\eta_P = 1 - (0.3 \cdot 1.2) = 0.64 \qquad (35)$$

Execution Time/Latency: The pattern accelerates the processing and has therefore a positive effect on the application's runtime. The overall execution time of an application is difficult to predict if power consumption levels are changing dynamically during runtime.

Consequences: Developers have to consider other peripheral devices (e.g. timers) when adjusting the frequency of a processor, because they may use the same clock generators. Clock-rate changes can also lead to negative side-effects and undefined behavior when timer-related intervals are used. The application has to be designed without blocking accesses and waiting periods, because they cannot be parallelized and are reducing the overall efficiency.

5   Discussion

The design pattern framework has been evaluated by achieving a uniform description of various design patterns. The *power-timing diagram* sketches the behavior of each pattern focusing on power consumption during runtime. The introduced metrics are a helpful tool to quantifiably describe power-related aspects and to compare the energy efficiency of a pattern implemented on different systems. While the framework enables the described advantages, it currently also has two limitations. First, the *efficiency factor* is not suitable for comparing different patterns used on the same hardware configuration. Second, meta-design patterns like energy-aware user interfaces (e.g. energy-adaptive displays) are currently not supported the framework.

6   Conclusion

In this paper, we presented a novel approach to include power consumption in the description of software design patterns for embedded systems. First, we identified power consumption characteristics and described the impact of software on those characteristics. Second, a framework to describe energy-aware software design patterns has been proposed. The approach extends well-known pattern descriptions with attributes related to power consumption and time behavior, which are also part of the proposed *power-timing diagram* as a uniform graphical behavior description. Additionally, we introduced two metrics *energy balance* EB_P and *efficiency factor* η_P to express the effectiveness of a design pattern for a given use case. EB_P describes the difference between the ability to save energy and additional energy consumption. η_P makes possible energy savings quantifiable and can describe the trade-off between energy savings and energy overhead of a pattern. The introduced design pattern framework can be used by both researchers and software developers. Researches can uniformly document new design patterns using the provides framework structure, metrics, and power-timing diagram while software developers use the introduced design pattern catalog to address energy-related problems. Furthermore, the uniform representation achieved by the framework can help to speed-up the selection of best-fitting design pattern and the overall decision-making process.

Future work following the current results includes an analysis of the impact on power consumption in situations where more than one pattern is used simultaneously. Additionally, we want to extend framework description for energy-aware user interfaces.

References

1. Abd El-Mawla, N., Badawy, M., Arafat, H.: Iot for the failure of climate-change mitigation and adaptation and IIot as a future solution. World J. Environ. Eng. **6**(1), 7–16 (2019). https://doi.org/10.12691/wjee-6-1-2
2. Abdulsalam, S., Lakomski, D., Gu, Q., Jin, T., Zong, Z.: Program energy efficiency: The impact of language, compiler and implementation choices. In: International Green Computing Conference (IGCC), pp. 1–6. IEEE, Piscataway (2014)
3. Albers, S., Antoniadis, A.: Race to idle. ACM Trans. Algorithms **10**(2), 1–31 (2014). https://doi.org/10.1145/2556953
4. Armoush, A.: Design patterns for safety-critical embedded systems. Ph.D. thesis, Aachen (2010). http://publications.rwth-aachen.de/record/51773
5. Banerjee, A., Chattopadhyay, S., Roychoudhury, A.: On testing embedded software. In: Advances in Computers, vol. 101, pp. 121–153. Elsevier (2016)
6. Bunse, C., Höpfner, H.: Resource substitution with components - optimizing energy consumption. In: ICSOFT - Proceedings of the 3rd International Conference on Software and Data Technologies, Volume SE/MUSE/GSDCA, Porto, Portugal, 5–8 July, pp. 28–35. INSTICC Press (2008)
7. Douglass, B.P.: Real-Time Design Patterns: Robust Scalable Architecture for Real-Time Systems. The Addison-Wesley Object Technology Series. Addison-Wesley, Boston, London (2003)
8. Douglass, B.P.: Design Patterns For Embedded Systems in C: An Embedded Software Engineering Toolkit. Newnes/Elsevier, Oxford and Burlington (2011)
9. EventHelix.com Inc.: High speed serial port design pattern (2019). http://www.eventhelix.com/RealtimeMantra/PatternCatalog/high_speed_serial_port.htm. Accessed 03 Aug 2020
10. Feitosa, D., Alders, R., Ampatzoglou, A., Avgeriou, P., Nakagawa, E.Y.: Investigating the effect of design patterns on energy consumption. J. Softw. Evol. Process **29**(2), e1851 (2017). https://doi.org/10.1002/smr.1851
11. Gamma, E., Helm, R., Johnson, R., Vlissides, J.M.: Design Patterns: Elements of Reusable Object-Oriented Software. Addison-Wesley Professional, Bosto (1994)
12. Grunwald, A., Schaarschmidt, M., Westerkamp, C.: Lorawan in a rural context: Use cases and opportunities for agricultural businesses. In: Mobile Communication - Technologies and Applications; 24. ITG-Symposium, pp. 134–139. VDE-Verl. GmbH, Berlin (2019)
13. Hammadi, A., Mhamdi, L.: A survey on architectures and energy efficiency in data center networks. Comput. Commun. **40**, 1–21 (2013)
14. Jiang, H., Marek-Sadowska, M., Nassif, S.R.: Benefits and costs of power-gating technique. In: International Conference on Computer Design. pp. 559–566. IEEE Computer Society, Los Alamitos (2005)
15. Kim, N.S., et al.: Leakage current: Moore's law meets static power. Computer **36**(12), 68–75 (2003). https://doi.org/10.1109/MC.2003.1250885

16. Landau, H.J.: Sampling, data transmission, and the Nyquist rate. Proc. IEEE **55**(10), 1701–1706 (1967). https://doi.org/10.1109/PROC.1967.5962
17. Lim, C., Ahn, H.T., Kim, J.T.: Predictive dvs scheduling for low-power real-time operating system. In: 2007 International Conference on Convergence Information Technology, pp. 1918–1921. IEEE Computer Society, Los Alamitos (2007)
18. Litke, A., Zotos, K., Chatzigeorgiou, A., Stephanides, G.: Energy consumption analysis of design patterns. Int. J. Electr. Comput. Energ. Electron. Commun. Eng. **1**(11), 1663–1667 (2007)
19. Maleki, S., Fu, C., Banotra, A., Zong, Z.: Understanding the impact of object oriented programming and design patterns on energy efficiency. In: 8th International Green and Sustainable Computing Conference (IGSC), pp. 1–6. IEEE (2017)
20. Miśkowicz, M.: Event-Based Control and Signal Processing. Embedded Systems. CRC Press, Boca Raton (2016)
21. Noureddine, A., Rajan, A.: Optimising energy consumption of design patterns. In: Proceedings of the 37th International Conference on Software Engineering, ICSE 2015, vol. 2, pp. 623–626. IEEE Press, Piscataway (2015)
22. NXP Semiconductors: An11783 - clrc663 pluslow power card detection (2017). https://www.nxp.com/docs/en/application-note/AN11783.pdf
23. Object Management Group: Unified Modeling Language, Version 2.5.1. OMG Document Number formal/17-12-05 (2017). https://www.omg.org/spec/UML/2.5.1/
24. Oshana, R., Kraeling, M.: Software Engineering for Embedded Systems: Methods, Practical Techniques, And Applications. Newnes/Elsevier, Waltham (2013)
25. Pang, C., Hindle, A., Adams, B., Hassan, A.E.: What do programmers know about software energy consumption? IEEE Softw. **33**(3), 83–89 (2016)
26. Patterson, D.A., Hennessy, J.L.: Computer Organization and Design: The Hardware/Software Interface. The Morgan Kaufmann Series in Computer Architecture and Design. Elsevier/Morgan Kaufmann, Amsterdam and Boston (2014)
27. Pering, T., Burd, T., Brodersen, R.: The simulation and evaluation of dynamic voltage scaling algorithms. In: Chandrakasan, A., Kiaei, S. (eds.) Proceedings. pp. 76–81. ACM Order Dept, NY (1998). https://doi.org/10.1145/280756.280790
28. Procaccianti, G., Lago, P., Bevini, S.: A systematic literature review on energy efficiency in cloud software architectures. Sustain. Comput. (SUSCOM) **7**(9), 2–10 (2015). https://doi.org/10.1016/j.suscom.2014.11.004
29. Reinfurt, L., Breitenbücher, U., Falkenthal, M., Leymann, F., Riegg, A.: Internet of things patterns for devices. In: 2017 Ninth international Conferences on Pervasive Patterns and Applications (PATTERNS), pp. 117–126 (2017)
30. Reinfurt, L., Breitenbücher, U., Falkenthal, M., Leymann, F., Riegg, A.: Internet of things patterns for devices: Powering, operating, and sensing. Int. J. Adv. Internet Technol. **10**, 106–123 (2017)
31. Rossi, D., Loi, I., Pullini, A., Benini, L.: Ultra-low-power digital architectures for the internet of things. In: Alioto, M. (ed.) Enabling the Internet of Things, pp. 69–93. Springer, Cham (2017). https://doi.org/10.1007/978-3-319-51482-6_3
32. Schaarschmidt, M., Uelschen, M., Pulvermüller, E., Westerkamp, C.: Framework of software design patterns for energy-aware embedded systems. In: Proceedings of the 15th International Conference on Evaluation of Novel Approaches to Software Engineering, vol. 1: ENASE. pp. 62–73. INSTICC, SciTePress (2020)
33. Shu, T., Xia, M., Chen, J., Silva, C.D.: An energy efficient adaptive sampling algorithm in a sensor network for automated water quality monitoring. Sensors **17**(11), 2551 (2017). https://doi.org/10.3390/s17112551

34. Svennebring, J., Logan, J., Engblom, J., Strömblad, P.: Embedded multicore: An introduction (2009). https://www.nxp.com/files-static/32bit/doc/ref_manual/ EMBMCRM.pdf
35. Tan, T.K., Raghunathan, A., Jha, N.K.: Software architectural transformations: a new approach to low energy embedded software. In: Design, Automation, and Test in Europe Conference and Exhibition. pp. 1046–1051. IEEE Computer Society, Los Alamitos (2003). https://doi.org/10.1109/DATE.2003.1253742
36. Tobola, A., et al.: Sampling rate impact on energy consumption of biomedical signal processing systems. In: IEEE 12th International Conference on Wearable and Implantable Body Sensor Networks (BSN), pp. 1–6. IEEE (2015)
37. Uelschen, M., Schaarschmidt, M., Fuhrmann, C., Westerkamp, C.: Powermonitor: design pattern for modelling energy-aware embedded systems. In: Proceedings of the International Conference on Embedded Software Companion, EMSOFT 2019, ACM, New York (2019). https://doi.org/10.1145/3349568.3351551
38. Urard, P., Vučinić, M.: IoT nodes: system-level View. In: Alioto, M. (ed.) Enabling the Internet of Things, pp. 47–68. Springer, Cham (2017). https://doi.org/10.1007/ 978-3-319-51482-6_2
39. Yu, K., Han, D., Youn, C., Hwang, S., Lee, J.: Power-aware task scheduling for big.LITTLE mobile processor. In: International SoC Design Conference (ISOCC), 2013, pp. 208–212. IEEE (2013)
40. Zurawski, R.: Embedded Systems Handbook: Networked Embedded. Network Embedded Systems, Systems. CRC Press, Boston (2017)

Towards Evolvable Ontology-Driven Development with Normalized Systems

Marek Suchánek[1,2(✉)] 📙, Herwig Mannaert[2,3] 📙, Peter Uhnák[4] 📙, and Robert Pergl[1] 📙

[1] Faculty of Information Technology, Czech Technical University in Prague, Thákurova 9, Prague, Czech Republic
marek.suchanek@fit.cvut.cz, robert.pergl@fit.cvut.cz
[2] Faculty of Business and Economics, University of Antwerp, Prinsstraat 13, Antwerp, Belgium
herwig.mannaert@uantwerpen.be
[3] Normalized Systems Institute, University of Antwerp, Prinsstraat 13, Antwerp, Belgium
[4] NSX bvba, Wetenschapspark Universiteit Antwerpen, Galileilaan 15, 2845 Niel, Belgium
peter.uhnak@nsx.normalizedsystems.org

Abstract. Normalized Systems (NS) enables sustainable software development and maintenance using code generation of evolvable information systems from models of so-called NS Elements. To promote semantic interoperability with other conceptual models, RDF and OWL technologies can be used for knowledge representation in NS as it is common within the Semantic Web and Linked Open Data domains. Previous research resulted in initial NS-OWL bi-directional transformation and a prototype tool for its execution. In this extended paper, these efforts are further elaborated into an evolvable solution based on NS Expanders. The transformation utilizes RDF to encode all domain-specific structural knowledge of an NS model to ensure bi-directionality. In addition, it also maps entities of NS metamodel to OWL concepts to serve as an ontology for underlying data. Because of the metacircular NS metamodel, any NS model including the metamodel itself, can be transformed. Moreover, the transformation of application data to or from RDF is also possible. Having the NS metamodel, NS models, and potentially also data in RDF opens further research possibilities in terms of analysis and integrations. The use of NS Expanders caused that the solution can be easily extended and refined, e.g. when the metamodel is updated. The results of our research are expected to help with the design of real-world information systems, including the NS tooling and the metamodel.

Keywords: Normalized systems · Ontology engineering · Model-driven development · Transformation · RDF · Expanders

© Springer Nature Switzerland AG 2021
R. Ali et al. (Eds.): ENASE 2020, CCIS 1375, pp. 208–231, 2021.
https://doi.org/10.1007/978-3-030-70006-5_9

1   Introduction

Normalized Systems (NS) theory [20] describes how to build evolvable systems as fine-grained modular structures. The theory is applicable to any domain related to building some systems, for example, electrical or civil engineering. However, it also describes how to build evolvable-proven software using so-called Elements. NS theory is used already in practice to build, maintain, and evolve various real-world and large-scale information systems [8,22]. The realization of the NS theory exists in the form of code expanders and related tools to support their execution, modelling NS Elements, and manage systems as applications and their instances. The expanders are used to produce evolvable enterprise information systems from models of its components, custom code fragments, and technological settings. When change occurs in a model or technologies, the application can be easily expanded again with the new modifications [7,15].

The NS models currently tie domain-specific knowledge (entities, their attributes, processes, or views on entities) together with implementation-specific configurations (data validation, form-rendering, attributes visibility, schedule triggers, or integrations with external systems). The import and export functionalities use XML format that is convenient to store data but not efficient for integration and analysis. This is where help can be sought in ontologies that are widely used in the software engineering domain to describe the meaning of data in a machine-actionable and yet flexible format [3]. We aim to eliminate the issues using the Resource Description Framework (RDF) and the Web Ontology Language (OWL). More specifically, our goal is to devise bi-directional transformation between NS models and OWL ontologies and to implement a tool for executing this transformation similarly to the existing custom-XML import and export. Having RDF representation of the NS model will allow to (re-)use many of existing tools and techniques widely used in the Semantic Web and Linked Data domains.

This paper extends the previous [27], where we designed initial bi-directional transformation between Normalized Systems Elements and OWL domain ontologies. It also describes how we implemented a prototype using Java technologies. The extension first focuses on an essential issue of our previous work – evolvability. The prototype tested and proved the possibilities of exchanging OWL ontologies and NS Elements models (including the NS metamodel), but as a standalone tool with dependencies of NS-related Java libraries, it would be unsustainable for the longer term when changes in NS metamodel occurs. Moreover, we deal also with other issues, such as violation of the "Don't Repeat Yourself" (DRY) principle, that we discuss further. All those issues are solved using the transition from the standalone tool into NS expanders. Finally, valuable comments from experts on the transformation are incorporated.

The paper first introduces relevant topics and related work together with our previous research in Sect. 2. Then, we describe our approach in three parts. Section 3 clarifies the design of the transformation for both directions between OWL and NS as well as shows the differences from the original transformation. Then, Sect. 4 explains the transition from standalone Java tool to NS Expanders for running the transformation. The transformation is then demonstrated in the example case in Sect. 5. Various aspects of our solution, together with the comparison between the current and the previous tools are discussed in Sect. 6. Finally, Sect. 7 suggests possible future steps.

2   Related Work

In this section, we provide a brief overview of the relevant topics together with references that are vital for our research. The overview provides a necessary context for our approach and describes the previous work done on the transformation between NS and OWL.

2.1   RDF and OWL Technologies

An ontology in terms of computer science is a definition of concepts together with their taxonomies, properties, and relationships. Sometimes it is also defined as a "specification of a conceptualization", which shows the relations to conceptual models [12]. Both ontologies and conceptual models share the same goal to capture the semantics of a particular domain. The Web Ontology Language (OWL) is a declarative language for expressing ontologies, i.e. sets of precise descriptive statements [14]. OWL is built on top of the Resource Description Framework (RDF); however, OWL is a higher conceptual language and provides additional semantics not available in RDF. OWL provides a machine-actionable and straightforward way of describing a domain using classes, properties, and individual using so-called triples: statement with subject, predicate, and object. International resource identifiers (IRIs) are commonly used for unique and persistent identification of concepts [3].

Ontology engineering is a discipline dealing with designing and building ontologies. It encompasses various formal methods and languages for expressing ontologies and extending their capabilities, there not just well-known RDF and OWL – but also SHACL, ShEx, OntoUML, Gellish, and others. The versatility and generality of these technologies allow them to be applied in any field to solve the semantic interoperability problems and to bring semantic clarity for different use cases. Currently, the most significant uses of ontology engineering are observable in fields that are data-intensive, require a lot of data integration, or are based on artificial intelligence method, e.g., life sciences or computational linguistics [13]. By *RDF/OWL*, we denote a model represented as RDF knowledge graph that also contains OWL constructs to form an ontology from that model.

2.2   Normalized Systems

Normalized Systems (NS) theory [20] explains how to develop highly evolvable systems by eliminating combinatorial effects or by putting them systematically under control. It is based on well-known engineering concepts, including basic combinatorics, theoretic stability, or thermodynamic entropy. The book [20] describes avoiding combinatorial effects in the system using four elementary principles: Separation of Concerns, Data Version Transparency, Action Version Transparency, and Separation of States. It results in a fine-grained modular structure composed of so-called Elements. The theory is already applied in practice for several years to develop and maintain evolvable enterprise information systems for various organisations.

To achieve evolvable information systems, it applies a code generation technique producing skeletons from the NS model and custom code fragments. In NS context, the code generators are called Expanders as they expand the system from the NS model, custom code fragments, technological (e.g. Java version) and other configuration options. An Expander is simply said a string template and a definition of mapping to NS model, i.e., what is used from the model in the template. Custom code is then inserted during the expansion to places marked by anchors. Such anchors also exist for so-called expander features that are making even expanders themselves easily extensible. A system can be then built executing various expanders based on the configuration options, e.g., use expanders for Java 1.8, PostgreSQL, and UI styling specific to the organisation. To automate the whole process, Prime Radiant tool serves to design the models in components, configure the application, and maintain deployments. Still, executing expanders and other tasks is possible to do using prepared scripts directly as well [21].

NS theory defines five types of NS Elements: Data, Task, Flow, Connector, and Trigger. Data Elements carry structural information about entities and their attributes and relationships. The current implementation defines Components as re-usable modules describing a specific part of a system, e.g., *account* is a generic component for user accounts and permissions. An Application is then a collection of used components together with additional metadata such as a name or version. Transformation of Data Elements and Components is the primary concern of our work, whereas remaining Elements are concerned with behaviour, orchestration, and interaction. The core of NS metamodel describes these NS Elements and is itself described by them, thus forming a metacircular model (e.g. the Data Element in metamodel is an instance of Data Element). There are various utility tools and libraries that are expanded directly from the NS metamodel that keep them evolvable. For example, the Prime Radiant tool is itself also an evolvable application [19, 21].

2.3   Ontology-Based Information Systems

Similarly to the use of conceptual models in the Model-Driven Development (MDD), ontologies as a domain description can be used in the software development cycle in various ways. First, some libraries and frameworks, e.g. RDF4J [10], Apache Jena [31], rdflib [24], allow to efficiently query and use OWL and RDF specifications to in software. Then, there are persistence libraries for integrating data classes with OWL ontologies or other RDF data and use triplestores as storage similarly to the concept of Object-Relational Mapping (ORM) and relational databases. Example of such approach is, for instance, JOPA [18].

Moreover, ontologies can directly serve as a mean for the design and specification of a software information system itself [17]. That can lead to more precise semantics provided to multiple applications and to controlled correctness of data integration.

There is a whole specialized field on ontology mapping and semantic integration that strives to allow simple and generic re-use, linking, and transformations of ontologies as well as underlying data [26]. In the terms of transformations between various conceptual models (in different language) to OWL ontologies and back, several attempts for UML and especially its Class Diagrams has been made in [11,25], and [32]. There is also a working transformation from ontology-based conceptual modelling language OntoUML (UML profile) to OWL and SWRL [2]. Even closer to our work is the transformation of Extended ER models into OWL described in [30]. These related works represent potential for integration with our bi-directional conversion between NS and OWL.

2.4   Bi-directional Transformations

Bi-directional transformations (often abbreviated as *BX*) are designed for maintaining consistency between two or more representations of the same or overlapping information [6]. If a transformation is bijective can be tested using executing forth and back, and comparison of result with input. Various aspects of transformation can be then evaluated to measure its quality, e.g., completeness, that is subject of benchmarking [1]. There are multiple languages and methods for the specification of bi-directional transformations between models using their respective metamodels.

The most of the existing methods focus on information captured using XML, for example, biXid [16] that is based on *programming-by-relation* paradigm for relations over XML documents, or Multifocal [23] incorporated algebraic rewrite system to transform XML using XSD schemas. In the field of model-driven development, the Janus Transformation Language (JTL) [5] supports non-bijective transformations, including change propagation. The last example, BOTL [4] uses a unique approach to focus on the transformation of objects. As our requirements and goals are very specific and implementation follows certain constraints, it prevents using the existing methods. Nevertheless, the methods of designing BX are a valuable source of information for our design. Naturally, developing a custom tool for transformation is often the most viable solution for custom formats or special needs. In our case, the special need is relating the transformation to specific metamodel whilst retaining its evolvability.

2.5   Transformation Between OWL and NS

In our original work [27], we presented an initial bi-directional transformation between NS Elements models and OWL ontologies. The transformation has been designed for all domain-specific parts of the NS Metamodel (mainly components, data elements and related entities such as fields, projections, and several types of options). To maintain consistency, every construct of NS model is recorded in the ontology as an individual – an instance of its type from NS metamodel ontology (or meta-ontology). It allows transforming NS models to OWL and back without losing any domain-specific information. Then to form a real OWL ontology, it was identified how classes, datatype properties, and object properties together with certain constraints, should be created from the NS model. However, those constructs are ignored for the other direction, and the NS model from OWL is built purely from individuals.

The transformation has been implemented as a prototype standalone application using Java, Apache Jena, and NS packages to manipulate with NS models and their XML representation. We extend the previous work both in transformation rules and implementation as the target is to use NS Expanders to achieve evolvability and increase usability that was limited with the standalone transformation tool. We highlight the additions to the previous research in the respective parts as modifications are done in both transformation design and implementation.

3   Transformation Between RDF/OWL and NS

Our approach first targets the analysis and mapping of NS metamodel and OWL constructs. The mapping is then the basis for designing rules of the bi-directional transformation.

3.1   Transformation Requirements and Resources

To design the desired mapping and transformation, it is needed to specify requirements, i.e., define expectations and available resources. There are significant additions to the previous work [27] as working with the XML representation of NS models is no longer a target and implementation as NS Expanders is pursued. Furthermore, we also refined the existing requirements as follows:

1. Essential parts of the NS metamodel that hold domain-specific structural information must be identified and will be subject of the transformation.
2. The transformation must be lossless, i.e., when the NS model is transformed to RDF/OWL, and back, the essential parts stay the same.
3. The RDF/OWL output of transformation must be related to RDF/OWL of NS metamodel (as it is also an NS model).
4. There must not be any limitations with respect to the size or structure of an NS model, i.e., the transformation must be usable with any valid NS model and any valid RDF/OWL that encodes an NS model.
5. The transformation must be executable without further user intervention, i.e. must be fully automated.

By RDF/OWL we denote that the transformation does not target to produce only OWL-ontologies. We do transform the core of the NS models as OWL (OWL DL). However, when applied in practice, we have quickly discovered that we would like to attach additional information to the models during the transformation itself. For example, attaching version control system information when mining extracting the model files. For such additional information, RDF proven to be sufficient for our current needs.

3.2   Domain-Specific Parts

The first goal is to identify the domain-specific parts of the NS metamodel, i.e. the entities, relations, and attributes that carry the semantics of the domain and are not implementation-related details. We focus purely on the structural part of an NS model as the behavioural part (tasks and flows) is currently tied to the implementation and also does not have a direct counterpart in basic OWL. The essential entities are:

- *Application* ties together Components for some particular purpose and also metadata such as name, version, or description among implementation details. An example would be the Flight Booking App with components Booking, Application, Workflow, etc.
- *Component* is a reusable encapsulation of a model that can be bound to multiple Applications. Besides its metadata, it may specify Component Dependencies and collection of its Data Elements. For example, Booking component can have Finance component as its dependency.
- *Data Element* represents a structural entity or a concept, for instance, Flight, Passenger, or Airline. In NS systems, a Data Element is never represented directly – i.e. there is no `Flight.java` class. Instead, it is always represented by *Data Projections*.
- *Fields* are properties of a Data Element and are the most complicated from the selected entities. Each Field is either Link Field (relationship with a Data Element) or Value Field (traditional attribute with a certain datatype). Moreover, Value Field can be Calculated Field, which is similar to a derived attribute in UML (e.g. `age` calculated using `birthdate` and current date).
- *Data Projection* defines a view on a Data Element to change (usually limit) its Fields, i.e. it specifies a subset of original Fields using Reference Field and can add new Calculated Fields. For example, a *Data projection* (e.g. `FlightData.java`) is concerned with database persistence, and a *Tree projection* (e.g. `FlightTree. java`) is concerned with external interchange (import/export). We will be using this Tree projection as a basis for our transformation. From the NS theory perspective, we can even view the resulting ontology as a projection (an *OWL projection*).
- *Options* of Components, Data Elements, and Fields allow to encode name-value pairs tied to the related entity. Although Options serve for implementation details (enumerated names of such options), they can be used to store custom domain knowledge as well.
- *Types* of Data Elements, Fields, Link Fields, and Value Fields are used to categorize its instances, i.e. form taxonomies semantically. A Value Field Type specifies a datatype, whereas a Link Field Type is used to distinguish types of association between data elements (one-to-many, many-to-many, and directions).

As the transformation must handle the listed entities, it has to be ready for extension and changes in the future. For example, when Tasks and Flows will be adjusted, their incorporation into the transformation must not cause a ripple effect.

3.3 Mapping Between NS and RDF/OWL

The next step is to map the identified entities of the NS metamodel from the previous subsection to constructs in RDF and OWL. The mapping must enable bi-directional transformation without information loss. That is done directly by encoding every domain-specific information from an NS model into an individual of its type from NS metamodel ontology. For example, a data element Aircraft is transformed to an individual of RDF type NS:DataElement and its field callSign will be an individual of NS:Field and NS:ValueField. As every domain-specific information is encoded in RDF, it is then always possible to create back NS model with identical domain-specific part (the implementation-specific information that is not transformed is deliberately lost).

Table 1. Mapping between NS metamodel and OWL constructs.

NS metamodel	RDF/OWL (rdf:type)
Component	OWL:Ontology
Component dependency	OWL:imports
Data element	OWL:Class
Value field	OWL:DatatypeProperty
Link field	OWL:ObjectProperty
Value field type	RDF:datatype (mapping instances)
* (all)	NS:* (individuals)

To form an OWL ontology, some entities of the NS metamodel are additionally mapped to OWL concepts [14]. The mapping is summarized in Table 1. Each transformed NS Component forms a single ontology that can be linked using OWL imports to its dependencies. The metadata of the component annotate the ontology in a de-facto standard way using Dublin Core [9] (e.g. as dcterms:title) A data element becomes an OWL:Class. alue Fields and Link Fields of a Data Element then naturally form OWL:DataTypeProperty and OWL:ObjectProperty respectively. The rdfs:range and rdfs:domain of those properties are used to capture both sides of the relationship: two data elements, or the data element with a datatype. A relationship requires also mapping on the level of individual data types, for example, String from NS will be xsd:string.

With an NS model transformed into OWL ontology (together with its direct RDF representation), it is possible to encode even application instance data as RDF related to the OWL ontology. For example, if there is an instance of the data element Aircraft named myAircraft with field callSign having BEL812, it would result in RDF illustrated in Fig. 1.

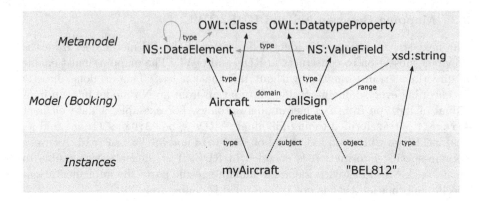

Fig. 1. Example of relations between instance, model, and metamodel.

3.4   Overall Architecture

The defined mapping allows us to define the architecture for the transformation execution. By using NS Expanders to generate the transformation based on the prototype, the overall architecture is significantly enhanced when compared to the previous work. Expanding an NS model to OWL, i.e. developing just string templates for RDF output, would be straightforward and yet evolvable but not bi-directional. Instead, the tool to perform the bi-directional transformation based on an NS model (or metamodel) will be expanded.

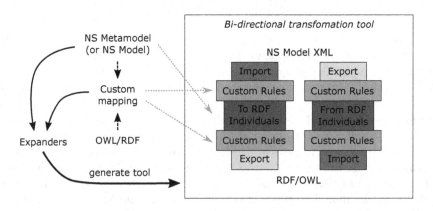

Fig. 2. Architecture of generated transformation tool.

The expanded and therefore, evolvable transformation tool works practically the same as the previous prototype. For the NS → RDF/OWL direction, model from XML is loaded together with relations to the metamodel, individuals are created (optionally together with additional OWL constructs) according to the Table 1, and finally the ontology is exported. For the other direction, an

RDF/OWL file is loaded, and an NS model is reconstructed based on the individuals related to NS metamodel ontology. It is exported again to XML format.

3.5   RDF/OWL Identifiers

A crucial element in building RDF/OWL are identifiers [13]. Although names in OWL are International Resource Identifiers (IRIs), for the time-being we restrict ourselves to Uniform Resource Identifier (URI) subset for compatibility reasons. The identifiers are commonly shortened using defined prefixes, and we do so in provided examples. There are two possibilities of how to create such identifiers for entities. The first is to generate them randomly, e.g. a data element Aircraft would have identifier `booking:bdfe35fe-eeeb-47c9-837e-7bfcf275cb08`. It allows keeping the same identifier even when the entity name changes; however, it is not readable, and more importantly, it would require storing the identifier directly in the NS model to make it persistent. The second option is to compose it from names that further specify it's location and meaning, for example https://example.com/booking/Aircraft/callSign. It plainly captures "what it is" and "where it is" but may cause problems upon renaming.

For the current transformation, the second way of creating identifiers will be used. Even though storing random and unique identifiers would be possible using Options of entities in an NS model, it should be done directly when they are created and not when the transformation is triggered as it may cause consistency issues. Also, for our purposes, the readable and hierarchical identifiers are more convenient. Nevertheless, it should be possible to change the identification mechanism easily in the future.

For our current use, we have opted for the second variant combined with DataRefs of NS models. DataRefs are name-based identifiers utilized by NS models to uniquely identify a particular instance among all instances of an element. For example a Field has a DataRef <`componentName`>::<`dataElement Name`>:: <`fieldName`> (e.g. Field `booking::Aircraft::callSign`). Thus the current naming scheme for the core URI identifiers is https://example.com/projects/bookingApp/v2/field#booking::Aircraft::callSign or https://example.com/projects/bookingApp/v2/application#bookingApp::v2.

Producing consistent URIs based on DataRefs allows us to generate additional RDF data in other tools *independently* of the transformation, as we are able to attach the data without any extra work necessary, such as requiring OWL:sameAs, or maintaining an ID database. Nevertheless, this approach is more appropriate for the metamodel and models. For instance, data, which is typically orders of magnitude larger in volume, using UUIDs or similar may be more appropriate. For this reason, our URI generator is pluggable and can be modified to produce different identifiers without requiring any changes to the transformation code itself.

3.6   NS Metamodel Transformation

The described design of the transformation and the homoiconicity of NS meta-model [19] result in some interesting consequences that deserve to be pointed out. In the NS Elements metamodel, all of the domain-specific parts are modelled as Data Elements. With the mapping in Table 1, the resulting RDF/OWL should contain Data Element (from NS metamodel) both as an OWL Class `DataElement` and an RDF Individual of type OWL Class `DataElement`, i.e. itself. This meta-modelling technique of using a Class at the same time as an Instance is named *punning* [14]. Using a metamodel as a model of itself causes the "Chicken and Egg" problem – NS metamodel in OWL (as a vocabulary) is needed to produce NS metamodel RDF/OWL. To solve the problem, a minimal subset of the vocabulary used to be bootstrapped manually for the first iteration. With NS Expanders we can easily the new solution can expand the full vocabulary of NS metamodel directly.

Another important note must be made concerning the absence of inheritance in NS models. NS models do not permit the use of classical inheritance as it produces high coupling between the involved classes and causes unstable combinatorial effects [20]. Therefore models are "flat", i.e. without any class hierarchy, which is typical for OWL ontologies. However, there are Taxonomy Data Elements as specifications of certain entity types; for example, each instance of Data Element Type defines a specific type of Data Elements. The metamodel also specifies taxonomies, for instance, a Data Element can be of a certain type (e.g. Primary, History, or Directory) and it needs to be a subject of transformation as well.

4   Evolvable Transformation Using NS Expanders

This section focuses the implementation of the transformation as NS Expanders. The solution is put in contrast to the previous standalone traditional Java tool that is described in [27] further denoted as *prototype*.

4.1   Structuring Project

Because the NS codebase is using Java, it is for maintainability reasons used in this project as well just as was in the previous prototype. It allows us to easily convert (although manually) the code fragments of the prototype into expanders. The expanders (code templates and mappings) in our case are used to generating Java classes based on data elements of given NS model. When we want to produce a transformation tool for NS models, the input model for the generation is the NS metamodel. However, it would allow creating a transformation tool for any NS model (e.g. for the Flight Booking App model).

The newly developed tool is composed of two modules. The first module contains only expanded transformation and vocabulary classes. The second module contains hand-written code responsible for loading/writing NS models (from/to XML) and RDF/OWL models, defining URI builder, and other configuration, and

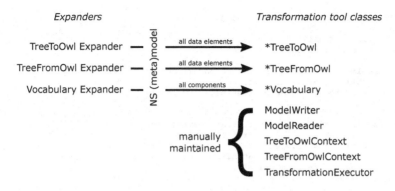

Fig. 3. Parts of transformation tool project.

invoking the transformation module. The entire solution can be used both as a tool (i.e. feed it model and get an RDF/OWL output) or as a library. For example, in one of our use cases, we utilize only a specific subset of transformation classes and invoke them directly from a different codebase. The critical parts of the projects and their relations are depicted in Fig. 3 and further explained below.

4.2   Vocabulary Expander

As explained, to build or read an RDF representation of an NS model, vocabulary of concepts and relationships from the NS metamodel is required. The prototype used the trivial solution: manually hard-coded vocabulary in the form of a Java class. It was just a duplication of the information provided by the

```
public class Elements {

    private static final Model m =
    ↪   ModelFactory.createDefaultModel();

    public static final String NS =
    ↪   "https://example.com/elements#";

    // anchor:dataElements:start
    public static final Resource Application =
    ↪   createResource("Application");
    public static final Property Application_name =
    ↪   createProperty(Application, "name");
    public static final Property Application_components =
    ↪   createProperty(Application, "components");
    //...
}
```

Fig. 4. Example of expanded vocabulary for the core Elements component.

```
public class %dataElement.name%TreeToOwl {

  private final TreeToOwlnContext context;
  private final OntModel model;

  public %dataElement.name%TreeToOwl(TreeToOwlContext context) {
    this.context = context;
    this.model = treeToOwlContext.getModel();
  }

  public Individual project(%dataElement.name%Tree
  ↪   %dataElement.name.firstToLower%Tree) {
    String %dataElement.name.firstToLower%Uri =
    ↪   context.getUri(%dataElement.name.firstToLower%Tree);
    // anchor:custom-uri:start
    // anchor:custom-uri:end

    // anchor:custom-project-before:start
    // anchor:custom-project-before:end

    Individual individual =
    ↪   model.createIndividual(%dataElement.name.firstToLower%Uri,
    ↪   %componentName.firstToUpper%.%dataElement.name%);
    individual.addProperty(NSX.dataRef,
    ↪   %dataElement.name.firstToLower%Tree.getDataRef().toString());

    // anchor:value-fields:start
    %valueFields:valueField(); separator="\n"%
    // anchor:value-fields:end

    // anchor:link-fields:start
    %linkFields:linkField(); separator="\n"%
    // anchor:link-fields:end

    // anchor:custom-project:start
    // anchor:custom-project:end

    return individual;
  }
}
```

Fig. 5. Part of the TreeToOwl expander.

metamodel. Therefore, it is an easy task to design an expander to generate this Java class with vocabulary. The expander is usable for any component, and for each component of given NS model, it results in a class similar to example in Fig. 4. The vocabulary class is then used both by the expanded transformation classes, as well as any additional custom code.

4.3   TreeToOwl Expander

The second expander generates *TreeToOwl classes that handle transformation of an entity from input NS model to its OWL/RDF representation (e.g. DataElement TreeToOwl). It based on the *TreeToOwl classes from the prototype with several improvements as shown in Fig. 5. First, all objects that are necessary for executing the transformation (output OntModel[1] model, URI builder,

---

[1] OntModel is an instance of OWL model in Apache Jena.

```
public Individual project(ComponentTree componentTree) {
  String componentUri = projectionContext.getUri(componentTree);
  // anchor:custom-uri:start
  // anchor:custom-uri:end

  // anchor:custom-project-before:start
  Ontology ontology = model.createOntology(componentUri + "/ontology");
  ontology.addProperty(DC.title, componentTree.getName());
  ontology.addProperty(DC.description, componentTree.getDescription());
  ontology.addProperty(OWL.versionInfo, componentTree.getVersion());
  // anchor:custom-project-before:end

  Individual individual = model.createIndividual(componentUri,
  ↪   Elements.Component);
  individual.addProperty(NSX.dataRef, componentTree.getDataRef().toString());

  // anchor:value-fields:start
  individual.addProperty(Elements.Component_name,
  ↪   componentTree.getName().toString());
  [...]
  // anchor:value-fields:end

  // anchor:link-fields:start
  for (DataElementTree dataElement : componentTree.getDataElements()) {
    individual.addProperty(Elements.Component_dataElements,
    ↪   projectionContext.getUri(dataElement.getDataRef()));
  }
  [...]
  // anchor:link-fields:end

  // anchor:custom-project:start
  // anchor:custom-project:end

  return individual;
}
```

Fig. 6. Example of ComponentTreeToOwl.java file.

or lookup table) are passed together as `TreeToOwlContext`. For every data element of the input NS model, a `*TreeToOwl` class is created with a single `project` `NSElementTree` → `Individual` method that implements transformation of the Tree projection onto an OWL projection (as described in Sect. 3). During the projection, the Individual is populated with data and object properties based on the source value fields and link fields.

The additional constructs that need to be added to the `OntModel` based on Table 1 are handled using harvested custom code. For example, to add Ontology information for Components, as shown in Fig. 6, we utilize `custom-project-before` anchor that is injected from a so-called harvest file during a code expansion – here namely `ComponentTreeToOwl.java.harvest` (Fig. 7). This custom code is also harvested (extracted) from the source code; thus developers can write the code directly in the generated files. Using `custom-*` anchors is the primary way we inject additional statements into expanded code. Necessary Java imports (here for the Dublin Core (DC) vocabulary), are also injected from the harvest file. It further enhances the evolvability and versatility of the transformation.

```
-- anchor:custom-imports:start
import org.apache.jena.ontology.Ontology;
import org.apache.jena.vocabulary.DC;
import org.apache.jena.vocabulary.OWL;
-- anchor:custom-imports:end
-- anchor:custom-project-before:start
Ontology ontology = model.createOntology(componentUri +
  ↪  "/ontology");
ontology.addProperty(DC.title, componentTree.getName());
ontology.addProperty(DC.description,
  ↪  componentTree.getDescription());
ontology.addProperty(OWL.versionInfo,
  ↪  componentTree.getVersion());
-- anchor:custom-project-before:end
```

Fig. 7. Example of ComponentTreeToOwl.java.harvest file.

4.4   TreeFromOwl Expander

The TreeFromOwl expander is in its logic and structure very similar to the TreeToOwl expander, just for the other direction of transformation. It is used to generate *TreeFromOwl classes based on its predecessor from the prototype. Again, the context container is used to pass all required objects. The main method accepts an individual of the corresponding RDF:type and returns an NS model object. For example, DataElementTreeFromOwl is used for individuals of type NS:DataElement for which it returns DataElementTree. The related entities are recursively linked to the returned entity. For instance, to return DataElementTree, all related fields are found in the RDF model and added as FieldTree objects.

4.5   Non-expanded Code

As explained, the transformation tool also uses code that is not expanded. It is everything that needs to be present for executing the transformation but is not related to the model. This part of the project consists of the two classes for the contexts (one per direction), reader and writer helper classes (working with XML and RDF files), and a single class that executes the transformation based on user's command and options. Based on the selected transformation direction together with provided input and output file/folder, it loads the model, executes the transformation by expanded classes, and stores the result. Although the code is manually written and maintained, it is only a small fraction of the entire code base, thus significantly reducing the overall maintenance burden.

5   Demonstration Case

In this section, we show how the transformation tool (generated using the NS metamodel) can be used in a simple use case. The example demonstrates usage of both directions of the transformation and use of existing tools for both NS models and OWL ontologies. The results are further discussed in Sect. 6. With respect to the prototype [27], the provided example did not significantly change as the outputs of the transformation are the same.

5.1   Flight Booking NS Model

For this example, we use a simple model of *Flight Booking* domain that is used across this paper. In the NS terminology, it is a single component with six data elements where each has several fields (both link and value) as shown in Fig. 8. The model includes both many-to-many and one-to-many relationships. Also, various types of value fields are being used, including Date, String, Boolean, or Double. As such and notwithstanding its size, the example model contains most commonly used structural types.

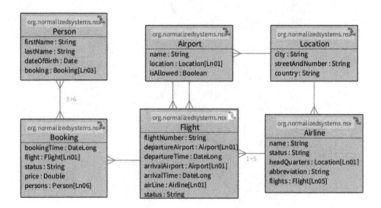

Fig. 8. The example NS model for flight booking domain [27].

5.2   Flight Booking NS Ontology

Figure 9 is an example of transformation output in RDF Turtle format. Figure 10 shows the result of NS-to-OWL transformation in WebVOWL tool. All six data elements became classes (light blue circles) with is-a relationship to external *DataElement* from the metamodel ontology (dark blue circle). The link fields (i.e. relationships) are also present in the ontology as object properties with navigation between classes, e.g. *headQuarters* between *Airline* and *Location*. Both bi-directional relationships (*Person-Booking* and *Flight-Airline*) are present and connected as inverse object properties. Finally, matching datatypes (yellow boxes) were used for generated datatype properties based on value fields.

```
<https://example.com/demobookingapp/V2/application#bookingApp::1.0>
a elements:Application ;
gp:branch <https://example.com/demobookingapp/branch/V2> ;
# ...
elements:Application_baseVersion    "" ;
elements:Application_description    "" ;
elements:Application_disabled       "" ;
elements:Application_name           "bookingApp" ;
elements:Application_releasePeriod  "Wed Feb 28 08:40:00 CET 2018" ;
elements:Application_shortName      "bookingApp" ;
elements:Application_version        "1.0" ;
nsx:dataRef                         "bookingApp::1.0" .
```

Fig. 9. Example of Turtle RDF file for the Booking App.

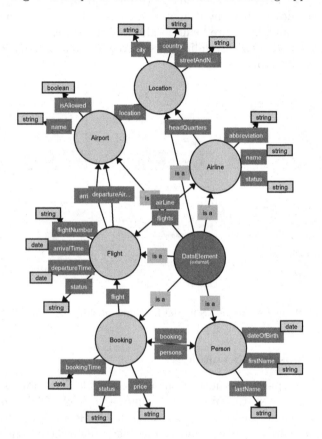

Fig. 10. The generated OWL ontology for flight booking domain [27]. (Color figure online)

5.3   Refining RDF/OWL

With an RDF representation of the Booking component, we can take advantage of various existing tools for managing OWL ontologies and RDF data. To show this in practice, we refine *streetAndNumber* property to two using well-known

Protégé. First, we rename the existing property to *street* (alternatively we could create a new and delete the old one). Then, we add a new datatype property *number* with domain *Location* and range *xsd:int*. To enable transformation back to an NS model, we need to do the same with the corresponding individuals of type *ValueField* according to the metamodel ontology. The final step is to transform it back to the NS model. Like this, we could change also object properties, classes, or change any NS-related individuals.

5.4   Information System Generated from RDF

When the refinements are done, we can proceed to expand an enterprise information system for flight booking management from the model or ontology (as they are now interchangeable). The current NS tools allow to expand the application, build the application, and then even manage the application instance efficiently using a single user interface. The refinement within *Location* entity where *street* and *number* replaced *streetAndNumber* is visible in Fig. 11. Thanks to Normalized Systems, the model (or ontology) can be continually refined, and the application can be re-generated.

After the regeneration of an existing application instance, data are automatically migrated as long as the naming is preserved. For example, with the change that we made, all records of *Location* would remain with its *city* and *country*, *streetAndNumber* would disappear and both *number* and *street* would be empty. To handle such change, data migration must be handled separately.

Fig. 11. Screenshot from generated NS application [27].

6   Evaluation

We summarize the key aspects of our work and evaluate fulfilment of the requirements in this section. The main focus is evolvability of the solution that was demonstrated in Sect. 5. Further empirical evaluation requires long-term use in various real-world scenarios. As a benefit of the design, potential refinements can be easily adopted in the implementation and distributed through NS applications.

6.1   Transition from Traditional Utility to Expanders

It is evident that the transition from standalone Java tool (the prototype) to partially-expanded tool significantly improved the solution. By using the NS Expanders to generate the transformation tool, it automatically covers all entities captured as Data Elements in the (meta)model. For the Elements component of the NS metamodel, the generated tool for bi-directional NS-OWL transformation consists of 175 generated classes (87 per direction and one vocabulary) using three expanders and just five custom classes for execution and input/output operations. As a result, we need to maintain only a small set of 10 classes, and small sections of custom code harvests instead of incurring the full cost of developing and maintaining hundreds of classes. A change in the NS metamodel can be easily reflected in the transformation tool just by re-generating it.

All of the OWL concepts that are mapped in Table 1 are covered. No additional OWL constructs are mapped to as of yet, and are subject to further exploration. Finally, the use of expanders enabled to create the transformation tool not just for the NS metamodel, but for any NS model.

6.2   Evolvability of Transformed Ontology

The other level of evolvability aside from the tool is the evolvability of the transformed ontology. It can be transformed again via XML representation when there is a change in an NS model and vice versa. In case of a change in the NS metamodel, first, the tool must be re-generated, and then ontology can be transformed with the new NS metamodel relations. Despite the absence of a mechanism for merging independent changes in both representations, correct OWL handling can avoid some conflicts. First, the version number of an NS component is used for versioning its OWL counterpart. Then, by using principles of linked data, no changes should be made directly in the generated ontology, unless they are intended. Instead, additional statements and annotations of the NS model in OWL should be made externally, and attached using OWL imports. For the future, it may be needed to implement consistency checking and even merging the changes when loading both an NS model and related OWL ontology using comparison and user interaction.

6.3   Consistency and Integrity

All information from an NS model that is modelled in the metamodel as a Data Element is during the transformation encoded in RDF. That covers all the domain-specific entities listed in Sect. 3 (e.g. a Component is a Data Element in the metamodel). Moreover, it includes any other information, including Task Elements, Flow Elements, etc. Everything that is transformed in RDF can be then also transformed back to an NS model. For the other direction, one can compose RDF according to the NS metamodel ontology, transform it into an NS model and back. Any entity that is not related to the NS metamodel well be ignored. The transformation is bi-directional and consistent on the defined constructs by the NS metamodel ontology. With both directions possible, it is feasible to maintain integrity between an NS model and corresponding RDF/OWL side-by-side.

7   Future Work

This section outlines the possibilities of subsequent research and work based on the results presented in the paper.

7.1   Extending NS Meta-ontology

The metamodel of NS models, i.e., NS Elements model, can change over time when there is a need to incorporate new concepts or to refine existing (for instance, adding a particular type of relationships for aggregation). Such changes are, of course, made carefully to maintain compatibility with existing systems. There are additional constructs and concepts in different conceptual or systems modelling languages the we are interested in incorporating into Normalized Systems metamodel in a way compliant with the NS theory. One example of this is the inheritance that is very common on the conceptual level but causes combinatorial effects on the implementation of level [20, 28].

In RDF and OWL, it is an essential technique to refine concepts by adding statements about and relate them together with others. In the future, we want to extend the ontology of NS metamodel with additional concepts (such as inheritance). Firstly, that will enhance possibilities of semantic integration with other models where such concept exists with the same or at least similar semantics. Secondly, it will provide a simple description of how the new (or changed) concept is related to the existing metamodel that can be used as a description for adoption. Finally, additional information can be added for documentation or other purposes, e.g., that some construct is deprecated.

7.2   Integrations with Conceptual Models

The use of flexible and interoperable format elevates possibilities in terms of semantic integration. There are various attempts and solutions for transforming conceptual models in different modelling languages to and from RDF or OWL (for example, we reviewed these possibilities for UML [29]). It is, therefore, possible to map or even translate multiple domain models on the level of OWL ontologies together with Normalized System models. That can be used, for example, to generate Normalized Systems from UML models.

Such integration would also be possible with the XML format with use of XSLT rules, but that would lack flexibility and evolvability. Moreover, incorporating interoperability of new modelling language (or its standard) would cause a combinatorial effect. The ontological layer serves as a generic interface for integration, and each modelling language can be "plugged in" independently. This topic surely requires further research with experiments on real-world scenarios to achieve consistent integration between NS and conceptual model (e.g. in UML). Nevertheless, the advantages are evident – the possibility to directly generate an evolvable enterprise information system from a conceptual model. Directly from analysis, one could get a prototype of the system where changes in the model are propagated to the implementation just by clicking a button.

7.3   Analysis of Real-World Systems

With the use of RDF and OWL, there are also other advantages aside from the semantic integration and linked data. Using the RDF representation of a Normalized System, it can be easily analysed with SPARQL queries. It could answer simple questions such as how many data elements are in the component to more advanced, e.g., find all duplicate attributes in terms of name, type, and options across the component. The queries are not limited only to one system, and analysis can be done to compare two or more systems or even to find some similarities in order to design some common components. Other queries can be related to systems data and for example, count usage of the relationship between data elements in the real use. Finally, SPARQL queries could also be used to update the model of a system, e.g., when there is a need to change multiple models in the same way.

Again, such queries or similarity analysis of multiple systems could be done on an XML level but with significantly more effort. With NS models encoded in RDF, existing tooling designed for big/linked data analysis and semantic inference can be used easily. We plan to use SPARQL and other related technologies to analyse and improve real-world, large-scale systems in the future. Design of queries for analysis purposes will be the subject of future research. We already utilize a subset of the generated RDF data and use SPARQL to draw insights across our projects.

8   Conclusion

In this extended paper, we followed on the previous work. The initial NS-OWL transformation has been proposed together with the standalone prototype tool in Java. The transformation no longer focuses mainly on OWL as an output, but rather on the RDF description of an NS model that was previously used as a necessary addition for assuring bi-directionality. The most significant step forward is re-using the prototype and developing NS Expanders to generate it from the NS metamodel (or any NS model). It makes the whole solution extensible for the future development related to the metamodel enrichment as we explained in the evaluation. The bi-directional transformation has been demonstrated on an example that concludes by generating an NS application and produces the same results as with the previous prototype. Refining the solution into the form of NS Expanders helped to make it evolvable, versatile, and maintainable (e.g. by avoiding code duplication), yet offering the same desired outputs. Other advances of the solution, as well as new open research paths for the future, were discussed. The transformation and expanders are ready to be used with real-world, large-scale NS applications for analysis, interoperability, or other purposes.

Acknowledgements. The research was performed in collaboration of Czech Technical University in Prague, University of Antwerp, and NSX bvba. The research was supported by Czech Technical University in Prague grant No. SGS20/209/OHK3/3T/18.

References

1. Anjorin, A., Diskin, Z., Jouault, F., Ko, H.S., Leblebici, E., Westfechtel, B.: BenchmarX reloaded: a practical benchmark framework for bidirectional transformations. In: Proceedings of the 6th International Workshop on Bidirectional Transformations co-located with The European Joint Conf. on Theory and Practice of Software, BX@ETAPS 2017, Uppsala, Sweden, 29 April 2017. CEUR Workshop Proceedings, vol. 1827, pp. 15–30. CEUR-WS.org
2. Barcelos, P.P.F., dos Santos, V.A., Silva, F.B., Monteiro, M.E., Garcia, A.S.: An Automated Transformation from OntoUML to OWL and SWRL. Ontobras **1041**, 130–141 (2013)
3. Bhatia, M., Kumar, A., Beniwal, R.: Ontologies for software engineering: past, present and future. Indian J. Sci. Technol. **9**(9), 1–16 (2016). https://doi.org/10.17485/ijst/2016/v9i9/71384
4. Braun, P., Marschall, F.: Transforming object oriented models with BOTL. Electron. Notes Theor. Comput. Sci. **72**(3), 103–117 (2003). https://doi.org/10.1016/S1571-0661(04)80615-7
5. Cicchetti, A., Di Ruscio, D., Eramo, R., Pierantonio, A.: JTL: a bidirectional and change propagating transformation language. In: Malloy, B., Staab, S., van den Brand, M. (eds.) SLE 2010. LNCS, vol. 6563, pp. 183–202. Springer, Heidelberg (2011). https://doi.org/10.1007/978-3-642-19440-5_11
6. Czarnecki, K., Foster, J.N., Hu, Z., Lämmel, R., Schürr, A., Terwilliger, J.F.: Bidirectional transformations: a cross-discipline perspective. In: Paige, R.F. (ed.) ICMT 2009. LNCS, vol. 5563, pp. 260–283. Springer, Heidelberg (2009). https://doi.org/10.1007/978-3-642-02408-5_19
7. Bruyn, P.: Towards designing enterprises for evolvability based on fundamental engineering concepts. In: Meersman, R., Dillon, T., Herrero, P. (eds.) OTM 2011. LNCS, vol. 7046, pp. 11–20. Springer, Heidelberg (2011). https://doi.org/10.1007/978-3-642-25126-9_3
8. De Bruyn, P., Mannaert, H., Verelst, J., Huysmans, P.: Enabling normalized systems in practice – exploring a modeling approach. Bus. Inf. Syst. Eng. **60**(1), 55–67 (2017). https://doi.org/10.1007/s12599-017-0510-4
9. Dublin Core Metadata Initiative and others: Dublin Core Metadata Element Set, version 1.1 (2012)
10. Eclipse Foundation: rdf4j (2019). https://rdf4j.org
11. Gasevic, D., Djuric, D., Devedzic, V., Damjanovi, V.: Converting UML to OWL oOntologies. In: Proceedings of the 13th International Conference on World Wide Web - Alternate Track Papers and Posters, WWW2004, New York, USA, 17–20 May 2004, pp. 488–489. ACM. https://doi.org/10.1145/1013367.1013539
12. Guarino, N., Oberle, D., Staab, S.: What is an ontology? In: Staab, S., Studer, R. (eds.) Handbook on Ontologies. IHIS, pp. 1–17. Springer, Heidelberg (2009). https://doi.org/10.1007/978-3-540-92673-3_0

13. Hitzler, P., Gangemi, A., Janowicz, K.: Ontology Engineering with Ontology Design Patterns: Foundations and Applications, Studies on the Semantic Web, vol. 25. IOS Press (2016)
14. Hitzler, P., Krötzsch, M., Parsia, B., Patel-Schneider, P.F., Rudolph, S., et al.: OWL 2 web ontology language primer. W3C Recomm. **27**(11), 123 (2009)
15. Huysmans, P., Verelst, J.: Towards an engineering-based research approach for enterprise architecture: lessons learned from normalized systems theory. In: Franch, X., Soffer, P. (eds.) CAiSE 2013. LNBIP, vol. 148, pp. 58–72. Springer, Heidelberg (2013). https://doi.org/10.1007/978-3-642-38490-5_5
16. Kawanaka, S., Hosoya, H.: biXid: A Bidirectional Transformation Language for XML, pp. 201–214 (2006). https://doi.org/10.1145/1159803.1159830
17. Křemen, P., Kouba, Z.: Ontology-driven information system design. IEEE Trans. Syst. Man Cybern. Part C (Appl. Rev.) **42**(3), 334–344 (2011). https://doi.org/10.1109/TSMCC.2011.2163934
18. Ledvinka, M., Kostov, B., Křemen, P.: JOPA: efficient ontology-based information system design. In: Sack, H., Rizzo, G., Steinmetz, N., Mladenić, D., Auer, S., Lange, C. (eds.) ESWC 2016. LNCS, vol. 9989, pp. 156–160. Springer, Cham (2016). https://doi.org/10.1007/978-3-319-47602-5_31
19. Mannaert, H., De Cock, K., Uhnak, P.: On the realization of meta-circular code generation: the case of the normalized systems expanders. In: ICSEA 2019, The Fourteenth International Conference on Software Engineering Advances. IARIA (2019)
20. Mannaert, H., Verelst, J., De Bruyn, P.: Normalized Systems Theory: From Foundations for Evolvable Software Toward a General Theory for Evolvable Design. Koppa, Kermt, Belgium (2016)
21. NSX bvba NS Foundation (2019). https://primeradiant.stars-end.net/foundation/
22. Oorts, G., Huysmans, P., De Bruyn, P., Mannaert, H., Verelst, J., Oost, A.: Building evolvable software using normalized systems theory: a case study. In: 2014 47th Hawaii International Conference on System Sciences, pp. 4760–4769. IEEE (2014). https://doi.org/10.1109/HICSS.2014.585
23. Pacheco, H., Cunha, A.: Multifocal: a strategic bidirectional transformation language for XML schemas. In: Hu, Z., de Lara, J. (eds.) ICMT 2012. LNCS, vol. 7307, pp. 89–104. Springer, Heidelberg (2012). https://doi.org/10.1007/978-3-642-30476-7_6
24. RDFLib Team: RDFLib (2019). https://github.com/RDFLib/rdflib
25. Sadowska, M., Huzar, Z.: Representation of UML Class diagrams in OWL 2 on the background of domain ontologies. e-Informatica **13**(1), 63–103 (2019). https://doi.org/10.5277/e-Inf190103
26. Salamon, J.S., Reginato, C.C., Barcellos, M.P.: Ontology integration approaches: a systematic mapping. In: Proceedings of the XI Seminar on Ontology Research in Brazil and II Doctoral and Masters Consortium on Ontologies, São Paulo, Brazil, October 1st-3rd, 2018. CEUR Workshop Proceedings, vol. 2228, pp. 161–172. CEUR-WS.org (2018)
27. Suchánek, M., Mannaert, H., Uhnák, P., Pergl, R.: Bi-directional transformation between normalized systems elements and domain ontologies in OWL. In: Proceedings of the 15th International Conference on Evaluation of Novel Approaches to Software Engineering 2020, vol. 2020, pp. 74–85. INSTICC, SciTePress, Prague, Czech Republic, May 2020. https://doi.org/10.5220/0009356800740085

28. Suchánek, M., Pergl, R.: Evolvability evaluation of conceptual-level inheritance implementation patterns. In: PATTERNS 2019, The Eleventh International Conference on Pervasive Patterns and Applications, vol. 2019, pp. 1–6. IARIA, Venice, Italy, May 2019

29. Suchánek, M., Pergl, R.: Case-study-based review of approaches for transforming UML class diagrams to OWL and vice versa. In: 22nd IEEE Conference on Business Informatics (CBI 2020), vol. 2020, pp. 270–279. IEEE Computer Society, Antwerp, June 2020. https://doi.org/10.1109/CBI49978.2020.00036

30. Telnarova, Z.: Transformation of extended entity relationship model into ontology. In: Nguyen, N.T., Hoang, D.H., Hong, T.-P., Pham, H., Trawiński, B. (eds.) ACIIDS 2018, Part II. LNCS (LNAI), vol. 10752, pp. 256–264. Springer, Cham (2018). https://doi.org/10.1007/978-3-319-75420-8_24

31. The Apache Software Foundation: Apache Jena: A free and open source Java framework for building Semantic Web and Linked Data applications (2019). https://jena.apache.org

32. Zedlitz, J., Jörke, J., Luttenberger, N.: From UML to OWL 2. In: Lukose, D., Ahmad, A.R., Suliman, A. (eds.) KTW 2011. CCIS, vol. 295, pp. 154–163. Springer, Heidelberg (2012). https://doi.org/10.1007/978-3-642-32826-8_16

Improving Node-RED Flows Comprehension with a Set of Development Guidelines

Diego Clerissi[1]([⊠]), Maurizio Leotta[2], and Filippo Ricca[2]

[1] Dipartimento di Informatica, Sistemistica e Comunicazione (DISCO),
Università di Milano-Bicocca, Milan, Italy
diego.clerissi@unimib.it
[2] Dipartimento di Informatica, Bioingegneria,
Robotica e Ingegneria dei Sistemi (DIBRIS), Università di Genova, Genoa, Italy
{maurizio.leotta,filippo.ricca}@unige.it

Abstract. The recent technological advancements has pointed the interest of developers, researchers, and end-users towards the Internet of Things (IoT) domain, whose plethora of services naturally arises to improve the human life. As the IoT becomes more and more involved in our everyday activities, we are personally encouraged to experiment it in practice.

Node-RED tool has emerged as a practical solution to develop IoT systems in a simple manner. The tool was inspired by the flow-based programming paradigm and is built on top of Node.js framework. Its simplicity relies on the visual interface providing built-in functionalities and large customization. Moreover, the Node-RED community is quite active and inclined to offer support and share solutions to integrate within existing systems, therefore it is expected that the produced Node-RED flows are easy to comprehend and re-use. However, to the best of our knowledge, no consolidated approaches or guidelines to develop comprehensible Node-RED flows currently exist.

For this reason, in this paper we, first, propose a set of guidelines aimed at helping Node-RED developers in producing flows easy to comprehend and re-use. Then, we report on an experiment to evaluate the effect of such guidelines on Node-RED flows comprehension. Results show that the adoption of the guidelines has a significant positive effect on both the number of errors and the time required to comprehend Node-RED flows. Finally, we describe an analysis of the Top-100 most downloaded Node-RED flows to discuss about their compliance (or not) with the proposed guidelines.

Keywords: Node-RED · Guidelines · Comprehension · IoT Web based systems · Visual development

© Springer Nature Switzerland AG 2021
R. Ali et al. (Eds.): ENASE 2020, CCIS 1375, pp. 232–260, 2021.
https://doi.org/10.1007/978-3-030-70006-5_10

1   Introduction

In the context of the Internet of Things (IoT), Node-RED has become a practical solution to the development of working solutions and artefacts sharing. Node-RED is a visual Web-based tool inspired by the flow-based programming paradigm [13] and built on top of the Node.js framework. The basic concept of the tool is the *node*, representing part of a service logics and largely configurable. Groups of nodes, called *flows*, collaborate and communicate together when virtually or physically connected.

Nodes are black-box components that hide all the implementation details (i.e., basically, JavaScript functions and graphical features), as suggested by the flow-based programming paradigm [13]. Hence, the developer can select the nodes she desires and wire them together in order to implement the desired system, without having to know their implementation details. Every day, developers participating in the Node-RED community develop and upload new nodes and flows on the Node-RED library (over 2000 nodes in 2020[1]). They represent solutions to general or specific problems, and anyone can download part of this content to integrate it within existing systems. Nodes can execute a variety of tasks, from storing daily weather forecasting data into a database to performing sentiment analysis on the feeds received from a Twitter account. Node-RED gives the developer the freedom of choosing her own *programming style* for the implementation of new nodes and flows, similarly to any other programming tool and language. Given that Node-RED is a visual tool, along with the programming style, the **comprehensibility factor** related to the adopted *graphical style* must also be carefully considered. Such factor can be influenced by the way the nodes are wired together and by the names they are provided with. In general, this is a more frequent problem at design stage. The lack of a disciplined approach for the development of Node-RED flows could result in messy "spaghetti" artefacts that are generally very hard to comprehend and use. This could lead to unexpected outcomes when they are integrated into further complicated systems, without mentioning the problem of maintaining and testing them. Looking at the literature and the practitioner's web sites, no consolidated approaches supporting Node-RED developers in producing reusable and comprehensible flows has been yet proposed, and only few basic and unofficial attempts of defining best practices and design patterns have been made so far[2].

In this paper, we define a set of guidelines aimed at producing Node-RED flows that are easier to comprehend (by construction), and also more suitable to reuse, maintain and test. We have evaluated the benefits of adopting our guidelines through of a controlled experiment involving ten master students, where two selected Node-RED systems, each one developed with and without our guidelines, are compared in a comprehension scenario. Moreover, to determine the compliance with our guidelines of the most used Node-RED flows produced by external sources, we collected and analysed the Top-100 Most Downloaded

---

[1] https://flows.nodered.org/.

[2] https://medium.com/node-red/node-red-design-patterns-893331422f42.

Table 1. Node-RED essential terms and definitions.

Term	Definition
Node	The basic Node RED component, representing (part of) the logics of a service/functionality
	Each node has a type describing its general behaviour and a set of custom properties
Conditional Node	A node specifically designed to check over data and activate alternative scenarios
Flow	The logical way the nodes are wired, expressing how they collaborate by exchanging messages
Sub-Flow	Each self-contained logical portion of a flow, contributing to its completion
Wire	The edge used to graphically connect two nodes in a flow
Pin	The input/output port of a node where a wire enters/leaves
Message	A data object exchanged by some nodes, characterized by a sequence of configurable properties
Global/Flow Variable	A variable defined in a node and visible by all the flows or by just the one containing that node

Node-RED flows from the official repository. This paper is a substantially revised version of our original proposal presented in a conference paper [5]. The main extensions are: (1) a more detailed guidelines description, also with the help of multiple examples (Sect. 2), and (2) an analysis of the Top-100 most downloaded Node-RED flows, to understand their compliance with the guidelines (Sect. 4) together with a discussion of the reasons why some guidelines are satisfied more often than others in the considered flows.

In Sect. 2 the guidelines are described. The experiment investigating the benefits of adopting our guidelines and the corresponding results are discussed in Sect. 3, together with some Node-RED comprehensibility issues pertaining the two selected Node-RED systems showing how the guidelines can be applied on them. Section 4 reports an analysis of the Top-100 most downloaded Node-RED flows from the official web site and their compliance with the guidelines is discussed. Finally, related work are presented in Sect. 5, and the conclusions are discussed in Sect. 6.

2   Proposed Guidelines

The guidelines we propose in this paper address some common Node-RED comprehensibility issues, which may emerge while developing flows or trying to understand and integrate flows provided by an external source (e.g., the Node-RED community library). Issues may concern confusing nodes names, hidden loops and loss of messages, lack of conditional statements, unexpected inactive nodes, and more. More details about issues are provided in Sect. 3.2. The guidelines aim at supporting Node-RED developers in producing flows that are easy to comprehend by construction, and suitable for future reuse, maintenance and testing activities.

The guidelines have been inspired by several design works addressing systems quality using UML and BPMN [1,12,16,18,20], and by our experience in IoT systems design and Node-RED flows development [4,8]. UML is one of the most used notational languages [17], and differs to Node-RED in many aspects: while UML works at design level and describes the static and dynamic details of a system, Node-RED is an executable visual language used to implement, execute and deploy a working system. The constructs they use are quite different, as well as their syntax and semantics. Nevertheless, we have experimented in practice that some design and technology-independent principles can be inherited from UML even to solve specific Node-RED issues [4,8].

To better comprehend the Node-RED terminology and the issues that our guidelines try to address, in Table 1 we recap a short list of terms and definitions, extracted and elaborated from the Node-RED official documentation[3].

The guidelines we propose can be classified into four types, based on the comprehensibility issues they address: **Naming**, **Missing Data**, **Content**, and **Layout**.

2.1 Naming

Node Name Behaviour (NNB). Each Node-RED node should have a unique (unless a duplicate of another existing node) and meaningful name, suggesting its high-level behaviour [7]. The name of a node should make explicit the *action(s)* performed by the node and the *object(s)* receiving such *action(s)*. An *object* may refer to a message property or a global/flow variable, written in upper-case to be more visible within the flow [18]. The name of a node should be concise, otherwise it may indicate that the node is performing too many tasks and has to be simplified. There should not exist two or more nodes having the same name but different behaviours, otherwise this may bring to a comprehensibility issue that has to be solved by renaming the nodes properly. The nodes following a conditional node should make explicit the condition they satisfy, in order to clarify the scenarios they start (e.g., *if VALUE > 10, print VALUE*). Nodes names should avoid any jargonic terminology or overly technical detail. To reach the larger set of Node-RED users, nodes names should be formulated in English. An example of **NNB** applied on a node that receives weather forecasting data

Fig. 1. Node Name Behaviour (NNB) applied.

---

[3] https://nodered.org/docs/.

and parses just the date and the description is shown in Fig. 1; on the left, the original node name is shown, while on the right it is properly renamed.

Flow Name Behaviour (FNB). Each Node-RED flow should have a unique and meaningful name, summarizing in a very concise way its high level behaviour [7]. The name of a flow should provide enough details that, even at a first glance, is able to explain what the flow does. This may include the device the flow communicates with (e.g., Sensor Monitor), the entity or data it manages (e.g., Office Lights Switch), or the environment it lives within (e.g., Kitchen Room). As for nodes, the name of a flow should be formulated in English and avoid any complicated terminology. An example of **FNB** applied is shown in Fig. 2, where the flow name appears in a browser-like tab within the Node-RED environment. Since the flow should elaborate weather forecasting data and report them via SMS and MQTT, its name is changed from left to right.

Fig. 2. Flow Name Behaviour (FNB) applied.

2.2 Missing Data

Node Effective Contribution (NEC). By adapting to Node-RED the terms used by Ambler [1], there should neither exist *black hole* nodes nor *miracle* nodes. A black hole node is a node with no leaving wires but output pins > 0, which means that the node output might be lost or unused by the flow, while a miracle node is a node with no entering wires but input pins > 0, which means that the node cannot be explicitly activated or is missing some data. Besides actual problems in the flow, which may require to address the issue by introducing sub-flows to handle the forgotten black hole or miracle node, the presence of such kind of nodes may also indicate that a previous debugging stage occurred, which isolated some undesired nodes during the process and left them disconnected once completed. An example of **NEC** applied on a node is shown in Fig. 3. The node transforms tweets into colours to later instrument remote LEDs, but is missing the output wires, resulting in lost messages (top

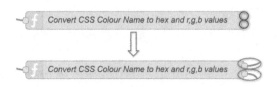

Fig. 3. Node Effective Contribution (NEC) applied. (Color figure online)

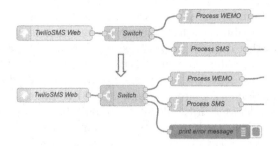

Fig. 4. Conditions Consistency and Completeness (CCC) applied.

red circles). By applying **NEC**, the black hole node is detected and its output handled as desired, by adding the wires that will properly route the output messages (bottom green circles).

Conditions Consistency and Completeness (CCC). The conditions of every conditional node, like the switch node (i.e., a core Node-RED node basically implementing the switch/if constructs of every programming language, and used to route the messages by evaluating a set of conditional statements over global/flow variables or message properties[4]) should not overlap and be complete (i.e., their disjunction returns true) [1,18], in order to handle separately all the possible scenarios. The suggested way for guaranteeing the conditions completion in a flow is to introduce the 'otherwise' statement as ultimate condition within every conditional node, in order to cover any unexpected/wrong alternative scenario. Clearly, this newly additional scenario will likely have to be developed as well (e.g., by simply providing a sub-flow catching and notifying the error once the 'otherwise' condition is matched). An example of **CCC** applied on a Node-RED flow is shown in Fig. 4. The flow receives Twilio[5] calls and manages them either as SMS or WEMO commands[6] (i.e., to control electronic home devices remotely); in the original flow (top) a conditional node considers only the SMS and WEMO alternatives, while the application of **CCC** (bottom) introduces a 'otherwise' alternative to handle unexpected scenarios with a simple debug node printing an error message if, e.g., due to network issues the Twilio request is null or wrongly formatted.

2.3 Content

Sub-Flows Relatedness (SFR). The sub-flows composing a flow should be logically related among each others [7], following the design principle of high cohesion and low coupling [11]. Two sub-flows F1 and F2 are logically related if, e.g.: F1 and F2 describe (part of) the behaviour of the same device; F1 and F2

---

[4] https://nodered.org/docs/user-guide/nodes#switch.
[5] https://www.twilio.com/.
[6] https://www.wemo.com/.

receive/send data from/to the same device; F1 and F2 act in the same environment; F1 and F2 contribute to the same service/functionality; F1 and F2 share some variables or other data; F1 is activated by F2 or vice versa.

The presence of several input sources activating a flow or output destinations receiving the outcome of a flow, or even large nodes or sub-flows performing heterogeneous functionalities, are all hints of a **SFR** failure. **SFR** is just an indicator of a possible issue in the flow, that should be considered the moment the flow has to be restructured, by isolating the unrelated sub-flows and produce equivalent independent flows. An example of a possible **SFR** failure is shown in Fig. 5. The flow takes in input a very generic data structure that can be received from a variety of input sources (red circles), like MQTT and TCP ports, and parses it for a later storage. The presence of such heterogeneous input sources suggests that the flow may have to be restructured as mentioned above.

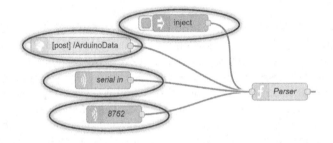

Fig. 5. Sub-Flows Relatedness (SFR) applied to detect possible unrelated sub-flows.

Flow Content (FC). If a flow is overpopulated, its content should be simplified [1, 12, 20], by identifying some of its sub-flows, and either: (a) physically split and virtually connect them together through link nodes (i.e., a core Node-RED node used to add a virtual wire between two sub-flows[7]), or, (b) collapse them into corresponding sub-flow nodes (i.e., a core Node-RED node used to collect sub-flows to favour reuse and reduce layout complexity[8]). Since Node-RED flows design and development phases are strongly related due to the visual nature of the tool, as in the case of more general design activities, there is a positive correlation between flows size and complexity. A flow is then classified as overpopulated if the number of nodes it contains is equal or above 50 [12]. An example of **FC** applied on a flow is shown in Fig. 6. The original flow (on top) is rather simple i.e., it retrieves the content of a file and alternatively defines a new file template and sends it via MQTT (sub-flow 1) or modifies and saves it locally (sub-flow 2). Even though the flow is not overpopulated and does not actually need a simplification, the application of **FC** is provided just as an example. As shown in Fig. 6, the simplification can occur via sub-flow nodes, collapsing

---

[7] https://nodered.org/blog/2016/06/14/version-0-14-released.
[8] https://nodered.org/docs/user-guide/editor/workspace/subflows.

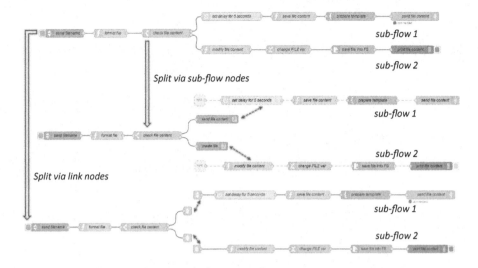

Fig. 6. Flow Content (FC) applied via sub-flow or link nodes.

into them the sub-flows 1 and 2, or via link nodes, hence physically separating sub-flows 1 and 2 from the main sub-flow to keep just virtual connections with them.

2.4 Layout

Wiring Style Consistency (WSC). The wires connecting the nodes should follow a consistent wiring style, to differentiate main/correct scenarios from exceptional/wrong ones [1,16,18,20]. Since Node-RED flows may handle several scenarios, as it happens for classic programming languages concerning conditional statements, different wiring styles may be adopted within the same flow. For example, a "straight, from left to right, top-down" style to wire all the nodes participating in a correct scenario, and a "cascade" style to wire all the nodes participating in a wrong scenario. An example of **WSC** applied on a flow is shown in Fig. 7. The flow tracks local air traffic and, even if quite simple, it adopts an inconsistent wiring style, moving from up to down with no actual meaning. The original wiring style (top) can be reworked in order to produce a more consistent straight flow (bottom).

Wiring Style Tidiness (WST). The wires connecting the nodes should be long enough to clearly show the starting/ending nodes and avoid any overlapping, whether possible [1]. Wires should be drawn in the order they enter/leave a node. The node joining multiple wires should be placed at the level of the node where such wires originated. An example of **WST** applied on a flow is shown in Fig. 8. The large node named *Route Messages* of the original flow (top) routes several measures and information pertaining the inside of a shed, like

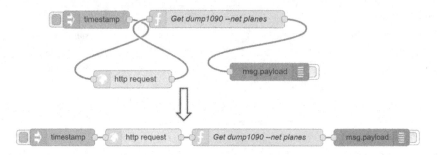

Fig. 7. Wiring Style Consistency (WSC) applied.

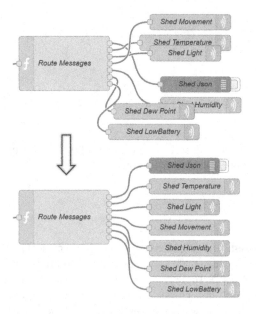

Fig. 8. Wiring Style Tidiness (WST) applied.

temperature, humidity, and light intensity, to a likewise number of devices connected via the MQTT protocol. It is evident that there are several overlapping nodes and entangled wires, all hindering the flow comprehensibility and making hard to track which MQTT node receives what message. The flow is made tidier (bottom) by rearranging the nodes placements and the wires connecting them.

3   Empirical Evaluation of the Comprehension Improvement

Based on the Goal Question Metric (GQM) template [21], the main aim of our experiment can be defined as follows: "Evaluate the effect of the guidelines in Node-RED flows comprehension", with the purpose of understanding if the guidelines are able to improve the *comprehension level* of Node-RED flows and the *time* required to complete tasks pertaining such flows; therefore, consequently, the overall *efficiency* is computed as: *comprehension level* ÷ *time*. The *perspective* is of: a) Node-RED developers, using it for their own purpose and/or sharing artefacts with the community, who may be interested to consider a disciplined technique to develop Node-RED flows using our guidelines; b) teachers and instructors interested to offer courses and tutorials on Node-RED and c), researchers interested in focusing their research activities and study improvements or constraints to the Node-RED language. Thus, our research questions are:

Table 2. Overview of the Experiment.

Goal	Evaluate the effect of the guidelines in Node-RED flows comprehension
Quality focus	Pertaining Node-RED tasks, we evaluate: (i) Comprehension, (ii) Time, (iii) Efficiency
Context	**Objects**: DiaMH and WikiDataQuerying Node-RED systems **Participants:** 10 Computer Science master students
Null Hypotheses	No effect on (i) comprehension, (ii) time, (iii) efficiency
Treatments	Non-compliant ($^-$) and Compliant ($^+$) Node-RED flows
Dependent variables	(i) TotalComprehension to complete Node-RED tasks (ii) TotalTime to complete Node-RED tasks (iii) TotalEfficiency to complete Node-RED tasks

RQ1. Does the comprehension level of Node-RED flows vary when our guidelines are applied?

RQ2. Does the comprehension time of Node-RED flows vary when our guidelines are applied?

RQ3. Does the efficiency of completing tasks pertaining Node-RED flows vary when our guidelines are applied?

To quantitatively investigate the research questions, we used ad-hoc questionnaires containing 16 comprehension questions for each experimental object. We measured the comprehension level of Node-RED flows as the number of correct answers on the total, the time required to provide such answers, and the efficiency as the ratio between the comprehension level and the time required to provide such answers (i.e., the number of correct answers divided by the time is a proxy for measuring the efficiency construct).

Table 2 summarizes the main elements of the experiment, following the guidelines by Wohlin *et al.* [22].

In the following, we describe in detail: treatments, objects, participants, experiment design, hypotheses, variables, procedure, and other aspects of the experiment.

3.1   Treatments

Our experiment has one independent variable (main factor) and two treatments: *Non-compliant* and *Compliant* Node-RED flows. Non-compliant Node-RED flows (in the following, characterized by symbol ⁻) are those produced without following our guidelines, while compliant Node-RED flows (in the following, characterized by symbol ⁺) are those produced following our guidelines.

3.2   Objects

To conduct the experiment we selected two existing Node-RED systems that were developed by former students of the master course Data Science and Engineering (Genova, Italy), as part of the last year project.

The systems, named **DiaMH** and **WikiDataQuerying**, present some common Node-RED comprehensibility issues derived from an undisciplined and basic Node-RED usage (i.e., the teacher of that course was not involved in our research and thus students developed the systems without following any guideline).

DiaMH System. DiaMH is a simulated Diabetes Mobile Health IoT system which monitors a diabetic patient by collecting glucose values using a wearable sensor, sends notifications to the patient's smartphone about the monitored data, and, based on some logical computations involving a cloud-based healthcare system and realistic data patterns, determines the patient's health state (i.e., Normal, More Insulin required, or Problematic) and, when needed, orders insulin injections to a wearable insulin pump. It consists of 71 nodes and 63 wires.

WikiDataQuerying System. WikiDataQuerying is a web query service used to select textual geospatial questions from a predefined list shown in an HTML page, and query WikiData[9] knowledge base, by first restructuring the selected questions into SPARQL query language and formatting them using a Prolog grammar. The results of the queries can be triples adhering to the Resource Description Framework (RDF) language or boolean answers. It consists of 25 nodes and 27 wires.

Applying Guidelines to Node-RED Systems. For the selected Node-RED systems, only some of the aforementioned guidelines have to be applied. However, even such simple systems can hide several comprehensibility issues. Despite their simplicity, involving mainly core Node-RED nodes, DiaMH works in the thorny context of the healthcare and WikiDataQuerying must provide prompted feedback to the user's requests. Therefore, producing Node-RED flows that adhere to our proposed guidelines may improve the comprehensibility level during flows inspection and development, and facilitate the subsequent engineering stages, such as maintainability and testing.

---

[9] https://www.wikidata.org.

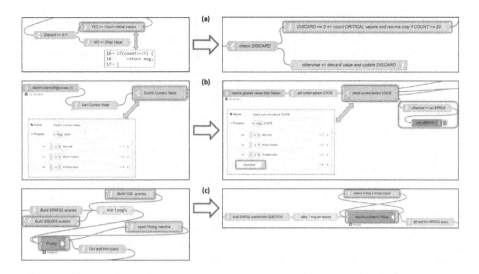

Fig. 9. Issues in Node-RED Systems and Guidelines Application (see [5]).

Just few of the issues we found from a high-level flows analysis of the systems are shown in Fig. 9 and discussed in the following. Most of the nodes names do not clarify their behaviours, forcing the developer to inspect the nodes contents and settings in order to comprehend them. Therefore, **NNB** can be applied to clarify the nodes purposes, by making explicit in their names the performed actions and the used variables in uppercase (see nodes names in Fig. 9, changed from left to right). Sub-flow **(a, left)** of Fig. 9 presents the function node (i.e., a core Node-RED node used to implement customized JavaScript functions[10]) named *Yes =>* *Count critical values*, which performs several actions and then sends a message to subsequent nodes (not shown in Fig. 9) only when a certain condition holds (i.e., `if count >= 20`, see lines 15–17 in Fig. 9 left associated with the node); from an unaware Node-RED developer perspective, this may unexpectedly block the execution of the sub-flow until the condition is satisfied, even if the nodes are graphically connected by means of wires. This comprehensibility issue emerged in several topics posted on the main Node-RED forum[11] and can be solved by applying **NNB**, as previously mentioned, by renaming the function node as, e.g., *DISCARD == 0 => count CRITICAL values and returns only if COUNT* *>= 20*, in order to make explicit the condition it satisfies from the preceding switch node (i.e., *DISCARD == 0*), the core behaviour (i.e., *count CRITICAL* *values*), and the hidden condition for the message to return (i.e., *returns only* *if COUNT >= 20*). Sub-flow **(a, right)** of Fig. 9 is the result. In sub-flow **(b,** **left)** of Fig. 9, the switch node *Switch Current State* hides a severe issue: it considers only three possible values for the `msg.state` variable, but the check will fail and idle the sub-flow execution if any unexpected event sets the variable

---

[10] https://nodered.org/docs/user-guide/nodes#function.

[11] https://discourse.nodered.org/t/function-node-stopping/7017.

to a different value before the switch node. This problem was solved in the dawn era of Node-RED[12] by introducing an "otherwise" entry to handle all the alternative conditions, but the average Node-RED developer may still miss to use it in favour of a more explicit, but incomplete set of conditions[13]. By applying **CCC**, the "otherwise" condition is added to the switch node (see the change in the configuration panel from left to right in Fig. 9), while the application of **WSC** displays in a cascaded wiring style the newly introduced exceptional scenario. Sub-flow **(b, right)** of Fig. 9 is the result. Sub-flow **(c, left)** of Fig. 9 presents several issues. First, the wires do not follow any consistent wiring style (e.g., build the flow by wiring nodes from top to bottom or from left to right, avoiding crossing wires), which reduces the overall comprehensibility[14]. Second, a loop is generated between *Prolog* and *send Prolog newline* nodes; although in this scenario finding the loop is rather simple, it may be harder to detect and produce a weird outcome or overheat the CPU, when more wires are involved[15]. Third, the sub-flow shows three function nodes connected through output pins to *limit 1 msg/s* node, but only *Build SPARQL queries* actually contributes to the flow, since the other two nodes have no entering wires, making them inactive; this case in particular is easy to detect, but could be hard to understand for a novel Node-RED developer, in case she forgets to trace a wire between two nodes to specify the input source or the output destination of a node, without receiving any explicit warning from the Node-RED environment. This issue often arises when there is a need for debugging a flow and some nodes have to be temporary disconnected from it[16]. By applying **WSC** and **WST**, a more consistent and tidier wiring style is generated, to highlight the loop and avoid further entangles, while **NEC** is used to remove the miracle nodes originally named *Build SQL queries* and *Build SQLGIS queries* (i.e., those having input pins but no entering wires, in fact inactive). Sub-flow **(c, right)** of Fig. 9 is the result.

Preparation for the Experiment. We limited each object to just a comparable (in size and complexity) flow of the original behaviour, consisting of 20 nodes and 23 wires for DiaMH and 21 nodes and 21 wires for WikiData-Querying, employing mostly Node-RED core nodes. We carefully inspected and tested both the flows of the systems; these two flows correspond to the non-compliant treatment ($^-$), since our guidelines were not adopted during their implementations. Then, an author of the paper applied the guidelines discussed in Sect. 2 to the initial flows, producing two equivalent compliant versions ($^+$), while another author double checked the newly produced flows. In total, we used four Node-RED flows for executing the experiment: DiaMH$^-$, DiaMH$^+$, WikiDataQuerying$^-$, WikiDataQuerying$^+$.

---

[12] https://github.com/node-red/node-red/issues/88.

[13] https://discourse.nodered.org/t/switch-node-not-consistent/11908.

[14] https://discourse.nodered.org/t/help-simplifying-flow/8765.

[15] https://discourse.nodered.org/t/cpu-hogging-to-100/2944.

[16] https://discourse.nodered.org/t/how-to-comment-out-a-node/1106.

3.3   Participants

We involved ten Computer Science master students of the University of Genova (Italy), that were attending a course on advanced software engineering. The total number of students enrolled in the course was 15, which is basically the average number of students enrolled in any Computer Science Master Course in Genova. They had average knowledge of Software Engineering, UML and JavaScript (the Node-RED core programming language), and few experience in Node-RED and flow-based programming, that was provided in another course related to Node-RED development.

3.4   Experiment Design

Before the experiment, all the participants were involved in a 4-hours lecture split in two days about Node-RED theory and practice using the tool. Participants were provided with material to understand the main Node-RED core nodes, samples of flows and sub-flows to reproduce/change, and questions to answers about comprehensibility issues of the flows similar to those we asked for the later experiment. Participants were not informed about the guidelines, and therefore, about the treatments. Due to the limited number of participants (only ten), we adopted a counterbalanced experiment design ensuring each participant to work in two tasks on the two different objects, receiving each time a different treatment. Since participants had the same experience in Node-RED, acquired by attending another course, we randomly split them into four groups (see Table 3), balancing the representatives for each group. Each participant had to work first on **Task 1** on an object with a treatment, then in **Task 2** on the other object with the other treatment.

Table 3. Experimental Design: $^{+}$ Compliant treatment, $^{-}$ Non-Compliant treatment (see [5]).

	Group A	Group B	Group C	Group D
Task 1	DiaMH^{+}	DiaMH^{-}	WikiDataQuerying^{+}	WikiDataQuerying^{-}
Task 2	WikiDataQuerying^{-}	WikiDataQuerying^{+}	DiaMH^{-}	DiaMH^{+}

3.5   Dependent Variables and Hypotheses Formulation

Our experiment had three dependent variables, on which the treatments were compared measuring three different constructs to answer our three research questions: (a) *Comprehension* of the Node-RED flows (measured by variable *TotalComprehension*), (b) *Time* required to answer the questions pertaining the Node-RED flows (measured by variable *TotalTime*), (c) *Efficiency* in completing the tasks pertaining the Node-RED flows (measured by variable *TotalEfficiency*). For each treatment:

- *TotalComprehension* was computed by summing up the number of correct answers of each participants;
- *TotalTime* was computed as the difference between the stop time of the last question and the start time of the first question, where timing was tracked down in the time sheet by each participant;
- *TotalEfficiency* was derived by the two previously computed variables, as:

$$TotalEfficiency = TotalComprehension/TotalTime$$

Since we could not find any previous empirical evidence pointing out a clear advantage of one treatment versus the other, we formulated the following three null hypotheses as non-directional, with the objective to reject them in favour of alternative ones:

- H_{0a}: $TotalComprehension^- = TotalComprehension^+$
- H_{0b}: $TotalTime^- = TotalTime^+$
- H_{0c}: $TotalEfficiency^- = TotalEfficiency^+$

3.6 Material, Procedure and Execution

To estimate the comprehensibility of the tasks to provide to the participants and the time required to complete them, we conducted a pilot experiment with three participants: two master students in Computer Science not involved in the experiment and one of the authors of this paper. On average, the time required to complete both tasks was about 105 min, with 5 errors. Given such results, we tried to remove any ambiguity from the questions. Then, we uploaded the material on the Moodle module of the course from which the participants were selected, consisting, for each group of Table 3, of: two Node-RED flows (one per system/treatment), two questionnaires containing 16 questions each, and a post-questionnaire to fill after the completion of the two questionnaires containing seven further questions. Each questionnaire presented exactly 7 open questions and 9 multiple choices questions, in order to keep the perceived complexity of both tasks as equivalent as possible. Questions ranged from comprehending the general behaviour of the provided Node-RED flows, like identifying the names and the number of nodes involved in certain activities, detecting the presence of loops and missing conditions in switch nodes, counting the number of intersections among wires, to listing some simple maintenance tasks to do on the flows. Concerning multiple choices questions, only one answer among the proposed was correct and counted 1 point each, while for open questions we gave 1 point to totally correct answers and 0 otherwise. For each object (i.e., DiaMH and WikiDataQuerying), the questions asked to the participants were exactly the same, independently from the treatment that had occurred (i.e., non-compliant or compliant). The participants had to complete each task in the order defined by the group they were assigned to, and to stop each task only when completed. For each task, participants had to import the corresponding Node-RED flow into Node-RED and, for each question, track start time, answer the question,

Table 4. Descriptive statistics per treatment and results of paired Wilcoxon test (see [5]).

Dependent variable	Non-compliant treatment ($^-$)			Compliant treatment ($^+$)			p-value	Cliff's delta
	Median	Mean	St. Dev.	Median	Mean	St. Dev.		
Total comprehension	9.500	9.600	2.319	13.500	12.800	2.044	0.00903	−0.69 (L)
Total time	58.500	71.100	38.484	57.000	59.100	25.291	0.04883	+0.17 (S)
Total efficiency	0.180	0.179	0.109	0.254	0.253	0.100	0.00586	−0.36 (M)

and track stop time. Finally, the participants were asked to complete the post-experiment questionnaire, to collect insights about their skills and motivations for the obtained results. Questions were about the perceived complexity of the two tasks, the exercise usefulness, the feelings and the preferences between the styles of the two flows, and the competencies required to complete the tasks. Answers were provided on a Likert scale ranging from one (Strongly Agree) to five (Strongly Disagree).

3.7 Analysis

Because of the sample size and mostly non-normality of the data (measured with the Shapiro–Wilk test [19]), we adopted non-parametric test to check the three null hypotheses.

Since participants answered to the questions on the two different objects (DiaMH and WikiDataQuerying) with the two possible treatments (non-compliant and compliant), we used a paired Wilcoxon test to compare the effects of the two treatments on each participant. To measure the magnitude of the effects of the two treatments, we used the non-parametric Cliff's delta (d) effect size [6], which is considered small (S) for $0.148 \leq |d| < 0.33$, medium (M) for $0.33 \leq |d| < 0.474$, and large (L) for $|d| \geq 0.474$. We decided to accept the customary probability of 5% of committing Type-I-error [22], i.e., rejecting the null hypothesis when it is actually true.

3.8 Results

In this section, the effect of the main factor on the dependent variables (*Total-Comprehension, TotalTime,* and *TotalEfficiency*), as resulted from the experiment, and the post-experiment questionnaires are discussed. Table 4 summarizes the essential *Comprehension, Time,* and *Efficiency* descriptive statistics (i.e., median, mean, and standard deviation) per treatment, and the results of the paired Wilcoxon analysis conducted on the data from the experiment with respect to the three dependent variables.

H_{0a}: **Comprehension (RQ1).** Figure 10 (left) summarizes the distribution of *TotalComprehension* by means of boxplots. Observations are grouped by treatment (non-compliant or compliant). The y-axis represents the average comprehension measured as number of correct answers on the 16 questions for each treatment, where score = 16 represents the maximum value of comprehension and corresponds to provide correct answers to all the 16 questions. The boxplots show that the participants achieved a better comprehension level when working on the compliant Node-RED flows (median 13.5) with respect to those working on non-compliant flows (median 9.5). By applying a Wilcoxon test (paired analysis), we found that the difference in terms of comprehension is statistically significant, as testified by p-value = 0.00903. Therefore, we can reject the null hypothesis H_{0a}. The effect size is large ($d = -0.69$). *To answer RQ1*: The adoption of the guidelines significantly improves the level of comprehension of the Node-RED flows.

H_{0b}: **Time (RQ2).** Figure 10 (center) summarizes the distribution of *TotalTime* by means of boxplots, where the y-axis represents the total time to answer the 16 questions for each treatment. The boxplots show that the participants needed slightly more time to answer the questions pertaining the objects with the non-compliant treatment w.r.t. those answering the questions pertaining the objects with the compliant treatment (58.5 versus 57.0 min respectively in the median case). By applying a Wilcoxon test (paired analysis), we found that the overall difference is marginally significant (p-value = 0.04883). Therefore, we can reject the null hypothesis H_{0b}. The effect size is small (d= 0.17). *To answer RQ2*: The adoption of the guidelines marginally reduces the time required to answers the questions pertaining the Node-RED flows.

H_{0c}: **Efficiency (RQ3).** Figure 10 (right) summarizes the distribution of *Total-Efficiency* by means of boxplots. The boxplots show that participants working on the objects with the compliant treatment outperformed in terms of efficiency those working with the objects with the non-compliant treatment (medians 0.254 versus 0.180, respectively). By applying a Wilcoxon test (paired analysis), we found that the overall difference is statistically significant, as shown by the p-value (p-value = 0.00586). Therefore, we can reject the null hypothesis H_{0c}. The effect size is medium ($d = -0.36$). *To answer RQ3*: The adoption of the guidelines increases the overall efficiency in the comprehension of the Node-RED flows.

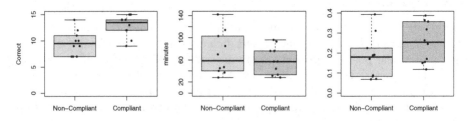

Fig. 10. Boxplots of Comprehension, Time, and Efficiency.

3.9   Post Experiment

When participants had to fill the post-experiment questionnaire, they were unaware of the guidelines and, therefore, of the two treatments. For this reason, the actual questions were formulated as a comparison between the flows they had worked on in the two tasks, keeping track of which treatment occurred on them, according to the group the participants were assigned to. Thus, for instance, question PQ1 was originally formulated as *Comprehending the Node-RED flow in Task 1 was harder than the Node-RED flow in Task 2*. In Table 5 the post-experiment questionnaire has been adjusted in order to clarify the purpose of our experiment. Table 5 reports also the medians of the answers given by the participants. The possible choices for each answer, on a 5-point Likert scale, were: Strongly Agree, Agree, Unsure, Disagree, Strongly Disagree.

As the Table 5 shows, participants did not perceive any difference in the complexity while trying to comprehend the Node-RED flows using each treatment (PQ1), but believed that developing and maintaining such flows may result more complex with the non-compliant treatment (PQ2-3). The names of the nodes and of the used variables in the two treatments had no significant impact in the overall comprehension (PQ4), whereas the wiring style was better perceived in the case of the compliant treatment (PQ5). In general, participants found the exercise useful (PQ6) to the course of their studies, and fitting their knowledge in Node-RED (PQ7), in part acquired by attending the 4-hours lecture preceding the experiment.

Table 5. Adjusted post-experiment questionnaire (see [5]).

ID	Question	Median
PQ1	Comprehending the non-compliant Node-RED flow was harder than the compliant one	Unsure
PQ2	In your opinion, developing the non-compliant Node-RED flow is harder than the compliant one	Agree
PQ3	In your opinion, maintaining the non-compliant Node-RED flow is harder than the compliant one	Agree
PQ4	The names of the nodes and the variables in the non-compliant Node-RED flow were less useful for the comprehension than in the compliant one	Unsure
PQ5	The wiring style to connect nodes in the non-compliant Node-RED flow was less useful for the comprehension than in the compliant one	Agree
PQ6	I found the exercise useful	Agree
PQ7	I had enough knowledge to answer the questions	Agree

3.10   Discussion on the Experiment

Given the results of the experiment, all null hypotheses can be rejected. The guidelines are generally beneficial to the comprehension level and reduce the time required to complete Node-RED tasks. Consequently, the overall efficiency is also positively affected.

One of the main reasons of success of the guidelines was producing flows that follow a consistent and tidy wiring style, by means of **WSC** and **WST**, which improved the capability of detecting loops and reduced entangles among wires. This is corroborated by **PQ5** of Table 5. In fact, the questions pertaining comprehensibility issues about wires and loops presented generally better outcomes for the flows compliant with our guidelines. For example, a question in both questionnaires requires identifying the number of intersections between wires. While we had only 1 error for the flows compliant with our guidelines, for the non-compliant flows the errors amounted to 8.

On the other hand, by the feeling of the participants (**PQ4**), giving proper names to nodes was not so relevant for the comprehension. This is contradicted by the results of the experiment, since the importance of names, given by **NNB** guideline, resulted to be helpful in indirectly answering several questions on both systems. For instance, we had two open questions specifically asking the names of the nodes responsible for a certain behaviour (e.g., *Which node (provide name) displays on a web page the WikiData answer to the user's question?*), which resulted in a total of 4 errors for the flows compliant with our guidelines against 10 for the non-compliant ones . We had also two questions in both questionnaires asking about which data was changed/returned after the completion of a certain activity (e.g., *Which data are saved just after the HTTP request to URL?*): while we had just 1 error in the flows compliant with our guidelines, 5 errors were counted for the non-compliant cases. One question asked about the effective contributions of the nodes in a selected portion of the flows (i.e., if they were able to transform the message they had received); by using **NEC** guideline, the inactive nodes (e.g., those added for debugging purposes) were removed from the flows compliant with the guidelines, but not from the non-compliant flows. In this case, while participants easily identified the contributions of the remaining nodes, they failed (4 errors) in identifying the inactive ones in the non-compliant flows. Finally, there was a question asking to list all the files in the file system used by the flows, which resulted in 1 error for the flows compliant with our guidelines against 4 for the non-compliant ones. Indeed, by following our guidelines, the nodes names were formulated to make their behaviours more explicit, as well as the main used variables, hence reducing the overall errors in the comprehension, as summarized by the statistics data of Table 4.

From **PQ1**, participants did not have a clear opinion on which treatment was easier to comprehend, while they agreed that flows produced without following our guidelines would be harder to develop and maintain (**PQ2-3**). Concerning comprehensibility complexity, we speculate that the uncertainty of the participants is due to the domain of the two systems: while DiaMH presents the MQTT node (i.e., a core Node-RED node used to establish a communication from/to entities and flows using the MQTT protocol[17]) as the most complex node, Wiki-DataQuerying refers to WikiData repository and to Prolog and SPARQL languages, which could deviate from their average academic background. Finally, the participants recognized that the tasks they completed did not require excessive knowledge of Node-RED and were helpful for their current/next academic studies (PQ6-7).

To conclude, the proposed guidelines resulted useful in terms of comprehension level, time, and overall efficiency. This may suggest Node-RED developers to apply them to reduce the comprehensibility issues of the flows they will produce, deploy and share. At the same time, the guidelines may turn useful to the designers of the Node-RED language, who may want to fix some of the issues exposed in the paper, by introducing additional features in future Node-RED releases. Just to mention few possible additions: (i) nodes resizing in height and width, to highlight the most important nodes and make long names more readable, (ii) general warnings, to notify the presence of unused variables, incomplete conditions within switch nodes, and loops, and (iii) jumps between wires, to graphically handle colliding wires.

3.11 Threats to Validity of the Experiment

The threats to validity that could affect our experimentation are: internal, construct, conclusion and external [22].

Internal Validity Threats: these threats concern factors which may affect the dependent variables. The participants had to complete two tasks; therefore, a fatigue/learning effect may have intervened. However, since they had a break between the two tasks and they previously completed some exercises about Node-RED comprehensibility issues, we expect this effect to be limited. Another threat is the subjectivity in the objects selection. The objects were flows chosen from a list of systems developed by former master students of another course related to Node-RED, and were comparable in size and complexity and composed of mostly Node-RED core nodes.

Construct Validity Threats: these threats concern how comprehension and time were measured. The correctness of the answers was checked by one of the authors, who also measured the execution time, based on the time sheets filled by the participants. The statistics data (i.e., median, mean, and standard deviation) and the results of the paired Wilcoxon analysis were computed using Excel and R^{18}.

Conclusion Validity Threats: these threats concern the limited sample size of the experiment (ten master students), which may have affected the statistical tests. Unfortunately, this is the average number of students of any Computer Science Master Course in Genova, so it is difficult for us to conduct experiments with more participants.

---

[17] https://cookbook.nodered.org/mqtt/.

[18] https://www.r-project.org/.

External Validity Threats: these threats can limit the generalization of the results and, in our case, concern the use of students as experimental participants. Our participants had few knowledge of Node-RED, therefore more expert Node-RED developers may produce a different outcome. We intend to replicate our experiment with more complex systems and more expert developers.

4   Analysis of the Top-100 Most Downloaded Flows

To determine the compliance with our guidelines of existing Node-RED flows produced by external sources, we consulted the official Node-RED flows library[19] and collected a sample consisting in the 'Top-100 Most Downloaded Node-RED Flows'. In Table 6 the collected flows are listed and briefly described. Each flow was manually analysed to determine its behaviour, its size as number of nodes, and its compliance (✓ for success, ✗ for failure) with the proposed guidelines. The flows come from disparate domains and involve a large number of services, including weather forecasting, coordinates management, social networking, physical/virtual devices communication, sentiment analysis, and custom nodes implementation to enhance Node-RED core behaviour. The analysis of the flows and their compliance with the guidelines was firstly conducted by one author of the paper, then reviewed by the other authors to avoid any mistake.

From Table 6, it emerges that, on average, the flows include about 9.54 nodes, with a minimum of 1 unique node in 4 cases (flows *#29 Rate Limiter, #64 Twitter scrape and count triggers signal, #80 AmberTweets,* and *#94 Calculate 'feels like temperature' for weather models*) and a maximum of 63 nodes in a single case (flow *#27 Input and Output controls for Pibrella on Raspberry Pi*). The number of failed guidelines by Top-100 most downloaded flows is the following: 6 flows have no fails, the majority of flows fail one or two guidelines (32 flows for both cases), then 20 flows fail exactly three guidelines, followed by 9 flows failing four guidelines, finally 1 flow fails five guidelines.

The 6 flows with no fails are: *#9 Forecast.io rain prediction , #31 Live Google Maps Update - Websockets, #41 Alert if NO motion is detected, #81 Read SunSprite values, #87 Light switch off timer, #94 Calculate 'feels like temperature' for weather models*. All these flows do not involve complicated scenarios and their names clarify their intentions. Their nodes are assigned with semantically meaningful names (e.g., flow *#9 Forecast.io rain prediction* presents a node named *Is weather unsafe* to check if the weather forecasting data may suggest a potentially dangerous situation) and the wires are connected avoiding any entangle and following a generally consistent wiring style. Moreover, they do not include conditional nodes or they include them by covering all possible alternative scenarios (e.g., the 'otherwise' condition). One of these flows, *#94 Calculate 'feels like temperature' for weather models*, is actually a unique node, therefore cannot fail guidelines addressing wires or nodes population of the flow. Instead, the flow with the highest number of fails is *#28 Flow GPS raw from your Raspberry to websocket*; although this flow is rather simple, containing 13 nodes only, the

---

[19] https://flows.nodered.org/search?type=flow, consulted in August 2020.

Table 6. Top-100 Most Downloaded Node-RED Flows and Guidelines Compliancy.

#	Flow name	Description	# nodes	NNB	FNB	NEC	CCC	SFR	FC	WSC	WST
1	SunSprite Calendar View web service	it displays a SunSprite calendar view for light exposure	18	✗	✓	✓	✓	✓	✓	✗	✓
2	Node-RED Current Cost XML Parser	it parses XML temperatures data to JSON	7	✗	✓	✗	✓	✓	✓	✗	✓
3	Get UK Power Demand	it fetches UK electricity power demand	5	✗	✓	✓	✓	✓	✓	✓	✓
4	Stock Price Alerts	it notifies about stock price quotes	5	✗	✓	✓	✓	✓	✓	✓	✗
5	Twitter Sentiment Analysis	it performs sentiment analysis on tweets	3	✗	✗	✗	✗	✓	✓	✓	✓
6	PiLite output	it sends payloads to Ciseco PiLite serial output	2	✗	✓	✓	✓	✓	✓	✓	✓
7	JQuery Mobile Web Page	it serves mobile web pages from HTTP requests	3	✗	✗	✓	✓	✓	✓	✓	✓
8	Tweet your location with MQTTitude	it tweets user's location based on MQTTitude service	4	✗	✓	✓	✓	✓	✓	✓	✓
9	Forecast.io rain prediction	it calls Forecast.io service to predict next rainfall	14	✗	✓	✓	✓	✓	✓	✓	✓
10	Sensor hub for JeeNode / Open Energy Monitor	it bridges MQTT topics to remote sensors	24	✓	✓	✓	✓	✗	✓	✓	✓
11	Parsing JeeNode Room Board	it parses JeeNode room board messages and routes data	13	✓	✓	✓	✓	✗	✓	✗	✗
12	Aurora visibility	it gets geomagnetic activity from NOAA agency	6	✗	✓	✓	✓	✓	✓	✓	✓
13	Earthquake monitor	it creates earthquakes reports from USGS data	5	✗	✓	✓	✓	✓	✓	✓	✓
14	Flow that makes a new flow	it generates output flows from input JSON objects	8	✗	✓	✓	✓	✓	✓	✗	✓
15	Siemens Logo8 - Example Node-RED	it shows how to use Node-RED with Siemens Logo8	7	✗	✗	✓	✓	✓	✓	✓	✓
16	Parsing Open Energy Monitor emonTH sensor	it parses raw data from an Open Energy Monitor sensor	10	✓	✓	✓	✓	✗	✓	✓	✗
17	Weather reports to SMS and MQTT topic	it reports via SMS/MQTT weather forecast from BBC	10	✓	✓	✓	✓	✓	✓	✓	✗
18	CurrentCost to LEDborg energy monitor	it activates LEDs based on an energy monitor	13	✗	✓	✓	✓	✓	✓	✓	✓
19	FRITZ!box router to PiLite Caller ID Display	it routes incoming calls data to a PiLite display	7	✗	✗	✓	✓	✓	✓	✗	✗
20	Owntracks Geofence Notifications via Pushover	it routes Owntracks location messages to Pushover	8	✗	✓	✓	✗	✓	✓	✗	✓
21	Process Twilio SMS request	it routes received SMS to TwiML service	7	✗	✓	✓	✗	✓	✓	✓	✓
22	MQTT-SN buffer formatter	it creates a MQTT-SN buffer formatter	4	✗	✓	✓	✓	✓	✓	✓	✓
23	Air/ground frost alerts via wunderground.com	it provides warnings of overnight frosts	9	✓	✓	✓	✓	✓	✓	✓	✗
24	Plane spotting with RTL-SDR and Dump1090	it tracks local air traffic	5	✗	✓	✓	✓	✓	✗	✗	✗
25	Daily weather forecast based on OwnTracks location	it returns weather forecast from OwnTracks locations	12	✓	✓	✗	✗	✓	✓	✓	✗
26	Flow to shut down a Raspberry Pi	it enables a cleanly shut down of a Raspberry Pi	2	✓	✓	✗	✓	✓	✓	✓	✓
27	Input and Output controls for Pibrella on Raspberry Pi	it controls Pibrella LEDs via gpio-in and gpio-out nodes	63	✗	✓	✓	✗	✗	✗	✓	✓
28	Flow GPS raw from your Raspberry to websocket	it routes Raspberry GPS data to websocket	13	✗	✓	✗	✓	✗	✓	✗	✗
29	Rate Limiter	it drops intermediate messages of a rated flow	1	✓	✗	✓	✓	✓	✓	✓	✓
30	Tweet to latitude / longitude coordinates	it returns the coordinates of a tweet original location	15	✗	✓	✓	✓	✓	✓	✗	✓
31	Live Google Maps Update - Websockets	it updates Google Maps coordinates via websockets	10	✓	✓	✓	✓	✓	✓	✗	✗
32	Send content to Little Printer Direct Print API	it sends commands to a Little Printer using Direct Print API	6	✗	✓	✓	✓	✓	✓	✗	✗
33	Flash a Hue lamp with Twitter hashtags	it flashes a Hue lamp when a given Twitter hashtag is detected	4	✗	✓	✗	✓	✓	✓	✓	✓
34	Pinocchio Command Flow	it sends commands for controlling dynamics of robotic models	10	✗	✗	✗	✓	✓	✓	✓	✓
35	Tweet IP address upon bootup	it tweets IP address when a Raspberry Pi has powered up	7	✗	✗	✓	✓	✓	✓	✓	✓
36	Counter	it counts the number of message passing in a flow	4	✗	✓	✓	✓	✓	✓	✓	✓
37	Simple Twilio based IVR	it handles Twilio Voice calls	11	✓	✗	✓	✓	✓	✓	✓	✓
38	Routing with External Business Rules	it performs switch routing using IBM Decision Manager	8	✓	✓	✗	✗	✓	✓	✓	✗
39	Dynamic Word Cloud	it generates a Word Cloud from a Twitter feed	6	✓	✓	✓	✓	✓	✓	✗	✗
40	Turn off HDMI connected TV when leaving WIFI	it turns off TV when a phone is disconnected from WIFI	8	✓	✓	✓	✓	✓	✓	✗	✗
41	Alert if NO motion is detected	it alerts if no motion is detected at a certain place	8	✓	✓	✓	✓	✓	✓	✓	✓
42	Alert if Public IP address changes	it sends an alert if home IP address changes	4	✗	✓	✗	✓	✓	✓	✓	✓
43	Calculate how far away from the ISS you are.	it computes the distance to the International Space Station	5	✓	✓	✓	✓	✓	✓	✗	✓
44	Control a PiGlow using Node-RED	it controls PiGlow LEDs of a Raspberry Pi	2	✗	✓	✗	✓	✓	✓	✓	✓
45	SONOS TTS	it plays a sound on a SONOS speaker when batteries are low	5	✗	✗	✗	✗	✓	✓	✓	✓
46	Update Dynamic DNS service when IP changes	it notifies Dynamic DNS when IP address changes	12	✗	✓	✗	✓	✓	✓	✓	✗
47	Push data to Google Spreadsheet	it pushes a data source to Google Spreadsheet	6	✗	✓	✗	✓	✓	✓	✓	✓
48	Convert timestamp to array	it converts a timestamp into an array	5	✗	✓	✓	✓	✓	✓	✓	✓
49	no-ip.com update client	it notifies No-IP Free Dynamic DNS when IP address changes	7	✓	✓	✗	✓	✓	✓	✗	✓
50	AirPi with Node-RED	it listens on a UDP port and publishes data to Xively service	4	✓	✗	✓	✓	✓	✓	✓	✓
51	DuckDNS dynamic DNS update client	it notifies DuckDNS Dynamic DNS when IP address changes	13	✓	✗	✓	✓	✓	✓	✗	✓
52	Notify on public IP change	it saves IP address in a file and notifies when it changes	30	✗	✓	✗	✓	✓	✓	✓	✗
53	UDP Request response	it handles UDP requests and responses	7	✗	✓	✓	✓	✓	✓	✗	✗
54	Data in -> MySql and Google Spreadsheet out	it stores input in MySQL database and Google Spreadsheet	17	✗	✓	✗	✓	✗	✓	✓	✓
55	Gmaps experiment + earthquake experiment	it provides Google Maps and EarthQuake monitor examples	11	✗	✗	✓	✓	✓	✓	✗	✗
56	Google Spreadsheet in	it connects to a Google Spreadsheet and outputs its cells	5	✗	✗	✓	✓	✓	✓	✗	✓
57	AC CONTROL	it controls and returns the temperature of a CPU	7	✗	✗	✓	✗	✓	✓	✓	✓
58	Filter which drops 'seenbefore' items	it filters out duplicate data in a flow	4	✗	✓	✓	✓	✓	✓	✓	✓
59	Loop with start, stop and toggle actions	it handles loops in a flow	9	✗	✓	✓	✓	✓	✓	✓	✓
60	Parse weather data from NOAA Weather Centre	it saves data from NOAA Weather Centre in a CSV file	6	✗	✓	✓	✓	✓	✓	✓	✓
61	Simple UK Sky+ satellite receiver control	it allows to control a UK Sky+ satellite box	20	✗	✓	✓	✓	✗	✗	✗	✗
62	Run coffee-script	it processes CoffeeScript commands	5	✗	✓	✓	✓	✓	✓	✓	✓
63	Thirteen cases: node-red-contrib-jsonpath	it provides examples of JSONPath usage	29	✗	✗	✓	✓	✓	✓	✓	✓

(*continued*)

Table 6. (*continued*)

#	Flow name	Description	# nodes	NNB	FNB	NEC	CCC	SFR	FC	WSC	WST
64	Twitter scrape and count triggers signal	it counts the tweets having a given hashtag	1	✓	✗	✓	✓	✓	✓	✓	✓
65	IoT Example	it monitors the temperature of a device	7	✗	✗	✓	✗	✓	✓	✓	✓
66	for-loop (simple iterating over an array)	it handles array loops iterations	2	✗	✓	✓	✓	✓	✓	✓	✓
67	HTTP Monitor check	it classifies web pages as available/down based on content	6	✓	✗	✓	✓	✓	✓	✓	✓
68	Integrating KNX+ZWave, v0.01	it integrates KNX installation with Z-Wave device	24	✗	✓	✓	✓	✗	✓	✓	✗
69	z-wave <-> mqtt bridge and examples of usage	it provides examples of using Z-Wave	11	✗	✓	✓	✓	✓	✓	✓	✓
70	z-wave context.global.zwavenodes object builder	it handles global variables of Z-Wave devices	29	✗	✓	✓	✓	✗	✓	✓	✓
71	Use sipgate.io to log and send phone calls	it sends incoming calls notifications via sipgate service	5	✗	✓	✓	✓	✓	✓	✗	✓
72	Simple flow which controls a Tesla electric car	it controls a Tesla Model S electric car	11	✗	✓	✓	✓	✓	✓	✓	✗
73	GetStatus - Denkovi	it gets the status of a Denkovi board device	5	✗	✗	✓	✓	✓	✓	✗	✓
74	SetAction - Denkovi	it sets the action to execute by a Denkovi board device	7	✗	✗	✓	✓	✓	✓	✗	✗
75	Yandex Weather[20]	it parses daily Yandex weather forecasting in Moscow	9	✓	✗	✓	✓	✓	✓	✓	✓
76	Using the collector node to generate XML	it provides Collector node example to collects inputs data	7	✗	✓	✓	✓	✓	✓	✓	✓
77	1-wire to MQTT bridge	it reads a sensor temperature and publishes it via MQTT	5	✗	✓	✓	✓	✓	✓	✓	✗
78	Wait for and combine multiple inputs to a node	it combines input from multiple sources	9	✓	✓	✓	✓	✓	✓	✓	✓
79	7 Segment decoder	it converts numbers from an Arduino 6 segment decoder	24	✗	✗	✓	✓	✓	✓	✓	✓
80	AmberTweets	it forwards Twitter messages to a IRC channel	1	✗	✗	✓	✓	✓	✓	✓	✓
81	Read SunSprite values	it reads data from SunSprite service	11	✓	✓	✓	✓	✓	✓	✓	✓
82	Boxcar Push Notification to iOS	it shows how to push iOS notifications with Boxcar platform	6	✗	✓	✓	✓	✓	✓	✗	✗
83	REST API using MongoDB + CoffeeScript	it uses MongoDB and CoffeeScript via REST API	13	✗	✓	✓	✓	✓	✓	✗	✗
84	@Cheerlights to various RGB devices	it routes a Twitter stream to various RGB devices	8	✗	✗	✗	✗	✓	✓	✗	✓
85	Google Map With BART Stations Using Websockets	it points all public transport locations in San Francisco	7	✗	✓	✓	✓	✓	✓	✓	✓
86	Milight control via MQTT	it controls wireless lights via MQTT	5	✓	✓	✓	✓	✓	✓	✓	✓
87	Light switch off timer	it turns lights switch on and off	8	✓	✓	✓	✓	✓	✓	✓	✓
88	Database examples - insert and select using binding	it provides examples of using a database	13	✗	✓	✓	✓	✗	✓	✓	✓
89	Freeboard load/save to file	it loads/saves Freeboard configuration from/to a file	7	✗	✓	✓	✓	✓	✓	✓	✓
90	Metro	it provides a sub-flow example to turn LEDs on and off	4	✗	✗	✗	✗	✓	✓	✗	✗
91	Blinking LEDS on Raspberry Pi	it sends inputs to Raspberry Pi LEDs to make them blink	8	✗	✓	✓	✓	✗	✓	✗	✗
92	Control a projector via the PJLink protocol	it controls projectors using PJLink protocol	21	✗	✓	✓	✓	✓	✓	✓	✓
93	Get your monthly bandwidth usage with TekSavvy ISP	it provides bandwidth usage with TekSavvy service provider	3	✗	✓	✓	✓	✓	✓	✓	✓
94	Calculate 'feels like temperature' for weather models	it elaborates weather data from a METAR weather report	1	✓	✓	✓	✓	✓	✓	✓	✓
95	HTTP-based chat server	it implements a basic chat server	16	✗	✓	✓	✓	✓	✓	✓	✓
96	Simple way to pulse output n times	it periodically returns up to N outputs from a flow	4	✗	✓	✓	✓	✓	✓	✓	✓
97	Function that dumps all context.global vars to debug	it dumps all global variables to the debug panel	7	✓	✓	✓	✓	✗	✓	✓	✓
98	Bluemix-GameStopHackathon #16	it performs sentiment analysis on GameStop tweets	27	✓	✗	✓	✗	✓	✗	✗	✗
99	Node red flow for Fight Match	it manages the state of GameStop stores	9	✗	✗	✓	✓	✓	✓	✓	✓
100	Bluemix-GameStopHackathon #17	it performs sentiment analysis on GameStop tweets	15	✓	✗	✓	✓	✓	✗	✓	✓

names of the nodes are very generic or include technical details and acronyms. There is a conditional node missing to cover the 'otherwise' condition and with an output pin with no leaving wires, resulting in a possible loss of the output messages. Finally, the wiring style presents several entangles and is not consistent to differentiate the occurring scenarios.

Table 7 shows the success rate statistics for the proposed guidelines in the collected Node-RED flows. The guideline presenting the highest success rate is **FC**; this can be easily explained by the fact that only one among the considered flows slightly exceeded the upper bound limit of 50 nodes, as described in Sect. 2 concerning **FC** guideline. It is flow *#27 Input and Output controls for Pibrella on Raspberry Pi* with 63 nodes, which may require a simplification even if it satisfies both **WSC** and **WST** guidelines.

Three guidelines are above 80% of success rate: **NEC**, **CCC**, and **SFR**, with 82%, 89%, and 87%, respectively. Very few flows presented black hole or miracle nodes (i.e., nodes with input/output pins and no entering/leaving wires), therefore **NEC** guideline rarely failed, but when it happened it was mostly due to a function node that was missing an output wire. Even though this is

Table 7. Guidelines Success Rate in Top-100 Most Downloaded Node-RED Flows.

Guideline	Success rate %
Node Name Behaviour (NNB)	30%
Flow Name Behaviour (FNB)	72%
Node Effective Contribution (NEC)	82%
Conditions Consistency and Completeness (CCC)	89%
Sub-Flows Relatedness (SFR)	87%
Flow Content (FC)	99%
Wiring Style Consistency (WSC)	73%
Wiring Style Tidiness (WST)	71%

not necessarily an error, since not sending an output message might be the expected behaviour, it is not the case of flow *#51 DuckDNS dynamic DNS update client*, which includes a function node that checks over a variable with two possible outcomes, but only one is actually covered by the flow and the other output pin is missing the wire leaving from it. Concerning **CCC**, only a limited number of flows included conditional nodes routing messages to different possible scenarios; the majority of those who had included at least one conditional node also considered the 'otherwise' condition to cover any unexpected alternative. An example of **CCC** failure is given by flow *#25 Daily weather forecast based on OwnTracks location*, which includes a conditional node that checks over a string value but does not consider a 'otherwise' scenario if the value is, for instance, null. Finally, **SFR** is more oriented to complex flows, hence not just partial solutions or simplified examples as some of the selected flows, which rarely included unrelated sub-flows; an example of a possible **SFR** failure is given by flow *#10 Sensor hub for JeeNode / Open Energy Monitor*, which handles remote sensors placed at different locations in the house, like loft, garage, or shed, that could be treated separately. Another case is flow *#11 Parsing JeeNode Room Board*, which contains a large node routing environmental heterogeneous sensors data to a likewise number of MQTT nodes.

Another cluster of results includes **FNB**, **WSC**, and **WST** guidelines, all ranging between 71% and 73% success rate. Even though this is not always true, the bigger the flow is the harder it is to comprehend. The comprehension of complicated/large flows can be supported by **FNB**, since the developer has to name a flow properly to provide hints about its general behaviour. Fails can occur when the given name is, for instance, too generic or too technical. Some examples are flows *#65 IoT example* and *#90 Metro*, that have too generic names, flow *#75 Yandex Weather* that was originally formulated in Russian alphabet, and flow *#19 FRITZ!box router to PiLite Caller ID Display* that uses some technical details. Other interesting instances are flows from *#98* to *#100* that describe the context of their creation, that are software development events (i.e., Gamestop hackathons), without providing details about their content. **WST** guideline is also important to produce comprehensible flows. In many cases there were overlapping nodes that required to move them to make the flow fully readable, e.g., in flows *#17 Weather reports to SMS and MQTT topic* and *#23 Air/ground frost alerts via wunderground.com*, while in other cases the problem was in the twisted wires, e.g., in flows *#11 Parsing JeeNode Room Board* and *#24 Plane spotting with RTL-SDR and Dump1090*. The consistency of wiring styles, granted by **WSC**, was neglected in several cases, producing alternative scenarios that did not follow any rational, jumping between straight wires to cascaded wires with no distinction, like flow *#61 Simple UK Sky+ satellite receiver control*.

Finally, **NNB** guideline was the one that failed the most, satisfied only by 30% of the considered flows. This is explained by the frequency of the comprehensibility issue (i.e., nodes naming) it addresses, that can be scattered along the whole flow and inhibit its comprehension. Indeed, there could be nodes that are assigned with default meaningless names (e.g., in flow *#13 Earthquake monitor* a very generic 'csv' node is present to convert CSV earthquake data into Javascript), empty names (e.g., in flow *#20 Owntracks Geofence Notifications via Pushover* there is a function node with no name transforming the received message content), or even jargonic, too technical or mysterious names (e.g., acronyms and names not in English are frequent but the flow *#77 1-wire to MQTT bridge* wins the challenge by naming a node with the indecipherable string '28.D8FE434D9855').

In conclusion, this analysis reveals that on average NODE-RED developers, although unaware of our guidelines, adopt a disciplined approach to the flows development. This is testified by the average of the computed guidelines success rate in Top-100 most downloaded Node-RED flows which exceeds 75%. The success rate of the guideline **NNB** is an exception, which stands at 30%. As in traditional programming, we believe that it is very important to adopt meaningful names of nodes and follow naming conventions also in NODE-RED development to facilitate understanding.

5   Related Work

As anticipated in Sect. 2, several works on UML and BPMN concerning the quality of the produced models have inspired our guidelines. However, none specifically treats guidelines for developing comprehensible Node-RED flows. To the best of our knowledge, only a simple set of principles[20] is provided as guidance to Node-RED developers that have to implement nodes: they include suggestions like nodes should be "simple to use" and "consistent" in their behaviour, and few unofficial design patterns[21] to make flows easier to understand and reuse.

Bröring et al. in a recent industrial work [2] propose an approach to automatically collect metadata from Node-RED flows and nodes, and feed a knowledge base for future analyses, such as nodes quality ratings, downloads data, and nodes dependencies. That work does not provide to users any development

---

[20] https://nodered.org/docs/creating-nodes.

[21] https://medium.com/node-red/node-red-design-patterns-893331422f42.

guideline even if it considers several quality aspects of Node-RED, like selecting the most suitable solutions to integrate within a system. Prehofer and Chiarabini [15] identify the differences between mash-up tools for IoT systems, like Node-RED, and model-based approaches for the IoT, and propose an approach to exploit both their benefits: the simplicity of mash-up tools in systems development and the strengths of models to formalize a behaviour and have it checked by a model checker. However, in that paper, the quality checks of IoT systems are not oriented to the comprehensibility issues that may emerge during flows development using mash-up tools.

Mendling et al. [12] defined 7 guidelines, built on empirical insights, as a response to the lack of practical solutions to improve the quality of business process models. In the current work, we adopted some of these guidelines. For instance, "Use verb-object activity label" (G6), to reduce the ambiguity of the constructs in a model, particularly useful for the large number of nodes collaborating within Node-RED flows, as well as "Use as few elements in the model as possible" (G1) and "Decompose a model with more than 50 elements" (G7), to reduce flows complexity.

In the book [20], Unhelkar has a particular focus on syntax, semantics and aesthetic checks of UML 2.0 diagrams. UML is quite different from Node-RED in many aspects: indeed it operates at a design stage and involves constructs that are not comparable to Node-RED nodes and wires, but in the book there are some aesthetic checks concerning activity diagrams that we have included in our guidelines. For example, it is important to adopt a consistent style to differentiate regular from exceptional scenarios and to balance overpopulated diagrams by redistributing the included constructs.

Reggio et al. [16,18] face the problem of quality in business process modelling. They propose an empirical method aimed at helping the modeller in selecting among five business process modelling styles, that differ in terms of abstraction and precision. For instance, a more precise style requires each construct to declare all the participants, the objects and the used data in capital letters, as in our guidelines, to make explicit the data used by each node.

Ambler proposes [1] several guidelines addressing both general and UML-specific modelling issues, with the goal of improving the effectiveness of the produced models. Some of them can be also adopted in Node-RED, since they use very general terms and descriptions. In the context of UML, activity diagrams represent sequences of actions similarly to Node-RED flows. The guidelines suggest, for instance, to avoid black-hole and miracle nodes (i.e., nodes without a leaving/entering line), that may indicate a missing interaction , and to check that the guards within decision points are always complete.

Several works investigate software repositories for improving the quality of newly produced or existent software and evaluating the compliance w.r.t. different quality criteria (e.g., patterns application) [3,9,10,14].

Ozbas-Caglayan and Dogru [14] investigate on Design-Code compliance to support development and maintenance activities. Livshits and Zimmermann propose DynaMine [10], a tool for history mining of source code to detect bugs and common error patterns. Li and Zhou propose the PR-Miner method [9] to automatically extract programming rules from large software code, without employing constrained rule templates, and an algorithm to detect rules violation that may bring to bugs in software. Rules violation is also addressed by Campos et al. [3] to inspect Stack Overflow repository and detect issues in Javascript code snippets provided as solutions to the users.

All these works rely on software repository mining and automated detection and evaluation of rules violation. In our work, we manually employed software repository mining to select and evaluate the Top-100 most downloaded Node-RED flows, aimed at determining Node-RED flows compliance with our proposed guidelines. Our evaluation required to carefully inspect the produced artefacts both in terms of code and from a visual perspective.

6   Conclusion and Future Work

In this paper, we have proposed a set of guidelines to address some common Node-RED comprehensibility issues and help Node-RED developers in producing flows that are easy to comprehend and re-use, as well as being suitable for future maintenance and testing activities.

The effectiveness of the guidelines has been evaluated by an experiment involving ten master students. The results of the experiment mark that our guidelines are able to improve Node-RED flows comprehension, with the double benefit of reducing the number of errors and the time required to complete the Node-RED tasks assigned to the experiment participants. We have also analyzed the Top-100 most downloaded Node-RED flows to discuss about their compliance (or not) with the guidelines. This additional analysis reveals that Node-RED developers are quite disciplined during development except in the choice of node names.

The proposed guidelines also pinpoint some Node-RED comprehensibility issues that might be fixed in future tool releases, by introducing functionalities, such as, nodes resizing to highlight the most important nodes and make long names more readable, graphical jumps to handle collisions between wires, and notifications to inform the developer about, e.g., unused variables, missing wires, incomplete conditions within switch nodes, and loops.

We are planning to address further Node-RED comprehensibility issues that did not emerge from the Node-RED systems we chose; for instance, how to avoid loops by transforming graph-based Node-RED flows into tree-based ones. As future work, we intend to replicate the experiment on the evaluation of the guidelines with more participants, including also Node-RED designers. Moreover, we plan to implement a checker tool able to automatically detect the comprehensibility issues from the Node-RED flows failing our guidelines, and fix them accordingly. Also, the tool will be used to replicate the manually conducted Top-100 most downloaded Node-RED flows compliance evaluation, by automatically mine the official Node-RED flows repository and determine the compliance of the submitted flows with our guidelines.

References

1. Ambler, S.W.: The elements of UML (TM) 2.0 style. Cambridge University Press, Cambridge (2005)
2. Bröring, A., Charpenay, V., Anicic, D., Püech, S.: NOVA: a knowledge base for the Node-RED IoT ecosystem. In: Hitzler, P., et al. (eds.) ESWC 2019. LNCS, vol. 11762, pp. 257–261. Springer, Cham (2019). https://doi.org/10.1007/978-3-030-32327-1_45
3. Campos, U.F., Smethurst, G., Moraes, J.P., Bonifácio, R., Pinto, G.: Mining rule violations in Javascript code snippets. In: 2019 IEEE/ACM 16th International Conference on Mining Software Repositories (MSR), pp. 195–199. IEEE (2019)
4. Clerissi, D., Leotta, M., Reggio, G., Ricca, F.: Towards an approach for developing and testing Node-RED IoT systems. In: Proceedings of EnSEmble@ESEC/SIGSOFT 2018, pp. 1–8 (2018). https://doi.org/10.1145/3281022.3281023
5. Clerissi, D., Leotta, M., Ricca, F.: A set of empirically validated development guidelines for improving Node-RED flows comprehension. In: Proceedings of the 15th International Conference on Evaluation of Novel Approaches to Software Engineering, ENASE, vol. 1, pp. 108–119. INSTICC, SciTePress (2020). https://doi.org/10.5220/0009391101080119
6. Grissom, R.J., Kim, J.J.: Effect Sizes for Research: A Broad Practical Approach. Lawrence Erlbaum Associates Publishers, Hillsdale (2005)
7. Lange, C.F.J., DuBois, B., Chaudron, M.R.V., Demeyer, S.: An experimental investigation of UML modeling conventions. In: Nierstrasz, O., Whittle, J., Harel, D., Reggio, G. (eds.) MODELS 2006. LNCS, vol. 4199, pp. 27–41. Springer, Heidelberg (2006). https://doi.org/10.1007/11880240_3
8. Leotta, M., et al.: An acceptance testing approach for internet of things systems. IET Softw. **12**(5), 430–436 (2018). https://doi.org/10.1049/iet-sen.2017.0344
9. Li, Z., Zhou, Y.: PR-miner: automatically extracting implicit programming rules and detecting violations in large software code. ACM SIGSOFT Softw. Eng. Notes **30**(5), 306–315 (2005)
10. Livshits, B., Zimmermann, T.: Dynamine: finding common error patterns by mining software revision histories. ACM SIGSOFT Softw. Eng. Notes **30**(5), 296–305 (2005)
11. Martin, R.C.: Agile Software Development: Principles, Patterns, and Practices. Prentice Hall PTR, Upper Saddle River (2003)
12. Mendling, J., Reijers, H.A., van der Aalst, W.M.: Seven process modeling guidelines (7PMG). Inf. Softw. Technol. **52**(2), 127–136 (2010)
13. Morrison, J.P.: Flow-Based Programming: A New Approach to Application Development. CreateSpace, Scotts Valley (2010)
14. Ozbas-Caglayan, K., Dogru, A.H.: Software repository analysis for investigating design-code compliance. In: 2013 Joint Conference of the 23rd International Workshop on Software Measurement and the 8th International Conference on Software Process and Product Measurement, pp. 231–234. IEEE (2013)
15. Prehofer, C., Chiarabini, L.: From Internet of Things mashups to model-based development. In: Proceedings of COMPSAC 2015, vol. 3, pp. 499–504. IEEE (2015)
16. Reggio, G., Leotta, M., Ricca, F.: "Precise is better than light" A document analysis study about quality of business process models. In: Proceedings of EmpiRE 2011, pp. 61–68. IEEE (2011). https://doi.org/10.1109/EmpiRE.2011.6046257

17. Reggio, G., Leotta, M., Ricca, F.: Who knows/uses what of the UML: a personal opinion survey. In: Dingel, J., Schulte, W., Ramos, I., Abrahão, S., Insfran, E. (eds.) MODELS 2014. LNCS, vol. 8767, pp. 149–165. Springer, Cham (2014). https:// doi.org/10.1007/978-3-319-11653-2_10

18. Reggio, G., Leotta, M., Ricca, F., Astesiano, E.: Business process modelling: five styles and a method to choose the most suitable one. In: Proceedings of EESS-Mod@MoDELS 2012, pp. 8:1–8:6. ACM (2012). https://doi.org/10.1145/2424563.2424574

19. Shapiro, S.S., Wilk, M.B.: An analysis of variance test for normality (complete samples). Biometrika **52**(3/4), 591–611 (1965)

20. Unhelkar, B.: Verification and Validation for Quality of UML 2.0 Models, vol. 42. Wiley, Hoboken (2005)

21. Van Solingen, R., Basili, V., Caldiera, G., Rombach, H.D.: Goal Question Metric (GQM) approach. Encycl. Softw. Eng. (2002, online)

22. Wohlin, C., Runeson, P., Höst, M., Ohlsson, M.C., Regnell, B., Wesslén, A.: Experimentation in Software Engineering. Springer, Heidelberg (2012). https://doi.org/10.1007/978-3-642-29044-2

A Study of Maintainability in Evolving Open-Source Software

Arthur-Jozsef Molnar$^{(\boxtimes)}$ ⓘ and Simona Motogna ⓘ

Faculty of Mathematics and Computer Science, Babeş-Bolyai University,
Cluj-Napoca, Romania
{arthur,motogna}@cs.ubbcluj.ro
http://www.cs.ubbcluj.ro

Abstract. Our study is focused on an evaluation of the maintainability characteristic in the context of the long-term evolution of open-source software. According to well established software quality models such as the ISO 9126 and the more recent ISO 25010, maintainability remains among key quality characteristics alongside performance, security and reliability. To achieve our objective, we selected three complex, widely used target applications for which access to their entire development history and source code was available. To enable cross-application comparison, we restricted our selection to GUI-driven software developed on the Java platform. We focused our examination on released versions, resulting in 111 software releases included in our case study. These covered more than 10 years of development for each of the applications. For each version, we determined its maintainability using three distinct quantitative models of varying complexity. We examined the relation between software size and maintainability and studied the main drivers of important changes to software maintainability. We contextualized our findings using manual source code examination. We also carried out a finer grained evaluation at package level to determine the distribution of maintainability issues within application source code. Finally, we provided a cross-application analysis in order to identify common as well as application-specific patterns.

Keywords: Software quality · Software metrics · Software maintainability · Software evolution · Maintainability index · SQALE model · Technical debt · Open-source

1 Introduction

Maintenance includes all activities intended to correct faults, update the target system in accordance to new requirements, upgrade system performance and adapt it to new environment conditions. As a consequence, maintenance effort becomes very costly, especially in the case of large-scale complex applications, especially since in many cases they include third party components sensitive to updates.

© Springer Nature Switzerland AG 2021
R. Ali et al. (Eds.): ENASE 2020, CCIS 1375, pp. 261–282, 2021.
https://doi.org/10.1007/978-3-030-70006-5_11

The causes of high maintenance costs can be tracked to multiple reasons. The first such reason regards the inherent complexity of code comprehension tasks, due to the fact that maintenance teams are different from the development team, causing further delays for understanding source code and locating software defects. Another important issue is that maintenance is approached only during the late stages of the development lifecycle, when issues have already built up in the form of technical debt [11]. These reasons can be overcome by considering maintainability issues earlier in the development process and employing existing tool support that can help identify future maintenance "hotspots", namely those parts of code that can generate more problems. If we consider agile practices, then integration of maintenance tasks with development processes becomes a necessity. When these issues are not addressed at the right moment they tend to accumulate in the form of technical debt that can later lead to crises during which development is halted until the bulk of the issues are addressed [29].

The focus of this study regards the long term assessment of maintainability in large software applications; software evolution plays an important part that is observed through the release of a consistent number of software versions. In many of these applications we find that complexity is increased by functionalities end-users rely on. They are usually implemented as plugins, which can create additional dependencies on the main code base. Our empirical investigation targets open source applications where full access to the source code was available over the entire application life span. This not only allows the usage of quantitative quality models based on software metrics, but also facilitates the manual examination of source code, which can be used to understand the rationale behind observed changes to application architecture and structure.

Previous studies have identified some of the existing relations between the maintainability characteristic and software metric values [9,17,18,23,25,27]. Our goal is to employ several quantitative models having well studied strengths and weaknesses [34] in order to determine some of the patterns in the evolution of open-source software, to understand the rationale behind important changes to source code, as well as to improve our understanding of the quality models and their applicability.

The present study continues our existing research regarding the maintainability of open-source software [34] and brings the following novel contributions: (a) a longitudinal study of software maintainability that covers the entire development history of three complex, open-source applications; (b) a detailed examination of the relation between maintainability, expressed through several quantitative models and software size measured according to several levels of granularity; (c) an examination of sudden changes to maintainability as well as "slopes" - significant modifications that occur over the span of several releases; (d) a finer-grained analysis at package and class level regarding software maintainability and its evolution; (e) an analysis of the maintainability models themselves as applied to real-life open-source software systems.

2   Software Quality Models

The importance of software quality continues to pose a key interest in both the academic and industry communities after more than 50 years of research and practice. Furthermore, as the number of complex networked systems and critical infrastructures relying on them is increasing, it is expected to remain an issue of continued interest in software research, development and maintenance. Previous research into software quality resulted in a large number of quality models. Most of them describe a set of essential attributes that attempt to characterize the multiple facets of a software system from an internal (developer-oriented), external (client-oriented) or both perspectives.

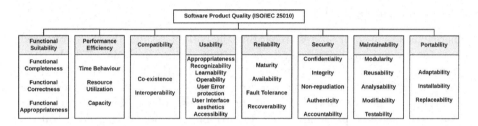

Fig. 1. ISO 25010 hierarchical quality model (from [35]).

The introduction of the first software quality model is attributed to McCall in 1976, followed by the Dromey model which improved it [1]. Later on, these initial contributions became a part of the ISO 9126 standard, which expressed software quality using a hierarchical model of six characteristics that are comprised of 31 sub-characteristics. The ISO 25010 model [19] illustrated in Fig. 1 represents the current version, and it considers maintainability as the ensemble of six sub-characteristics: *Modularity, Reusability, Analysability, Modifiability* and *Testability*. Like its previous versions, ISO 25010 does not provide a methodology to evaluate quality characteristics or to improve them, which precludes practitioners from using them directly. However, this shortcoming can be overcome using software metrics, which measure different properties of source code and related artefacts. Basic metrics such as lines of code, number of functions or modules have been widely used and in turn, superseded by the introduction of the object oriented paradigm and its related set of metrics. Nowadays we find a multitude of object oriented metrics [9] defined and used to detect code smells, design flaws or in order to improve maintainability. These metrics were also harnessed by researchers to evaluate software quality in general. However, these tasks have remained difficult and tedious in the context of large-scale software systems.

Authors of [42] study the relation between object-oriented metrics and software defects. They report the response for a class (RFC) and weighted method count (WMC) as most suited for identifying defect potential. A similar study using the Mozilla application suite [16] showed the coupling between objects (CBO) and lines of code (LOC) as accurate fault predictors. These findings were backed by [45], where a NASA data set was the target of defect estimation efforts, and [7], where evaluation was carried out using eight C++ applications. This also leads to the issue of the target application's programming language, with authors [23] claiming that metric value expectations have to be adapted to each language in particular. The over-arching conclusion of metric-based evaluations is that further work is required before definitive expectations can be formalized regarding the relation between software quality characteristics and metric values.

3 Maintainability Models

3.1 Maintainability Index

There exists long-term interest regarding the correct estimation of the required effort for maintaining software systems. Initially defined in the late '70, the computational formula for the Maintainability Index (MI) was introduced in 1992 [38]. The formula takes into consideration source code size, measured according to variants of the lines of code metric and two views of complexity expressed in terms of the modular paradigm; they are the number of operations and operators, also known as the Halstead volume and the number of possible execution paths generated by existing conditional and loop statements. The variant employed in our research is [38]:

$$MI = 171 - 5.2 * ln(aveV) - 0.23 * aveG - 16.2 * ln(aveSTAT)$$

where $aveV$ denotes average Halstead volume, $aveG$ is the number of possible execution paths (cyclomatic complexity) and $aveSTAT$ is the average number of statements. Several versions of this formula exist, such as considering the LOC metric instead of statement counts, or including the number of lines of comments into the formula. The presented version returns values between 171 (best maintainability) and negative numbers, which are evaluated as very poor maintainability. Several implementations [30] normalize the formula to return values in the $[0, 100]$ range by translating all negative values to 0. Different development, metric or code inspection tools compute the MI [24,30,41,43], and some provide good practices [30], stating that values below 20 correspond to poor maintainability.

Several criticisms to this maintainability assessment formula have been reported in the literature [12,17,44]. They are related to the fact that average values are used in the computation, ignoring the real distribution of values, or that the defined threshold values are not very accurate. Also, the index was defined for modular and procedural programming languages, thus not taking into consideration object oriented features that defined new relations such as inheritance, coupling and cohesion. These have been reported to have a considerable effect on maintainability [9,23,27,31].

3.2   ARiSA Compendium Model

The *Compendium of Software Quality Standards and Metrics*[1] was created by ARiSA and researchers from the Linnaeus University. It aims to study the relation between software quality characteristics and software metric values. The Compendium models software quality according to the ISO 9126, an older version in the ISO family for software quality standards. Like the more recent ISO 25010 incarnation, it is a hierarchical model made up of six characteristics, which in turn have 27 sub-characteristics. Similar with ISO 25010, *Maintainability* is one of the characteristics, with sub-characteristics *Analyzability*, *Changeability*, *Compliance*, *Stability* and *Testability*. For each characteristic, with the notable exception of Compliance, the set of influencing metrics is provided. For each metric influence, the Compendium details the direction and strength of the influence, as detailed using Table 1. The direction of the influence can be direct, or inverse, represented using upward, or downward chevrons, respectively. These illustrate whether increased values for the given metric lead to an improvement or degradation of maintainability. The number or chevrons represent the strength of this correlation, with two chevrons representing a stronger relation. For example, the weighted method count (WMC) metric relates strongly and inversely with analyzability, changeability and testability, and inversely (but not strongly) with stability.

The VizzMaintenance [3] Eclipse plugin implements a quantitative model of class-level maintainability. It is based on the relations from the Compendium and uses a number of structural, complexity and design class-level object-oriented metrics that are shown in Table 1. They are the coupling between objects (CBO), data abstraction coupling (DAC), depth of inheritance tree (DIT), locality of data (LD), lack of cohesion in methods (LCOM) and its improved variant (ILCOM), message pass coupling (MPC), number of children (NOC), tight class cohesion (TCC), lines of code (LOC), number of attributes and methods (NAM), number of methods (NOM), response for class (RFC), weighted method count (WMC), number of classes in cycle (CYC) length of names (LEN) and lack of documentation (LOD). They are formally defined within the Compendium [3] and were used in previous research [6,36].

The proposed quantitative model relies on the relations presented in Table 1 and the extracted metric values. The level of maintainability is calculated for each class on a $[0, 1]$ scale, with smaller values representing improved maintainability. First, the percentage of metric values within the top or bottom 15% of each metric's value range across all classes is calculated. Then, they are aggregated across the four criteria according to the direction and strength of the relations shown in Table 1, resulting in the maintainability score of the class. As such, a score of 0 means that none of the metrics has an extreme value for the given class, while a value of 1 is obtained when all metric values belong in the top (or bottom) 15%. As an example, let us consider a class having a single metric value in the top 15%, that of the WMC. The analyzability score for WMC is $\frac{2}{33}$.

---

[1] http://www.arisa.se/compendium/.

Table 1. Metric influences on maintainability according to the ARiSA Model [3].

	CBO	DAC	DIT	LD	LCOM	ILCOM	MPC	NOC	TCC	LOC	NAM	NOM	RFC	WMC	CYC	LEN	LOD
Analyzability	⌄	⌄	⌄	⌃	⌄	⌄	⌄	⌄	⌃	⌄	⌄	⌄	⌄	⌄	⌄	⌄	⌄
Changeability	⌄	⌄	⌄	⌃	⌄	⌄	⌄	⌄	⌃	⌄	⌄	⌄	⌄	⌄	⌄	⌄	⌄
Stability	⌄	⌄	⌄	⌃	⌄	⌄	⌄	⌄	⌃	⌄	⌄	⌄	⌄	⌄	⌄	⌄	⌄
Testability	⌄	⌄	⌄	⌃	⌄	⌄	⌄	⌄	⌃	⌄	⌄	⌄	⌄	⌄	⌄	⌄	⌄
	Structure									Complexity					Design		

The numerator is the weight WMC has for analyzability, and the denominator is the sum total of weights for that criteria (the number of chevrons). The influence of WMC in Changeability is $\frac{2}{34}$, in Stability it is $\frac{1}{26}$ and in testability it is $\frac{2}{33}$. As such, the maintainability score will be calculated as $\frac{\frac{2}{33}+\frac{2}{34}+\frac{1}{26}+\frac{2}{33}}{4} \approx 0.0546$, or 5.46%.

When compared with the MI, the ARiSA model employs a wider selection of metrics. In addition to the commonly used LOC metric, it also employs the WMC as a complexity metric, together with many well-known object-oriented ones, covering object-oriented concerns such as cohesion, coupling and inheritance. While the MI can be calculated at several granularity levels, by default the ARiSA model is limited to class level. In order to scale it to system level, we calculate its geometric mean value across all system classes.

3.3   SQALE Model

The SQALE (Software Quality Assessment Based on Lifecycle Expectations) methodology was first introduced by J.L. Letouzey [22] as a method to evaluate the quality of application source code, in an independent way from programming language or analysis tools. SQALE is tightly linked with the measurement of technical debt[2], especially in the context of Agile development methodologies. The first definition for technical debt was provided in 1992 [11] and predates the SQALE model. Cunningham borrowed terminology from the financial sector and compared shipping immature code with *"going into debt"*, and opined that doing so was fine *"so long as it is paid back promptly with a rewrite"* [11]. More recently, Fowler agreed that the presence of technical debt showed that delivering functionality to customers was prioritized above software quality [15]. Given the focus from both researchers and practitioners on controlling software quality resulted in several tools that implement SQALE in order to produce a quantitative assessment of code quality.

Perhaps the most well-known such tool is the SonarQube platform for code quality and security. Its entry-level *Community Edition* is free and open-source. Analysis support is provided through language-specific plugins, with the free version providing the required plugins for analyzing source code in 15 languages including Java, XML and HTML. Support for additional languages or features can be deployed in the form of plugins; for instance, C++ code can be analyzed

---

[2] Found as design debt in some sources.

using a free, community developed plugin[3]. Plugins usually include a number of rules[4], against which the source code's abstract syntax tree is checked during analysis.

Each rule is characterized by the programming language it applies to, its type, associated tags and severity. Rule type is one of *maintainability* (code smell), *reliability* (bug) or *security* (vulnerability). Tags serve to provide a finer-grained characterization, each rule being associated with one or more tags[5] such as *unused, performance* or *brain-overload* (e.g. when code complexity is too high). Breaking a rule results in an *issue*, which inherits its characteristics from the rule that was broken. For example, Java rule *S1067* states that *"Expressions should not be too complex"*. It generates critical severity issues that are tagged with *brain-overload* for expressions that include more than 3 operators. The time estimated to fix the issue is a 5 min constant time to which 1 min is added for each additional operator above the threshold.

An application's total technical debt is calculated as the sum of the estimated times required to fix all detected issues. SonarQube normalizes the level of technical debt relevant to application size using the *Technical Debt Ratio* (TDR), with $TDR = \frac{TD}{DevTime}$; TD represents total technical debt quantified in minutes, while $DevTime$ represents the total time required to develop the system, with 30 min of time required to develop 1 line of production level code. The application is graded according to the SQALE rating between A (best value, $TDR < 5\%$) and E (worst value, $TDR \geq 50\%$). SQALE provides a high-level, evidence-backed and easy to understand interpretation of the system's internal quality. In our case study we calculate SQALE ratings using SonarQube version 8.2, which integrates the Eclipse Java compiler and uses more than 550 rules to detect potential issues in source code.

While SonarQube and similar tools provide quantitative models of software quality, existing research also pointed out some existing pitfalls. Authors of a large-scale case study [26] showed that many of the reported issues remained unfixed, which could be the result of these tools reporting many false-positive, or low-importance results. A study of SonarQube's default rules [21] also showed most of them having limited fault-proneness. These findings are also mirrored in our work [33], where we've shown that issue lifetimes are not correlated with severity or associated tags.

4   State of the Art

The role and impact of maintainability as a software quality factor was investigated in existing literature [13, 17, 18, 37]. The SIG Maintainability model [13, 17] is based on the idea of relating different source code properties such as volume, complexity and unit testing with the sub-characteristics of maintainability as described according to the ISO 9126 model [20]. The SIG Maintainability model

---

[3] https://github.com/SonarOpenCommunity/sonar-cxx.

[4] https://docs.sonarqube.org/latest/user-guide/rules/.

[5] https://docs.sonarqube.org/latest/user-guide/built-in-rule-tags/.

was evaluated on a large number of software applications. Authors of [18] proposed a framework in which quality characteristics defined according to the ISO 25010 model [19] could be assessed directly or indirectly by associated measures that can be easily computed using existing software tooling. The framework remains a proof of concept with more measures required for consideration before the measurement of quality characteristics such as maintainability becomes possible.

The ARiSA model [25; 39] detailed in Sect. 3.2 remains one of the most exhaustive studies that analyzes the relations between a significant number of software metrics and quality factors and sub-factors as defined according to ISO 9126.

The influence object-oriented metrics have on maintainability received a continuous interest in the research community ever since their introduction [9], with existing research showing the existence of a relation between maintainability, coupling and cohesion [2,10,23,28,31]. The influence different metrics have on maintainability has also received intense scrutiny. However, we find that in many cases author conclusions are limited to the identified relation between a singular metric and target system maintainability [23,39]. While important in itself, these do not provide a definitive quantitative model for maintainability, partly due to their strong empirical nature. Thus, in order to develop more precise and easily applicable methods for assessing software quality characteristics we find that more investigations need to be carried out and reported.

As such, the distinctive feature of our study is that it describes and analyzes three approaches of different complexity that enable an evaluation of maintainability in the case of large applications. Furthermore, we analyze and compare results across the application versions and maintainability models themselves in order to improve our understanding of the evolution of open-source applications on one hand, as well as the applicability, strengths and weaknesses of maintainability models on the other.

5   Case Study

The presented case study is the direct continuation of the work presented in [34]. The work was organized and carried out according to currently defined best practices [40,46]. We started by stating the main objective of our work, which we distilled into four research questions. We structured the current section according to Höst and Runeson's methodology [40]. We first discuss the selection of target applications, after which we present the data collection process. We used Sect. 5.4 to discuss the results of our analysis, after which we address the threats to our study's validity.

5.1   Research Questions

We defined our work's main objective using the goal-question-metric approach [8] to be *"study the maintainability of evolving open-source software using quantitative software quality models"*. We refined our stated objective into four research questions. They serve to guide the analysis phase of the study, as well as to provide an in-depth view when compared with our previous work [34].

RQ_1: *What is the Correlation between Application size and Maintainability?* In our previous work [34] we have disproved the naïve expectation that lower maintainability is reported for larger applications. However, we employ RQ_1 to ensure that maintainability scores reported using the proposed quantitative models are not excessively influenced by software size. While in our previous work [34] we have examined this relation using the number of classes as a proxy for system size, we extend our investigation to cover the number of packages, methods and lines of code. We aim to employ system size measurements in order to study their effect on reported maintainability, as both the MI and ARiSA models include class and line counts in their assessment.

RQ_2: *What Drives Maintainability Changes between Application Versions?* In our previous study we identified important changes in the maintainability scores reported for the target applications. We expect the answer to RQ_2 will help us identify the rationale behind the large changes in maintainability reported in each of the target applications studied in our previous work. We aim to triangulate collected data [40] by carrying out a cross-application examination. We expect this will facilitate identifying common causes and help alleviate external threats to our study. In order to properly contextualize observed changes to maintainability, we carry out a detailed manual source code examination.

RQ_3: *How are Maintainability Changes Reflected at the Package Level?* We employ RQ_1 in order to study the relation between reported maintainability and software size, each measured according to several quantitative metrics. Then, the answer to RQ_2 helps determine the amplitude and rationale behind the reported changes. We take the following step via RQ_3, where we carry out a finer grained analysis at package level, in order to improve our understanding of the impact software evolution has on application component maintainability.

RQ_4: *What are the Strengths and Weaknesses of the Proposed Maintainability Models?* In our previous research we determined the TDR to be the most relevant quantitative model from a software development perspective [34]. However, we also discovered that both the ARiSA model and the MI can provide actionable information in the right context. This is especially true since the ARiSA model was created for class-level usage, while the MI works from system down to method levels. As such, as part of our data analysis we examine our answers to RQ_2 and RQ_3 and highlight the insight that each model can provide together with its drawbacks.

5.2   Target Applications

Since the present paper builds upon and expands our previous research [34], we maintained our selection of target applications. In this section we reiterate our rationale and briefly discuss inclusion criteria. Our main goal was to select a number of complex, widely-used and open-source applications that facilitate

Table 2. Information about the earliest and latest target application versions in our study.

Application	Version	Release date	Statements	Maintainability rating		
				MI	ARiSA	SQALE
FreeMind	0.0.3	July 9, 2000	1,359	81.30	0.22	3.10
	1.1.0Beta2	Feb 5, 2016	20,133	73.92	0.19	3.2
jEdit	2.3pre2	Jan 29, 2000	12,150	73.38	0.16	3.00
	5.5.0	April 9, 2018	43,875	66.90	0.17	3.50
TuxGuitar	0.1pre	June 18, 2006	4,863	71.53	0.12	2.10
	1.5.3	Dec 10, 2019	51,589	75.99	0.17	1.20

evaluating maintainability in the context of software evolution. Previous empirical research in open-source software has shown that many of these systems go through development hiatuses, or are abandoned by the original developers [5]. In other cases, available source code is incomplete, with missing modules or libraries, or contains compile errors [6]. Other applications include complex dependencies which are required to compile or run them, such as Internet services, database servers or the presence of additional equipment.

Taking these considerations into account, we set our inclusion criteria to applications with a long development history and no external dependencies. In order to allow comparing results across applications and in order to alleviate external threats to our study, we limited ourselves to GUI-driven applications developed using the Java platform.

Our selection process resulted in three Java applications. Each of them is available under permissive open-source licensing, has a fully documented development history including an important number of version releases and a consistent user base. They are the FreeMind[6] mind mapper, the jEdit[7] text editor and the TuxGuitar[8] tablature editor. Table 2 provides relevant information for the first and last target application version included in our case study. We refer to all releases included in our study using the version numbers assigned to them by developers. We believe this provides additional context on the magnitude of expected changes between versions, and facilitates replicating our results, as it allows third parties to unambiguously identify them within the code base. Furthermore, as we identified several hiatuses in the development of the studied applications, we found version numbers were more representative than release dates.

FreeMind is a mind-mapping application with a consistent user base, rich functionalities and support for plugin development and integration. The first version in our study is 0.0.3. Released in July, 2000, it consisted of around 1,350 code statements and around 60 classes, which make it the smallest release in our study. This is reflected on a functional level, with early versions of Free-

---

[6] http://freemind.sourceforge.net/wiki/index.php/Main_Page.

[7] http://jedit.org.

[8] http://www.tuxguitar.com.ar.

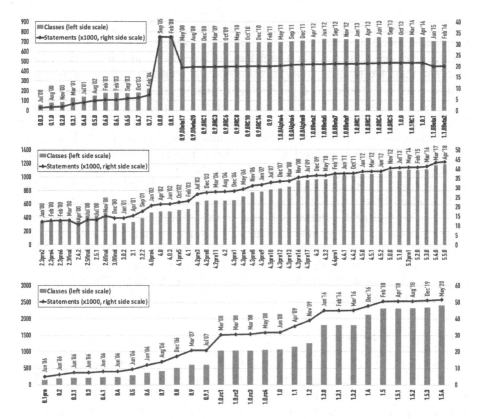

Fig. 2. Size and release date information for FreeMind (top), jEdit (middle) and Tux-Guitar (bottom) versions included in our study.

Mind having limited functionalities, in contrast with later versions. We take this into account in our research when studying the difference between early and mature application versions. Several of its versions were used in previous empirical research [4]. Figure 2 illustrates the development across the versions in our case study using system size and release dates. Versions 0.8.0 and 0.8.1 show an important increase in system size, which is tempered in version 0.9.0Beta17, after which system size remains stable. We also note the $2\frac{1}{2}$ years of hiatus between versions 0.8.0 and 0.8.1. Major changes are recorded for version 0.9.0Beta17, released only 3 months after the previous one. While the most recent version released at the start of 2016, FreeMind maintained a consistent user base, with 681k application downloads during last year and over 21 million over its lifetime[9].

jEdit is a plugin-able text-editor targeted towards programmers. As shown in Fig. 2, its first public version, 2.3pre2 was released in January 2000. Having over 300 classes and 12,000 statements, it is the most polished entry version in our

---

[9] Download data points from https://sourceforge.net/, only consider application releases. Recorded August 25th, 2020.

study. In opposition to FreeMind, we did not record multi-year hiatuses during the development of jEdit. Class and statement counts showed a gradual, but steady increase version to version, which we found reflected at the user experience and functional levels. jEdit was also the subject of software engineering research that targeted GUI testing [4, 47] and software quality [31, 36]. The application has managed to maintain a large user base, having over 92k application downloads last year and over 5.8 million over its lifetime.

TuxGuitar is a tablature editor with multi-track support, which support data import and export across multiple formats. This is implemented in the form of plugins that are included in the default code distribution, which we included in our case study. TuxGuitar was developed with support for several GUI toolkits, and we selected to use its SWT implementation across all versions. As illustrated in Fig. 2, TuxGuitar's evolution is similar to that of jEdit, with a steady increase in application size across most versions. While its development seemed to be halted between versions 1.2 and 1.3.0, its latest version was released in 2020, with the project being actively developed. TuxGuitar also has a consistent user base, recording 266k application downloads during the last year and over 6.9 million over its lifetime.

5.3   Data Collection

We limited our selection to publicly released versions in order to address the risk of compiler errors or missing libraries, as reported by previous research [6]. We handled the case of many incremental version releases in the span of days by only considering the last of them, which helps keep the number of versions manageable. This resulted in 38 releases of FreeMind, 45 releases of jEdit and 28 releases of TuxGuitar included in our study. Each release was then imported into an IDE, where a manual examination of its source code was carried out. A common recurring issue concerned the presence of library code shipped together with application source code. Several jEdit versions included code for the *com.microstar.xml* parser or *BeanShell* interpreter. Our solution was to extract these into a separate library that was added to the application classpath. FreeMind and jEdit source code was analyzed without any plugin code, although both applications provide plugin support. In the case of TuxGuitar, we kept the data import/export plugins included in the official distribution.

Metric data was extracted using the VizzMaintenance plugin for Eclipse, which was also used to calculate the ARiSA maintainability score of each class. We employed the Metrics Reloaded plugin for IntelliJ to calculate the components of the MI, while the SQALE rating was obtained using the community edition of SonarQube 8.2.

5.4   Analysis

In this section we present the most important results of our analysis, structured according to the research questions defined in Sect. 5.1. In order to facilitate

Table 3. Spearman rank correlation between software size according to package, class, method or statement count and system maintainability. FreeMind data on top row, jEdit on middle row and TuxGuitar on bottom row.

	Package	Class	Method	Statement
MI	−0.46	−0.67	−0.71	−0.77
	−0.32	−0.29	−0.40	−0.45
	0.76	0.71	0.69	0.57
ARiSA	−0.29	−0.49	−0.53	−0.62
	−0.51	−0.53	−0.54	−0.55
	0.64	0.63	0.64	0.69
SQALE	−0.23	0.10	0.19	0.38
	0.12	0.14	0.21	0.24
	−0.68	−0.73	−0.74	−0.79

replicating or extending our results, we made available the entire set of collected and processed metric data [32].

RQ$_1$: What is the Correlation between Application size and Maintainability? In our previous research [31,34] we showed that maintainability measured according to quantitative metrics was not correlated with software size, at least not when the latter was expressed using the number of the system's classes. We extended our investigation to also cover the number of a system's packages, methods and statements[10]. Since target applications were developed using Java, there was a strong and expected correlation between class and source file counts, so this evaluation was omitted.

We first carried out a Spearman rank correlation between the size measures for each application. We found very high correlation between all measures for application size ($\rho \geq 0.8$), especially between the number of classes, methods and statements ($\rho \geq 0.96$) for each target application.

We repeated the correlation analysis between the size measurements and reported values for maintainability, which we report using Table 3. Note that higher scores correspond to a decrease in maintainability according to the ARiSA and SQALE models, and an increase according to the MI. Results for FreeMind and jEdit show similarity across all three models. We note that increased values for the MI are accounted for by joint increases across its components (statement count, Halstead volume and cyclomatic complexity). Values produced by our generalization of the ARiSA model are skewed by small files added in later software versions; these keep mean values low, leading to what we believe are under-reported changes to maintainability. The SQALE model is driven by static analysis of the abstract syntax tree, and is not directly influenced by size-related metric values. This also explains the weak correlation with the number of statements, which is the lowest-level size metric considered.

---

[10] Collected using the Metrics Reloaded plugin for IntelliJ.

As shown in Fig. 3, TuxGuitar was evaluated as having very good maintainability [34]. All releases remained well below the 5% threshold required to receive an A rating according to SQALE. We believe this to be the result of a conscientious effort on the behalf of its developers. Important increases to system size, such as those for versions 1.0rc1, 1.3 and 1.5 did not have an important effect on measured maintainability. In version 1.0rc1, an increase in system size was actually coupled with improved maintainability according to SQALE.

Our analysis showed the MI and ARiSA models to be influenced by software size, which is known to have a confounding effect [14]. The SQALE model did not appear to have been influenced by it, as it does not rely on size-related software metrics.

RQ_2: *What Drives Maintainability Changes between Application Versions?* We base our answer to RQ_2 on the data from Fig. 3, which shows system-level maintainability according to the three models. Data is normalized to the [0, 100] range. Our previous research [34] showed that of the proposed quantitative models, technical debt was the most suitable for evaluating system-

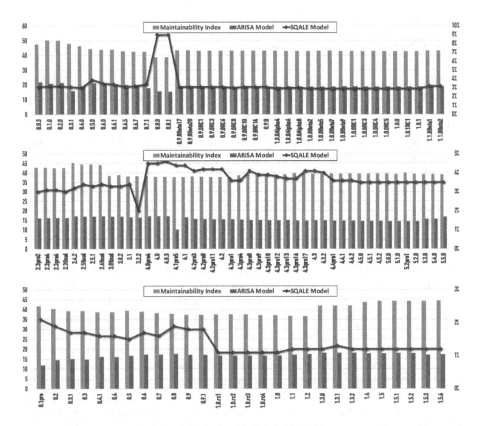

Fig. 3. Maintainability of FreeMind (top), jEdit (middle) and TuxGuitar (bottom) versions in our study. SQALE model uses the scale on the right side.

level quality. As such, we focus on the SQALE rating to quantify system-level maintainability [34]. According to it, most application versions have good maintainability, with most studied versions receiving an A rating; the only exceptions were FreeMind versions 0.8.0 and 0.8.1, which earned a B SQALE rating. We also note that most TuxGuitar versions have a $TDR \leq 2\%$, as during our previous evaluation we found evidence of concerted developer action to improve software quality.

Examining the data in Fig. 3 revealed that system-level maintainability did not suffer major changes across most versions. As such, we identified key versions [34] during which quantitative changes were detected. In the case of FreeMind, versions 0.8.* were the result of significant application development that increased application size from 12.5k LOC to 65.5k LOC, with an additional 370 days worth of technical debt added [33,34]. Most of the added debt was fixed in version 0.9.0Beta17 with no loss to functionality; our detailed analysis of subsequent versions only revealed small-scale maintainability changes [33].

Our evaluation of jEdit version 4.0pre4 revealed that additional functionalities such as improved management of the text area, buffer events and the document model, implemented using 11k LOC added an extra month of technical debt. However, our detailed examination [33] revealed that versions after 4.0 gradually reduced the level of debt and the addition of significant additional quality issues appears to have been avoided.

Most of the changes observed within TuxGuitar were of smaller significance, as it already presented very good maintainability. The most significant version shown in Fig. 3 is 1.0rc1; here, we observed that extensive refactoring efforts on existing debt were coupled with the introduction of additional issues [33], most likely as part of the additional support for the song collection browser and the inclusion of new plugins. Overall, technical debt was improved to a level that was maintained until the most recent released version.

RQ_3: How are Maintainability Changes Reflected at the Package Level? Our previous evaluation [34] revealed that among studied models, SQALE was the one best suited for system and package-level quality assessment. As such, we used SonarQube's estimation of required maintainability effort at package level for each of the application versions in our study. We identified core packages that existed within all studied versions, as well as packages introduced at some point and removed at a later time. We found this to be typical of TuxGuitar, for which we counted a total of 354 packages across all versions. On the other hand, jEdit's entire code base consisted of 30 packages, while the FreeMind code base covering all releases was comprised of 41 packages.

We represent the estimated time to address at least half the total maintainability effort for each application in Fig. 4. We show that most maintainability issues were concentrated on a small subset of application packages. For instance, the six packages represented for jEdit account for almost 80% total maintenance effort, while the 24 packages illustrated for TuxGuitar cover half the required effort.

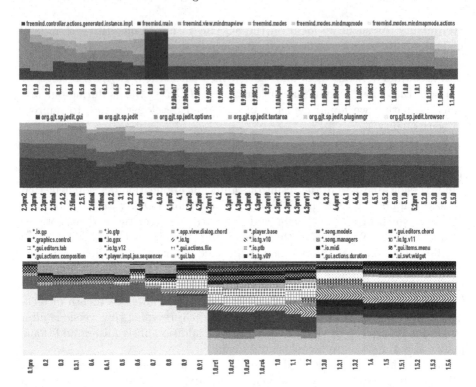

Fig. 4. Estimated maintainability effort at package level according to the SQALE model for FreeMind (top), jEdit (middle) and TuxGuitar (bottom, * stands for *org.herac.tuxguitar*) versions. Represented packages account for at least half of total effort per application.

Figure 4 shows FreeMind and jEdit versions to be very stable with regards to the distribution of the required maintenance effort. In the case of FreeMind, we discovered it was mainly generated code from the *[...].generated.instance.impl* package that caused the severe decrease in maintainability, while in the remaining application packages the maintenance effort did not change significantly. For TuxGuitar, we noted the changes in versions 1.0rc1 and 1.3.0. While our previous evaluation already showed system maintainability to be affected within these versions [34], it was package-level examination that revealed changes to plugin code from the *org.herac.tuxguitar.io.gp* package as the cause of changes in version 1.0rc1.

Figure 4 also reveals information about application architecture. Both FreeMind and jEdit were built around a relatively small, but constant set of packages and suffered most changes during the development of their early versions [31]. In the case of TuxGuitar, we found each plugin to have a separate package, with many input-output plugins maintaining separate packages for each implementation versions. This resulted in a more complex and change-prone hierarchy.

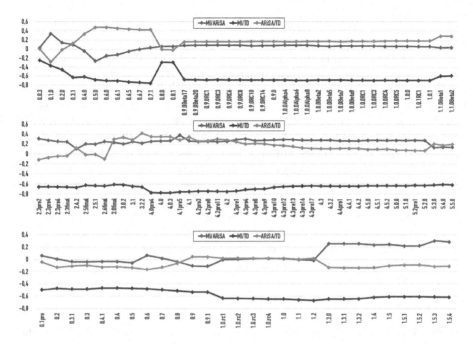

Fig. 5. Value of the Spearman correlation coefficient between maintainability models applied at class level for FreeMind (top), jEdit (middle) and TuxGuitar (bottom) versions.

We found that the main advantage of drilling down to package level regarded the precise identification of the locations and dimensions of the maintenance effort. When combined with a longitudinal analysis [33], a package-level evaluation can help with program comprehension and testing, as it can be used to discard application areas that have not undergone changes.

RQ_4: **What are the Strengths and Weaknesses of the Proposed Maintainability Models?** Our answer for RQ_4 takes into account our existing research in software maintainability [31,34] and the long-term evolution of technical debt [33], as well as the results of the detailed examination carried out for RQ_2 and RQ_3. We found that the SQALE model, and its implementation in the form of technical debt to be the most accurate quantitative quality measure among those studied. Technical debt evaluation provides a general assessment of a given system, but can also be employed at a finer level of granularity to uncover the root causes of detected issues [33]. However, existing criticism outlined in Sect. 3.3 point against using it without prejudice to evaluate software quality.

The ARiSA model is strictly based on the evaluation of extreme values for class level object-oriented metrics. We found that aggregating class-level scores did not produce useful results, as in many cases quality issues were masked, or completely countered by large numbers of small, low complexity classes that influenced mean values. The same criticism can be brought against the MI, computing which is limited to three metrics, none of which specific to the object-oriented domain. The important advantage of the MI is that it remains language-independent and has a straightforward implementation. As such, in order to examine its potential for usage at a finer-grained level, we carried out a Spearman rank correlation between the result produced using the proposed models at class level, as shown in Fig. 5. The only consistent correlation observed occurred between the MI and technical debt with $\rho \approx -0.6$. We believe this is an indication that the MI can be employed to quickly discover code complexity issues at method and class levels. However, a more detailed examination is required in order to fully describe and characterize this result.

We believe the ARiSA model remains well suited to discovering quality hot spots within the context of a singular application [34]. While it employs an important number of object-oriented measurements, the model derives value thresholds from the evaluated system's context, making it unsuitable for cross-application and cross-version comparisons.

5.5   Threats to Validity

We structured the case study according to existing best practices [40]. First, the main objective and research question were defined, after which target application selection took place. This was followed by the data collection and analysis phases. We carried out a manual examination of source code in order to complement the results from the quantitative models, and open-sourced the data to facilitate replicating or extending our study [32].

Internal threats were addressed by complementing automated evaluation with a manual examination of the source code; this step was also assisted by source code in order to prevent any observer bias. Data analysis was carried out using previously used research tooling [31,33,34,36] to avoid the possibility of software defects influencing evaluation result.

Quantitative models employed were selected according with their previous use in research and practice, as well as varying implementation complexity. MI values were calculated using both statement count and LOC, while for the ARiSA model we studied the effect of calculating the final value using all three Pythagorean means.

We addressed external threats by limiting target application selection to GUI-driven Java applications. While this limited the applicability of our study's conclusions, it also enabled data triangulation and directly comparing results across applications. To the best of our knowledge, there were no overlaps between target application development teams. Furthermore, neither of the present study's authors were involved with their development.

The entire data set of extracted metric values together with versions processed by our tooling are open-sourced and freely available. We believe this to be the most important step required in order to solidify our results and encourage further work to extend them.

6   Conclusion and Future Work

In the present paper we continued our empirical research targeting the relation between metric values and software product quality [31, 33, 34, 36]. We confirmed our initial findings regarding the independence of maintainability effort from software size [34]. We also confirmed initial expectations regarding the gradual, but sustained increase in application size during development. However, we could also identify key versions where extensive refactoring kept application size and complexity in check. Another interesting observation was that mature application versions no longer introduced significant quality issues. We first observed this when studying software metric values [35, 36] and confirmed it through evaluating the data summarized in Fig. 3. We believe this can be explained through an already matured application architecture, together with the existence of a core of experienced contributors.

Our evaluation also uncovered the existence of milestone versions, characterized by significant changes at source code level and the addition of many new features. Versions such as FreeMind 0.8.0, jEdit 4.0pre4 or TuxGuitar 1.0rc1 are such examples, where changes to the application had an important effect on software quality. The case of TuxGuitar 1.0rc1 is especially worth mention, as a development milestone was coupled with refactoring efforts that lowered maintenance effort. With regards to the root causes of changes to maintainability, we consistently found the main drivers to be significant changes to application presentation, functionality and extensive refactoring.

Most of the existing research is limited to evaluating software quality at system level. In our study, we carried out a finer grained analysis at application package level in order to improve our understanding of the distribution and evolution of the maintenance effort. Figure 4 illustrates this for the most maintenance-heavy application packages. This allowed us to discover the root cause of the maintenance spike in FreeMind 0.8.0, as well as the effects of the plugin-centered architecture on the distribution and evolution of maintenance effort for TuxGuitar. Especially in the case of TuxGuitar, Fig. 4 illustrates how maintenance effort was redistributed across the packages in versions with significant changes to source code.

Finally, our study provided an opportunity to examine the maintainability models themselves. We found the MI to remain useful at a very fine granularity level, and can be used at method or class level to ensure code complexity remains in check. We found the ARiSA model to be useful at application level, but its particularities preclude it from being useful when comparing applications. This can be achieved using the SQALE methodology and its implementations, which provide a language agnostic measurement scale.

Further directions targeting this research topic include extending the evaluation from two perspectives. First, to consider other types of software systems, such as mobile or distributed applications. Second, to investigate the effect the development platform and programming language have on maintenance effort.

References

1. Al-Qutaish, R.E., Ain, A.: Quality models in software engineering literature: an analytical and comparative study. Technical report 3 (2010). http://www.americanscience.org. editor@americanscience.org166
2. Almugrin, S., Albattah, W., Melton, A.: Using indirect coupling metrics to predict package maintainability and testability. J. Syst. Softw. **121**, 298–310 (2016). https://doi.org/10.1016/j.jss.2016.02.024. http://www.sciencedirect.com/science/article/pii/S016412121600056X
3. ARISA Compendium, VizzMaintenance: Technical documentation of the VizzMaintenance metric extraction tool (2019). http://www.arisa.se/products.php?lang=en
4. Arlt, S., Banerjee, I., Bertolini, C., Memon, A.M., Schaf, M.: Grey-box GUI testing: efficient generation of event sequences. CoRR abs/1205.4928 (2012)
5. Avelino, G., Constantinou, E., Valente, M.T., Serebrenik, A.: On the abandonment and survival of open source projects: an empirical investigation. In: 2019 ACM/IEEE International Symposium on Empirical Software Engineering and Measurement (ESEM), pp. 1–12 (2019)
6. Barkmann, H., Lincke, R., Löwe, W.: Quantitative evaluation of software quality metrics in open-source projects. In: 2009 International Conference on Advanced Information Networking and Applications Workshops, pp. 1067–1072, May 2009. https://doi.org/10.1109/WAINA.2009.190
7. Basili, V.R., Briand, L.C., Melo, W.L.: A validation of object-oriented design metrics as quality indicators. IEEE Trans. Software Eng. **22**(10), 751–761 (1996). https://doi.org/10.1109/32.544352
8. Caldiera, V.R.B.G., Rombach, H.D.: The goal question metric approach. Encycl. Softw. Eng. 528–532 (1994)
9. Chidamber, S., Kemerer, C.: A metric suite for object- oriented design. IEEE Trans. Software Eng. **20**(6), 476–493 (1994)
10. Counsell, S., et al.: Re-visiting the 'Maintainability Index' metric from an object-oriented perspective. In: 2015 41st Euromicro Conference on Software Engineering and Advanced Applications, pp. 84–87 (2015)
11. Cunningham, W.: The WyCash portfolio management system. SIGPLAN OOPS Mess. **4**(2), 29–30 (1992). https://doi.org/10.1145/157710.157715. http://doi.acm.org/10.1145/157710.157715
12. van Deursen, A.: Think twice before using the maintainability index (2014). https://avandeursen.com/2014/08/29/think-twice-before-using-the-maintainability-index/
13. Döhmen, T., Bruntink, M., Ceolin, D., Visser, J.: Towards a benchmark for the maintainability evolution of industrial software systems. In: 2016 Joint Conference of the International Workshop on Software Measurement and the International Conference on Software Process and Product Measurement (IWSM-MENSURA), pp. 11–21 (2016)
14. Emam, K.E., Benlarbi, S., Goel, N., Rai, S.N.: The confounding effect of class size on the validity of object-oriented metrics. IEEE Trans. Softw. Eng. **27**(7), 630–650 (2001). https://doi.org/10.1109/32.935855
15. Fowler, M.: Technical debt (2019). https://martinfowler.com/bliki/TechnicalDebt.html
16. Gyimothy, T., Ferenc, R., Siket, I.: Empirical validation of object-oriented metrics on open source software for fault prediction. IEEE Trans. Software Eng. **31**(10), 897–910 (2005). https://doi.org/10.1109/TSE.2005.112

17. Heitlager, I., Kuipers, T., Visser, J.: A practical model for measuring maintainability. In: Quality of Information and Communications Technology, 6th International Conference on the Quality of Information and Communications Technology, QUATIC 2007, Lisbon, Portugal, 12–14 September 2007, Proceedings, pp. 30–39 (2007). https://doi.org/10.1109/QUATIC.2007.8
18. Hynninen, T., Kasurinen, J., Taipale, O.: Framework for observing the maintenance needs, runtime metrics and the overall quality-in-use. J. Softw. Eng. Appl. **11**, 139–152 (2018). https://doi.org/10.4236/jsea.2018.114009
19. ISO/IEC 25010: Software quality standards (2011). http://www.iso.org
20. ISO/IEC 9126–1: Software quality characteristics (2001)
21. Lenarduzzi, V., Lomio, F., Huttunen, H., Taibi, D.: Are SonarQube rules inducing bugs? In: 2020 IEEE 27th International Conference on Software Analysis, Evolution and Reengineering (SANER) (2020). https://doi.org/10.1109/saner48275.2020.9054821. http://dx.doi.org/10.1109/SANER48275.2020.9054821
22. Letouzey, J.L.: The SQALE method for evaluating technical debt. In: Proceedings of the Third International Workshop on Managing Technical Debt, MTD 2012, pp. 31–36. IEEE Press (2012). http://dl.acm.org/citation.cfm?id=2666036.2666042
23. Li, W., Henry, S.: Maintenance metrics for the object oriented paradigm. In: IEEE Proceedings of the First International Software Metrics Symposium, pp. 52–60 (1993)
24. Metrics library, N.: (2019). https://github.com/etishor/Metrics.NET
25. Lincke, R., Lundberg, J., Löwe, W.: Comparing software metrics tools. In: Proceedings of the 2008 International Symposium on Software Testing and Analysis - ISSTA 2008 (2008). https://doi.org/10.1145/1390630.1390648
26. Marcilio, D., Bonifácio, R., Monteiro, E., Canedo, E., Luz, W., Pinto, G.: Are static analysis violations really fixed? A closer look at realistic usage of SonarQube. In: Proceedings of the 27th International Conference on Program Comprehension,ICPC 2019, pp. 209–219. IEEE Press (2019). https://doi.org/10.1109/ICPC.2019.00040. https://doi.org/10.1109/ICPC.2019.00040
27. Marinescu, R.: Measurement and quality in object oriented design. Ph.D. thesis, Faculty of Automatics and Computer Science, University of Timisoara (2002)
28. Marinescu, R.: Measurement and quality in object-oriented design, vol. 2005, pp. 701–704, October 2005. https://doi.org/10.1109/ICSM.2005.63
29. Martini, A., Bosch, J., Chaudron, M.: Investigating architectural technical debt accumulation and refactoring over time. Inf. Softw. Technol. **67**(C), 237–253 (2015). https://doi.org/10.1016/j.infsof.2015.07.005
30. Microsoft VS Docs (2020). https://docs.microsoft.com/en-us/visualstudio/code-quality/code-metrics-values
31. Molnar, A., Motogna, S.: Discovering maintainability changes in large software systems. In: Proceedings of the 27th International Workshop on Software Measurement and 12th International Conference on Software Process and Product Measurement, IWSM Mensura 2017, pp. 88–93. ACM, New York (2017). https://doi.org/10.1145/3143434.3143447. http://doi.acm.org/10.1145/3143434.3143447
32. Molnar, A.J.: Quantitative maintainability data for FreeMind, jEdit and TuxGuitar versions, September 2020. https://doi.org/10.6084/m9.figshare.12901331.v1. https://figshare.com/articles/dataset/Quantitative_maintainability_data_for_FreeMind_jEdit_and_TuxGuitar_versions/12901331
33. Molnar, A.J., Motogna, S.: Long-term evaluation of technical debt in open-source software (2020). https://dl.acm.org/doi/abs/10.1145/3382494.3410673

34. Molnar., A., Motogna, S.: Longitudinal evaluation of open-source software maintainability. In: Proceedings of the 15th International Conference on Evaluation of Novel Approaches to Software Engineering - Volume 1: ENASE, pp. 120–131. INSTICC, SciTePress (2020). https://doi.org/10.5220/0009393501200131
35. Molnar, A.-J., Neamţu, A., Motogna, S.: Evaluation of software product quality metrics. In: Damiani, E., Spanoudakis, G., Maciaszek, L.A. (eds.) ENASE 2019. CCIS, vol. 1172, pp. 163–187. Springer, Cham (2020). https://doi.org/10.1007/978-3-030-40223-5_8
36. Molnar, A., Neamçu, A., Motogna, S.: Longitudinal evaluation of software quality metrics in open-source applications. In: Proceedings of the 14th International Conference on Evaluation of Novel Approaches to Software Engineering - Volume 1: ENASE, pp. 80–91. INSTICC, SciTePress (2019). https://doi.org/10.5220/0007725600800091
37. Motogna, S., Vescan, A., Serban, C., Tirban, P.: An approach to assess maintainability change. In: 2016 IEEE International Conference on Automation, Quality and Testing, Robotics (AQTR), pp. 1–6 (2016). https://doi.org/10.1109/AQTR.2016.7501279
38. Oman, P., Hagemeister, J.: Metrics for assessing a software system's maintainability. In: Proceedings Conference on Software Maintenance 1992, pp. 337–344 (1992). https://doi.org/10.1109/ICSM.1992.242525
39. Lincke, R., Lowe, W.: Compendium of Software Quality Standards and Metrics (2019). http://www.arisa.se/compendium/quality-metrics-compendium.html
40. Runeson, P., Höst, M.: Guidelines for conducting and reporting case study research in software engineering. Empir. Softw. Eng. (2009). https://doi.org/10.1007/s10664-008-9102-8
41. SonarSource: SonarQube (2019). https://www.sonarqube.org
42. Tang, M.H., Kao, M.H., Chen, M.H.: An empirical study on object-oriented metrics. In: Proceedings of the 6th International Symposium on Software Metrics, METRICS 1999, pp. 242–249. IEEE Computer Society, Washington (1999). http://dl.acm.org/citation.cfm?id=520792.823979
43. Virtual Machinery: Discussion on measuring the Maintanability Index (2019). http://www.virtualmachinery.com/sidebar4.htm
44. Welker, K.: Software Maintainability Index revisited. J. Defense Softw. Eng. (2001). https://www.osti.gov/biblio/912059
45. Xu, J., Ho, D., Capretz, L.F.: An empirical validation of object-oriented design metrics for fault prediction. J. Comput. Sci. 4, 571–577 (2008)
46. Yin, R.K.: Case Study Research and Applications - Design and Methods. SAGE Publishing, Thousand Oaks (2017)
47. Yuan, X., Memon, A.M.: Generating event sequence-based test cases using GUI run-time state feedback. IEEE Trans. Softw. Eng. 36(1), 81–95 (2010). http://doi.ieeecomputersociety.org/10.1109/TSE.2009.68

Risk Treatment: An Iterative Method for Identifying Controls

Roman Wirtz$^{(\boxtimes)}$ and Maritta Heisel

University of Duisburg-Essen, Duisburg, Germany
roman.wirtz@uni-due.de

Abstract. Due to the increasing number of security incidents in the last years, the consideration of security during software development becomes more and more important. A certain level of security can be achieved by applying suitable countermeasures. The ISO 27001 standard demands a risk-based selection of countermeasures, i.e. controls, for information security. Risk serves as a prioritization criterion for selecting controls. To reduce the development effort, security should be addressed as early as possible in the software development lifecycle.

In this paper, we present an iterative and risk-based method to select controls during requirements engineering, following the principle of security-by-design. We select controls based on unacceptable risks and the related functional requirements. Each risk and control is described by attributes that allow an evaluation of the control's effectiveness based on the Common Vulnerability Scoring System. The evaluation is supported by a web-based tool. A distinguishing feature of our method is that during iteration, we consider new incidents that may occur when applying a control. For documenting the results, we present a metamodel that ensures consistency and traceability between requirements and security aspects.

Keywords: Security risk · Risk management · Risk treatment · Controls · Requirements engineering · Model-based · Patterns

1 Introduction

Due to the increasing number of security incidents in the last years, the consideration of security during software development becomes more and more important [6]. A security incident describes an event or state that leads to harm for a stakeholder, e.g. in terms of financial or reputation loss [17]. To achieve a certain level of security, it is necessary to select appropriate controls addressing those incidents. By considering controls as early as possible during software development, the development effort can be reduced significantly. Concerning information security, the ISO 27001 standard [14] demands a risk-based selection of controls. Risk is defined by an incident's likelihood and the corresponding impact, and applying a control can reduce that risk to an acceptable level.

© Springer Nature Switzerland AG 2021
R. Ali et al. (Eds.): ENASE 2020, CCIS 1375, pp. 283–310, 2021.
https://doi.org/10.1007/978-3-030-70006-5_12

We aim to support security engineers in all phases of a risk management process as described in the ISO 27005 standard [15]. Following the principle of security-by-design [12], we work in the context of requirements engineering as one of the earliest phases of software development.

In previous work, we have developed methods to identify and evaluate security risks during requirements engineering. Our model-based approach based on *Problem Frames* [16] and *CORAS* [19] ensures consistency between the requirements model and the security model. To make knowledge reusable, we developed a template to describe incidents [28]. Using CORAS, we document those incidents in the context of functional requirements [29]. The attributes used in the template are based on the *Common Vulnerability Scoring System (CVSS)* [9], and they allow us to evaluate and prioritize the risks which arise in the context of an incident [26].

We further provide a template-based method to select and evaluate suitable controls for unacceptable risks [25,30]. It describes an aspect-oriented approach to integrate controls into the requirements model. The extended model serves as the input for the design phase, thus helping to create an architecture that takes security into account right from the beginning.

The previously developed method does not consider that the application of controls may lead to new incidents. For example, when applying an encryption mechanism, an attacker may break it. In this paper, we extend the method in such a way that it is carried out iteratively to identify and treat those incidents, too. To capture knowledge about new possible incidents when applying a control, we extend our control specification template with a new section.

To support the application of the method, we provide tool support for the documentation and evaluation of controls. First, we extend our metamodel for risk evaluation [26] with elements for risk treatment. The extension formalizes the relation between the CVSS attributes, the elements of the CORAS language, and the requirements model. By instantiating that model, the results of risk treatment can be documented systematically, at the same time ensuring traceability and consistency. Second, we provide a web-based tool for pre-filtering and evaluating suitable controls. For filtering controls, the tool takes the CVSS attributes into account. Furthermore, it systematically presents a control's details required for carrying out the manual steps of the method. It can be accessed from any browser via a graphical user interface. We further provide a REST API to connect our metamodel with the application.

The remainder of the paper is structured in the following way: In Sect. 2, we present necessary background knowledge, namely problem frames and CORAS, and we introduce our previous work in Sect. 3. Section 4 contains the metamodel for documentation, which is followed by our iterative method in Sect. 5. To exemplify its application, we show a case study in Sect. 6, and we describe our tool in Sect. 7. Finally, we discuss our findings in Sect. 8, present related work in Sect. 9, and provide an outlook on future research directions in Sect. 10.

2   Background

In this section, we introduce necessary background knowledge, i.e. Jackson's problem frames approach and the CORAS language.

2.1   Problem Frames

For modeling requirements, we make use of problem diagrams which consist of domains, phenomena, and interfaces [16]. We make use of Google's Material Design[1] to illustrate the diagrams in a user-friendly way [27].

Machine domains (⌑) represent the piece of software to be developed.

Problem domains represent entities of the real world. There are different types: biddable domains with an unpredictable behavior, e.g. persons (☻), causal domains (❀) with a predictable behavior, e.g. technical equipment, and lexical domains (▤) for data representation. A domain can take the role of a connection domain (⊞), connecting two other domains, e.g. user interfaces or networks.

Interfaces between domains consist of phenomena. There are symbolic phenomena, representing some kind of information or a state, and causal phenomena, representing events, actions, and commands. Each phenomenon is controlled by exactly one domain and can be observed by other domains. A phenomenon controlled by one domain and observed by another is called a shared phenomenon between these two domains. Interfaces (solid lines) contain sets of shared phenomena. Such a set contains phenomena controlled by one domain indicated by $X!\{...\}$, where X stands for an abbreviation of the name of the controlling domain.

A problem diagram contains a statement in form of a functional requirement (represented by the symbol ▣) describing a specific functionality to be developed. A requirement is an optative statement that describes how the environment should behave when the software is installed.

Some phenomena are *referred to* by a requirement (dashed line to controlling domain), and at least one phenomenon is *constrained* by a requirement (dashed line with arrowhead and italics). The domains and their phenomena that are *referred to* by a requirement are not influenced by the machine, whereas we build the machine to influence the *constrained* domain's phenomena in such a way that the requirement is fulfilled.

In Fig. 1, we show a small example describing a functional requirement for updating some information. A *Person* ☻ provides information to *Software* ⌑ to be updated. We make use of a lexical domain *Information* ▤ to illustrate a database. The functional requirement *Update* ▣ refers to the phenomenon *updateInformation* and constrains the phenomenon *information*.

---

[1] Google Material - https://material.io (last access: February 20, 2020).

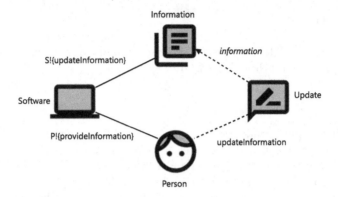

Fig. 1. Example of a problem diagram [30].

2.2 CORAS

CORAS is a model-based method for risk management [19]. It consists of a stepwise process and different kinds of diagrams to document the results. Each step provides guidelines for the interaction with the customer on whose behalf the risk management activities are carried out. The results are documented in diagrams using the CORAS language. The method starts with the establishment of the context and ends with the suggestion of treatments to address the risk.

Identified risks can be documented in a so-called threat diagram of which we show an example in Fig. 2. A threat diagram consists of the following elements: An *Asset* is an item of value. There are *Human-threats deliberate*, e.g. a network attacker, as well as *Human-threats accidental*, e.g. an employee pressing a wrong button accidentally. To describe technical issues there are *Non-human threats*, e.g. malfunction of software. A threat *initiates* a *Threat scenario* with a certain likelihood, and a threat scenario describes a state, which may *lead to* an unwanted incident with another likelihood. An *Unwanted incident* describes the action that actually *impacts* an asset, i.e. has a negative consequence for it.

In the following, we will use the term *incident scenario* as given in the ISO 27005 standard [15]. In the context of CORAS, an incident scenario describes

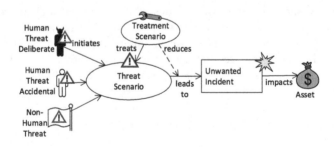

Fig. 2. CORAS threat diagram [30].

the path between threat and asset and the related elements, i.e. threat scenario and unwanted incident. It can be further specified using our template which we describe in Sect. 3.1.

To describe controls, there are *Treatment Scenarios*. The solid arrow points to the element which the control treats, e.g. the threat scenario. Additionally, we introduce a dashed arrow that points to the likelihood or consequence which will be reduced, e.g. the likelihood that a threat scenario leads to an unwanted incident. The template given in Sect. 3.2 allows describing controls in a systematic way.

3   Our Previous Work

In previous work, we developed two templates to determine an incident's risk level and the applicability of controls.

3.1   Template for Incident Scenarios

In previous work, we proposed a pattern that describes an incident scenario based on the base metrics of the CVSS [28]. Table 1 shows the relevant excerpt of a pattern instance for the scenario *Database Injection*. In the following, we explain the different metrics and corresponding values. For each attribute, we state its relation to the different elements and relations of the CORAS language.

The first set of attributes can be used to specify the likelihood that a threat scenario leads to an unwanted incident.

The *Threat Vector* (called *attack vector* in CVSS) describes possible ways how to realize a threat scenario. There are four different values: (1) *network,*

Table 1. Description of *Database Injection* [30].

Incident Information	
LeadsTo Likelihood	
Threat Vector	☐ Network ☑ Adjacent ☐ Local ☐ Physical
Complexity	☑ Low ☐ High
Privileges Required	☐ None ☑ Low ☐ High
User Interaction	☑ None ☐ Required
Threat Scope	☐ Unchanged ☑ Changed
Consequences	
Confidentiality Impact	☐ None ☐ Low ☑ High
Integrity Impact	☑ None ☐ Low ☐ High
Availability Impact	☑ None ☐ Low ☐ High

which means access from an external network; (2) *adjacent*, which means a local network; (3) *local*, which means direct access to the computer; and (4) *physical*, which describes access to the hardware.

The *Complexity* of a scenario is defined by two possible values: *low* and *high*. A high effort is required when a threat needs some preparation to realize the threat scenario and that the scenario cannot be repeated an arbitrary number of times.

To state whether privileges are required to successfully realize the threat scenario, we make use of the corresponding attribute. There are three possible values: (1) *None*; (2) *Low*, e.g. a user account; and (3) *High*, administrative rights.

A realization may require some *User Interaction*, for example by confirming the installation of malicious software.

The *Threat Scope* denotes the range of a scenario. A changed scope means that the part being attacked is used to reach other parts of software. For example, an attacker uses the wireless connection to access the database.

The impact on confidentiality, integrity, and availability is measured using qualitative scales. The used scale consists of three values: *None*, *Low* and *High*. In the context of CORAS, the value states the consequences that unwanted incidents have for an asset.

In previous work, we developed a method that allows evaluating risks using the CVSS metrics [26]. We will use the calculated severities to determine the effectiveness of controls. In Sect. 7, we also present a web-based tool for supporting the evaluation.

3.2   Template for Controls

We further provide a pattern that allows to describe controls in a similar way as incident scenarios [25]. In Table 2, we provide an example of the control *Encrypted Storage*. It allows encrypting data before storing them persistently.

First, we informally describe the context in which a control can be applied, e.g. a special type of distributed system. Each control can be used to support the protection of security properties. Furthermore, we state the functional requirement in the form of a problem diagram for which the control is suitable. Figure 3(a) shows the corresponding diagram of the example. For applying the control, it is necessary that a *Storage Machine* ▢ stores data persistently in a *Database* ▣. The corresponding requirement constrains the lexical domain.

Furthermore, we distinguish between the benefits and liabilities of a control, and we provide an aspect-oriented integration into the requirements model.

Benefits. For specifying the benefits, we use a set of attributes according to the CVSS specifications, e.g. *Modified Complexity*. Each attribute is a counterpart of the one used in incident descriptions. For example, after applying a control, the new complexity for an incident is high. The range of values for each attribute is the same as for the attributes of the incident description. Additionally, there is the value *not defined* which means that the control does not influence that

Table 2. Description of *Encrypted Storage*.

Context	
Description	The control can be applied for software where data shall be stored persistently.
Supported Security Property	☑ Confidentiality ☐ Integrity ☐ Availability
Functional Requirement	The problem diagram is given in Fig. 3(a).
Benefits	
Reduction of leadsTo likelihood	
Modified Complexity	☑ Not defined ☐ Low ☐ High
Modified Privileges Required	☑ Not defined ☐ None ☐ Low ☐ High
Modified User Interaction	☑ Not defined ☐ None ☐ Required
Modified Threat Scope	☑ Not defined ☐ Unchanged ☐ Changed
Reduction of impact	
Modified Confidentiality Impact	☐ Not defined ☑ None ☐ Low ☐ High
Modified Integrity Impact	☑ Not defined ☐ None ☐ Low ☐ High
Modified Availability Impact	☑ Not defined ☐ None ☐ Low ☐ High
Reduction of initiates likelihood	
Hints	The likelihood for initiating the threat scenario cannot be reduced.
Liabilities	
Costs	Since there are many open source libraries that can be used to implement the control, the costs do not increase significantly.
Usability	There is no impact on the usability.
Performance	Depending on the size of data, the performance may decrease. The higher the size of data, the lower the performance.
Integration	
Aspect diagram	The aspect diagram is given in Fig. 3(b).

specific attribute, i.e. the value specified by the incident description will stay the same after applying the control.

The *leadsTo* likelihood can be reduced by increasing the complexity, by requiring higher privileges, by requiring a user interaction, or by modifying the threat scope. The impact can be reduced separately for confidentiality, integrity, and availability. In Sect. 5.2, we use the values to evaluate the effectiveness of a control concerning incidents to be treated.

The CVSS specification does not provide attributes to specify the likelihood that a threat initiates a threat scenario. Therefore, we provide a textual description of how a control affects that likelihood. These are given as hints in the last section of the specification of benefits.

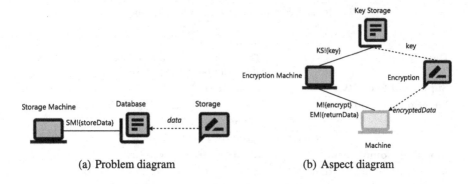

(a) Problem diagram   (b) Aspect diagram

Fig. 3. Diagrams of *Encrypted Storage* [30].

Liabilities. We distinguish between costs, usability, and performance. In Sect. 5.2, we use the hints together with the context description to validate the applicability of a control for a concrete software development project.

Integration. To integrate controls into the requirements model, we make use of an aspect-oriented approach that has been proposed by Faßbender et al. [8]. For each control, we provide an aspect diagram which has a similar notation as problem diagrams. In addition to problem domains, there are placeholders called *join points* (marked in light gray). Problem domains of an aspect diagram will be added to the requirements model, whereas a placeholder will be instantiated with an existing domain. For the *Encrypted Storage*, we provide an aspect diagram in Fig. 3(b). *Encryption Machine* ⌑ and *Key Storage* 🖻 are problem domains, *Machine* ⌑ is a join point. The requirement for encryption refers to the key and constrains the encrypted data. In Sect. 5.3, we describe the integration of controls into the requirements model in more detail.

4 Metamodel

To document requirements and the results of the risk management process, we make use of two models: (i) Security Model and (ii) Requirements Model. Based on the *Eclipse Modeling Framework* [21], we provide metamodels that formalize the semantics of these models. Furthermore, these models serve as the foundation for creating a graphical editor for problem diagrams and CORAS diagrams, as well as to document the results of risk treatment consistently.

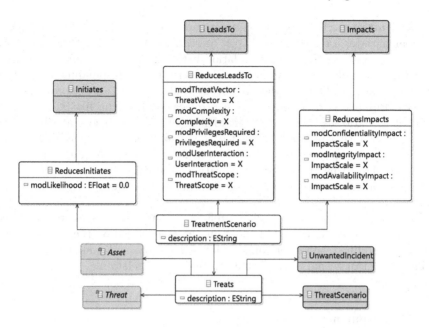

Fig. 4. Security metamodel.

4.1   Security Model

To document incidents with CORAS and to store the information provided by the templates, we described a metamodel in previous work [26]. We now extend that model with necessary elements to document selected controls. Figure 4 provides an overview of those new elements and their relations to the existing ones (marked in gray).

Treatment Scenario. In CORAS, we use a *Treatment Scenario* to illustrate a control. A treatment scenario can have different types of associations with other elements. For each of those references, we add a class to the metamodel containing the related attributes.

Treats. A control can address risks in several ways. The corresponding *treats* reference can point to an asset, a threat, a threat scenario, or an unwanted incident.

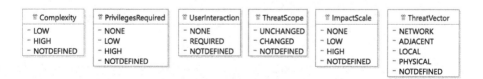

Fig. 5. Datatypes of metamodel.

ReducesInitiates. By applying a treatment scenario, the likelihood that a threat initiates a threat scenario can be reduced. In that case, the treatment scenario points to the *initiates* relation between threat and threat scenario. The modified likelihood can be described with the corresponding attribute.

ReducesLeadsTo. Our template to specify controls (see Table 2) provides several attributes to describe how a control can reduce the likelihood that a threat scenario leads to an unwanted incident. We use those attributes for the reference that points from the treatment scenario to the *leadsTo* relation. In Fig. 5, we show the possible values in form of enumerations. Those values are defined by the CVSS specification. The default value is *not defined (X)* which means that the control does not reduce the risk regarding this attribute.

ReducesImpacts. We also provide a reference that describes the reduction of the impact of an unwanted incident on an asset. Based on the template, we provide modified values for confidentiality, integrity, and availability impact. The treatment scenario then points to the *impact* relation.

4.2   Requirements Model

In previous work [31], we presented a metamodel to document functional requirements. Jackson's problem frames approach (see Sect. 2.1) serves as the basis for the metamodel. An instance of the metamodel contains the functional requirements of software, thus serving as the initial input for the control selection.

In Fig. 6, we show the relation between the requirements model and the security model. Those relations are also part of the metamodel. The elements of the requirements model are given in light gray.

A threat scenario occurs in the context of a *Statement*. For example, an attacker can misuse a user input for injecting malicious queries. Therefore, the threat scenario (part of the security model) holds a reference to the corresponding class. A statement can either be a (functional) *Requirement* or *Domain Knowledge*. As domain knowledge, we consider indicative statements about the environment of software to be developed.

As mentioned in Sect. 3.2, we document controls in the requirements model. For example, an encryption mechanism leads to a new functional requirement. Therefore, a treatment scenario (part of the security model) holds a reference

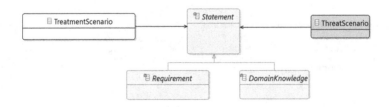

Fig. 6. Requirements metamodel.

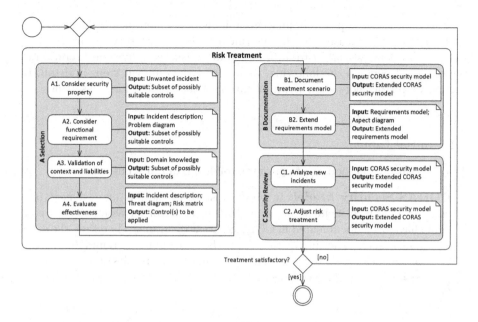

Fig. 7. Overview for risk treatment method.

to a statement. Controls concerning the environment can be documented using domain knowledge, e.g. the training of employees.

The provided references ensure consistency and traceability between the results of the risk management process and the requirements model. In Sect. 7, we describe a web-based tool that can be connected with the metamodel.

5   Iterative Risk Treatment

In the following, we present our iterative method to treat risks during requirements engineering. It is an extension of the method, we presented in previous work [30].

Figure 7 provides an overview of the structure of the method, which consists of eight steps. These steps can be divided into three phases. For our method, we assume that the risk assessment including risk identification, risk analysis, and risk evaluation has already taken place. We described methods for those steps in previous work [26, 28, 29].

Selection. The first four steps deal with the selection of an appropriate control including its evaluation.

Documentation. The documentation part consists of two steps for extending the security model and requirements model.

Security Review. In the last part of our method, we review the selected controls with regard to security, i.e. we analyze new incidents that may arise due to a control's application.

We carry out these steps for all unacceptable risks, i.e. identified incident scenarios to be treated. In case that the treatment is not satisfactory for an incident, e.g. new incidents still lead to an unacceptable risk, we require an iteration of the risk treatment. In the following, we describe the different steps in detail. In Sect. 6, we furthermore show the application of the method for a case study.

5.1   Initial Input

To carry out our method, we require the following initial input:

1. **CORAS Security Model:** In previous steps of the risk management process, we identified incidents that might lead to harm for assets. Those incidents have been documented in CORAS threat diagrams. Therefore, the security model serves as an input, as well as, the corresponding template description for the incidents (see Sect. 3.1). We document the results of the treatment process in the security model using the metamodel extension we presented in Sect. 4.
2. **Catalog of Controls:** Controls that shall be considered for our selection process have to be specified with the template we described in Sect. 3.2. We describe a new extension of the template in this section. The catalog of controls is an implicit input for all steps of the method.
3. **Requirements Model:** To decide about the applicability of controls, we take a requirements model as an input. That model shall be based on Jackson's problem frames approach (see Sect. 2.1) for which we already described a metamodel [31]. The selected controls will be integrated in that model, too.

5.2   Part A: Selection

In the following, we describe the four steps of the selection part.

Step A1: Consider Security Property. We consider the security property as the first criterion to filter suitable controls. The unwanted incident denotes the harmed security property. We search for controls that help to preserve that property. The control specification template (see Table 2) states the properties that a control supports.

For further consideration, we therefore take those controls from the catalog into account that support the harmed security property. Our tool supports that step and automatically suggests suitable controls.

Step A2: Consider Functional Requirement. A control is applicable in the context of specific functional requirements, e.g. controls for data transmission vs. controls for data storage. Therefore, the functional requirement in the context of which the incident occurs is another criterion for filtering suitable controls. As described in Sect. 4, a threat scenario holds a reference to its corresponding functional requirement. We compare the problem diagram of that requirement with the control description. A control is possibly relevant when the problem diagram contains the domains, domain interfaces, and requirement references (*constrains* and *refers to*) given in the description. Note, that a problem diagram may contain additional elements in comparison to the control description, since the description only contains the minimal set of necessary elements.

All controls that fulfill that condition are taken into consideration. The step can be automated based on the metamodels we presented in this paper.

Step A3: Validation of Context and Liabilities. In the third step, we validate the context and liabilities of controls to decide about their applicability. This step requires the interaction with domain experts, for example, the software provider. Such an expert provides further necessary domain knowledge. The control description template states details about the context, as well as details about liabilities, i.e. costs, usability, and performance. Those attributes have to be compared with the environment in which the software under development will be integrated later. For example, software running on small servers does not provide much computational power for strong encryption mechanisms. Furthermore, it is necessary to consider the costs for implementing a control compared to the asset value to be protected.

Only those controls that are suitable regarding the context and the liabilities are further considered.

Step A4: Evaluate Effectiveness. In the fourth step, we evaluate the effectiveness of the controls filtered so far. The effectiveness states the risk reduction that can be achieved by applying a control. For the evaluation, we make use of a control's description and the risk matrix which has been defined during risk evaluation. In previous work, we provide a method to evaluate risks using the CVSS [26]. The first dimension of the risk matrix is the frequency per year that a threat initiates a threat scenario (see y-axis of Table 4). For estimating the reduction of that frequency, our template provides specific hints, e.g. that security checks for employees are performed before hiring them.

The second dimension is the severity of an incident scenario (see x-axis of Table 4). The severity is defined by the likelihood that a threat scenario leads to an unwanted incident and the impact. The qualitative scale for the severity is defined by the CVSS [9]. The incident description contains the metrics which are required to calculate the initial severity based on formulas.

A control can also be used to reduce that severity. The reduction is specified by the modified metrics given in a control's description. Using those metrics and the initial metrics of the incident, we calculate the new severity. The CVSS provides formulas for that purpose. Note that a control does not necessarily reduce both, the severity and the likelihood for initiating a threat scenario.

For evaluating the risk reduction, i.e. the effectiveness of a control, we use the risk matrix. If the combination of the new frequency and the new severity leads to an acceptable risk, indicated by a white cell, we consider the control as effective. Sometimes, a single control does not lead to a sufficient risk reduction, thus making it necessary to consider combinations of controls. For example, the first control reduces the severity, whereas the second one reduces the frequency. In that case, we combine the risk reduction of both controls. The evaluation yields one or more controls providing a sufficient risk reduction.

If there is more than one control or control combination to achieve a sufficient risk reduction, it is necessary to finally select those controls that shall be applied. Different criteria can be used for that task, e.g. the maximum reduction or the costs for implementation.

In the case that no suitable control has been found, the following steps for documentation and review can be skipped. However, it is still necessary to document that a sufficient reduction is not possible.

Our tool allows to calculate an incident's severity, as well as, the reduced severity when applying a control.

5.3 Part B: Documentation

After selecting suitable controls, we document the results in the security model and requirements model.

Step B1: Document Treatment Scenario. After a suitable control has been selected, we document the corresponding treatment scenario in the security model using the CORAS language. The treatment scenario points to the element of the diagram that the control treats (*treats* relation). Furthermore, we document the resulting likelihood or consequence reduction (*reduces* relation). The arrows can have an *initiates*, *leadsTo*, or *impacts* relation as target. The control description denotes which likelihoods or consequences can be reduced, and the arrows have to be added accordingly.

The metamodel we presented in Sect. 4 provides formal rules to document treatment scenarios and risk reductions. Those rules ensure traceability and consistency. By providing a graphical editor, the instantiation of the metamodel can be supported.

Step B2: Extend Requirements Model. The second step of the documentation phase integrates the functional requirements of selected controls in the requirements model. An integration is required for those controls that are realized as an additional software functionality, e.g. encryption mechanisms. To integrate controls into the requirements model, we follow an aspect-oriented approach for problem frames [8]. As input for this step, we consider the problem diagram related to the threat scenario and the aspect diagram given in the control description.

We add the control to the problem diagram in the following way: The aspect diagram contains domains, join points, and the functional requirement for the control. We add the domains to the problem diagram along with the corresponding domain interfaces. Since a join point represents a placeholder for a domain of the problem diagram, we instantiate it accordingly. Furthermore, we add the functional requirement for the control and the requirement references.

The resulting requirements model can be used in the subsequent design phase. An architecture that can be created based on that model considers security right from the beginning.

Controls that only influence the environment, e.g. security training for employees, will not be considered in this step. We document those controls only in the CORAS security model since they do not need to be considered for software design decisions.

5.4   Part C: Security Review

The application of controls may lead to new incidents with regard to security. We, therefore, extend our method with a new part called *Security Review* that allows us to identify those incidents.

Step C1: Analyze New Incidents

Template Extension. To document new incidents that may occur due to the application of a control, we extend the control specification template (cf. Sect. 3.2) in the following way: For each new incident, we add a new entry referring to its specification. The incident's details can then be looked up in the incident catalog. Furthermore, we propose three new keywords to express the relation to the initial incident which has already been addressed by the control. The keywords help to adjust the security model in the next step.

after. The new incident occurs after using the control, e.g. breaking the encryption will be initiated <u>after</u> the encryption itself.
before. The new incident is realized before using the control, e.g. an attacker has to steal the credentials <u>before</u> using the authentication mechanism.
independent. There is no relation regarding the time between control and incident.

Along with the keyword, we briefly describe the incident and its (negative) influence with regard to security in terms of CVSS attributes. Optionally, the template contains a description of how the control may already address the new incident.

Table 3. New incidents of *Encrypted Storage* (cf. Table 2).

New Incidents	
Ref.	Break Encryption
{after}	The attacker may break the encryption to retrieve the plaintext [confidentialityImpact=HIGH].
Refinement	By choosing a strong encryption algorithm, the complexity to break the encryption increases [modComplexity=HIGH].

In Table 3 we show the extension for the control *Encrypted Storage*. When encrypting data, an attacker may try do break the encryption. That happens after the attacker gains access to the encrypted data. Since breaking the encryption will lead to disclosure of plaintext, the resulting impact on confidentiality is *high*. This issue may be addressed by the control itself by using a strong encryption algorithm, since breaking a strong algorithm has a *high* complexity.

The analyst has to decide whether the incident is relevant or not. To document the related incident in our security model, we make use of the CORAS language again. The defined keywords help to integrate the new threat scenario in the right place in the threat diagram. It defines the order of threat scenarios regarding the time. For example, stealing the data may lead to breaking the encryption, thus the new threat scenario occurs after the initial one (see Fig. 12). Furthermore, it is necessary to specify and document the threat that initiates the scenario along with corresponding likelihood.

The documentation for this step is supported by our metamodel. Furthermore, our tool shows the references and associated values for new incidents.

Step C2: Adjust Risk Treatment. In the case that the control is able to treat the new incident, we adjust the risk treatment accordingly. For the documentation, we add a *treats* relation between treatment scenario and threat scenario. Furthermore, we document the resulting risk reduction by adding a corresponding *reduces* relation along with the corresponding values.

The residual severity can be calculated in the following way: In a chain of threat scenarios, there are multiple *leads to* relations, each of them having different annotated values, e.g. for complexity. We collect all relations, and for each attribute, we choose the most critical value to calculate the overall severity. For example, a low complexity leads to a higher risk than a high complexity, and we choose value *low* for the calculation. The criticality of the different values is defined by the CVSS [9]. Here, we also take into account when a value has been reduced by applying a control for which we consider the modified value. Afterwards, we follow the procedure as described in step *A4* for evaluating the residual risk. In the case that the risk is not acceptable due to new incidents, we require an iteration of the risk treatment.

For this step, our tool supports the evaluation of new incidents.

5.5   Decision Point: Treatment Satisfactory?

Finally, we decide whether the risk treatment was successful or not. To do so, we check if all identified risks have been reduced to an acceptable level. If this is not the case, it is necessary to perform another iteration of the method until a sufficient risk reduction has been achieved.

If a reduction is not possible, e.g. because no suitable control has been found, the method terminates, too. In that case, it is necessary to adjust the risk evaluation criteria, e.g. by adjusting the risk matrix. Otherwise, the software cannot be deployed with the desired security level.

6 Case Study

In the following, we show the application of our method on a small case study.

Description and Initial Input. We consider a smart grid scenario. A smart grid is an intelligent power supply network, which also allows measuring a customer's power consumption remotely. Since such networks are critical infrastructures, they are often subject to attacks, and due to their complexity, it is hard to analyze their security [18,22].

1. Requirements Model: The software to be developed is the *Communication Hub*, which serves as the gateway between a customer's home and the energy supplier. In this paper, we focus on the functional requirement for storing personal data of a customer. We show the corresponding problem diagram in Fig. 8. A customer can store his/her personal data in the communication hub's internal database.
2. CORAS Security Model: The personal data shall be protected against disclosure to an attacker. We show the CORAS threat diagram in Fig. 9, which is part of the security model. An attacker may inject malicious database queries via the customer's interface to disclose the data. In this scenario, the command to store the personal data (*FR:Store PD*) will be replaced with a query. In Table 1, we presented the template-based description for the incident.

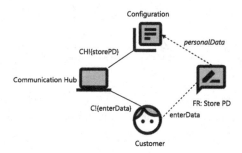

Fig. 8. Case study: problem diagram of *Store personal data* [30].

Fig. 9. Case study: injection to disclose personal data (adapted from [30]).

3. Catalog of controls: For reasons of simplicity, we only use the control *Encrypted Storage* in this example. In Table 2, we presented the corresponding description.

In the following, we apply our method to the case study.

Step A1: Consider Security Property. The unwanted incident given in Fig. 9 defines an impact on the confidentiality of personal data. The control *Encrypted Storage* supports the confidentiality. Therefore, we consider the control as relevant.

Step A2: Consider Functional Requirement. The control description (cf. Fig. 3(a)) states a functional requirement for storing data. The problem diagram contains a *Storage Machine* ⌑ and a *Database*. The requirement constrains the lexical domain. The machine and the lexical domain are connected via a domain interface, and the annotated phenomenon is controlled by the machine. The problem diagram from our scenario given in Fig. 8 contains those elements. Therefore, the control is applicable in the context of the requirement.

Step A3: Validation of Context and Liabilities. Considering the control description given in Table 2, there are no liabilities concerning costs and usability. Since a customer's personal data has a small data size, there is also no major impact on performance. The control will be further considered for an application.

Step A4: Evaluate Effectiveness. In Table 4, we show the risk matrix we consider to determine the risk reduction, i.e. a control's effectiveness. We use *Inject* as an abbreviation for the risk that an attacker injects malicious database queries.

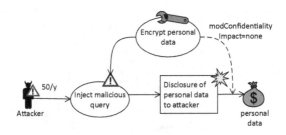

Fig. 10. Case study: treatment documentation (adapted from [30]).

During risk evaluation, a frequency of **50 times per year (frequently)** has been estimated that the attacker injects malicious database queries. The attributes' values given in Table 1 lead to a severity of **6.8 (medium)** for the incident. The combination of likelihood and severity denotes an unacceptable risk marked with a gray cell in the matrix.

The control description is given in Table 2 and does not state any reduction of the frequency. Next, we consider the modified values. The control's application results in a modified impact on confidentiality. Since an attacker cannot disclose plaintext, there is no impact on confidentiality after applying the control. The new severity is **0.0 (none)** which we evaluate using the risk matrix. The risk after applying the control is acceptable ($Inject_{treat}$). Therefore, the effectiveness of the control is sufficient, and we select the control to treat the risk of injection.

Step B1: Document Treatment Scenario. For the control we selected, we document the treatment scenario *Encrypt personal data* in the initial threat diagram (cf. Fig. 10). The control treats the threat scenario which is related to the functional requirement for storing the personal data. The control description given in Table 2 states a modified confidentiality impact. The *reduce* relation points to the *impacts* relation which indicates the impact reduction. In Fig. 10, we show the resulting diagram.

Step B2: Extend Requirements Model. Figure 8 shows the problem diagram in which the control shall be integrated. The aspect diagram is given in Fig. 3(b). It contains two additional domains and one joint-point. We instantiate the joint-point with the *Communication Hub* ⌑, and we add all other domains and interfaces to the problem diagram. Last, we add the functional requirement and the requirement references. The new *Encryption Machine* ⌑ has to be developed to provide an encryption mechanism for securely storing personal data.

Table 4. Case study: risk matrix.

	None 0.0	Low 0.1–3.9	Medium 4.0–6.9	High 7.0–8.9	Critical 9.0–10.0
Never 0 times					
Seldom ≤ 20 times					
Frequently ≤ 50 times	$Inject_{treat}$		Inject Inject+$Break_{treat}$		
Often > 50 times					

Figure 11 shows the final problem diagram containing both functional requirements and related domains.

Step C1: Analyze New Incidents. In Table 3, we showed the template extension for the control *Encryption*. There is a new incident regarding breaking the encryption that is relevant for our scenario. In Fig. 12, we show the threat diagram in which we integrated the new threat scenario *Break encryption* which occurs in the context of the functional requirement for encryption. After stealing the encrypted data, an attacker may initiate the threat scenario of breaking the encryption. By breaking the encryption, the attacker can disclose the plain data, thus leading to a high impact on confidentiality. The resulting severity is

6.8 (medium). Next, we estimate the percentage of attackers that try to break the encryption after performing the injection. The value denotes the likelihood of the new *initiates* relation. We estimate that **50%** of them try to break the encryption. In our scenario, the frequency that attackers initiate both threat scenarios is then **25 times per year (frequently)**, thus indicating an unacceptable risk. We try to adjust the risk treatment in the next step.

Step C2: Adjust Risk Treatment. Table 3 shows that the new incident can be addressed by selecting a strong algorithm. Therefore, we adjust the treatment as shown in Fig. 12. The control now treats both threat scenarios, and it reduces the likelihood that the threat scenario leads to the unwanted incident. Due to the strong algorithm, the modified complexity is high. The resulting severity is **5.8 (medium)**, and the likelihood remains the same (**25 times a year (frequently)**). The risk matrix in Table 4 still denotes an unacceptable risk (*Inject+Break$_{treat}$*) when only applying the encryption mechanism.

Decision Point: Treatment Satisfactory? For deciding if the treatment is satisfactory, we consider two different cases:

1. When considering the injection of data in isolation (see Fig. 10), the risk reduction was successful. An iteration is not necessary.
2. In the case that an attacker tries to break the encryption, the risk regarding that incident is not acceptable. Furthermore, it cannot be reduced only by applying an encryption mechanism. Therefore, our method requires an iteration.

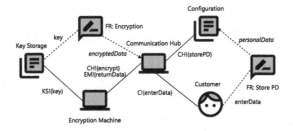

Fig. 11. Case study: problem diagram including encryption requirement [30].

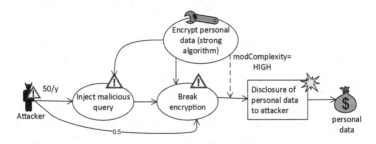

Fig. 12. Case study: threat diagram with adjusted treatment.

Since the iteration for the second case follows the schema of risk treatment we already presented, we do not show it here.

7 Tool Support

We present a web-based tool to support the application of our method. The focus lays on the steps A1, A4, C1, and C2. It pre-filters suitable controls based on the CVSS attributes and helps to evaluate their effectiveness.

7.1 Functionalities

The main functionalities that our tool provides are the following:

Calculate an Incident'S Severity: Based on the formulas provided by the CVSS, the tool allows to calculate the severity of an incident. Users have to enter the required values to the tool. The calculation of an incident's severity is used in the steps A4, C1, and C2.

Set up a Catalog of: We provide a data structure to set up a catalog of controls. It is derived from the template we presented in Sect. 3.2. The common structure allows us to share the catalog between software development projects. By specifying new controls, the catalog can be extended continuously. The catalog of controls is an implicit input for all steps of the method and therefore supports all of them. For the tool, we use it for automatic calculations, as well as, to present the required information for manual steps of the control selection.

Calculate the New Severity: Based on an incident's severity and the modified values contained in a control specification, our tool allows us to calculate the new severity when applying a control. The modified values are taken from the control specifications defined by the catalog's data structure. With the calculation, we support the steps A4, C1, and C2.

Pre-filter Suitable Controls: To assist analysts as much as possible in selecting suitable controls, we provide a filtering mechanism in our tool. After entering an incident's values, our tool suggests suitable controls from the catalog regarding the supported security property (step A1) and their effectiveness (step A4). For the effectiveness-based filtering, we consider the new severity and the likelihood reduction of the *initiates* relation. A control is irrelevant when it neither reduces the severity sufficiently (new severity ≥ old severity) nor the likelihood. The control will not appear in the list of suitable controls. For finally deciding about the effectiveness, one has to manually enter the new severity and likelihood to the risk matrix.

In the following, we describe how we realized those functionalities in more detail, as well as, how we connected our metamodels (see Sect. 4) with the tool. We follow the model-view-controller pattern [10].

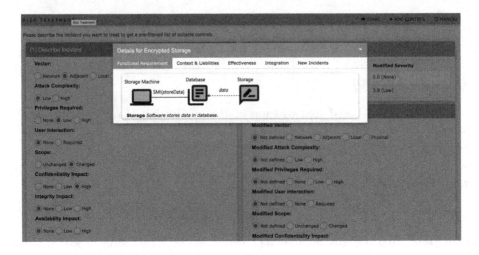

Fig. 13. Tool: graphical user interface.

7.2 Frontend

We provide a user-friendly graphical interface for the tool. In Fig. 13, we show a screenshot of the main window. We build it using web standards like HTML, CSS, and JavaScript to ensure compatibility with modern web browsers.

We provide an input form to enter the incident's values for calculating its severity. After providing the values, the tool presents a list of pre-filtered controls. For each of them, it states the new severity. Users can request more details about the control by clicking on a control's name. The detailed description contains all information specified in the control description template. For the functional requirement and integration, we provide an image of the corresponding problem diagram and aspect diagram, respectively. For structuring the representation of a control, we make use of tabs. Each tab contains the part of the information that is required for a specific step of the method, e.g. integration. The control descriptions are contained in a database that is part of the backend.

When selecting a control, it is also possible to adjust its attributes, for example regarding new incidents. The severity is recalculated accordingly.

Finally, we provide a form to add new controls to the catalog.

7.3 Backend

Besides our frontend which is the view to the user, we provide a server application that handles the requests to the database.

We decided to use Node.js[2] for deploying the server. The *Forum of Incident Response and Security Teams* (FIRST) provides a JavaScript library that

---

[2] https://nodejs.org/en/ (last access: August 8, 2020).

implements the formulas specified by the CVSS. We embedded this library in our tool for calculating the different severities. Besides, we implemented the previously mentioned pre-filtering rules. To store the control catalog, we make use of an SQL database. Based on the control description template, we developed a database schema. The diagrams are stored separately in the server's file system.

For combining our metamodel with our server application, we specified and implemented a REST API. The Eclipse Modeling Framework, with which we created our models, automatically translates the metamodel into Java classes. We extended those classes with methods to connect to the API and to send requests to it. When instantiating the models, it is possible to directly calculate a severity based on the model information or to request information about suitable controls. The API contains the following types of request:

incident-severity. It returns the severity for a specific incident.

show-controls. Based on the provided incident's parameters, the server returns a list of suitable controls. The list contains the name and id of the controls.

get-control-details. When providing the id of a control, the request returns the details of a control which are selected from the database. The API does not support returning diagrams.

evaluate-effectiveness. It returns the new severity when providing the required attributes for an incident and a control.

We make use of vector strings as defined by the CVSS specification for formatting a request's parameters. For example, the request for evaluating the control *Encryption* (see Fig. 10) is the following: *https://localhost:3000/evaluate-effectiveness?vector= CVSS:3.1_AV:A_AC:L_PR:L_UI:N_S:C_C:H_I:N_A:N_MC :N*. It returns a new severity of *0.0*.

8   Discussion

Based on the description of our method in Sect. 5 and the application to the case study, we discuss the benefits and limitations of our method. The metamodel and tool we introduced in the present paper provide additional benefits. In the following, we consider usability, scalability, and precision.

8.1   Usability

For selecting and evaluating controls, we make use of templates to describe incident scenarios and controls. The templates describe incident scenarios and controls consistently and systematically, based on well-known concepts such as the CVSS. We extended the template for controls with a reference to new incidents. The extension supports the iteration when applying our method. Security engineers do not need to fill the templates on their own but can use existing catalogs. Furthermore, the required input and provided output of our method are documented in a user-friendly way, i.e. in problem diagrams and CORAS diagrams. We already provide tools for creating problem frame models and CORAS security models. By extending the existing metamodels we allow to document selected controls in a precise manner. With our tool, we further support the selection and evaluation of controls.

The control selection still needs some manual effort, e.g. for analyzing the context. The descriptions we provide with our templates support security engineers in this process.

8.2 Scalability

The complexity of our method mainly depends on the number of unacceptable risks and the number of controls contained in the catalog. On the one hand, a larger catalog improves the results because there are more possibly suitable controls. On the other hand, the complexity increases with the number of controls. Since we reduce the set of relevant controls with each step, the complexity of the steps decreases. Therefore, the complete catalog only needs to be considered for the first step.

We designed all steps in a way that they can be automated as much as possible to limit the manual effort for engineers to carry out the method. For calculating the severity of an incident and to evaluate the effectiveness of a control, we presented a tool in this paper. The provided API allows us to directly send requests from the model to the server application. Our metamodel defines clear semantics between security aspects and requirements. Furthermore, the different diagram types, namely problem diagrams and threat diagrams, help to structure views on larger models and to focus on relevant aspects.

8.3 Precision

For evaluating the effectiveness of controls, we use the CVSS. The defined metrics are widely accepted by the community and the industry to estimate severities. The corresponding formulas to calculate the severity of incidents have been defined by security experts based on real use cases. Although the metrics and formulas have been defined on sound expertise, there are limitations in their precision. The usage of qualitative scales helps to improve usability. In contrast to quantitative scales, those values are less precise. The values do not consider a concrete context in which an incident may be realized or where a control shall be applied. To address this issue, we decided to perform a step that requires manual interaction and validates the context and liabilities of controls (cf. Sect. 5.2). By replacing the CVSS with other scales, the precision can be improved. As a liability, a qualitative scale may impact the usability.

9 Related Work

In the following, we focus on related work dealing with control selection and evaluation in the context of risk management. Furthermore, we consider related work that may complement or support our method.

The CORAS method [19], which we use to model incident scenarios, suggests so-called structured brainstorming sessions to identify appropriate controls. Our method partially relies on brainstorming sessions, e.g. for validating the liabilities and the context of controls. For the other steps, we provide systematic guidance based on patterns.

There is an empirical study on the role of threat and control catalogs in the context of risk assessment [11]. The study revealed that non-security experts who made use of catalogs identified threats and controls of the same quality as security experts who did not use any catalog. We further support non-security experts by providing guidance with our method in using catalogs.

[3] proposed a quantitative model for risk management. The model covers the identification and analysis of possible threats to security, and it supports the identification and evaluation of controls. The authors do not propose a systematic method, and the application of the model requires specific expertise. However, the consideration of a quantitative evaluation of controls can improve precision (see Sect. 8).

[2] proposed a formalized approach to select and evaluate information security controls. To evaluate the effectiveness, the authors follow a model-based approach. Besides the evaluation of effectiveness to sufficiently reduce risks, the method also considers the assurance of operation during run-time. By embedding selected controls into the requirements model, we ensure the consideration of controls in the following steps of software development.

In the context of business process modeling, there is a standardized representation of controls [24]. The representation shall serve as an input for automated risk treatment. The same authors proposed an automated approach to determine and evaluate security configurations based on feature modeling and constraint programming [23].

[1] described an extension of the Tropos language [4] for a goal-driven risk assessment during requirements engineering. The method analyzes risks along with stakeholders' interests based on three layers: (i) assets, (ii) events, and (iii) treatments. [13] proposed a risk management method based on business goals. Selected controls are linked to specific business goals. Furthermore, the method allows to prioritize controls and to justify security experts' decisions. Since we mainly focus on functional requirements for software, the consideration of goal-oriented approaches can complement our work.

There are many official resources for controls. For example, the *Bundesamt für Sicherheit in der Informationsbranche* provides the *IT-Grundschutz-Kompendium* which contains a list of countermeasures to treat security risks [5]. The *National Institute of Standards and Technology* published the special publication 800-53 which offers descriptions for security and privacy controls [20]. Independently of national regulations, standards like the *Common Criteria* [7] provide control specifications, as well. Those resources can be used as input for our method, thus providing a wide range of controls.

10 Conclusion

Summary. In this paper, we extended our method for risk treatment. First, we extended our control specification template with a new section. This section contains incidents that may arise when applying the control to the software. Based on the extended template, we added new steps to our method to analyze those incidents. The method is then carried out iteratively to identify all relevant incidents. To document the results, we provide a metamodel that bridges the gap between security and functional requirements. It ensures consistency and traceability through all steps of risk management process. Since it is realized as an EMF metamodel, the model can easily be instantiated. Besides, we presented a web-based tool to simplify the application of our method. It allows to set up a catalog of controls and to evaluate their effectiveness. Based on the CVSS attributes, it pre-filters suitable controls. The provided details of each control support the manual selection. A REST API allows to directly connect instances of the metamodel with the server application.

Outlook. As mentioned in Sect. 8, the CVSS may lead to unprecise evaluation results. We therefore plan to perform a systematic comparison with other scales for risk evaluation. The results of that comparison can be used to improve our templates and also the precision of the method.

Furthermore, we only consider confidentiality, integrity, and availability in our method. We plan to extend our templates with additional security attributes, e.g. *Authenticity* and *Non-Repudiation*. Since the CVSS does not consider those attributes, the extension requires to adjust the scales and formulas, as well.

Concerning our tool, we plan to bring more features to the web. For example, we plan to add aspect diagrams that users can download from the server. By using the structures of the metamodel, users can add the aspect to their requirements model.

While we only consider security in our method, privacy is another important aspect, too. We will investigate how the results obtained in our risk management process can be used to analyze and preserve privacy. For example, confidentiality is an overlapping concept in both areas.

References

1. Asnar, Y., Giorgini, P., Mylopoulos, J.: Goal-driven risk assessment in requirements engineering. Requir. Eng. **16**(2), 101–116 (2011). https://doi.org/10.1007/s00766-010-0112-x
2. Barnard, L., von Solms, R.: A formalized approach to the effective selection and evaluation of information security controls. Comput. Secur. **19**(2), 185–194 (2000). https://doi.org/10.1016/S0167-4048(00)87829-3. http://www.sciencedirect.com/science/article/pii/S0167404800878293
3. Bojanc, R., Jerman-Blažič, B.: A quantitative model for information-security risk management. Eng. Manage. J. **25**(2), 25–37 (2013). https://doi.org/10.1080/10429247.2013.11431972

4. Bresciani, P., Perini, A., Giorgini, P., Giunchiglia, F., Mylopoulos, J.: Tropos: an agent-oriented software development methodology. Auton. Agents Multi-Agent Syst. **8**(3), 203–236 (2004). https://doi.org/10.1023/B:AGNT.0000018806.20944. ef

5. BSI: IT-Grundschutz-Kompendium. Bundesamt für Sicherheit in der Informationstechnik (2019)

6. BSI: State of IT Security in Germany 2019 (2019). https://www.bsi.bund.de/EN/Publications/SecuritySituation/SecuritySituation_node.html

7. Common Criteria: Common Criteria for Information Technology Security Evaluation v3.1. Release 5. Standard (2017). http://www.iso.org/iso/catalogue_detail?csnumber=65694

8. Faßbender, S., Heisel, M., Meis, R.: Aspect-oriented requirements engineering with problem frames. In: Proceedings of the 9th International Conference on Software Paradigm Trends, ICSOFT-PT 2014. SciTePress (2014). https://doi.org/10.5220/0005001801450156

9. FIRST.org: Common Vulnerability Scoring System v3.1: Specification Document (2019). https://www.first.org/cvss/v3-1/cvss-v31-specification_r1.pdf

10. Gamma, E., Helm, R., Johnson, R., Vlissides, J.M.: Design Patterns: Elements of Reusable Object-Oriented Software, 1st edn. Addison-Wesley Professional, Boston (1994)

11. de Gramatica, M., Labunets, K., Massacci, F., Paci, F., Tedeschi, A.: The role of catalogues of threats and security controls in security risk assessment: an empirical study with ATM professionals. In: Fricker, S.A., Schneider, K. (eds.) REFSQ 2015. LNCS, vol. 9013, pp. 98–114. Springer, Cham (2015). https://doi.org/10.1007/978-3-319-16101-3_7

12. Haskins, B., Stecklein, J., Dick, B., Moroney, G., Lovell, R., Dabney, J.: Error cost escalation through the project life cycle. INCOSE Int. Symp. **14**, 1723–1737 (2004)

13. Herrmann, A., Morali, A., Etalle, S., Wieringa, R.: RiskREP: risk-based security requirements elicitation and prioritization. In: 1st International Workshop on Alignment of Business Process and Security Modelling, ABPSM 2011. Lecture Notes in Business Information Processing. Springer, Verlag (2011)

14. ISO: ISO 27001:2018 Information technology - Security techniques - Information security risk management. International Organization for Standardization (2018)

15. ISO: ISO/IEC 27005:2018 Information security management. International Organization for Standardization (2018)

16. Jackson, M.: Problem Frames: Analyzing and Structuring Software Development Problems. Addison-Wesley, Boston (2001)

17. Kaspersky Lab: The Kaspersky Lab Global IT Risk Report (2019). https://media.kaspersky.com/documents/business/brfwn/en/The-Kaspersky-Lab-Global-IT-Risk-Report_Kaspersky-Endpoint-Security-report.pdf

18. Kumar, P., Lin, Y., Bai, G., Paverd, A., Dong, J.S., Martin, A.P.: Smart grid metering networks: a survey on security, privacy and open research issues. IEEE Commun. Surv. Tutor. **21**(3), 2886–2927 (2019). https://doi.org/10.1109/COMST.2019.2899354

19. Lund, M.S., Solhaug, B., Stølen, K.: Model-Driven Risk Analysis. The CORAS Approach. Springer, Heidelberg (2010). https://doi.org/10.1007/978-3-642-12323-8

20. NIST: Special Publication 800–53 Rev. 4. National Institute of Standards and Technology (2013)

21. Steinberg, D., Budinsky, F., Paternostro, M., Merks, E.: EMF: Eclipse Modeling Framework 2.0, 2nd edn. Addison-Wesley Professional, Boston (2009)

22. Tellbach, D., Li, Y.F.: Cyber-attacks on smart meters in household nanogrid: modeling, simulation and analysis. Energies **11**(2), 316 (2018). https://doi.org/10.3390/en11020316

23. Varela-Vaca, A.J., Gasca, R.M.: Towards the automatic and optimal selection of risk treatments for business processes using a constraint programming approach. Inf. Softw. Technol **55**(11), 1948–1973 (2013). https://doi.org/10.1016/j.infsof.2013.05.007

24. Varela-Vaca, A.J., Warschofsky, R., Gasca, R.M., Pozo, S., Meinel, C.: A security pattern-driven approach toward the automation of risk treatment in business processes. In: Herrero, Á., et al. (eds.) International Joint Conference CISIS'12-ICEUTE'12-SOCO'12 Special Sessions. Advances in Intelligent Systems and Computing, Ostrava, Czech Republic, 5–7 September 2012, vol. 189, pp. 13–23. Springer, Heidelberg (2012). https://doi.org/10.1007/978-3-642-33018-6_2

25. Wirtz, R., Heisel, M.: Managing security risks: template-based specification of controls. In: Sousa, T.B. (ed.) Proceedings of the 24th European Conference on Pattern Languages of Programs, EuroPLoP 2019, Irsee, Germany, 3–7 July 2019, pp. 10:1–10:13. ACM (2019). https://doi.org/10.1145/3361149.3361159

26. Wirtz, R., Heisel, M.: Model-based risk analysis and evaluation using CORAS and CVSS. In: Damiani, E., Spanoudakis, G., Maciaszek, L.A. (eds.) ENASE 2019. CCIS, vol. 1172, pp. 108–134. Springer, Cham (2020). https://doi.org/10.1007/978-3-030-40223-5_6

27. Wirtz, R., Heisel, M.: RE4DIST: model-based elicitation of functional requirements for distributed systems. In: van Sinderen, M., Maciaszek, L.A. (eds.) Proceedings of the 14th International Conference on Software Technologies, ICSOFT 2019, Prague, Czech Republic, 26–28 July 2019, pp. 71–81. SciTePress (2019). https://doi.org/10.5220/0007919200710081

28. Wirtz, R., Heisel, M.: A systematic method to describe and identify security threats based on functional requirements. In: Zemmari, A., Mosbah, M., Cuppens-Boulahia, N., Cuppens, F. (eds.) CRiSIS 2018. LNCS, vol. 11391, pp. 205–221. Springer, Cham (2019). https://doi.org/10.1007/978-3-030-12143-3_17

29. Wirtz, R., Heisel, M.: Risk identification: from requirements to threat models. In: Furnell, S., Mori, P., Weippl, E.R., Camp, O. (eds.) Proceedings of the 6th International Conference on Information Systems Security and Privacy, ICISSP 2020, Valletta, Malta, 25–27 February 2020, pp. 385–396. SCITEPRESS (2020). https://doi.org/10.5220/0008935803850396

30. Wirtz, R., Heisel, M.: Systematic treatment of security risks during requirements engineering. In: Ali, R., Kaindl, H., Maciaszek, L.A. (eds.) Proceedings of the 15th International Conference on Evaluation of Novel Approaches to Software Engineering, ENASE 2020, Prague, Czech Republic, 5–6 May 2020, pp. 132–143. SCITEPRESS (2020). https://doi.org/10.5220/0009397001320143

31. Wirtz, R., Heisel, M., Wagner, M.: Distributed frames: pattern-based characterization of functional requirements for distributed systems. In: van Sinderen, M., Maciaszek, L.A. (eds.) ICSOFT 2019. CCIS, vol. 1250, pp. 81–107. Springer, Cham (2020). https://doi.org/10.1007/978-3-030-52991-8_5

Combined Similarity Based Automated Program Repair Approaches for Expression Level Bugs

Moumita Asad[✉], Kishan Kumar Ganguly, and Kazi Sakib

Institute of Information Technology, University of Dhaka, Dhaka, Bangladesh
{bsse0731,kkganguly,sakib}@iit.du.ac.bd

Abstract. Automated program repair aims at finding the correct patch of a bug using a specification such as test cases. An existing study found that almost 82.40% repair actions are associated with expressions such as method invocation or assignment expression. However, handling expression level bugs enhances the search space and increases the probability of finding incorrect plausible patches before the correct one. Consequently, existing program repair approaches either avoid or limitedly focus on expression level bugs. This study proposes two automated program repair approaches that extensively deals with expression level bugs. The devised techniques combine syntactic and semantic similarities to handle the enlarged search space and rank the correct patch higher. Genealogical and variable similarity are used to measure semantic similarity since these are good at differentiating between correct and incorrect patches. Two popular metrics namely normalized longest common subsequence and token similarity are considered individually for capturing syntactic similarity. To evaluate the proposed techniques, these are compared with baseline approaches that use either semantic or syntactic similarity. Single line bugs from Defects4J and QuixBugs benchmark are used for comparison. Result reveals that the proposed techniques can correctly repair 22 and 21 expression level bugs which are higher than approaches using only semantic or syntactic similarity. Furthermore, the devised approaches obtain 64.71% and 61.76% precision and outperform the baseline program repair techniques.

Keywords: Syntactic similarity · Semantic similarity · Patch prioritization · Automated program repair · Expression level bugs

1 Introduction

A patch is the modifications applied to a program for fixing a bug [2]. Automated program repair finds the correct patch based on a specification, e.g., test cases [30]. It works in three steps namely fault localization, patch generation and patch validation [21]. Fault localization identifies the faulty code where the bug resides. Patch generation modifies the faulty code to fix the bug. Finally, by

© Springer Nature Switzerland AG 2021
R. Ali et al. (Eds.): ENASE 2020, CCIS 1375, pp. 311–335, 2021.
https://doi.org/10.1007/978-3-030-70006-5_13

executing test cases, patch validation examines whether the bug has been fixed or not. Since the search space is infinite, numerous patches can be generated [13]. Besides, a plausible solution - patch that passes all the test cases - can be incorrect, which is known as overfitting problem [42]. To limit the search space, most of the program repair techniques rely on redundancy assumption, which states that the patch of a bug can be found elsewhere in the application or other projects [6]. The existing code element that is reused for generating the patch, is called the fixing ingredient [42]. The redundancy assumption has already been validated by existing studies [3,28]. Martinez et al. found that 3–17% of the commits are redundant at the line level, whereas it is 29–52% at the token level [28]. Another study on 15,723 commits reported that approximately 30% fixing ingredients exist in the same buggy file [3].

Although the redundancy assumption limits the search space, in practice it is too large for exploring exhaustively especially for working at a finer granularity like expression level [6]. For example, there is only one buggy line in Listing 1.1, however, existing fault localization techniques mark 187 statements from 7 source files as buggy. If fixing ingredients are collected from the corresponding buggy files, 1081 statements are retrieved. Hence, the number of patches generated will be almost $187 * 1081 = 202147$. On the other hand, if the expression level granularity is used, 591 expressions are labeled as buggy and 4451 expressions are obtained as fixing ingredients. In this case, the number of patches generated will be around $591 * 4451 = 2630541$, which is 13 times larger compared to statement level granularity. Each of these patches needs to be compiled and validated by executing test cases, which is time consuming [6,35]. In addition, an existing study found that enhancing the search space increases the probability of generating incorrect plausible patches rather than correct ones [25]. Consequently, it becomes challenging for automated program repair techniques to handle expression type bugs such as *assignment expression, method invocation*, etc.

Listing 1.1. A Sample Bug *Chart_9* from Defects4J Benchmark.

```
public TimeSeries createCopy(RegularTimePeriod start,
                             RegularTimePeriod end) {
-    if (endIndex < 0)
+    if ((endIndex < 0) || (endIndex < startIndex))
}
```

Nevertheless, a study on 16,450 bug fix commits from 6 open-source projects such as Apache Mahout, Solr, etc reported that around 82.40% repair actions are related to expressions [20]. To understand the importance of handling expression type bugs, the current study also analyzes the CodRep dataset [6]. This dataset contains 58,069 one-line replacement bugs and corresponding fixes from 29 projects such as Apache Log4j, Spring Framework, etc. For each sample from this dataset, the differences between the buggy and the fixed version files are identified at the expression level. Result demonstrates that 42,856 out of 58,069 bugs (73.80%) are fixed by replacing an expression with another. Due to the importance of handling expression type bugs, an automated program repair approach needs to be devised that rigorously deals with these types of bug. The devised technique should incorporate a strategy to find the correct patch from the expanded search space within the allocated time and rank it before incorrect plausible ones.

Existing program repair approaches either avoid or limitedly work on expression level bugs. To keep the search space tractable, GenProg [19] and RSRepair [31] only work at the statement level [42]. Similarly, fix pattern based program repair approaches PAR [16], ELIXIR [35] and CapGen [42] define only a few templates related to expressions for preventing search space explosion [22]. Although PAR [16] can modify *conditional expressions*, it cannot solve other frequently occurring expression type bugs such as *class instance creation* expression or *variable name* modification [20]. ELIXIR [35] extensively deals with method invocation related bugs, however, it can not repair *assignment* or *class instance creation* expression bugs, which are also prevalent [20]. Likewise, CapGen [42] cannot handle bugs related to *class instance creation* or *number literal* expression [22]. Other approaches SimFix [13] and LSRepair [23] operate at a coarse granularity, which are a code snippet of 10 lines and method level respectively. Hence, the searching strategy used by these techniques are suitable for identifying only coarse-grained fixing ingredients [39,40].

In this context, the current study proposes two automated program repair approaches that extensively deals with expression level bugs. Through an empirical study on patch prioritization, the authors found that when the faulty location is known, combining syntactic and semantic similarities helps to rank the developer-written patch higher [2]. Hence, the proposed techniques integrate syntactic and semantic similarity to constrain the expanded search space caused by expression and prioritize the correct patch over incorrect plausible ones. The proposed techniques use genealogical and variable similarity for measuring semantic similarity since these are effective in distinguishing between correct and incorrect patches [2]. To calculate syntactic similarity, two widely-used metrics namely normalized longest common subsequence and token similarity are considered separately [2]. Thus, two bug fixing approaches namely *ComFix-L* and *ComFix-T* are proposed respectively. Genealogical similarity checks whether faulty code and fixing ingredient are frequently used with the same type of code elements (e.g., inside *for* statement) [2]. Variable similarity examines the name and type of variables accessed by the faulty code and fixing ingredient. Normalized longest common subsequence calculates maximum similarity at character level. Token similarity measures to what extent same tokens (e.g., *identifiers*) exist in the faulty code and fixing ingredient, regardless of its position.

The proposed approaches take a buggy program and a set of test cases with at least one failing test as input and output a program passing all the test cases. At first, the line-wise suspiciousness scores (0–1) of the buggy program are calculated using the execution traces of the test cases [17]. Next, these scores are mapped to *Expression* type abstract syntax tree nodes and those with a suspiciousness score above 0, are considered as faulty. These faulty nodes are replaced with fixing ingredients to generate patches. The fixing ingredients are collected from the corresponding buggy files, as followed in [16,22,42]. To validate potentially correct patch earlier, patches are ordered using a ranking score (0–3). To calculate the ranking score, the suspiciousness score is multiplied by the similarity score (0–3), which is obtained by incorporating genealogical, variable similarity with normalized longest common subsequence or token similarity. For limiting the search space, only patches with a ranking score greater than 0 are considered as candidate patches. Finally, the correctness of these patches are validated by executing test cases. Patch validation continues until a plausible patch is found or the predefined time-limit exceeds.

To evaluate the proposed approaches, these are compared with baseline techniques that use either semantic or syntactic similarity for handling expression level bugs. The is because the proposed approaches target a different defect class (expression level bugs) from the existing program repair approaches [29]. For comparison, single line bugs from Defects4J [14] and QuixBugs [47] benchmark are chosen as a representative of large and small buggy projects respectively. Next, the results are examined based on three metrics namely the number of bugs correctly fixed, precision (the ratio of correct and incorrect plausible patches) and repairing time [18,42,45]. To assess the correctness of the plausible patches, both manual and automated analysis are performed, as suggested by [48]. The result demonstrates that the proposed techniques correctly repair 22 and 21 bugs from these benchmarks, which are higher compared to approaches using only semantic or syntactic similarity. Furthermore, the proposed approaches obtain a precision of 64.71% and 61.76% respectively and outperform the baseline approaches that use only syntactic or semantic similarity. It indicates that the combination of syntactic and semantic similarities contributes to detect the correct patch over incorrect plausible patches. Through Wilcoxon Signed-Rank test, it is found that combining similarities does not significantly increase the bug fixing time. For the devised approaches, the average repairing time is 8.19 and 7.96 min for the commonly fixed bugs.

2   Background

This section creates the knowledge base for understanding automated program repair. At first, software bugs and associated terms, e.g., faulty code, patch, test cases are presented. Next, terminologies related to source code such as statement, expression, abstract syntax tree, are explained.

2.1   Concepts Related to Software Bug

Since automated program repair deals with software bug, a clear concept of bug and associated terminologies (test case, faulty code, patch and fixing ingredient) is necessary before understanding automated program repair. The definitions and examples of those terms as well as their relevance with automated program repair are presented in this subsection.

Software Bug. It is a deviation between the expected and the actual behavior of a program execution [30]. Listing 1.2 shows a method that finds maximum between two integers. It is expected that if a and b are set to 3 and 4 respectively, the method will output 4. However, the method returns 3, which indicates there is a bug. Bugs can cause financial loss as well as loss of human lives [51]. For example, in 2001, 28 patients received overdose of radiation due to incorrect calculation provided by a treatment-planning software [51]. Therefore, it is necessary to fix bugs.

Listing 1.2. Buggy Version of *max()* Method.

```
1: int max(int a, int b)
2: {
3:      if(a>b)
4:          return a;
5:      else
        // buggy statement
6:          return a;
7: }
```

Listing 1.3. Fixed Version of *max()* Method.

```
1: int max(int a, int b)
2: {
3:      if(a>b)
4:          return a;
5:      else
        // fixed statement
6:          return b;
7: }
```

Although it is important to find and fix bugs, doing it manually is a difficult, time-consuming and expensive task [19]. A study found that the median time to solve a bug manually is around 200 days [51]. Most of the time human resources are not enough to solve even known bugs. For example, Windows 2000 was shipped with more than 63000 known bugs due to lack of human resources [16]. Furthermore, globally 312 billion dollars are spent in a year for general debugging [42]. Hence, automated program repair is needed to reduce the time and cost.

Test Case: It is a specification that states a set of inputs, execution conditions and expected outputs [5]. Test cases are developed for a particular objective such as executing a specific program path or detecting bugs. Listing 1.4 presents a sample test case for the method *max()* (shown in Listing 1.2). It will check whether the output of *max(6,5)* is equal to the expected output 6. If these are not equal, the test case will fail. Test cases can be divided into two categories based on the outcome of a test execution. The categories are:

1. **Passing Test Case:** A test case for which a program's actual output matches with the expected one, is called a passing test case [15]. For the test case in Listing 1.4, the output of *max(6,5)* is 6, which is the same as expected output. Hence, it is a passing test case.
2. **Failing Test Case:** A test case for which a program's actual output is different from the expected output, is called a failing test case [15]. The test case in Listing 1.5 is a failing test case since the expected and actual output do not match. The actual output of *max(3,4)* (shown in Listing 1.2) is 3, whereas the expected output is 4.

Apart from buggy source code, automated program repair takes test cases with at least one failing test as input. These test cases are used for two purposes: (1)

to identify the buggy source code location and (2) to check the correctness of a generated solution.

Listing 1.4. A Passing Test Case for Method *max()*.

```
@Test
public void test() {
    assertEquals(6,max(6,5));
}
```

Listing 1.5. A Failing Test Case for Method *max()*

```
@Test
public void test2() {
    assertEquals(4, max(3,4));
}
```

Faulty Code. It refers to the source code fragment where the bug resides. For example, in Listing 1.2, line 6 represents the faulty code. The line should be *return b;*, as depicted in Listing 1.3. In automated program repair, faulty code is identified by the execution results of test cases [17]. If a program element (statement or predicate) is frequently executed by the failing test cases and rarely executed by the passing test cases, it is likely to be faulty. Based on this assumption, a suspiciousness score is assigned to the program elements.

Patch. It refers to the modifications applied to a program for fixing a bug [2]. Patches can be generated in numerous ways such as inserting a new statement, replacing or deleting the faulty code fragment. For Listing 1.2, the correct patch is replacing variable *a* in line 6 with variable *b*, as illustrated in Listing 1.3. Automated program repair aims at finding the correct patch of a bug. However, it faces the following two challenges, as identified by prior literature [23,42,45].

1. **Determining the Search Space:** Since the search space is infinite, automated program repair approaches can produce numerous patches [13]. Nevertheless, search space should be constrained for scaling automated program repair to large projects. On the contrary, this may result into the unavailability of the correct patches in the search space. In such case, it becomes impossible to repair a bug successfully.
2. **Identifying the Correct Patch over Incorrect Plausible Ones:** A patch that passes all the test cases is called a plausible patch [32,46]. In real world projects, the test cases are unable to completely specify the program behaviors [47]. Due to the weaknesses of the test suite, incorrect plausible patches occur that pass all the given test cases but fail to be generalized, which is known as overfitting problem [47]. Although correct patches are sparse in the search space, incorrect plausible patches are densely distributed [25]. Thus, it is challenging to identify the correct patch over incorrect plausible ones.

Fixing Ingredient. It refers to existing code elements that can be reused to generate the patch of a bug [12,42]. In Listing 1.3, variable *a* at line 6 is replaced with variable *b* for generating the correct patch. Here, variable *b* is the fixing ingredient. Fixing ingredients can be collected from the buggy source file or the whole project [27]. Considering the whole project increases the chance of including the correct fixing ingredient in the search space. However, it enlarges the search space and thereby makes it difficult to find the correct fixing ingredient earlier [25]. On the contrary, considering only the buggy source file helps to reduce the bug fixing time by finding the correct fixing ingredient earlier. Nevertheless, it may cause unavailability of the correct fixing ingredient in the search space [23].

2.2 Concepts Related to Source Code

Almost 90% of the reported bugs reside in source code [51]. Hence, knowledge of source code related terminologies (statement, expression and abstract syntax tree) is needed before understanding automated program repair. In this subsection, the definitions and examples of those terms as well as their relevance with automated program repair are described.

Statement and Expression. Statement is the fundamental unit of execution that denotes some action to carry out [9]. Statements are of various types such as if statement, while statement, break statement, etc. An expression is a construct made up of variables, operators, or method invocations that evaluates to a single value [9]. Expressions are used in a statement or as part of another expression. In Listing 1.3, $a>b$, *return a*, *a*, *return b* and *b* all are expressions. Automated program repair mostly collects fixing ingredient at statement or expression level to generate patches [42].

Abstract Syntax Tree. An Abstract Syntax Tree (AST) is a tree that represents syntactic structure of a source code while hiding details such as parentheses or semicolons [50]. The corresponding AST of the method *max()* is presented in

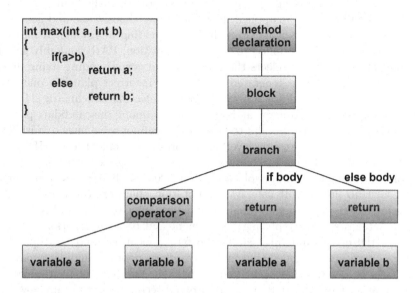

Fig. 1. Abstract Syntax Tree for *max()* Method.

Fig. 1. In automated program repair, AST is a way of representing the source code. This AST is traversed to collect fixing ingredients (statements or expressions) [42]. Additionally, patches are generated by modifying the AST [16].

3   Related Work

Recently, automated program repair has drawn the attention of researchers due to its potentiality of minimizing debugging effort [10]. Existing program repair approaches can be broadly divided into two categories based on the patch selection strategy. The first category is stochastic patch selection based approaches [16,19,31,41]. These techniques generate and select patches for validation using a randomized algorithm. GenProg [19], PAR [16], RSRepair [31], HDRepair [18] fall into this category. GenProg is the first generic automated program repair approach [19]. It uses genetic programming to find the correct patch. It randomly modifies (insert, replace, delete) a faulty statement by reusing statements from the buggy project. It calculates the fitness of the generated program variants using the weighted average of the positive and negative test cases. However, it collects fixing ingredients at statement level, which is too coarse-grained to find the correct ones in the search space [42]. Furthermore, GenProg randomly selects the mutation operator and fixing ingredients. As a result, most of the patches generated by GenProg are incorrect plausible patches [32].

Similar to GenProg, PAR also uses genetic programming. Unlike GenProg, PAR uses ten pre-defined templates (e.g., null pointer checker) to generate patches [16]. These templates are extracted from manually inspecting 62,656 human-written patches. For a faulty location, PAR checks which templates can be applied to it by inspecting its context (code surrounding the faulty location). If multiple templates can be applied, PAR randomly chooses one and generates a patch using fixing ingredients from the corresponding buggy file. If multiple fixing ingredients can be applied to the faulty location, PAR randomly selects one. Since PAR randomly selects the template and corresponding fixing ingredient, most of the patches generated by PAR are incorrect plausible ones. For example, the precision of PAR is only 15.9% on Defects4J benchmark [24].

Another approach RSRepair randomly searches among the candidate patches to find the correct one [31]. Similar to GenProg, it cannot solve bugs requiring fix at a finer granularity (expression level) as it works at statement level. HDRepair is the first repair technique to incorporate historical bug-fix patterns for patch selection [18]. These patterns are obtained from 3000 bug-fixes across 700+ large, popular GitHub projects. It uses twelve mutation operators taken from mutation testing or existing program repair techniques GenProg [19] and PAR [16] to generate patches such as replacing a statement and boolean negation. At each iteration, HDRepair randomly selects the faulty locations and corresponding mutation operators for generating an intermediate pool of candidate patches. From this pool, patches that occur frequently in the bug-fix history are selected. Similar to other stochastic patch selection based techniques, it obtains low precision namely 26.09% [22]. It indicates that considering only historical bug-fix patterns is not enough to eliminate incorrect plausible patches. Furthermore, HDRepair assumes that the faulty method is known, which may not always be true [21].

The second category is patch prioritization based approaches [13,35,42]. These techniques rank and select patches for validation based on their likelihood of correctness [46]. These techniques can be further divided into two groups based on the information used for prioritization. The first group [13,45] uses patch related attributes, e.g., the number of modifications. One of such approaches ssFix performs syntactic code search from a codebase containing the faulty program and other projects [45]. At first, ssFix extracts the faulty code along with its context, which is called target chunk (*tchunk*). A similar process is followed to retrieve fixing ingredients and their contexts from the codebase, which are called candidate chunks (*cchunks*). The *tchunk* and *cchunks* are tokenized after masking project-specific code (e.g., variable names). Next, *cchunks* are prioritized based on its syntax-relatedness to the tchunk, calculated using TF-IDF. Currently, ssFix uses maximum 100 top *cchunks* for generating patches. These patches are next prioritized using the type and size of modifications. For example, patches generated by replacement or insertion are ranked higher than those generated by deletion. However, ssFix obtains only 33.33% precision.

Another approach SimFix considers three metrics - structure, variable name and method name similarity to collect syntactically similar fixing ingredients, called the donor snippets [13]. Structure similarity extracts a list of features related to AST nodes (e.g., number of *if* statements). Variable name similarity tokenizes variable names (e.g., splitting studentID into student and ID) and calculates similarity using Dice coefficient [38]. Method name similarity follows the same process as variable name similarity. To generate patches, SimFix selects top 100 donor snippets based on the similarity score. To further limit the search space, only patches with frequently occurring modifications are considered. Lastly, these patches are sorted based on their attributes such as number and type of modifications (insertion/replacement). However, SimFix sometimes fails to find fine-grained fixing ingredients such as expressions since it identifies donor snippets at a coarse-granularity (10 lines) [40]. After executing SimFix on 192 additional bugs from 8 open-source projects, Ghanbari et al. found that SimFix can not repair any of the bugs since it can not find donor snippets [11]. All these demonstrate that the granularity and similarity metrics for identifying donor snippets need to be further improved.

The second group uses similarity between faulty code and fixing ingredient to prioritize patches. ELIXIR [35], CapGen [42] and LSRepair [23] belong to this group. ELIXIR is the first object-oriented program repair technique that makes extensive use of method invocation [35]. ELIXIR uses eight templates including modification and insertion of method invocation for generating patches. It considers four features including contextual and bug report similarities to prioritize patches. Contextual and bug report similarity compare fixing ingredients with the faulty location's context and bug report respectively to measure syntactic similarity. For assigning different weights to these similarities, logistic regression model is used. The approach validates only the top 50 patches generated from each template. Although ELIXIR can handle *method invocation* expression, it can not repair *assignment* or *class instance creation* expression bugs due to the design of the templates, which are also prevalent [20].

CapGen defines 30 mutation operators such as replacing conditional expression to generate patches [42]. It uses three models based on genealogical structures, accessed variables and semantic dependencies to capture context similarities at AST node level. These models mainly focus on semantic similarities between faulty code and fixing element to prioritize patches. The precision of this approach is higher (84.00%), however, it relies on the program dependency graph to calculate semantic dependency which does not scale to even moderate-size programs [8]. Besides, Ghanbari et al. executed CapGen on 192 additional bugs from 8 open-source projects and found that the mutation operators used by CapGen are ineffective for these bugs [11]. It indicates that the mutation operators used by CapGen lack generalizibility.

Another technique, LSRepair performs both syntactic and semantic code search to collect fixing ingredients [23]. To limit the search space, LSRepair works at the method level. At first, it searches for methods that are syntactically similar to the faulty method. If this strategy fails, LSRepair looks for semantically similar methods. LSRepair can correctly fix 19 out of 395 bugs from Defects4J benchmark [14]. Among these bugs, 10 were not fixed by any automated program repair technique before LSRepair. It indicates that LSRepair is complementary to other approaches. However, due to working at method level, it cannot fix bugs occurring outside method body such as *field declaration* related bugs. In addition, it achieves a precision of 51.35%, which is lower than ELIXIR [35], CapGen [42] and SimFix [13].

The above discussion indicates that existing program repair techniques either avoid or limitedly work on expression level to prevent search space explosion and incorrect plausible patch generation. However, a study on 16,450 bug fix commits from 6 open-source projects found that almost 82.40% repair actions are related to expressions [20]. Due to the importance of handling expression level bugs, an automated program repair approach needs to be devised that extensively deals with expression level bugs.

4   Methodology

This study proposes two combined similarity based automated program repair approaches that work at the expression level. Through empirical study, it is found that when the faulty location is known, combining syntactic and semantic similarities helps to rank the developer-written patch higher [2]. Therefore, the devised techniques integrate syntactic and semantic similarity to handle the enlarged search space, which occurred due to working at the expression level as well as identify the correct patch over incorrect plausible ones within the allocated time budget. These techniques take a buggy program and test cases with at least one failing test as input and output a program passing all the test cases. These approaches work in four steps namely fault localization, patch generation, patch prioritization and patch validation. The details of these steps are given below:

1. **Fault Localization.** This step calculates suspiciousness scores of *Expression* type AST nodes. This score indicates an expression's probability of being faulty (0–1). At first, the line-number wise suspiciousness scores of a program are computed using spectrum-based fault localization technique [17]. For this purpose, Ochiai metric is used, as followed in [13,42]. Given a line of code (l), Ochiai metric uses Eq. (1) to calculate the suspiciousness score based on the number of passing and failing tests that execute it.

$$suspiciousness\ score(l) = \frac{failed(l)}{\sqrt{total\ failed * (failed(l) + passed(l))}} \quad (1)$$

Where, *total failed* indicates the total number of failing test cases. $failed(l)$ and $passed(l)$ denote the number of failing and passing test cases that execute the line l. Since the proposed approaches work at the expression level, these line-number wise scores are mapped to *Expression* nodes. Listing 1.6 shows a sample bug *Math_70* from Defects4J benchmark. Here, the suspiciousness score of line number 72 is 1, calculated using Ochiai metric. Consequently, all the expressions at line 72 *solve(min, max), solve, min, max* are assigned the suspiciousness score 1.

Listing 1.6. Buggy Statement, Fixed Statement and Fixing Ingredient of Bug *Math_70*.

```
public double solve(double min, double max, double initial)
{
    59: return solve(f, min, max); // fixing ingredient
}

public double solve(final UnivariateRealFunction f, double
                    min, double max, double initial)
{
    72: - return solve(min, max); // buggy statement
    72: + return solve(f, min, max); // fixed statement
}
```

2. **Patch Generation.** In this step, faulty nodes are modified to generate patches. *Expression* nodes whose suspiciousness score are above 0, are considered as faulty [42]. These faulty nodes are replaced with fixing ingredients for patch generation. Similar to [16,22,42], this study collects fixing ingredients from the corresponding buggy source file. *Expression* nodes from the buggy source file are considered as fixing ingredients. In Listing 1.6, since the expression *solve(min, max)* at line 72 has a suspiciousness score of 1, it is considered as faulty. A sample patch can be replacing this expression with *solve(f, min, max)* at line 59.

3. **Patch Prioritization.** After generating patches, those are prioritized to find potentially correct patches earlier. For prioritization, the suspiciousness score of a faulty node as well as similarity between faulty node and fixing ingredient are used. To measure similarity between faulty node and fixing ingredient, both semantic and syntactic similarity are considered. To calculate semantic similarity, genealogical and variable similarity are used since these are effective in differentiating between correct and incorrect patches [42]. For capturing syntactic similarity, two widely-used metrics namely normalized longest common subsequence and token similarity are considered individually [33]. Thus, two combined similarity based bug fixing approaches namely *ComFix-L* and *ComFix-T* are proposed.

Genealogical Similarity. Genealogical structure indicates the types of code elements, with which a node is often used collaboratively [42]. For example, node *solve(min, max)* at line 72 resides inside *return* statement. To extract the genealogy contexts of a node residing in a method body, its ancestor as well as sibling nodes are inspected. The ancestors of a node are traversed until a method declaration is found. For sibling nodes, nodes having a type *Expressions* or *Statements* within the same block of the specified node are extracted. Next, the type of each node is checked and the frequency of different types of nodes (e.g., number of *for* statements) are stored. Nodes of type *Block* are not considered since these provide insignificant context information [42]. On the other hand, for nodes outside method body such as *field declaration statement*, only its respective type is stored. The same process is repeated for the faulty node (fn) and the fixing ingredient (fi). Lastly, the genealogical similarity (gs) is measured using Eq. (2).

$$gs(fn, fi) = \frac{\sum_{t \in K} min(\phi_{fn}(t), \phi_{fi}(t))}{\sum_{t \in K} \phi_{fn}(t)} \tag{2}$$

where, ϕ_{fn} and ϕ_{fi} denote the frequencies of different node types for faulty node and fixing ingredient respectively. K represents a set of all distinct AST node types captured by ϕ_{fn}.

Variable Similarity. Variables (local variables, method parameters and class attributes) accessed by a node provide useful information as these are the primary components of a code element [42]. In Listing 1.6, both the faulty node *solve(f, min, max)* and the fixing ingredient *solve(f, min, max)* access the same variables *min* and *max*. To measure variable similarity, two lists containing names and types of variables used by the faulty node (θ_{fn}) and the fixing ingredient (θ_{fi}) are generated. Next, variable similarity (vs) is calculated using Eq. (3).

$$vs(fn, fi) = \frac{|\theta_{fn} \cap \theta_{fi}|}{|\theta_{fn} \cup \theta_{fi}|} \tag{3}$$

Two variables are considered same if their names and types are exact match. To measure variable similarity of nodes that do not contain any variable such as *boolean* or *number literal* type nodes, only their respective data types are matched [42].

Normalized Longest Common Subsequence. Longest Common Subsequence (LCS) finds the common subsequence of maximum length by working at character-level [6]. This study computes normalized longest common subsequence (nl) between faulty node (fn) and fixing ingredient (fi) at AST node level using Eq. (4).

$$nl(fn, fi) = \frac{LCS(fn, fi)}{max(|fn|, |fi|)} \quad (4)$$

where, $max(|fn|, |fi|)$ indicates the maximum length between fn and fi.

Token Similarity. Unlike normalized longest common subsequence, token similarity ignores the order of text [6]. It only checks whether a token such as *identifiers* or *literals*, exists regardless of its position. For example, both the faulty node *solve(f, min, max)* and the fixing ingredient *solve(f, min, max)* in Listing 1.6 have the *solve* token in common. To calculate token similarity, at first, the faulty node and fixing ingredient are tokenized. Similar to [35], camel case identifiers are further split and converted into lower-case format. Next, token similarity (ts) is computed using Eq. (5).

$$ts(fn, fi) = \frac{|\theta_{fn} \cap \theta_{fi}|}{|\theta_{fn} \cup \theta_{fi}|} \quad (5)$$

where, θ_{fn} and θ_{fi} represent the token set of the faulty node and fixing ingredient respectively.

Each of the above mentioned metrics outputs a value between 0 and 1. To calculate the similarity score, *ComFix-L* and *ComFix-T* integrate genealogical and variable similarity with normalized longest common subsequence and token similarity respectively, as presented in Eq. (6) and (7).

$$\text{For } \textbf{\textit{ComFix-L}}, similarity\ score(fn, fi) = gs + vs + nl \quad (6)$$

$$\text{For } \textbf{\textit{ComFix-T}}, similarity\ score(fn, fi) = gs + vs + ts \quad (7)$$

where, $similarity\ score(fn, fi)$ is the similarity score between faulty node (fn) and fixing ingredient (fi). This similarity score is multiplied by the faulty node's suspiciousness value to compute the patch ranking score, as shown in Eq. (8).

$$ranking\ score = suspiciousness\ score(fn) * similarity\ score(fn, fi) \quad (8)$$

where, $suspiciousness\ score(fn)$ is the suspiciousness value of the faulty node fn. To constrain the search space, only patches with a ranking score above 0, are considered as candidate patches. To remove duplicate candidate patches, only patch with the highest ranking score is kept. These candidate patches are next sorted in descending order based on the ranking score.

4. **Patch Validation.** This step examines the correctness of the candidate patches by executing test cases. To validate a patch, at first, the failing test cases are executed, as followed in [13,42]. If it passes those test cases, the passing test cases are executed. Patch validation continues until a patch passing all the test cases is found or the predefined time-limit exceeds. If a patch that passes all the test cases is found, this step outputs that patch.

5 Experiment

This section discusses the implementation and experimentation of the study. At first, the language and tools used for implementing the proposed approaches are presented. After that, the experimentation dataset as well as the evaluation metrics are described.

5.1 Implementation

Similar to recent program repair techniques [13,35,42], the proposed approaches are implemented in Java. The following tools are used for implementation:

– **Eclipse JDT Parser.** It is used for parsing and manipulating AST[1].
– **GZoltar.** To localize fault, GZoltar tool (version 0.1.1) is used [4]. It is widely used by existing automated program repair techniques [27,42,45]. It takes the class files of the buggy source code and the test cases as input and outputs line-number wise suspiciousness scores of the program.
– **Javalang.** It tokenizes code which is used for calculating token similarity[2]. It takes Java source code as input and provides a list of tokens as output.

To understand the impact of combining similarities, the proposed approaches are compared with baseline techniques that use either semantic or syntactic similarity for repairing expression level bugs. Consequently, this study further implements the following semantic or syntactic similarity based bug fixing approaches:

1. **Semantic Similarity Based Approach (SSBA).** It uses genealogical similarity (gs) and variable similarity (vs) along with faulty node's suspiciousness value to calculate patch ranking score, as shown in Eq. (9).

$$ranking\ score = suspiciousness\ score(fn) * (gs + vs) \qquad (9)$$

2. **LCS Based Approach (LBA).** It multiplies the value of normalized longest common subsequence (nl) with faulty node's suspiciousness score to measure patch ranking score, as presented in Eq. (10).

$$ranking\ score = suspiciousness\ score(fn) * nl \qquad (10)$$

3. **Token Based Approach (TBA).** It considers token similarity (ts) and faulty node's suspiciousness value for computing patch ranking score, as displayed in Eq. (11).

$$ranking\ score = suspiciousness\ score(fn) * ts \qquad (11)$$

Except ranking score calculation, all of these approaches follow the same repairing process as the combined ones. The implementations of these techniques are publicly available at GitHub[3].

---

[1] https://github.com/eclipse/eclipse.jdt.core/blob/master/org.eclipse.jdt.core/dom/org/eclipse/jdt/core/dom/ASTParser.java.

[2] https://github.com/c2nes/javalang.

[3] https://github.com/mou23/Combined-Similarity-Based-Automated-Program-Repair-Approaches-for-Expression-Level-Bugs.

5.2 Dataset

To evaluate the proposed approaches, those are executed on Defects4J [14] and QuixBugs [47] benchmarks. Defects4J is the most widely used benchmark in automated program repair [7,24]. It contains 395 bugs from six large, open-source Java projects, e.g., JFreeChart, Apache Commons Lang, etc. From this benchmark, bugs that fulfill the following criteria are selected:

- **Require Fixing at a Single Line.** Similar to [35,42], this study focuses on repairing single line bugs. Therefore, only the single line bugs are chosen from the benchmark, as followed in [35]. The list of single line bugs is obtained from the study of Sobreira et al. [37].
- **Unique.** To avoid bias, only unique bugs are chosen. If both the buggy and fixed version files of two bugs are the same, those are called duplicates. In Defects4J, *Closure_63* and *Closure_93* are duplicates of *Closure_62* and *Closure_92* respectively, which are removed.
- **Localizable at Line Level.** A bug is localizable at line level if the output list of the fault localization technique contains the actual buggy line [21]. From the dataset, unlocalizable bugs such as *Chart_8* and *Mockito_5* are eliminated since those are impossible to fix correctly.

After filtering, it results in 64 bugs. To ensure generalizability, automated program repair techniques should be effective for both large and small projects. However, existing studies [7,11] found that most of the program repair approaches are evaluated using only Defects4J and biased towards this benchmark. These techniques perform better for the projects of Defects4J compared to other projects. To ensure generalizability, this study uses QuixBugs benchmark [47] apart from Defects4J. This benchmark comprises single line bugs belonging to 40 small programs whose average lines of code is 190 [7]. These bugs are of diverse types such as incorrect method call, missing arithmetic expression, etc [47]. Furthermore, space and time complexity of these bugs are significant. For example, 14 programs contain recursion. From this dataset, GZoltar fails to produce output for 3 programs - *bitcount, find_first_in_sorted* and *sqrt* since these bugs generate infinite loop [1]. Hence, these 3 bugs are excluded from the experiment. The experiment is run on an Ubuntu server with Intel Xeon E5-2690 v2 @3.0GHz and 64GB physical memory. For each bug of these two benchmarks, the time budget is set to 90 min, as followed in [18,35,42].

5.3 Evaluation Metrics

For evaluating the proposed techniques, the following metrics are inspected:

- **Number of Bugs Correctly Fixed.** If an approach fixes more bugs correctly, it is considered more effective [18].
- **Precision.** It indicates the percentage of correct patches out of the plausible ones [24]. It is calculated using Eq. (12).

$$precision = (\frac{total\ correct\ patches}{total\ plausible\ patches}) * 100 \qquad (12)$$

where, *total correct patches* and *total plausible patches* denote the total number of the correct and plausible patches generated respectively. If precision is high, developers do not have to manually analyze the solutions generated by the technique [42,46].

– **Elapsed Time to Generate Correct Patches.** The less time a technique takes to generate correct patches, the better it is [18].

To assess the correctness of a plausible patch, both manual and automated analysis are performed, as suggested by [48]. For automated analysis, EvoSuite tool generated test cases are used since it is the most effective tool for identifying overfitting patches [47]. The test cases for Defects4J and QuixBugs benchmark are obtained from the study [48] and [47] respectively. These tests are generated using 30 trials of EvoSuite with 30 different seeds (1,2,...,30). From these test cases, flaky tests whose outcome (pass/fail) are depended on the environment, are removed [36]. To detect flaky tests, all the tests are executed 3 times on the fixed versions of the buggy projects, as followed in [48]. Next, tests that failed at least one time on the fixed version projects, are marked as flaky. After removing the flaky tests, the remaining tests are executed on the plausible patches generated by *ComFix-L*, *ComFix-T*, *SSBA*, *LBA* and *TBA*. Next, patches that passed all the test cases are manually examined to check whether those are semantically equivalent to the developer-written patches (provided with the benchmarks). For example, a plausible patch, presented in Listing 1.7, passes all the Evosuite test cases and thereby it is labeled as correct by automated analysis. Through manual inspection, the patch is found to be incorrect. When x is set to any valid double value and y is *NAN*, this patch produces a different result from the correct one. However, such project specific input can not always be covered by EvoSuite [47].

Listing 1.7. An Incorrect Plausible Patch for Bug *Math_63*.

```
public static boolean equals(double x, double y) {
-     return (Double.isNaN(x) && Double.isNaN(y)) || x == y;
+     return (!Double.isNaN(x) && Double.isNaN(y)) || x == y;
}
```

6 Result Analysis

Table 1 and Table 2 present the results of *LBA*, *ComFix-L*, *SSBA*, *ComFix-T* and *TBA* on Defects4J and QuixBugs benchmarks respectively. Results demonstrate that both *ComFix-L* and *ComFix-T* can correctly fix more bugs of Defects4J than syntactic similarity based approaches *LBA* and *TBA*. For some bugs, there exists no textual similarity between the faulty code and the correct fixing ingredient. Hence, the correct fixing ingredient is not included in the search space of *LBA* or *TBA*. For example, the bug *Math_59* is fixed by replacing variable b with variable a, as shown in Listing 1.8. Neither *LBA* or *TBA* can repair this bug due to lack of syntactic similarity (both normalized LCS and token similarity are 0).

Table 1. Results of Different Approaches on Defects4J Benchmark.

Approach	Number of bugs correctly fixed	Number of bugs incorrectly fixed	Precision (%)
LBA	10	12	45.45
ComFix-L	11	7	61.11
SSBA	11	7	61.11
ComFix-T	11	7	61.11
TBA	8	10	44.44

Table 2. Results of Different Approaches on QuixBugs Benchmark.

Approach	Number of bugs correctly fixed	Number of bugs incorrectly fixed	Precision (%)
LBA	10	4	71.43
ComFix-L	11	5	68.75
SSBA	9	7	56.25
ComFix-T	10	6	62.50
TBA	6	4	60.00

Listing 1.8. A Correct Sample Patch for Bug *Math_59*.

```
public static float max(final float a, final float b) {
-    return (a <= b) ? b : (Float.isNaN(a + b) ? Float.NaN : b);
+    return (a <= b) ? b : (Float.isNaN(a + b) ? Float.NaN : a);
}
```

Listing 1.9. A Correct Sample Patch for Bug *Lang_59*.

```
878: public StrBuilder appendFixedWidthPadRight(Object obj,
                                int width, char padChar) {
884: -    str.getChars(0, strLen, buffer, size);
884: +    str.getChars(0, width, buffer, size);
895: }
```

Listing 1.10. An Incorrect Plausible Patch Generated by *LBA* and *TBA* for Bug *Lang_59*.

```
878: public StrBuilder appendFixedWidthPadRight(Object obj,
                                int width, char padChar) {
880: -    ensureCapacity(size + width);
880: +    ensureCapacity(size + 4);
895: }
```

In Defects4J, *ComFix-L* and *ComFix-T* outperform *LBA* and *TBA* in terms of precision as well. The values are 61.11%, 61.11%, 45.45% and 44.44% correspondingly. For bug *Lang_59*, the actual faulty line is 884 and the correct patch is replacing variable *strLen* at line 884 with variable *width*, as shown in Listing 1.9. However, fault localization technique assigns both line 880 and 884 a suspiciousness score of 0.58. Both *LBA* and *TBA* generate an incorrect plausible patch before the correct one by replacing *ensureCapacity(size + width)* at line 880 with *ensureCapacity(size + 4)*, as shown in Listing 1.10. This is because syntactic similarity between the faulty code and the fixing ingredient is higher for the incorrect plausible patch than the correct one. For the correct patch, normalized LCS and token similarity are 0.17 and 0 respectively, whereas those are 0.82 and 0.75 for the incorrect plausible patch. On the other hand, both *ComFix-L* and *ComFix-T* can rank the correct patch over the incorrect plausible one due to incorporating genealogical and variable similarity. Genealogical and variable similarity are 1 for the correct patch while those are respectively 0.53 and 0.50 for the incorrect plausible patch.

Listing 1.11. An Incorrect Plausible Patch Generated by *ComFix-T* for Bug *flatten*.

```
13: public static Object flatten(Object arr) {
21: -    result.add(flatten(x));
21: +    result.add(x);
29: }
```

Listing 1.12. A Correct Sample Patch for Bug *flatten*.

```
13: public static Object flatten(Object arr) {
26: -    result.add(flatten(arr));
26: +    return arr;
29: }
```

Listing 1.13. An Incorrect Plausible Patch Generated by *ComFix-L* and *ComFix-T* for Bug *quicksort*.

```
public static ArrayListInteger quicksort(ArrayListInteger arr) {
-       else if (x > pivot) {
+       else if (x > 0) {
           greater.add(x);
       }
}
```

In QuixBugs benchmark, *ComFix-L* outperforms *LBA* and *TBA* in terms of correctly fixed bugs. *ComFix-T* performs better than *TBA* and as good as *LBA*. For *ComFix-T*, there is a tie between incorrect plausible (shown in Listing 1.11) and correct patch (shown in Listing 1.12) for the bug *flatten*. Although *ComFix-L* and *ComFix-T* achieve higher precision than *TBA*, *LBA* performs better than these two techniques. For the bug *quicksort*, both *ComFix-L* and *ComFix-T* generate a plausible patch by replacing a variable *pivot* with a number literal *0*, as illustrated in Listing 1.13. Nevertheless, this type of plausible patches can be eliminated by using historical bug fix patterns while generating patches [42], which is out of scope of this study.

Listing 1.14. A Correct Sample Patch for Bug *next_palindrome.*

```
public static String next_palindrome(int[] digit_list) {
-    otherwise.addAll(Collections.nCopies(digit_list.length,0));
+    otherwise.addAll(Collections.nCopies(digit_list.length-1,0));
}
```

Listing 1.15. A Correct Sample Patch for Bug *mergesort.*

```
public static ArrayListInteger mergesort(ArrayListInteger arr) {
-    if (arr.size() == 0) {
+    if (arr.size()/2 == 0) {
       return arr;
    }
}
```

Table 1 further reveals that semantic similarity based technique *SSBA* performs as good as *ComFix-L* and *ComFix-T* for Defects4j bugs. Similar to *ComFix-L* and *ComFix-T*, *SSBA* correctly repairs 11 bugs and obtains a precision of 61.11%. However, both *ComFix-L* and *ComFix-T* outperform *SSBA* in QuixBugs benchmark, as listed in Table 2. In case of *SSBA*, there exists a tie between incorrect plausible and correct patch for the bugs *flatten* and *next_palindrome*. For the bug *next_palindrome*, *ComFix-L* and *ComFix-T* can rank the correct patch at first position through incorporating syntactic similarity, as displayed in Listing 1.14. Similarly, for the bug *mergesort*, *ComFix-L* and *ComFix-T* rank the correct solution (shown in Listing 1.15) higher than *SSBA* due to considering syntactic similarity. *SSBA* ranks the correct patch at 463, whereas *ComFix-L* and *ComFix-T* rank it at 17 and 14 respectively.

To compare the repairing time of correctly fixed bugs, Wilcoxon Signed-Rank test is used since no assumption regarding the distribution of samples has been made [43]. Table 3 reports the statistical significance of the result using significance level = 0.05. For comparing two approaches, their commonly fixed bugs are used. For example, *ComFix-L* and *SSBA* have 20 correct fixes in common. The mean repairing time of these bugs are 8.59 and 7.71 min for *ComFix-L* and *SSBA* respectively. Result shows that these mean times are not significantly different since the p-value is 0.18. Similar result is obtained for all the other approaches. It indicates that although *ComFix-L* and *ComFix-T* considers more similarity metrics than other techniques, it does not significantly increase the bug fixing time. *ComFix-T* calculates 3 similarity metrics (genealogical, variable and token similarity) for each patch, whereas TBA computes only 1 similarity metric (token similarity). However, result implies that calculation of those additional metrics do not take significantly extra time.

In summary, *ComFix-L* and *ComFix-T* can correctly fix more bugs compared to syntactic or semantic similarity based techniques and achieve higher precision, as displayed in Table 4. In a previous study, the authors found that when the faulty location is known, the developer-written patch can be ranked higher by combining syntactic and semantic similarities [2]. Through the current study, it

Table 3. Differences between Mean Repairing Time (In Minutes) of Different Approaches.

Compared groups	Mean		P-value
ComFix-L and SSBA	ComFix-L	SSBA	0.18
	8.59	7.71	
ComFix-T and SSBA	ComFix-T	SSBA	0.55
	8.35	7.71	
ComFix-L and LBA	ComFix-L	LBA	0.27
	2.74	3.87	
ComFix-T and LBA	ComFix-T	LBA	0.98
	3.56	4.11	
ComFix-L and TBA	ComFix-L	TBA	0.92
	2.68	2.79	
ComFix-T and TBA	ComFix-T	TBA	0.77
	2.76	2.79	
ComFix-L and ComFix-T	ComFix-L	ComFix-T	0.24
	8.19	7.96	
SSBA and LBA	SSBA	LBA	0.39
	4.92	4.39	
SSBA and TBA	SSBA	TBA	0.16
	5.25	3.09	
LBA and TBA	LBA	TBA	0.15
	9.99	8.52	

[1]P-value < 0.05 denotes the mean difference in time is statistically significant

Table 4. Overall Result of Different Approaches.

Approach	Total number of bugs correctly fixed	Total number of bugs incorrectly fixed	Precision (%)
LBA	20	16	55.56
ComFix-L	22	12	64.71
SSBA	20	14	58.82
ComFix-T	21	13	61.76
TBA	14	14	50.00

is evident that the combination of similarities is effective even when the faulty code is unknown. It can contribute to find the correct patch from the enhanced search space caused by expressions and rank it over incorrect plausible patches. Furthermore, the combined similarity based approaches calculate more similarity metrics for each patch, however, it does not significantly increase the bug repairing time.

7 Threats to Validity

This section discusses the threats which can affect the validity of the proposed approaches. The threats are identified from two perspectives namely threats to external and internal validity.

- **Threats to External Validity.** The external threat of this study is the generalizability of the obtained result [18]. To minimize the threat of generalizability, bugs belonging to both large and small projects are used for experimentation. As the representative of large projects, Defects4J is chosen since it is the most widely used benchmark in automated program repair [7,24]. On the other hand, QuixBugs is selected as the representative of small projects because it contains diverse types of bugs such as incorrect method call, missing condition, etc [47]. In addition, space and time complexity of these bugs are significant [47].
- **Threats to Internal Validity.** The first threat to internal validity is error in the implementation of the study. This study uses GZoltar tool (version 0.1.1) for fault localization [4]. The results of the GZoltar tool are directly incorporated in this study without checking whether there is any defect in the tool. However, GZoltar tool is widely used by existing automated program repair approaches [27,42,45]. The second threat to internal validity lies in setting the experimentation time budget. The time budget is set to 90 min, as followed in [18,35,42]. Changing the time budget may impact the obtained result. The third threat to internal validity comes from an error in assessing the patch correctness. Assessing the patch correctness is itself a research, which is explored by [44,46,49]. However, this study performs both manual and automated analysis to evaluate the correctness of a patch, as suggested by [48]. For automated analysis, test cases generated from 30 trials of the EvoSuite tool are used. These test cases are used by existing studies as well, for assessing patch correctness [47,48]. On the other hand, determining patch correctness based on manual inspection is a common practice in automated program repair [13,18,35,42].

8 Conclusion and Future Work

This study proposes two automated program repair approaches that work at the expression level. However, considering expression level enlarges the search space and thereby decreases the probability of finding the correct patch [25]. To address this problem, the proposed approaches combine syntactic and semantic similarity to limit the search space as well as prioritize the generated patches. To calculate semantic similarity, genealogical and variable similarity are used. For capturing syntactic similarity, normalized longest common subsequence and token similarity are used individually. These techniques take a buggy program, a set of test cases as input and generate a program passing all the test cases as output. At first, the suspiciousness score of *Expression* type nodes are calculated using spectrum-based fault localization [17]. Next, patches are generated by replacing the faulty nodes with the fixing ingredients. To validate potentially correct patch earlier, patches are prioritized based on suspiciousness score and similarity score. The similarity score is measured by integrating genealogical, variable similarity with normalized longest common subsequence or token similarity. Finally, the correctness of a patch is validated by executing test cases.

To understand the impact of combining similarities, the proposed approaches are compared with techniques that use either semantic or syntactic similarity. For comparison, 64 and 37 out of 395 and 40 bugs from Defects4J and QuixBugs benchmark are selected through preprocessing. Results show that combined similarity based techniques correctly fix more bugs than approaches using either semantic or syntactic similarity. In addition, combined similarity based approaches obtain a precision of 64.71% and 61.76% on these benchmarks, which is higher than syntactic or semantic similarity based bug fixing approaches. The result further reveals that although combined similarity based techniques consider more similarity metrics than other approaches, it does not significantly increase the bug fixing time.

In future, these combined similarity based approaches can be further explored using other benchmarks such as Bears [26], Bugs.jar [34], etc. Besides, common fix patterns for expression type bugs such as replacing method or variable name, can be identified and integrated with these techniques to check whether it can further constrain the search space and eliminate incorrect plausible patches.

Acknowledgement. This research is supported by the fellowship from Information and Communication Technology Division, Bangladesh. No-56.00.0000.028.33.093.19-427; Dated 20.11.2019. The virtual machine facilities used in this research is provided by the Bangladesh Research and Education Network (BdREN).

References

1. Asad, M., Ganguly, K.K., Sakib, K.: Impact of similarity on repairing small programs: a case study on quixbugs benchmark. In: Proceedings of the 42nd International Conference on Software Engineering Workshops (ICSEW), pp. 21–22. ACM (2020)
2. Asad, M., Ganguly, K.K., Sakib, K.: Impact of combining syntactic and semantic similarities on patch prioritization. In: Proceedings of the 15th International Conference on Evaluation of Novel Approaches to Software Engineering (ENASE), pp. 170–180. SCITEPRESS (2020)
3. Barr, E.T., Brun, Y., Devanbu, P., Harman, M., Sarro, F.: The plastic surgery hypothesis. In: Proceedings of the 22nd International Symposium on Foundations of Software Engineering (FSE), pp. 306–317. ACM (2014)
4. Campos, J., Riboira, A., Perez, A., Abreu, R.: Gzoltar: an eclipse plug-in for testing and debugging. In: Proceedings of the 27th International Conference on Automated Software Engineering (ASE), pp. 378–381. ACM (2012)
5. Chauhan, N.: Software Testing: Principles and Practices. Oxford University Press, Oxford (2010)
6. Chen, Z., Monperrus, M.: The remarkable role of similarity in redundancy-based program repair. Computing Research Repository (CoRR) abs/1811.05703 (2018). http://arxiv.org/abs/1811.05703

7. Durieux, T., Madeiral, F., Martinez, M., Abreu, R.: Empirical review of Java program repair tools: a large-scale experiment on 2,141 bugs and 23,551 repair attempts. In: Proceedings of the 27th Joint Meeting on European Software Engineering Conference and Symposium on the Foundations of Software Engineering (ESEC/FSE), pp. 302–313. ACM (2019)

8. Gabel, M., Jiang, L., Su, Z.: Scalable detection of semantic clones. In: Proceedings of the 30th International Conference on Software Engineering (ICSE), pp. 321–330. ACM (2008)

9. Gallardo, R., Hommel, S., Kannan, S., Gordon, J., Zakhour, S.B.: The Java Tutorial: A Short Course on the Basics. Addison-Wesley Professional (2014)

10. Gazzola, L., Micucci, D., Mariani, L.: Automatic software repair: a survey. IEEE Trans. Softw. Eng. (TSE) **45**, 34–67 (2017)

11. Ghanbari, A., Benton, S., Zhang, L.: Practical program repair via bytecode mutation. In: Proceedings of the 28th International Symposium on Software Testing and Analysis (ISSTA), pp. 19–30. ACM (2019)

12. Ji, T., Chen, L., Mao, X., Yi, X.: Automated program repair by using similar code containing fix ingredients. In: Proceedings of the 40th Annual Computer Software and Applications Conference (COMPSAC), vol. 1, pp. 197–202. IEEE (2016)

13. Jiang, J., Xiong, Y., Zhang, H., Gao, Q., Chen, X.: Shaping program repair space with existing patches and similar code. In: Proceedings of the 27th International Symposium on Software Testing and Analysis (ISSTA), pp. 298–309. ACM (2018)

14. Just, R., Jalali, D., Ernst, M.D.: Defects4j: a database of existing faults to enable controlled testing studies for java programs. In: Proceedings of the International Symposium on Software Testing and Analysis (ISSTA), pp. 437–440. ACM (2014)

15. Ke, Y., Stolee, K.T., Le Goues, C., Brun, Y.: Repairing programs with semantic code search. In: Proceedings of the 30th International Conference on Automated Software Engineering (ASE), pp. 295–306. IEEE (2015)

16. Kim, D., Nam, J., Song, J., Kim, S.: Automatic patch generation learned from human-written patches. In: Proceedings of the 2013 International Conference on Software Engineering (ICSE), pp. 802–811. IEEE (2013)

17. Le, T.D.B., Thung, F., Lo, D.: Theory and practice, do they match? A case with spectrum-based fault localization. In: Proceedings of the International Conference on Software Maintenance (ICSM), pp. 380–383. IEEE (2013)

18. Le, X.B.D., Lo, D., Le Goues, C.: History driven program repair. In: Proceedings of the 23rd International Conference on Software Analysis, Evolution, and Reengineering (SANER), vol. 1, pp. 213–224. IEEE (2016)

19. Le Goues, C., Nguyen, T., Forrest, S., Weimer, W.: GenProg: a generic method for automatic software repair. IEEE Trans. Softw. Eng. (TSE) **38**(1), 54–72 (2011)

20. Liu, K., Kim, D., Koyuncu, A., Li, L., Bissyandé, T.F., Le Traon, Y.: A closer look at real-world patches. In: Proceedings of the International Conference on Software Maintenance and Evolution (ICSME), pp. 275–286. IEEE (2018)

21. Liu, K., Koyuncu, A., Bissyandé, T.F., Kim, D., Klein, J., Le Traon, Y.: You cannot fix what you cannot find! an investigation of fault localization bias in benchmarking automated program repair systems. In: Proceedings of the 12th IEEE Conference on Software Testing, Validation and Verification (ICST), pp. 102–113. IEEE (2019)

22. Liu, K., Koyuncu, A., Kim, D., Bissyandé, T.F.: TBAR: revisiting template-based automated program repair. In: Proceedings of the 28th International Symposium on Software Testing and Analysis (ISSTA), pp. 31–42. ACM (2019)

23. Liu, K., Koyuncu, A., Kim, K., Kim, D., Bissyande, T.F.D.A.: LSRepair: live search of fix ingredients for automated program repair. In: Proceedings of the 25th Asia-Pacific Software Engineering Conference (APSEC), pp. 658–662 (2018)

24. Liu, K., et al.: On the efficiency of test suite based program repair: a systematic assessment of 16 automated repair systems for Java programs. In: Proceedings of the 42nd International Conference on Software Engineering (ICSE) (2020)
25. Long, F., Rinard, M.: An analysis of the search spaces for generate and validate patch generation systems. In: Proceedings of the 38th International Conference on Software Engineering (ICSE), pp. 702–713. IEEE (2016)
26. Madeiral, F., Urli, S., Maia, M., Monperrus, M.: Bears: an extensible Java bug benchmark for automatic program repair studies. In: Proceedings of the 26th International Conference on Software Analysis, Evolution and Reengineering (SANER), pp. 468–478. IEEE (2019)
27. Martinez, M., Monperrus, M.: Astor: exploring the design space of generate-and-validate program repair beyond GenProg. J. Syst. Softw. **151**, 65–80 (2019)
28. Martinez, M., Weimer, W., Monperrus, M.: Do the fix ingredients already exist? An empirical inquiry into the redundancy assumptions of program repair approaches. In: Companion Proceedings of the 36th International Conference on Software Engineering (ICSE), pp. 492–495. ACM (2014)
29. Monperrus, M.: A critical review of "automatic patch generation learned from human-written patches": essay on the problem statement and the evaluation of automatic software repair. In: Proceedings of the 36th International Conference on Software Engineering (ICSE), pp. 234–242 (2014)
30. Monperrus, M.: Automatic software repair: a bibliography. ACM Comput. Surv. (CSUR) **51**(1), 17 (2018)
31. Qi, Y., Mao, X., Lei, Y., Dai, Z., Wang, C.: The strength of random search on automated program repair. In: Proceedings of the 36th International Conference on Software Engineering (ICSE), pp. 254–265. ACM (2014)
32. Qi, Z., Long, F., Achour, S., Rinard, M.: An analysis of patch plausibility and correctness for generate-and-validate patch generation systems. In: Proceedings of the International Symposium on Software Testing and Analysis (ISSTA), pp. 24–36. ACM (2015)
33. Ragkhitwetsagul, C., Krinke, J., Clark, D.: A comparison of code similarity analysers. Empir. Softw. Eng. **23**(4), 2464–2519 (2018)
34. Saha, R., Lyu, Y., Lam, W., Yoshida, H., Prasad, M.: Bugs.jar: a large-scale, diverse dataset of real-world Java bugs. In: Proceedings of the 15th International Conference on Mining Software Repositories (MSR), pp. 10–13. IEEE (2018)
35. Saha, R.K., Lyu, Y., Yoshida, H., Prasad, M.R.: Elixir: effective object-oriented program repair. In: Proceedings of the 32nd International Conference on Automated Software Engineering (ASE), pp. 648–659. IEEE (2017)
36. Shamshiri, S., Just, R., Rojas, J.M., Fraser, G., McMinn, P., Arcuri, A.: Do automatically generated unit tests find real faults? An empirical study of effectiveness and challenges. In: Proceedings of the 30th International Conference on Automated Software Engineering (ASE), pp. 201–211. IEEE (2015)
37. Sobreira, V., Durieux, T., Madeiral, F., Monperrus, M., de Almeida Maia, M.: Dissection of a bug dataset: anatomy of 395 patches from defects4j. In: Proceedings of the 25th International Conference on Software Analysis, Evolution and Reengineering (SANER), pp. 130–140. IEEE (2018)
38. Thada, V., Jaglan, V.: Comparison of Jaccard, Dice, Cosine similarity coefficient to find best fitness value for web retrieved documents using genetic algorithm. Int. J. Innov. Eng. Technol. **2**(4), 202–205 (2013)

39. Wang, S., Mao, X., Niu, N., Yi, X., Guo, A.: Multi-location program repair strategies learned from successful experience (S). In: Perkusich, A. (ed.) Proceedings of the 31st International Conference on Software Engineering and Knowledge Engineering (SEKE), pp. 713–777. KSI Research Inc. and Knowledge Systems Institute Graduate School (2019)
40. Wang, S., Wen, M., Mao, X., Yang, D.: Attention please: consider Mockito when evaluating newly proposed automated program repair techniques. In: Proceedings of the Evaluation and Assessment on Software Engineering (EASE), pp. 260–266. ACM (2019)
41. Weimer, W., Nguyen, T., Le Goues, C., Forrest, S.: Automatically finding patches using genetic programming. In: Proceedings of the 31st International Conference on Software Engineering (ICSE), pp. 364–374. IEEE (2009)
42. Wen, M., Chen, J., Wu, R., Hao, D., Cheung, S.C.: Context-aware patch generation for better automated program repair. In: Proceedings of the 40th International Conference on Software Engineering (ICSE), pp. 1–11. ACM (2018)
43. Wilcoxon, F.: Individual comparisons by ranking methods. In: Kotz, S., Johnson, N.L. (eds.) Breakthroughs in Statistics. SSS, pp. 196–202. Springer, New York (1992). https://doi.org/10.1007/978-1-4612-4380-9_16
44. Xin, Q., Reiss, S.P.: Identifying test-suite-overfitted patches through test case generation. In: Proceedings of the 26th International Symposium on Software Testing and Analysis (ISSTA), pp. 226–236. ACM (2017)
45. Xin, Q., Reiss, S.P.: Leveraging syntax-related code for automated program repair. In: Proceedings of the 32nd International Conference on Automated Software Engineering (ASE), pp. 660–670. IEEE (2017)
46. Xiong, Y., Liu, X., Zeng, M., Zhang, L., Huang, G.: Identifying patch correctness in test-based program repair. In: Proceedings of the 40th International Conference on Software Engineering (ICSE), pp. 789–799. ACM (2018)
47. Ye, H., Martinez, M., Durieux, T., Monperrus, M.: A comprehensive study of automatic program repair on the quixbugs benchmark. In: Proceedings of the 1st International Workshop on Intelligent Bug Fixing (IBF), pp. 1–10. IEEE (2019)
48. Ye, H., Martinez, M., Monperrus, M.: Automated patch assessment for program repair at scale. arXiv preprint arXiv:1909.13694 (2019)
49. Yu, Z., Martinez, M., Danglot, B., Durieux, T., Monperrus, M.: Alleviating patch overfitting with automatic test generation: a study of feasibility and effectiveness for the nopol repair system. Empir. Softw. Eng. **24**(1), 33–67 (2019)
50. Zhang, J., Wang, X., Zhang, H., Sun, H., Wang, K., Liu, X.: A novel neural source code representation based on abstract syntax tree. In: Proceedings of the 41st International Conference on Software Engineering (ICSE), pp. 783–794. IEEE (2019)
51. Zhong, H., Su, Z.: An empirical study on real bug fixes. In: Proceedings of the 37th International Conference on Software Engineering (ICSE), vol. 1, pp. 913–923. IEEE (2015)

A Multi-engine Aspect-Oriented Language with Modeling Integration for Video Game Design

Ben J. Geisler[1][(⊠)] and Shane L. Kavage[2]

[1] Saint Norbert College, De Pere, WI 54115, USA
benjamin.geisler@snc.edu
[2] University of Wisconsin, La Crosse, WI 54601, USA

Abstract. Video game programming is a diverse, multi-faceted endeavor involving elements of graphics programming, systems programming, UI, HCI, and other software engineering disciplines. Game programmers typically employ a new "codebase" per software artifact which often means a unique choice of game engines and scripting languages. Non-portable code is exacerbated by a lack of a shared language and a lack of translation utilities between languages. Meanwhile, many game programming tasks occur time and time again. Aspect-oriented programming was largely developed to assist software engineers in decoupling tasks while maintaining software reuse. GAMESPECT is a language that promotes software reuse through aspects while also providing a platform for translation of software artifacts which has enabled it to be used in multiple game engines across multiple projects. Code reuse on these projects has been high and our methodologies can be summarized by discussing three tenants of GAMESPECT: 1) composition specifications, which define source to source transition properties 2) pluggable aspect interpreters and 3) high level language constructs and modeling language constructs (MDAML) which encourage designer friendly terminology. By comparing accuracy, efficiency, pluggability, and modularity, these three tenants are demonstrated to be effective in creating a new game programming language.

Keywords: Video game programming · Game engines · Game design · Metaprogramming · Domain specific languages · Aspect-oriented programming

1 Introduction

There are two main bodies of work in this paper. The first, and most documented, is aspect insertion via source to source transformation languages using composition specifications [1–5]. This topic relates to interpreter and compiler design and has contributed a new language to the research/industrial community called GAMESPECT [13]. The second body of work of this paper is that of game balance and game design as it relates to common toolsets. Wherein we ask the fundamental question: how can we better allow

© Springer Nature Switzerland AG 2021
R. Ali et al. (Eds.): ENASE 2020, CCIS 1375, pp. 336–359, 2021.
https://doi.org/10.1007/978-3-030-70006-5_14

for developers to make games "fun". The second question, that of "fun", has been studied but lacks an end-to-end solution for a game design framework [6–9].

This paper is based upon a conference paper given at the ENASE 2020 conference, entitled "Aspect Weaving for Multiple Video Game Engines using Composition Specifications" [13]. However, since then research has continued: we continued refining our experimental results and applying GAMESPECT to new balancing tasks. Also, the new work since the conference focuses on game balance and GAMESPECT's innate ability to exploit aspect-oriented programming to create more robust and successful software artifacts; this new version of GAMESPECT is called GAMESPECT 1.01 and includes a game design modeling language which is introduced in Sect. 4.4.

1.1 Shortcomings of Game Design Tools

Much work has been done to categorize, demonstrate and catalog game design principles. Researchers, journalists, and practitioners in video game development have tried many times to quantify what constitutes a "fun" video game and specifically how to make one [10]. We believe this is a tool problem: most designers intuitively know what a "fun" game is when they see one, but they lack the proper tools to describe, tweak and implement changes quickly to address any shortcomings [11]. This is not a paper about how to automatically make a "fun" video game with no designer input. Creativity is perhaps a uniquely human trait and the synthesis of fun is as elusive for researchers as it has ever been, which means that game design should be left to professionals with an artistic talent for such things. However, they need good tools to do their jobs and the industry has struggled for some time to create these tools. Sometimes the tools are non-existent, sometimes they are in massive spreadsheets that are illegible, and almost always they are not integrated to development toolsets [12]. There is no real solution for the problem of how to balance a game. Meanwhile, there has been very little academic work on the subject. We believe that quality software starts with solid research, which is the motivating factor of this paper.

To further demonstrate the lack of tooling, let us examine a typical process of designing a video game. Developers begin creating the game, with programmers and level designers laboriously programming each individual entity. At some point the designers play the game and decide the proper values for all the entities in terms of balancing the game for difficulty. At this stage, many designers will record all these values in a massive spreadsheet [12]. But the spreadsheet is not incorporated into any software because the entry points for each value are not recorded and are scattered. This is less than ideal since it requires hunting and pecking for the right spot to get at the value, and some may be missed. Also, the iteration time is greatly reduced with a game designer needing to work with a game programmer to get proper results. Not to mention that there is no permanent home to "game balance" in this system.

It might help to consider an actual example development cycle. *Noise Paradox* is an independent game for iOS, Android and Nintendo Switch. Designed over the course of 2–3 years, the traditional approach of *Noise Paradox* development mirrors most other game development initiatives. We started with a design document, which was very high level and contained explanatory text (no code or modeling language). The developers then began in Unreal Engine 4 and continued implementing systems, artwork, etc. *Noise*

Paradox used the original GAMESPECT 1.00 as setup by Geisler and Kavage [13]. For GAMESPECT 1.00, at no time was there a distinct bridge between gameplay systems we had envisioned and the design documentation. During the creation of GAMESPECT 1.01 (which incorporates a design modeling language, as discussed in Sect. 4), we were able to get rid of the laborious "spreadsheet" method described above. The original GAMESPECT 1.00 had already added the ability to summarize multiple target languages [13], but GAMESPECT 1.01 added this ability to bridge the gap in game design tools and balance methodologies. We will summarize GAMESPECT 1.0′s contribution within a general context as well as the context of *Noise Paradox* (as an example), and we will also describe the contributions of GAMESPECT 1.01.

1.2 Introduction to GAMESPECT

As far as we know, at least the following programming and scripting languages are being used to create modern video games: C++, C, C#, Java, Python, LUA, Blueprints (UE4), Assembly, Switch, Objective-C, Boo (Unity), Javascript. Game engines typically write the low-level graphics code in a highly efficient version of C/C++, and provide a scripting language which sits on top the lower level language. This implements an abstraction which allows for game designers to focus on more important tasks such as high level game design concerns [14].

GAMESPECT is a metaprogramming language that builds on similar ideas from a number of works, including the AWESOME language and composition specifications [5]. It also uses ideas of source to source transformation languages from the influential TXL language [16]. As it stands, GAMESPECT (both version 1.00 and 1.01) is the only production domain specific aspect language (DSAL) we know of that translates from one common source language to multiple target languages. While there are others such as XAspects, LARA and Awesome, which accept multiple source languages, there are none that support the other direction: from one source language to multiple targets [15]. GAMESPECT is also the only known DSAL which accepts design framework terminology such as shown in Robin Hunicke's MDA (Mechanics, Design, Aesthetics) framework [9], which is covered in later sections.

1.3 Organization of This Paper

This paper loosely follows a background, literature review, methodology, results structure. The motivation section is first, in which we discuss further the problems of game balance and lack of a common language. Furthermore, we will discuss the lack of a source-to-source, one-to-many metaprogramming language and the need for GAME-SPECT. As this paper is also meant to be practical, we will review some of the literature surrounding game balance as well as compiler implementation and composition specifications surrounding similar languages such as Awesome. In this way, curious readers could implement their own many-to-many solutions across multiple target domains (other than gaming). Our methodology section largely focuses on how to tie together the moving parts of GAMESPECT, but we also propose a method for evaluating the endeavor, patterned off work done by Kojarski and Pinto [4, 15]. There many code examples given which show the relative benefits of GAMESPECT over "vanilla" approaches (e.g. straight blueprints/C++ in Unreal Engine 4). This largely gives way to a results discussion driven by our previously states goals of efficiency, pluggability, accuracy and modularity. We realize that if GAMESPECT lacks in any of these areas, it would prevent wide-scale adoption of both the technology itself as well as the new applications of composition specifications, and the new methodology of creating a one-to-many solution.

2 Background

2.1 Design Tools

A game engine (also known as simply the "engine" in this text) is a codebase of existing routines, algorithms and functions which allows for an expedited development of a game. Decades ago, developers realized that many types of tasks were being done over and over again. In the 1990's, researchers and professionals alike began developing game engines [14]. As of 2018, the engines Unity and Unreal Engine 4 composed approximately 80% of all games made on the market. With 2,400 games a year being created, this is around 1,900 games alone created on these engines.

Fig. 1. Market share of game engines [19].

Engine Architecture. Game engine architecture is built upon the idea of layers. Loosely speaking, an engine is a framework that has a collection of utilities and components, some built on each other, that provides for common rendering, physics and object interactions in a game [17].

An engine consists of the compile time tools such as programming (script) language parsers, generators and runtime components. The complete discussion of each component of a game engine is an exhaustive text and best left for books on the subject, such as Gregory's penultimate "Game Engine Architecture" book [14]. Figure 2 is a compact summary from his book.

In a typical engine architecture, the gameplay specific systems are usually thought to be the highest level, followed by the front-end and the setup for any state machine systems. Animations, visual effects, and audio make up a mid level- along with networking routines. At the bottom-most level is the renderer and physics calculations. GAMESPECT savings take advantage of the fact that the Game Specific Subsystems are the major changing factor from game to game. Depending on the engine- most or all of the game specific systems are done in a scripting language (which is at the foundations level). This leaves plenty of room for lines of code savings.

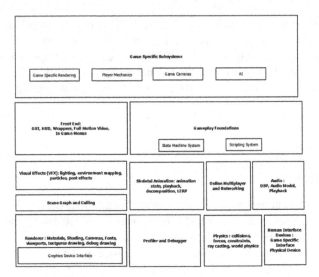

Fig. 2. A typical game engine architecture.

Room for Savings. If you factor in the average game codebase size of 2 million lines of code, this means there are approximately 3.8 trillion lines of code written each year from the gaming industry. Typically, 1/2 of a game codebase is the "engine" [14]. Which means 1.9 trillion unique lines of code are being written. Which 50% is a good savings, this is still wasteful especially considering the common tasks that are done in each codebase. For example, a first-person shooter will have spawning code for enemy players, as will a third-person game or a strategy game [17].

2.2 Metaprogramming, Aspect-Oriented Programming and DSAL's

The topics of metaprogramming, aspect-oriented programming, and domain specific languages (DSL's) all have impressive amounts of current and past research. We will summarize each and then explain the relevance to GAMESPECTT.

Metaprogramming. The specific type of metaprogramming we are interested in is "macro systems", which allow high level languages to be interpreted and translated to either other high level languages or low level languages. Metaprogramming languages describe operations at an abstract level which are then compiled down to usable code, for example CoffeeScript, Nim, and Scala Macros. In general, a source to source compiler is needed for these languages: in the case of CoffeeScript it compiles to Javascript. Our language GAMESPECT follows a similar paradigm in that its also source to source, but it compiles to multiple distinct pieces of source code in different languages, instead of just one [13].

For example, consider the CoffeeScript below and the resulting JavaScript. In this example, we want to manually search for a value in an array. Once found, we return the array position. If we get past the beginning of the list, we return a negative value.

Doing this in Javascript involves a do-while loop with variables being updated inside the loop. In CoffeeScript it is called "pattern-matching" to match the new parameters of the function with the old values and rerun the loop; essentially this is a macro that expands to the Javascript code provided (Figs. 3 and 4).

```
1    findNumber = (x, i, list) ->
2      [x, i, list] = [x, i-1, list] until (i<0 || list[i] == x)
3      i
```

Fig. 3. CoffeeScript findNumber.

```
1    findNumber = (x, i, list) => {
2        do {
3            if(list[i] == x)
4                return i
5            i = i - 1
6        } while (i >= 0)
7        return i
8    }
```

Fig. 4. Javascript findNumber: the above CoffeeScript code is transformed to Javascript.

Aspect-Oriented Programming. Aspect-oriented programming was created to solve inherent problems that exist in object-oriented programming related to issues of decoupling, composition and cohesion [19]. One classic example is logging. For example, in a game engine, every game system as indicated from Fig. 1 could possibly send out log messages to the developer: perhaps we wish to print how much memory is available, or we'd like to print when the boss monster attacks. Printing to the log device is very useful but occasionally certain preparations must be made. For example, when printing to an iOS device the device must either print to the remotely connected computer or to a file since there is no command terminal available on iOS. The logic for this decision could potentially be repeated over and over in each type of log message. Or we could extract the processing of where the output goes to a function which determines it for us. Aspect-oriented programming allows us to form a pattern for these log messages, match them and perform what's called "advice". Advice can be pre-function call, synchronous with the actual call, or post-function call (later in this paper we'll refer to this advice as BEFORE, DURING or AFTER advice).

In the case of our example, aspect-oriented programming would remove the need for two function calls at each call-site (one for remote-printing, one for log file). This is because aspect-oriented programming will allow for the programmer to specify an "aspect" which scans for the name of the function call, in this case "LogMessage" (see Fig. 5). Alternatively, aspect-oriented programming would allow for a new level of abstraction which allows for the aspect to call both types of logs (see Fig. 6).

Domain Specific Languages (DSLs). Domain specific languages are a fairly straight forward approach to programming that involves the creation of a new language for a specific purpose, as opposed to using a general programming language such as C++.

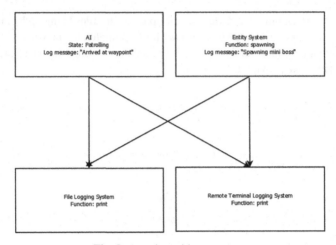

Fig. 5. Logging without aspects.

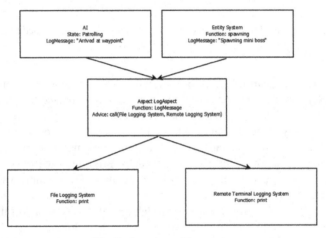

Fig. 6. Logging with aspects.

Unix shell languages such as BASH are a good example of domain specific languages. These languages provide logic functionality but also utilities for controlling processes, jobs, etc. Game engines serve as a major source of DSLs, for example the following engines all use some type of DSL: GameMaker, Unreal Engine 4, Unity, Torque, Ogre, Lumberyard. In fact, almost every known engine uses some type of "scripting language" to setup its gameplay components and other systems.

One particular Domain Specific Language we will focus on is SkookumScript, this is because GAMESPECT uses SkookumScript as an intermediary runtime solution. SkookumScript is a perfect example of a DSL because it was written just for Unreal Engine 4 (UE4), as a plugin to the same. It contains the ability to influence almost every system inside UE4, with deep integrations into the other scripting system in UE4, which is known as blueprints. It has been used on shipped games and is suitable for production quality; an example snippet of code can be seen below (Fig. 7). This code snippet is from the game *Noise Paradox,* a professional game being created for iOS and Android devices as well as Nintendo Switch. *Noise Paradox* is a beatmatching game similar to *Patapon* or *Rockband.* As such, hitting objects to the beat is important: the code in Fig. 7 shows part of this logic.

```
1     ()
2     [
3         !lastMarker1 : char.GetLastMarker1()
4         !lastMarker2 : char.GetLastMarker1()
5         !currentTimeDelta : world.abs(lastMarker1, lastMarker2)
6         !total : 0.0f;
7
8         char.InsertLastDeltaTimes(currentTimeDelta);
9         loop [
10            for(!delta : !char.lastDeltaTimes)
11            [
12                !total : total + delta
13            ]
14        ]
15
16        !char.TrackTimeDelta :s char.lastDeltaTimes.Num();
17        if [char.TrackTimeDelta >= 1000]
18            !char>TrackTimeDelta : 999.9f;
19
20        !char.TrackTimeDelta = char.TrackTimeDelta - 200;
21        if [char.lastDeltaTimes.Num() > 7]
22            !char>lastDeltaTimes.Pop()
23
24        !char.GetLastMarker1() : world.cycle();
25        !diff : char.TrackTimeDelta;
26    ]
```

Fig. 7. SkookumScript example: setting up timing on a marker in a beat-matching game.

3 Similar Languages and Frameworks

3.1 Similar Metaprogramming Languages

Over the course of the last decade, a few initiatives for source-to-source compilers in the aspect-oriented domain have come forth [1, 3, 4, 15]. That said, none of them provide for a one-to-many solution and none of them have been applied on a large codebase such as a game project (over one million lines of code). Nonetheless, they serve as inspiration and groundwork for GAMESPECT. To understand the new GAMESPECT system it's helpful to consider the thesis of our designs. XAspect, Awesome and LARA are the three most influential frameworks to our new game programming language.

XAspect. XAspect was an initiative to add a domain specific aspect language on top of AspectJ, an existing aspect-oriented language. The XAspect system was created as a plugin to the AspectJ system, made to be used in the Eclipse IDE [3]. Developers that wished to use this system were required to override a class called *AspectPlugin* if they wished to have a DSL that worked in AspectJ. Essentially this was a way to specify the translation rules between their custom high level language(s) and AspectJ. XAspects is a "many to one" solution, meaning developers could create more than one DSL, all of which could be used in AspectJ.

Awesome/SPECTACKLE. The work of Lorenz and Kojarski seeks to incorporate multiple aspect languages into one common aspect-oriented target language, which is ultimately responsible for runtime behaviors. With this work, a developer can create "composition specifications" which enable a novel aspect-oriented domain specific language (AODSL) to be "plugged" into the Awesome framework [4, 14] (Fig. 8).

Fig. 8. Pluggable aspect languages ([14]).

Often, aspect-oriented programming requires the idea of a wrapper, which is responsible for creating code in the underlying platform to "weave in" aspects. This work is done in Awesome by "composition specifications". The key idea is to extract common language tasks to a tool, known as SPECKTACKLE, and allow for composition specifications to dictate exact nuances in syntax, ordering and priority of the various aspects which are advising. The main goal of Lorenz's work in SPECTACKLE was to alleviate foreign advising collisions between aspect languages [14]. In SPECKTACKLE, Cool, AJ, Spring, AspectWerks or AspectJ can be used as a source language, as long as specifications are created to decide how they function to the weaver. Although the goals of Awesome are different than the goals of GAMESPECT, an analogy can be drawn between what GAMESPECT does and what SPECKTACKLE does. That said, composition specifications and weavers are more complex for GAMESPECT since the underlying language itself might be different. In other words, Awesome went from many source languages to one target language. As stated before, our language is translating to multiple target languages. This means the weavers must be different for each, and the composition specifications become more complex- needing an additional set of technology and tools [13, 14].

A portion of our work can be seen as an extension of composition specifications with more compiler directives. Future sections of this paper will discuss GAMESPECT's composition specifications. We will explore how crucial these specifications are to the underlying weaver of the system.

LARA. LARA is a framework which allows developers to more easily create weavers for source language and compile them to other target languages [15]. The main languages used by LARA for testing were MATLAB, C and Java. In addition, performance testing, efficiency calculations and modularity have been performed- making this a great fit for comparisons to GAMESPECT. In most the research papers on LARA, researchers take an existing tool named MANET and perform the actual weaving for C, Java or any other target language. Of course, this implies that a lot of custom weaving code is needed per language and it is unclear if any shared code exists between weavers. Despite this, LARA is a great tool to draw inspiration from, as there are many similarities. The notable exception is that GAMESPECT is being advised by the aforementioned composition specifications. The following transformation is possible with LARA and is useful to look at as we consider the transformation task for GAMESPECT (Fig. 9).

```
1  aspectdef LogCall
2
3    select function.call end
4    apply
5     $call.insert before %{
6       printf("[[$function.name]]->[[$call.name]]\n");
7     }%;
8    end
9
10  end
```

```
1  import lara.inst.Logger;
2
3  aspectdef LogCall
4    call logger : NewLogger();
5
6    select function.call end
7    apply
8      logger.log($call, 'before',
9          $function.name+'->'+$call.name);
10   end
11  end
```

Fig. 9. An example LARA transformation [15].

3.2 Similar Game Balancing Frameworks

In 2004, Robin Hunicke introduced a new way of analyzing, creating and balancing gameplay. Since then, mostly in academic circles but also in practice, this has become the default system chosen when thinking about mechanics and balance. The method is called MDA, standing for "mechanics, dynamics and aesthetics". In her framework, mechanics are the runtime low level components. Meanwhile dynamics are interactions that occur due to mechanics and their results. Aesthetics are emotional responses from the players of the game [4].

A game designer builds from mechanics towards the aesthetics, but in the case of the player, she looks at everything from a different angle: from aesthetics towards mechanics.

1. **Sensation** Game as sense-pleasure
2. **Fantasy** Game as make-believe
3. **Narrative** Game as drama
4. **Challenge** Game as obstacle course
5. **Fellowship** Game as social framework
6. **Discovery** Game as uncharted territory
7. **Expression** Game as self-discovery
8. **Submission** Game as pastime (Hunicke et al., 2004).

Fig. 10. MDA framework categories for aesthetics.

All levels must be considered for careful game design, but the starting point is aesthetics, which can be defined as eight broad categories: sensation, fantasy, narrative, challenge, fellowship, discovery and expression. Any one particular game need not have all of these aesthetics, but this is the toolbox from which design can be pulled (Fig. 10).

More recently, a group of researchers at University of Southern California proposed a modeling language for game mechanic design called Game System Modeling Language (GSML). GSML is largely a flowcharting system that connects game entities to actions (verbs) and produces events [20]. For example see the following chart which explains the mechanics of Tetris (Fig. 11):

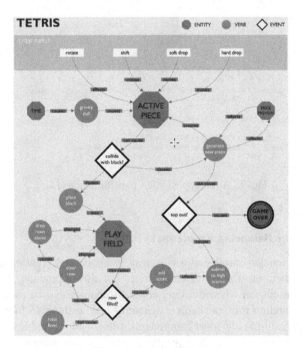

Fig. 11. Tetris in GSML.

However, GSML is distinct and separate from MDA: it doesn't use shared terminology. The two most well known frameworks of this type are Hunicke's model and Bartles. GSML doesn't adopt either and leaves out crucial components such as aesthetics [8]. We feel that is a mistake: Hunicke's work has been cited over 2,000 times and Bartle's Taxonomy has been sited over 2,800 times. That doesn't alone doesn't imply they are perfect but it does imply relative perceived utility. The problem with Bartle's Taxonomy is that it was written for MUDs (Multi-user Dungeons). Bartle categorizes four types of players and their reasons for playing MUDs: exploration, socialization, imposition and achievement [8]. Notably left out of this list are elements revolving around quick reflexes (other challenges), expression/fantasy and narrative. MUDs didn't have a story, the story was built by the players. MUDs were also text based only, so reflexes were out of the question: modern gaming has moved well past text based gaming. Hunicke's work was made with modern trappings of the video game industry in mind, many of which were implemented at Electronic Arts during her collaborative work on The Sims [21].

Although we can see that the work of GSML is slightly lacking MDA fundamentals, we also note that it's the only approach that offers a programmatic, flow-chart based approach to mechanics design. Therefore, as part of this paper we have implemented a hybrid approach: Mechanics, Dynamics, Aesthetics Modeling Language (MDAML).

4 Development Methodology

Aspect-weaving refers to the process of taking "advice" and wrapping it into source code, making sure that it is called either at run time or compiled-in (statically). Luckily, there is precedence for aspect weaving in other research works [4].

The weaving process should output a new set of source code that can be executed at runtime by the game engine. In the case of GAMESPECT this must be more than one target language since we intend to support both Unreal Engine 4 and Unity, and each of those engines also has multiple scripting languages.

Weaving is the process of inserting advice code at certain join points inside the original code. The output of the weaving process is a new set of source code or binary code which performs the original code as modified by the aspect code [23]. For example if we consider Fig. 1, we can see that the advice code makes an additional call to take damage. This call would increase the damage taken; by virtue of an additional call being made it would increase the damage by a multiple of two (Fig. 12).

```
1    Aspect AIDamage (Events)
2    {
3        declare Pointcut BEFORE decHealth(
4            float damage, Entity e)
5        {
6            if(Skookum.GetDifficulty() == "Hard")
7            {
8                e.takeDamageInternal(damage);
9            }
10       }
11   }
```

Fig. 12. Aspect code for increasing damage.

This code must be generated for Skookum Script (or C# in the case of Unity) as shown in Fig. 1. Of course, the original call site also had to be modified to call this extra bit of code. But this match is not straight forward because the calling site could occur in C++, Blueprints, or SkookumScript. This is where composition specifications fit into the overall architecture of GAMESPECT. We will cover composition specifications shortly (Fig. 13).

```
1    (damage, e:Entity) : void
2    [
3        if GetDifficulty() == ("Hard")
4        [
5            e.TakeDamage(damage)
6        ]
7    ]
```

Fig. 13. Generated Skookum Script code.

4.1 GAMESPECT Architecture

To demonstrate that the GAMESPECT methodology works we need to create an entire, extensible system for weaving. The framework is therefore made as an API with all the hooks needed for new language integration. The core idea is that GAMESPECT will sit on top of all an engine's languages, and the API will provide for hooks, composition specifications and other utilities to make weaving possible (Fig. 14).

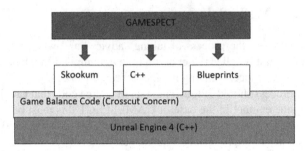

Fig. 14. GAMESPECT architecture.

4.2 External Tools

The work needing to be done for this research involved creation of a new high-level domain specific aspect language. To expedite this process, we used the open source

```
1    grammar org.xtext.example.gamespect.GameSpect with org.eclipse.xtext.common.Terminals
2
3    generate gameSpect "http://www.xtext.org/example/gamespect/GameSpect"
4
5
6    Aspect:
7        'Aspect' name=ID '(' type=ID ')' '{'
8            joinpoints += JoinPoint*
9            callingspecscpp += CallingSpecCPlusPlus*
10           callingspecslua += CallingSpecLua*
11           callingspecssk += CallingSpecSk*
12           callingspecsbp += CallingSpecBp*
13           declares += DeclareVar*    /*this is for declaring variables */
14           variables += Variable* /*this is for variable assignment */
15           methods += Declare* /* this is for declaring and implementing methods */
16           '}';
17
18   VarName:
19       name=ID;
20
21   Variable:
22       name=ID '=' exp=Expression |
23       fun=FunctionCall;
24
25   Expression:
26       expr=BooleanExpression;
27
28   BooleanExpression returns Expression:
29       comp=Comparison
30       (({BooleanExpression.left=current} op=("||"|"&&")) right=Comparison)*;
31
32   Comparison returns Expression:
33       eq=Equals
34       (({Comparison.left=current} op=("<") ) right=Equals)*;
35
36   Equals returns Expression:
37       ad=Addition
38       (({Equals.left=current} op=("==") ) right=Addition)*;
39
40   Addition returns Expression:
41       mu=Multiplication
42       (({Plus.left=current} '+' | {Minus.left=current} '-')
43           right=Multiplication)*;
44
```

Fig. 15. XText grammar for GAMESPECT.

XText language creation system [22]. This allows us to create a grammar in XText, and generate code generators- ultimately these generators are compiled down to Java. The other main tool employed in GAMESPECTS pipeline is TXL. Developed by Dr. James Cordy, TXL provides for source to source transformations provided that the grammar is known for both the target and the source. GAMESPECT turns composition specifications into TXL specifications which are then run offline to perform code injection for the aspects (Fig. 15).

4.3 Weaving Process

To GAMESPECT, a composition specification is a set of rules which sit on top of TXL to be used for generation of a TXL template, which ultimately allows for transformation of the language. But this explanation simplifies the overall process: not only do we need to find the calling sites for the aspects, we need to be able to call extra code. For this we looked to the work of Lorenz [5]. In their research they identified four processes needed for creating an aspect weaver: reification, matching, ordering and mixing. We must use these four processes as well.

GAMESPECT is significantly different from the other metaprogramming initiatives discussed in Sect. 3.1 in that a shared codebase: C++, exists on top of all the original source languages. Also, we have the ability to use one of our target languages at execution time. For this reason, we modified the four step process and redefined the steps as follows:

- Reify: Build time directives using TXL to find the specific script calling locations and flag all incoming calls as potential sites for advice
- Match: Finds the exact calling spots, modifies the code to provide table lookup for calling advice, and continues the build process.
- Order: Runtime directives which find calling advice which is supposed to be executed against the table lookup.
- Mix: Actually perform the advice at runtime calling the GAMESPECT script [24].

Reification. During reification we use GAMESPECT glue code— a C# API program written to make calls to utility functions such as TXL. The main work is done by TXL which goes through thousands of engine files looking for call sites as determined by the composition specifications. Composition specifications are in the following format:

$$\text{SPECIFIER MATCH FUNCTION\_NAME} \tag{1}$$

For example, in Fig. 16, we see a number of calling specifications. Each of these is a C++ callsite. For example, *UTableUtil::call* is the call which is made from C++ for all

```
1   BEFORE void UTableUtil::call(*) decHealth incHealth addPowerup DropItem
2
3   BEFORE int  ue_lua_pcall(lua_State *L, int nargs, int nresults, int errfunc) decHealth incHealth
4       addPowerup DropItem
5
6   BEFORE void push_and_call(int32, int32, FFrame&) decHealth incHealth addPowerup DropItem
7
8   DURRING decHealth(*)
```

Fig. 16. Example composition specifications.

Skookum Script functions, and *ue_lua_pcall* is for all LUA functions. The composition specification is used during reification to search on any of these named functions.

Matching. Three important sub-steps are done during the matching phase. First, we call the GAMESPECT glue code API to generate TXL directives from the composition specification, this results in TXL replacement code as shown in Fig. 17. Notice on line 48 the presents of the *UTableUtil::call* method, this was populated from the compositions specification by the GAMESPECT API. A complete description of TXL is beyond the scope of this paper, but essentially TXL is a text replacement system which operates on the rules of the grammar provided.

The second sub-step of matching is that of creating a mapping between named functions in the composition specification and a custom generated function in SkookumScript that is to be executed at runtime. We call this the *"hashmatcher"* in GAMESPECT. The *hashmatcher* is a simple function inside the codebase which matches to calls which should be made at runtime, in the mixer. In Fig. 17, this is visible on lines 67–83, where we add functions to call based on the aspect definitions which have actually been presented. The key line which adds the functions is as follows:

$$\text{'SkMind::add\_to\_funcs\_to\_call(std::string(get\_name\_cstr()));} \qquad (2)$$

```
46    rule addSkookumCalls
47        construct InterestingFunctionIds [repeat id]
48            'UTableUtil::call'
49        replace $ [function_definition]
50            Specifiers [opt decl_specifiers] Pointer [repeat pointer_operator] DeclaredItem [declared_item]
51                Extensions [repeat declarator_extension+] CtorInitializer [opt ctor_initializer]
52                Exceptions [opt exception_specification]
53            Body [function_body]
54        deconstruct * [id] DeclaredItem
55            FunctionId [id]
56        deconstruct * [id] InterestingFunctionIds
57            FunctionId
58        construct StringFunctionId [stringlit]
59            _ [+ FunctionId]
60        by
61            Specifiers Pointer DeclaredItem Extensions
62            CtorInitializer
63            Exceptions
64            Body [addSkookumCall StringFunctionId]
65    end rule
66
67    function addSkookumCall String [stringlit]
68        replace * [compound_statement]
69        '{
70            Statements [repeat statement+]
71        '}
72        by
73        '{
74            'if (get_scope())
75            '{
76                'if (SkMind::pointcuts.Find(FString(get_name_cstr())) != INDEX_NONE)
77                '{
78                    'SkMind::add_to_funcs_to_call(std::string(get_name_cstr()));
79                '}
80            '}
81            Statements
82        '}
83    end function
```

Fig. 17. Generated TXL code for Skookum Script.

Ordering and Mixing. Ordering is a runtime operation which orders the function to be called at the calling site. In the current version of GAMESPECT, ordering only works for BEFORE and DURING advice. BEFORE advice is what occurs in Fig. 17, and this happens automatically at runtime once matching phase has recompiled the codebase. DURING advice simply spawns off a new process as part of the inserted code (this would be inserted between likes 77 and 79 on Fig. 17, for example). AFTER advice waits until the function has ended and then calls the matched aspect advice (Fig. 18).

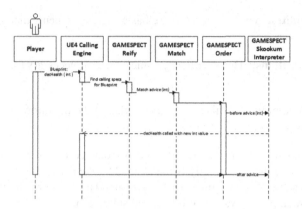

Fig. 18. Compile time and run-time calls of GAMESPECT modules.

4.4   MDAML Extensions for GAMESPECT

As mentioned, it would be desirable if the game mechanic descriptions of the popular MDA framework are incorporated into a usable framework. To date, all the MDA-like frameworks and other attempts at game design, have been devoid of implementable options [6, 7]. It is intended that MDAML (Mechanics, Design, Aesthetics Modeling Language) be described in concrete terms inside GAMESPECT (.gs) files. This allows for more descriptive power during implementation of the game as well as descriptive power during planning.

To motivate this, we created the MDAML specification language (based of Hunicke's MDA) and implemented it alongside an existing game, *Noise Paradox*.

In MDAML there are three types of constructs: Mechanics, Dynamics and Aesthetics (MDA). Each of these categories has subtypes, which are important for the resulting MDAML diagrams. The subtypes are as follows:

Mechanics, Entities: Items in the game which represent objects or things. For example a player character is actually a "mechanic".

Mechanics, Properties: Properties are held by entities, and refer to the low level details of that object. Forr example a player might have a certain jump height. In MDA this is important because tuning is a special consideration.

Mechanics, Verbs: This concept is borrowed from GSML and added to MDAML. It is the idea that all entities can also perform certain actions.

Dynamics, State Actions: State actions are events that cause a change in state of some sort. For example, maybe the player goes from running to walking.

Dynamics, Property Changes: Property changes are actions that change property in the aforementioned mechanics of objects/players/entities.

Dynamics, Conditionals: Conditionals are basic logic statements that some decision hinges upon.

Aesthetics, Transitions: These are the dynamic situations necessary to complete levels or fail at levels.

Aesthetics, Informational: This represents tutorials and other information-only items given to the player.

Aesthetics, Purpose: This is the original category defined by Hunicke which defines the sense of purpose that is currently being elicited by the active dynamics. More than one "purpose" can be active at a time. These correspond to: sensation, fantasy, narrative, challenge, fellowship, discovery, expression and submission.

GAMESPECT 1.01: In the newest version of GAMESPECT we have begun to allow for MDAML design terminologies to be used in our aspects. We feel this is an expressive power that will be useful to game designers. For example, in our above "taking damage" scenario, certain MDAML items would be flagged. Anything which is listed in the dynamics category has the potential of being a pointcut with associated advice (Fig. 19).

```
1    Aspect AIDamage (Dynamic)
2    {
3        MDAML
4        {
5            SubType: PropertyChange
6        }
7        declare Pointcut BEFORE decHealth(float damage, Entity e)
8        {
9            if(Skookum.GetDifficulty() == "Hard")
10           {
11               e.TakeDamage(damage);
12           }
13       }
14   }
15   Aspect Player(Mechanic)
16   {
17       MDAML
18       {
19           SubType: Entity
20       }
21   }
```

Fig. 19. GAMESPECT 1.01 with MDAML.

The advantage of this encoding is that during game creation, designers should create complete MDAML diagrams. In doing so they can then identify potential point cuts by looking at the important actions in a game. Since there is no automatic process of finding potential aspects, this is very important. For example, consider our take damage code above. During game creation, there would have been a step that realizes that enemies and players can be damaged. This would encourage developers to fill in the gaps in

GAMESPECT by investigating the code and seeing where these pointcuts happen. In this way the game becomes far more tunable, game balance has a place to "live" and we reduce the complexity all the code base.

MDAML Partial Example. To help for future work, we are providing a partial description of the game *Noise Paradox*. The hope is that, in seeing how easy it is to diagram these mechanics, more practitioners will take this approach. The first step is to plan out all the game interactions in the form of MDAML, cataloging the various objects in the game and what they can do to each other. With GAMESPECT 1.01 it's also possible to define aesthetics, although they probably won't appear in any aspects. A brief description of *Noise Paradox* follows, to help contextualize the given MDAML diagrams.

Noise Paradox is about the experience of being a DJ. It's about taking multiple songs and combining them albeit briefly to sound like a completely new song. It's a game about influencing AI actions via this beatmatching. Friendly AI are known as "Beat Spirits". There's also enemy AI, known simply as Automaton; cold and unfeeling, they seek to stop the player's beatmixes and stop the beat spirits. Through correctly beatmatching, the player is rewarded. Failure means the song doesn't match up and more automaton are attacking you, eventually defeating you. Success means you spawn beat spirits to fend off the attacking automaton and protect you, eventually passing the level and going on to beatmatch more. DJ battles will occur at the end of key areas, which are in-place battles but with complementary mechanics (Fig. 20).

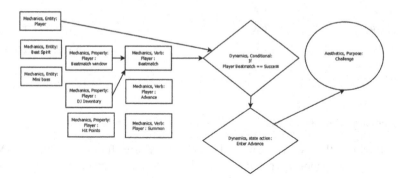

Fig. 20. MDAML for Noise Paradox (partial).

In practice, we have found that it's very convenient to have new systems mapped out in MDAML because it translates directly to code that can be written for GAMESPECT. In this way, its an apriori step of denoting all the possible callsites that are going to be questioned and potentially tuned during development. This is much easier than typical methods which involve hunting and pecking or keeping track of massive spreadsheets, as described in Sect. 1.1.

5 Results

5.1 Testing Process

The goal of testing GAMESPECT across multiple software projects and codebases was to verify accuracy, efficiency, pluggability and modularity. A process was established to enable comparisons. Namely, it was necessary to create two versions of every test: one using the standard game design methodology (without GAMESPECT and without MDAML) and the other with GAMESPECT and MDAML. In addition, to demonstrate pluggability it was necessary to create a second version of the game which was running on a separate game engine. Table 1 shows the test matrix employed for verification during this phase of development.

With GAMESPECT 1.00 our process was to use Visual Studio Assist to find the pointcuts and moments for game balance "advice". But with GAMESPECT 1.01 we used MDAML to find these point cuts.

Table 1. High level test matrix for GAMESPECT.

Engine	Languages	Versions
Unreal Engine 4 (OOP)	LUA, SkookumScript, C++, Blueprints	Vanilla
Unreal Engine 4 (AOP)	LUA, SkookumScript, C++, Blueprints	GAMESPECT 1.01
Unity (OOP)	C#, LUA	Vanilla
Unity (AOP)	C#, LUA	GAMESPECT 1.00
Unity (AOP)	C#, LUA	GAMESPECT 1.01

5.2 Accuracy Measurements

As seen in Table 1, there were five individual codebases tested for this version of GAME-SPECT. This was a laborious process of keeping the code separate, in different repositories, etc. Also, if some logic was updated in one code base, it needed to be merged to the others. We used Perforce for this due to its ability to handle non-text based binary files such as various pieces of art assets.

All five "products" listed above were run through a quality assurance process using the bug tracking tool "HackNPlan". As the days went on in the production cycle, we tracked number of bugs, with the goal being to reach zero bug regression (ZBR). If the new GAMESPECT version of the product roughly matches the vanilla version, then we can expect that accuracy is maintained. As Fig. 21 shows, the deviation in bug counts is nearly nonexistent.

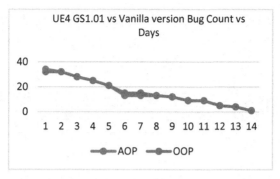

Fig. 21. Comparing bug counts AOP versions vs OOP versions.

5.3 Efficiency Measurements

The benefit we are expecting of GAMESPECT is to reduce the total lines of code. For example, the code at the join point, if it is used more than once is pulled out and therefore a savings is possible because multiple call sites exist for each piece of advice- hence duplicating code. It has been found by other research that smaller lines of code counts leads to easier maintenance, so this is desirable [25].

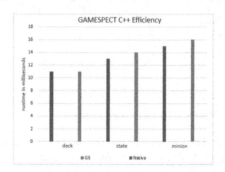

Fig. 22. Runtime performance of GAMESPECT.

We present Table 2, Table 3, and Table 4 to show the summary of lines of code testing. The range of savings varied from 9% to 40%. Other research in the field has showed that the target LOC savings, to be considered impactful, is around 10% [25]. Also, according to studies done on the LARA metaprogramming language, their savings was in the 10–20% range [15]. We are well within that range on this project.

Given the extra calls made at runtime it was also necessary to gauge performance. Therefore, we also ran a runtime analysis to ensure there was no performance impact (Fig. 22). Similar to LARA, GAMESPECT has virtually no performance impact [13, 15].

Table 2. LOC Comparisons for C#, GAMESPECT Test Suite 1 [13].

	total lines	GAMESPECT lines	Destination Lines Total	Savings	
beatNow (C#)	36	3	30	6	16.00%
calculateBPM (C#)	75	5	53	22	29.33%
spawnAtPlayer	75	6	41	24	32.00%
CharacterDeckComponent (C#)	50	3	45	5	10.00%
StateManagerComponent (C#)	10	1	6	4	40.00%
MinionController (C#)	29	1	25	4	13.79%

Table 3. LOC Comparisons for C++, Sk, UE4, GAMESECT Test Suite 2.

	original lines	original files	total lines	GAMESPECT lines	Destination Lines Total	Savings in Lines	Savings Percent
AIStateAdvancing (CPP)	10	2	20	3	17	3	15%
PlayerStateAdvancing (CPP)	14	3	42	5	26	16	38%
LevelStateAdvancing (CPP)	8	5	40	8	13	27	68%
SyncTracks (SK)	5	3	15	4	13	2	13%
FastFoward (SK)	4	3	12	2	5	7	58%
Rewind (SK)	4	3	12	2	5	7	58%

Table 4. LOC for C++, Sk, UE4, GAMESPECT Test Suite 3: including MDAML.

	original lines	original files	stotal lines	GAMESPECT LINES	GAMESPECT LINES w/MDAML	Savings Percent
beatDetect (CPP)	8	2	16	9	15	44%
spawnFX (CPP)	4	4	16	7	16	56%
hitSpark (CPP)	9	2	18	8	19	56%
activatePower (CPP)	5	5	25	20	25	20%

5.4 Pluggability and Modularity Measurements

In addition to accuracy and efficiency, we wanted to demonstrate pluggability and modularity. These two are related: pluggability refers to the ability to plug into a new system with a new language. Modularity refers to the API's ability to compartmentalize and quickly scale up to a new implementation of the language.

One way modularity/pluggability can be shown is by looking at the efficiency comparison across engines, in this way if the system was made modular enough to be applied to a completely new codebase, we'd expect there to be relatively few issues. It turns out this is the case, as shown in Fig. 23. Another way is just by looking at the huge number of transformations made possible by using GAMESPECT. In fact, we can compare the number of source transformations created by our system to the number of transformations made possible by Cool/Awesome, XAspects and LARA. This is shown in Fig. 24.

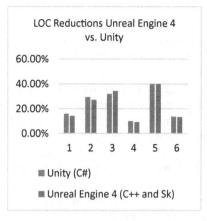

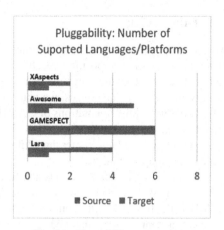

Fig. 23. LOC unity vs UE4.   **Fig. 24.** Pluggability comparison.

6 Summary

6.1 Summary

This research is impactful for a number of areas including aspect-oriented programming, DSLs and game design/balance. In terms of aspect-oriented programming we have demonstrated that it is possible to perform aspect weaving in a "pluggable", modular way and yet with great efficiency. Furthermore, it's possible to support multiple languages using the idea of composition specifications. GAMESPECT also shows that there need not be a single target language with respect to the source-to-source transformation languages. Indeed, by using tools such as TXL and some GAMESPECT API code (i.e. the *hashmatcher*) it's possible to support one-to-many scenarios. Previous to this work, LARA demonstrated that a one-to-one translation was possible [3]. Likewise, Awesome and SPECTACKLE provided a many-to-one solution [2]. As far as we know this is the only contribution with a one-to-many solution which uses an intermediate composition specification scheme.

The other segment of work which is impactful is that of game balance and game design. There are many frameworks which provide for game balancing concepts and terminology, but nothing is standardized. MDA seems to be the most prolific, but it lacks the low level of details needed to express it as a modeling language. Meanwhile, projects such as GSML provide for detailed connections and descriptors but ignore the hierarchy setup by MDA. Our work in GAMESPECT has combined these into MDAML. We have used MDAML in our "test suite 3" and the results are summarized in Table 4. By looking at this table, it's clear to see that test suite 3 is no different from the other test suites, in all cases the lines of code savings were significant. That said, the extra descriptive power of MDAML comes at a cost: once we add it into the GAMESPECT language (1.01), we return to baseline in terms of lines of code used. However, this is to be expected- and may be mitigated once constructs are shared between aspects in MDAML (see future work section).

6.2 Future Work

When an appropriate TXL template must be selected, the user has to set a language enumeration in the composition specification. This is actually needless, since we could automatically detect the language. This should work 90% of the time, and in cases we get ambiguity of languages, we could report back to the user. Also, the Unity and Unreal Engine 4 implementations of GAMESPECT do not share interpreters. However, they have languages in common: LUA, Javascript. In the future a language should be chosen for the shared interpreter that eliminates the need to maintain two GAMESPECT codebases, and two binaries.

The final area of improvements and future work is that of game balance. Firstly, an initiative should be taken to investigate the time savings in enumerating game mechanics in MDAML. Intuitively, it should save developers time during implementation phase once the mechanics are ironed out. But this has yet to be verified.

Now that the project incorporates MDAML we feel that much work is possible in terms of enumerating types of constructs which need game balance, and studying the best ways to go about designing, iterating and tuning. In addition, topics such as auto-balancing of difficulty level could be attempted since it's possible that GAMESPECT code (.gs files) themselves could be generated, or at least tuned quickly by play testers. We believe the biggest promise of GAMESPECT lies in it's ability to quickly iterate on design solutions. By exposing gameplay constructs via GAMESPECT and MDAML we allow designers a chance to make their games better. This hasn't been capitalized on yet, and could be the subject of future work.

References

1. Bispo, J., Cardoso, J.M.: Clava: C/C++ source-to-source compilation using LARA. SoftwareX **12**, 100565 (2020)
2. Kojarski, S., Lorenz, D.H.: Pluggable AOP: designing aspect mechanisms for third-party composition. ACM SIGPLAN Not. **40**, 247–263 (2005)
3. Shonle, M., Lieberherr, K., Shah, A.: XAspects: an extensible system for domain-specific aspect languages. In: Companion of the 18th Annual ACM SIGPLAN Conference on Object-Oriented Programming, Systems, Languages, and Applications, pp. 28–37 (2003)
4. Kojarski, S., Lorenz, D.H.: Awesome: an aspect co-weaving system for composing multiple aspect-oriented extensions. ACM SIGPLAN Not. **42**, 515–534 (2007)
5. Lorenz, D.H., Mishali, O.: SPECTACKLE: toward a specification-based DSAL composition process. In: Proceedings of the 7th Workshop on Domain-Specific Aspect Languages, pp. 9–14 (2012)
6. Walk, W., Görlich, D., Barrett, M.: Design, dynamics, experience (DDE): an advancement of the MDA framework for game design. In: Korn, O., Lee, N. (eds.) Game Dynamics, pp. 27–45. Springer, Cham (2017). https://doi.org/10.1007/978-3-319-53088-8_3
7. Zohaib, M.: Dynamic difficulty adjustment (DDA) in computer games: a review. Adv. Hum. Comput. Interact. **2018**, 12 (2018)
8. Bartle, R.: Hearts, clubs, diamonds, spades: players who suit MUDs. J. MUD Res. **1**, 19 (1996)
9. Hunicke, R., LeBlanc, M., Zubek, R.: MDA: a formal approach to game design and game research. In: Proceedings of the AAAI Workshop on Challenges in Game AI, p. 1722 (2004)

10. Koster, R.: Theory of Fun for Game Design. O'Reilly Media Inc., Newton (2013)
11. Blow, J.: Game development: harder than you think. Queue **1**, 28–37 (2004)
12. Adams, E., Dormans, J.: Game Mechanics: Advanced Game Design. New Riders, Indianapolis (2012)
13. Geisler, B.J., Kavage, S.L.: Aspect weaving for multiple video game engines using composition specifications. In: ENASE, pp. 454–462 (2020)
14. Gregory, J.: Game Engine Architecture. CRC Press, Boca Raton (2018)
15. Pinto, P., Carvalho, T., Bispo, J., Cardoso, J.M.: LARA as a language-independent aspect-oriented programming approach. In: Proceedings of the Symposium on Applied Computing, pp. 1623–1630 (2017)
16. Cordy, J.R.: The TXL source transformation language. Sci. Comput. Program. **61**, 190–210 (2006)
17. Sherrod, A.: Ultimate 3D Game Engine Design & Architecture. Charles River Media Inc., Newton (2006)
18. Kiczales, G., et al.: Aspect-oriented programming. In: Akşit, M., Matsuoka, S. (eds.) ECOOP 1997. LNCS, vol. 1241, pp. 220–242. Springer, Heidelberg (1997). https://doi.org/10.1007/BFb0053381
19. Moby Games Stats (n.d.). https://www.mobygames.com/
20. Emms, R., Wixon, D., Wiscombe, S., Malaika, Y.: Spatializing play structures and interaction flow using GSML (Game System Modelling Language). Comput. Games J. **3**(2), 40–53 (2014). https://doi.org/10.1007/BF03395951
21. Gee, J.P., Hayes, E.: No quitting without saving after bad events: gaming paradigms and learning in The Sims. Int. J. Learn. Media **1**, 49–65 (2009)
22. Eysholdt, M., Behrens, H.: Xtext: implement your language faster than the quick and dirty way. In: Proceedings of the ACM International Conference Companion on Object Oriented Programming Systems Languages and Applications Companion, pp. 307–309 (2010)
23. Courbis, C., Finkelsteiin, A.: Towards aspect weaving applications. In: Proceedings of the 27th International Conference on Software Engineering, pp. 69–77 (2005)
24. Geisler, B.J.: GAMESPECT: a composition framework and meta-level domain specific aspect language for unreal engine 4 (2019)
25. Polo, M., Piattini, M., Ruiz, F.: Using code metrics to predict maintenance of legacy programs: a case study. In: Proceedings IEEE International Conference on Software Maintenance, ICSM 2001, pp. 202–208. IEEE (2001)

Model-Based Timing Analysis of Automotive Use Case Developed in UML

Padma Iyenghar[(⊠)] [iD], Lars Huning, and Elke Pulvermueller

Software Engineering Research Group, University of Osnabrueck, Osnabrück, Germany
{piyengha,lhuning,elke.pulvermueler}@uos.de

Abstract. Development of AUTOSAR-based systems using UML tools is gaining significant attention in the automotive industry. In this context, incorporating an early and automated model-based timing analysis of such systems in state-of-the-practice timing analysis tools is a significant step towards automated tooling for Verification & Validation (V&V) in the AUTOSAR-based development process; nevertheless is missing. Addressing this aspect, a workflow for early model-based timing analysis of AUTOSAR models is outlined. A detailed discussion of the model transformations for extracting a timing analysis model from a timing annotated AUTOSAR-based design model is presented in this book chapter. Further, a detailed case study of an automotive use case is presented and evaluated step-by-step by employing the outlined workflow. An early model-based timing analysis of the use case developed in UML is discussed in detail.

Keywords: Model-based tool support · Automation · Timing analysis · Automotive software · AUTOSAR · UML · V&V

1 Introduction

Software quality is now fundamental to the automotive industry. All stakeholders, from top-level automotive manufacturers through multiple tiers of component suppliers, need to give quality assurance to their customers along with delivery of high-quality and compliant systems and components. In the automotive domain, the Electronic Control Units (ECUs)[1] are used for various tasks such as controlling the vehicle dynamics and providing advanced driver assistance systems. With autonomous cars on the horizon, the functionality provided by the ECUs is deemed to increase ever more. This implies that there are risks towards (1) exhausting the processing resources of the existing ECUs (2) delayed execution of potentially safety-critical and timing-relevant functions and (3) increase in manufacturing costs (e.g. because of adding more ECUs). Reflecting the increasing complexity of the embedded software domain, automated tooling for checking and monitoring software quality (e.g. timing) is growing more sophisticated and serving a wider community of stakeholders.

---

[1] An embedded system that controls one or more of the electrical systems or subsystems in a vehicle.

© Springer Nature Switzerland AG 2021
R. Ali et al. (Eds.): ENASE 2020, CCIS 1375, pp. 360–385, 2021.
https://doi.org/10.1007/978-3-030-70006-5_15

1.1 Model-Based Development of Automotive Software

Model-based techniques are gaining rapid attention in the field of Embedded Software Engineering (ESE). They provide systematic, cost-effective development processes which help reduce the time-to-market and development costs, while also enhancing the embedded software quality [25]. Models of the software and hardware architecture can be reused in multiple development phases to automate the process, e.g. by generating code from a design model. Therefore, for automotive embedded software systems which are rich in timing critical functions, it is imperative to integrate quality (e.g. timing) analysis into the model-based ESE development process, as early as possible. In this context, AUtomotive Open System ARchitecture (AUTOSAR) is already a de facto industry standard for the design and implementation of software for automotive applications. Further, development of AUTOSAR-based embedded systems using Unified Modeling Language (UML) such as Rhapsody [14], Enterprise Architect [9] tools and Matlab/Simulink [23] is gaining significant attention in the automotive industry.

1.2 Model-Based Timing Analysis

In automotive embedded architectures, many functions are time critical due to safety requirements. Some other functions could have timing constraints for certain performance guarantee. In order to perform a timing analysis of such a system, its timing analysis model with timing properties, should be available. Based on this information, timing analysis in state-of-the-practice tools such as Timing Architect [31], T1. Timing [11] and Inchron [15], can predict the execution behavior of the system with respect to overall timing analysis and specific parameters such as end-to-end delay. Incorporating an early and automated model-based timing analysis of such systems in state-of-the-practice timing analysis tools, is a significant step towards, automated tooling for Verification and Validation in the AUTOSAR-based ESE development process; nevertheless is missing.

1.3 Relation to Author's Previous Work and Novel Contributions

In the above context, a systematic series of steps towards incorporating an early, automated extraction and synthesis of timing analysis models in AUTOSAR-based embedded system design models which are developed in UML tools has been presented in [18]. Similarly, an automated end-to-end timing analysis of AUTOSAR-based causal event chains of automotive software developed using UML is described in [17]. In this book chapter, the work in [17] is extended and the following novel contributions are presented.

- An elaboration of various transformation rules for synthesis of AUTOSAR-based timing analysis model with examples.
- Detailed evaluation of the proposed series of steps, for automated model-based timing analysis of AUTOSAR-based use case, employing an elaborate automotive case study.

In the remainder of this paper, background and related work is presented in Sect. 2. A systematic series of steps for early timing analysis introduced in [18] is outlined in Sect. 3. A detailed automotive case study is presented in Sect. 4. In Sect. 5, an elaborate discussion on the application of the proposed workflow in Sect. 3 on the use case described in Sect. 4 is presented. Model transformations are detailed with examples in Sect. 6. Results of timing analysis are discussed in Sect. 7. Section 8 concludes the paper.

2   Background and Related Work

Model Driven Development (MDD) [26] methodology employing UML has been increasingly used for design and development in ESE, especially for modeling automotive embedded software systems. It has also been applied for Non-Functional Properties (NFR) analysis, such as timing, energy and reliability analysis [16]. Further, development of AUTOSAR-based systems using UML tools is gaining significant attention in the automotive industry. In this context, a brief background and related work on the AUTOSAR framework, timing modeling and analysis in AUTOSAR models is provided in this section.

2.1   AUTOSAR Framework

A comprehensive and well- established solution used in the automotive sector is the AUTOSAR standard [6]. The various components of the AUTOSAR framework are illustrated together with the mapping of software components to ECUs, in the system configuration step, in Fig. 1. AUTOSAR uses a component-based software architecture, with central modeling elements called *Software Components* (SWCs or SW-Cs).

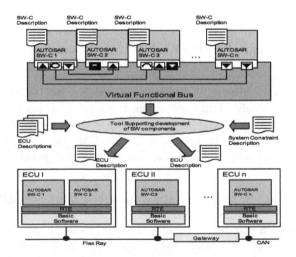

Fig. 1. Components of AUTOSAR framework [6, 17].

The SWCs (e.g., *SW-C1* seen at the top of Fig. 1) are used to structure the AUTOSAR model and group functionality into individual components. These components can be connected together, oblivious of the hardware they are running on. This is handled by the *Virtual Function Bus* (VFB), which provides an abstraction layer for the SWC to SWC communication.

Components distributed over different ECUs however, may use the network bus for communication (e.g., *ECUs 1, 2..n* communicating over FlexRay and CAN buses in lower part of the Fig. 1). This is determined automatically by the *Run-Time Environment* (RTE), which is a communication interface for the software components. In each ECU, the RTE provides interfaces between SW-Cs (e.g. AUTOSAR SWC 1 and AUTOSAR SWC 2 in ECU 1 in lower part of Fig. 1) and between SW-C and Basic Software (BSW). In this paper, the design model is created using the AUTOSAR framework and the timing properties are annotated using AUTOSAR-TE.

2.2 Timing Modeling

Modeling and Analysis of RealTime and Embedded Systems (MARTE) [22] is a standardized UML profile, which extends UML and provides support for modeling the platform, software and hardware aspects of an application [1]. Non-UML time modeling alternatives include *SystemC* [8] and Event-B[2] to name a few.

AUTOSAR-Timing Extensions. The AUTOSAR-Timing Extensions (TE) metamodel feature an event-based model for the description of the software's temporal behavior and can be defined on top of a system architecture. The AUTOSAR release with timing extensions and its own timing model find extensive usage in the automotive industry [27] and [10]. The TE metamodel provides five different views for timing specification, depending on the kind of timing behavior described in the AUTOSAR model [5]. The five views are *VfbTiming*, *SwcTiming* (describes internal behavior timing of SWC), *SystemTiming*, *BswModuleTiming* and *EcuTiming*. In the experimental evaluation, the *SwcTiming* view is employed, because the system configuration and timing specification steps use the SWCs. For further explanation of AUTOSAR methodology and AUTOSAR-TE, interested readers are referred to [6].

AUTOSAR-Based Causal Event Chain. In component-based ESE, individual subsystems are modeled with chains of components that are translated to chains of tasks for scheduling analysis. The timing requirements of such chains, which we coarsely refer to as the end-to-end delay can be specified in the component model and also estimated/analyzed during a timing analysis.

Figure 2 shows an event chain end-to-end timing describing the causal dependency between "Sensor" and "Actuator". The sequence of event chain segments shows the details of end-to-end timing according to the AUTOSAR timing views. A timing event chain describes a causal order for a set of functionally dependent timing events. Each event chain defines at least the relationship between two differing events, its stimulus

---

[2] http://www.event-b.org/index.html.

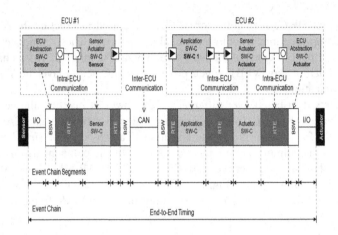

Fig. 2. End-to-End timing of a AUTOSAR-based causal event chain [5, 17].

and response which describe its start and end point respectively. This means that if the stimulus event occurs then the response event occurs after. One way to guarantee that the system meets its timing requirements is to perform pre-run-time analysis of it (e.g. already during design level), using end-to-end timing analysis. Such analysis can validate the timing requirements without performing exhaustive testing. In [7], methods to compute end-to-end delays based on different levels of system information is presented and evaluated in an industrial case study. An evaluation of this work is carried out in an automotive industrial case study, using a commercial tool chain, Rubus-ICE. Similarly, [24] targets the challenges that are concerned with the unambiguous refinement of timing requirements, constraints and other timing information among various abstraction levels. However, the aforementioned works concentrates on usage of EAST-ADL and Rubus Component Model and does not concentrate on AUTOSAR, AUTOSAR-TE modeling in UML tool or automated tooling for (end-to-end) timing analysis.

2.3   Model-Based Timing Analysis

The timing behavior specified in the design model can be analyzed using dedicated timing analysis tools. There are several open source tools such as Cheddar [29] and MAST [12]. Some popular proprietary timing analysis tools include chronSIM [15], Gliwa T1. timing suite [11] and Timing Architect [31]. These tools are independent of the modeling languages used. Therefore, they require the timing specifications to be in a particular format, although some provide import functions for common modeling languages. However, the timing analysis carried out in such tools are very late it in the development process. It is imperative to note that the design errors realised from such late timing analysis would be costly to fix at a later development stage. Hence, an early model-based timing analysis is necessary to overcome this drawback.

On the other hand, there is no tool support for automated synthesis and export of AUTOSAR-based timing analysis model (from AUTOSAR-based application design model in UML tools) to these timing analysis tools. In the literature, AUTOSAR-TE were used for a model-based timing analysis in works such as [19] and [28]. Further, a review of the literature shows that there is no systematic model-based approach for timing or energy analysis of AUTOSAR-based systems. Except for [18], there exists no related work on early synthesis of timing models for model-based timing analysis of AUTOSAR-based systems.

2.4 Research Gap and Challenge

Thus, on examining the related literature and state-of-the-practice tools, it can be stated that several related work deal with examination of the required timing properties for end-to-end timing analysis. Many industrial tools implement the end-to-end delay/timing analysis for event chains. These exist as island solutions without an automated integrated workflow from timing specification in design model to timing analysis. They further require manual creation and/or export of *timing-analysis-model artifacts* in the analysis tool, for timing analysis. Thus, automated timing analysis of AUTOSAR-based systems described in UML tool [14] in state-of-the-practice timing analysis tool [11,21] is missing.

3   Early Timing Analysis of Automotive Use Cases Developed in UML

The proposed workflow for integrating timing requirements in the AUTOSAR-design model and the automated synthesis of an AUTOSAR-based timing analysis model, introduced in [18], is shown in Fig. 3 and elaborated in brief in this section. It comprises of the following steps:

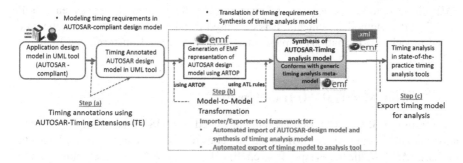

Fig. 3. Systematic series of steps for early timing analysis in AUTOSAR-based ESE [17].

1. In the first step (step (a) in Fig. 3), it is considered that an initial AUTOSAR-based design model of the automotive embedded software application under consideration is already modeled in an UML/SysML tool [9,14]. Note that step-(a) in Fig. 3 is applied in an early stage of development process. It involves the specification of the timing requirements in the AUTOSAR-based design model using AUTOSAR-TE. The output of this step is a timing annotated AUTOSAR-based design model.

2. Based on the input from step-(a) in Fig. 3, given the timing annotated design model as input, Model-to-Model (M2M) transformations are implemented for extracting the timing properties. This results in the synthesis of the AUTOSAR-based timing analysis model (conforming to a generic timing metamodel [18]). Thus, the output model from step (b) may be exported as shown in step (c) in Fig. 3, for instance in XML format, to industry standard timing analysis tools [11,31].

3.1   Generic Timing Metamodel

As seen in Fig. 3, a generic timing metamodel comprising a set of timing properties is required for model transformations in step (b). A generic custom-defined metamodel for timing analysis of AUTOSAR-models is introduced already in [18]. This is employed in this paper to synthesize the timing analysis model for AUTOSAR-based embedded software systems developed using UML/SysML tools. This metamodel bears similarity to the AUTOSAR metamodel with respect to the software and hardware architecture elements. It can be termed as a generic metamodel as it closely adheres with the timing models used in several timing validation tools [11,31]. Please note that in place of the custom-defined but generic metamodel used in this paper, an open source metamodel namely, AMALTHEA[3], may be employed for M2M related to timing properties.

3.2   Mapping Among Metamodels for Timing Properties

The relevant metamodel elements from the custom-defined intermediate timing-energy metamodel are mapped to their counterparts in the AUTOSAR-TE metamodel [4] in step-(c) in Fig. 3. The AUTOSAR Tool Platform[4] provides an EMF model, which contains the element names as per specification. An evaluation version of this AUTOSAR EMF model is used in this paper for mapping the timing metamodel elements to the AUTOSAR metamodel elements. It is also used as an input metamodel for the automated model transformations implemented using the Atlas Transformation Language (ATL) [3].

3.3   Model-to-Model (M2M) Transformations

As seen in Fig. 3, after step (a), a timing annotated AUTOSAR-based design model is now available in the UML/SysML tool under consideration. It can be exported from the tool as an *ARXML* file [4] as input for step (b) in Fig. 3. Note that while employing M2M transformations, both source and target models must conform with their respective metamodels. Here the *source model* is the *timing annotated AUTOSAR design model* obtained from the system description specification in the UML/SysML tool in ARXML format. This conforms with the AUTOSAR metamodel [4]. The *target metamodel* is the *custom-defined generic timing metamodel*. In this work, the ATLAS transformation language (ATL) [3] is used for implementing the M2M transformations.

---

[3] https://www.eclipse.org/app4mc/.

[4] https://www.artop.org/.

The next step after synthesis of timing analysis model in the proposed workflow in Fig. 3 is the automated export of this model to a state-of-the-art timing analysis tool such as [15,31] for timing analysis. Note that an importer/exporter framework for this step (i.e., step (c) in Fig. 3) has already been introduced in [17], therefore it is not discussed in detail in this book chapter.

4 Autonomous Emergency Braking System (AEBS)

According to German federal statistics[5], in 2019 approximately 30% of all road traffic accidents with personal injury happened in parallel traffic. These accidents comprise of head-on and rear-end collisions. At high speeds, these collisions get more dangerous, because of high impact forces. Therefore an early braking in case of an imminent crash is critical for avoiding casualties. An advanced driver assistance system may help the driver to reduce the reaction time or to amplify the brakeforce, in order to lower the speed and thus the kinetic force of the car.

An Autonomous Emergency Braking Systems (AEBSs) that additionally warns the driver and automatically applies the brakes in emergency situations are available since 2003 [30]. Also, in order to be effective in preventing casualties, these systems need to react as fast as possible. For instance, a hard deadline on the timing behavior would be the average reaction time of a human driver. Hence there are strict timing requirements (e.g. between a stimulus event and a response event, thus representing a causal event chain) that must be taken into account when developing such systems.

The main purpose of an AEBS is to warn the driver in case of an imminent frontal collision. This commonly happens through visual and acoustic warning signals as a first step. The next level of warning is often a tactile warning. The AEBS in cars use the Time-To-Collision (TTC) value [13,20] to estimate the danger of the situation. It is defined as the time left until a collision happens, if every object (e.g. both cars) continues to move at the same speed. To calculate TTC, AEBS needs data such as the distance to frontal objects (e.g. from radar sensors) and wheel speed sensor input at certain speed ranges. In this paper, based on the systems used in current automobiles, a simplified version of an AEBS is modeled as an use case and used for experimental evaluation.

4.1 Requirements Specification

To have an exact description of the functionality provided by AEBS, several Functional (FR) and Non-Functional Requirements (NFR) were implemented for this use case. They are elaborated below:

---

[5] https://www.destatis.de/.

Functional Requirements (FR)

FR 1 The Assistant Shall Support the Driver in Avoiding Frontal Collision. By reducing the driver's reaction time and supporting the driver in emergency brake situations, the chance of a frontal collision while driving shall be mitigated.

FR 2 The System needs Constant Information about the Car's Speed. In order to deactivate the system at low speed conditions, information about the car's speed is needed constantly.

FR 3 The Distance to the Next Car in the Same Lane Shall be Measured Constantly. The distance to the next car is needed to determine an imminent collision. If it is measured constantly, the relative speed of a preceding object and thus the TTC can be calculated from consecutive measurements.

FR 4 The Assistant Shall Prepare the Brake System when TTC falls below 6s. To reduce the response time of a possible brake application, the brake system can be pre-filled by increasing the hydraulic pressure and bringing the brake pads closer to the brake discs. Additionally, the brake force is increased according to the danger of the situation, if the driver applies the brakes too hesitantly.

FR 5 The Assistant Shall Warn the Driver when the TTC falls below 5 Seconds: Before intervening with an autonomous braking, the assistant needs to warn the driver in multiple stages of the imminent danger, so that the driver can react appropriately. These stages are entered consecutively with decreasing TTC.

> **FR 5.1 Visual: Warning Light (TTC = 5s)** A warning lamp or warning icon in the instrument cluster or head-up display shall provide a first visual warning.

> **FR 5.2 Accoustic: Warning Sound (TTC = 4s):** An audible signal shall provide a second warning.

> **FR 5.3 Tactile: Warning Jolt (TTC = 3s):** A warning jolt shall precede initiation of a full brake.

FR 6 The Assistant Shall Engage an Emergency Braking when the TTC falls below 1.5 Seconds: If the system determines that it is too late to avoid a collision, an emergency braking is engaged autonomously to reduce the car's remaining speed and thus weaken the impact force.

Non-functional Timing Requirements. The following presents a list of non-functional timing requirements of the AEBS, which are later validated using the proposed approach in Sect. 7.

NFR 1 The System must Estimate the TTC every 50 ms. The AEBS needs to estimate the danger of the situation with a period of 50 ms. This is to make sure that the need to brake is recognized sufficiently fast.

NFR 2 The Relative Speed of the Next Car must be Calculated every 50 ms. After the distance values have been filtered, the relative speed of the next car must be calculated from consecutive measurements every 50 ms.

NFR 3 The Speed of the Car must be Sampled every 10 ms. In order to average multiple speed sensor values, the speed of the car must be read every 10 ms and provided to the system every 50 ms after sensor noise has been filtered out.

NFR 4 The Distance to the Next Car must be Sampled every 10 ms. In order to average multiple distance sensor values, the distance to the next car must be read every 10 ms and provided to the system every 50 ms after sensor noise has been filtered out.

NFR 5 The Load on the ECU Processing Cores must Not Exceed 80%. In order to reserve some processing resources as a buffer (e.g., for future software updates or a performance decrease over time), the AEBS must not occupy its processing resources more than 80% of the time.

NFR 6 New Sensor Data must Influence the TTC Computation after a Maximum Delay of 200 ms. The system needs to react fast to sudden speed changes, so the end-to-end response time from sensor measurements to a reaction needs to be below 200 ms.

4.2 Control Flow

The AEBS use case is connected to sensors such as speed and radar sensors and actuators such as the warning LED, speaker and brakes via a software interface. Thus information such as the speed of the car in ms^{-1} (from *wheel speed sensor*), distance in m and relative speed in ms^{-1} (from *radar sensor*) are provided as inputs to the AEBS system. The system is connected to the output actuators such as, *Warning LED* (with on/off state), *speaker* (with the ability to create an acoustic warning signal) and *brakes* (need to have a preparation, warning brake and an emergency brake functionality) for respective output action.

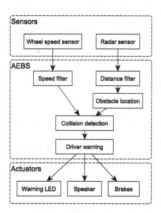

Fig. 4. Control flow and modules of the AEBS [17].

The AEBS basic control flow shown in Fig. 4 illustrates the aforementioned sensors and actuators as system input and output, as well as the AEBS modules. The sensor values are both processed by filter modules (*Speed filter* and *Distance filter*), which retrieve them periodically, filter outliers and smooth the sensor noise. The distance information from the radar sensor is then further processed by the *Obstacle location* module. It stores the filtered distance values of consecutive measurements and calculates the relative speed of a proceeding car from the change of distance over time. These values are used in the *Collision detection* module, to estimate the TTC. If the filtered speed sensor value is above a certain threshold, indicating a normal driving state, the TTC is sent to the *Driver warning* module. This triggers different stages of warnings, depending on the criticality of the TTC value, or sets off an emergency braking as last resort respectively. If the warning measures are successful and the TTC rises above the thresholds again, the corresponding warnings are cancelled.

4.3   Timing Behavior

In order to perform a timing analysis of the AEBS and verify the results against the timing requirements from Sect. 4.1, the timing behavior of the AEBS has to be captured. Anssi et. al. [2] identify a basic set of features necessary for a scheduling analysis of system models:

- Execution/transmission time for functions/messages
- Activation patterns for functions
- Function/end-to-end deadlines
- Processor scheduler
- Task type/priority
- Allocation of functions to tasks
- Allocation of tasks to processors

Thus, for a scheduling analysis of the AEBS, a more detailed division of the modules in functions and a specification of their Core Execution Time (CET) is needed. The functions also need to be allocated to fixed priority tasks, which in turn are allocated to processing cores.

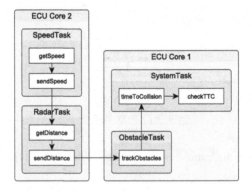

Fig. 5. AEBS architecture and end-to-end execution path [17].

This detailed architecture of the AEBS can be seen in Fig. 5. The system is distributed over two processing cores on one ECU. The *ECU Core 2* is responsible for handling the sensor tasks, which consist of a function for retrieving the data (*getSpeed*, *getDistance*) and filtering/sending the data (*sendSpeed*, *sendDistance*). The *ECU Core 1* handles the *ObstacleTask* and *SystemTask*, which handle the tracking of obstacles and calculating/checking the TTC value. The complete end-to-end flow of the system, from sensor input to possible actuator output, is depicted by the arrow function path.

Table 1 lists the detailed timing properties of the functions and tasks. It shows the guaranteed minimum and maximum CET of the functions, which can be obtained using experience values or independent run-time measurements of already implemented functions. The periodic activation of the functions is taken from the timing requirements and they are grouped into fixed priority tasks, responsible for the function execution. The priority values are assigned depending on the importance of the task, where higher values correspond to more important tasks. For example, the *RadarTask* has a higher priority than the *SpeedTask*, because the distance values are used for the decision whether an emergency brake is needed.

5 AUTOSAR Model of AEBS Use Case

Based on the control flow in Fig. 4 and the architecture in Fig. 5, the AUTOSAR-based system description of the AEBS is elaborated in detail in this section. The AUTOSAR-based design of the AEBS use case is modeled using a state-of-the-practice MDD tool in automotive industry, namely IBM Rational Rhapsody Developer [14]. As the tool is originally UML-based, the AUTOSAR model is also stored as a stereotyped UML model in the background. There is, however, a dedicated perspective that abstracts from the UML concepts and provides graphical AUTOSAR modeling elements, corresponding to the representation in the AUTOSAR specification [6]. The first step is to define the software components the system is composed of, which is described in Sect. 5.1. Next, the internal behavior of the components is defined and described in Sect. 5.2. Section 5.3 gives an overview of the software composition and Sect. 5.4 shows a mapping of the software components to ECUs. Section 5.5 describes the system mapping and root software composition. Finally, the timing annotation of the design model and task configuration are described in Sects. 5.6 and 5.7.

Table 1. Timing behavior of system functions [17].

Module	Function	min–max CET (ms)	Period (ms)	Task	Task priority
Speed filter	getSpeed	1–2	10	SpeedTask	0
	sendSpeed	4–6	50		
Distance filter	getDistance	1–2	10	RadarTask	1
	sendDistance	4–6	50		
Obstacle location	trackObstacles	6–10	50	ObstacleTask	2
Collision detection	timeToCollision	5–7	50	SystemTask	5
Driver warning	checkTTC	3–5	50		

5.1 Software Components

This subsection describes the software components of the AEBS model. For every module of the AEBS group in the control flow diagram (see Fig. 4) there is a software component created in the AUTOSAR model. Figure 6 shows the software component diagram in Rhapsody. The sensor filter modules on the left-hand side are modeled as *SensorActuatorSwComponentTypes*. They have client ports (*speedSensorPort, radarSensorPort*) to be able to connect to the corresponding sensors. These ports are typed by *ClientServerInterfaces* that provide an operation for retrieving the sensor value. This is illustrated by the association between the ports and the interfaces, which is stereotyped as a *portType*. The rest of the modules are modeled as *ApplicationSwComponentTypes*, as they do not directly represent a sensor or an actuator.

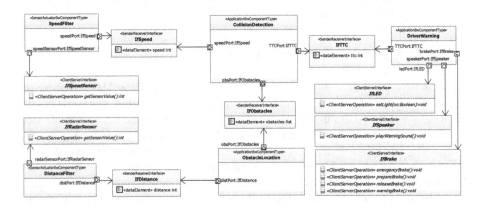

Fig. 6. AEBS software components [17].

The communication between the sensor filters and the *CollisionDetection* and *ObstacleLocation* components happens through sender/receiver ports. The filtered *dataElements* get sent to the processing components. Equally, the *ObstacleLocation* sends a list of obstacles (comprising of distance and relative speed) to the *CollisionDetection*. Note that in this simplified AEBS use case, only one obstacle will be tracked. But in case multiple radar sensors in different angles are attached to the car and used as input, the system would be able to track multiple obstacles, e.g. in different driving lanes. The communication between *CollisionDetection* and *DriverWarning* is also typed as sender/receiver and the corresponding *dataElement* is the TTC value.

In the end, the *DriverWarning* component is connected by client ports (*ledPort, speakerPort* and *brakePort*) to the three actuators. The corresponding interfaces provide the necessary operations for the different levels of driver warning, e.g., setting the warning LED light status (*setLight*), playing a warning sound (*playWarningSound*) or performing an emergency brake (*emergencyBrake*).

5.2   Internal Behavior

To further specify the functionality and behavior of the software components described in Sect. 5.1, AUTOSAR uses *SwcInternalBehavior* elements contained in the components. These are modeled as internal behavior diagrams in [14] for the AEBS use case.

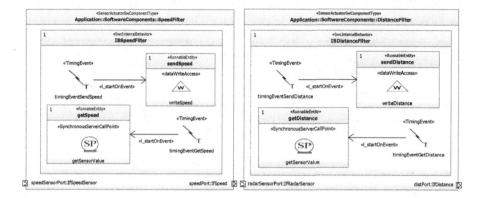

Fig. 7. Internal behavior of sensor filters (speed and distance) software components.

Sensor Filters: The *SpeedFilter* and *DistanceFilter* software components have a similar internal behavior as can be seen in Fig. 7(a) and (b). Both feature two *RunnableEntities*: *getSpeed* and *sendSpeed*, or *getDistance* and *sendDistance* respectively.

The respective get-operation is supposed to call the *ClientServerOperation getSensorValue* of the corresponding sensor client port (*radarSensorPort* or *speedSensorPort*), which is to be implemented by the sensor, to retrieve the sensor value and store it in a fixed-size FIFO queue. Hence a *SynchronousServerCallPoint* assigned to these runnables that link to the corresponding operation of the client/server interface (*IfSpeedSensor* or *IfRadarSensor*).

The respective send-operation is supposed to apply a filter to the queue of sensor-values and send the filtered value to the corresponding sender port (*speedPort* or *distPort*). Therefore, these runnables are assigned a *dataWriteAccess* linking to the *dataElements* of the corresponding sender/receiver interface (*IfSpeed* or *IfDistance*) for implicit sending of the sensor value.

All runnable entities are triggered by periodic *TimingEvents*, linked to the runnables by the *l_startOnEvent* association. The *getSpeed* and *getDistance* runnables are triggered every 10 ms. On the other hand, the *sendSpeed* and *sendDistance* runnables are triggered every 50 ms, so as to provide enough distinct measurements for the filter algorithm.

Obstacle Location: The internal behavior of the *ObstacleLocation* software component is shown in the first figure in Fig. 8. It contains the *RunnableEntity trackObstacles* that reads the latest distance value from the *distPort* and stores it in an obstacle object.

The read access is made possible by adding a *dataReadAccess* to the runnable and linking it to the *dataElement* distance of the *distPort*. By comparing the new distance value to the previously stored value, the runnable entity also calculates the relative speed of the obstacle and stores it in the same object. Finally, by specifying a *dataWriteAccess* linking to the obstacles list of *obsPort*, the obstacle object is sent implicitly through this port. This behavior is triggered every 50 ms by a periodic *TimingEvent*.

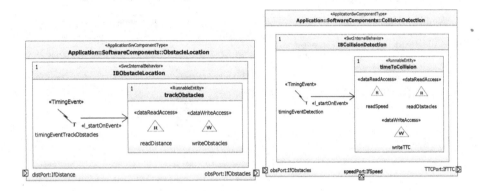

Fig. 8. Internal behavior of *ObstacleLocation* & *CollisionDetection* software component.

Collision Detection: The internal behavior of the *CollisionDetection* software component is shown in Fig. 8. It contains one *RunnableEntity timeToCollision* that calculates the TTC value and is invoked by a periodic *TimingEvent* every 50 ms. It has two *dataReadAccess* elements linked to the speed value of the *speedPort* and the obstacle list of the *obsPort*. If the speed value is too low, the operation stops at this point. Otherwise, the TTC is computed using the values of the obstacle object. This TTC value is afterwards implicitly sent through the *TTCPort*, which is linked by the *dataWriteAccess* element of the runnable entity. Please note that due to space limitations, the internal behavior of the *driver warning* software component is not described in detail here.

5.3   Software Composition

After the software component types and their internal behavior are defined, they are instantiated by *SwComponentPrototypes* and aggregated in a top-level *CompositionSwComponentType* shown in Fig. 9.

The corresponding prototype ports of the same interface are linked by *AssemblySwConnectors* (e.g. *speedPort* of *speedFilter* to *speedPort* of *collisionDetection*) to express the data flow between those prototypes. The sensor and actuator client ports (*radarSensorPort*, *ledPort*, etc.) are connected by *DelegationSwConnectors* to corresponding client ports on the top-level software composition. This highlights the external communication of the prototypes with the sensors and actuators. As the *AEB-SComposition* is the top-most composition, it represents the system boundary of the AEBS. The outgoing ports are thus also the system interface to the AEBS.

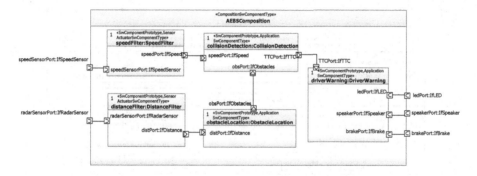

Fig. 9. Top-level software composition of the AEBS.

5.4 ECU Description

So far in this example, the AUTOSAR model is independent of the underlying hardware. But in order to conduct a timing analysis, information about the number of available ECUs and their processing units is needed. Every software component prototype can only be mapped to one ECU processing core and executes on this core only. Thus, it can make a difference in the system timing behavior, if the number of cores or the distribution of prototypes to cores changes.

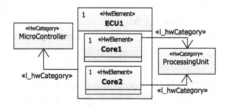

Fig. 10. ECU diagram of hardware elements.

The hardware architecture can be specified in Rhapsody using ECU diagrams. Figure 10 shows the hardware architecture of the AEBS use case. ECUs and their processing cores are modeled using *HwElements* of specific *HwCategories*. For example, the *ECU1* is linked to the category *MicroController* with the *l_hwCategory* association. The processing cores, *Core1* and *Core2*, are contained in the ECU and linked to the category *ProcessingUnit*. The mapping of software component prototypes is part of the system mapping described in the following subsection.

5.5 System Description

The top level software composition of the AEBS from Sect. 5.3 is associated to a *System* element as the *rootSoftwareComposition*. Normally, the root composition would comprise of every subordinate composition and software components of the whole vehicle.

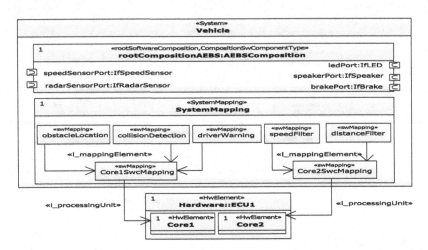

Fig. 11. System diagram containing system mapping & root software composition [17].

This means that every software subsystem (e.g. the AEBS) would be connected to the other subsystems in a nested software composition. But as this use case concentrates on the timing behavior of the AEBS, it can be viewed independent of the other subsystems. Thus, the root composition of the system is the top-level composition of the AEBS.

The corresponding system diagram is shown in Fig. 11. It also contains a *SystemMapping* element, which maps the software components to ECUs or to ECU cores respectively. The mapping is necessary for conducting a timing analysis, because it also maps the runnables of the software component's internal behavior to an ECU or an ECU core respectively and indicates, which function will be executed on which processing unit later on.

In the system mapping, for every processing core, a *swMapping* element linking to the corresponding *hwElement* from the ECU diagram with *l_processingUnit* is created. Then, for every software component prototype, a *swMapping* that links to the core mappings with *l_mappingElement* is created. These prototype mapping elements reference the component prototypes with their tagged value *component*.

5.6 Timing Attributes

The timing descriptions and constraints of the AEBS, specified as the timing behavior in Sect. 4.3, are added to the model with the help of AUTOSAR-TE.

Figure 12 shows one such diagram with a latency constraint for the *checkTTC* runnable entity of the *DriverWarning* software component. An *SwcTiming* is created for each software component in the AEBS, which link to the component's internal behavior with the *l_behavior* association. Inside these elements, two *TD-EventSwcInternalBehaviors* are defined for each runnable entity (in this case, *checkTTC* of *IBDriverWarning*).

The first event highlights the activation of the runnable, while the second highlights the termination. This is defined by setting the tag *tdEventSwcInternalBehaviorType* of

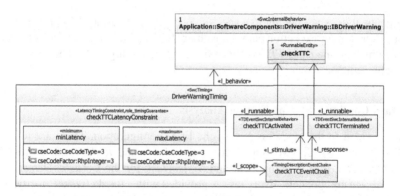

Fig. 12. Timing attributes for the *checkTTC* runnable entity [17].

the timing event to either *runnableEntityActivated* or *runnableEntityTerminated*. Both these events are used to form a *TimingDescriptionEventChain*, in which the event chain stimulus is the runnable activation and the event chain response is the runnable termination.

Finally, the core execution time of the runnable *checkTTC* is specified by the *checkTTCLatencyConstraint* that links to its event chain with *l_scope*. The *role_timing Guarantee* stereotype declares that this constraint is the expected execution time instead of a requirement (*role_timingRequirement*). The related timing information can be given as maximum and minimum execution time and is specified by ASAM-CSE[6] codes. The *cseCode* specifies the time base (e.g., $2 = 100\,\mu s$, $3 = 1\,ms$ and $4 = 10\,ms$) and the *cseCodeFactor* determines an integer scaling factor. Thus, in this case, the execution time of the *checkTTC* runnable entity lies between 3ms and 5ms. Note that every runnable entity in the model is similarly specified with their respective timing requirements.

Causal Event Chain Example: Given the timing annotated AUTOSAR-design model, the time critical path of AEBS system is identified. Let us consider **NRF 6** which states that, *new sensor data must influence the TTC computation after a maximum delay of 200ms*. Thereby, the system needs to react fast to sudden speed changes, so the end-to-end response time (delay) from sensor measurements to a reaction needs to be below 200 ms. The end-to-end flow of the AEBS system Fig. 4, from sensor input to *possible* actuator output, in which the **NRF 6** needs to be satisfied, is an example of a causal event chain. This is referred hereafter as **systemEventChain:**. It is depicted by the function path in Fig. 5, namely **getSpeed → sendSpeed → getDistance → sendDistance → trackObstacles → timeToCollision → checkTTC**. This describes the time critical path between the event *requesting the speed of the vehicle (stimulus)* and the event *making available the determined TTC value (response)*.

During timing modeling, this event chain is modeled as an end-to-end execution path through the system. As this path spans over runnables from different software

---

[6] https://www.asam.net/.

components, it does not belong to a specific *SwcTiming*. Thus, a *VfbTiming* element is created to contain the execution path event chain. It comprises of a sequence of runnable event chains (e.g. the *checkTTCEventChain* in Fig. 12) to highlight the execution path of runnable entities.

5.7   Task Configuration for Timing Analysis

Tasks are added to the model as part of the ECU configuration. There are four tasks specified in the AEBS. Two sensor tasks, *SpeedTask* and *RadarTask*, *ObstacleTask* for the *ObstacleLocation* component and *SystemTask* for the *CollisionDetection* and *DriverWarning* components. Every task is provided with a fixed *OsTaskPriority*, where higher values indicate a more important task, and an *OsTaskSchedule* parameter, which indicates if the task is preemptible or not.

Table 2. Task properties and mapped runnable entities [17].

Task	Priority	Period	Preemptible	Runnable entities
SpeedTask	0	10 ms	Yes	getSpeed sendSpeed
RadarTask	1	10 ms	Yes	getDistance sendDistance
ObstacleTask	2	50 ms	Yes	trackObstacles
SystemTask	5	50 ms	Yes	timeToCollision checkTTC

To annotate the period of the tasks, an *OsCounter* is first added to the model, which provides an *OsSecondsPerTick* value of 0.001s/tick or 1ms/tick. This counter is referenced in *OsAlarms* that are added for each task and specify at which counter value the task will be executed, which corresponds to the period of the task. For example, the obstacle task has an *OsAlarmCycleTime* of 50ticks. This means, after a counter cycle time of $50ticks * 1$ ms/tick = 50 ms the task will be triggered. Finally, the runnables of the software components need to be mapped to the tasks. This happens by linking the *RTEEvent* activating the runnable entity (see Sect. 5.2) to the *OsTask* with an *RteEvent-ToTaskMapping* in the *RteSwComponentInstance* parameter container, belonging to the *Rte* configuration module. In this mapping, the position of the runnable in the task can also be specified. The respective task properties and the mapping of runnables to tasks in their specified order are shown in Table 2. At this point, there is sufficient information contained in the model, to analyze the timing behavior of the AEBS. The model is now exported from the UML representation in the UML tool to an interchangeable ARXML file [6].

6   Model-to-Model (M2M) Transformations

A general outline of the transformations were provided in [17]. In this book chapter, an elaborate description of the transformations (in line with novelties listed in Sect. 1.3) and their performance attributes are discussed. The generic M2M transformations are implemented in an ATL module, *autosar2Timing.atl*. It can be applied to any use case (e.g. AEBS) which satisfies the source and target model criteria as in the workflow in Fig. 3. In this *autosar2Timing.atl* module, there are 9 matched rules for all conditional mappings and 8 lazy rules for all unconditional mappings. In addition, 15 helpers are implemented which may be invoked by the transformation rules. An example for each type of rule (matched and lazy) and helper, from the prototype implementation of the M2M transformations in *autosar2Timing.atl* is described below.

6.1   Matched Rule

A simple example of an ATL matched rule is shown in Listing 1.1. The rules consist of a source pattern in the `from` section and a target pattern in the `to` section. The source pattern specifies the type of the source model element to be matched and the target pattern contains the output model element that will be created by the transformation for each source element. In the ATL module *autosar2Timing.atl*, for synthesis of timing analysis models, the matched rules are used for source elements such as model, package, classes and for the elements with applied stereotypes from AUTOSAR profile [17].

Listing 1.1. An example of an ATL matched rule.

```
1   -- @atlcompiler emftvm
2   -- @path Timing=/de.uos.te.model/model/timing.ecore
3   -- @nsURI UML=http://www.eclipse.org/uml2/5.0.0/UML
4   -- @nsURI AR=http://autosar.org/schema/r4.0/autosar40
5   module autosar2Timing;
6   create OUT: Timing, from IN : AR
7   rule AtomicSWC2SWComponent extends
8   Identifiable2ICATObject{
9   from
10      input : AR!AtomicSwComponentType
11  to
12      output : Timing!SoftwareComponent(
13  runnables <- input.internalBehaviors
14      ->collect(ib | ib.runnables)
15      -> flatten())}
```

In Listing 1.1, the various paths of the metamodels invoked in the ATL module are specified in lines 2–4. The `AtomicSWC2SWComponent` rule `extends` the parent rule `Identifiable2ICATObject` and thus, its target pattern is inherited. This means that, the target element `SoftwareComponent` automatically receives the name and description attributes from parent rule (i.e., `Identifiable2ICAT-Object`-not listed here). In this matched rule (lines 7–12), a software component in the source AUTOSAR (meta) model (`AR!AtomicSwComponentType`) is matched to a target software component element (`Timing!SoftwareComponent`) in the timing (meta) model. Thereby, an instance of the target element (i.e., a software component corresponding to the timing analysis metamodel) is created. As the above output is a two-dimensional list, the `flatten` operation (lines 13–15) ensures that a list directly containing the runnables is returned and assigned to the `runnables` attribute.

6.2 Lazy Rule

Lazy rules are used for source elements that satisfy specific conditions and must be called explicitly for creating target elements. Listing 1.2 shows an example of an ATL lazy rule which is used to create a `timeValue` from a `Real` number. It may be recalled that the time values are specified in the tag values of the respective AUTOSAR stereotype (cf. Sect. 5.6). The ATL rule in Listing 1.2 converts this specified time value from a `real` number to a corresponding model element `timeValue` in the generic metamodel.

Listing 1.2. An example of an ATL Lazy rule.

```
1  lazy rule createTimeValue {
2    from
3      input : Real
4    to
5      output : Timing!TimeValue (
6        unit <- #ms, value <- input) }
```

6.3 Helpers

Helpers can be used to define (global) variables and functions. Some examples of include *setter()*, *getter()* methods and functions to resolve attributes involving repetitive pieces of code in one place (e.g. resolving metric units). Helper functions are Object Constraint Language (OCL) [26] expressions. They can call each other by recursion or they can be called from within rules.

Listing 1.3. An example of an ATL Helper.

```
1  helper context AR!TimingDescriptionEventChain def:
2  getNestedRunnables() : Sequence(AR!RunnableEntity) =
3    if not self.hasPathElements() then
4      if self.isRunnableEventChain() then
5        if self.isActivatedToTerminated() then
6          self.getRunnable()
7        else Sequence{}
8        endif
9      else Sequence{}
10     endif
11   else
12     self.segments->collect(s | s.getNestedRunnables()).flatten()
13   endif;
```

Listing 1.3 provides an example of a helper to obtain the sequence runnables in an event chain. It may be recalled that an example of an AUTOSAR-based causal event chain for our AEBS use case, namely *systemEventChain* is described in Sect. 5.6. Invoking helper in Listing 1.3 for the above examples provides the output with the set of runnables in the event chain, i.e., a sequence with runnables *getSpeed, sendSpeed, getDistance, sendDistance, trackObstacles, timeToCollision* and *checkTTC*.

6.4 Synthesis of Timing Analysis Model

The synthesized AUTOSAR-timing analysis model of the AEBS use case is shown in Fig. 13.

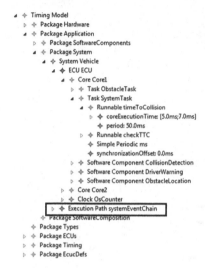

Fig. 13. Synthesized timing model of AEBS use case [17].

The necessary elements for a timing analysis were extracted from the AUTOSAR design model annotated with timing properties (cf. Fig. 6, 12). As seen in Fig. 13, the AEBS model is structured by different *Packages* and the *System* element contains the complete software and hardware elements in a hierarchy. For example, the runnable *timeToCollision* with its corresponding execution time can be seen, allocated to the *SystemTask*, which is in turn allocated to *Core1* of the ECU. The execution path *systemEventChain* in Fig. 13 is the causal event chain **systemEventChain** described in Sect. 5.6.

Note that the resulting timing analysis model is automatically exported to the timing analysis tool SymTA/S [21] for a detailed timing analysis, including end-to-end timing analysis. This is carried out using an importer/exporter tool framework which is described in [17], thus not detailed in this book chapter. If the import was successful, a new project is created with the corresponding elements from the timing model in the SymTA/S representation. The same elements from the timing model, annotated with timing properties, are now available inside the timing analysis tool.

7 Results of the Timing Analysis

Once the timing model (from Sect. 3.3) is exported to SymTA/S, timing analysis can be carried out and results can be visualized graphically in the tool. For the AEBS use

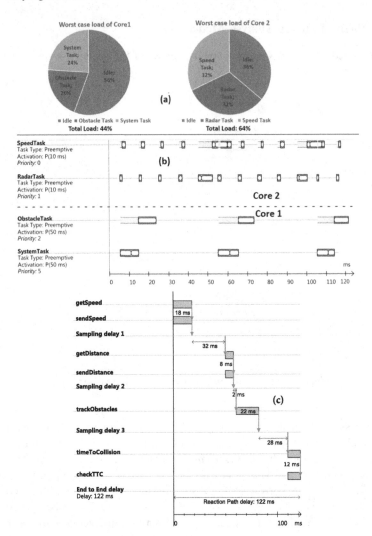

Fig. 14. (a) Worst case load of processing cores 1 & 2 (b) Exemplary task scheduling for system distribution analysis and (c) Worst case response time for the causal event chain **systemEventChain** modeled in use case (ref. Sect. 5.6) [17].

case, the results from processor utilization analysis, worst-case scheduling analysis and end-to-end latency analysis are described below.

Figure 14(a) shows the worst case processor workload as pie charts for processing cores 1 and 2. It is seen that, even in the worst case, the system is schedulable and both cores still have resources left (56% idle time for core1 and 36% idle time for core 2). Thus, the timing requirement **NRF 5** in Sect. 4.1 is satisfied for this set of function execution times.

The detailed scheduling of the AEBS tasks for the cores is seen in a Gantt chart by Fig. 14-(b). It provides an exemplary iteration of the system distribution analysis. The upper half shows the scheduling of *Core2* and the lower one shows the scheduling of *Core1*, which are independent of each other. Each task has different activation periods and priorities and executes a set of runnables, which are depicted as blocks on the timeline. If a task is preempted, e.g., because of a higher priority task, this is expressed by a yellow backdrop in the timeline.

As seen in Fig. 14(b), the *SpeedTask* tries to execute the *getSpeed* runnable every 10 ms. But as the *RadarTask* also executes its *getDistance* function every 10 ms and has a higher priority this is delayed until the end of the *RadarTask* execution. The same applies for the *sendSpeed* operation, which is to be executed every 50ms, but has to wait for the *sendDistance* operation. Thus, this provides an extensive overview of the possible scheduling behavior of the software system. It also confirms that the ECU will be able to schedule the system and obstacle tasks every 50ms, and the sensor tasks every 10 ms. Hence, the timing requirements **NRF 1** to **NRF 4** from Sect. 4.1 are satisfied.

The worst case response times for end-to-end execution paths as evaluated during timing analysis is shown in Fig. 14(c). It shows the *systemEventChain* as specified in the AUTOSAR model in a Gantt chart. The runnables of the AEBS contained in the event chain are executed consecutively. This leads to a worst case response time of 122ms, which satisfies the system end-to-end path timing requirement **NRF 6** from Sect. 4.1.

8 Conclusions

The work presented in this book chapter brings us one step closer to the goal of developing a seamless tool chain for AUTOSAR-based development of embedded systems in industry standard UML modeling tools and support for early timing analysis in state-of-the-practice timing analysis tools.

Some future directions include (a) investigating how the results from timing analysis tool could be back-annotated to the AUTOSAR model and modeling tools, thereby presenting it to the user/developer for an automatic verification of timing requirements, (b) AUTOSAR-based design and timing modeling of distributed ECU (software) and their timing analysis employing the proposed approach and (c) integrated timing and safety (ISO26262) analysis of AUTOSAR-based systems developed in UML.

Acknowledgements. This work is supported by grants ZF4447201BZ7 and KF2312004KM4 from BMWi-ZIM co-operation, Germany.

References

1. Anssi, S., Gérard, S., Kuntz, S., Terrier, F.: AUTOSAR vs. MARTE for enabling timing analysis of automotive applications. In: Ober, I., Ober, I. (eds.) SDL 2011. LNCS, vol. 7083, pp. 262–275. Springer, Heidelberg (2011). https://doi.org/10.1007/978-3-642-25264-8_20
2. Anssi, S., Tucci-Piergiovanni, S., Kuntz, S., Gérard, S., Terrier, F.: Enabling scheduling analysis for AUTOSAR systems. In: ISORC 2011, pp. 152–159. IEEE (2011)
3. Atlas Transformation Language (ATL) Technology. https://www.eclipse.org/atl/. Accessed 20 June 2020

4. Automotive Open System Architecture. http://www.autosar.org/. Accessed 16 June 2020
5. AUTOSAR: Specification of timing extensions (2017). https://www.autosar.org/fileadmin/user_upload/standards/classic/4-3/AUTOSAR_TPS_TimingExtensions.pdf. Accessed Jan 2020
6. AUTOSAR: Release 4.4.0: Methodology and templates (2018). https://www.autosar.org/standards/classic-platform/classic-platform-440/. Accessed Nov 2019
7. Becker, M., Dasari, D., Mubeen, S., Behnam, M., Nolte, T.: End-to-end timing analysis of cause-effect chains in automotive embedded systems. J. Syst. Archit. **80**, 104–113 (2017)
8. Bhasker, J.: A SystemC Primer. Star Galaxy (2010)
9. Enterprise Architect tool. http://www.sparxsystems.com/. Accessed 25 June 2020
10. Ficek, C., Feiertag, N., Richter, K., Jersak, M.: Applying the AUTOSAR timing protection to build safe and efficient ISO 26262 mixed-criticality systems. In: Proceedings of ERTS (2012)
11. GLIWA Embedded Systems-Timing suite T1. https://www.gliwa.com/. Accessed 20 June 2020
12. Harbour, M.G., García, J.G., Gutiérrez, J.P., Moyano, J.D.: Mast: modeling and analysis suite for real time applications. In: 13th Euromicro Conference on Real-Time Systems, pp. 125–134. IEEE (2001)
13. van der Horst, R., Hogema, J.: Time-to-collision and collision avoidance systems. In: Proceedings of the 6th ICTCT Workshop (1993)
14. IBM Software: IBM rational rhapsody developer. https://www.ibm.com/products/systems-design-rhapsody. Accessed 25 June 2020
15. INCHRON: chronSIM (2019). https://www.inchron.com/tool-suite/chronsim.html. Accessed Nov 2019
16. Iyenghar, P., Pulvermueller, E.: A model-driven workflow for energy-aware scheduling analysis of IoT-enabled use cases. IEEE Internet Things J. **5**(6), 4914–4925 (2018). https://doi.org/10.1109/JIOT.2018.2879746
17. Iyenghar, P., Huning, L., Pulvermüller, E.: Automated end-to-end timing analysis of autosar-based causal event chains. In: Proceedings of the 15th International Conference on Evaluation of Novel Approaches to Software Engineering, ENASE, Czech Republic, pp. 477–489 (2020)
18. Iyenghar, P., Huning, L., Pulvermüller, E.: Early synthesis of timing models in autosar-based automotive embedded software systems. In: Proceedings of the 8th International Conference on Model-Driven Engineering and Software Development, MODELSWARD 2020, pp. 26–38. SCITEPRESS (2020)
19. Kim, J.H., Kang, I., Kang, S., Boudjadar, A.: A process algebraic approach to resource-parameterized timing analysis of automotive software architectures. IEEE Trans. Ind. Inform. **12**(2), 655–671 (2016)
20. Kusano, K.D., Gabler, H.: Method for estimating time to collision at braking in real-world, lead vehicle stopped rear-end crashes for use in pre-crash system design. SAE Int. J. **4**(1), 435–443 (2011)
21. Luxoft - Symtavision: Timing analysis solutions (2019). https://auto.luxoft.com/uth/timing-analysis-tools/. Accessed Nov 2019
22. MARTE profile. https://www.omg.org/spec/MARTE/About-MARTE/. Accessed 25 June 2020
23. Mathworks Products. https://www.mathworks.com/. Accessed 20 June 2020
24. Mubeen, S., Nolte, T., Sjödin, M., Lundbäck, J., Lundbäck, K.L.: Supporting timing analysis of vehicular embedded systems through the refinement of timing constraints. J. Softw. Syst. Model. **18**, 36–69 (2019). https://doi.org/10.1007/s10270-017-0579-8
25. Navet, N., Simonot-Lion, F. (eds.): Automotive Embedded Systems Handbook. CRC Press, Boco Raton (2009)

26. Object Management Group. http://www.omg.org. Accessed 25 June 2020

27. Peraldi-Frati, M.A., Blom, H., Karlsson, D., Kuntz, S.: Timing modeling with AUTOSAR - current state and future directions. In: DATE (2012)

28. Scheickl, O., Ainhauser, C., Gliwa, P.: Tool support for seamless system development based on AUTOSAR timing extensions. In: Proceedings of Embedded Real-Time Software Congress (ERTS) (2012)

29. Singhoff, F., Legrand, J., Nana, L., Marcé, L.: Cheddar: a flexible real time scheduling framework. In: ACM SIGAda Ada Letters, vol. 24–4. ACM (2004)

30. Sugimoto, Y., Sauer, C.: Effectiveness estimation method for advanced driver assistance system and its application to collision mitigation brake system. In: 19th International Technical Conference Enhanced Safety Vehicles (2005)

31. Timing Architects Tool. https://www.timing-architects.com/. Accessed 20 June 2020

Internal Software Quality Evaluation of Self-adaptive Systems Using Metrics, Patterns, and Smells

Claudia Raibulet$^{(\boxtimes)}$, Francesca Arcelli Fontana , and Simone Carettoni

DISCo-Dipartimento di Informatica, Sistemistica e Comunicazione,
Universitá degli Studi di Milano-Bicocca, Viale Sarca 336, Milan, Italy
`raibulet@disco.unimib.it`, `francesca.arcelli@unimib.it`,
`s.carettoni@campus.unimib.it`

Abstract. Quality has a key role in the functioning, maintenance, and longevity of software. To evaluate the software quality, different points of view and mechanisms may be adopted, e.g., quality attributes, runtime performances. In this paper, we are interested in the internal quality of self-adaptive systems (SAS). SAS are more complex than non-self-adaptive systems (NSAS) because they implement also the mechanisms to monitor the execution environment, to analyze the gathered data about the environment, to plan adaptation strategies and to execute necessary adaptations required by the current state of the system. The available evaluation approaches for SAS focus mainly on the runtime performances achieved through the self-adaptive mechanisms. We consider that also the internal quality of SAS is equally important for their evaluation as for any other software. Therefore, we analyze 20 SAS using 4 different quality evaluation mechanisms: software metrics, design patterns, code and architectural smells. To discuss the quality of SAS, in our analysis we have considered 20 NSAS as a quality reference. Hence, we compare the quality of SAS with the quality of NSAS, and discuss the possible reasons behind the identified quality issues.

Keywords: Self-adaptive systems · Quality evaluation · Software metrics · Design patterns · Code smells · Architectural smells

1 Introduction

Software quality is one of the fields of software engineering which focuses on the attributes of software products. These attributes may concern the degree of software to meet its specifications and requirements, and the degree of software to meet the users needs and expectations. As established by the ISO/IEC25010:2011 [17], there are various aspects concerning the software quality.

A software characterized by a good quality is easier to be comprehended, extended, evolved, and maintained during its whole life-cycle. In addition, a good software is more likely to be used and reused. This is particularly important

© Springer Nature Switzerland AG 2021
R. Ali et al. (Eds.): ENASE 2020, CCIS 1375, pp. 386–419, 2021.
https://doi.org/10.1007/978-3-030-70006-5_16

for software which has to address and manage internal and external changes during its execution due to the variabilities in its execution environment. Self-adaptive systems (SAS) represent an example of such software [12]. There are various definitions of SAS as summarized by Danny Weyns in [33]. The main idea behind these definitions is that SAS are able to do modifications in their behaviour or structure at runtime autonomously to address variations in their execution environment or inside themselves [22,23].

In this paper, we analyze SAS with the objective to provide an overview of their internal quality. This analysis is useful for the developers of SAS because it helps them to improve their software, and for the potential software engineers interested in using available SAS to understand their quality and possible design issues. To achieve our objective we analyzed 20 systems dealing with self-adaptivity: 10 artifacts made available by the SEAMS community[1], 6 frameworks identified based on our previous knowledge in the self-adaptive domain, and 4 student projects developed during their academic studies at the University of Würzburg in Germany. We also analyzed 20 NSAS available in the QualitasCorpus[2] and MavenRepository[3]. The analyzed NSAS have been often considered in software quality studies [7,21,30]. In this paper, they represent a quality reference for the discussion of the SAS internal software quality.

We have analyzed SAS and NSAS from various points of view. We have computed Chidamber and Kemerer (CK) [6] and Robert Martin (RM) [15] software metrics, which provide quantitative indicators about the software quality. We have detected several design patterns defined by Gamma et al. [9] because their presence indicate often good solutions and help understanding the rationale behind the applied solutions due to their semantic [1,2]. We have detected smells at the code [32] and architectural levels [16]. Smells are indicators of possible issues in the implementation and design of software, issues which may lead to increasing problems in the software evolution and maintenance if not properly addressed.

In our previous work [25] we have done a preliminary analysis of 11 SAS by detecting code and architectural smells, as well as design patterns. In addition, we have started an analysis and comparison of 6 SAS and 6 NSAS based on code and architectural smells, and design patterns in [26]. In this paper, we extend the number of analyzed systems, i.e., 20 SAS and 20 NSAS, and we consider also software metrics for the analysis and comparison of the two types of systems.

The contribution of this paper may be summarized as follows. First, it extends the number of analyzed SAS and NSAS considered in our previous work to confirm our previous results. Second, it extends the analysis by using also software metrics often used for NSAS evaluation.

The rest of the paper is organized as follows. Section 2 addresses some related work. Section 3 describes our study design. The results are summarized in Sect. 4. The paper ends with a discussion and concluding remarks in Sect. 6.

---

[1] SEAMS Artifacts - https://www.hpi.uni-potsdam.de/giese/public/selfadapt/exemp lars/.

[2] QualitasCorpus - http://qualitascorpus.com/.

[3] MavenRepository - https://mvnrepository.com/.

2   Related Work

Software quality assessment can be done by taking into account several issues, such as metrics, code violations, code and design/architectural smells of different kinds, bugs, defects, and change evolution.

Many works have been done in the literature on the well-known Chidamber and Kemerer (CK) metrics [6] or other software quality metrics [15], by studying their evolution, thresholds, correlations with further issues as bugs or code smells.

Some studies considered code smells or anti-patterns. For example, Romano et al. [28] use anti-patterns to predict code changes and they found that classes affected by anti-patterns change more frequently along the evolution of a system. Olbrich et al. [18] investigated historical data on some code smells detection and they show that code smell-infected components have a higher change frequency. Chatzigeorgiou et al. [5], and Peters et al. [19] considered selected properties of code smells, e.g., their evolution and longevity. They observed that the number of code smells in software systems increases over time and developers almost never invest significant effort in removing them. This result was further confirmed by [4], who observed that code smells frequently persist in source code for a long time and developers withheld from refactoring them to avoid API modifications.

Various works have also considered the impact of design patterns on software quality, by considering metrics and code smells [32]. Only few works analyzed, evolved, or correlated architectural smells for software quality aims. Generally, the works have been mainly focused on the detection of these smells, even if few tools are currently freely available [3,13]. The above studies have analyzed software projects of different categories or domains without focusing on the analysis of SAS.

The available evaluation approaches for the quality assessment in SAS use quality attributes, software metrics, and design patterns [23]. Some of these approaches exploit the mechanisms applied for the evaluation of NSAS concerning performance, dependability, robustness, security, safety, complexity of self-adaptive systems. Most of the approaches introduce novel mechanisms, which aim to capture the specificity of self-adaptivity, i.e., degree of autonomy, time for adaptivity, quality of response, adaptivity metric, adaptability of services, support for detecting anomalous system behavior.

Furthermore, one of the first catalogs identifying 12 adaptation-oriented design patterns which capture the adaptation expertise is presented in [27]. This catalog proposes patterns concerning the monitoring (e.g., reflective monitoring, sensor factory, content-based routing), decision making (e.g., adaptation detector, case-based reasoning), and reconfiguring (e.g., component insertion/removal, server reconfiguration, decentralized reconfiguration) steps of self-adaptivity.

In this paper we provide an evaluation of various issues, e.g., software metrics, code smells, architectural smells, and design patterns in SAS and NSAS and a comparison of the quality of SAS in front of NSAS. As far as concerns our knowledge, this is the first study to address the internal software quality of SAS from such a wide internal quality point of view.

3   Main Elements of Our Analysis

Self-adaptive mechanisms increase the dimension and the complexity of SAS. In this analysis, we evaluate 20 SAS and 20 NSAS (all written in the Java programming language and freely available or open source) to observe the difference in terms of internal quality of SAS in front of NSAS. Hence, our analysis was guided by the following research questions (RQ):

RQ1: How can SAS be evaluated in terms of software metrics? Which is the difference between SAS and NSAS based on software metrics evaluation?

RQ2: How can SAS be evaluated in terms of design patterns? Which is the difference in terms of design patterns presence in SAS and NSAS?

RQ3: How can SAS be evaluated in terms of code smells? Which is the difference in terms of code smells presence in SAS and NSAS?

RQ4: How can SAS be evaluated in terms of architectural smells? Which is the difference in terms of architectural smells presence in SAS and NSAS?

3.1   SAS Analyzed Examples

In our analysis we have considered 20 SAS: 10 artifacts presented during the SEAMS editions, 6 frameworks for the development of SAS, and 4 student projects implementing self-adaptive solutions. The analyzed projects are heterogeneous and cover a wide range of SAS examples.

The 10 artifacts are (in alphabetical order):

Adasim: is a simulator for the Automated Traffic Routing Problem (ATRP), built as an agent-based system. Self-adaptivity deals with the scalability issues and the unexpected changes (e.g., an accident, a closed street).

DeltaIoT: enables the evaluation and comparison of self-adaptivity for Internet of Things (IoT). It monitors the network (e.g., transmission power, spreading factor) to reduce energy consumption and maintain performances.

Hogna: is an artifact for cloud management that can automatically deploy a topology, add/remove instances, configure each instance and provide tools for monitoring them.

Intelligent Ensembles (IE): is an artifact for dynamic cooperation groups, such as those specific to the smart cyber-physical systems. It is built to describe dynamic cooperation in applications specific to smart cities and smart mobility.

JDEECo: is a component system (model and runtime platform) that provides the architecture abstractions of autonomous components and dynamic component groups (called ensembles) on top of which different adaptation techniques can be deployed.

K8-Scalar: is a workbench, which implements and evaluates various self-adaptive approaches to autoscaling container-orchestrated services. It extends Scalar, a generic test bed for evaluating the scalability of large-scale systems.

Lotus (Lotus@Runtime): uses models@runtime to verify self-adaptive systems at runtime. It monitors the execution traces and annotates the probabilities of occurrence of each action. It checks if a set of reachability properties are performed against a probabilistic model.

mRUBiS: is an exemplar for model-based architectural self-healing and self-optimization. It simulates the adaptable software and maintains an architectural runtime model of the software, which can be directly used by adaptation engines to implement and perform self-adaptation.

Tele Assistance System (TAS): is a health-care service-based application for distance assistance to elderly and chronically ill people. The self-adaptive mechanisms address the issues concerning the uncertainties generated by third-party services (e.g., service failure, variable response time).

UNDERSEA: helps researchers to develop, evaluate and compare new self-adaptation solutions in unmanned underwater vehicles. It has predefined oceanic surveillance UUV missions, adaptation scenarios, and a reference controller implementation, all of which can easily be extended or replaced.

The 6 frameworks for SAS development are:

ATLAS[4] (Personalized-Travel-Assistant): acts as a navigator and assists the user in all phases of the journey. It allows the definition of value-added mobility services by enhancing interoperability among the existing services, supporting their execution via run-time adaptation, through the definition of multi-channel front-end applications.

EUREMA[5] (Executable Runtime Megamodels): provides a modeling language for feedback loops, the coordination of feedback loops, and the adaptation engine, as well as an interpreter for EUREMA models to execute the loops.

FESAS[6] (Framework for Engineering Self-Adaptive Systems): is a model-driven framework offering reusable components and design patterns. It is equipped with a tool set and includes a middleware that controls system deployment.

iCASA[7]: is a set of integrated tools for the development and autonomic administration of pervasive applications. It provides a simulated environment (e.g., for a smart home) enabling complete control of the environment and time.

Rainbow[8]: is a framework for the development of self-adaptive systems. It offers support to add self-adaptive mechanisms at the architectural level, i.e., feedback control loops which implement the MAPE-K (monitoring, analyzing, planning, executing using appropriate knowledge) steps.

---

[4] https://github.com/das-fbk/ATLAS-Personalized-Travel-Assistant.

[5] https://www.hpi.uni-potsdam.de/giese/public/mdelab/mdelab-projects/software-engineering-for-self-adaptive-systems/eurema/.

[6] https://fesas.bwl.uni-mannheim.de/.

[7] http://adele.imag.fr/icasa-a-dynamic-pervasive-environment-simulator/.

[8] https://github.com/cmu-able/rainbow.

StarMX[9]: is an architecture-based framework for dynamic adaptation behavior in Java EE enterprise systems and for the development of self-managing applications. It uses JMX features and can be integrated with different policy/rule engines to enable self-management capabilities.

Table 1. Number of classes in SAS artifacts.

ARTIFACTS	Adasim	DeltaIoT	Hogna	IE	JDEECo	K8-Scalar	Lotus	mRUBiS	TAS	UNDERSEA
NO. of Classes	64	82	865	825	1105	32	51	82	765	77

The 4 students projects are:

Code Offloading: is a software that proposes a version of the standard work that usually is performed by a scheduler with priority queues using a self-adaptive architecture.

Fall Detection: is a tool whose purpose is to understand and identify possible falls of animated or inanimate objects within an environment. It implements self-adaptive techniques for learning and mapping the surrounding environment.

Platooning Coordination: simulates an environment for coordination of multiple autonomous vehicles into convoys or platoons through a multi-agent system in which each agent captures the "autonomous decisions" carried out by each vehicle. The platoon formation is characterized by the string of vehicles traveling with small separation distances that need to be kept through communication among vehicles.

Vacuum Cleaner and Simulation: is a simulation software for coverage problems in planar environments. The simulation allows to choose different scenarios and algorithms to learn and map the environment.

The number of classes of all the SAS systems is shown in Table 1, 2, and 3.

Table 2. Number of classes in SAS frameworks.

FRAMEWORKS	ATLAS	EUREMA	FESAS	iCASA	Rainbow	StarMX
NO. of Classes	85	240	75	143	1707	88

Table 3. Number of classes in SAS student projects.

STUDENT PROJECTS	Code Offload	Fall Detection	Platoon Coord	Vacuum Simulator
NO. of Classes	169	284	257	134

---

[9] https://sourceforge.net/projects/starmx/.

3.2   NSAS Analyzed Examples

The NSAS systems considered in this analysis are available in the QualitasCorpus and in the MavenRepository websites. They are split into three categories: 4 parsers, 8 tools, and 8 software utilities as introduced in the following.

The 4 parsers generators are:

Apache Ant: is a Java library and command-line tool which drives processes described in built files as targets and extension points dependent on each other.

ANTLR (ANother Tool for Language Recognition): is a parser generator for reading, processing, executing, or translating structured text or binary files.

NekoHTML: is a HTML scanner and tag balancer that enables application programmers to parse HTML documents and access the information using standard XML interfaces.

SableCC: generates fully featured object-oriented frameworks for building compilers, interpreters and other text parsers.

The 8 tools are:

Cobertura: calculates the percentage of Java code that can be covered by test implementation. It is based on JScoverage.

DrawSWF: is a drawing application written in Java. It generates animated SWF Files, which redraw everything drawn with the mouse in the editor.

JGraph: is a Java Swing diagramming (graph visualisation) library for the development of workflow, BPM, org charts, UML, ER, and network diagrams.

JHotDraw: is a two-dimensional graphics framework for structured drawing editors written in Java.

Marauroa: is an open source multiplayer online framework which provides support to create games.

ProGuard: is a class file shrinker, optimizer, obfuscator, and preverifier.

Sunflow: is a rendering system for the synthesis of photorealistic images through the implementation of global illumination algorithms.

Velocity: is a Java-based template engine. It permits anyone to use a simple yet powerful template language to reference objects defined in Java code.

The 8 software utilities are:

Apache PDFBOX: is an open source library that can be used to create, render, print, split, merge, edit, and extract text and metadata from PDF files.

Checkstyle: is a development tool to help programmers write Java code that adheres to a coding standard. It automates the process of checking Java code to spare humans of this task.

Emma: is an open-source toolkit for measuring and reporting Java code coverage. It has a unique feature combination: support for large-scale enterprise software development while keeping individual developer work fast and iterative.

Hibernate (ORM): is an object-relational mapping tool for Java. It is a framework for mapping an object-oriented domain model to a relational database.

JUnit: is a unit testing framework for Java used in test-driven development.

PicoContainer: is a tiny embeddable container for Constructor Dependency Injection (CDI) Inversion of Control (IoC) Java components.

Quartz: is an application framework for rich and highly-integrated Java applications for any operating system that supports Java.

Quilt: is a Java software development tool which measures coverage, the extent to which testing exercises the software under test.

The number of classes of all the NSAS systems is shown in Table 4, 5 and 6.

Table 4. Number of classes in NSAS parsers.

PARSER	ANT	ANTLR	NekoHTML	SableCC
NO. of Classes	962	280	47	246

Table 5. Number of classes in NSAS tools.

TOOL	Cobertura	DrawSWF	JGraph	JHotDraw	Marauroa	ProGuard	Sunflow	Velocity
NO. of Classes	172	321	179	346	209	707	209	262

Table 6. Number of classes in NSAS software utilities.

SW Utilities	PdfBOX	Checkstyle	Emma	Hibernate	JUnit	Pico	Quartz	Quilt
NO. of Classes	388	410	17	588	276	250	284	115

3.3 Evaluation Mechanisms

We have analyzed SAS and NSAS by considering four different evaluation mechanisms: software metrics, design patterns, code smells, and architectural smells. Software metrics and design patterns represent indicators of good design, while code and architectural smells indicate possible issues in the code and design.

Software Metrics. Software metrics [6, 15] represent indicators of the quality of a system helping to estimate the progress and health of a software. They can be computed at package or class level. A brief description of the metrics considered in this analysis is following.

- **Chidamber and Kemerer Metrics (CK)** [6]:
  - Weighted Methods for Class (WMC): is the sum of complexities of methods defined in a class. It represents the complexity of a class and it is used to indicate the development and maintenance effort for the class.
  - Depth of Inheritance Tree (DIT): is the maximum length of a path from a class to a root class in the inheritance structure of a system. DIT measures how many super-classes can affect a class.
  - Number of Children (NOC): is the number of immediate subclasses subordinated to a class in the class hierarchy.
  - Coupling Between Objects (CBO): counts the number of classes coupled to a particular class i.e., where the methods of one class call the methods or access the variables of the other classes. These calls need to be counted in both directions so the CBO of class A is the size of the set of classes that class A references and those classes that reference class A. Since this is a set, each class is counted only once even if the reference operates in both directions.
  - Response For Class (RFC): represents the size of the response set of a class, i.e., a set of methods that can potentially be executed in response to a message received by an object of that class, i.e., all the methods in the class and all the methods that are called by methods in that class. As it is a set, each called method is counted once no matter how many times it is called.
  - Lack of Cohesion of Methods (LCOM): measures the dissimilarity of methods in a class via instanced variables.
- **Robert Martin Metrics (RM)** [15]:
  - Afferent couplings (CA): represents the number of classes in other packages that depend upon classes within the package; it is an indicator of the package responsibility. Afferent couplings signal inward.
  - Efferent couplings (CE): represents the number of classes in other packages that the classes in a package depend upon; it is an indicator of the package dependence on externalities. Efferent couplings signal outward.
  - Abstractness (A): represents the ratio of the number of abstract classes (and interfaces) in the analyzed package to the total number of classes in the analyzed package. Its range is 0 to 1, with $A = 0$ indicating a completely concrete package and $A = 1$ indicating an abstract package.
  - Instability (I): represents the ratio of efferent coupling (CE) to total coupling (CE + CA), i.e., $I = CE/(CE + CA)$. It is an indicator of the package resilience to change. Its range is 0 to 1, with $I = 0$ indicating a completely stable package and $I = 1$ indicating an unstable package.
  - Distance from the main sequence (D): represents the perpendicular distance of a package from the idealized line $A + I = 1$. D is calculated as

$D = |A+I-1|$. It is an indicator of the package balance between abstractness and stability. A package squarely on the main sequence is optimally balanced with respect to its abstractness and stability. Ideal packages are either completely abstract and stable ($I = 0$, $A = 1$) or completely concrete and unstable ($I = 1$, $A = 0$). Its range is 0 to 1, with $D = 0$ indicating a package that is coincident with the main sequence and $D = 1$ indicating a package that is as far as possible from the main sequence.

Design Patterns. Design patterns may provide significant hints on the development and quality of a system by capturing indications about the design decisions due to the semantic behind them. Design patterns provide enhanced and already verified solutions to a common design problem [9]. Hence, their detection may be very useful for the understanding, maintaining, and evolving a system [1,2].

In our analysis, we have considered the GoF's design patterns [9]. In particular, we have considered the following 13 design patterns in the three categories:

- *Creational*: Factory Method, Prototype, Singleton.
- *Structural*: Bridge, Composite, Decorator, Object Adapter, Command, Proxy.
- *Behavioral*: Chain of Responsibility, Observer, State-Strategy, Template Method, Visitor.

Observation: State and Strategy have identical structures, with different behaviors, thus in this analysis they are considered together, as a single pattern.

Code Smells. Code smells are indicators of possible problems at the code or design level (e.g., large classes or methods) [8]. They provide hints on parts of code which may be characterized by a poor quality, and may lead to negative effects on the maintenance and evolution of the software. We introduce below all the code smells that we have considered in our analysis. These definitions and further details are available on the plug-in[10] web site for their detection.

- *AntiSingleton (AS)*: a class that provides mutable class variables, which consequently could be used as global variables.
- *BaseClassKnowsDerivedClass (BCKDC)*: a class that invokes or has at least binary-class relationship pointing to one of its subclasses.
- *BaseClassShouldBeAbstract (BCSBA)*: a class with many subclasses without being abstract.
- *Blob (B)*: a large controller class depending on data stored in surrounding classes. A large class declares many fields and methods with a low cohesion.
- *ClassDataSouldBePrivate (CDSBP)*: a class that exposes its fields, thus violating the principle of encapsulation.
- *ComplexClass (CC)*: a class that has (at least) one large and complex method, in terms of cyclomatic complexity and lines of code.

---

[10] https://github.com/davidetaibi/sonarqube-anti-patterns-code-smells.

- *FunctionalDecomposition (FD)*: a main class, i.e., a class with a procedural name, such as Compute or Display, in which inheritance and polymorphism are scarcely used, that is associated with small classes, which declare many private fields and implement only few methods.
- *LargeClass (LC)*: a class that has grown too large in term of lines of code.
- *LazyClass (LzzC)*: a class that has few fields and methods.
- *LongMethod (LM)*: a class that has (at least) a very long method in terms of lines of code.
- *LongParameterList (LPL)*: a class that has (at least) one method with a too long list of parameters in comparison to the average number of parameters per methods in the system.
- *ManyFieldAttributesButNotComplex (MFABNC)*: a class that declares many attributes but which is not complex and, hence, more likely to be a kind of data class holding values without providing behaviour.
- *MessageChains (MC)*: a class that uses a long chain of method invocations to implement (at least) one of its functionality.
- *RefusedPatternBequest (RPB)*: a class that redefines inherited methods using empty bodies, thus breaking polymorphism.
- *SpaghettiCode (SC)*: a class with no structure, declaring long methods with no parameters, and using global variables.
- *SpeculativeGenerality (SG)*: a class that is defined as abstract having few children, which do not make use of its methods.
- *SwissArmyKnife (SAK)*: a complex class that offers a high number of services, e.g., a complex class implementing a high number of interfaces.
- *TraditionBreaker (TB)*: a class that inherits from a large parent class but that provides little behaviour and without subclasses.

Architectural Smells. An architectural smell results from a common architectural decision, intentional or not, that negatively impacts on the internal software quality [10] with significant effects on software maintainability [14]. The architectural smells considered in our analysis are:

- *Unstable Dependency (UD)*: describes a subsystem (component) that depends on other subsystems less stable than itself. This may cause a ripple effect of changes in the system. UD is detected on packages.
- *Hub-Like Dependency (HL)*: arises when an abstraction has (outgoing and ingoing) dependencies with a large number of other abstractions [29]. HL is detected on classes.
- *Cyclic Dependency (CD)*: refers to a subsystem (component) involved in a chain of relations that break the desirable acyclic nature of a subsystem dependency structure. The subsystems involved in a dependency cycle can be hardly released, maintained, or reused in isolation. CD has been detected on classes. The cycles are detected based on their shapes (tiny, star, clique, circle, chain) as described in [3].

We have considered these architectural smells since they represent critical problems related to dependency issues. Components highly coupled and with a high number of dependencies cost more to maintain and hence can be considered more critical. For example, the Cyclic Dependency smell is one of the most common and considered more critical by the developers [16].

3.4 Tool Support

To collect automatically the data related to the evaluation mechanisms described above we exploited the following tools:

- **Understand**[11]: used for the computation of the Chidamber and Kemerer metrics. It is a very well known tool able to detect a very large number of metrics and to analyze the code. Most of the metrics in Understand can be categorized as complexity, volume, and object-oriented metrics.
- **DPDT (Design Pattern Detection Tool)** [31]: used for the detection of design patterns. It exploits the similarity scoring between graph vertices for patterns detection. This enables the detection of most of the pattern variants. DPDT is freely available and detects most of the GoF's patterns (see Sect. 3). It is one of the most used tools for patterns detection ([20]).
- **SonarQube**[12]: used to detect the code smells. It is one of the most diffused tools for quality assessment. It is used in more than 85000 organizations as indicated on the tool web site. It becomes more and more popular also in the academic world [11,24]. For the code smell analysis presented in this work we have used an external plug-in[13], not present in the default version of the tool, but integrable and compatible stating from SonarQube version 6.3.
- **Arcan** [3]: used to detect architectural smells in Java projects. It relies on graph database technology. Once a project has been analyzed by Arcan, a new graph-database is created containing the structural dependencies of the projects. It is then possible to run detection algorithms on this graph to extract information about the analyzed project. It is also used to calculate the Robert Martin's metrics.

4   Results of SAS and NSAS Analysis

The results concerning the evaluation mechanisms about the various categories of SAS and NSAS are presented in this section. The values shown in the tables of this section have been normalized with respect to the size, i.e., the number of classes, of each system so that the observations and comparisons can be made easily. For the Unstable Dependency architectural smell the normalization has been done based on the number of packages because this smell is computed at the package level. The normalization has been done to enable the comparison

---

[11] https://scitools.com/.

[12] https://www.sonarqube.org.

[13] https://github.com/davidetaibi/sonarqube-antipatterns-code-smells.

between SAS and NSAS because, for example, the presence of one smell in a system with 20 classes may be significantly different than the presence of one smell in a system with 200 classes. The size of SAS and NSAS can be found respectively in Table 1, 2, 3 for SAS and 4, 5, 6 for NSAS.

4.1 Software Metrics Computation Results

The results obtained from the computation of the software metrics proposed by Chidamber and Kemerer (C&K) and by Robert Martin (RM) for SAS and NSAS are shown in Table 7, 8, 9, 10, 11, 12 for C&K, and in Table 13, 14, 15, 16, 17, 18 for RM. Figure 1 and 2 show the Box Plots associated to the results in these tables.

Chidamber and Kemerer Software Metrics. Chidamber and Keremer offer different software metrics to analyze the state of a system based on its classes and the interaction among these classes [6]. WMC, CBO and LCOM metrics provide quantitative information about the quality of a system. High values associated to these three metrics usually correspond to lower overall quality of a system. We note that the analyzed SAS are characterized by higher values for WMC and also for CBO with respect to NSAS. High values for CBO are not desired because high coupling means high inter-class dependencies. Dependecies have a negative impact on the modularity and also on the reuse of a system. High coupling makes code difficult to maintain, i.e., an alteration of code in one area leads to a high risk of affecting code in another liked area. High values for WMC indicate that a class is complex and therefore harder to reuse and maintain. This results also from the RFC related values. So, in terms of complexity, the category of SAS seems to be characterized by higher values than NSAS.

The values of DIT and NOC are similar in SAS and NSAS (see Fig. 1). These metrics are indicators of code reusability, i.e., greater is the number of children, greater is the level of reuse, inheritance being a form of reuse.

Finally, the LCOM values (indicating the cohesion) in NSAS are a bit higher than in SAS, being however overall low. Low values of LCOM indicate a high cohesion, a positive result.

Table 7. Chidamber and Kemerer metrics computed in SAS frameworks.

FRAMEWORK	ATLAS	EUREMA	FESAS	iCASA	Rainbow	StarMX
WMC	0.067	0.014	0.086	0.04	0.014	0.049
DIT	0.988	0.45	0.453	0.184	0.28	0.274
NOC	0.012	0.0036	0.0016	0.02	0.006	0.0056
CBO	0.104	0.158	0.183	0.17	0.08	0.143
RFC	0.145	0.163	0.086	0.241	0.03	0.365
LCOM	0.359	0.252	0.312	0.252	0.22	0.358

Table 8. Chidamber and kemerer metrics computed in SAS artifacts.

ARTIFACT	Adasim	DeltaIoT	Hogna	IE	JDEECo	K8-Scalar	Lotus	mRUBiS	TAS	UNDERSEA
WMC	0.058	0.039	0.122	0.014	0.011	0.089	0.053	0.035	0.003	0.02
DIT	0.4	0.50	0.549	0.72	0.298	0.5	0.79	0.463	0.032	0.669
NOC	0.06	0.02	0.044	0.02	0.01	0	0.07	0.041	0.019	0.053
CBO	0.22	0.12	0.262	0.06	0.063	0.271	0.29	0.228	0.04	0.24
RFC	0.34	0.30	0.239	0.15	0.143	0.152	0.22	0.474	0.21	0.376
LCOM	0.20	0.31	0.404	0.25	0.25	0.21	0.27	0.523	0.18	0.401

Table 9. Chidamber and Kemerer metrics computed in SAS student projects.

STUDENT PROJECTS	Code Offload	Fall Detection	Platoon Coord	Vacuum Simulator
WMC	0.052	0.076	0.06	0.063
DIT	0.592	0.409	0.462	0.413
NOC	0.028	0.014	0.013	0.031
CBO	0.15	0.218	0.18	0.229
RFC	0.334	0.038	0.052	0.057
LCOM	0.297	0.348	0.314	0.195

Table 10. Chidamber and Kemerer metrics computed in NSAS parsers.

PARSER GENERATOR	ANT	ANTLR	NekoHTML	SableCC
WMC	0.007	0.002	0.012	0.004
DIT	0.29	0.057	0.574	0.075
NOC	0.007	0.015	0.06	0.015
CBO	0.15	0.067	0.195	0.077
RFC	0.05	0.147	0.362	0.273
LCOM	0.41	0.442	0.411	0.273

Table 11. Chidamber and Kemerer metrics computed in NSAS tools.

TOOL	Cobertura	DrawSWF	JGraph	JHotDraw	Marauroa	ProGuard	Sunflow	Velocity
WMC	0.033	0.006	0.004	0.009	0.007	0.02	0.04	0.003
DIT	0.038	0.654	0.384	0.25	0.329	0.22	0.51	0.285
NOC	0.07	0.032	0.055	0.046	0.014	0.007	0.02	0.021
CBO	0.18	0.154	0.111	0.11	0.171	0.06	0.1	0.104
RFC	0.05	0.136	0.096	0.07	0.2	0.10	0.04	0.129
LCOM	0.49	0.356	0.435	0.32	0.461	0.30	0.25	0.331

Table 12. Chidamber and Kemerer metrics computed in NSAS software utilities.

SW UTILITIES	PdfBOX	Checkstyle	Emma	Hibernate	JUnit	Pico	Quartz	Quilt
WMC	0.053	0.002	0.024	0.003	0.016	0.008	0.005	0.009
DIT	0.39	0.399	0.5	0.239	0.326	0.259	0.489	0.435
NOC	0.01	0.005	0.071	0.039	0.028	0.035	0.025	0.003
CBO	0.20	0.079	0.202	0.065	0.139	0.077	0.092	0.239
RFC	0.04	0.051	0.497	0.168	0.196	0.139	0.167	0.174
LCOM	0.32	0.511	0.345	0.332	0.224	0.133	0.398	0.443

Robert Martin Software Metrics. RM metrics focus on the relation between the packages in a project. The results obtained in SAS and NSAS are summarized in Table 13, 14, 15 for SAS and in Table 16, 17, 18 for NSAS. Figure 2 shows also the box-plots associated to the values in these tables.

We can observe from the results that the value of CE and CA are similar, although the CA values are a little bit higher in SAS than in NSAS. Overall the value of the CE is a bit high with respect to the optimal value, i.e., < 20. This may lead to some issues because making changes on a class that has a high CE

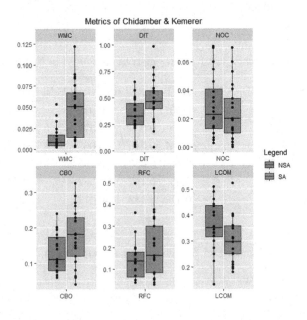

Fig. 1. Box-Plot results for Chidamber and Kemerer metrics for SAS and NSAS.

Table 13. Robert Martin metrics computed in SAS frameworks.

FRAMEWORK	ATLAS	EUREMA	FESAS	iCASA	Rainbow	StarMX
CA	0.273	0.081	0.228	0.023	0.04	0.262
CE	0.267	0.44	0.113	0.078	0.14	0.269
A	0.1	0.234	0.094	0.38	0.15	0.244
I	0.528	0.743	0.241	0.543	0.43	0.543
D	0.252	0.278	0.381	0.243	0.16	0.428

can be difficult and risky because of its complexity. The I (Instability) index has values higher than the average especially in NSAS.

The A (Abstractness) index is under the average, especially in SAS. This denotes the presence of packages that are mostly concrete, with a high degree of instability especially in NSAS. The values of the D (Distance from the main sequence) index may be a direct consequence of the relationship between A (Abstractness) and I (Instability). Hypothetically, the value of this metric should be as low as possible so that the components are located close to the main sequence. The values for both the categories are comparable and still low.

4.2 Design Patterns Detection Results

The detected creational design patterns are summarized in Table 19, 20, 21 for SAS and in Table 22, 23, 24 for ·NSAS. Three SAS implement no creational patterns: Adasim, DeltaIoT, and Lotus. Rainbow implements all the considered

Table 14. Robert Martin metrics computed in SAS artifacts.

ARTIFACT	Adasim	DeltaIoT	Hogna	IE	JDEECo	K8-Scalar	Lotus	mRUBiS	TAS	UNDERSEA
CA	0.18	0.49	0.164	0.04	0.034	0.24	0.27	0.078	0.42	0.112
CE	0.2	0.36	0.264	0.06	0.02	0.25	0.42	0.40	0.37	0.19
A	0.13	0.35	0.127	0.27	0.229	0.122	0.34	0.177	0.18	0.175
I	0.48	0.37	0.374	0.26	0.077	0.499	0.48	0.630	0.58	0.542
D	0.34	0.4	0.292	0.22	0.238	0.267	0.21	0.252	0.43	0.275

Table 15. Robert Martin metrics computed in SAS student projects.

STUDENT PROJECTS	Code Offload	Fall Detection	Platoon Coord	Vacuum Simulator
CA	0.326	0.103	0.032	0.219
CE	0.305	0.128	0.066	0.294
A	0.167	0.126	0.105	0.131
I	0.45	0.457	0.496	0.538
D	0.242	0.219	0.136	0.211

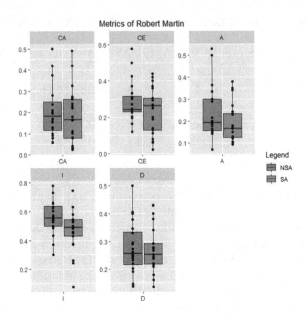

Fig. 2. Box-Plot results for Robert martin metrics for SAS and NSAS.

creational patterns. The most detected pattern is Singleton that, except for the three systems mentioned before, is present in all the other projects. This result may be mostly due to the implementation of the managers of the various steps of the MAPE-K loop. The less used pattern is Prototype: it occurs only in Rainbow.

Looking at NSAS, NekoHTML and Emma implement no creational patterns. They are small systems, as shown in Table 4 and 6. With respect to SAS there are two systems that implement all the creational patterns i.e., Quartz and JHotDraw. Also in NSAS, the most detected pattern is Singleton, while the less detected one is Prototype.

The detected structural design patterns are summarized in Table 25, 26, 27 for SAS and in Table 28, 29, 30 for NSAS. Three systems implement no instances of any structural pattern: ATLAS, FESAS and JDEECo. In EUREMA, DeltaIoT, Hogna, mRUBiS, UNDERSEA, and Code Offloading only the Object Adapter has been detected.

Table 16. Robert Martin metrics computed in NSAS parsers.

PARSER GENERATOR	ANT	ANTLR	NekoHTML	SableCC
CA	0.09	0.419	0.375	0.281
CE	0.12	0.425	0.333	0.577
A	0.30	0.364	0.333	0.529
I	0.55	0.663	0.625	0.661
D	0.33	0.346	0.405	0.378

Table 17. Robert Martin metrics computed in NSAS tools.

TOOL	Cobertura	DrawSWF	JGraph	JHotDraw	Marauroa	ProGuard	Sunflow	Velocity
CA	0.17	0.21	0.195	0.20	0.153	0.21	0.13	0.28
CE	0.37	0.197	0.247	0.24	0.234	0.31	0.23	0.271
A	0.20	0.163	0.144	0.15	0.152	0.16	0.15	0.299
I	0.54	0.433	0.655	0.37	0.56	0.49	0.57	0.485
D	0.14	0.192	0.233	0.29	0.261	0.40	0.24	0.221

Table 18. Robert Martin metrics detected in NSAS software utilities.

SW Utilities	PdfBOX	Checkstyle	Emma	Hibernate	JUnit	Pico	Quartz	Quilt
CA	0.06	0.058	0.5	0.159	0.123	0.099	0.078	0.239
CE	0.24	0.243	0.5	0.227	0.163	0.301	0.202	0.233
A	0.07	0.159	0.5	0.215	0.289	0.215	0.178	0.188
I	0.63	0.778	0.5	0.542	0.603	0.526	0.731	0.303
D	0.25	0.146	0.5	0.273	0.296	0.245	0.138	0.202

Table 19. Creational Design patterns detected in SAS frameworks.

FRAMEWORK	ATLAS	EUREMA	FESAS	iCASA	Rainbow	StarMX
Factory Method	0	0.0041	0	0.1888	0.0052	0
Prototype	0	0	0	0	0.0050	0
Singleton	0.0235	0.0333	0.0933	0.6363	0.0193	0.0227

Table 20. Creational design patterns detected in SAS artifacts.

ARTIFACT	Adasim	DeltaIoT	Hogna	IE	JDEECo	K8-Scalar	Lotus	mRUBiS	TAS	UNDERSEA
Factory Method	0	0	0.0232	0.0878	0	0.03125	0	0	0.0013	0
Prototype	0	0	0	0	0	0	0	0	0	0
Singleton	0	0	0.0465	0.0218	0.0090	0.1250	0	0.0731	0.0039	0.0129

Table 21. Creational design patterns detected in SAS projects.

STUDENT PROJECTS	Code Offload	Fall Detection	Platoon Coord	Vacuum Simulator
Factory Method	0	0	0.0389	0
Prototype	0	0	0	0
Singleton	0.0355	0.950	0.0622	0.0149

Table 22. Creational design patterns detected in NSAS parsers.

PARSER GENERATOR	ANT	ANTLR	NekoHTML	SableCC
Factory Method	0	0.0071	0	0
Prototype	0	0	0	0
Singleton	0.0062	0.0142	0	0.0528

Table 23. Creational design patterns detected in NSAS tools.

TOOL	Cobertura	DrawSWF	JGraph	JHotDraw	Marauroa	ProGuard	Sunflow	Velocity
Factory Method	0	0.0031	0.0055	0.084	0.0047	0.070	0.1913	0.0114
Prototype	0	0	0	0.2528	0	0	0	0
Singleton	0.0116	0.0404	0.0223	0.0056	0.1674	0.1145	0.0478	0

Table 24. Creational design patterns detected in NSAS software utilities.

SW UTILITY	PdfBOX	Checkstyle	Emma	Hibernate	JUnit	Pico	Quartz	Quilt
Factory Method	0.051	0	0	0.0204	0.0217	0.012	0.0176	0
Prototype	0	0	0	0	0	0	0.0070	0
Singleton	0.0180	0.0048	0	0.0170	0.0217	0.024	0.0176	0.0173

We have Object Adapter and Decorator in StarMX for Framework, Object Adapter with Bridge and Composite respectively for Adasim and Lotus for the Artifacts, and finally, Object Adapter and Proxy in Fall Detection and Vacuum Simulator for the Student Projects. In IE and TAS, instances of three structural patterns have been detected: Object Adapter, Bridge, and Decorator. Platoon Coordination has four instances of design patterns: Object Adapter, Bridge, Composite, and Decorator. iCASA and Rainbow implement all the structural patterns considered. The most detected structural pattern is Adapter, while the less detected ones are Composite and Proxy.

Looking at the NSAS, there are, as for SAS, three systems in which there are no instances of structural patterns: NekoHTML, SableCC, and Emma. Cobertura and Quilt implement Adapter. JHotDraw, ProGuard. Hibernate, and JUnit implement all the structural patterns considered. The most detected structural design pattern is Adapter, while, the less detected ones are Composite and Proxy followed by the Decorator and Bridge.

The detected behavioral design patterns are summarized in Table 31, 32, 33 for SAS and in Table 34, 35, and 36 for NSAS. Several systems implement instances of one behavioral pattern: State-Strategy (Adasim, DeltaIoT, Lotus, mRUBiS, UNDERSEA), Observer (ATLAS, Platoon Coordination), Template Method (FESAS) or Chain of Responsibility (JDEECo). Two instances of State-Strategy and Template Method patterns have been detected in: EUREMA and StarMX for the Framework, K8-Scalar for Artifacts, Fall Detection for Student

Projects. There are systems with two instances of patterns: IE with Observer and State-Strategy, Vacuum Simulator with State-Strategy and Chain of Responsibility. Rainbow, for the Framework category, and Code Offloading, for the Student Projects, are the projects implementing all the behavioral patterns considered. The remaining systems implement three instances of patterns between Chain of Responsibility, Observer, State-Strategy, Template Method. The most detected pattern is State-Strategy followed by the Template method, while the less detected are Chain of Responsibility and Visitor followed by the Observer.

Table 25. Structural design patterns detected in SAS frameworks.

FRAMEWORK	ATLAS	EUREMA	FESAS	iCASA	Rainbow	StarMX
Object Adapter	0	0.0541	0	0.8041	0.0527	0.1931
Bridge	0	0	0	0.1608	0.0046	0
Composite	0	0	0	0.0279	0.0005	0
Decorator	0	0	0	0.2797	0.0076	0.01136
Proxy	0	0	0	0.0769	0.0011	0

Table 26. Structural design patterns detected in SAS artifacts.

ARTIFACT	Adasim	DeltaIoT	Hogna	IE	JDEECo	K8-Scalar	Lotus	mRUBiS	TAS	UNDERSEA
Object Adapter	0.0156	0.0121	0.0116	0.0484	0	0.0.625	0.0052	0.1219	0.0052	0.0129
Bridge	0.0156	0	0	0.0012	0	0	0	0	0.0013	0
Composite	0	0	0	0	0	0	0.0196	0	0	0
Decorator	0	0	0	0.0036	0	0	0	0	0.0006	0
Proxy	0	0	0	0	0	0	0	0	0	0

Table 27. Structural design patterns detected in SAS student projects.

STUDENT PROJECTS	Code Offload	Fall Detection	Platoon Coord	Vacuum Simulator
Object Adapter	0.0236	0.0176	0.1789	0.0223
Bridge	0	0	0.0622	0
Composite	0	0	0.0038	0
Decorator	0	0	0.0194	0
Proxy	0	0.0035	0	0.0311

Table 28. Structural design patterns detected in NSAS parsers.

PARSER GENERATOR	ANT	ANTLR	NekoHTML	SableCC
Object Adapter	0.0166	0.0071	0	0
Bridge	0.0010	0	0	0
Composite	0	0	0	0
Decorator	0.0010	0.0035	0	0
Proxy	0	0	0	0

Table 29. Structural design patterns detected in NSAS tools.

TOOL	Cobertura	DrawSWF	JGraph	JHotDraw	Marauroa	ProGuard	Sunflow	Velocity
Object Adapter	0.0290	0.9034	0.1508	0.0730	0.1674	0.1145	0.2344	0.0763
Bridge	0	0.0031	0	0.0365	0.0047	0.0014	0.0047	0.0190
Composite	0	0	0	0.0056	0	0.0099	0	0.0038
Decorator	0	0.0093	0.0167	0.0117	0.0047	0.1131	0.0239	0.0114
Proxy	0	0	0.0034	0.0055	0	0.0248	0.0143	0

Looking at NSAS, two systems, NekoHTML and Quilt, implement one behavioral pattern: State-Strategy. State-Strategy and Template Method patterns have been detected in: ANTLR for the Parsers, Cobertura, DrawSWF, JGraph, Marauroa for the Tools, and Emma for software utilities. Three systems implement four behavioral patterns: Sunflow, Velocity, and Quartz. ProGuard is the only system implementing instances of all the behavioral patterns considered in this analysis. The remaining systems implement three patterns among Observer, State-Strategy, Template Method, and Visitor. The most detected behavioral patterns are State-Strategy and Template Method, while the less detected ones are Chain of Responsibility and Visitor. We observe that SAS implement more instances of the creational design patterns with respect to NSAS; while NSAS use more structural and behavioral design patterns with respect to SAS.

Figure 3 shows the box-plots associated to all the categories of design patterns for SAS and NSAS.

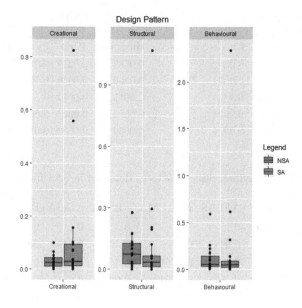

Fig. 3. Box-plot results for design patterns for SAS and NSAS.

4.3 Code Smells Detection Results

The code smells detected in the SAS and NSAS are summarized in Table 37, 38, and 39 for SAS and in Table 40, 41, and 42 for NSAS. From the 18 code smells considered in this analysis, and detectable by the SonarQube (with the external plug-in), the following 6 code smells have not been detected in any of the projects: BaseClassKnowsDerivedClass, Blob, FunctionalDecomposition, ManyFilesAttributesButNoComplex, SpeculativeGenerality, and TraditionBreaker. The most detected code smells present in all SAS are: ComplexClass, LongMethod, and LongParameterList. The less detected code smells are: BaseClassShouldBeAbstract and RefusedParentBequest revealed only in the IE artifact.

Looking at NSAS, there are 3 code smells present, i.e., LargeClass, MessageChains, and SwissArmyKnife in addition to the ones detected in SAS. As in SAS, also in NSAS the most present code smells are: ComplexClass, LongMethod, and LongParameterList. The first two are present in all NSAS analyzed, while the third i.e., LongParameterList is not present in NekoHTML and PicoContainer. The less present code smells are: LargeClass, MessageChains, RefusedParentBequest, SpachettiCode and SwissArmyKnife. Figure 4 shows the box-plots for the six code smell values most detected in Table 37, 38, 39, 40, 41, and 42 associated to all SAS and all NSAS. We observe that the numbers of the detected code smells in the two category of systems are comparable. We also observe that the number of LongMethod smells in SAS is higher than in NSAS, while the number of LongParameterList smells in NSAS is higher than in SAS.

Table 30. Structural design patterns detected in NSAS software utilities.

SW UTILITY	PdfBOX	Checkstyle	Emma	Hibernate	JUnit	Pico	Quartz	Quilt
Object Adapter	0.0154	0.0292	0	0.0782	0.0217	0.016	0.0915	0.0782
Bridge	0	0.0024	0	0.0306	0.0036	0.008	0.0140	0
Composite	0	0	0	0.0017	0.0072	0	0.0105	0
Decorator	0	0.0024	0	0.0085	0.0326	0.0064	0.0176	0
Proxy	0.0051	0.0024	0	0.0034	0.0036	0.012	0	0

Table 31. Behavioral design patterns detected in SAS frameworks.

FRAMEWORK	ATLAS	EUREMA	FESAS	iCASA	Rainbow	StarMX
Chain of Responsibility	0	0	0	0	0	0.0489
Observer	0.0117	0	0	0.0419	0.0082	0
State-Strategy	0	0.0166	0	1.2937	0.050	0.0795
Template Method	0	0.0041	0.0266	0.9510	0.0222	0.01136
Visitor	0	0	0	0	0.0005	0

Table 32. Behavioral design patterns detected in SAS artifacts.

ARTIFACT	Adasim	DeltaIoT	Hogna	IE	JDEECo	K8-Scalar	Lotus	mRUBiS	TAS	UNDERSEA
Chain of Responsibility	0	0	0	0	0.03125	0	0	0	0.0039	0
Observer	0	0	0.0581	0.7636	0	0	0	0	0	0
State-Strategy	0.0312	0.0609	0.0116	0.0084	0	0.0625	0.1372	0.0243	0.0013	0.519
Template Method	0	0	0.0116	0	0	0.2187	0	0	0.0156	0
Visitor	0	0	0	0	0	0	0	0	0	0

Table 33. Behavioral design patterns detected in SAS student projects.

STUDENT PROJECTS	Code Offload	Fall Detection	Platoon Coord	Vacuum Simulator
Chain of Responsibility	0.0059	0	0	0.0038
Observer	0	0	0.0233	0
State-Strategy	0.0059	0.0105	0.5136	0.0223
Template Method	0.0118	0.0035	0.0972	0
Visitor	0.0177	0	0	0

Table 34. Behavioral design patterns detected in NSAS parsers.

PARSER GENERATOR	ANT	ANTLR	NekoHTML	SableCC
Chain of Responsibility	0	0	0	0.0040
Observer	0.0031	0	0	0
State-Strategy	0.0155	0.035	0.0638	0.0203
Template Method	0.0051	0.0035	0	0.0040
Visitor	0	0	0	0

Table 35. Behavioral design patterns detected in NSAS tools.

TOOL	Cobertura	DrawSWF	JGraph	JHotDraw	Marauroa	ProGuard	Sunflow	Velocity
Chain of Responsibility	0	0	0	0	0	0.0028	0.0095	0
Observer	0	0	0	0.0056	0	0.1032	0	0.0038
State-Strategy	0.0232	0.0342	0.0949	0.1432	0.0526	0.1060	0.1722	0.1030
Template Method	0.0058	0.0155	0.0167	0.0337	0.0095	0.0198	0.0813	0.0267
Visitor	0	0	0	0	0	0.0919	0.3301	0.1297

Table 36. Behavioral design patterns detected in NSAS software utilities.

SW UTILITIES	PdfBOX	Checkstyle	Emma	Hibernate	JUnit	Pico	Quartz	Quilt
Chain of Responsibility	0	0	0	0	0	0	0.0040	0
Observer	0	0.0024	0	0.0102	0.0036	0	0.0105	0
State-Strategy	0.0128	0.0170	0.0588	0.0850	0.0036	0.0056	0.0704	0.0347
Template Method	0.0154	0.0170	0.1776	0.0357	0.0398	0.012	0.0281	0
Visitor	0.0257	0	0	0	0	0.028	0	0

Table 37. Code smells detected in SAS frameworks.

FRAMEWORK	ATLAS	EUREMA	FESAS	iCASA	Rainbow	StarMX
AntiSingleton	0	0.0208	0.0533	0	0.0058	0
BaseClassShouldBeAbstract	0	0	0	0	0	0
ClassDataShouldBePrivate	0.358	0.0083	0.0533	0	0.0117	0.0113
ComplexClass	0.2352	0.15	0.0933	0.0559	0.0386	0.7954
LazyClass	0.352	0.0083	0	0	0.0110	0
LongMethod	0.058	0.1958	0.1466	0.0419	0.0287	0.2272
LongParameterList	0.0941	0.0333	0.0266	0.0139	0.0093	0.5681
RefusedParentBequest	0	0	0	0	0	0
SpaghettiCode	0	0.0041	0	0	0	0

Table 38. Code smells detected in SAS artifacts.

ARTIFACTS	Adasim	DeltaIoT	Hogna	IE	JDEECo	K8-Scalar	Lotus	mRUBiS	TAS	UNDERSEA
AntiSingleton	0.03100	0.0121	0	0.0157	0.0153	0	0	0	0.0078	0.077
BaseClassShouldBeAbstract	0	0	0	0.0012	0	0	0	0	0	0
ClassDataShouldBePrivate	0	0.0243	0.0348	0.7878	0.0877	0	0	0	0.0156	0.090
ComplexClass	0.1718	0.1341	0.0697	0.1393	0.1194	0.1562	0.0980	0.0731	0.2610	0.1948
LazyClass	0.0625	0.0609	0.0232	0.0157	0.0217	0	0	0.0121	0.0052	0
LongMethod	0.2187	0.0975	0.2674	0.0921	0.1203	0.2812	0.1372	0.2073	0.0209	0.116
LongParameterList	0.0156	0.0853	0.1976	0.0387	0.0361	0.0625	0.0392	0.0731	0.0156	0.0259
RefusedParentBequest	0	0	0	0.0012	0.0009	0	0	0	0	0
SpaghettiCode	0	0	0	0	0	0	0	0	0	0.0129

4.4 Architectural Smell Detection Results

The architectural smells detected in SAS and NSAS are summarized in Table 43, 44, 45 for SAS and in Table 46, 47, 48 for NSAS. Observing the results obtained

Table 39. Code smells detected in SAS student projects.

STUDENT PROJECTS	Code Offload	Fall Detection	Platoon Coord	Vacuum Simulator
AntiSingleton	0.01775	0.0352	0.0820	0
BaseClassShouldBeAbstract	0	0	0	0
ClassDataShouldBePrivate	0.0236	0.0201	0.0350	0.0074
ComplexClass	0.2130	0.1478	0.1712	0.0820
LazyClass	0.0295	0.0774	0.0194	0.0223
LongMethod	0.1656	0.1302	0.1361	0.1044
LongParameterList	0.0710	0.0950	0.1789	0.0074
RefusedParentBequest	0	0	0	0
SpaghettiCode	0.0118	0	0.0077	0

Table 40. Code smells detected in NSAS parsers.

PARSER GENERATOR	ANT	ANTLR	NekoHTML	SableCC
AntiSingleton	0.0031	0.0607	0.0425	0.0162
BaseClassShouldBeAbstract	0.0176	0	0	0
ClassDataShouldBePrivate	0.0093	0.1714	0	0.0447
ComplexClass	0.1434	0.1428	0.1063	0.1463
LargeClass	0	0	0.0212	0
LazyClass	0.0363	0.075	0.0425	0.1219
LongMethod	0.1663	0.0571	0.1063	0.1585
LongParameterList	0.0301	0.0107	0	0.1504
MessageChains	0	0	0	0
RefusedParentBequest	0.1850	0	0	0
SpaghettiCode	0	0.0071	0	0.0121
SwissArmyKnife	0.0010	0	0	0

Table 41. Code smells detected in NSAS tools.

TOOL	Cobertura	DrawSWF	JGraph	JHotDraw	Marauroa	ProGuard	Sunflow	Velocity
AntiSingleton	0.0174	0.0373	0.1284	0	0.0047	0.014	0	0.0114
BaseClassShouldBeAbstract	0	0.0031	0	0.0028	0.0023	0.0169	0	0
ClassDataShouldBePrivate	0.1511	0.0218	0.1340	0.0056	0.0287	0.1244	0.0191	0.0419
ComplexClass	0.2325	0.1651	0.1229	0.1797	0.1961	0.2531	0.1961	0.1374
LargeClass	0	0	0	0	0	0	0	0
LazyClass	0.0523	0.0062	0.0502	0	0	0	0	0
LongMethod	0.1744	0.1651	0.1675	0.1882	0.1913	0.1753	0.1776	0.1641
LongParameterList	0.0406	0.0280	0.0446	0.0702	0.0669	0.0664	0.1052	0.1374
MessageChains	0	0	0	0	0.0047	0	0	0
RefusedParentBequest	0	0.0031	0	0	0.2631	0.1244	0	0
SpaghettiCode	0	0	0	0	0	0	0	0
SwissArmyKnife	0	0	0	0	0	0.0990	0	0

and summarized in Fig. 5 with the box-plots, we note that there is a higher number of UD and HL smells in all analyzed SAS than in all analyzed NSAS. The results concerning the CD smells are comparable in the two category of systems. However, we outline that, for example, the number of CD smells in the iCASA framework (the highest value among the SAS analyzed examples) is more than double with respect to ANTLR (the highest value among the NSAS analyzed examples), even if the number of classes in ANTLR is almost double the number of classes in iCASA. This result may ask for a particular attention

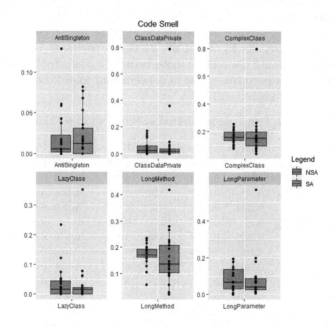

Fig. 4. Box-plot results for code smells in SAS and NSAS.

due to that fact that a single change or bug in a package/class may have a significant effect on other classes in a system, with increased maintenance and refactoring costs.

The presence of UD and HL smells in SAS more than in NSAS may be also due to the nature of SAS. The UD smell indicates a subsystem that depends on other subsystems less stable than itself. This instability may raise from the adaptation of SAS based on the variability of the internal or external parameters, meaning that the various classes and packages should be characterized by a high degree of flexibility. In addition, SAS operate in dynamic environments and need to analyze and adapt to changes in the environment to ensure the quality of the provided services. This is a possible explanation for the number of HD smells detected in SAS.

5   Threats to Validity

This analysis extended our work initially introduced in [26], where we have analyzed 6 SAS and 6 NSAS. Hence, we extended the number of analyzed systems by considering 20 from each category, all written in the Java programming language. However, one of the threats to validity may be related to the limited number of analyzed systems usually considered in other research areas. This is due to the limited number of SAS available.

Considering the results validity of the tools, we have used widely-adopted ones, such as Understand and SonarQube, or tools for which papers on the validity of their results have been published, e.g., DPDT [31] and Arcan [3,16]. From the results point of view on the detection of the design patterns, we have used DPDT, which detects 13 out of the 24 GoF's patterns. To detect all the GoF's patterns we should use various tools, because a single tool recognizes only a subset of the GoF's patterns, as far as concerns our knowledge.

Table 42. Code smells detected in NSAS software utilities.

SW UTILITIES	PdfBOX	Checkstyle	Emma	Hibernate	JUnit	Pico	Quartz	Quilt
AntiSingleton	0	0.0024	0.0588	0.0051	0.0036	0	0	0.0052
BaseClassShouldBeAbstract	0.0154	0	0	0.0017	0.0072	0	0	0
ClassDataShouldBePrivate	0	0.0024	0.0588	0.0068	0.0036	0	0.0070	0.060
ComplexClass	0.2164	0.1658	0.1776	0.2125	0.0797	0.096	0.1443	0.0782
LargeClass	0	0	0	0	0	0	0	0
LazyClass	0.0128	0.0243	0.2352	0.0153	0.0108	0.016	0.0211	0
LongMethod	0.2164	0.2268	0.2352	0.1989	0.1666	0.128	0.1478	0.2
LongParameterList	0.1932	0.0268	0.1764	0.1190	0.0036	0	0.1373	0.1478
MessageChains	0	0	0	0	0	0	0	0
RefusedParentBequest	0.0128	0	0	0	0.0036	0	0	0
SpaghettiCode	0	0.0024	0	0.0034	0.0036	0	0	0
SwissArmyKnife	0	0	0	0	0	0	0	0

Table 43. Architectural smells detected in SAS frameworks.

FRAMEWORK	ATLAS	EUREMA	FESAS	iCASA	Rainbow	StarMX
UD	0	0.0083	0.0266	0.0559	0.0005	0.0113
HL	0.0588	0.0083	0.0133	0.2727	0.0193	0.4545
CD	1.1058	0.3625	0.1333	52.804	0.5530	0.7045

Table 44. Architectural smells detected in SAS artifacts.

ARTIFACT	Adasim	DeltaIoT	Hogna	IE	JDEECo	K8-Scalar	Lotus	mRUBiS	TAS	UNDERSEA
UD	0.0156	0.0126	0.0232	0.0036	0	0.0937	0.0196	0.0243	0.0013	0.0779
HL	0.0781	0.0361	0.0116	0.0278	0	0.1875	0.0784	0.0243	0.0130	0.2337
CD	0.5384	0.4024	0.1395	0.4048	0.0036	8.2812	0.5490	0.7317	0.1241	37.428

Table 45. Architectural smells detected in SAS student projects.

STUDENT PROJECT	Code Offload	Fall Detection	Platoon Coord	Vacuum Simulator
UD	0	0.0070	0.0194	0.0074
HL	0.0650	0.0492	0.0739	0.0223
CD	1.207	0.3732	5.684	0.1716

Table 46. Architectural smells detected in NSAS parsers.

PARSER GENERATOR	ANT	ANTLR	NekoHTML	SableCC
UD	0.0062	0.0142	0	0.0040
HL	0.0062	0.0142	0.0212	0.0040
CD	0.8492	27.560	0.2340	0.1707

Table 47. Architectural smells detected in NSAS tools.

TOOL	Cobertura	DrawSWF	JGraph	JHotDraw	Marauroa	ProGuard	Sunflow	Velocity
UD	0.0058	0.0062	0.0223	0.0084	0.0143	0.0028	0.0143	0.0114
HL	0.0406	0.0373	0.0223	0.0196	0.0478	0.0198	0.0430	0.3053
CD	0.2965	1.1152	3.6592	0.7556	0.7272	0.4031	5.148	2.8167

Table 48. Architectural smells detected in NSAS software utilities.

SW UTILITY	PdfBOX	Checkstyle	Emma	Hibernate	JUnit	Pico	Quartz	Quilt
UD	0.0257	0.0073	0	0.0068	0.0108	0.004	0	0
HL	0.0412	0.0097	0	0.0238	0.0434	0.016	0.0316	0.0173
CD	2.0644	2.502	0.9411	1.3248	0.8478	0.5	0.8239	0.6086

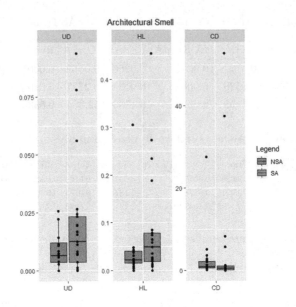

Fig. 5. Box-plot results for architectural smells.

The results may be influenced also by the NSAS analyzed projects. To limit this type of influence we have chosen systems from well-known public repositories. In addition, these NSAS projects are usually considered in studies focused on software quality assessment.

Furthermore, advanced statistical techniques may be exploited for results comparison. Here, the comparison is straightforward because of the limited number of analyzed systems.

6   Discussion and Concluding Remarks

In this section, we provide the answers to the RQ which guided our analysis and comparison and which have been mentioned in Sect. 3. Furthermore, we present our concluding remarks and future developments.

RQ1: How can SAS be evaluated in terms of software metrics? Which is the difference between SAS and NSAS based on software metrics evaluation?

Answer RQ1: We have considered two sets of software metrics, i.e., CK and RM, for the evaluation of SAS in front of NSAS. These two sets of metrics provide a complementary view on the analyzed systems.

Two of the CK metrics results, i.e., WMC and RFC are greater in SAS than in NSAS. They indicate a higher complexity in SAS than in NSAS. This results also from the values of CBO and DIT in a less significant manner than from WMC and RFC. While, NOC and LCOM have associated slightly lower values in SAS than in NSAS.

Three of the MR metrics results, i.e., CA, CE, and D (Distance from the main sequence) are very similar in SAS and NSAS. This indicates that SAS package design has minimum or non influence from the point of view of self-adaptivity. The A (Abstractness) index is lower in SAS than in NSAS and it has also low values. This indicates the use of concrete packages in SAS. The I (Instability) index is lower in SAS than in NSAS being at a half way between completely stable and completely unstable packages.

To summarize, the CK metrics capture differences between SAS and NSAS design by focusing on class level aspects, while RM metrics indicate similar results for SAS and NSAS by focusing on package level aspects. These are somehow expected results due to the nature of SAS concerning their ability to address changes at runtime.

RQ2: How can SAS be evaluated in terms of design patterns? Which is the difference in terms of design patterns presence in SAS and NSAS?

Answer RQ2: In our analysis we detected several GoF design patterns. The detection results in SAS are comparable to the results in NSAS, which in our opinion is a positive result. All the considered patterns are present both in SAS and NSAS. The most detected patterns are Singleton, Adapter, and State-Strategy both in SAS and NSAS; the less detected patterns are Prototype, Composite, Proxy, Chain of Responsibility, and Visitor both in SAS and NSAS. In SAS, more instances of creational patterns have been detected, while in NSAS more instances of structural and behavioral patterns. This result may be due also to the fact that SAS use self-adaptive specific structural and behavioral patterns, not considered in this analysis.

To summarize, the results on design patterns detection is similar in the two types of systems, with a prevalence of creational patterns in SAS.

RQ3: How can SAS be evaluated in terms of code smells? Which is the difference in terms of code smells presence in SAS and NSAS?

Answer RQ3: The results of code smell detection indicate that only 9 out of 18 considered smells have been identified in SAS, while 3 more code smells have been identified in NSAS. This is a positive result because (1) only half of the considered smells are present in SAS, and (2) in SAS were identified less different smells than in NSAS. The most present code smells in SAS are: AntiSingleton, ComplexClass, LongMethod, and LongParameterList. This may be due to the classes implementing the steps of a MAPE-K loop and being more complex with long methods and parameter lists. The less present code smells are BaseClassShouldBeAbstract, RefusedParentBequest, and SpaghettiCode.

To summarize, the results on code smells detection are comparable in SAS and NSAS and sometimes even better in SAS than in NSAS (in terms of number of different smells detected and of number of instances detected).

RQ4: How can SAS be evaluated in terms of architectural smells? Which is the difference in terms of architectural smells presence in SAS and NSAS?

Answer RQ4: We have detected all the three kinds of architectural smells both in SAS and in NSAS. There have been identified more UD and HL in SAS with respect to NSAS. Attention should be given to the possible false positives instances, that may represent not real problems to be removed in SAS.

To summarize, the SAS developers should consider the presence of the architectural smells and try to minimize their effect on the maintenance and evolution effort.

The analysis described in this paper may be useful in particular to the SAS developers who may rely on the feedback resulted from the software metrics computation to improve their solutions. In addition, they may apply the most used and appropriate GoF design patterns to implement SAS. The patterns represent also a documentation of the reasons concerning the design choices. This analysis can be also very important for the identification of the most common anomalies in the software through code smells and architectural smells. The SAS developers nay try to detect and remove them in order to avoid a progressive internal quality erosion [7], as this is usually done for NSAS. This analysis of SAS and the comparison of results with NSAS suggest that evaluation mechanisms currently used for NSAS can be successfully adopted and applied for SAS too. Further work may concern various tasks. From the software metrics points of view, the analysis may be extended to consider also software metrics defined for the evaluation of self-adaptivity (e.g., [24]).

In this analysis we have considered the design patterns defined by GoF because there is an available tool support for automating this task. There are also design patterns specifically defined for self-adaptivity. However, currently their automatic detection is not supported by tools, as far as concerns our knowledge. A possible future work may concern the detection of self-adaptive specific design patterns as well as other GoF's patterns not detectable through DPDT.

Moreover, we plan to analyze how the refactoring of the different kinds of smells, at code and architectural level, can impact on a set of software quality metrics. In addition, a future work will concern the identification of smells or anti-patterns specific to SAS.

References

1. Arcelli Fontana, F., Maggioni, S., Raibulet, C.: Understanding the relevance of micro-structures for design patterns detection. J. Syst. Softw. **84**(12), 2334–2347 (2011). https://doi.org/10.1016/j.jss.2011.07.006
2. Arcelli Fontana, F., Maggioni, S., Raibulet, C.: Design patterns: a survey on their micro-structures. J. Softw.: Evol. Process **25**(1), 27–52 (2013). https://doi.org/10.1002/smr.547
3. Arcelli Fontana, F., Pigazzini, I., Roveda, R., Tamburri, D.A., Zanoni, M., Nitto, E.D.: Arcan: a tool for architectural smells detection. In: International Conference on Software Architecture Workshops, Sweden, 5–7 April 2017, pp. 282–285 (2017). https://doi.org/10.1109/ICSAW.2017.16

4. Arcoverde, R., Garcia, A., Figueiredo, E.: Understanding the longevity of code smells: preliminary results of an explanatory survey. In: Fourth Workshop on Refactoring Tools 2011, WRT 2011, Honolulu, USA, pp. 33–36 (2011). https://doi.org/10.1145/1984732.1984740

5. Chatzigeorgiou, A., Manakos, A.: Investigating the evolution of bad smells in object-oriented code. In: 2010 Seventh International Conference on the Quality of Information and Communications Technology, pp. 106–115. IEEE (2010). https://doi.org/10.1109/QUATIC.2010.16

6. Chidamber, S.R., Kemerer, C.F.: Towards a metrics suite for object oriented design. In: Paepcke, A. (ed.) Conference on Object-Oriented Programming Systems, Languages, and Applications (OOPSLA 1991), Sixth Annual Conference, Phoenix, Arizona, USA, 6–11 October 1991, Proceedings, pp. 197–211. ACM (1991). https://doi.org/10.1145/117954.117970

7. Fontana, F.A., Roveda, R., Zanoni, M., Raibulet, C., Capilla, R.: An experience report on detecting and repairing software architecture erosion. In: 13th Working IEEE/IFIP Conference on Software Architecture, WICSA 2016, Venice, Italy, 5–8 April 2016, pp. 21–30. IEEE Computer Society (2016). https://doi.org/10.1109/WICSA.2016.37

8. Fowler, M.: Refactoring: Improving the Design of Existing Code. Addison-Wesley, Boston (1999)

9. Gamma, E., Helm, R., Johnson, R.E., Vlissides, J.M.: Design Patterns: Elements of Reusable Object-Oriented Software. Addison-Wesley, Boston (1994)

10. Garcia, J., Popescu, D., Edwards, G., Medvidovic, N.: Identifying architectural bad smells. In: CSMR 2009. pp. 255–258. IEEE, Germany (2009). https://doi.org/10.1109/CSMR.2009.59

11. Kozik, R., Choraś, M., Puchalski, D., Renk, R.: Platform for software quality and dependability data analysis. In: Zamojski, W., Mazurkiewicz, J., Sugier, J., Walkowiak, T., Kacprzyk, J. (eds.) DepCoS-RELCOMEX 2018. AISC, vol. 761, pp. 306–315. Springer, Cham (2019). https://doi.org/10.1007/978-3-319-91446-6_29

12. Krupitzer, C., Roth, F.M., VanSyckel, S., Schiele, G., Becker, C.: A survey on engineering approaches for self-adaptive systems. Pervasive Mob. Comput. **17**, 184–206 (2015). https://doi.org/10.1016/j.pmcj.2014.09.009

13. Le, D.M., Behnamghader, P., Garcia, J., Link, D., Shahbazian, A., Medvidovic, N.: An empirical study of architectural change in open-source software systems. In: 2015 IEEE/ACM 12th Working Conference on Mining Software Repositories, pp. 235–245 (2015). https://doi.org/10.1109/MSR.2015.29

14. Macia, I., Arcoverde, R., Cirilo, E., Garcia, A., von Staa, A.: Supporting the identification of architecturally-relevant code anomalies. In: Proceedings of 28th IEEE International Conference on Software Maintenance (ICSM 2012). IEEE, Trento (2012). https://doi.org/10.1109/ICSM.2012.6405348

15. Martin, R.: OO design quality metrics: an analysis of dependencies (1994). http://gerritbeine.de/assets/downloads/OODesignQualityMetrics-Martin,RobertC_.pdf. Accessed Sept 2020

16. Martini, A., Fontana, F.A., Biaggi, A., Roveda, R.: Identifying and prioritizing architectural debt through architectural smells: a case study in a large software company. In: Cuesta, C.E., Garlan, D., Pérez, J. (eds.) ECSA 2018. LNCS, vol. 11048, pp. 320–335. Springer, Cham (2018). https://doi.org/10.1007/978-3-030-00761-4_21

17. de Normalisation O.I.: ISO/IEC 25010:2011, systems and software engineering - systems and software quality requirements and evaluation (square) - system and software quality models (2017)

18. Olbrich, S., Cruzes, D.S., Basili, V., Zazworka, N.: The evolution and impact of code smells: a case study of two open source systems. In: 2009 3rd International Symposium on Empirical Software Engineering and Measurement, pp. 390–400 (2009). https://doi.org/10.1109/ESEM.2009.5314231

19. Peters, R., Zaidman, A.: Evaluating the lifespan of code smells using software repository mining. In: 16th European Conference on Software Maintenance and Reengineering, pp. 411–416. IEEE (2012). https://doi.org/10.1109/CSMR.2012.79

20. Pettersson, N., Löwe, W., Nivre, J.: Evaluation of accuracy in design pattern occurrence detection. IEEE Trans. Softw. Eng. **36**(4), 575–590 (2010). https://doi.org/10.1109/TSE.2009.92

21. Raemaekers, S., van Deursen, A., Visser, J.: The maven repository dataset of metrics, changes, and dependencies. In: Zimmermann, T., Penta, M.D., Kim, S. (eds.) Proceedings of the 10th Working Conference on Mining Software Repositories, MSR 2013, San Francisco, CA, USA, 18–19 May 2013, pp. 221–224. IEEE Computer Society (2013). https://doi.org/10.1109/MSR.2013.6624031

22. Raibulet, C.: Facets of adaptivity. In: Morrison, R., Balasubramaniam, D., Falkner, K. (eds.) ECSA 2008. LNCS, vol. 5292, pp. 342–345. Springer, Heidelberg (2008). https://doi.org/10.1007/978-3-540-88030-1_33

23. Raibulet, C., Arcelli Fontana, F.: Evaluation of self-adaptive systems: a women perspective. In: 11th European Conference on Software Architecture, UK, 11–15 September 2017, pp. 23–30 (2017). https://doi.org/10.1145/3129790.3129825

24. Raibulet, C., Arcelli Fontana, F.: Collaborative and teamwork software development in an undergraduate software engineering course. J. Syst. Softw. **144**, 409–422 (2018). https://doi.org/10.1016/j.jss.2018.07.010

25. Raibulet, C., Arcelli Fontana, F., Carettoni, S.: A preliminary analysis and comparison of self-adaptive systems according to different issues. Softw. Qual. J. **28**, 1213–1243 (2020). https://doi.org/10.1007/s11219-020-09502-5

26. Raibulet, C., Fontana, F.A., Carettoni, S.: SAS vs. NSAS: analysis and comparison of self-adaptive systems and non-self-adaptive systems based on smells and patterns. In: Ali, R., Kaindl, H., Maciaszek, L.A. (eds.) Proceedings of the 15th International Conference on Evaluation of Novel Approaches to Software Engineering, ENASE 2020, Prague, Czech Republic, 5–6 May 2020, pp. 490–497. SCITEPRESS (2020). https://doi.org/10.5220/0009513504900497

27. Ramirez, A.J., Cheng, B.H.C.: Design patterns for developing dynamically adaptive systems. In: ICSE Workshop on Software Engineering for Adaptive and Self-Managing Systems, South Africa, pp. 49–58 (2010). https://doi.org/10.1145/1808984.1808990

28. Romano, D., Raila, P., Pinzger, M., Khomh, F.: Analyzing the impact of antipatterns on change-proneness using fine-grained source code changes. In: Proc. 19th Working Conference on Reverse Engineering (WCRE 2012), pp. 437–446. IEEE, Canada (2012). https://doi.org/10.1109/WCRE.2012.53

29. Suryanarayana, G., Samarthyam, G., Sharma, T.: Refactoring for Software Design Smells, 1 edn. Morgan Kaufmann, Burlington (2015)

30. Tempero, E.D., et al.: The qualitas corpus: a curated collection of java code for empirical studies. In: Han, J., Thu, T.D. (eds.) 17th Asia Pacific Software Engineering Conference, APSEC 2010, Sydney, Australia, 30 November–3 December 2010, pp. 336–345. IEEE Computer Society (2010). https://doi.org/10.1109/APSEC.2010.46

31. Tsantalis, N., Chatzigeorgiou, A., Stephanides, G., Halkidis, S.T.: Design pattern detection using similarity scoring. IEEE Trans. Softw. Eng. **32**(11), 896–909 (2006). https://doi.org/10.1109/TSE.2006.112
32. Walter, B., Alkhaeir, T.: The relationship between design patterns and code smells: an exploratory study. Inf. Softw. Technol. **74**, 127–142 (2016). https://doi.org/10.1016/j.infsof.2016.02.003
33. Weyns, D.: Software engineering of self-adaptive systems. In: Cha, S., Taylor, R., Kang, K. (eds.) Handbook of Software Engineering, pp. 399–443. Springer, Cham (2019). https://doi.org/10.1007/978-3-030-00262-6_11

A Workflow for Automatic Code Generation of Safety Mechanisms via Model-Driven Development

Lars Huning[✉], Padma Iyenghar, and Elke Pulvermüller

Institute of Computer Science, University of Osnabrück, Wachsbleiche 27,
49090 Osnabrück, Germany
{lhuning,piyengha,epulverm}@uni-osnabrueck.de

Abstract. Due to the increasing size and complexity of embedded systems, software quality is gaining importance in such systems. This is especially true in safety-critical systems, where failure may lead to serious harm for humans or the environment. Model-Driven Development (MDD) techniques, such as model representation with semi-formal design languages and automatic code generation from such models may increase software quality and developer productivity. This paper introduces a workflow for automatically generating safety mechanisms from model representations. In summary, safety mechanisms are specified in class diagrams of the Unified Modeling Language (UML) via stereotypes alongside the remainder of the application. In a subsequent step, these model representations are used to perform model-to-model transformations. The resulting model contains all the information required to automatically generate source code for the application, including the specified safety mechanisms. Then, common MDD tools may be used to generate this productive source code. We demonstrate the application of our workflow by applying it to the automatic code generation of timing constraint monitoring at runtime.

Keywords: Code generation · Embedded software engineering · Embedded systems · Functional safety · Model-driven development

1 Introduction

The size and complexity of embedded software systems is increasing steadily [39]. This trend affects the software quality of the developed systems, e.g., because the complexity makes the system harder to understand or because the increased size leads to more programming errors. A potential solution for dealing with the increasing complexity of systems is the use of semi-formal design languages, such as Unified Modeling Language (UML) [14,15]. The number of programming errors may be reduced by automatic code generation features. This also has the advantage of increasing developer productivity, thus reducing the total costs of the developed systems. Both techniques, semi-formal design languages

© Springer Nature Switzerland AG 2021
R. Ali et al. (Eds.): ENASE 2020, CCIS 1375, pp. 420–443, 2021.
https://doi.org/10.1007/978-3-030-70006-5_17

and automatic code generation, are part of Model-Driven Development (MDD). This development paradigm promotes the use of models as central artifacts in the development process. Such models may be specified with the aforementioned semi-formal design languages. Furthermore, if the level of detail in the models is sufficient, productive source code may be generated automatically from these models. This paper introduces a workflow to model software safety mechanisms in a semi-formal design language and to automatically generate productive source code from these model representations in a subsequent step.

As described above, the usage of semi-formal design languages and automatic code generation may increase software quality. Furthermore, software safety mechanisms may also contribute to software quality. In the context of safety-critical systems, which are a category of systems whose failure may harm humans or the environment [35], the use of specific safety mechanisms to mitigate potential hazards is even required [19]. These requirements are described in safety standards, such as IEC 61508 [19] or ISO 26262 [20]. In many safety-critical domains, certification for the domain-relevant safety standard is required for admission to market. Modeling and automatic code generation of safety mechanisms, as proposed by our approach, may contribute to meet the requirements of these safety standards. Furthermore, the two key concepts of our approach, the use of semi-formal design languages and automatic code generation, are also encouraged by the safety standard IEC 61508 [19], which is a generic safety standard for electrical/electronic/programmable electronic safety-related systems.

In summary, our approach consists of the following steps: Developers create an application model of their system with UML. Afterwards, they apply a set of stereotypes to their application. These stereotypes model safety mechanisms from IEC 61508 or another relevant safety standard. These model representations are parsed in a subsequent step. The obtained information serves as the input to model-to-model transformations. The resulting model, which we call *intermediate* model in this paper, contains UML model elements for the safety mechanisms that were specified via the respective stereotypes. We use statecharts and opaque behavior for the generated safety mechanisms to capture the required amount of detail, so that common MDD tools, such as IBM Rational Rhapsody [32] or Enterprise Architect [9], may be used to generate productive source code from the intermediate model. This paper does not only describe the above process in detail, but also provides guidelines on how to represent safety mechanisms via UML stereotypes and how to generate code for these mechanisms efficiently. Last but not least, we also provide a generic workflow for the model transformation process for the safety mechanisms.

This paper is an extended version of a previously published paper [18]. It provides a more in-depth discussion of the workflow initially conceived in [18]. Furthermore, it presents a novel, non-trivial application of this workflow by presenting an approach to the automatic code generation of timing constraint monitoring via MDD.

The remainder of this paper is organized as follows: Sect. 2 presents some background regarding the development lifecycle of safety-critical systems and code generation via MDD. Afterwards, we present an extended discussion of the workflow initially described in [18] in Sect. 3. In Sect. 4 we present a novel application of this workflow for the automatic code generation of timing constraint monitoring mechanisms via MDD. Sections 5 presents an updated version of related work compared to the initially published paper [18]. Section 6 concludes this paper and presents future work.

2   Background

This section provides some background knowledge regarding the development of safety-critical systems relevant to our approach. In these systems, safety is a nonfunctional quality requirement. First, we discuss the IEC 61508 lifecycle in order to show in which development context our approach is located (cf. Sect. 2.1). Afterwards, we discuss code generation within MDD and on which technologies our approach depends (cf. Sect. 2.2).

2.1   IEC 61508 Lifecycle

IEC 61508 is a safety standard for "Functional safety of electrical/electronic/ programmable electronic safety-related systems" [19]. The terms *electrical/ electronic/programmable electronic* are often abbreviated as *E/E/PE*. IEC 61508 is the basis for many domain specific safety standards, such as ISO26262 in the automotive domain. As our approach is not limited to any specific domain, we choose the safety recommendations of IEC 61508 as the basis for our work.

IEC 61508 defines a safety lifecycle for safety-related systems, which is illustrated in Fig. 1. The steps 1–5 are concerned with the overall safety of the systems, not yet limited to E/E/PE aspects. For example, they may also consider mechanical safety aspects. At the end of step 5, a safety requirements allocation exists that describes which safety aspects are covered by which parts of the developed system. This is used in step 9, which explicitly formulates the safety requirements for the E/E/PE system. Based on these requirements, the E/E/PE system is realized in step 10. Steps 6–8 are executed in parallel to steps 9 and 10. They are concerned with planning further aspects of the lifecycle, e.g., validation and maintenance of the system. The results of this planning are used in steps 12–14, in which the system is installed, validated and subsequently maintained. Step 15 foresees the potential modification of the system after it is in use. The safety lifecycle ends with step 16, in which the system is decommissioned.

The contributions of this paper are conceptually located in step 10 of the safety lifecycle, i.e., during the realization of the E/E/PE system. We assume that a (correct) safety requirements specification related to the E/E/PE system exists (step 9 of the lifecylce). This safety requirements specification contains a set of safety mechanisms that are to be included within the final application. Our approach enables developers to model the safety mechanisms via UML and automatically generate the source code for these safety mechanisms afterwards. This may decrease the number of manual implementation errors and provide productivity gains.

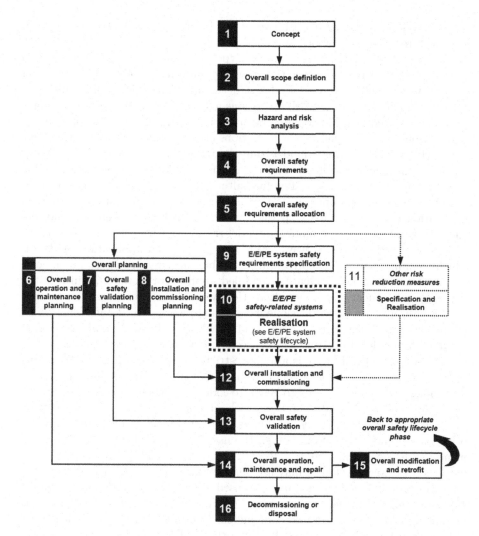

Fig. 1. Safety lifecycle of IEC-61508 [19]. The dotted box around step 10 was added and indicates in which step of the safety-lifecycle this paper is conceptually located.

2.2   Model-Driven Development

There exist integrated development environments that allow for the creation of UML models and subsequent code generation from these models, e.g., [9, 28,32]. Most of these tools are capable of generating code for UML elements that have a 1:1 mapping in object-oriented programming languages, e.g., classes. Some of them also provide the ability to generate code for UML diagrams and elements where such a 1:1 mapping does not exist. For example, [32] allows the code generation from statecharts by introducing a suitable framework for that purpose. Our approach builds upon these tools and assumes that they are used by the developers. We distinguish two types of usages of these MDD tools, both of which are supported by our approach.

The first type of usage is a "pure" type of usage of the MDD tools. The entire application is modeled within the tool and all source code is generated directly from the tool. This includes structural and behavioral diagrams. The opaque behavior feature of UML operations allows developers to write any manual code they require. This opaque behavior is then automatically copy-pasted into the source code of the specific operations that are generated by the tool. Our approach (cf. Sect. 3.1) uses model-to-model transformations in order to generate safety mechanisms. For this first type of usage, these model transformations may be applied in two ways. The first alternative is to execute the model-to-model transformations once on the developer model A and obtain a modified application model B with which the developers work from then on. The second alternative is that the model-to-model transformations are executed before each code generation. This way, developers work on an application model A, which contains the model representation of the safety mechanisms. The model-to-model transformations create a modified application model B, which is the input for subsequent code generation. However, as the transformation from A to B is entirely automatic, developers continue to work with the model A. Both approaches have their merits and depend on whether the additional abstraction provided by model A over model B is seen as benefit by the developers.

The second type of usage is a more restricted use of the MDD tools. In this scenario, only a structural model of the application, i.e., a class diagram, is created. The MDD tools are used to generate code skeletons from this UML model, i.e., classes, variables and operations without implementation. The implementation is written manually by developers in a subsequent step and may involve other development technologies, e.g., the use of text-based integrated development environments like Eclipse IDE [37]. For this second type of usage, there is only one way how developers may use our approach. The model-to-model transformations described in this paper are used to create a modified UML model B that includes the safety mechanisms. Afterwards, code is generated from this modified model. This generated code includes the safety mechanisms that have previously been added to the model B via the model-to-model transformations. Thus, the developers may start their manual implementation not only with a code skeleton of the classes, attributes and operations, but also with the safety mechanisms already implemented for them.

3   Workflow

This section first describes a high-level overview of the approach presented in this paper (cf. Sect. 3.1). Afterwards, the approach itself is described in Sect. 3.2.

3.1   High-Level Overview of the Approach

This section presents the high-level concept of our approach to preserve the non-functional requirement "safety". We also show, how this approach may be applied to the development of a fire detection system. Figure 2(a) shows the generalized concept of our approach, while Fig. 2(b) shows how this concept is applied to the fire detection system.

Step (A1) of Fig. 2(a) marks the start of our approach, in which a UML model of the system is realized on the basis of the functional requirements specification. In step (B1) of Fig. 2(b) we show a simplified version of this model for a fire detection system. For the purpose of illustration, the fire detection example is extremely simplified. It consists of a single class with a `smokeThreshold` variable that represents the maximum carbon monoxide concentration in the air before the system sounds an alarm. The `checkFire()` method is used to periodically measure the carbon monoxide concentration and raise an alarm if the measured value is greater than `smokeThreshold`. This model contains the functional features of the fire detection system, i.e., measuring the carbon monoxide concentration and raising an alarm when appropriate. However, it does not contain any specific safety mechanisms yet. The specification of such safety mechanisms is added in step (A2) of Fig. 2(a), in which appropriate stereotypes are added to the UML model based on the safety requirements specification. Step (B2) of Fig. 2(b) shows an example for one such stereotype. A mechanism for timing constraint monitoring is added to the `checkFire()` operation by applying the <<TimingMonitoring>> stereotype to the operation. This stereotype models that the `checkFire()` operation has to execute within a certain time frame, e.g., one second. If the operation executes for longer than this time frame, an error in the system is likely and thus the system should give an appropriate warning, e.g., a maintenance tone. For example, such errors may be programming errors leading to infinite loops or malfunctioning sensors that temporarily block the execution thread, as no data can be read.

After the safety mechanisms have been specified in the UML model, these features may be automatically realized via model-to-model transformations, resulting in an intermediate model that contains these features (step (A3) of Fig. 2(a)). The specific structure of the intermediate model depends on the safety mechanism that is realized. Step (B3) of Fig. 2(b) shows an example for the timing check safety mechanism. The fire detection class contains a composition to a `TimingMonitoringWatchdog` class, which is responsible for checking the execution duration of the `checkFire()` method. The details of this approach are explained in Sect. 4. As the intermediate model already contains all required safety mechanisms, automatic code generation mechanisms from existing MDD tools, such as [9, 28, 32] may be employed to generate corresponding source code (cf. steps (A4) and (B4) of Fig. 2). Finally, this generated source code may be translated into binary code by employing a suitable compiler. Depending on the realized safety mechanism, additional source code for the safety mechanism may need to be linked (cf. steps (A5) and (B5) of Fig. 2).

3.2 Enabling the Automatic Code Generation of Safety Mechanisms

While Sect. 3.1 gives an overview of how our approach is intended to be used, this section describes how to model safety mechanisms and generate code from

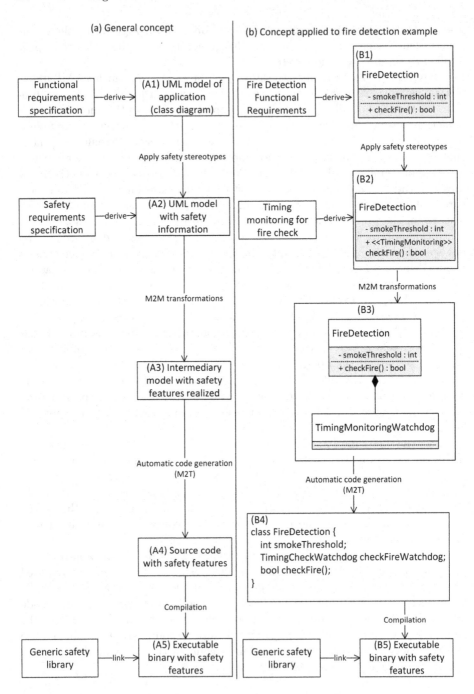

Fig. 2. High-level concept of the proposed approach for the generation of safety mechanisms via MDD. Vertical arrows show transitions from one code generation step to another. Horizontal arrows indicate the use of additional, external elements that are not part of the application model.

these model representations. For this, we present a workflow in Fig. 3 that has previously been presented in the original conference paper [18]. In the beginning (cf. action 1 in Fig. 3), a safety mechanism has to be identified for modeling and automatic code generation. Once such a safety mechanism has been found, existing model representations and software architectures for the mechanism may be researched (cf. action 2 in Fig. 3). Based on the acquired information model representations and software architectures may be adapted for the purpose of automatic code generation (cf. action 3 and 4 in Fig. 3). These two actions may be carried out concurrently, as the software architecture may influence the model representation and vice versa. Finally, a set of model-to-model transformations is required that receive the model representation of the safety mechanism as the input and produce the intermediate model with all the required safety elements as the output (cf. action 5 in Fig. 3). In the following, we discuss each of these steps in detail.

Action 1: Identify a Safety Mechanism. In action 1 of Fig. 3, a safety mechanism suitable for automatic code generation has to be identified. Such safety mechanisms may be identified during industry collaboration, i.e., safety mechanisms designed to prevent a specific hazard inside an application. Some classes of hazards and their corresponding safety mechanisms are well known. These mechanisms are actively encouraged or even mandated by safety standards, e.g., IEC 61508. Therefore, safety standards may be another source of information for finding potential safety mechanisms.

Last but not least, the literature on safety is steadily evolving. Some approaches, such as [34], already describe safety mechanisms and their possible software architectures, but do not present an approach to modeling and/or automatic code generation. Therefore, these approaches are another source for enabling modeling and automatic code generation of safety mechanisms.

Action 2: Gather Relevant Information. In the second action of Fig. 3, knowledge about the safety mechanism identified in action 1 has to be gathered. At a high-level, this includes existing model representations and software architectures of the mechanism. Even if these existing representations are unsuited for automatic code generation, they may serve as a basis for actions 3 and 4 of Fig. 3.

At a more fine-grained level, this includes detecting the configuration parameters of the safety mechanism. As these may change between different applications, it is important that these values are known and considered during the design of the model representation (cf. action 3 of Fig. 3).

Besides configuration parameters, there may also be several safety mechanisms that are similar to the one selected. For example, there exist different types of voting approaches that differ only in their specific method of voting [18]. The general process, however, i.e., multiple input sources being voted on and producing one output, is the same. Thus such related approaches may also be

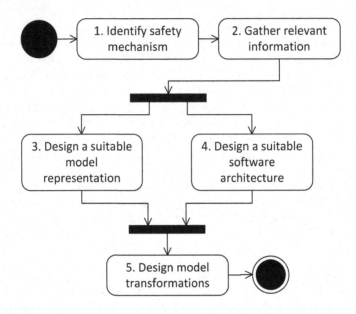

Fig. 3. UML 2.5 activity diagram showing a workflow for providing automatic code generation of safety mechanisms based on UML stereotypes. This figure is taken from the initial publication [18].

considered during the design of the model representation and software architecture (cf. actions 3 and 4 of Fig. 3).

Action 3: Design a Suitable Model Representation. In the third action of Fig. 3, a suitable model representation for the safety mechanism has to be found. This model representation has to enable a level of detail that enables the automatic code generation. In this paper, we focus on model representations based on UML stereotypes.

For a model representation of a safety mechanism based on UML stereotypes, a suitable UML model element needs to be identified to which the stereotype may be applied. As a rule of thumb, the UML model element that should be protected by the safety mechanism is a good candidate for this. For example, [16] applies stereotypes to attributes for a safety mechanism that protects these attributes from spontaneous bit-flips. Another example is shown in Sect. 4, where operations should be protected. There, the stereotype is applied to the operation that should be protected.

Configuration parameters for the safety mechanism may usually be represented as key-value pairs via the tagged values of the stereotype. However, for some safety mechanisms, this is not sufficient. This is the case when the safety mechanism depends on multiple input sources and where each input source may have its own configuration values. In this case, a second stereotype that is applied to each input source may be necessary. An example for this is the voting mechanism described in [18], where a second stereotype is applied to the associations between a voter class and the input classes for the voting process.

In case a safety mechanism exists in a group of related approaches that differ not only in their configuration values, but also in the number of parameters, stereotype inheritance may be used to represent these variants. An example for this is shown in Sect. 4.

All stereotypes that are part of the model representation may be grouped in an appropriate UML profile.

Action 4: Design a Suitable Software Architecture. In the fourth action of Fig. 3, a suitable software architecture for the safety mechanism has to be found. In the context of this paper, this means that the software architecture has to be suitable for automatic code generation. This includes several key points that have to be taken into consideration:

No Manual Developer Actions Required: In order to keep the code generation truly automatic, no manual developer actions should be required besides applying the stereotype that represents the safety mechanism. If this is not possible, e.g., due to inherent application-specific characteristics of the safety mechanism, the number of manual developer actions for code generation should be minimized.

Localized Changes: The model transformations in action 5 of Fig. 3 change the application model. In general, a single change may result in a large number of subsequent additional changes that need to be performed. For example, if the number of constructor parameters of a class x is changed, the entire application model has to be scanned for invocations of this constructor and the additional parameters need to be added to the constructor invocation. This might entail even more changes, as the constructor parameters for x might have to be initialized by the instantiating class y. Such chains of changes quickly become difficult to manage. Therefore, it is important that the software architecture for the safety mechanism is as localized as possible, i.e., avoids such chains of changes.

Low Overhead: Safety-critical systems often operate in the context of embedded systems. In these systems runtime and memory constraints are a common requirement. Therefore, the software architecture should minimize the overhead the safety mechanism imposes on runtime and memory.

Programming Standards in Safety Domains: Due to the nature of the safety mechanisms, the software architecture should respect programming standards intended for safety-critical domains. For example, the MISRA[1]-C++ standard [24], prohibits the use of dynamic heap memory allocation, which has consequences for the software architecture.

---

[1] Motor Industry Software Reliability Association.

Action 5: Design Model Transformations. In the fifth and final action of Fig. 3, model-to-model transformations have to be designed. The input of these transformations is the model representation designed in action 3 of Fig. 3 and the output is the software architecture designed in action 4 of Fig. 3. These model transformations may be implemented in an extensible manner, so that new variants of the safety mechanism may easily be integrated into the approach. This may be achieved by dividing the transformation process into two steps. In the first step, the information from the stereotype in the models is parsed and stored temporarily. In the second step, an interface is used to actually transform the model with the parsed information. New variants may be added as realizations of this interface.

Another aspect of the model transformations is their scalability. For example, the configuration parameters of the safety mechanism are modeled by the UML stereotype, i.e., they are known at compile time. As the constructor of the transformed class should not be changed (cf. description of action 4), this leaves two alternatives for the realization of the parameters in source code. The first is the use of constant member variables within a class that represent the configuration values. The second alternative is the use of template classes and specifying the configuration values as template parameters. The first alternative requires the creation of a new class in the model for each set of unique configuration parameters for the safety mechanism. The second alternative, on the other hand, only requires the creation of a single template class during model transformation. The different template instantiations are later inserted by the compiler. Thus, the template alternative performs fewer steps in code generation and therefore results in a lower execution time for the model transformations.

From a theoretical perspective, the model transformations should require a linear runtime, depending on the number of elements within the UML application model. This runtime occurs, because in the beginning of the model transformations, each model element has to be checked for whether it contains a relevant safety stereotype. Then, a usually fixed number of modifications are performed on the identified model elements. These theoretical observations have been supported by experimental measurements in the original paper [18], which we omit to reproduce due to space constraints.

4   Application Example: Generation of Timing Constraint Monitoring Mechanisms

This section applies the workflow presented in Sect. 3.2 to enable the model-driven code generation for timing constraint monitoring during runtime. The structure of this section resembles the workflow steps described in Sect. 3.2.

4.1   Need for Timing Constraint Monitoring at Runtime

Some safety-critical applications have to react to external events within a certain time frame to ensure safety, e.g., the brakes within a car [22,23]. Because timing is such an issue within safety-critical embedded systems, the timing behavior of the system is often modeled and analyzed in early design phases [21,22]. These analyses aim to ensure that the finished application satisfies the timing constraints. However, due to the uncertainty of the operating environment, some authors argue that runtime monitoring of these timing constraints is also required [1,26]. While these authors represent their own approach to monitoring timing constraints, they either provide no integration in a MDD process [1,26] or only consider animation and not the generation of productive source code [7]. Thus, an automated approach for the generation of timing constraint monitoring that is integrated within a MDD process is a research gap.

4.2 Information on Timing Constraint Monitoring

As timing is an important issue in many safety-critical embedded systems, many approaches to timing analysis during the system design phase exist. There are multiple modeling languages for timing analysis, e.g., [2,27] and (semi-) automated approaches for creating timing analysis models, e.g., [18,21]. While these approaches have their relevance in the whole development process, they are not intended for modeling additional timing checks during runtime. This is also reflected by the modeling overhead of approaches such as [2,27], which require extensive modeling of certain timing characteristics. For their intended purpose, i.e., timing analysis before the system is actually fully developed, this is a good approach. However, for the purpose of only modeling timing constraints that should be observed during runtime, these modeling languages contain unnecessary complexity. Therefore, a reduced model representation for timing constraints, without this unnecessary complexity, is beneficial (cf. Sect. 4.3).

On the software architecture level, several approaches for the monitoring of timing constraints during runtime have been proposed. A survey of these approaches has been published in [1]. These approaches may serve as inspiration for the software architecture designed in Sect. 4.4.

Another relevant issue for monitoring timing constraints during runtime is during which points in time the timing should be monitored. In timing analysis, an end-to-end execution path of the software refers to the chain of system activities in between obtaining a sensor input and executing an according response with an actuator. Such an execution path may consist of several tasks, which in turn may consist of several runnables. Runnables may be mapped directly to executable elements of the software source code, i.e., methods (operations) of classes [21]. This direct mapping facilitates automatic code generation, thus, we choose to provide runtime monitors for the timing constraints of individual runnables. While this does not consider latencies between the execution of runnables and other timing effects, our approach still detects when an individual runnable violates its timing constraints. Future work could extend our approach to include monitoring of task elements and execution paths.

4.3   A Model Representation for Timing Constraint Monitoring

This section presents a UML profile for modeling the runtime monitoring of timing constraints. The profile is shown in Fig. 4. A top-level stereotype (<<TimingMonitoring>>) contains relevant information that is focused on the timing constraint itself. These include the maximum time limit before the operation has failed its timing constraint, as well as the unit in which this time is specified. Additionally, developers may also specify the name of an operation that is invoked for error handling in case a timing constraint has been violated.

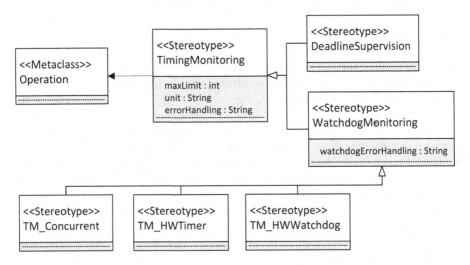

Fig. 4. UML 2.5 profile for modeling runtime monitoring mechanisms of timing constraints.

The stereotypes that represent the different monitoring mechanisms extend the <<TimingMonitoring>> stereotype. This differentiates the monitoring mechanisms at the model-level, while allowing mechanism-specific tagged values to be included. We identify four different monitoring mechanisms to observe timing constraints of operations during runtime. These include classic deadline supervision that checks whether the timing constraint has been met only after the operation has ended (<<DeadlineSupervision>>), as well as watchdog-inspired mechanisms that may generate an alarm as soon as a timing constraint has been violated, even if the monitored operation is not yet finished. These watchdog-inspired mechanisms inherit from the <<Watchdog-Monitoring>> stereotype. They differ in their preconditions and probe overhead. They are based on threads (<<TM_Concurrent>>), hardware timers and interrupts (<<TM_HWTimer>>), as well as dedicated watchdog hardware (<<TM_HWWatchdog>>). The <<WatchdogMonitoring>> stereotype has an additional tagged value, which is a second error handling mechanism. The need for this additional error handling mechanism is further explained in Sect. 4.4.

4.4   A Model-Driven Software Architecture for Monitoring Timing Constraints at Runtime

This section describes a software architecture that is suited for the automatic code generation of the timing monitoring mechanisms modeled in Sect. 4.3. Here, we differentiate between the relatively simple deadline supervision and the more complex watchdog variants. The basis for the software architecture in both cases is a UML class with an operation that has been stereotyped with one of the stereotypes from the profile presented in Fig. 4. Additionally, the class may contain a method for error handling. Naturally, the class may contain other attributes and operations that are independent of our approach but relevant for the application logic. Figure 5 shows a UML class diagram of this basis. Representative for the timing monitoring stereotypes from the profile shown in Fig. 4, the <<DeadlineSupervision>> stereotype is applied to the checkFire() method. An annotation shows the tagged values for the stereotypes, e.g., that the checkFire() method has to finish its execution within 1000 ms. The operation errorHandlingOp is to be invoked in case this timing constraint is not met.

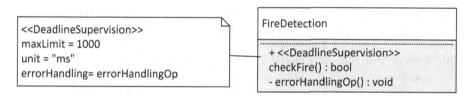

Fig. 5. UML 2.5 class diagram showing the model of the protected operation, before code generation is applied.

Software Architecture for Deadline Supervision. Adding deadline supervision to an operation is relatively straightforward. This is shown in Fig. 6, where Fig. 6 (a) shows the original operation body and Fig. 6 (b) shows the modified operation body after code generation. At the beginning of the operation body, the current time is measured and stored temporarily. At the end of the operation, just before the return statement, the current time is measured again. Now, the execution time of the operation may be calculated and the error handling operation may be executed in case the timing constraint has been violated.

This approach assumes a single return statement within the operation. This is in line with programming standards such as MISRA C++ [24]. However, multiple return statements may also be accommodated by our approach, by inserting the relevant code lines before every return statement within the operation.

```
checkFire(){

    /*
     * User-defined operation body
     */

    return;
}
```

```
checkFire(){
    startTime = systemTime();

    /*
     * User-defined operation body
     */

    endTime = systemTime();
    if(endTime - startTime > maxTimeLimit){
        errorHandlingOp();
    }
    return;
}
```

(a) Operation as
defined by user

(b) Operation after code
generation

Fig. 6. Pseudocode for the body of the protected operation before code generation (a) and after code generation (b). The highlighted code in (b) has been added automatically during code generation.

Software Architecture for Watchdog Mechanisms. Generating code for the watchdog variants of our approach is more complex than the deadline supervision described above, as the method of starting and stopping the watchdog may be dependent on system hardware. For example, the concurrent watchdog shown in Fig. 4 requires the use of different thread classes, depending on the operating system. For the <<TM_HWTimer>> variant, the application programming interface (API) for invoking interrupts and working with timers may differ between different microcontrollers. Furthermore, the <<TM_HWWatchdog>> stereotype requires different method calls for individual controllers, as the hardware watchdog requires a method of address unique to the controller.

In order to deal with this type of variability, we introduce the TimingMonitoringWatchdog interface. A realization of this interface is automatically added to the class with the protected operation during code generation. This status after code generation is shown in Fig. 7. The concurrent version of the watchdog is used as a representative. The interface contains a method for starting and stopping the watchdog. The specific implementation of how to start and stop the watchdog, is left to the realizations of this interface.

While the interface realizations of TimingMonoitoringWatchdog may be implemented anew for each application, they may also make use of abstraction mechanisms to be usable on several systems. For example, in our implementation of the concurrent watchdog (<<TM_Concurrent>> in Fig. 4), we use the thread abstraction provided by the MDD tool IBM Rational Rhapsody [32] to keep the implementation operating system independent (provided Rhapsody contains a thread abstraction for this operating system). A similar abstraction may be found for the watchdog that makes use of timers and interrupts (<<TM_HWTimer>> in Fig. 4). For this variant, hardware abstraction layers may be used to implement this watchdog for a broad range of different microcontrollers. In theory, this approach is also applicable to the hardware

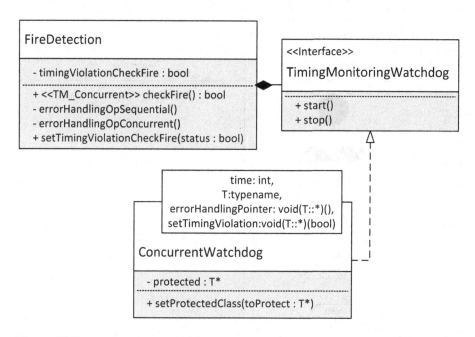

Fig. 7. UML 2.5 class diagram of the watchdog code generation. The attributes and operations are discussed in Sect. 4.5.

watchdog variant (<<TM_HWWatchdog>> in Fig. 4). However, the variability between the hardware watchdogs between different microcontrollers is larger than for timers and interrupts. Therefore, such a hardware abstraction layer may be harder to create (and to the best of the authors' knowledge, does not exist at the time this paper is written).

Runtime Behavior of the Software Architecture for Watchdog Mechanisms. The runtime behavior of the generated watchdog classes is shown in Fig. 8 for the case of a single protected operation. Initially, the program runs in its main thread (action 1 in Fig. 8). At the same time, the watchdog waits for its activation (signal reception 7 in Fig. 8). Depending on the type of watchdog (cf. Fig. 4), this waiting occurs concurrently (<<TM_Concurrent>>), interrupt-based (<<TM_HWTimer>>) or in parallel on extra hardware (<<TM_HWWatch dog>>). For legibility purposes, we only refer to the concurrent variant in the remainder of this section. The other variants work analogously. Once the main thread of the application calls an operation *op* to which one of the stereotypes inheriting from <<WatchdogMonitoring>> (cf. Fig. 4) is applied, the watchdog is activated (cf. action 2 and signal 3 in Fig. 8). Now, the watchdog and the main thread execute concurrently. We will first describe the behavior of the watchdog, before we describe the behavior of the main thread.

Once the watchdog starts, it activates a timer that corresponds to the maximum execution time specified in the stereotype that is applied to the operation.

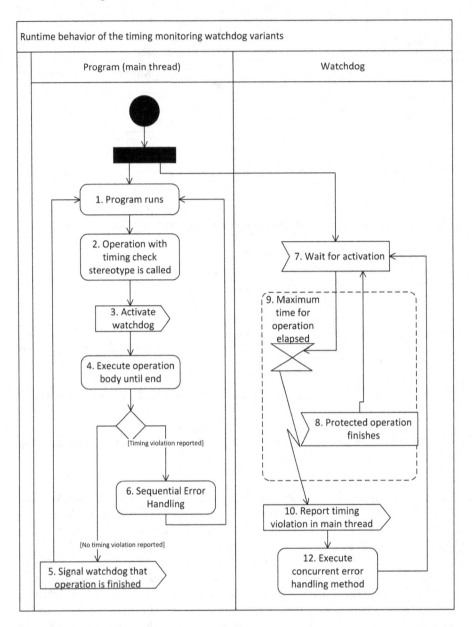

Fig. 8. UML 2.5 activity diagram showing the runtime behavior of the generated watchdogs.

Either this time elapses (time event 9 in Fig. 8) or the operation *op* finishes prior to the elapsed time (signal reception 8 in Fig. 8). If the operation finishes before the time has elapsed, then the watchdog returns to its waiting mode until operation *op* is called again. If the time elapses before operation *op* is finished, then the watchdog has detected a violation of a timing constraint. In this case, this violation is reported to the main thread by changing a boolean variable within the class in which operation op is located (signal 10 in Fig. 8). Afterwards, the watchdog thread may execute an error handling method that is concurrent to the main thread (action 12 in Fig. 8). This is further explained in Sect. 4.4.

Concurrently to the watchdog behavior, the main thread executes the protected operation op. Once this operation is finished (including all sub-operations that are called by op), a boolean variable b within the class in which op is located is checked. This variable b represents whether the watchdog for the operation op has detected a timing violation. In case a timing violation has been detected, a sequential error handling method is executed. We assume, that this method restores the system to a safe state (cf. Sect. 4.4). Afterwards, as the system is in a safe state again, the main thread continues its normal execution. In case b indicates that no timing violation has occurred, the corresponding watchdog is informed that the operation has finished. Afterwards, the main thread continues its normal execution.

Error Handling. Error handling for the deadline supervision described above is straightforward: in case a timing violation is detected at the end of the operation, a previously specified error handling operation is called within the same thread. For the watchdog variant, this behavior is more complex, as the timing violation is detected in a concurrent thread. This offers the chance to react to the timing violation as soon as it has occurred, instead of waiting for the operation op that violated the timing constraint to finish. This may offer a crucial timing advantage, especially when the operation op requires a lot of additional time to finish, or even contains an endless loop.

At the same time, concurrent error handling may only influence the execution of the main thread in a limited fashion. This is especially important in case the operation op_v that violated the timing constraint quickly finishes after the violation of the timing constraint. In this case, the concurrent error handling method may not yet be finished before the main thread resumes its operation. For these reasons, we also include a sequential error handling operation in the main thread, after the operation op_v has finished. This also allows for greater changes in the control flow of the main thread, e.g., by modifying the return value or throwing an exception.

For this reason, the stereotypes inheriting from <<TimingMonitoringWatchdog>> (cf. Fig. 4 in Sect. 4.3) allow to specify two error handling operations. One that is executed concurrently (tagged value "watchdogErrorHandling"), while the other is executed sequentially (tagged value "errorHandling"), as described above. The tagged values only refer to the names of these operations. As error handling is heavily application dependent, developers are required to implement these methods manually (`errorHandlingOpSequential()` and `errorHandlingOpConcurrent()` in Fig. 7).

Regardless of the type of error handling, our approach assumes that this error handling brings the system to a safe state. In the worst case, this may mean stopping the application in systems where fail-stop is an acceptable behavior.

4.5   Model Transformations for the Automatic Code Generation of Timing Constraint Monitoring at Runtime

This section describes the model transformations that transform the stereotypes introduced in Fig. 4 to the software architecture described in Sect. 4.4.

Model Transformations for Deadline Supervision. Similar to the software architecture for deadline supervision, the model transformations are relatively straightforward for this type of timing monitoring. Initially, each operation in each class of the application model is checked for whether the <<DeadlineSupervision>> stereotype (cf. Fig. 4) is applied to it. Each operation, for which this is the case, is modified as shown in Fig. 6. At the beginning of the operation code is added that measures the current time, which is evaluated at the end of the operation. If the timing constraint is violated, the previously specified error handling operation is executed.

Model Transformations for Watchdog Variants. This section describes the model transformations that realize the watchdog variants of the timing monitoring mechanisms. Similar to the model transformations for deadline supervision, all operations in the application model are checked for whether a stereotype inheriting from <<WatchdogMonitoring>> (cf. Fig. 4 in Sect. 4.3) is applied to them. For each operation op where this is the case, the class C in which op resides is modified to contain an instance of the `TimingMonitoringWatchdog` interface (cf. Fig. 7 in Sect. 4.4). The specific instance this interface is realized with depends on the specific stereotype that is applied to op. For example, in Fig. 7, the interface is realized with the class `ConcurrentWatchdog`, as the <<TM_Concurrent>> is applied to the `checkFire()` operation. The template parameters of the `ConcurrentWatchdog` class correspond mostly to the tagged values specified in the <<TM_Concurrent>> stereotype. An exception is the `setTimingViolation` function pointer, as the operation this pointer refers to is added automatically and thus is not specified by the developer.

Besides adding the `TimingMonitoringWatchdog` to the class C, an additional boolean variable b is added to C, alongside a setter method for this variable (`timingViolationCheckFire` and `setTimingViolationCheckFire()`in Fig. 7). Furthermore, the operation op is also modified. At the beginning of the operation, the `start()` method of the `TimingMonitoringWatchdog` interface is called. At the end of the method, just before the return statement, the `stop()` method of the same interface is called. Moreover, the variable b is checked for whether a timing violation has been detected. If this is the case, the sequential error handling operation inside C is called (method `errorHandlingSequential()` in Fig. 7.

5   Related Work

This section discusses research approaches that are related to our work. This includes related work on improving the development of safety-critical systems (cf. Sect. 5.1) and general code generation via model-driven development (cf. Sect. 5.2). Furthermore, the workflow presented in this paper has already been applied for the generation of some safety mechanisms, i.e., memory protection [16], graceful degradation [17] and voting [18].

5.1   Related Work on Improving the Development of Safety-Critical Systems

In Sect. 2.1 we describe the safety development lifecycle as defined by IEC 61508. While our approach targets the actual realization, i.e., implementation, of the system, many other approaches focus on earlier stages of the safety lifecycle, e.g., hazard and risk analysis or defining safety requirements. For example, [36,40] focus on specifying safety hazards and safety analysis, while [3] focus on specifying safety requirements. These approaches are complimentary to ours and may help to decide which safety mechanisms the application should contain. Once a set of safety mechanisms for the application has been decided, our approach may be used to model and automatically generate these safety mechanisms.

Besides related research that focuses on other phases of the safety lifecycle, there is also some research aiming to improve the realization of the system, similar to ours. These usually focus on automatically generating a single selected safety mechanism, e.g., [5,6,29] for the issue of memory protection. These approaches often do not consider modeling or code generation from models and are therefore separate from our approach, which uses models at its core. However, depending on the specific approach, they might be adapted to fit within the workflow presented in Sect. 3.2.

Some approaches, such as [39] or [30], consider the generation of safety mechanisms at a general application level, similar to the idea presented in this paper. The approach presented in [39] presents its own, text-based domain-specific modeling language for the generation of safety mechanisms in the automotive industry. Our approach, in contrast, uses UML as its modeling language, whose notation and syntax are more familiar to developers. Furthermore, UML allows for a graphic representation of the application model, which we believe to be an advantage. The approach presented in [30] introduces a pattern-based approach for the generation of safety mechanisms in fail-operational systems. However, as stated by the authors, their approach only allows for partial code generation, while our approach enables full code generation.

There also exists research that provides improvements for the development of safety-critical systems at more of a system level, while our approach focuses on the application level. Thus, the approaches may be used in a complementary fashion. Some examples include approaches for the operating system level, e.g., [8,31], the network level, e.g., [25,38] or timing issues in multicore environments, e.g., [10–12].

5.2 Related Work on Code Generation via Model-Driven Development

Code generation from UML models is commonplace, e.g., in commercial tools, such as [9,32], or in open source tools, e.g., [28]. These tools usually provide mappings between UML and source code, e.g., a mapping between a UML class and a class in C++. This works well for object-oriented programming languages, as UML is an object-oriented modeling language and therefore many 1:1 mappings exist. Some tools, such as [32], go a step further and provide code generation for UML concepts where no 1:1 mapping exists, e.g., code generation for statecharts. However, they focus on providing code generation for basic UML, which does not contain any safety mechanisms a priori. Therefore, these tools are not capable of generating safety mechanisms a priori. Our approach provides model representations in UML to model safety mechanisms and describes the model transformations required to generate code from them. Therefore, our approach enables the aforementioned tools to automatically generate safety mechanisms. Conversely, our approach assumes that developers make use of some type of MDD tool that is capable of generating code from UML.

UML itself has been extended with the MARTE profile for the development of embedded systems [27]. However, it does not consider safety mechanisms or code generation. Some dependability and rudimentary safety aspects have been provided by the profile presented in [4]. However, its level of detail is too low to be usable for code generation. The same applies to the approach presented in [33], which provides modeling for safety and security in combination.

Aside from UML, model-driven code generation is also discussed for other modeling languages, e.g., [13]. We chose to build our approach atop UML, as it is far more widespread than these other modeling languages and thus our approach is potentially more useful to a wider range of developers.

6 Conclusion

Safety standards, such as IEC 61508, define a number of safety mechanisms that mitigate the risk in safety-critical systems. Many of these safety mechanisms are at least partially application independent and may therefore be automatically generated. Such an automatic code generation may decrease the number of bugs in system and increase developer productivity. This is especially important, as the size and complexity of safety-critical embedded systems is steadily increasing.

We propose a model-driven approach for the automatic code generation of safety mechanisms. UML stereotypes are used to model the safety mechanisms with a UML application model. Model-to-model transformations take the information from these stereotypes and generate the safety mechanisms within the application model. In a subsequent step, with the help of common MDD tools, source code that contains these safety mechanisms is generated automatically.

We demonstrate our approach by applying it to the automatic generation of runtime timing monitoring. This enables the observation of timing constraints for individual operations within the application. In case such a timing constraint is violated, this violation is detected automatically and a predefined error handling operation is executed.

Future work may combine our approach with requirements engineering in order to automatically apply safety stereotypes to the UML application model based on the requirements specification. This may further be leveraged to improve safety certification. Furthermore, more safety mechanisms may be provided for automatic generation with our approach.

Acknowledgments. This work was partially funded by the German Federal Ministry of Economics and Technology (Bundesministeriums fuer Wirtschaft und Technologie-BMWi) within the project "Holistic model-driven development for embedded systems in consideration of diverse hardware architectures" (HolMES). The authors would also like to thank Nikolas Wintering for software development assistance.

References

1. Asadi, N., Saadatmand, M., Sjödin, M.: Run-time monitoring of timing constraints: a survey of methods and tools. In: The Eighth International Conference on Software Engineering Advances (ICSEA) (2013)
2. AUTOSAR: Specification of timing extensions (2017). https://www.autosar. org/fileadmin/user_upload/standards/classic/4-3/AUTOSAR_TPS_TimingExtens ions.pdf. Accessed 20 Aug 2020
3. Beckers, K., Côté, I., Frese, T., Hatebur, D., Heisel, M.: Systematic derivation of functional safety requirements for automotive systems. In: Bondavalli, A., Di Giandomenico, F. (eds.) SAFECOMP 2014. LNCS, vol. 8666, pp. 65–80. Springer, Cham (2014). https://doi.org/10.1007/978-3-319-10506-2_5
4. Bernardi, S., Merseguer, J., Petriu, D.: A dependability profile within MARTE. Softw. Syst. Model. **10**, 313–336 (2011). https://doi.org/10.1007/s10270-009-0128-1
5. Borchert, C., Schirmeier, H., Spinczyk, O.: Generative software-based memory error detection and correction for operating system data structures. In: Proceedings of the 2013 43rd Annual IEEE/IFIP International Conference on Dependable Systems and Networks (DSN), pp. 1–12. IEEE Computer Society, Washington, DC (2013). https://doi.org/10.1109/DSN.2013.6575308
6. Chen, D., et al.: JVM susceptibility to memory errors. In: Proceedings of the 2001 Symposium on JavaTM Virtual Machine Research and Technology Symposium, vol. 1. USENIX Association, Berkeley (2001)
7. Das, N., Ganesan, S., Jweda, L., Bagherzadeh, M., Hili, N., Dingel, J.: Supporting the model-driven development of real-time embedded systems with run-time monitoring and animation via highly customizable code generation. In: Proceedings of the ACM/IEEE 19th International Conference on Model Driven Engineering Languages and Systems, MODELS 2016, pp. 36–43. Association for Computing Machinery, New York (2016). https://doi.org/10.1145/2976767.2976781
8. Elektrobit. EB tresos Safety (2020). https://www.elektrobit.com/products/ecu/eb-tresos/functional-safety. Accessed 20 Aug 2020
9. Enterprise Architect (2020). https://sparxsystems.com/products/ea/index.html. Accessed 20 Aug 2020

10. Fernandez, G., et al.: Seeking time-composable partitions of tasks for COTS multicore processors. In: 2015 IEEE 18th International Symposium on Real-Time Distributed Computing, pp. 208–217 (2015). https://doi.org/10.1109/ISORC.2015.43

11. Fernandez, G., Jalle, J., Abella, J., Quinones, E., Vardanega, T., Cazorla, F.J.: Computing safe contention bounds for multicore resources with round-robin and FIFO arbitration. IEEE Trans. Comput. (2016). https://doi.org/10.5281/zenodo.165812

12. Girbal, S., Jean, X., Le Rhun, J., Pérez, D.G., Gatti, M.: Deterministic platform software for hard real-time systems using multi-core COTS. In: 2015 IEEE/AIAA 34th Digital Avionics Systems Conference (DASC) (2015). https://doi.org/10.1109/DASC.2015.7311481

13. Harrand, N., Fleurey, F., Morin, B., Husa, K.E.: ThingML: a language and code generation framework for heterogeneous targets. In: Proceedings of the ACM/IEEE 19th International Conference on Model Driven Engineering Languages and Systems, MODELS 2016, pp. 125–135. Association for Computing Machinery, New York (2016). https://doi.org/10.1145/2976767.2976812

14. Hatcliff, J., Wassyng, A., Kelly, T., Comar, C., Jones, P.: Certifiably safe software-dependent systems: Challenges and directions. In: Proceedings of the Conference on The Future of Software Engineering, FOSE 2014, pp. 182–200. ACM, New York (2014). https://doi.org/10.1145/2593882.2593895

15. Heimdahl, M.P.E.: Safety and software intensive systems: challenges old and new. In: 2007 Future of Software Engineering, FOSE 2007, pp. 137–152. IEEE Computer Society, Washington (2007). https://doi.org/10.1109/FOSE.2007.18

16. Huning, L., Iyenghar, P., Pulvermueller, E.: UML specification and transformation of safety features for memory protection. In: Proceedings of the 14th International Conference on Evaluation of Novel Approaches to Software Engineering, pp. 281–288. INSTICC, SciTePress, Heraklion (2019)

17. Huning, L., Iyenghar, P., Pulvermueller, E.: A UML profile for automatic code generation of optimistic graceful degradation features at the application level. In: Proceedings of the 8th International Conference on Model-Driven Engineering and Software Development, MODELSWARD, vol. 1, pp. 336–343. INSTICC, SciTePress (2020). https://doi.org/10.5220/0008949803360343

18. Huning, L., Iyenghar, P., Pulvermueller, E.: A workflow for automatically generating application-level safety mechanisms from UML stereotype model representations. In: Proceedings of the 15th International Conference on Evaluation of Novel Approaches to Software Engineering, ENASE, vol. 1, pp. 216–228. INSTICC, SciTePress (2020). https://doi.org/10.5220/0009517302160228

19. IEC 61508 Edition 2.0. Functional safety for electrical/electronic/programmable electronic safety-related systems (2010)

20. ISO 26262 Road vehicles - Functional safety. Second Edition (2018)

21. Iyenghar, P., Pulvermueller, E.: A model-driven workflow for energy-aware scheduling analysis of IoT-enabled use cases. IEEE Internet Things J. 5(6), 4914–4925 (2018)

22. Iyenghar, P., Huning, L., Pulvermueller, E.: Automated end-to-end timing analysis of autosar-based causal event chains. In: Proceedings of the 15th International Conference on Evaluation of Novel Approaches to Software Engineering, ENASE, vol. 1, pp. 477–489. INSTICC, SciTePress (2020). https://doi.org/10.5220/0009512904770489

23. Iyenghar., P., Huning., L., Pulvermueller., E.: Early synthesis of timing models in autosar-based automotive embedded software systems. In: Proceedings of the 8th

International Conference on Model-Driven Engineering and Software Development, MODELSWARD, vol. 1, pp. 26–38. INSTICC, SciTePress (2020). https://doi.org/10.5220/0009095000260038

24. MISRA C++2008 Guidelines for the use of the C++ language in critical systems (2008)

25. Moestl, M., Thiele, D., Ernst, R.: Invited: towards fail-operational ethernet based in-vehicle networks. In: 2016 53nd ACM/EDAC/IEEE Design Automation Conference (DAC), pp. 1–6 (2016). https://doi.org/10.1145/2897937.2905021

26. Mok, A.K., Liu, G.: Efficient run-time monitoring of timing constraints. In: Proceedings Third IEEE Real-Time Technology and Applications Symposium, pp. 252–262 (1997)

27. A UML Profile for MARTE: Modeling and Analysis of Real-Time Embedded Systems. Technical report, Object Management Group (2008)

28. The Eclipse Foundation. Eclipse Papyrus Modeling Environment (2020). https://www.eclipse.org/papyrus. Accessed 20 Aug 2020

29. Pattabiraman, K., Grover, V., Zorn, B.G.: Samurai: protecting critical data in unsafe languages. In: Proceedings of the 3rd ACM SIGOPS/EuroSys European Conference on Computer Systems 2008, pp. 219–232. ACM, New York (2008). https://doi.org/10.1145/1352592.1352616

30. Penha, D., Weiss, G., Stante, A.: Pattern-based approach for designing fail-operational safety-critical embedded systems. In: 2015 IEEE 13th International Conference on Embedded and Ubiquitous Computing, pp. 52–59 (2015). https://doi.org/10.1109/EUC.2015.14

31. Vector. PrEEVision (2020). https://www.vector.com/int/en/products/products-a-z/software/preevision/. Accessed 20 Aug 2020

32. IBM. Rational Rhapsody Developer. https://www.ibm.com/us-en/marketplace/uml-tools. Accessed 20 Aug 2020

33. Architecture models and patterns for safety and security. Deliverable D2.2 from EU-research project SAFURE (2017). https://safure.eu/publications-deliverables. Accessed 3 Feb 2020

34. Saridakis, T.: Design patterns for graceful degradation. In: Noble, J., Johnson, R. (eds.) Transactions on Pattern Languages of Programming I. LNCS, vol. 5770, pp. 67–93. Springer, Heidelberg (2009). https://doi.org/10.1007/978-3-642-10832-7_3

35. Storey, N.: Safety-Critical Computer System. Addison-Wesley, Harlow (1996)

36. Tanzi, T.J., Textoris, R., Apvrille, L.: Safety properties modelling. In: 2014 7th International Conference on Human System Interactions (HSI), pp. 198–202. IEEE Computer Society (2014). https://doi.org/10.1109/HSI.2014.6860474

37. The Eclipse Foundation: Eclipse IDE. https://www.eclipse.org/eclipseide/. Accessed 20 Aug 2020

38. Thiele, D., Ernst, R., Diemer, J.: Formal worst-case timing analysis of Ethernet TSN's time-aware and peristaltic shapers. In: 2015 IEEE Vehicular Networking Conference (VNC), pp. 251–258. IEEE (2016). https://doi.org/10.5281/zenodo.55528

39. Trindade, R.F.B., Bulwahn, L., Ainhauser, C.: Automatically generated safety mechanisms from semi-formal software safety requirements. In: Bondavalli, A., Di Giandomenico, F. (eds.) SAFECOMP 2014. LNCS, vol. 8666, pp. 278–293. Springer, Cham (2014). https://doi.org/10.1007/978-3-319-10506-2_19

40. Yakymets, N., Perin, M., Lanusse, A.: Model-driven multi-level safety analysis of critical systems. In: 9th Annual IEEE International Systems Conference, pp. 570–577. IEEE Computer Society (2015). https://doi.org/10.1109/SYSCON.2015.7116812

HumaniSE: Approaches to Achieve More Human-Centric Software Engineering

John Grundy⊙, Hourieh Khalajzadeh$^{(\boxtimes)}$⊙, Jennifer McIntosh⊙,
Tanjila Kanij⊙, and Ingo Mueller⊙

HumaniSE Lab, Faculty of IT, Monash University, Clayton, VIC 3800, Australia
{John.Grundy,Hourieh.Khalajzadeh,Jenny.McIntosh,Tanjila.Kanij,
Ingo.Mueller}@monash.edu
https://www.monash.edu/it/humanise-lab

Abstract. A common problem with many existing software systems and the approaches to engineering them is their lack of the *human aspects* of their target end users. People are different - with diverse characteristics including age, gender, ethnicity, physical and mental challenges, personality, technical proficiency, emotional reactions to software systems, socio-economic status, educational attainment, language, and so on. In this paper we describe our work at looking to better consider these characteristics by incorporation of *human aspects* throughout the software engineering lifecycle. We are developing a co-creational *living lab* approach to better collect human aspects in the software requirements. We are using *domain-specific visual languages*, themselves a more human-centric modelling approach, to capture these diverse human aspects of target software systems. We are working on incorporating these human aspects into design models to support improved *model-driven engineering,* and thereby to better support both code generation and run-time adaptation to different end user human characteristics. Finally we are working on better ways to support *continuous evaluation* of human aspects in the produced software, and to provide improved feedback of user reported defects to developers.

Keywords: Model-driven engineering · Human-centric software engineering · Human factors

1 Introduction

Modern software systems are extremely complex, currently hand-crafted artefacts, which leads them to be extremely brittle and error prone in practice. We continually hear about issues with security and data breaches (due to poorly captured and implemented policies and enforcement); massive cost over-runs and project slippage (due to poor estimation and badly captured software requirements); hard-to-deploy, hard-to-maintain, slow, clunky and even dangerous solutions (due to incorrect technology choice, usage or deployment); and hard-to-use

R. Ali et al. (Eds.): ENASE 2020, CCIS 1375, pp. 444–468, 2021.
https://doi.org/10.1007/978-3-030-70006-5_18

software that does not meet the users' needs and causing frustration (due to poor understanding of user needs and poor design) [7,47,61]. This leads to huge economic cost, inefficiencies, not fit-for-purpose solutions, and dangerous and potentially even life-threatening situations. Software is designed and built primarily to solve human needs. Many of these problems can be traced to a lack of understanding and incorporation of these *human aspects* during the software engineering process [23,41,57,59]. This includes aspects such as age, gender, language, culture, emotions, personality, education, physical and mental challenges, and so on.

Current software engineering approaches ignore many of these human aspects, or address them in piece-meal, ad-hoc ways [4,7,23,47,59]. For example, in Model-driven Software Engineering (MDSE), user requirements for the software are captured and represented by a variety of abstract requirements models. These are then refined to detailed design models to describe the software solution. These design models are then transformed by a set of generators into software code to implement the target system [52]. However, currently almost no human aspects are captured, reasoned about, designed in or used when generating or testing the software produced in this way [41,61]. We need to more fully integrate these *human aspects* into model-driven software development.

This paper is an extended version of an earlier one that appeared at ENASE 2020 [19]. In this paper we describe in more detail, by using a number of example projects, how we are addressing these issues using several complementary approaches, as outlined below:

Use a Co-creational, Agile Living Lab-Based Approach: Our idea here is to better enable software teams to provide better ways for software engineers to work with stakeholders to capture and reason about under-represented, under-used, under-supported yet critical human-centric requirements of target software. Our Living Lab is designed to provide a co-creational space for investigating socio-technological aspects of software engineering activities. Our focus is on enabling software development teams to capture and reason about critical human-centric aspects of software.

Develop a New Set of Human-Centric Requirements Modelling Languages: Understanding software stakeholder needs is essential for a successful software development project. However, software developers tend to focus much more on technological aspects and therefore often do not sufficiently capture the complete human context concerning, for example, software user age, accessibility challenges, ethnicity, language or gender. We want to enable software engineers to more effectively elicit and model diverse human aspects. Along with this we need new approaches for obtaining and extracting such human-centric software requirements from a wide variety of sources e.g. Word, PDF, natural language, videos, sketches, and so on.

Augment Conventional Model-Driven Engineering Design Models with Human-Centric Requirements: We want to be able to use human-centric aspects during MDSE, along with techniques to verify the completeness, correctness and consistency of these models, and proactively check them against best practice models and principles. We believe that incorporating more human-centric aspects into software design will lead to more useful, usable and desirable software. We work towards this goal by creating new notations, techniques and tools to augment software design models with human-centric aspects. We also need to develop new techniques to incorporate these human aspects in design models into MDSE-based software code generators, enabling target software to dynamically adapt to differing user needs at run-time.

Use of these Human-Centric Requirements During Software Testing: Software testing and evaluation is an essential software development activity which is aimed at ensuring that requirements have been implemented correctly and completely and that user needs are met. We focus on the testing of human-centric aspects and techniques for receiving better user feedback on human-centric defects in their software solutions. We need to better support human-centric requirements-based testing of software systems, along with techniques that give developers better feedback from users on the human aspects-related defects in their software solutions.

The rest of this paper is organised as follows. Section 2 presents a motivating example for this work, along with a review of key related work. Section 3 provides an overview of our approach. Section 4 discusses our development of a co-creational living lab approach, and Section 5 the use of human aspects during requirements engineering. Section 6 presents some projects we are undertaking enhancing design and model-driven software engineering to incorporate human aspects of end users. Section 7 discusses approaches to evaluating software as to how well (or poorly) it supports human asepcts, and some key exemplar application domains for our work. Finally, Section 8 concludes this paper.

2   Motivation and Related Work

2.1   Motivating Example: A Smart Home for Ageing

Consider a "smart home" aimed at providing ageing people with technology-based support for physical and mental challenges so they are able to stay in their own home longer and feel safe and secure [7,17,20]. To develop such a solution, the software team must deeply understand technologies like sensors, data capture and analysis, communication with hospital systems, and software development methods and tools. However, they must also deeply understand and appreciate the human aspects of their stakeholders: ageing people, their families and friends, and clinicians/community workers. These include the *Technology Proficiency and Acceptance* of ageing people – likely to be much older than the software designers. The development of "Smart homes" technology should factor in the *Emotional* – both positive and negative – reactions to the smart home e.g. daily interaction is potentially positive but being monitored potentially negative. The *Accessibility* of the solutions for people with e.g. physical tremors, poor eyesight, wheel-chair bound, and cognitive decline. Within this, personality

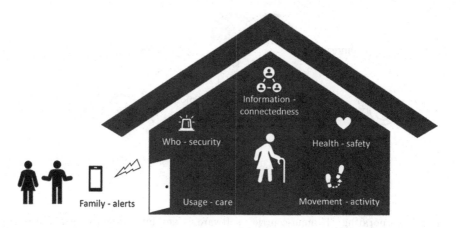

Fig. 1. Simple example of a smart home to support ageing people.

differences may be very important e.g. those wanting flexible dialogue compared to those needing directive dialogue with the system. The *Usability* of the software for a group of people with varied needs e.g. incorporating the use of voice or gestures or modified smart phone interface. Figure 1 shows an example of such a smart home.

The ageing population is diverse and therefore smart home technology must accommodate for the different *Ages, Genders, Cultures* and *Languages* of users including appropriate use of text, colours, symbols. This is particularly important as one quarter of the elderly in Australia are non-native English speakers and the majority women, but by far the majority of software developers are 20-something years old English-speaking men [32]. Failure to incorporate human aspects into the development of Smart Home software has the potential to result in a home that is unsuitable for who it is designed to help, by introducing confusing, possibly unsettling and invasive, and even potentially dangerous technology.

2.2 Model-Driven Software Engineering

Key aspects of Model-Driven Software Engineering (MDSE) are outlined in Fig. 2. MDSE captures high-level models about software requirements i.e. what users need their software to do (a). MDSE then refines these models to detailed designs about how the software solution is organised, composed and its appearance (b). Model transformation then turns these models into software code (c). This is in contrast with most current software development methods which use informal and imprecise models, hand-translation into code via error-prone, and time-consuming low-level hand-coding. Advantages of MDSE-based approaches include capture of formal models of a software system at high levels of abstraction, being able to formally reason about these high-level models and more quickly locate errors, and being able to generate lower-level software artefacts, such as code, without overheads and errors of traditional hand-translating

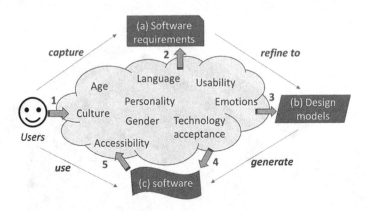

Fig. 2. Incorporating "Human-centric" software issues into Model-Driven Software Engineering (from [19]).

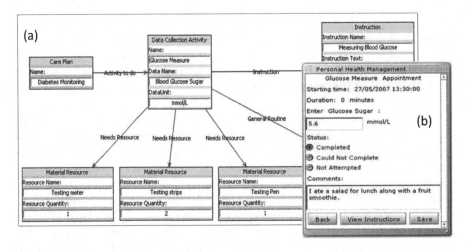

Fig. 3. A clinician-oriented Domain-specific Visual Language for care plan modelling and using Model-driven Engineering to generate an eHealth app ((c) IEEE, from [36]).

informal models. However, most MDSE approaches use generic requirements and design languages e.g. the Unified Modelling Language (UML) and extensions [11,33]. These have the disadvantages of being overly complex and are very difficult to use by non-software engineering domain experts [25]. Further MDSE limitations include the often very high level of abstraction of incorporated DSVLs. Necessary customisations or configurations to suit concrete requirements result in the need to implement code-level extensions of the underlying model transformation approach and the code generator.

2.3   Domain-Specific Visual Languages

Domain-specific Visual Languages (DSVLs) provide a more accessible approach to presenting complex models for domain experts [55]. DSVLs use one or more visual metaphors, typically derived from the domain experts, to represent the model(s). They enable domain experts to understand and even create and use the models directly, rather than rely on software engineers. These DSVLs are then used to generate software code and configuration artefacts to realise a software solution via MDSE approaches. This approach provides higher abstractions and productivity, improves target software quality, provides for repeatability, and supports systematic reuse of best practices [25,33,52,55].

There are many DSVLs for MDSE tools [2,39,55]. A representative example is shown in Fig. 3: (a) a custom DSVL designed for clinicians is being used to model a new patient care plan for diabetes and obesity management. Then (b) a model transformer takes the care plan and generates a mobile app to assist the patient to implement their plan [36]. This is a major improvement on developing software using conventional techniques. However, the approach fails to model or incorporate into the mobile app a range of critical human aspects, resulting in its failure in practice. Patient-specific, human-centric needs are not captured e.g. technology acceptance and emotional reactions e.g. some patients react negatively to the remote monitoring approach used. Some users are not proficient in English and hence need labels and inputs in their preferred language. Our evaluation found that some of the colours and care plan model language used in the app are confusing for many older users. Users with eyesight limitations find the app too hard to see and too fiddly to interact with. The app can not adapt to different contexts of use or preferences of the users e.g. it can not use their smart home sensors or each patient's particular mobile app dialogue preferences. The app displays a euro-centric terminology about wellbeing, which may put off some users who prefer e.g. a Buddhist, Confucius or Pacifika view of health concepts from following their care plan [29]. We need to incorporate these human aspects into MDE [4].

2.4   Human Aspects of Software

There has been increasing interest in the human aspects of complex software and how to better incorporate and support these during software development. Agile methods, design thinking and living lab approaches [12,18,24,26] all try and incorporate a human element both in eliciting software requirements and in involving end users of software in the development process [9,26,45]. However, none capture human aspects in any systematic way and therefore the software fails to address several critical aspects of the human users. Some new approaches have tried to capture limited human-centric software issues. Emotional aspects of software usage include identifying the emotional reactions of users e.g. when engaging with health and fitness apps or for gaming. Work has been done modelling these Emotional Requirements and applying them to challenging eHealth domains [7,41].

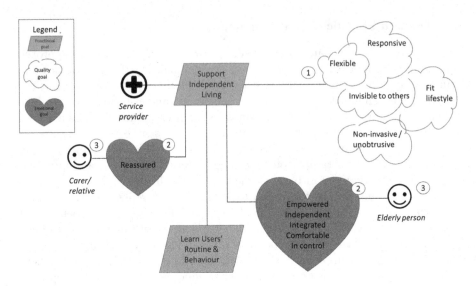

Fig. 4. A Human-centric, Emotion-oriented Domain-specific Visual Language (from [19]).

Figure 4 shows a representative example using an emotion-oriented requirements DSVL to design better smart homes [20]. Here a conventional goal-based
DSVL (1) has been augmented with a set of "emotional goal" elements (2) specific to different users (3). Human characteristics like age, gender, culture and
language can dramatically impact aspects of software, especially in the user interface presented by the software and the dialogue had with the user [23,57,59].
Limited support for the capture of some of these has been developed. Another
example is a multi-lingual requirements tool providing requirements modelling in
English and Bahasa Malaysia, including supporting linguistic and some cultural
differences between users [31].

Usability testing has long been studied in Human Computer Interaction
(HCI) research and practice. However, usability defect reporting is very under-
researched in the context of software engineering [61]. Similarly, a lot of work
has been done on accessibility in HCI e.g. sight, hearing or cognitively impaired
[57,59], and health IT e.g. mental health challenges when using mobile apps
[8]. However, little has been done to evaluate the extent to which physical and
mental challenges are properly addressed in engineering software development,
and is also poorly supported in practice. Personality, team climate and organisational issues relating to people have been heavily researched in Management,
Information Systems, and the personality of programmers and testers in software development [46,54]. However, little attention has been paid to how to
go about supporting differing personality, team climate or organisational or user
culture in software, nor to capture requirements relating to these human aspects.
Traditional software requirements and design models have very limited (or no)
ability to capture these sorts of human-centric software issues, and approaches
are ad-hoc, inconsistent, and incomplete.

Software is fundamentally produced by people, for people. People - and the organisations they work for or that provide them with services - inherently have a set of "values", which differ from person to person and organisation to organisation. Values represent the guiding principles that influence our decision-making processes as individuals, groups and organisations; and they describe what an individual or a group thinks is valuable or important [13]. Such values include but are not limited to openness, transparency, competitiveness, privacy, accessibility, inclusivity, independence, politeness, ambition, respect for authority, and so on. Some approaches have been developed to specify some human values and their relationship to software engineering methods and teams [10].

Current software engineering processes lack consistent, coherent ways to address this range of increasingly important human-centric software issues and thus they are often very incompletely supported or in fact are usually ignored [19,58]. To date only isolated human aspects have been addressed and often confined to one phase of software development. There are no modelling principles, DSVL-based model design principles, nor widely applicable, practical modelling tools to capture human-centric software issues at requirements or design levels. While a DSVL provides a more human-centric engineering approach, it fails to capture and support the key human aspects in the target software itself. Current MDSE tools, while providing significant software engineering benefits do not support modelling and using these critical human aspects.

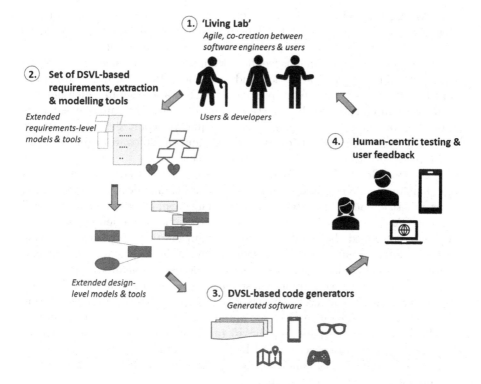

Fig. 5. Our overall HumaniSE approach.

3   Our Approach

Figure 5 illustrates the new human-centric, model-driven software engineering approach we are working to produce. We have identified a set of key approaches that are needed to achieve this vision. We aim to employ several innovative approaches to (i) systematically capture and model a wide range of human-centric software requirements and develop a novel integrated taxonomy and formal model for these; (ii) promote a wide range of human-centric requirements for first-class consideration during software engineering by applying principles for modelling and reasoning about these human-centric requirements using DSVLs; (iii) support a wide range of human-centric requirements in model-driven engineering during software generation and run-time reconfiguration via MDSE techniques; and (iv) systematically use human-centric requirements for requirements-based software testing and reporting human-centric software defects. This approach improves model-driven software engineering by placing crucially important, but to date often forgotten, human-centric aspects of software as first-class considerations in model-driven software engineering. The critical importance of this is really only just becoming recognised, due to the increasing breadth of uses of IT in society and the increasing recognition that understanding and incorporating the very diverse needs of our very diverse software end users is essential. Key features of this approach include:

(1) **An Agile, Living Lab Approach** is being used to co-locate the software team and target end users [20]. This provides a co-creational environment to elicit human-centric requirements, model and capture with human-centric DSVLs, and receive continuous feedback from users. The Living Lab concept's design thinking, agile, co-creation and continuous feedback mechanisms are critical. These are then used to provide an MDSE approach in which human-centric requirements can be effectively and efficiently captured, treated as priorities by the software team, users can quickly report defective software violating these human-centric requirements, and the software team can work effectively with these end users to co-design changes.

(2) **A New Set of DSVL Tools** are being developed to capture and model the human-centric requirements, validate them against design principles and best practice modelling patterns, and translate them to extended design-level models. A set of principles for domain-specific visual modelling languages is being developed that enables software engineers to better capture a wide range of human-centric aspects of software: including user's age, gender, cultural preferences, language needs, emotional needs, personality and cognitive characteristics, and accessibility constraints, both physical and mental. These and other human end user characteristics are essential to prioritise during both software development and software deployment to ensure a useful and usable end product results for a broad range of end users. These principles are used to design a range of novel DSVLs that fully support the capture of many of the important human-centric aspects and model them as the critical requirements issues that they are.

(3) A Set of MDSE-based Code Generators are used to generate software applications – code, configurations, etc. Augmented design models are used to ensure modelled human-centric requirements are preserved for use at design-time to ensure that MDSE-based solutions take them into account appropriately when generating software applications. Unlike existing generators, our extended MDSE generators take into account variations of end-users as specified in the human-centric requirements, producing either multiple versions of the target software applications and/or reconfigurable applications that adapt to each end user's differing human-centric needs.

(4) A Combination of Human-centric Requirements Testing and Continuous Defect Feedback are fed to the development team. We are developing a new framework for human-centric, requirements-based testing of software that can verify whether the constructed software systems meet these critical human-centric requirements. By leveraging the Living Lab concept, this enables both faster feedback and defect correction, but also better evolution and modelling of the human-centric requirements over time. Lessons are fed into the improvement of the DSVL tools, best practice patterns and MDSE generators.

Ultimately we want to translate our learning into industry practices and Software Engineering education. To do this we are working with several industry partners, our students, and colleagues teaching Software Engineering courses.

In the following sections, we are explaining these four key features in the format of different projects we are working on across human-centric agile Living Lab, human aspects in requirements engineering, using human aspects in design and implementing software, and evaluating and applying human aspects in software engineering.

4   A Human-Centric Agile Living Lab

Human-centric requirements have to be elicited from target end users (or stakeholders), captured (or modelled) using our DSVL-based tools, used by extended MDSE solutions to generate software, and then the software tested and user feedback accepted and actioned to correct requirements and design model problems. A new approach is needed to effectively support the software team in achieving this. We are investigating the *Living Lab* co-creation concept that has become popular in digital health software development [20, 26].

We are establishing this lab with a domain-specific focus with partner companies and target end users and the software team co-located as in Agile customer-in-team approaches [9, 46]. Target end users and developers closely collaborate to elicit, capture, test, use and refine the human-centric software requirements. The DSVL modelling tools, MDSE generators and testing tools all need to support collaborative capture, discussion and refinement of the human-centric requirements for this to be most effective. We plan to do this by extending our current work on developing digital health technologies [20], human-centric software engineering processes in software teams, including personality and team climate [49], and collaborative DSVL-based modelling tools [16].

In the following subsections we describe some of our projects that aim to make this living lab for Human-centric Software Engineering a reality.

4.1 Review of Human Aspects in Other Disciplines

We are conducting reviews of the notion of "human aspects" and how they are studied in other disciplines outside software engineering. This includes HCI/UX, information systems, business, design, engineering, psychology, sociology, anthropology, etc. Our objective is to learn from existing bodies of knowledge and to apply relevant theories, notions and findings to build a more complete understanding of human aspects and their implications on software engineering practices. The expected outcome of this project is a more complete, useful and practical taxonomy and ontology of human aspects for use in software engineering.

4.2 Review of How Human Aspects Impact Developers

We are conducting reviews of software engineering research literature to better understand - (i) what human aspects have been studied in software engineering to date (ii) how these issues inter-relate and impact software engineer performance; and (iii) where there are key gaps, limitations and need for further studies of human aspects impact on software engineers. From this we aim to determine the range of ways explored to date of how human aspects impact software engineering teams. We then plan to conduct our own studies of under-researched human aspects on software engineers.

4.3 Survey of How Developers Currently Handle End User Human Aspects

To complement the review of works done to understand human aspects impacting software engineers, we are conducting a survey of developers and follow-up interviews to better understand: (i) what are the key human aspects that they encounter when developing software, especially for "challenged" end users (ii) what are the more common, challenging to elicit, challenging to address human aspects for their end-users (iii) how do they currently meet these challenges (iv) are their current best practices we can learn from and disseminate to the wider software engineering community; and (v) what are key practice gaps and challenges that need further R&D to address. From the outcome of this survey and interview study we plan to focus the work described in the following sections on the particularly important and difficult under-supported end user human aspects for software development.

4.4   Analysis of How Human Aspects of Software Are Currently Discussed by Software Engineers

Software development and issue tracking systems such as GitHub, Stackoverflow, Atlassian Jira, Bugzilla, etc. provide tools for developers to discuss bugs and development related issues with each other. However, whether human aspects are getting discussed among hundreds of issues developers discuss together, is questionable. On the other hand, software users leave reviews for the apps to share their issues and experiences in using the apps with the other users and developers. Issue tracking and reporting software has many uses for customer service teams, one of which is bug reporting and fix tracking. This software is meant for internal bug tracking, so when team members find bugs and issues while testing products, they can report it to product development.

We are working on mining software repositories and app reviews to better understand whether human aspects are discussed in these platforms. We are also interested to explore what issues developers currently discuss or do not discuss about human aspects in software engineering and how they are currently talked about. At the same time, we are interested in what human aspects do users discuss in app reviews, and how they discuss them. These would enable us to analyse the differences in the discussions across human aspects in software engineering, how the discussions vary between different platforms, e.g. Stack Overflow, GitHub, how discussions vary based on human factor, project, person, etc., and how discussions vary in different fields and applications.

Analysis from this data collection will give us better insights into how discussions vary between developers and users, whether developers address human aspects discussed by the users, and finally, whether developers address what they discuss about the human aspects in software development.

4.5   A Taxonomy of Human-Centric Software Requirements

To the best of our knowledge, no taxonomy of human-centric software requirements or even informal definition exists at this time. We are working on developing a new, rich taxonomy of human-centric requirements for software systems. The taxonomy includes different human-centric concepts relating to computer software, and draws on other disciplines including HCI, usability, psychology, sociology, and others to build the conceptual model, and provide detailed relationships and trade-offs between different human-centric requirements.

We are applying this to a number of representative requirements examples to test and refine it, and use the outcomes to inform the development of DSVLs, DSVL tools and MDSE solutions in other activities. This is critical research as it provides software engineers with a lexicon, a set of principles and conceptual model to model and reason about these kinds of requirements. We are conducting a detailed analysis of several representative real-world software applications from eHealth apps [18], smart homes [20], community service apps [21], educational apps [1], and other heavily human-centric requirements critical domains.

From these we are developing a framework and model for prioritising human-centric software issues. This characterises complex trade-offs and other relationships between different human aspects that make supporting one issue problematic for other issues, similar to the Cognitive Dimensions framework [15]. We plan to use a set of focus groups comprising end users and developers to refine and validate our taxonomy. The taxonomy is being tested on real-world example requirements to gain feedback from both developers and end users to demonstrate its effectiveness. We are drawing on our extensive previous work developing taxonomies for design critics [2], emotion-oriented requirements [7], usability defects [61], and team climate [54].

5   Human Aspects in Requirements Engineering

5.1   Extracting Human Aspects from Requirements

Software requirements need to be elicited from end users and these are typically held in a variety of documents and can be obtained in a variety of ways. In the context of the Living Lab we are developing new tools to enable extraction of diverse human-centric requirements from diverse sources, including Powerpoint, Word, Excel, PDF, audio transcripts, images and video. A number of works have addressed different parts of this problem, including extracting requirements using light weight and heavy weight natural language processing [3,38]. However, none have specifically addressed the extraction of a wide range of human-centric requirements. We are developing, trialing and will then refine a set of extraction tools leveraging existing approaches but focused on human-centric requirements capture and representation using our DSVLs, within our living lab approach, and leveraging our human-centric requirements taxonomy. These tools will also be refined as these other related activities are refined and extended, and applying these tools to representative real-world requirements artefacts will help us to test and extend the outputs of these other tasks. We are focusing on developing leading-edge tools for extracting requirements for goal-directed and multi-lingual models [31,38], and requirements checking and improvement [3].

5.2   Human Aspects Impacting Requirements Engineers in Agile Teams

We are interested in a range of human aspects in the requirements engineering (RE) domain, particularly those impacting agile requirements engineering teams. These include but are not limited to: (i) how do requirements engineers handle requirements changes during agile software development, from both technical and behavioural/emotional reaction perspectives; (ii) how are agile requirements defined, talked about, is there a taxonomy of "agile" requirements changes; (iii) how do human aspects impact requirements engineering team members and stakeholders; and (iv) how can we improve RE practices and outcomes by better understanding and taking into account human aspects of team members and stakeholders. To this end we are carrying our studies with RE teams to better understand these issues, design techniques and tools to better evaluate human aspects impacting on RE processes and outcomes, and trial these with partner organisations.

5.3 How Are Human Aspects Discussed in Requirements Engineering Documents

Requirements elicitation and specification play an important role in the software development life cycle. Human aspects are often neglected in the early stages of development, i.e., requirements engineering. If human aspects are not taken into account from the early stages of the software development, these issues can impact the final product and make it not tailored toward the diverse range of end-users. Not taking human-centric requirements of users into account can lead to serious impacts to the software under development.

We are working on initially analysing existing requirement engineering documents to explore whether human aspects are discussed/noted, including epics, user stories, use cases, discussion transcripts, feature outlines, and so on. Using the taxonomy of human aspects discussed earlier, we aim to develop guidelines and tools using Natural-Language Processing and Machine Learning techniques to identify relevant human aspects in requirements specifications. This will lead to an improved human aspects-driven requirement engineering process, and an automated tool for identifying human aspects in system artefacts and guiding analysts in deliberately considering these issues during the requirements engineering phase.

5.4 New DSVLs to Model Human-Centric Requirements

While DSVLs have been an active research area for at least 20 years, remarkably few principles exist for design and evaluation of effective DSVLs [43]. We are developing a set of new design principles and associated DSVL evaluation approaches to provide more rigorous principles and design steps for specifically human-centric DSVL development. This will require us to identify a range of human-centric software requirements and design issues identified in the taxonomy built. We need to determine how we can best model these, use appropriate visual metaphors to represent the models, how we can support interaction with the visual models, and how we can reason about the suitability of these visual models in terms of usability and effectiveness. We are drawing upon the work on DSVL design tools to achieve this [2,16,39], as well as work on 'Physics' of Notations [43] and Cognitive Dimensions [15] to develop these DSVL design principles for modelling human-centric software issues.

We are developing a range of new and augmented DSVLs to model a wide variety of human aspects at the requirements level for software systems. Some of these DSVLs extend existing requirements modelling languages – in successively more principled ways than currently – e.g. goal-directed requirements languages such as i*, use cases and essential use cases, target user personas, user stories, etc.

However, others may provide wholly novel requirements modelling techniques and diagrams that are then linked to other requirements models. We envisage novel requirements capture for things like identifying cultural, age, accessibility and personality aspects of target end users. Where multiple target end users for the same software application have differing human-centric requirements, multiple or composite models may be necessary. Even partial progress here will be very useful for both researchers and practitioners well beyond the scope of our research.

We are building on a wide range of DSVLs, including for design tools, requirements, reporting, business processes, surveys, performance testing, and many others [2,16,31] as well as digital health software [20] and work on modelling usability defects and emotional and multi-lingual requirements [7].

5.5 Capturing Human Aspects with Personas

We are investigating the use of personas in requirements engineering with a view to working out ways to better use these during software engineering. To this end we are looking into (i) how personas are currently used in RE and SE; (ii) how to build personas that represent effectively a wide range of human aspects; (iii) how to validate these personas; and (iv) how to use these personas during design and evaluation of software systems. This may include improved ways of defining personas, incorporating specific human aspects into personas, generating personas, and using persona models to support RE, design and evaluation.

6 Using Human Aspects in Design and Implementing Software

6.1 Software Design Decision Support

The objective of this project is to develop a decision-support system that systematically guides software developers through capturing selected human aspect needs and requirements. It aims to give developers better support for incorporating these aspects into the design of a software system. Design decisions, contextual information and other tacit information such as design rationales are planned to be formalised using techniques such as decision trees, Markov chains and Bayesian networks. The expected outcome is a demonstrable prototype implementation that can be used and evaluated by software developers. Software developers are humans, and they, therefore, might be subject to cognitive biases and other human challenges. We are studying and evaluating how such a decision-support system may assist developers to use more of System 2 or rational thinking in design [56].

6.2 Collaborative Human-Centric Domain-Specific Visual Languages

We aim to develop a collaborative browser-based domain specific visual languages platform for designing a variety of software tools and systems including data analytics applications, eHealth apps, etc. Multidisciplinary teams of users can design their applications based on their specific characteristics, such as age, gender, culture, personality, etc. Different users can work collaboratively at the same time through a browser-based drag-and-drop based tool in a visualised and programming-free way. Users will be able to store data in, for example, graph databases to enable them to get more specialised views based on their needs and preferences. Domain specific visual languages can be built on top of the existing model-driven approaches such as BiDaML [34], big data analytics modelling languages, and can be further extended by incorporating human-centric issue into the development of the notations. We are adding to our tool code and report generators to automatically generate source code, reports and documents from the visualised models.

6.3 Extending Design Models to Include Human Aspects

Model-driven software engineering tools typically use the Unified Modelling Language (UML) or similar design models. Even those using their own design models need to refine higher-level abstract requirements models into lower-level architectural, software design, interface, database and other models. We are working on different ways to effectively extend design-level models to capture necessary design-level human-centric properties, derived from higher level human-centric requirements-level properties [4]. For example, we want to capture design alternatives to achieve an application user interface for a target end user who has sight-impairment, prefers a gesture-based sensor interface to using a Smart phone, has limited mobility, and is quite "neurotic" about device feedback.

We are going to evaluate these different modelling solutions via our living lab with both software engineers and end users, in terms of needed design information and preserving critical human-centred end user needs respectively. Even partial successful outcomes here will be immediately of interest and applicable for software teams. We are extending design models with aspects [44], goal-use case model integration [38], and goal-models extended with emotions [7,20].

6.4 Human-Centric Design Critics and Modelling Patterns

Just because we add human aspects to our requirements and design models does not mean they may be correct or even appropriate. We are developing a set of proactive tool support systems to advise software engineers of errors or potentially incorrect/unintended issues with their models [2,48]. This will enable the DSVL toolsets for human-centric requirements and design models to provide proactive feedback to modellers. To enable these design critics are identifying a range of "human-centric requirements and design patterns". These will provide best-practice approaches to modelling complex requirements and design models mixed with human aspects. These features will be added to successive iterations of our prototype tools from above. This work is building on our approaches to develop DSVL design critics [2] and DSVL-based requirements and design pattern modelling tools [30].

6.5   Using Human Aspects in Model Driven Engineering

Once we have some quality design-level human aspects in models – incremental outcomes from the above activities – we can use these in model-driven engineering code and configuration generators. This research involves adding generators that consume design level models augmented with human-centric properties and synthesizing software applications that use these appropriately. For example, we might generate a gesture-based, passive-voice feedback solution for the target user from the smart home example described in Sect. 2. However, we might instead generate several interfaces for the same software feature, and at run-time configure the software either with pre-deployment knowledge, end user input, or even modify it while in use based on end user feedback. Thus for example a part of the software for our smart home example could adapt to different end users' current and changing needs (e.g. age, culture, emerging physical and mental challenges, personality etc.).

This work is being done incrementally, focusing on single issues first then looking at successively more complex combinations, adding support to the prototype tools and repeatedly trialling the tools. We are adding human aspects to MDSE code generators [4], generating adaptive user interfaces [37], adaptive run-time software [42], and DSVL-based MDSE solutions [55].

7   Evaluating and Applying Human Aspects in Software Engineering

We are addressing critically important issues of (i) testing whether the resultant software generated from our augmented MDSE approach actually meets the requirements specified; (ii) providing a feedback mechanism for end users to report defects in the software specifically relating to human aspects; and (iii) providing a feedback mechanism from software developers to users about changes made relating to their personal human aspects. We are developing human-centric requirements-based testing framework, techniques and tools. These enable human aspects to be used in acceptance tests to improve validation of software against these requirements. We are also developing new human-centric defect reporting mechanisms and developer review and notification mechanisms. These support continuous defect reporting, correction, and feedback via the living lab and remotely. Even partial outcomes would be of immediate benefit to the software engineering research and practice communities. This work is extending research on software tester practices and usability defect reporting [14,61] and requirements-based testing [31].

7.1   How Can We Provide Better Fixes for Human Aspect-Related Defects

We are working on characterising a mobile app model with the desired human values for its target end-users. We are then using these values to assist us in detecting what we term "values-violating defects" [58] in the target mobile apps. We then provide app developers with a set of recommendations for suggested fixes for these values-violating app defects.

This involves studying a large number of apps, their reviews, and how users feel various "human values" – such as transparency, integrity, privacy, trust, and other human values – may be violated by the apps. We are then identifying ways to (i) detect these "values violations", or values defects, in apps; (ii) identify possible fixes for these defects so that the human values are supported; and (iii) providing tools to developers to help them find and fix these values-related app defects. We hope to generalise this approach to other end user human aspects that need to be supported in apps, including accessibility, age and gender bias, and different end user language and culture.

7.2   Gender Bias in IT Job Ads

We are investigating whether gender is a crucial factor to be an IT professional. As a starting point, we are reviewing if IT job advertisements are more appealing to male candidates. We are using an automated word based gender bias checker to examine if there is any bias in IT job advertisements. We are also conducting a survey of IT hiring managers and IT professionals and/or IT candidates to collect their perception about gender bias in IT job advertisements. Finally, we are applying a cognitive walkthrough approach with gender based persona, proposed by GenderMag [6] tool, to find if male and female candidates react differently to IT job advertisements. The overall finding from this study will help us to identify if IT job advertisements are gender biased, and if yes, what areas need improvement to make those gender inclusive. This will address a critical human aspect where the software engineering profession lacks diversity.

7.3   How Age Affects Users' Interaction with Software

We are looking to generalise the GenderMag [6] approach to supporting other human aspects during evaluation. In this project we are designing new persona templates that include "facets" for different ages that have been shown to influence differently-aged users' interaction with technology. These templates will be customisable using different descriptions of the facets and will generate different persona representing users of different age groups. These enhanced age-related personas can then be used by software engineers to enhance requirements engineering, design and evaluation of software for ageing people [51], in a similar way to GenderMag. Again, we aim to generalise this work to other human aspects of end users.

7.4   eHealth Applications

We are trialing our approaches with real industry practitioners and organisations for whom human aspects are critical. Our approach is particularly suitable for eHealth applications with end users with challenging human aspects, such as physical or mental disability, English as second language, cognitive decline, very young or old, and needing software to adapt to their changing personal or contextual usage needs. Planned target application domains include digital health apps for community members, community educational apps, government service and transport apps and websites, and smart home and smart building management software.

7.5   How Developers Address Accessibility Issues in Mobile Apps

We are studying how developers address one common class of human aspects – accessibility – in mobile apps, by large-scale analysis of app reviews, change histories, and other associated app development and release information. We hope to identify areas where accessibility issues are well-supported and can be more widely adopted. We also hope to identify problematic accessibility issues for developers and use this to carry out targeted studies to improve its support. With mobile apps becoming increasingly widely used for an increasing number of tasks, those not supporting diverse end user accessibility challenges run a great risk of reducing access of many in our communities to critical services [21].

7.6   Developing Better Apps with Personas

We are exploring human-centric smart city development approaches. One of our case studies is the development of better "smart parking" apps. We are using personas to identify a range of parking app users, informed by review mining and other techniques. We are then using these personas to help evaluate existing apps and to then develop and refine requirements and to evaluate designs and prototypes from a range of human-centric perspectives. The idea is to generalise this approach to other smart living systems that by definition have a wide range of diverse end users. We aim to employ the results of adding human aspects to design models and MDE, as discussed above, to improve development of these apps in the future.

We are also exploring the how personas might be used in eHealth. We will use personas to inform the development of a website and eHealth resources for people who have experienced miscarriage. The personas will be developed from inductive qualitative analyses from extensive interviews with women who have had a miscarriage, partners of women who have had a miscarriage, and health practitioners who support women who have had a miscarriage [5, 28, 40] and will include relevant human aspects including users' personalities, age, background, culture, language, physical and mental challenges, comfort with technology and so on. The personas will inform the look and feel of the website and resources, and will be used to test the website during the development and design phases. The website and resources will be evaluated through surveys and where possible, interviews with people who access the website, and this will be used to validate the personas.

7.7   COVID-19 Apps

In response to the COVID-19 pandemic, there has been an exponential growth in contact tracing apps worldwide [50]. The apps were created very quickly and are designed to be used across often disparate groups within a population. We are interviewing COVID-19 app developers and conducting focus groups to explore if human-centric aspects suitably taken into account and if so how, or if not how might they be included in the development. This is particularly important for contact tracing apps given their effectiveness is dependent on a critical mass of people engaged with the app.

7.8   Environmental and Sustainability Software Applications

Coastal communities around the world feel the impact of climate change in the form of rising sea levels. Current observations and future projections indicate that sea levels will be significantly higher in the second half of this century [60] causing more frequent and prolonged flooding that pose "unique challenges to risk management decision processes" [22].

We are planning to create a DSVL and decision-support system in collaboration with bay-side communities of Melbourne, Australia, to enable the modelling and simulation of the impact of flooding events and to support automated risk assessments. The DSVL will support the modelling of the needs of the various affected stakeholder groups, e.g. people who live and work in affected areas while also providing means to model localised contextual information about infrastructure, topology as well as local knowledge. We will be following an iterative human-centred design (HCD) approach to devise and evaluate our human-centric decision support system.

7.9   Human Aspects in SE Education and Practice

As argued throughout this paper, we propose to put humans into the focus of SE. Software should adapt to user needs - not the other way round. To build software to do so, a culture change in the SE industry and the way SE is taught is required. Besides improving concepts and methods, we aim to change some terminology in order to explicitly support a new way of thinking, e.g. through redefining or replacing terms such as 'user', 'stakeholder' and 'requirement'.

The term 'user' does not fully convey the human nature and individual differences between people. The term 'stakeholder' is often too narrowly applied. Indirect stakeholders - those who are affected by software systems used by others - are too often overlooked, e.g. self-driving cars may put the safety of other road users at risk [53], facial recognition systems may misidentify innocent people as criminals [35]. We believe the term 'people' is better suited to express such socio-technical aspects and to break up traditional technology-centred thinking.

Similarly, the term 'need' may be used to overcome the strict separation between functional and non-functional requirements. This differentiation is not only detrimental as the latter are often treated as less important afterthoughts; it is also incomplete. For example, human aspects beyond usability are typically not covered [27].

Moreover, we aim to change the way SE is taught to better prepare future generations of software engineers for the development of successful human-centric software systems. Social sciences need to play a more prominent role in SE curricula. Students and practitioners need the soft skills required for the work in diverse teams and to more effectively elicit and model diverse requirements and perspectives. Various of the above mentioned research activities will inform our revision of SE education.

8   Conclusion

Human aspects that are necessary to incorporate into the development of complex software systems include different end user age, language, gender, ethnicity, physical and mental challenges, personality, socio-economic status, educational attainment, emotional reactions, technology proficiency and so on. We described a motivating example - a smart home to support ageing in place - showing how many of these human aspects of software systems need to be fully understood and incorporated by software engineers. To realise this, we described our current work to advance HumaniSE - Human-Centric Software Engineering. This includes the use of a co-creational living lab to better identify diverse end user requirements. The use of domain-specific visual models to improve capture and reasoning about these characteristics. The use of design thinking, extended design models and augmented model-driven engineering. Improving defect reporting to help developers better understand and fix these human aspect-related issues in their software. We are applying these approaches to a range of domains requiring full support of the diverse human aspects of end users. This includes a range of eHealth applications, smart city applications, education-related software, support for vulnerable community members to access and use government and employment services, and sustainability solutions. We very much welcome approaches to discuss collaboration on some of these directions and projects.

Acknowledgements. Support for this work from ARC Discovery Projects DP170101932 and DP200100020 and from ARC Laureate Program FL190100035 is gratefully acknowledged.

References

1. Abdelrazek, M., Ibrahim, A., Cain, A., Grundy, J.: Vision: mobile ehealth learning and intervention platform. In: Proceedings of the 5th International Conference on Mobile Software Engineering and Systems, pp. 252–256 (2018)

2. Ali, N.M., Hosking, J., Grundy, J.: A taxonomy and mapping of computer-based critiquing tools. IEEE Trans. Softw. Eng. **39**(11), 1494–1520 (2013). https://doi.org/10.1109/TSE.2013.32
3. Ali, R., Dalpiaz, F., Giorgini, P.: A goal-based framework for contextual requirements modeling and analysis. Requirements Eng. **15**(4), 439–458 (2010)
4. Ameller, D., Franch, X., Cabot, J.: Dealing with non-functional requirements in model-driven development. In: 2010 18th IEEE International Requirements Engineering Conference, pp. 189–198. IEEE (2010)
5. Bellhouse, C., Temple-Smith, M., Watson, S., Bilardi, J.: The loss was traumatic ... some healthcare providers added to that: women's experiences of miscarriage. Women Birth **32**(2), 137–146 (2019)
6. Burnett, M., et al.: Gendermag: a method for evaluating software's gender inclusiveness. Interact. Comput. **28**(6), 760–787 (2016)
7. Curumsing, M.K., Fernando, N., Abdelrazek, M., Vasa, R., Mouzakis, K., Grundy, J.: Emotion-oriented requirements engineering: a case study in developing a smart home system for the elderly. J. Syst. Softw. **147**, 215–229 (2019). https://doi.org/10.1016/j.jss.2018.06.077
8. Donker, T., Petrie, K., Proudfoot, J., Clarke, J., Birch, M.R., Christensen, H.: Smartphones for smarter delivery of mental health programs: a systematic review. J. Med. Internet Res. **15**(11), e247 (2013). https://doi.org/10.2196/jmir.2791
9. Dybå, T., Dingsøyr, T.: Empirical studies of agile software development: asystematic review. Inf. Softw. Technol. **50**(9), 833–859 (2008). https://doi.org/10.1016/j.infsof.2008.01.006. http://www.sciencedirect.com/science/article/pii/S0950584908000256
10. Ferrario, M.A., Simm, W., Forshaw, S., Gradinar, A., Smith, M.T., Smith, I.: Values-first SE: research principles in practice. In: 2016 IEEE/ACM 38th International Conference on Software Engineering Companion (ICSE-C), pp. 553–562. IEEE (2016)
11. Fontoura, M., Pree, W., Rumpe, B.: The Uml Profile for Framework Architectures. Addison-Wesley Longman Publishing Co., Inc., USA (2000)
12. Friedland, B., Yamauchi, Y.: Reflexive design thinking: putting more human in human-centered practices. Interactions **18**(2), 66–71 (2011)
13. Friedman, B., Kahn, P.H., Borning, A.: Value sensitive design and information systems. In: The Handbook of Information and Computer Ethics, pp. 69–101 (2008)
14. Garousi, V., Zhi, J.: A survey of software testing practices in Canada. J. Syst. Softw. **86**(5), 1354–1376 (2013)
15. Green, T.R.G., Petre, M.: Usability analysis of visual programming environments: a 'cognitive dimensions' framework. J. Vis. Lang. Comput. **7**(2), 131–174 (1996)
16. Grundy, J.C., Hosking, J., Li, K.N., Ali, N.M., Huh, J., Li, R.L.: Generating domain-specific visual language tools from abstract visual specifications. IEEE Trans. Softw. Eng. **39**(4), 487–515 (2013). https://doi.org/10.1109/TSE.2012.33
17. Grundy, J.: Human-centric software engineering for next generation cloud-and edge-based smart living applications. In: 2020 20th IEEE/ACM International Symposium on Cluster, Cloud and Internet Computing (CCGRID), pp. 1–10. IEEE (2020)
18. Grundy, J., Abdelrazek, M., Curumsing, M.K.: Vision: improved development of mobile ehealth applications. In: 2018 IEEE/ACM 5th International Conference on Mobile Software Engineering and Systems (MOBILESoft), pp. 219–223. IEEE (2018)
19. Grundy, J., Khalajzadeh, H., Mcintosh, J.: Towards human-centric model-driven software engineering. In: ENASE, pp. 229–238 (2020)

466   J. Grundy et al.

20. Grundy, J., et al.: Supporting diverse challenges of ageing with digital enhanced living solutions. In: Global Telehealth Conference 2017, pp. 75–90. IOS Press (2018)
21. Grundy, J., Grundy, J.: A survey of Australian human services agency software usage. J. Technol. Hum. Serv. **31**(1), 84–94 (2013)
22. Hall, J., et al.: Rising sea levels: helping decision-makers confront the inevitable. Coast. Manage. **47**(2), 127–150 (2019)
23. Hartzel, K.: How self-efficacy and gender issues affect software adoption and use. Commun. ACM **46**(9), 167–171 (2003)
24. Hoda, R., Salleh, N., Grundy, J.: The rise and evolution of agile software development. IEEE Softw. **35**(5), 58–63 (2018)
25. Hutchinson, J., Whittle, J., Rouncefield, M., Kristoffersen, S.: Empirical assessment of MDE in industry. In: Proceedings of the 33rd International Conference on Software Engineering, pp. 471–480 (2011)
26. Hyysalo, S., Hakkarainen, L.: What difference does a living lab make? Comparing two health technology innovation projects. CoDesign **10**(3–4), 191–208 (2014)
27. ISO/IEC: Iso/iec 25010 system and software quality models. Technical report (2010)
28. Jensen, K.L., Temple-Smith, M.J., Bilardi, J.E.: Health professionals' roles and practices in supporting women experiencing miscarriage: a qualitative study. Aust. N. Z. J. Obstet. Gynaecol. **59**(4), 508–513 (2019)
29. Joseph, A.J.: The necessity of an attention to eurocentrism and colonial technologies: an addition to critical mental health literature. Disabil. Soc. **30**(7), 1021–1041 (2015)
30. Kamalrudin, M., Hosking, J., Grundy, J.: Improving requirements quality using essential use case interaction patterns. In: 2011 33rd International Conference on Software Engineering (ICSE), pp. 531–540. IEEE (2011)
31. Kamalrudin, M., Hosking, J., Grundy, J.: MaramaAIC: tool support for consistency management and validation of requirements. Autom. Softw. Eng. **24**(1), 1–45 (2017)
32. Kenny, E.J., Donnelly, R.: Navigating the gender structure in information technology: how does this affect the experiences and behaviours of women? Hum. Relat. **73**(3), 326–350 (2020)
33. Kent, S.: Model driven engineering. In: Butler, M., Petre, L., Sere, K. (eds.) IFM 2002. LNCS, vol. 2335, pp. 286–298. Springer, Heidelberg (2002). https://doi.org/10.1007/3-540-47884-1_16
34. Khalajzadeh, H., Simmons, A., Abdelrazek, M., Grundy, J., Hosking, J., He, Q.: An end-to-end model-based approach to support big data analytics development. J. Comput. Lang. **58**, 100964 (2020)
35. Khalil, A., Ahmed, S.G., Khattak, A.M., Al-Qirim, N.: Investigating bias in facial analysis systems: a systematic review. IEEE Access **8**, 130751–130761 (2020)
36. Khambati, A., Grundy, J., Warren, J., Hosking, J.: Model-driven development of mobile personal health care applications. In: 2008 23rd IEEE/ACM International Conference on Automated Software Engineering, pp. 467–470. IEEE (2008)
37. Lavie, T., Meyer, J.: Benefits and costs of adaptive user interfaces. Int. J. Hum. Comput. Stud. **68**(8), 508–524 (2010)
38. Lee, J., Xue, N.L.: Analyzing user requirements by use cases: a goal-driven approach. IEEE Softw. **16**(4), 92–101 (1999)
39. Li, L., Grundy, J., Hosking, J.: A visual language and environment for enterprise system modelling and automation. J. Vis. Lang. Comput. **25**(4), 253–277 (2014)

40. Miller, E.J., Temple-Smith, M.J., Bilardi, J.E.: There was just no-one there to acknowledge that it happened to me as well: a qualitative study of male partner's experience of miscarriage. PLOS ONE **14**(5), e0217395 (2019)

41. Miller, T., Pedell, S., Lopez-Lorca, A.A., Mendoza, A., Sterling, L., Keirnan, A.: Emotion-led modelling for people-oriented requirements engineering: the case study of emergency systems. J. Syst. Softw. **105**, 54–71 (2015)

42. Almorsy, M., Grundy, J., Ibrahim, A.S.: Adaptable, model-driven security engineering for SaaS cloud-based applications. Autom. Softw. Eng. **21**(2), 187–224 (2014). https://doi.org/10.1007/s10515-013-0133-z

43. Moody, D.: The "physics" of notations: toward a scientific basis for constructing visual notations in software engineering. IEEE Trans. Softw. Eng. **35**(6), 756–779 (2009)

44. Mouheb, D., Talhi, C., Lima, V., Debbabi, M., Wang, L., Pourzandi, M.: Weaving security aspects into UML 2.0 design models. In: Proceedings of the 13th Workshop on Aspect-Oriented Modeling, pp. 7–12 (2009)

45. Mummah, S.A., Robinson, T.N., King, A.C., Gardner, C.D., Sutton, S.: Ideas (integrate, design, assess, and share): a framework and toolkit of strategies for the development of more effective digital interventions to change health behavior. J. Med. Internet Res. **18**(12), e317 (2016)

46. Pikkarainen, M., Haikara, J., Salo, O., Abrahamsson, P., Still, J.: The impact of agile practices on communication in software development. Empirical Softw. Eng. **13**(3), 303–337 (2008)

47. Prikladnicki, R., Dittrich, Y., Sharp, H., De Souza, C., Cataldo, M., Hoda, R.: Cooperative and human aspects of software engineering: CHASE 2013. SIGSOFT-Softw. Eng. Notes **38**(5), 34–37 (2013). https://doi.org/10.1145/2507288.2507321

48. Robbins, J.E., Redmiles, D.F.: Software architecture critics in the argo design environment. Knowl. Based Syst. **11**(1), 47–60 (1998)

49. Salleh, N., Hoda, R., Su, M.T., Kanij, T., Grundy, J.: Recruitment, engagement and feedback in empirical software engineering studies in industrial contexts. Inf. Softw. Technol. **98**, 161–172 (2018)

50. Samhi, J., Allix, K., Bissyandé, T.F., Klein, J.: A first look at Android applications in Google Play related to Covid-19. arXiv preprint arXiv:2006.11002 (2020)

51. Sarcar, S., et al.: Designing mobile interactions for the ageing populations. In: Proceedings of the 2017 CHI Conference Extended Abstracts on Human Factors in Computing Systems, pp. 506–509 (2017)

52. Schmidt, D.C.: Model-driven engineering. Computer **39**(2), 25 (2006)

53. Combs, T.S., Sandt, L.S., Clamann, M.P., McDonald, N.C.: Automated vehicles and pedestrian safety: exploring the promise and limits of pedestrian detection. Am. J. Prev. Med. **56**(1), 1–7 (2019)

54. Soomro, A.B., Salleh, N., Mendes, E., Grundy, J., Burch, G., Nordin, A.: The effect of software engineers' personality traits on team climate and performance: a systematic literature review. Inf. Softw. Technol. **73**, 52–65 (2016)

55. Sprinkle, J., Karsai, G.: A domain-specific visual language for domain model evolution. J. Vis. Lang. Comput. **15**(3–4), 291–307 (2004)

56. Stanovich, K., West, R.: Individual differences in reasoning: implications for the rationality debate. Behav. Brain Sci. **23**, 645–655(discussion 665) (2000). https://doi.org/10.1017/S0140525X00003435

57. Stock, S.E., Davies, D.K., Wehmeyer, M.L., Palmer, S.B.: Evaluation of cognitively accessible software to increase independent access to cellphone technology for people with intellectual disability. J. Intellect. Disabil. Res. **52**(12), 1155–1164 (2008)

58. Whittle, J.: Is your software valueless? IEEE Softw. **36**(3), 112–115 (2019)
59. Wirtz, S., Jakobs, E.M., Ziefle, M.: Age-specific usability issues of software interfaces. In: Proceedings of the IEA, vol. 17 (2009)
60. Wright, L., Syvitski, J., Nichols, C.: Sea level rise: recent trends and future projections. Coast. Res. Libr. **27**, 47–57 (2019)
61. Yusop, N.S.M., Grundy, J., Vasa, R.: Reporting usability defects: a systematic literature review. IEEE Trans. Softw. Eng. **43**(9), 848–867 (2016)

Finding and Use of Source Code Changes for Aspect-Oriented Software

Marija Katic$^{(\boxtimes)}$ (iD)

London, UK

Abstract. In aspect-oriented software, code contained in special constructs called pieces of advice is used to define cross-cutting functionalities. This code is separated from more purpose-specific code (base code) and applies to it at specified program execution points called join-points. Such mechanism of composing a program imposes new requirements for finding changes between two versions of aspect-oriented software. This particularly refers to finding changes in advice applications at join-points as these applications are rather implict due to the absence of syntactical dependence of the base code to pieces of advice. In our previous work, we proposed and evaluated a novel approach for finding changes in advice applications. In this paper, we overview that approach, provide more details about how it works and additional results of manual verification analysis. We also compare the state-of-the-art approaches for finding and use of changes between two aspect-oriented software versions, including our previous work. Finally, we introduce the implementation of the graphical user interface for presenenting the changes found with our approach. We discuss its perspective usage and other potential applications of our approach.

Keywords: Program differencing · Aspect-oriented programming · Software evolution

1 Introduction

The aspect-oriented programming (AOP) [18] has gained its popularity because of its simplicity to isolate cross-cutting concerns into separate modules. Thus, the program code becomes separated into two parts: the base code (BC) and the aspect code (AC). The base code is used for the core program functionalities, while the cross-cutting concerns are part of the aspect code.

As such, the AOP is used on the top of another programming paradigm [4,17]. The well-established AOP language, AspectJ [17], is built on top of the object-oriented programming paradigm (OOP). We base this paper on AspectJ. In an AspectJ program, and in general in AOP approaches, the main unit in the AC is *aspect*. Aspect contains *advice*, this is code executed at a point in the execution of a program such as method invocation or field access. Such a program execution point is called join-point (JP). There are three types of advice: `before` advice

© Springer Nature Switzerland AG 2021
R. Ali et al. (Eds.): ENASE 2020, CCIS 1375, pp. 469–493, 2021.
https://doi.org/10.1007/978-3-030-70006-5_19

that executes prior to the execution of a JP, **after** advice that executes following the execution of the JP, and **around** advice that can affect the execution of the JP. The BC and AC are merged via the process that is referred to as the aspect *weaving*. The rules for weaving or so called *pointcuts* specify JPs where pieces of advice apply.

In general, software is changed for reasons such as fixing bugs, adding new functionalities or changing running environments. The research area devoted to the exploration of activities that support software changes is known as *software evolution* [22]. Nowadays, it is well-known that in aspect-oriented (AO) program, modularity has improved for the price of hampered software evolution [23,29]. This can be attributed to the absence of the syntactical dependence of the BC to the AC, making the interactions between the two parts rather implicit [6,29].

In such a program, introducing changes in one part of the program can change the semantics of the other part of the program, which can result in a program failure. For example, when a method in the BC is renamed, pointcuts may incorrectly capture or miss capturing JPs that are related to the renamed method. This problem is known as the fragile pointcut problem [19]. Changes in the AC can also change program behavior in an undesired way. Consider an example of moving advice from one aspect to another; this can introduce an unwanted change in the order of advice execution at places where multiple pieces of advice apply to the same JP.

To alleviate software evolution tasks such as change impact analysis [36], regression testing [33] or dynamic software updating [12], researchers proposed approaches for finding changes between two versions of an AO program. Most of these approaches [13,15,16,26,33] focus on finding changes in interactions between the BC and the AC. Others [10,36] also study changes in these interactions, but give them less attention as they focus on finding changes in general for AO programs [10] or finding all program parts that are affected by changes and linking failed regression tests with responsible changes [36]. What is common to all of these approaches is that they work as an extension or complement to techniques for finding changes between object-oriented programs. This is because existing techniques for object-oriented programs still work for finding changes between the BC of two versions of AO programs.

For two versions of a program, original and modified, finding changes between them means the identification of differences and correspondences between their source code files [2]. This activity assumes classifying program entities from two program versions as deleted, added, and matched (modified or unchanged). This is also the lowest level of describing changes between two program versions. Using these results, the found changes can be described in different ways such as small or compound changes [7].

Describing or presenting found changes is important because of their use in software evolution tasks. For example, if changes found between two AO program versions are used for selecting regression tests to rerun such as in [33], then it is enough to present found changes in terms of added or deleted control-flow graph[1] (CFG) edges. On the other hand, if the found changes are used to facilitate program understanding so that a developer can fix a bug, then the graphical user interface (GUI) would be more convenient. An example of such GUI is a feature of EGit[2] for previewing the result of the comparison of files within the Eclipse IDE.

This paper is an extension of our previous work [13] for finding changes in advice applications between AO programs. In this paper, we overview that work. Additionally, we introduce illustrations of our technique for finding changes in advice applications thus providing more details of how the technique works. We also review the state-of-the-art approaches for finding and use of changes between two AO software versions and compare our technique to these approaches. We discuss the potential uses of our approach. For that reason, we extended the tool AjDiff, which we presented in our previous work [13], with a GUI component for presenting the found changes between AO programs at the source code level. The contribution of this paper are as follows:

- Comparison of the state-of-the-art approaches, including the work from [13], for finding changes between AO programs accross several criteria.
- Comparison of the actual usage and the perspective usage of state-of-the-art approaches, including the work from [13], for finding changes between AO programs. We also review the way in which these approaches present found changes.
- For our technique from [13], descriptive illustrations of how it works on an example. We also provide more details about the tool AjDiff proposed in [13] where the most important part refers to the graph model for storing methods and pieces of advice in an AO program.
- The GUI design, for the presentation of found changes between AO programs, that we implemented as an extension of AjDiff. This includes the discussion of the perspective usage of our approach.
- The qualitative analysis of the results of AjDiff on pairs of versions of Telecom and Tracing AO program examples from AspectJ example suite.

The rest of this paper is structured as follows. Section 2 describes a motivating example and short background knowledge. Section 3 brings out a comparison of the state-of-the-art approaches from the perspective of finding and use of changes. Section 4 gives an overview of our previous work, provide more details and illustrations of our approach and the AjDiff tool. In Sect. 5, we discuss the results of the evaluation of AjDiff including the details of the qualitative analysis. We present the design of the GUI component of AjDiff and its potential applications in Sect. 6. Section 7 gives conclusions and outlines the directions for future work.

---

[1] The CFG of a method m $CFG = (N, E, s, e)$ is a directed graph that represents all possible paths traversed though the method [1]. Nodes (set N) represent statements, and edges (set E) represent flow of control between statements. There are single entry node s and a single exit node e.

[2] https://www.eclipse.org/egit/.

2   Background and Motivating Example

In our previouse research [13], we presented an example that demonstrates how a change in AO program can negatively affect the application of pieces of advice at JPs. Here, we present that same example, but slightly modified in order to make the change more close to the real-world scenario. In particular, in our previous work we only assumed that the undesired change can happen during the refactoring pocess, but in this work we demonstrate the process of refactoring that includes moving advice from one aspect to another. We show how this can introduce an unwanted change in the order of advice execution at places where multiple pieces of advice apply to the same JP. Also, we introduce a picture that improves the clarity of our presentation.

Since the model of applying multiple pieces of advice at the same JP is crutial for understanding of the presented example, we shortly overview that model as in our previous research. The order of advice execution with respect to the JP is derived based on the advice type and precedence rules. Just as its name states, the type of advice suggests its execution order with respect to a JP: before, after, or around (surrounding) JP.

For pieces of advice from the same aspect, precedence rules are automatically derived from their position within the aspect. The general rule is that for two pieces of advice, advice that comes prior to another advice applies prior to another advice unless at least one is after advice in which case the advice that comes first has the lower precedence [33]. For pieces of advice from different aspects, the precedence rules must be explicitly defined (using declare precedence statement). The explicit definition is particularly important because for different versions of a compiler used, different precedence order among the different aspects may be derived if the order is not explicitly defined [20].

If the around advice has pecedence over some other advice, then the around advice affects its application at JPs where these two pieces of advice apply. This control is achieved with the use of the call to proceed within the body of the around advice. In particular, if it is desired behaviour to skip the execution of the advised JP and any lower-precedence advice (with respect to the around advice in question), proceed is omitted from the body of the around advice, and vice versa. If desired behaviour is that the advised JP is executed, then proceed must be invoked [20]. For the JP and for advice whose execution depends on the around advice, we say that they are *nested* within the around advice.

Our Telecom example, which represents a simple demonstration of a telephone system, includes an instance of a JP, with few pieces of advice whose order of execution is important for correct program behaviour. Originally, it was taken from the AspectJ example suite. We extended it with additional features and pieces of advice in order to account for the importance of inter-advice precedence. To simplify the presentation, we present only the most relevant excerpt of the AC (Fig. 1).

We did not introduce any changes between two versions on the BC. For the two main entities that interact with the program, a caller and a receiver, the features of our interest that we added to the Telecom's BC are: the caller can

```
1: aspect Aspect {/*...*/              1: aspect ControllingConn {/*...*/
                                       2: pointcut pcConn(Connection c):/*...*/
2: pointcut pcConn(Connection c):      3: void around(Connection c):pcConn(c){
   target(c)&& call(void                  /*...check conn...*/}
   Connection.establish());           4: }
                                       5: aspect Timing {/*...*/
3: after(Connection c): pcConn(c) {    6: pointcut pcConn (Connection c):/*...*/
   /*...timing advice...*/             7: after (Connection c): pcConn (c) {
4: }                                       /*...timing advice...*/}
5: void around(Connection c):pcConn(c){ 8: }
   /*... check conn..*/                9: aspect Recording {/*...*/
6: proceed(c);                         10: pointcut pcConn (Connection c):/*...*/
7: }                                   11: after (Connection c): pcConn (c){
8: }                                       /*...recording advice...*/}
            (a)                                        (b)
```

Fig. 1. AC for the original version (a) [13], and the modified version.

make a request for a call such that the call is established only if the receiver accepts to pay for it - this is named *conditional* call; for the conditional call, the receiver can accept or reject the call. The caller and receiver can communicate only if a connection between them is established. This is achieved via the invocation of the method **establish** from the class **Connection** in the BC. For conditional calls, the connection is also called *conditional* because it must not be established unless the receiver accepts to pay for the call.

Part (a) of Fig. 1 shows the original version of the AC with two pieces of advice that apply to the call JPs **establish**. The **around** advice checks whether a conditional connection can be established. Depending on the evaluation of the conditional call and connection, via **proceed**, it controls whether call JPs of **establish** will execute. It also controls the execution of the lower-precedence **after** advice. This **after** advice needs to be executed only if the connection has been established. The execution order for two pieces of advice is inferred from their position within the aspect **Aspect**. Part (a) of Fig. 2 illustrates the resulting execution order for two pieces of advice and the corresponding JP.

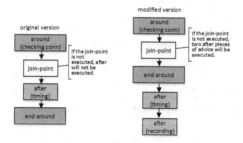

Fig. 2. The execution order for pieces of advice at the JP **establish**.

We refactored [9] the original AC as the aspect **Aspect** contains two pieces of advice with different purposes. This is the main difference with respect to our original example presented in our previous work [13]. We created two aspects with the aim that each contains pieces of advice of similar purpose. In addition, we added a new aspect and new advice for recording of calls. Part (b) of Fig. 1 shows the resulting three aspects in the modified version: `ControllingConn`, `Timing`, and `Recording`. Pieces of advice from those three aspects all apply to call JPs `establish`.

For the correct behaviour of the modified program, the precedence order of the `around` advice and the timing `after` advice should be the same as in the original version. Additionally, the `after` advice for the recording of calls needs to be executed only if the connection has been established. This means that the `around` advice should also have precedence over the `after` advice for recording.

As the three pieces of advice are placed in different aspects in the modified AC, we need to explicitly define the precedence among the aspects. This is only needed when the execution order for these pieces of advice at the call JP `establish` is important for program behaviour, which is the case in our example.

To demonstrate a faulty change, we assume that a developer has forgotten to define inter-aspect precedence. Part (b) of Fig. 2 presents the undesired execution order, which might be determined by a compiler, for the three pieces of advice with respect to the JP `establish`. We can see that the two pieces of `after` advice are not nested within the `around` advice, which is unexpected. Issues related to precedence between multiple pieces of advice referring to the same JP have been already recognized in the literature [27].

Because of this faulty change, when a caller makes a call that needs to be paid by a receiver and the receiver rejects such a call, the connection will not be established but the pieces of advice for timing and recording will be executed. This failure affects all the places in the source code where the method `establish` is called. In this paper we discuss how our approach detects such changes in advice applications. We also discuss the state-of-the-art approaches for the detection of such changes.

3   Changes of Aspect-Oriented Software

Change of an AO program can include source code addition, deletion or modification in AC, BC or both AC and BC. In general, these changes can be classified as the addition, deletion or modification of a method, class, interface, field, aspect, pointcut or advice. Pointcut and advice changes affect the BC via changes in advice applications at JPs. As already mentioned a change in the BC can silently change the pointcut semantics and thus affect the application of pieces of advice in an undesired way.

The existing proposals for finding changes between object-oriented programs such as [2,8,11] do not account for interactions between the BC and the AC. Therefore, equivalent approaches for AO programs focus on those interactions by extending or complementing proposals for object-oriented programs. In this section, we review these approaches from the two perspectives: (1) the finding or identifying changes and (2) the use or application of found changes.

Table 1. Approaches to finding changes for AO programs.

Problem, citation, year	Granularity	Program representation	Approach	What it finds
Pointcut fragility [19, 26], 2004/5	Coarse-grained changes: method-level	Directed acyclic graph for syntactic analysis and pointcut matching info from AspectJ compiler	Pointcut delta calculation for matched JPs heuristic for JP mapping based on the relevant program elements	Added and deleted pieces of advice for matched JPs and the reason (AC or BC change) for that change
Unsuitability of regression-test-selection technique from [11] for AspectJ programs; [33], 2007	Fine-grained changes: statement level	CFG representation that accounts for BC-AC interactions, extends the representation from [11]	Comparison of two CFGs that accounts for BC-AC interactions; extends the comparison from [11]	Changes in terms of different CFG edges for changes in BC, AC and/or advice applications
Manual effort in estimating the side-effects of changes; [36, 37], 2008	Coarse-grained changes: method level	AST static AspectJ call graph	Dynamic programming algorithm for comparing two ASTs; [35] dependence rules [38] to relate changes	*Atomic changes* [25] for BC and AC; advice application changes at JPs as *Advice Invocation Change*
Manual effort for general program differencing for AspectJ programs; [10], 2009	Fine-grained changes: statement level	CFG representation	Algorithm for comparing two CFGs from [2]; a new technique for comparing signatures at method-level	Added, deleted and matched CFG nodes; BC and AC atomic changes as defined by [25] and [36]
Pointcut fragility; detecting JPs where pieces of advice need to apply [15], 2012	Fine-grained changes: statement level	AST; concern graph for structural program representation	Heuristic for finding similarities among program elements common to JPs per pointcut	Recommends JPs (among added or modified BC) for inclusion within a scope of a pointcut
Pointcut fragility; detecting silently broken pointcuts after BC change [16], 2017	Fine-grained changes: statement level	AST representation	Probabilistic approach; finding patterns of similarities for JPs per pointcuts; uses diff algoritm [8]	Recommends pointcuts that potentially need to be changed because of added JPs in BC
Manual effort for general AO program differencing [13], 2019	Fine-grained changes: statement level	A new CFG representation that accounts for BC-AC interactions	*Artificial hammocks* matching; extends matching in [2]	BC, AC changes; added, deleted, modified pieces of advice for matched JPs

3.1 Finding Changes for Aspect-Oriented Programs

Table 1 presents the seven state-of-the-art approaches for finding changes between AO programs. For each approach, we briefly describe the *problem* that it tackles, the *granularity* of the approach, the *program representation* that it is based on, the details of the *approach* that works on the program representation, and *what it finds*.

Table 2. Use of identified changes for AO programs.

Citation year	Change preview	Actual usage	Potential usage
[19,26], 2004/5	PCDiff, an Eclipse IDE plug-in, shows changes in code using Eclipse marker mechanism; in GUI view, lists changes per advice and gives overview of changes	Providing insights in changes between versions	Understanding changes [28]; help with fixing bugs or detecting silently broken pointcuts between two versions; alleviate program evolution
[33], 2007	No GUI provided	For defining a set of test cases to rerun in a regression-test-selection technique	Static analyses such as change impact analysis [36], program slicing [32]; program understanding [28]
[36,37], 2008	Celadon, an Eclipse IDE plug-in, shows atomic changes, change impacted program parts, affected tests with responsible changes; GUI preview not found publicly	Automation of the change impact analysis for AspectJ programs	Help in detecting faulty code as it detects changes responsible for faulty tests; help in understanding of the impact of changes
[10], 2009	AJDiffer, Java app; GUI displays matched CFGs; preview not available publicly; API for other program analysis	Providing insights in changes between versions	Understanding changes [28]; help with fixing bugs; in analysis like CIA [36], regression testing [33]
[15], 2012	Rejuvenate Pointcut, Eclipse IDE plug-in; view, for single advice, lists suggested JPs for inclusion in a pointcut (manually)	For two versions, after BC changes, fix to AC by changing pointcut that need to include recommended JPs	Help to avoid mistakes while writing code (does not run in background) help with fixing bugs
[16], 2017	Fraglight, extension of the Mylyn Eclipse IDE plug-in, adds or removes pieces of advice for likely broken pointcuts to the Mylyn context and shows them in the *Package Explorer*	Simulation of adding JPs between two program versions and investigation of the accuracy of the pointcut breakage	For BC developers while writing fine-grained BC changes, shows broken pointcuts, hides unbroken pointcuts from the view; runs in backgorund
[13], 2019	No GUI provided; API for other program analyses	Providing insights in changes between versions	Understanding changes between two versions [28]; help with fixing bugs; in analysis like CIA [36], regression testing [33]

From Table 1, we can see that finding changes for AO software has been explored in several contexts: fragile pointcuts [15,16,19,26], regression testing [33], change impact analysis [36,37], and general program differencing [10,13].

Our approach [13], which we describe in this paper, is most similar to Gorg and Zhao's approach [10] as they both work at the statement level and extend the same object-oriented differencing algorithm. However, Gorg and Zhao do not relate changes in advice applications to their corresponding JPs, which is covered with our approach. Furthermore, our approach is similar to Koppen and Storzer's approach [19] as they both look for the differences between advice applications for matched JPs. But, Koppen and Storzer do not match program statements, and only match JPs based on the program elements (e.g. methods) that contain or reference JPs. The two approaches proposed in [15,16] can potentially complement ours as they can detect the semantic changes of pointcuts that are not reflected in the differences between advice applications at JPs and thus cannot be detected with our approach. For example, advice was expected to be deleted, but still applies or for added JPs advice does not apply, but should apply. Other two approaches work in the context of the another software engineering task, change impact analysis and regression testing and do not focus on the classification of differences in pieces of advice per JPs.

3.2   Use of Changes for Aspect-Oriented Programs

Table 2 presents the same seven state-of-the-art approaches as Table 1, but it presents them from the point of view of using these approaches in software engineering tasks. For each approach, we briefly describe the way it *previews the change*, the *actual usage* of the approach, and the *potential usage*. The actual usage refers to the approach evaluation that the authors described in the corresponding paper(s). The potential usage refers to the potential approach application as the authors described. In this case, the authors did not do research on that application.

Unlike most of the approaches given in Table 2, our approach from [13] does not provide the GUI for presenting identified changes. Similarly, the approach from [33] does not provide the GUI as its main purpose is to develop a new regression test selection technique rather then present identified changes.

It is worth mentioning that all these proposals work with AspectJ. The AspectJ Development Tools[3] support for the development of AO programs provides a feature that can mark the places in the code where pieces of advice apply. However, it only works on a single program version. Also, it is interesting to note that there are many potential usages for each approach, which opens possibilities for research on the application of the proposed techniques.

4   Approach to Finding Changes Between AO Programs

In our previous works [12–14], we proposed a differencing algorithm for AO programs (CalcDiffAO) as an extension of the differencing algorithm for OO programs (CalcDiff). In that work, we also proposed a CFG representation of a method in an AO program. That is *aspect-oriented control-flow graph* (AO-CFG). CalcDiffAO bases the comparison of methods on their AO-CFGs. In addition, we introduced a notion of an *artificial hammock* as a special type of a subgraph of an AO-CFG, which is used to mark the aspect part of the AO-CFG. In this way, artificial hammocks facilitate the comparison of advice applications at JPs that is done by CalcDiffAO. In this section, we briefly overview our previous work, provide more details and illustrations of our approach, and overview the high level architecture and process flow of our tool AjDiff for finding changes between two AO programs.

---

[3] https://www.eclipse.org/ajdt/.

The algorithm `CalcDiffAO` extends `CalcDiff` such that it compares two AO programs (original and modified). In further text, we refer to the original AO program version as P, and to the modified AO program version as P'. The Algorithm 1 highlights our extensions of `CalcDiff`. Program entities are classified in the following way: equal or modified entities are considered as matches, those entities that exist only in P are considered as deletions, and those entities that exist only in P' are considered as additions.

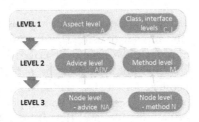

Fig. 3. Levels of comparison with `CalcDiffAO`.

In both algorithms the comparison is done in a top-down manner that is at the three levels (Fig. 3): level 1 - comparison of classes, interfaces, and, only in `CalcDiffAO`, comparison of aspects (Algorithm 1, lines 2, 3, 4); level 2 - comparison of methods, and, only in `CalcDiffAO`, comparison of pieces of advice (Algorithm 1, lines 5, 6, 12, 13); level 3 - comparison of statements for matched pairs of methods, and, only in `CalcDiffAO`, comparison of statements for matched pairs of pieces of advice and comparison of advice applications for matched pairs of JPs from matched methods (Algorithm 1, lines 7–11, 14–18).

At the level 1, the comparison is done for fully-qualified names of classes, interfaces and aspects. This name consists of package name followed by a class, interface or aspect name. At the level 2, fully-qualified method names are compared. This name consists of a fully-qualified class, interface or aspect name followed by a method signature. Pieces of advice are compared by using *advice identifiers* (aspect name followed by the advice declaration and pointcut specification) at the level 2.

The sets C, I, A, M, and ADV are given in the output of `CalcDiffAO`. The output also contains the set N that is populated based on the result of the comparison at the level 3 (Algorithm 1, line 18). Just like in `CalcDiff`, N consists of the matched pairs of CFG nodes that correspond to statements. Each node pair is accompanied with the change status (*modified* or *unchanged*). In addition, `CalcDiffAO` extends each element of N with a set of classified pieces of advice that are relevant to the element. Since we do not consider that advice applies to another advice, the set NA consists of pairs of nodes along with the variable that describes its change status (*modified* or *unchanged*);

When `CalcDiffAO` matches pieces of advice at matched JPs, we associate the information about a possible change in bodies of matched pieces of advice

---

Algorithm 1. Differencing algorithm for AO programs - extension from [2].

1: **procedure** CALCDIFFAO(P, P')
2:     Compare classes in P and P'; Add matched class pairs to C
3:     Compare interfaces in P and P'; Add matched interface pairs to I
4:     Compare aspects in P and P'; Add matched aspect pairs to A
5:     **for** each matched pair (a, a') in A **do**
6:         Compare pieces of advice; Add matched advice pairs to ADV
7:         **for** each matched pair (adv, adv') in ADV **do**
8:             create CFGs G and G' for advice adv and advice adv'
9:             identify, collapse hammmocks in G until max hammock node na left
10:            identify, collapse hammocks in G' until max hammock node na' left
11:            $NA \leftarrow NA \cup HmMatch(na, na', LH, S)$
12:    **for** each matched pair (c, c') in C, I, or A **do**
13:        Compare methods; Add matched methods pairs to M
14:        **for** each matched pair (m, m') in M **do**
15:            create AO-CFGs $AOCFG$ and $AOCFG'$ for methods m and m'
16:            identify, collapse hammocks in $AOCFG$ until max hammock node n left
17:            identify, collapse hammocks in $AOCFG'$ until max hammock node n' left
18:            $N \leftarrow N \cup ExtendedHmMatch(n, n', LH, S, NA)$

---

with a JP location where they apply. This provides additional view of AC change from the relevant BC location. For the information about the result of the comparison between advice bodies to be available during the comparison of JPs, the comparison of matched pieces of advice at the level 3 must be done before the comparison of JPs. For that reason, we compare all matched pieces of advice at the level 3 before starting the comparison of matched methods at that level (Algorithm 1, lines 7–11, 14–18). This is convenient because we assume that advice does not apply to another advice. Another approach is to apply the comparison $call - by - need$ for the matched pieces of advice, which is especially relevant when advice applies to another advice. With this comparison advice pairs would be compared as they appear in the application of method (advice) bodies during the comparison of method (advice) bodies.

In the following text, we overview how we create AO-CFGs, the notion of hammock, and how the procedures HmMatch and ExtendedHmMatch work.

4.1 Aspect-Oriented Control-Flow Graph

CalcDiff already works on a CFG representation of a method in an OO program. The main difference between the represenation of the method in the OO program and its representation in an AO program is in the representation of interactions between the BC and the AC as these interactions exist only in the AO program. These interactions are implicit at the source code level, and they are established via the compiler viewing mechanism. In their work, Xu et al. [33] experimentaly showed that when the compiler generates bytecode, it generates additional code that is used to establish BC-AC interactions, but that negatively affects the program analysis. For that reason, the authors suggested that the control-flow analysis of AO programs might be better performed on the source-code-based CFGs rather than the bytecode-based CFGs. Such CFGs are then compiler-independent.

In our previous work [13], we followed their approach and constructed our representation of an AO program by proposing AO-CFG as an extension of the traditional CFG representation in which we accounted for dynamic binding from [2]. In order to improve the understanding of that work, in this work, we bring the illustrations that represent the construction of the AO-CFG (parts (a) and (b) of Fig. 4). AO-CFG is the intra-procedural representation of a method.

In Fig. 4 (a), we can see the CFG representation of a method with a call JP establish within its body. The call JP refers to the invocation of a method establish from the abstract class Connection in the BC of the original version of Telecom from Sect. 2. Because of the dynamic binding, which is modelled as in [2], there are four nodes for the call JP (yellow nodes). This is because there are two classes Local and LongDistance that inherit from the class Connection.

For a JP, which is represented with one or more nodes in a CFG, and pieces of advice that apply to it (but are not represented with CFG), an AO-CFG is formed by creating nodes for these pieces of advice (advice nodes) and inserting them into the CFG at appropriate places around nodes for the JP. How the nodes of the CFG correspond to the JPs depends on a type of the JP. The AO-CFG accounts for the execution and call JPs. The execution JP encompasses the entire body of a method. Thus, all nodes of the CFG for the method correspond to the execution JP. The call JP refers to the invocation of a method as discussed above.

Figure 4 (b) illustrates the AO-CFG for a method from the original version of the BC of our motivating example. The method contains a call JP establish where two pieces of advice apply. As we discussed in Sect. 2, around and after pieces of advice apply to this JP. We can see the two aspect-related sub-graphs that AO-CFG defines: the *aspect graph* (AG) and the *around graph* (ARNG). The AG, with its entry node 2 and its exit node 10, marks the aspect-part of the CFG for the JP. The nodes 3 and 9 also denote the start and the exit node of the ARNG respectively, and thus mark the scope of the execution of the around advice. In this way, we can determine from the graph whether the around advice controls the execution of another advice. The after advice is represented with a single node 8 and its execution is controled by the around advice, as discussed in Sect. 2, which we can detect from the AO-CFG.

We can notice that the order of the execution for multiple pieces of advice that apply to the same JP is reflected in the control-flow of the AG. This order is derived from the advice nesting tree proposed in [33]. In the evaluation section we discuss some cases where our approach identifies changes in the advice execution order.

AO-CFG Limitations. The limitation of the AO-CFG is that it does not account for the *exception handling* constructs in a program. However, if the control-flow within a method is represented as if no exceptions are thrown or

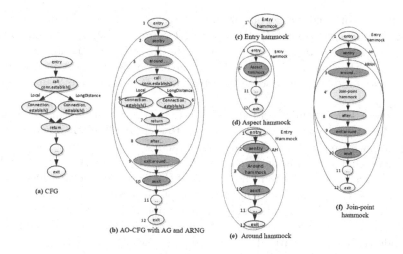

Fig. 4. AO-CFG and artificial hammocks.

catched, then the AO-CFG can be used for programs with exception handling constructs as well. The representation for exception handling proposed in [2] could be extended. However, this needs to be investigated additionally. For example, it needs to be investigated how to represent *exception handler execution JPs* (that represent the handler block of the exception type).

4.2   Comparison of Method Bodies

Since we assume that advice does not apply to another advice, bodies of pieces of advice are compared by using HmMatch procedure which was proposed as a part of CalcDiff. HmMatch is the algorithm which is the extension and the modification of the Laski and Szermer's algorithm [21] for finding isomorphism between CFGs of procedural programs.

For the comparison of method bodies, we extended HmMatch so that it compares pieces of advice for matched JPs. Here, we discuss the main details of the extended algorithm HmMatchAO from the perspective of the comparison of pieces of advice for a pair of matched call JPs establish from our motivating example in Sect. 2.

The main idea for the matching of nodes with HmMatch between two CFGs is the use of hammocks. A hammock $H = (N, E, n, e)$ for a CFG G is its sub-graph with the start node n in H and the exit node e not in H, such that all edges from (G/H) to H go to n and all edges from H to (G/H) got to e [5]. HmMatch bases the comparison on the identification of *minimal hammocks*. Minimal hammock is a sub-graph of CFG with the minimum number of nodes for its start and exit nodes.

To facilitate the comparison of advice applications for matched JPs with HmMatchAO, in [13], we defined the three types of artificial hammocks that satisfy the definition of a hammock, but are not necessarily minimal hammocks. These are the *aspect hammock* (AH), the *join-point hammock* (JPH), and the *around hammock* (ARNH). In part (b) of Fig. 4, the three hammocks are marked as follows: (1) AH with the start node 2 and the exit node 10; (2) ARNH with the start node 3 and the exit node 9; (3) JPH with the start node 4 and the exit node 7.

Parts (c), (d), (e) and (f) of Fig. 4 illustrate the process of creating these hammocks. Like with `CalcDiff`, the main idea is to identify all minimal and artificial hammocks within the AO-CFG and replace them with their corresponding hammock node that is then appropriately connected with the rest of the AO-CFG. In our approach, we start from the outside of the AO-CFG and first identify the entire AO-CFG as a hammock node (part (c)). Recursively, we identify all the innner minimal and artificial hammocks and appropriately connect their corresponding nodes. We can see the results as follows: in part (c), we can see the AH node (node 2'); in part (d), we can see the ARNH node (node 3'); in part (f), we can see the JPH node within the ARNH.

The comparison of two AO-CFGs is done with `ExtendedHmMatch` in a similar way as the comparison of CFGs with `HmMatch`. Two hammock nodes are recursively expanded and labels of the corresponding nodes of two graphs are compared. A pairwise graph traversal is done in a depth-first-search manner. The algorithm also accepts the values of the two parameters LH and S that can be used to improve the accuracy of the matching. LH is used to specify the depth in the graph until which a particular node is searched for. S is used to specify the desired similarity between two hammocks. For the comparison of two nodes out of which at least one is AH, the algorithm `HmMatchAO` is used. With two AHs, `HmMatchAO` does a pairwise comparison of advice nodes with respect to their order of application to the corresponding JP. It also removes nodes that are irrelevant for the comparison (entry and exit nodes of the AH and the exit node of the ARNH) but were useful for the construction of the artificial hammocks. Finally, `HmMatchAO` returns a pair of JPs and the sets with classified advice nodes (added, deleted, modified or unchanged).

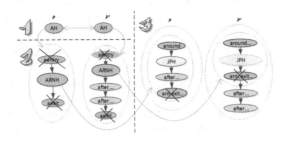

Fig. 5. Comparison of advice applications for a pair of call JPs `establish`, [13].

Figure 5 illustrates how `HmMatchAO` compares and classifies advice nodes for a pair of call JPs `establish`. In the first step, two AHs are expanded and in the second steps two ARNHs are expanded. When the irrelevant nodes are removed from the graph, the remaining nodes are appropriately connected so that the CFG structure is preserved. We illustrate the excerts from two graphs. In Sect. 2, we discussed that all the these pieces of advice are placed in different aspects in P and P'. For that reason, the comparison classifies the around and after pieces of advice from P as deleted, and the around and the two after pieces of advice as added. If we did not refactored the version P, and just placed two after pieces of advice into the same aspect in P' as in P, then the algorithm would classify two around pieces of advice as unchanged, after advice from P as deleted, and two after pieces of advice from P as added. In the final step, the algorithm would compare added and deleted pieces of advice and classify the matched pair as modified. In this way, it is detected a change in the control of the execution of the around advice over the after advice for timing (as discussed in Sect. 2).

4.3   Implementation Details

We implemented our approach in a tool called AjDiff. In previous work, we introduced the main components of AjDiff: *compilation, graph storage and data access layer*, and *change identification*. Here, we illustrate the high level architecture and the process flow of AjDiff. In addition, we introduce the graphical user interface component and give details of how we persisted graphs [12].

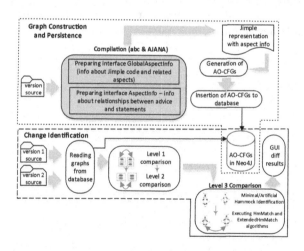

Fig. 6. High level overview and process flow of AjDiff.

AjDiff is run separately for graph construction and persistence and for the change identification as illustrated in Fig. 6. The compilation is done with *AspectBench (abc)* extensible compiler framework [3], which generates Jimple intermediate code representation [30] along with details for aspect weaving. To determine the advice order of application we used the implementation of the advice nesting tree [33] from AJANA framework [34]. In order to eliminate the overhead with the compilation, we stored AO-CFGs in the graph database created with Neo4J[4] (Fig. 7). Graph nodes are Jimple statements, and they are connected as follows.

- There is a root node for each AO program and a directed edge between the root and each program version.
- There is a directed edge between a node for each program version and a node for each class, aspect or interface that version contains.
- There is a directed edge between a node for a class, aspect or interface and a node for each method that it contains.
- There is a directed edge between a node for an aspect and a node for each advice that it contains.
- There is a directed edge between a node for a method and an entry node of its AO-CFG.
- There is a directed edge between a node for advice and an entry node of its CFG.
- Nodes for methods from interfaces are without outgoing edges.

The GUI was implemented using JFC/Swing API. The mapping between Jimple and source code statements is approximate. We used the information about source code line numbers from the object `SourceLnNamePosTag` from the Soot framework [31]. When the information about a line number is not available for a particular Jimple statement, we search for the closest Jimple statement with the available line number.

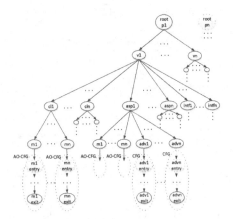

Fig. 7. Structure of the graph database with AO-CFGs.

---

[4] https://neo4j.com.

5   Evaluation of AjDiff

In our previous work [13], we run ajdiff on three pairs of versions of Telecom and three pairs of versions of Tracing programs from Aspectj example suite. More details about the setting of the run are available in that work. Here, we summarize those results and also introduce the results of additional experimentation with a change in a package name for a pair of versions of the Tracing program. Also, in this work, we present the most important details of our findings of the manual evaluation. These give better insights into the details of how our tool works on real examples of AO programs.

5.1   Quantitative Analysis

Table 3 presents a summary of program entities as they are classified in the four categories: *added*, *deleted*, *modified* and *unchanged*. For each of these categories, there are four columns that denote a compared version pair: first, second, third and fourth columns, respectively, refer to (v1, v2), (v1, v3), (v2, v3) and a pair with a changed package name (v2, v3). The pair with the changed package name is applicable only for the Tracing program.

The results of the comparison are shown in terms of the number of classified program entities for each of the three levels of the comparison. The numbers of added, deleted, and matched classes and aspects come from the result of the level 1 comparison. Similarly, the numbers of classified methods and pieces of advice come from the level 2 comparison, the numbers of classified call and execution JPs come from the level 3 comparison. It is worth mentionting that AjDiff uses the result of the comparison at the level 3 to inform the comparison at the level 2. Then comparison at the level 2 is combined with the result of the comparison at the level 3 to inform the comparison at the level 2. For that reason, a pair of classes or aspects with only one change within bodies of a pair of matched methods is considered as matched-modified pair. In this case, because of a change within method bodies (level 3), two pieces of methods are classified as matched-modified (level 2). Finally, two classes or aspects with those matched-modified methods are also classified as matched-modified (level 1) regardless of other possible changes between them.

In Tracing subject versions, only execution JPs exists, and in Telecom subject versions, only call JPs exist. As described in [13], we defined four categories for enumerating matched JP pairs depending on the outcome of the classification of the advice applications at those pairs: (1) pairs with only added advice, (2) pairs with only deleted advice, (3) pairs with at least one of deleted advice, or one of added advice, or a pair of matched-modified pieces of advice, and (4) pairs with only matched-unchanged pieces of advice. For (3) and (4) we count only matched JP types that is two call JPs or two execution JPs. We do not count JPs from deleted or added methods as these methods are not submitted to the comparisons at the node level.

For compared versions of Tracing, we can see that AjDiff identified 19 or 16 matched execution JPs with at least one pair of matched-modified pieces of advice. The total number of pieces of advice for all versions of Tracing is 4, which suggests the usefulness of AjDiff as for large programs it would not be trivial to identify such changes manually.

Table 3. Results of AjDiff for Tracing and Telecom [13] and for (v2,v3) of Telecom.

		Added				Deleted				Modified				Unchanged			
TRACING	Call	–	–	–	–	–	–	–	–	–	–	–	–	–	–	–	–
	Execution	–	–	–	–	–	3	3	3	19	16	16	16	–	–	–	–
	Class	–	–	–	–	1	1	–	–	3	3	3	3	1	1	1	1
	Aspect	2	2	2	–	1	1	2	–	–	–	–	2	–	–	–	–
	Advice	4	4	4	4	4	4	4	4	–	–	–	–	–	–	–	–
	Method	11	11	11	2	11	11	11	2	19	19	19	19	2	2	2	11
TELECOM	Call	2	2	–	NA	–	–	–	NA	–	–	1	NA	–	–	1	NA
	Execution	–	–	–	NA	–	–	–	NA	–	–	–	NA	–	–	–	NA
	Class	2	2	1	NA	1	1	1	NA	5	2	5	NA	1	4	2	NA
	Aspect	2	2	1	NA	–	–	1	NA	–	–	1	NA	–	–	–	NA
	Advice	3	4	2	NA	–	–	1	NA	–	–	–	NA	–	–	2	NA
	Method	26	17	8	NA	3	3	17	NA	5	5	6	NA	24	24	32	NA

5.2 Qualitative Analysis

In this section, we discuss several examples of where AjDiff detected changes as expected and vice versa. We draw examples from Tracing and Telecom subject programs as well as from our motivating Telecom example.

The main change between versions v1 and v2 of the Tracing program refers to the refactoring of the class `Trace` such that it becomes an abstract aspect in v2. Furthermore, four pieces of advice, which are placed in the aspect `TraceMyClasses` in v1, are moved to `Trace` in v2. Also, `TraceMyClasses` is changed in v2 so that it inherits from `Trace`. When we run AjDiff on (v1, v2), it classifies the aspect `TraceMyClasses` from v1 as deleted, and aspects from v2, `TraceMyClasses` and `Trace`, as added. This is expected behaviour because AjDiff compares entire strings of fully-qualified names of aspects at the level 1. This can be improved by using approaches for finding string similarity as suggested in [2]. As a consequence of this classification, but interestingly, AjDiff classifies all pieces of advice from `TraceMyClasses` as deleted, and from `Trace` as added even though these pieces of advice are the same in both aspects. It is worth noting that in this case an efficient approach could be using the Gorg and Zhao's proposal [10] which omits class or aspect level comparisons. That approach is suitable when there are lots of structural changes as it reduces the numbers of added and deleted program entities.

With the original setting in the AspectJ example suite, the v2 and v3 of Tracing are prepared such that classes are placed in the package named `tracing`, while two aspects `Trace` and `TraceMyClasses` are in the `tracing.version2` package in v2, and in the package `tracing.verison3` in v3. Table 3 shows the results of AjDiff when it is run on the original locations of aspects. Because of the difference in package names, and because AjDiff compares full strings of fully-qualified names at the level 1, the two aspects TraceMyClasses and Trace are classified as deleted in v1 and added in v2. In order to determine how AjDiff would work if these package names were the same, we renamed tracing.version3 into tracing.version2. Table 3 also shows the result of the run of AjDiff for these two versions. As expected, AjDiff matched the two pairs of aspects TraceMyClasses and Trace and classified them as modified pairs. However, the pieces of advice from these two aspects are still classified as deleted in v1 and added in v3 (that is the reason why these pairs of aspects are classified as modified). This is because of the change in pointcut declarations in v3 for all 4 pieces of advice. It is interesting to notice that no changes in the applications of advice were identified, which was expected as we have not changed any pointcut declaration compared to the run with different package names. However, even if it was the case that after renaming packages we found matched pieces of advice, we might not necessarily expect changes in applications of pieces of advice as advice matching at the level 1 does not implicitly mean matching for advice applications at the level 3 of the comparison.

The impact of inter-advice precedence among pieces of advice at a matched pair of call JPs appears for the pair (v2, v3) of Telecom. In v2, for aspects Billing and Timing, there is declared precedence in Billing such that all pieces of advice from Billing apply prior to pieces of advice from Timing. When we run AjDiff on v2 and v3, we found a matched pair of call JPs within the bodies of matched methods hangup from a matched pair of classes Call. In v2, there are two pieces of advice, Billing.after and Timing.after that apply to the invocation of a method drop, while in v3, there is only Timing.after advice that applies the counterpart call JP drop. As expected, AjDiff classifies Billing.after as deleted. Expected result is also that Timing.after is classified as matched-modified. However, from the user perspective, this might be better classified as matched-unchanged pair as there is no undesired change caused by deleting the advice Billing.after. Moreover, the deletion of Billing.after has already been reported. These changes in the order of the execution for pieces of advice are reported because AjDiff considers their order of the execution with respect to the JP to which they apply. Our tool can detect changes, but cannot detect whether these changes are desired or not.

In addition, the run of AjDiff on the original and modified (refactored) version of our motivating example shows that pieces of advice from v1 are classified as deleted (Aspects.around and Aspects.after), and pieces of advice from v2, Recording.after, Timing.after and ControllingConn.around, are classified as added. The main limitation for not classifying the same pieces of advice from different aspects comes again from the fact that AjDiff compares full strings of fully-qualified names. However, our tool is able to detect that the change exists. Improving its precision will be part of our future work.

Some of the limitations of AjDiff refer to the way it manipulates with the underlying technologies. For statement comparisons, AjDiff uses Jimple code generated by the Soot framework [31]. Numbering for local variables, which is

Jimple-specific might differ between two versions of the same program. Thus, for some statements that should be identified as the same, AjDiff would identify as different, again, because it compares the full strings of Jimple statements. Additionaly, there are some methods generated by the compiler that do not map directly to source code. For default constructor that does not exist within the class or aspect, compiler generates the `init` method. Also, for aspect, it generates `hasAspect` and `aspectOf` methods. These are not relevant from the source code view, but still they are present in the current version of AjDiff.

5.3   Threats to Validity

A threat to the external validity are small examples that we used for the evaluation. These examples have been also used by other researchers to evaluate their proposals [33,36]. A threat to the internal validity refers to errors in our implementation and possible oversights in the manual verification. To minimize them, we analyzed AjDiff textual and GUI outputs and performed code debugging.

6   Usage Example

One potential application of our approach is assisting a programmer during the process of understanding fine-grained changes between two versions of a program. Programmers need to understand code changes in order to fix bugs or to avoid them during development and maintenance tasks [28]. Program versions could be two different releases of a program or could be formed from different commits of a single program.

We argue that understanding changes for an AO program implies understanding differences in BC-AC interactions. This is because existing research [24] states that for understanding functionalities in the AO program programmers must understand the BC-AC interactions which implement these functionalities. An automated support, such as our tool AjDiff, for the classification of program entities (as deleted, added, or matched) including pieces of advice at JPs between two versions could facilitate the process of understanding program changes. In this section, we describe how AjDiff presents its results.

As already discussed, for two program versions, AjDiff detects their differences and correspondences at the three levels. Here, we discuss how AjDiff presents these results also at the three levels. The first differencing view that AjDiff shows is the result of differencing at the level 1. This view consists of several parts that list deleted classes and aspects, added classes and aspects, and matched classes and aspects. From this view, a user can access the results of the level 2 differencing for matched classes and aspects. For succinctness, we only show the screens of AjDiff for the results of the level 2 differencing for matched aspects (Fig. 8) and for the results of the level 3 differencing for matched methods (Fig. 9).

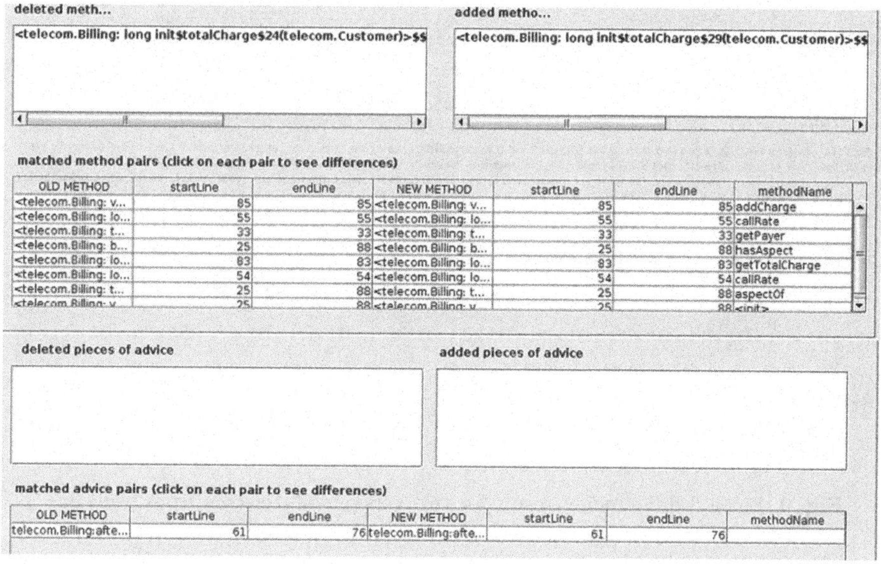

Fig. 8. Level 2 differencing result for two versions of Telecom from Sect. 2.

Figure 8 presents deleted, added and matched methods as well as deleted, added and matched pieces of advice for the aspect `Billing` which is matched between two Telecom versions from Sect. 2.

Figure 9 presents a screen that is accessed from a screen for matched pair of `Call` classes for the two Telecom versions from Sect. 2. We can see four parts that list classified pieces of advice for a matched pair of methods. Although AjDiff identifies changes at the statement level, it only approximately relates the classified pieces of advice to statements by highlighting the relevant statements. However, all the classified pieces of advice are available at the method level which is still expected to be very useful for the investigation of changes in advice applications between two matched methods.

In addition to applying our tool for differencing of versions, our tool could be used as a part of other software engineering activities such as code review. In code review, developers study code changes in order to detect mistakes. A tool presented in [39] demonstrates a comparison view of two files as a part of the tool developed for code review. When doing code review of AO programs, our tool can be used for the comparison view of two files. Furthermore, we applied our tool to derive changes for composing and applying dynamic updates for AO software [12].

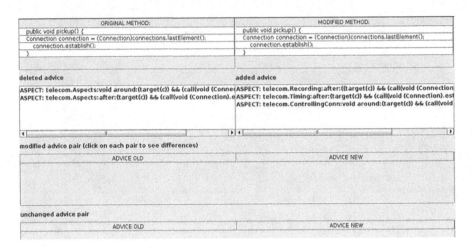

Fig. 9. Level 3 differencing result for two versions of Telecom from Sect. 2.

7   Conclusion

Finding and use of source code changes between two versions of AO software has already been in the focus of the existing research. The most attention has been devoted to finding changes in advice applications because BC changes can silently affect these applications in a negative way. In this paper we have discussed the technique for finding changes in advice applications from our previous work. Additionally, we introduced illustrations that provide more insights into the details of how the technique works, and the GUI extensions of our tool AjDiff. We discussed the potential usages of our approach by refering to the GUI design of AjDiff. Furthermore, we reviewed the state-of-the-art proposals for the comparison of AO programs from the two points of views: the finding changes and the use of changes. Compared to other proposals, our work is the first proposal that gives the most precise information about changes in advice applications at matched JPs that are matched using one of the state-of-the-art techniques for object-oriented programs. For all of the changes in advice applications that we detect, we cannot detect if the change has been desired or not. A developer needs to investigate the results of our technique. Still, the result of our technique can serve as guidance for the developer and thus reduce the amount of the manual work that is needed to check changes in advice applications. Although our analysis showed that our tool needs improvements, our results are promising.

In future, we are interested in comparing our technique with the approach used by Gorg an Zhao [10]. It would be interesting to investigate how artificial hammocks affect the accuracy of the comparison with respect to relating changes in advice applications to their respective JPs. Also, we plan to improve our tool and evaluate it on large AO programs to confirm our current findings.

Acknowledgements. I am grateful to Professor Kresimir Fertalj who provided me with the environment to work on this research under the project grant 036-0361983-2022 funded by the Ministry of Science, Education, and Sport, Republic of Croatia, as well as for valuable pieces of advice from Professor Fertalj.

References

1. Aho, A.V., Lam, M.S., Sethi, R., Ullman, J.D.: Compilers: Principles, Techniques, and Tools, 2nd edn. Addison-Wesley Longman Publishing Co., Inc., USA (2006)
2. Apiwattanapong, T., Orso, A., Harrold, M.J.: JDiff: a differencing technique and tool for object-oriented programs. Autom. Softw. Eng. **14**(1), 3–36 (2007)
3. Avgustinov, P., et al.: ABC: an extensible AspectJ compiler. In: Proceedings of the 4th International Conference on Aspect-Oriented Software Development, AOSD 2005, pp. 87–98. Association for Computing Machinery, New York (2005)
4. Coady, Y., Kiczales, G., Feeley, M., Smolyn, G.: Using AspectC to improve the modularity of path-specific customization in operating system code. In: Proceedings of the 8th European Software Engineering Conference Held Jointly with 9th ACM SIGSOFT International Symposium on Foundations of Software Engineering, ESEC/FSE-9, pp. 88–98. Association for Computing Machinery, New York (2001)
5. Ferrante, J., Ottenstein, K.J., Warren, J.D.: The program dependence graph and its use in optimization. ACM Trans. Program. Lang. Syst. **9**(3), 319–349 (1987)
6. Filman, R.E., Friedman, D.P.: Aspect-oriented programming is quantification and obliviousness. Technical report, RIACS (2000)
7. Fluri, B., Gall, H.C.: Classifying change types for qualifying change couplings. In: 14th IEEE International Conference on Program Comprehension (ICPC 2006), pp. 35–45 (2006)
8. Fluri, B., Wursch, M., PInzger, M., Gall, H.: Change distilling: tree differencing for fine-grained source code change extraction. IEEE Trans. Softw. Eng. **33**(11), 725–743 (2007)
9. Fowler, M.: Refactoring: improving the design of existing code. In: Wells, D., Williams, L. (eds.) XP/Agile Universe 2002. LNCS, vol. 2418, p. 256. Springer, Heidelberg (2002). https://doi.org/10.1007/3-540-45672-4_31
10. Görg, M.T., Zhao, J.: Identifying semantic differences in AspectJ programs. In: Proceedings of the Eighteenth International Symposium on Software Testing and Analysis, ISSTA 2009, pp. 25–36. Association for Computing Machinery, New York (2009)
11. Harrold, M.J., et al.: Regression test selection for java software. In: Proceedings of the 16th ACM SIGPLAN Conference on Object-Oriented Programming, Systems, Languages, and Applications, OOPSLA 2001, pp. 312–326. Association for Computing Machinery, New York (2001)
12. Katic, M.: Dynamic evolution of aspect oriented software. PhD thesis, University of Zagreb, Croatia (2013)
13. Katic, M.: Hammock-based identification of changes in advice applications between aspect-oriented programs. In: Proceedings of the 14th International Conference on Evaluation of Novel Approaches to Software Engineering, ENASE 2019, pp. 442–451. SCITEPRESS - Science and Technology Publications, Lda (2019)
14. Katic, M., Fertalj, K.: Identification of differences between aspect-oriented programs. Bern, Switzerland (2013)

15. Khatchadourian, R., Greenwood, P., Rashid, A., Xu, G.: Pointcut rejuvenation: recovering pointcut expressions in evolving aspect-oriented software. IEEE Trans. Softw. Eng. **38**(3), 642–657 (2012)
16. Khatchadourian, R., Rashid, A., Masuhara, H., Watanabe, T.: Detecting broken pointcuts using structural commonality and degree of interest. Sci. Comput. Program. **150**, 56–74 (2017)
17. Kiczales, G., Hilsdale, E., Hugunin, J., Kersten, M., Palm, J., Griswold, W.G.: An overview of AspectJ. In: Knudsen, J.L. (ed.) ECOOP 2001. LNCS, vol. 2072, pp. 327–354. Springer, Heidelberg (2001). https://doi.org/10.1007/3-540-45337-7_18
18. Kiczales, G., et al.: Aspect-oriented programming. In: Akşit, M., Matsuoka, S. (eds.) ECOOP 1997. LNCS, vol. 1241, pp. 220–242. Springer, Heidelberg (1997). https://doi.org/10.1007/BFb0053381
19. Koppen, C., Storzer, M.: PCDiff : attacking the fragile pointcut problem (2004)
20. Laddad, R.: Aspectj in Action: Enterprise AOP with Spring Applications. 2 edn. Manning Publications (2009)
21. Laski, J., Szermer, W.: Identification of program modifications and its applications in software maintenance. In: Proceedings Conference on Software Maintenance 1992, pp. 282–290 (1992)
22. Mens, T., Demeyer, S.: Software Evolution, 1st edn. Springer, Heidelberg (2008). https://doi.org/10.1007/978-3-540-76440-3
23. Przybyłek, A.: An empirical study on the impact of AspectJ on software evolvability. Empir. Softw. Eng. **23**(4), 2018–2050 (2018)
24. Rinard, M., Salcianu, A., Bugrara, S.: A classification system and analysis for aspect-oriented programs. In: Proceedings of the 12th ACM SIGSOFT Twelfth International Symposium on Foundations of Software Engineering, SIGSOFT 2004/FSE-12, pp. 147–158. Association for Computing Machinery, New York (2004)
25. Ryder, B.G., Tip, F.: Change impact analysis for object-oriented programs. In: Proceedings of the 2001 ACM SIGPLAN-SIGSOFT Workshop on Program Analysis for Software Tools and Engineering, pp. 46–53. PASTE 2001. Association for Computing Machinery, New York (2001)
26. Stoerzer, M., Graf, J.: Using pointcut delta analysis to support evolution of aspect-oriented software. In: 21st IEEE International Conference on Software Maintenance (ICSM2005), pp. 653–656 (2005)
27. Storzer, M., Forster, F.: Detecting precedence-related advice interference. In: Proceedings. 21st IEEE International Conference on Automated Software Engineering, pp. 317–322. IEEE Computer Society, Los Alamitos, September 2006
28. Tao, Y., Dang, Y., Xie, T., Zhang, D., Kim, S.: How do software engineers understand code changes? An exploratory study in industry. In: Proceedings of the ACM SIGSOFT 20th International Symposium on the Foundations of Software Engineering, FSE 2012. Association for Computing Machinery, New York (2012)
29. Tourwe, T., Brichau, J., Gybels, K.: On the existence of the AOSD-evolution paradox (2003)
30. Vallee-Rai, R., Hendren, L.J.: Jimple: simplifying java bytecode for analyses and transformations (1998)
31. Vallée-Rai, R. Co, P., Gagnon, E., Hendren, L., Lam, P., Sundaresan, V.: Soot - a java bytecode optimization framework. In: Proceedings of the 1999 Conference of the Centre for Advanced Studies on Collaborative Research, CASCON 1999, p. 13. IBM Press, Mississauga (1999)
32. Xu, B., Qian, J., Zhang, X., Wu, Z., Chen, L.: A brief survey of program slicing. SIGSOFT Softw. Eng. Notes **30**(2), 1–36 (2005)

33. Xu, G., Rountev, A.: Regression test selection for AspectJ software. In: 29th International Conference on Software Engineering (ICSE 2007), pp. 65–74 (2007)
34. Xu, G., Rountev, A.: AJANA: a general framework for source-code-level interprocedural dataflow analysis of AspectJ software. In: Proceedings of the 7th International Conference on Aspect-Oriented Software Development, AOSD 2008, pp. 36–47. Association for Computing Machinery, New York (2008)
35. Yang, W.: Identifying syntactic differences between two programs. Softw.: Pract. Exp. **21**(7), 739–755 (1991)
36. Zhang, S., Gu, Z., Lin, Y., Zhao, J.: Change impact analysis for AspectJ programs. In: 2008 IEEE International Conference on Software Maintenance, pp. 87–96 (2008)
37. Zhang, S., Gu, Z., Lin, Y., Zhao, J.: Celadon: a change impact analysis tool for aspect-oriented programs. In: Companion of the 30th International Conference on Software Engineering, pp. 913–914. Association for Computing Machinery, New York (2008)
38. Zhang, S., Zhao, J.: Locating faults in AspectJ programs (2007)
39. Zhang, T., Song, M., Kim, M.: Critics: an interactive code review tool for searching and inspecting systematic changes. In: Proceedings of the 22nd ACM SIGSOFT International Symposium on Foundations of Software Engineering, FSE 2014, pp. 755–758. Association for Computing Machinery, New York (2014)

Author Index

Printed in the United States
By Bookmasters